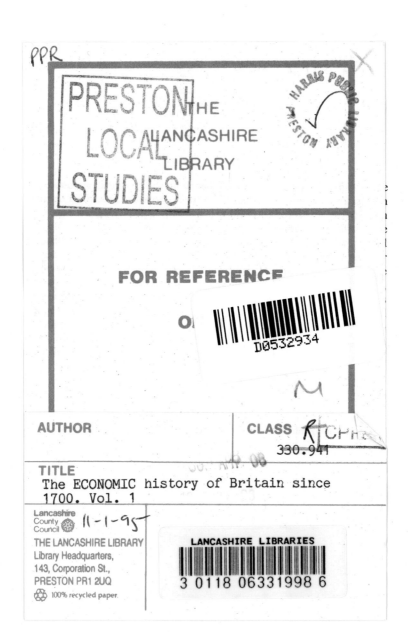

X

THE ECONOMIC HISTORY OF BRITAIN SINCE 1700

SECOND EDITION

Volume 1: 1700–1860

THE ECONOMIC HISTORY OF BRITAIN SINCE 1700

SECOND EDITION

Volume 1: 1700–1860

Edited by RODERICK FLOUD *and*
DONALD McCLOSKEY

CAMBRIDGE
UNIVERSITY PRESS

06331998

PPR

Published by the Press Syndicate of the University of Cambridge
The Pitt Building, Trumpington Street, Cambridge CB2 1RP
40 West 20th Street, New York, NY 10011–4211, USA
10 Stamford Road, Oakleigh, Melbourne 3166, Australia

First published 1981
Second edition 1994

Printed in Great Britain at the University Press, Cambridge

A catalogue record for this book is available from the British Library

Library of Congress cataloguing in publication data

The economic history of Britain since 1700 / edited by Roderick Floud and
Donald McCloskey. – 2nd ed.
    p.   cm.
Includes bibliographical references and index.
Contents: v. 1. 1700–1860 v. 2. 1860–1939 v. 3. 1939–1992.
1. Great Britain – Economic conditions. I. Floud, Roderick. II. McCloskey,
Donald N.
HC254.5.E27 1993   330.941′07   93-20093

ISBN 0 521 41498 9 (v. 1) 0 521 41499 7 (v. 2)
ISBN 0 521 42520 4 (v. 1 pb) 0 521 42521 2 (v. 2 pb)
ISBN 0 521 41500 4 (v. 3) 0 521 42522 0 (v. 3 pb)

ISBN 0 521 41498 9 hardback
ISBN 0 521 42520 4 paperback

UP

To Lydia, Sarah, Daniel and Margaret

Contents

Figures

Tables

Contributors

ROBERT ALLEN is Professor of Economics at the University of British Columbia

MAXINE BERG is Senior Lecturer in Economic History at Warwick University

NICK CRAFTS is Professor of Economic History at Warwick University

STANLEY L. ENGERMAN is Professor of Economics and of History at the University of Rochester

RODERICK FLOUD is Provost of London Guildhall University

KNICK HARLEY is Professor of Economics at the University of Western Ontario

ANN KUSSMAUL is Reader in Economic History at Oxford University

PETER H. LINDERT is Professor of Economics and Director of the Agricultural History Center at the University of California – Davis

DONALD McCLOSKEY is Professor of Economics and of History at the University of Iowa

JOEL MOKYR is Professor of Economics and of History at Northwestern University, Evanston, Illinois

LARRY NEAL is Professor of Economics at the University of Illinois at Urbana–Champaign

PATRICK O'BRIEN is Professor of Economic History and Director of the Institute of Historical Research, University of London

ROGER SCHOFIELD is Director of the SSRC Cambridge Group for the History of Population and Social Structure and Honorary Reader in Historical Demography at the University of Cambridge

NICK VON TUNZELMANN is Reader in the Economics of Science and Technology at the Science Policy Research Unit, University of Sussex

JEFFREY WILLIAMSON is the Laird Bell Professor of Economics at Harvard University

Introduction to first edition

Roderick Floud & Donald McCloskey

Economic history is an exciting subject, a subject full of problems and controversy. It is exciting because in economic history one is constantly forced to ask the question – why? Why were steam engines brought into use at a particular point during the industrial revolution? Why did so many millions brave great dangers to emigrate to the New World? Why were so many unemployed in the depression of the 1930s? Why do parents today have fewer children than parents 200 years ago? Economic history is not, therefore, a story – still less a chronological story, for most events in economic history cannot be neatly dated. Instead it is a list of questions; some can be answered, some cannot, but it is the search for answers, and for the best way to seek answers, which gives the subject both its justification and its interest. 'Economic history concerns the dullest part of human life. Sex, art, aberrant behaviour, politics, bloodshed – it is largely devoid of these' (Parker 1971). Yet it is concerned instead with how people live most of their lives, how many people are born and how they die, how they earn and how they spend, how they work and how they play.

At the same time, economic history can be hard, boring and frustrating, both to write and learn. Simply because it is concerned with how people have commonly lived, and why they have commonly behaved in a particular way, it is often difficult to discover relevant evidence; people, certainly most people, do not record in great detail for posterity what they buy or what they do at work, nor even how many children they have. The historian has to reconstruct the details of such behaviour from scattered and ambiguous evidence, and his reconstruction can often only be imprecise; few of the statements made in this book are, for that reason, entirely free from the possibility of error, and many represent only guesses. They are the best guesses made, when the book was written, by economic historians expert in their subject, but guesses nonetheless. Indeed, part of the fascination of economic history, although also one of the main causes of the controversies which rumble on for years in the scholarly journals of the subject, lies in making new guesses, and in working out what the effect on our knowledge of the past might be if we made different, but still sensible, guesses about the interpretation of evidence.

Even when we know, at least approximately, whether people ate white or brown bread, or at what age they married, they are very unlikely to have recorded for posterity why they ate white bread when their parents ate brown, or why they married at twenty-seven when their parents married at twenty-four. Even if they did so, their records would be inconclusive, for two reasons: first, people are poor at self-analysis; second, the factor which they choose as 'the' reason why is usually one among many joint reasons. In any case, the economic historian's interest is not normally in the behaviour of individuals, except as exemplars of the behaviour of society, or large groups within society, as a whole. While a political historian can reasonably hope to understand something of the political history of the nineteenth century by studying the life and thoughts of Queen Victoria or of Abraham Lincoln, the economic historian knows that the behaviour of any one individual has very little or no effect upon, and may even be totally different from, the observed behaviour of society as a whole. The fact that the marriage age in a parish is observed to have fallen from an average of twenty-seven in one generation to an average of twenty-four in the next does not show that all those who married did so at the age of twenty-four; nor, conversely, does the fact that two people married at twenty-nine invalidate the fact of the fall in the average.

The answer that we give to a question such as 'why did people marry at an earlier age than their parents' cannot therefore stem directly from the memories or writings of those who were doing the marrying. It can stem partly from such evidence, but only because such evidence helps to build up a set of the many possible reasons why people might have decided to marry earlier. This set of reasons, based partly on evidence from those who married and partly on the knowledge and common sense of the historian, is a necessary beginning to the task of explanation. Armed with it, the historian can begin to explore the evidence, and to see to what degree the behaviour which he observes fits best with one reason rather than another. He might begin, for example, with the belief that people are likely to marry if they are richer and can afford to set up house at an earlier age than their parents; if he finds after seeking for evidence of changes in income levels that on the contrary income levels fell at the same time as marriage became earlier, then that belief seems unlikely to be helpful, and another possible reason must be explored.

In other words, the historian uses evidence of the behaviour of individuals to help him to build up an expectation of how people might have behaved, against which he can contrast his observations of how they actually seem to have behaved. The expectation, or model as it is often called, is founded on assumptions about human behaviour, and therefore about the likely response of groups of individuals to changes in their circumstances. At its most simple, for example, the expectation might be that in general people buy less of a commodity as it becomes more expensive. The expectation may not always be correct for each individual, but it serves in general.

We need to have such expectations, or models, if we are to organise our thoughts and assumptions and apply them to the elucidation or solution of problems about what happened in history. If we do not, then we can only flounder in a mass of individual observations, unaware whether the individual behaviour which we observe is normal or aberrant. Models, therefore, cut through the diversity of experience and behaviour which we all know to characterise any human activity, and embody our judgement as to why people are likely to have behaved as they did.

If the models of historians are to be useful in analysing the past, then they must be carefully chosen. The economic and social historian deals in his work on past societies with subjects which are the concern of many analysts of contemporary society: economists, geographers, sociologists, political scientists. It is sensible for the historian to consider whether he may use their models to aid him in his work. In making the choice he must always be conscious that contemporary society is different from past society, and that a model may either have to be adapted to the requirements of historical analysis or, at the extreme, rejected as entirely inappropriate. But if the adaptation can be made then the historian is likely to gain greatly in his work from the insights of contemporary social scientists; these insights help him to expand and refine his model of the past.

These assertions are controversial. Not all historians accept that it is useful to apply models drawn from the social sciences to historical analysis. Not all, even today, would accept that the primary task of the historian is to explain; they would hold, instead, that description, the discovery of the record of what happened in the past, should be given pride of place. Most frequently, critics of the use of models and of the statistical methods which often accompany them claim that models cannot cope with the rich diversity of human behaviour in the past, that they simplify and therefore distort. Even mere statistical description – counting heads and calculating averages – has been attacked for dehumanising history and for replacing people by numbers.

Such attacks are based largely on misunderstanding. It is certainly true that models of human behaviour must simplify; indeed, that is their purpose, to enable the historian to concentrate on a restricted set of possible explanations for that behaviour, rather than being distracted by the diversity of individual deeds. It is also true that models concentrate on expectations of normal or average behaviour; again, this is deliberate and necessary if the normal is to be distinguished from the aberrant. The historian who uses models does not forget that diversity exists; indeed he makes use of that diversity, those different reactions to different circumstances, to help him to frame and then to improve his model. In some circumstances, no doubt, the diversity of the past may defeat the simplifying powers of the historian and the most complex of models, but such circumstances are no grounds for rejection of the use of models as a whole.

A more reasonable criticism of models and their application to history is that they are often themselves too simple, and that they embody unjustifiable assumptions about human behaviour. In later chapters of this book, for example, we make use of models which assume the existence of full employment, or of perfect mobility of labour; such models may lead to misleading results if such conditions do not obtain. Yet to criticise the use of one model in one set of circumstances does not show that all use of models is wrong. It shows simply that the historian, and the reader of this or any book, should be alert and critical and should not make silly errors; the same could be said of any scholarly work.

A third ground of criticism of the use of models and of statistical methods in history is better founded. Many social scientists use mathematical language to express their ideas and to formulate their models, while most historians, and even many social scientists, are not sufficiently familiar with mathematics to understand what is written. They do not appreciate that mathematics is often used merely as a shorthand, and are even less likely to appreciate that it is sometimes used merely to impress the unwary. Very reasonably, someone who does not understand may reject the ideas along with the language by which they are veiled, even though, in truth, the models can almost always be expressed in a language which is comprehensible to non-mathematicians.

This book has been written by economic and social historians who are expert in the use of models and of statistical methods in history, but are conscious of the fears, doubts and misunderstandings which such usage evokes. They wish to show that economic and social history is not diminished thereby but augmented, and that the results can be understood by anyone interested in historical problems. The economic and social history which they write, and which is discussed in this book, is sometimes called the 'new' economic and social history. The novelty of applying the methods of social science to history is by now about a quarter of a century old; it is often 'new' not so much in its aim nor even in its methods, but merely in the language which it uses. The results, however, are of great interest, and for this reason the authors have expressed their ideas in a language which any student of the subject can understand; where they have used a model or a statistical method which may be unfamiliar, it has been explained.

Together, the chapters in this book make up an economic history of England and Wales since 1700. The basic chronology and the evidence on which it is based are discussed, and the book as a whole provides a treatment of the most important themes in English social and economic history during the period of industrialisation and economic growth. Much has been left out, for the authors and editors have chosen to concentrate on the topics which are most problematical and yet where solutions to problems may be attainable. The book is divided into five overlapping chronological divisions, corresponding to the periods from 1700 to 1800, from 1780 to 1860, from 1860 to 1914, from 1900 to 1945, and from 1945 to the present day. Each division except the last begins with a general survey of the period, which is followed by a number of chapters which consider the main problems which have arisen in the historical interpretation of that period; each division except the first and last concludes with a chapter dealing with the social history of the period in relation to the economic changes which have been considered. The period since 1945 is treated as a whole in one, final, chapter. The book is divided into two volumes, with the break at 1860, although a number of chapters in both volumes bridge the break. Each volume has its own index and glossary, and its own bibliography; frequent references to sources and to further reading are given in the text, making use of the 'author–date' system of reference. In this system, books or articles are referred to in the text simply by the name of the author and the date of publication, for example (Keynes 1936); the bibliography is an alphabetical list of authors, with the date of publication immediately following the author's name. Thus (Keynes 1936) in the text has its counterpart as Keynes, J. M. 1936. *The General Theory of Employment, Interest and Money* in the bibliography.

The book has been planned and written by many hands. The Social Science Research Council of Great Britain generously made funds available both for an initial planning meeting and for a conference at which the first drafts of the chapters were discussed. The authors and editors are grateful to the SSRC for its generosity, and to Donald Coleman, Philip Cottrell, Jack Dowie, Malcolm Falkus, Jordan Goodman, Leslie Hannah, Max Hartwell, Brian Mitchell, Leslie Pressnell, John Wright and Tony Wrigley for attending the conference and making many helpful comments. Annabel Gregory, Alan Hergert, Nigel Lewis, and Ali Saad gave invaluable help in preparing the manuscript for publication.

Introduction to second edition

Roderick Floud & Donald McCloskey

The first edition, in 1981, had two volumes. This, the second, a dozen years later, has three. The change marks not only the expansion of the study of the last fifty years but also the acceleration of historical research on the British economy. From its beginnings in the late 1960s, with a thin, bright stream of predecessors back to the 1940s and before, the historical economics of Britain has flourished.

This edition, like the first, embodies a collaboration between British and North American authors which has been characteristic of the subject. Much of the underlying research, of which it is a synthesis, was first published in American journals such as *Explorations in Economic History* and the *Journal of Economic History*, as well as in the British *Economic History Review*. British and American economic historians have published their findings in those journals and, increasingly, in general interest journals of economics, reflecting a continuing interest among economists in the past of the first industrial nation. The British economy was the first to commercialise, industrialise, move to services and mature. Small wonder that economists have come to see Britain's history as a laboratory for economic science.

The materials used in that laboratory have become more varied during the 1980s. Two books in particular, each the product of years of research, have extended our knowledge of the fundamentals of the economy; Wrigley and Schofield (1981) have put *The Population History of England* on a firmer footing, while Matthews, Feinstein and Odling-Smee (1982) have given a magisterial account of *British Economic Growth*. But their work has been accompanied, on a lesser scale, by a host of economists and historians who have continued to explore both the central issues of economic history – growth, distribution, consumption – and the inter-connections between those issues and topics of social, demographic and other forms of historical enquiry.

These enquiries have often been controversial. A political emphasis on the role of markets which was common to Reagan's America and Thatcher's Britain in the 1980s led to studies of such diverse topics as child labour, education and inter-war unemployment. Monetarists tested the power of money to explain British experience. From the left, a generation of economically trained Marxists challenged the optimistic view of Victorian economic performance which had characterised the first generation of cliometricians. Research into the distribution of income, into the speed of Britain's growth and the alleged decline of the British economy and into demographic history and the history of nutrition, mortality and morbidity has given rise to fierce challenge.

These controversies are reflected in the pages which follow. There is no agreement on many topics in Britain economic history and it is right that differences should be exposed rather than glossed over. The 1980s have, however, seen much less controversy than in previous decades about the methods of enquiry; the role of economic theory, of statistics and computing, whose use in economic history had been challenged but which now underpins all the chapters in these volumes. Underpin is the right word, for there is much less explicit quantification and theorising than in the first edition; it is still there, but the authors feel less need to expose it and less need to parade technical expertise and technical language.

As with the first edition, the style of the book owes much to discussion between the authors at a conference at which first drafts were presented to a critical and constructive audience of the authors themselves and invited commentators. The commentators were Bernard Alford, Sue Bowden, Andrew Dilnot, Peter Mathias, Roger Middleton, Geoffrey Owen, George Peden, Peter Wardley, Katherine Watson, and Tony Wrigley; the authors and editors are grateful to all of them for their help. The conference was made possible by grants from the Economic and Social Research Council, from the British Academy and from Cambridge University Press and it benefited from the hospitality and the pleasant surroundings of St Catharine's College, Cambridge. The production of the book has been greatly aided by the enthusiasm of Richard Fisher and the copy-editing of Linda Randall, together with other staff of Cambridge University Press.

It is salutory to remember, in considering a book which is to a large extent about technical change, that the first edition was produced without the aid of word processors, fax machines or electronic mail. Twelve years later all have been used but the travails of editorship remain, together with our wish to acknowledge, in overcoming them, the support of our wives, Cynthia and Joanne, and of our children to whom this edition, like the first, is dedicated.

ATLANTIC

OCEAN

SHETLAND ISLANDS

ORKNEY
ISLANDS

North

SUTHERLAND

ROSS
AND
CROMARTY • Culloden

Inverness

• Aberdeen

Sea

SCOTLAND

Edinburgh

LOTHIANS

Glasgow

LOWLANDS

BORDERS

NORTH-EAST

• Newcastle

NORTHERN
IRELAND

ULSTER

• Belfast

Irish Sea

NORTH-WEST

Leeds •

Hull

CONNAUGHT

Boyne

Liverpool •

Manchester •

REPUBLIC

• Dublin

Sheffield •

NORTH

LEINSTER

WALES

EAST
MIDLANDS

OF IRELAND

• Limerick

WEST
MIDLANDS

EAST

MUNSTER

St George's Channel

WALES

• Birmingham

ANGLIA

ENGLAND

SOUTH WALES

HOME

Cardiff

Bristol Channel Bristol

London • Thames
Estuary

COUNTIES

SOUTH-EAST

SOUTH-WEST

Southampton •

• Portsmouth

0   50   100   150 km
0   50   100 miles

• Plymouth

ISLES of SCILLY

English Channel

FRANCE

HEBRIDES

HIGHLANDS

Firth of Clyde

XXV

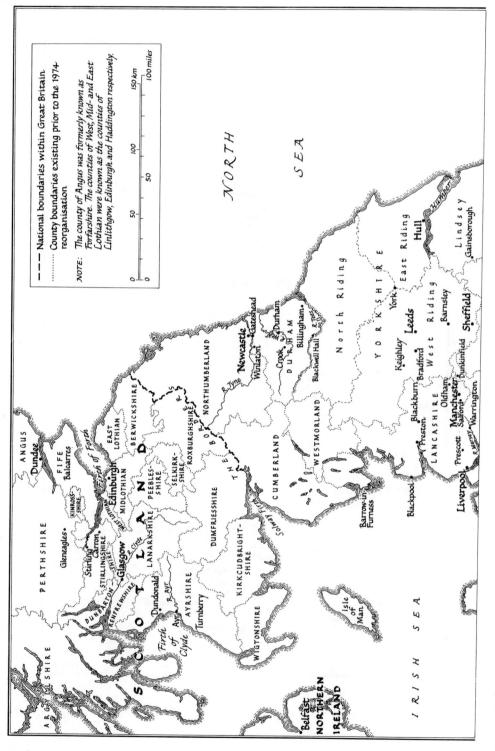

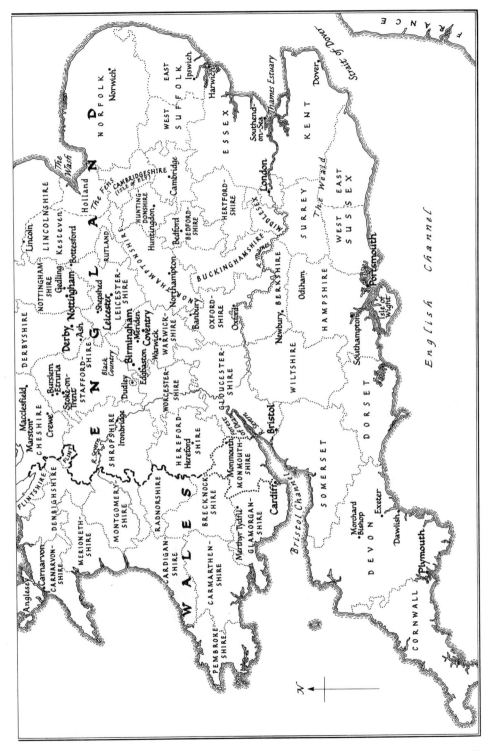

1   The pattern of work as the eighteenth century began

Ann Kussmaul

Introduction

The social and economic past remembered by men and women in the eighteenth century was not fixed; there was not a static World To Be Lost, as Peter Laslett found (1965). But the rapid pace of change in the world of work in the nineteenth century might well have excused a myopic view of earlier periods; the new industry and new techniques of the nineteenth century could then easily be seen as changes taking place on a fixed ground, The Past.

Much of the eighteenth century was spent in consolidating the gains made possible by the upsets of the seventeenth, which had seen even more turmoil than the Civil War and the execution of the monarch. At the start of the seventeenth century grain prices were still increasing, as they had from the recovery after their decline in the fourteenth and fifteenth centuries. Grain growing predominated in almost every area; it was fostered both by the continuation of rising grain prices in the first half of the century and by poor inter-regional connections and regional self-sufficiency in basic food-stuffs. By 1700, much of the west of Britain had forsaken the production of grain, principally for the raising of sheep and cattle and for manufacturing (Kussmaul 1986, 1990). Over the whole of the century, manufacturing continued a growth that had begun at least as early as the later sixteenth century, but that growth was also accompanied by an upsetting of regional orientations, especially over the second half of the century. Industry contracted in some regions, and grew rapidly in others. The century was one of the rearrangement of industrial locations and of agricultural specialisations.

Household and family

Which parts of the world of work of the seventeenth and eighteenth centuries were to be lost in the transition to the nineteenth century? What aspects of the eighteenth century more resembled the sixteenth and early

1

seventeenth centuries than the nineteenth? Laslett meant his title, *The World We Have Lost*, ironically: as he argued and as modern research has confirmed, nuclear families were no modern novelty (although see Chaytor 1980). But one of the things that was certainly to change was the meaning and role of the family. 'Family' was understood before the eighteenth century to include not only the parents and children, but also the workers temporarily hired into the household; these were servants and apprentices, usually youths and young adults (sometimes, but by no means always, from the families of neighbours), who acquired skills and savings before moving on either to new dependent positions or to fuller adulthood in their own new families. Apprenticeship and service were early modern institutional conveyors, moving people from their place of birth to new parishes, and from parish of employment to another, especially in the case of farm servants, who typically had one-year contracts (Kussmaul 1981a). Towns and cities, which were growing relative to rural populations despite their high mortality, also drew people, especially women, towards them (Wrigley and Schofield 1981: 415; Souden 1984).

In the eighteenth century, households were sites of production, not just sites of the reproduction of new generations; in any case, they were less procreative in 1700 than in either 1600 or 1800, judging by the lower rates of marital fertility and the higher ages at marriage found by Wrigley and Schofield for the start of the eighteenth century (1981). Farming and manufacturing were undertaken by households, and the world of work was thus very directly tied to the social world. Mothers and fathers supervised the life and work of their children and were surrogate parental supervisors to the youths who entered their households as servants or apprentices; they were responsible in law for their servant's actions (Humphries 1990).

Families were also the sites of education and of occupational training for most children, in the absence of formal schools, or of formal apprenticeship in the case of many adult occupations (Houston 1988). Religious nonconformity was a powerful reason to learn to read, in order to read the Bible; literacy was fostered in this manner more generally in all of Protestant northern Europe. As an example, in the very late eighteenth century one son of a Methodist, later Baptist, agricultural labourer and a lace maker learned enough, from his mother, his godmother, his village's Church of England Sunday School, the homes of his employing farmers and finally the militia, to be able to write the bitter memoirs of his difficult life (Kussmaul 1986).

Too close an attention to the structure and logic of families, even when they are understood to include servants or apprentices, risks ignoring the social and economic gulfs between households. Many were wholly dependent on a combination of wages, poor relief and Friendly Societies.

Some also still had access to their parish's commons, to keep a cow for their own consumption of dairy products, although such claims on the labourer's time were resented by farmers who wanted hired workers at their beck and call. Day-labourers had been thought to be 'the Feet of the Body Politique' in the seventeenth century (Kussmaul 1981b: 8); in the nineteenth century that perception of social ranking remained strong enough to lead observers (not yet in the mould of twentieth-century anthropometric studies such as that of Floud *et al.* 1990) to doubt the outcome of a measurement of schoolboy heights that had found the sons of the upper class to have been taller, but the sons of urban manufacturing workers shorter, than the sons of agricultural labourers (Szreter 1986).

Agriculture and manufacturing

Most farms, while large by the standards of modern Less Developed Countries or of much of the rest of eighteenth-century western Europe, were family operations, with farm servants and day-labourers hired in to expand the farm's labour force. Most farmers were tenants, and some of the land they farmed had been enclosed before, some of it long before, the early eighteenth century, but many open fields and much waste remained to be enclosed by Act of Parliament in that and the next century (Turner 1980; Wordie 1983).

Work in farming was seasonal, marked by a tight labour market in some seasons and underemployment or outright unemployment in others. Most manufacturing work was less driven by the solar year, but was, like agriculture, pursued in households, mostly rural. Textile production was the dominant manufacturing sector, whether measured by employment at spindles and wheels and at looms, or by value of output. Typical of most of the manufacturing of the time, the work was human powered, with mechanical help (Berg 1985 and ch. 2 below). The displacement of heavy woollens by New Draperies and cottons had actually displaced one use of non-human power: water-powered fulling mills had been associated with woollens production. There was much employment of women in rural manufacturing, especially in spinning.

But, by comparison with earlier periods, less manufacturing work was now done in association with agricultural work, in by-employed, or dual-employed, households (Levine 1977). Outright unemployment became more likely during swings in trade. This might, from our perspective, only have been short-term unemployment, but from theirs, to be unemployed was to have no income and to depend on parish poor relief (Levine 1983). Underemployment, by contrast, was endemic in agriculture. The spring was busy with ploughing and planting, and the autumn even busier with the harvest, but the harvest was followed by the slack winter season, with nothing associated with grain growing but threshing to offer employment; in stock rearing, the spring was a busy time for lambing, calving and foaling, but only sheep shearing, marketing or the harvesting of locally grown fodder offered much extra work in other seasons. Market gardening, with its variety of crops and overlap of harvest seasons (Thick 1985), was less sharply seasonal, as was dairying (except where cows were 'dried off' in winter) and fattening.

Where the family's labour was complemented by annually hired farm servants, all were underemployed together in the slack seasons. Farm servants were hired at the close of the year's busiest season, many of them at hiring fairs. Their receipt of the year's wages depended on their remaining in place through the year's work, to the end of their contracts. To the extent that farm servants were displaced by day-labourers in the later eighteenth and nineteenth centuries, as farms increased in size and labourers flooded home from the Napoleonic Wars, agricultural labour could then expect to be wholly unemployed in the slacker seasons of every year. Enclosure exacerbated their situation (Snell 1985). Labourers with rights to keep cows on common pasture or to cut turf for fuel, or with easy access to common fields for gleaning wheat for their bread and barley and beans for their cows had thus found unwaged work in slack seasons; they lost it with the enclosure of local common fields and waste (Humphries 1990), although there is much contrary opinion that the commons were purchased rather than stolen from the commoners.

Evidence of change

Imagine yourself to be standing in the early eighteenth century, viewing the economy of Britain. You would not be on a stable plain, but rocked by change, seeing the landscape of the eighteenth century being created all around you. Evidence of the changes in work and output that must have been happening is to be found in goods that were unlikely to have been produced for one's own consumption or imported; these are either goods written about at the time (McKendrick *et al.* 1982; Thirsk 1978) or goods listed in probate inventories (Weatherill 1988). There is evidence of increased internal trade or of increased wear on the roads carrying some of this trade (Spufford 1984; Chartres 1977). Rare census-like listings of occupations (for poll taxes or the like), or the occasionally recorded occupations of the buried, or of the parents of the baptised, in parish registers (Lindert 1980), can be counted and point to change. But in the absence of comprehensive occupational censuses, which were not compiled until well into the nineteenth century, these or other indirect methods are necessary to see late seventeenth- and early eighteenth- century changes.

Even more indirectly, economic change in England can be seen in the dent that different activities left in the timing of weddings, recorded in Church of England registers. Work-stopping weddings were infrequent when work was at its busiest, or risks at their highest, when there was the most to be lost, that is, from stopping work. Delayed weddings then accumulated, and were celebrated after the peak work/risk time ended. The late summer/early autumn harvest was the peak work/risk time for grain growing, while in regions of stock rearing it was the spring lambing, calving and foaling. Autumn marriages thus suggest arable farming and late spring marriages stock rearing. Since manufacturing was less seasonal than agriculture (though more seasonal than modern industry), weddings in industrial places were less likely to cluster in any one season. Dairying, fattening and market gardening were also less sharply seasonal in their work, risks and marriages than grain growing or stock rearing. When work in rural industry was integrated with farming as a by-employment, or as a more formal dual employment with agriculture, the stronger seasonality of the agricultural side of the operation often determined the timing of marriages.

Manufacturing work must have been the predominant activity in most parishes of non-seasonal marriages. It is especially unfortunate, however, given the great importance of women's work in rural household-based manufacturing, that this indirect measure reflects more clearly the grooms' rather than the brides' work and risks; male wages were so much higher that the new couple had more to lose if the groom rather than the bride stopped work to marry in an especially busy time.

The timing of weddings

Table 1.1 draws inferences from the seasonality of recorded weddings in a set of 406 largely rural English parishes; none of the parishes was in a town with a market charter. The parishes with at least twenty-four recorded marriages in the relevant forty-year period were divided into three classes: autumn-marrying arable, spring- or early summer-marrying pastoral and non-seasonal industrial. The table thus displays first the distribution of 'rural' (non-market town) English parishes among the three seasonal classes for each period. The penultimate column shows the number of parishes in market towns, and the last column estimates of population in England and Wales. Period 2 (1621–60) is anomalous, and enclosed in

Table 1.1. *Parishes by seasonality of marriages, 1581–1820*

		Percentages of totals (N) of non-market parishes					
		Seasonal		Non-seasonal		Parishes in English market towns	Population (million)
Period	Date	Arable parishes	Pastoral parishes	Industrial	N		
1	1581–1620	67	15	19	355	122	4·11
(2)	(1621–60)	(44)	(24)	(33)	(375)	132	5·09
3	1661–1700	42	30	28	385	134	4·93
4	1701–40	50	24	26	395	136	5·06
5	1741–80	51	15	33	401	136	5·15
6	1781–1820	54	13	33	398	135	8·66

Sources: Kussmaul (1990); Wrigley and Schofield (1981: 208–9).

parentheses: it includes the Interregnum, with its disordered Anglican record-keeping.

The relative number of autumn-marrying arable parishes at first declined, and then grew; the proportion of spring- and early summer-marrying parishes rose and then fell; the proportion of parishes that were non-seasonal in their marriages (the largely industrial parishes) more simply increased. The simplest explanations for these changes can be framed in terms of relative prices and real incomes. By the middle of the seventeenth century grain prices had been rising for more than a century, but they then declined relative to the prices of other products as population growth decelerated. This encouraged farmers to find products other than grains to produce and sell (products with less sharp late summer peaks of work and risks, as it happened). At the same time, the increase in real wages which was produced by the decline in grain prices strengthened the *demand* for products which had a higher income elasticity of demand than did grain, such as pastoral products and manufactured goods. In the middle of the eighteenth century, grain prices began to rise, and the proportion of parishes with arable-looking seasonality rose, but weakly: the proportion of parishes that were non-seasonal in their marriages (the largely industrial parishes) had more simply continued to increase.

The abandonment of grain growing in the later seventeenth and early eighteenth centuries was spatially ordered, as Table 1.2 indicates. It contrasts the seasonal patterns calculated for 1561–1640 with those calculated for 1661–1740. Parishes were divided into arbitrarily defined, rectilinear 'geoboxes', and then the proportion of the geoboxes' parishes

Table 1.2. *Distribution of 379 English parishes by seasonal pattern of marriages, 1561–1640 and 1661–1740, by geobox (parishes not in towns with market charters)*

GEOBOXES	south-west	marches	north-west	south central	south midlands	north midlands	north-east	south-east	East Anglia	east	total parishes	percentage of parishes
col.	1	2	3	4	5	6	7	8	9	10	11	12
distribution of parishes by region and season												
autumn 1561–1640	68	70	8	77	92	73	64	31	94	56	262	69·1
autumn 1661–1740	5	22	4	51	72	40	39	35	95	68	191	50·4
spring 1561–1640	11	13	26	8	5	14	25	28	4	36	55	14·5
spring 1661–1740	61	35	39	19	11	30	22	46	1	32	95	25·1
non-seasonal 1561–1640	21	22	65	12	3	13	11	40	3	8	62	16·4
non-seasonal 1661–1740	45	48	56	27	17	30	39	18	1	0	93	24·5
parishes in observation, both periods	38	23	23	26	58	30	36	45	75	25	379	

Source: Kussmaul (1990).

in each seasonal type was calculated for the two eighty-year periods that surround the Interregnum.

In 1561–1640, autumn seasonality predominated in all but two of the ten rectangular regions; by 1661–1740, three of the eastern geoboxes (columns 8, 9 and 10, 'south-east', 'East Anglia' and 'east') had recruited more autumn-marrying parishes, but every other region had lost parishes which exhibited the harvest-driven pattern. All the eastern geoboxes but one (column 8, 'south-east') lost parishes displaying the spring marriages of stock rearing; all other regions gained parishes dominated by spring marriages. It is likely that productivity increase came from this regional specialisation, as better use was made of land according to its soil, rainfall and distance from major markets (Kussmaul 1990).

The table also displays both regional industrialisation (in all but columns 3, 8 and 10), and regional deindustrialisation, especially in column 8, the

Table 1.3. *Proportion of sample's marriages celebrated in seasonal and non-seasonal parishes and in towns with market charters, 1581–1620 to 1781–1820*

Period	Dates	Non-seasonal	Seasonal	Market towns
1	1581–1620	0·125	0·392	0·483
(2)	(1621–60)	(0·237)	(0·280)	(0·479)
3	1661–1700	0·190	0·325	0·484
4	1701–40	0·209	0·295	0·495
5	1741–80	0·268	0·256	0·475
6	1781–1820	0·311	0·187	0·492

'south-east'. Industrialisation is especially found, in the table, in regions which were shifting from arable to pastoral seasonality (see especially columns 1, 2, 5 and 6, the 'south-west', 'marches' and the south and north midlands); the other strongly industrialising region, column 7, the 'north-east', more simply became less seasonal. The 'south-east' had been one of the two regions not dominated by autumn-marrying parishes in 1561–1620; it is the geobox containing the deindustrialising Weald.

If households were sites for the intergenerational transfer of skill, then the transfer mechanism would have been disrupted by the change in local economic opportunities. However, to the extent that skills were obtained in farm service or craft apprenticeships, the problem of intergenerational transfer would have been greatly lessened. Markets in capital stock, tools, improved land and livestock may similarly have eased the difficulty of adapting to the new orientations. But the rearrangement may also have necessitated a move to find areas where the old skills could still be employed. New pastoral practices also employed less labour than did earlier arable or industrial orientations, and prompted outmigration, often to new rural industry that was growing nearby.

In the same way as the seventeenth century is shown in Table 1.2 not to have been The Past, so different had the economic landscape become from that of the sixteenth century, so it was not a static past for the numbers involved in agriculture and manufacturing. The marriage seasons can be pressed into use to show this, by summing the numbers of marriages recorded according to the seasonality of the parishes, in each period. Table 1.3 uses the same six periods as Table 1.1. The total of marriages was summed, for each period, in three classes: (1) in the non-seasonal parishes, (2) in the seasonal parishes, the autumn- and the spring/early summer-marrying parishes and (3) in the parishes in market towns. The sums were then compared to the total of marriages over all three classes in each period, and the proportions of marriages recorded in the three classes calculated.

No meaning can be drawn from the value of any one proportion in the table; it cannot be said that '27 per cent of England's labour force was employed in rural manufacturing in 1741–80, and only 26 per cent in agriculture.' Instead, the table suggests that rural non-seasonal, predominantly industrial employment grew in a disconcertingly steady manner from the later sixteenth and early seventeenth centuries. Trends may be calculated from the logarithms of the seasonal (AG) and non-seasonal (X) proportions, transformed in percentages and excluding the second period, with its Interregnum-disordered records:

$$\ln (X_t) = 2.75 + 0.182 \text{ (period)} \quad r^2 = 0.9932 \tag{1.1}$$
$$(t = 20.92, \text{ significant at a } 0.0002 \text{ probability of error})$$
$$\ln (AG_t) = 4.24 - 1.30 \text{ (period)} \quad r^2 = 0.9398$$
$$(t = -6.85, \text{ significant at a } 0.0054 \text{ probability of error})$$

Table 1.3 assumes that (1) everyone in a rural non-seasonal parish was employed in manufacturing, and that no one in an agriculturally seasonal parish was; (2) the sample of parishes truly represented England; (3) the seasonal and non-seasonal marriage patterns truly reflected agricultural and industrial work; (4) similar proportions of the marriages pertained to marriages of people occupied in neither agriculture nor manufacturing (in services, principally) in both agricultural and non-agricultural parishes; and (5) rates of nuptiality were similar across all occupations. It is, however, not the absolute value of the proportions that is important to the argument that change was constant; all that is required is that the biases springing from differences in nuptiality, or services, or from the representativeness of the sample did not change over time.

The measures were driven by the main employment of most of the young adults of the parishes. The method is indirect, but it is interesting to know what most of the people were doing, rather than concentrating on exciting and productivity-increasing activity such as mechanisation and heroic individual initiative (Hoppit 1987). It was not the employment of 'most of the young adults' which drove the seasonality of weddings towards autumnal, or vernal, or non-seasonal patterns, it was that of 'most of the men', the young men. Women's wages were so much lower than male wages that their consequent lack of influence on the seasonal timing of their weddings is a lesson in itself.

There is nothing of a discontinuous industrial revolution about Table 1.3. Instead, it suggests a process of steady industrial growth in the seventeenth and eighteenth centuries, stemming from the redeployment of resources, in this instance of labour (Crafts 1985a; Hoppit 1990). Even if violently discontinuous industrial growth was a nineteenth-century phenomenon (Harley 1982), it lies outside the frame of this volume; human-powered manufacturing persisted well into the nineteenth century, showing up indirectly in the calculation in chapter 10 and more directly in the census (Wrigley 1988).

Conclusion

The constant increase in the proportion of marriages in the parishes that were non-seasonal, and the nearly as constant decline in the proportion of marriages in agriculturally seasonal parishes (see Table 1.2) are not without their implications, especially when this evidence is combined with the evidence of instability of industrial locations over time that the same source revealed in Table 1.2. To the extent that the increase in the non-seasonal proportion reflects increasing employment in manufacturing, and the decline in the seasonal proportion a relative decrease in the proportion employed in agriculture, two strong consequences follow.

Industrialisation is here revealing itself in the redeployment of factors of production, labour in this instance, whatever technological change was also occurring. Some of the increase in the non-seasonal proportion will have been produced by rural industry's emergence from its shell of by-employed invisibility; it can now be identified via the seasonality of its work and associated seasonality of its marriages. But even if all of the increase in the non-seasonal series, and the decline in the seasonal one, could be so explained, one form of rural industry (by-employment or dual-employment with agriculture) would have had to have been being displaced, at a constant rate, by another (simple industrial employment), over the 200 years of the table and the regression analyses. In that case, many more households must have learnt the new proto-industrial skills and tactics, skills and tactics that were to be of little help to the generations that followed, later in the nineteenth century.

Second, the absence of substantial imports of food must have placed increasing pressure on those who remained in agriculture. In this sample, with this indirect method, and waiving all the caveats against believing the calculated proportions, the proportion of English labour employed in agriculture would seem to have dropped from 0.392 to 0.187 between 1581–1620 and 1781–1820. This would suggest that towards the end of the eighteenth century, given the rate of productivity increase in agriculture, there was much less labour to squeeze out of agriculture in the way of redeployment. Population had begun to increase around mid-century, industry had kept growing and grain prices rose.

Some farmers responded by reverting to grain growing: twenty-one of the sample's non-market parishes that had been spring-marrying (pastoral) in 1661–1740 were autumn-marrying (arable) by 1741–1820, while only five parishes changed from autumn to spring patterns of marriages then. This would pose a new threat to the growth of industry: agriculture was now pulling labour back into grain growing, not pumping labour out to industry, and the shift back to grain growing was itself a response to the inability of the pastoral–arable mix of 1661–1740 to feed the growing non-agricultural numbers (Jackson 1985). The threat posed by the redeployment away from agriculture had been to the standard of living; now the threat was to the profits of manufacturing, as agriculture could release little more labour without labour-saving changes in techniques (which the nineteenth century would deliver). But redeployment proceeded so inexorably over the seventeenth and eighteenth centuries that the germ of the idea of Adam Smith and David Ricardo – that there must eventually be limits to Britain's growth – is not at all surprising. Gains from trade had already been garnered in the seventeenth-century specialisation, before coal and technological change brought Britain to a false dawn of limitless expansion (Wrigley 1988, 1990).

2   Technological change, 1700–1830

Joel Mokyr

Introduction

The acceleration of technological and economic changes that took place after about 1760 is collectively known as the industrial revolution. Changing technology is a tortuous, in some views even insidious, thing: it often takes place in out-of-the-way small workshops and dusty basements, far from the limelight. It may be many years, sometimes decades, before inventions find their way into the showrooms and national income accounts. The technological changes in Britain between 1760 and 1830 were no different. Consequently, the term 'industrial' revolution has led to some confusion, because the stream of inventions that rocked Britain in these years did not have much of an effect on living standards and national income until 1830 or even 1850. Adding to the confusion is the fact that the changes in technology reached far beyond the traditional domain of the economist into the structure of the family and the community, the nature of work, the location of residence, the division of political power and the relief of the poor, to name a few. One historian has aptly called it the 'more than Industrial Revolution' (Perkin 1969).

Technological progress is defined as the ability to extract more or better outputs from a given level of effort, equipment, fuel and other inputs. It is thus an improvement in the efficiency of our control of the physical environment, replacing known ways of putting food on the table and clothes on the body by better ones. 'Better' here is defined purely from the consumer's point of view: it means that innovation makes goods cheaper, better, longer-lasting or more pleasing in some other way for the consumer. This definition looks at the totality of the effect of change: if a change in technology can improve food output only by poisoning the ground water, more cautious evaluations of 'progress' must be employed. The consumer's point of view ('maximising utility') is not the only way of looking at the industrial revolution or indeed any case of technological progress, though it is the one that is most natural to modern economists. Marx, by contrast, was far more interested in the effects of technology on the labourer than on the consumer. While this is a legitimate point of view, it is not the one adopted here. As Adam Smith noted, 'consumption is the sole end and purpose of all production; the interest of the producer ought to be attended to only so far as it may be necessary for promoting that of the consumer' (1776: II, 660).

In some ways, the industrial revolution did not leave us much that is currently in use. Most of what surrounds consumers in the 1990s is made by technologies that came about much later: electronics, mass-produced apparel, synthetic materials, nuclear power, internal combustion engines and antibiotics – none date from the period of the industrial revolution. Even the great technological breakthroughs on which manufacturing in the later nineteenth century was based, such as cheap steel, chemicals and the railroad, came after the industrial revolution had run its course. In technology, however, as in the evolution of species, change begets change, and each generation stands on the shoulders of the preceding one. Just as the Descent of Man would be incomprehensible without knowing about our simian forefathers, so too would be the world of technology that emerged in the twentieth century, built on the new techniques of the industrial revolution.

What, then, was so special about what happened in Britain in those years? The short answer is: an acceleration in technological change. To be sure, change was not new in 1750: the previous century had witnessed some important breakthroughs, including a rudimentary steam engine and a flawed technique of using coke in blast furnaces. The industrial revolution marks a break, however, in that before 1760 stability was the rule and inventions the exception; afterwards, it was the other way around.

Some useful distinctions

Technological progress constitutes an important exception to the famous rule of economic science which states that scarcity lies at the very basis of economics, because technological progress is a clear-cut example of a free (or at least a very cheap) lunch. The nature of technological change and especially major inventions is that, although rarely wholly free, they often provide a stream of benefits that is out of proportion to the costs and efforts that went in to their creation. Such cost-benefit calculations are fraught with complications; many would-be inventors never invent a thing: should we count their time and resources as part of the social cost of technological progress?

Analysing technological change in this way requires making some distinctions. One old but useful dichotomy in the literature of technological change distinguishes between process and product innovation. Process innovation occurs when a good of given characteristics can be produced at lower cost. Product innovation occurs when a previously unavailable product can be made, or the quality of an existing product is improved. Of course, many innovations contain elements of both. A piece of coloured cotton cloth in 1830 cost a tiny fraction of its cost in 1750, yet was on the whole better made, more colour-fast and more evenly textured.

A second distinction in the economics of technological change is between invention (that is, the generation of new information) and diffusion (the adoption of technology generated elsewhere). For many purposes this is a useful distinction, but clearly in the narrowest economic framework it does not really matter if something that is new and useful is adopted from elsewhere or generated on the spot. As technology transfer was often accompanied by further innovation, the distinction is further complicated by techniques that required adaptation and modification to conform to local needs and constraints (Pacey 1990). Technology is site-specific in agricultural and other technologies that depend on topography and climate, such as water and wind power, water supply, drainage and construction. An iron water mill of the type built in England in the 1790s, for instance, could not be adapted to the rapid-flowing mountain streams of Switzerland without substantial modification. The sheep bred to thrive by grazing on the Scottish Highlands would not do well in Minnesota.

The need to modify technology blurs the sharp distinction between invention and diffusion. It is, in fact, fairly clear that similar factors govern the two. Moreover, as Landes (1969: 28) has pointed out, good innovators make good imitators. The reverse is equally true. Most successful technological societies – including medieval Europe and modern Japan – started as imitators and eventually evolved as innovators. As we shall see, this is also a good description of Britain during the industrial revolution. Closely related is the Schumpeterian distinction between invention and innovation. Schumpeter thought of them as two quite independent processes, but if invention is the creation or discovery of previously unknown techniques (improving *best*-practice techniques) and innovation the replacement of existing by superior techniques (improving *average*-practice techniques), the two are clearly complementary. Without invention, innovation will eventually run into diminishing returns when best-practice and average-practice techniques become very close. Without innovation, inventions remain as dormant as da Vinci's famous technical sketches. The creator of the *Mona Lisa* also left us with thousands of pages of sketches of machines and inventions, including aeroplanes, helicopters, tanks, elevators and diving suits – none of which were produced in his lifetime.

It is also customary among economists to distinguish between labour- and capital-saving innovations (see ch. 11). Some new techniques will decrease the ratio of labour to capital, while others will increase it. A technological change that decreases the ratio of labour to capital is said to have 'labour-saving bias'. These biases have been widely discussed, but at times they have created some confusion. First, even when the relative proportion of labour to capital declines, total output usually expands so as to more than compensate for this, so that 'labour-saving' inventions actually *increase employment*. Second, factor-saving biases can only be identified in models in which labour and capital are comparatively homogeneous. If technological change replaces skilled artisans with skilled proletarians, or replaces one form of capital with another, the measurement problems can become insuperable.

Third and most important, the discussion of factor biases in technological change has failed to emphasise that almost all technological change saves *all* factors of production relative to output, although it may save some more than others (von Tunzelmann 1990). It is therefore not necessarily correct that low-wage economies will be relatively less receptive to labour-saving innovations than high-wage economies. Even if labour is cheap, it always costs something. Thus, innovations that will save labour will reduce costs and increase efficiency, provided that the costs of installing the equipment which embodies the new techniques does not exceed the savings of labour. Moreover, labour is not like capital or land. Neoclassical economics ignores the fact that labour can strike, sabotage machinery, pick fights with other labourers and come to work on Monday with a hangover. Yet quite a few inventions in the industrial revolution were stimulated by workers' strikes, which prompted owners to replace labour by machines, not because machines were necessarily cheaper, but because they were more reliable and obedient (Bruland 1982).

Finally, inventions themselves can be usefully divided into door-opening breakthroughs, and gap-filling minor improvements in existing knowledge (Mokyr 1990a). In general, much of the popular literature is concerned with the great breakthroughs (macro-inventions), whereas economists seem widely agreed that most productivity gains are generated by the smaller improvements (micro-inventions).

The distinction between macro- and micro-inventions is to some extent arbitrary. Like the other distinctions listed above, there is a grey area in which the classification becomes subjective and ambiguous, but for most of the observed events a reasonable consensus seems plausible. The distinction is useful because of the fundamental complementarity of the two. If *all* inventions were small improvements on existing techniques, they would run into decreasing returns and eventually technological progress would peter out. No matter how you improve a horse-and-buggy, it will never become a bicycle. At the same time, very few macro-inventions succeeded without extended periods of improvement and refinement, during which a succession of minor improvements turned a curiosum into a major change in production technique. Moreover, micro-inventions occur at the margin and therefore seem to respond to economic stimuli, such as perceived needs and resource pressures, and are thus to some extent predictable. Macro-inventions, precisely because they consist of super-marginal changes and constitute a radical departure from established knowledge, often seem to defy economic logic. Yet macro-inventions open new avenues for subsequent research and create new 'technological paradigms' (Dosi 1988) and they remain the backbone of the industrial revolution.

The historical setting

Many scholars have tried to find some common denominator to the inventions that made the industrial revolution. In one view, mechanisation, the replacement of human physical exertion by machines, was the property of invention (Landes 1969). Others, such as Wrigley (1988) have emphasised the importance of substituting inorganic materials (coal and iron) for organic ones (animal power, wood). Cipolla (1965) has pointed to the steam engine and the energy revolution it entailed as the defining characteristic. Yet none of those distinctions captures the full richness of the thrust forward. As McCloskey and others have noted, the industrial revolution was not the age of cotton, of iron or of steam; it was the age of improvement (McCloskey 1985: 66). Before 1830, however, improvement was far from ubiquitous, and large sectors of the economy remained largely unaffected by technological progress.

In 1700, the vast bulk of national income in Britain was produced in or near people's homes. The home and the workplace were often indistinguishable. Shipping, shipbuilding, coal mining, brewing and a few specialised handicrafts were the exceptions to this rule, but otherwise it seems to apply quite generally to industries as disparate as textiles, chemical industries, charcoal making, and food processing. Even when capitalism had created large firms in which many workers were employed by merchant-manufacturers, the work itself typically was carried out in the labourer's home.

An old and by now discredited view of technological change has it that the household sector was incapable of sustained technological advances. Clearly, this was not the case: the flying shuttle, invented in 1733 by John Kay, is the best-known example of an innovation that was as useful in the workshop of a hand-loom weaver working at home as it was in larger 'proto-factories' in which workers were congregated under one roof. In iron, a similar invention was the 'oliver' or treddle hammer which doubled the productivity of the domestic nail maker (Rowlands 1989: 126). Berg (1985) in particular has argued that the cottage industries, of which most British manufacturing still consisted in the second half of the eighteenth century, generated many innovations which were capable of increasing productivity. All the same, technological progress engendered (and may itself again have been stimulated by) the beginning of the concentration of workers under one roof in factories and offices. While this concentration was not complete until the twentieth century, the industrial revolution began a set of changes that led to the eventual geographical divorce between household and firm, and between production and consumption.

Britain had a highly skilled labour force, perhaps more highly skilled than any other. But training was a strictly informal business. There was no formal education system that catered to the needs of industry, and the bulk of inventors were merchants or craftsmen whose remarkable ideas were often the result of luck, serendipity or inspiration. All the same, a small but highly distinguished class of technically skilled people emerged, whose mechanical abilities exceeded those of most mechanics and technicians. It is perhaps premature to speak of an 'invention industry' by this period, but clearly mechanical knowledge at a level beyond the reach of the run-of-mill artisan became increasingly essential to create the inventions associated with the industrial revolution. Engineers like Watt, Smeaton, Wilkinson, Rennie and Trevithick; chemists like Joshua Ward, John Roebuck and James Keir; watch and instrument makers like Benjamin Huntsman, Jesse Ramsden, Joseph Bramah and Henry Maudslay – none of these fit the convenient description of amateurs or gifted tinkerers. Though they lacked *formal* training, they thrived in an environment that encouraged and rewarded dexterity. A few of them were educated at Scottish universities or dissenting academies, but many were self-taught, through personal relations with masters, libraries, itinerant lecturers and so on (Musson 1972).

Yet the small number of inspired and creative minds that may be called inventors was not enough; what was needed, beyond the inventors, were the mechanics and craftsmen who could accurately build the devices according to specifications, using the correct dimensions and materials. Here more widely defined measures of human capital must have been of crucial importance. Britain may not have been much more literate than some other continental countries (e.g. Scandinavia, the Netherlands), but a higher emphasis on practical and mechanical skills among British workers may well have been a critical variable.

In addition, Britain provided considerable institutional support for technological progress. The political establishment, in London as well as in most of the provinces, recognised the importance of technological improvement as a source of progress for the nation. In addition to the patent system discussed below, private institutions encouraged the interaction between businessmen, scientists and practical persons with an interest in science and technology and a desire to use it to enrich themselves. In the two great London societies, the Royal Society (founded in 1662) and the Society of Arts (founded in 1754), as well as numerous smaller affairs in the provinces, information was exchanged, ideas compared and jealousies and rivalries were translated into emulation. By the middle of the eighteenth century, Britain contained an information network that created a well-lubricated machine that translated technological knowledge into more technological knowledge; a self-sustained engine of progress.

Technological change itself was concentrated in four main areas: textiles, energy utilisation, materials and 'miscellaneous'. However, all industries in which innovation was strong represented only a fraction of total industrial output and employment. Even when an activity or product was clearly transformed, the improvements of the industrial revolution rarely revolutionised an *entire* industry. At first innovations typically affected only a few stages or activities in an industry or activity, creating technological disequilibria between the branches where productivity increased and those in which nothing happened. But the spirit of improvement soon became epidemic. After the first stage, technological change spilled over into hitherto unaffected sectors, until mechanisation and rationalisation made the economy unrecognisable.

The textile industries

Traditionally, the cotton industry has been regarded as the central industry of the industrial revolution (Hobsbawm and Rudé 1968: 66ff). In many ways, however, cotton was atypical: starting as a local and rather marginal industry, it exploded into the most dynamic industry of Britain between 1760 and 1800. Despite the fact that the raw material had to come from long distances, the physical properties of the cotton fibre and fabrics were attractive. Cotton is a far more versatile and flexible fibre than linen or wool, easier to mechanise, and cotton fabrics are readily printed with the coloured patterns that people of the time desired. By the middle of the eighteenth century, south-eastern Lancashire was already deeply committed to cotton, although British spinners were still unable to spin as fine and strong a yarn as the Indian spinners. It was almost exclusively a domestic industry, carried out by workers toiling in their homes and small workshops, using spinning wheels, hand looms and manually operated printing presses. A few more substantial workshops, such as the ribbon industry and calico printing, employed more sophisticated equipment and thus contained what we would call today 'employees'. On the whole, however, this was a classical traditional industry, run on the principle of putting out work to labourers' homes.

The mechanisation of the cotton industry took place with unprecedented speed. The spinning of cotton was revolutionised in a short period of feverish invention. Until 1765, all yarn ever spun was twisted by human (usually female) fingers. Success in replacing human fingers was achieved first by Hargreaves, whose spinning jenny (1764) imparted the twist by rotating spindles, with the rovings guided by metal bars. It allowed the operator to spin a number of threads at the same time. The yarns were, however, not strong enough to serve as warps. Richard Arkwright's water frame (also known as throstle) used a set of rollers to draft out the fibres, an idea tried unsuccessfully in 1738 by Lewis Paul. The two machines were combined in 1779 in Crompton's mule, one of the most famous inventions ever made (Chapman 1972; Hills 1979). Mule spinning made it possible to spin finer and better yarns than could the Indian hand spinner, at a fraction of the cost. Soon combined with water and steam power, and made automatic with the invention of the self-actor in the 1820s, mules dominated the British cotton industry for more than a century.

Weaving was the obvious next locus of improvement. Previously, domestic weaving was largely a male occupation (as opposed to spinning which was predominantly female). Hand-loom weaving had become more productive with the introduction of the fly shuttle in the 1730s. Further mechanisation turned out to be difficult, and although Edmund Cartwright designed the first power loom in 1785, subsequent micro-inventions were slow in coming. Until 1820, power weaving remained experimental, with the predictable result that hand-loom weavers experienced a golden age between 1780 and 1820. After 1820 power looms were gradually improved so that they could weave finer and finer yarns. The decline of the hand-loom weaver in the 1830s was more protracted and painful than the decline of domestic spinning in the 1780s, but the outcome was just as inexorable.

Cotton manufacturing involved more than spinning and weaving. Many of the other stages of production experienced similar advances. The cotton gin, invented in the United States in 1793, did much to provide the rapidly growing industry with an elastically supplied raw material. Carding, which prepared the raw cotton bolls before the spinning by straightening the fibres through a combing-like procedure, was mechanised by the carding machine, employing cylinders patented by Arkwright in 1775. The carded cotton was then prepared into very rough and rudimentary 'pre-spun' yarn by a machine named the 'slubbing billy' which worked in a way similar to the jenny (invented in 1782). After weaving, the woven cotton cloth was usually a dirtyish grey, but consumers wanted white fabrics, and hence the woven fabric had to be bleached. Bleaching had traditionally been carried out on bleaching fields, using sunshine and primitive acids. An improvement was the use of vitriol (sulphuric acid) after the middle of the eighteenth century, once John Roebuck had replaced glass containers with lead chambers that were less fragile and could process larger quantities. The big breakthrough, however, came in 1784, when the French chemist Claude Berthollet discovered the bleaching properties of chlorine. The printing of coloured patterns on the bleached cloth, too, was mechanised. Copper printing cylinders, which printed coloured patterns by rolling action, were invented by Thomas Bell in 1783 and revolutionised the calico-printing industry.

Not every stage of cotton manufacturing was mechanised. The making of apparel remained a manual domestic industry, in which little changed until the invention of the sewing machine. At the other end of the production process, the planting and picking of cotton remained manual activities. All the same, the industry grew faster and its costs fell faster than any industry in previously recorded history. Chapman (1972) has calculated that the number of hours required to spin 100 lb of cotton fell from 50,000 by the Indian hand-spinning technology to 300 by machine in the 1790s. The price of a piece of cotton fell accordingly. Between 1779 and 1812, the costs of labour and capital (most of the value added) of cotton yarn declined by more than 85 per cent (Ellison 1886: 55). Recent research indicates that the money price of cotton goods remained about the same between 1770 and 1815, but because other prices had risen 50 per cent, this represents a substantial decline despite the fact that many stages of production, including weaving, had not yet been mechanised. By 1841, the price of a piece of cotton had fallen by two-thirds (Harley 1982: 271, 286–9). Prices are not a perfect indicator of improvements in technology, because costs of natural resources could have risen and because long-run supply curves are not flat so that demand could have affected prices. Yet as a first approximation it is a powerful indicator of the huge scale of the supply shift in the cotton industry.

Among the other textiles, silk, wool and linen experienced very different fates. Because silk requires very different physical manipulation than other fibres, the silk industry was the first to experience wholesale mechanisation. Silk is not spun into a fibre. Rather, the yarn is reeled off the silkworm cocoon by a process which is known as 'throwing'. Chinese and later Italian silk-throwing machines in the seventeenth century were, by the standards of the time, enormously complex. The silk-throwing works established in Derby by Thomas Lombe in 1717 contained a huge water wheel which drove thousands of smaller wheels and simultaneously threw and wound silk thread on a large scale. Further developments were slow in coming, however, and a century later the silk industry had fallen behind other textiles and was considered to be relatively backward (English 1958).

In the weaving of silk and other up-market textiles like worsted (a lighter fabric made of long-stapled wool that is combed rather than carded), a major breakthrough occurred in the form of the Jacquard loom, which automated the weaving of colours and patterns into the fabric. Unlike mass-produced cotton cloth which was printed, the up-market fabrics had the patterns woven into them using the so-called draw loom, which employed an assistant who manipulated pulleys and wires to make sure the right pattern was followed. Draw looms were laborious, expensive and often inaccurate. The Jacquard loom, invented in 1801 by Jean-Marie Jacquard, used coded punchcards, not unlike machine-readable computer cards, to control the patterns. These punchcards were probed by rods, and when a rod sensed a hole, it brought down another rod which activated the right coloured yarn. Thus, the need for the assistant was eliminated in one stroke and weaving became cheaper and more accurate. The binary coding whereby information was wholly conveyed by whether a rod detected a hole or not (equivalent to electronic circuits being in an 'on' or 'off' state) was revolutionary in manufacturing processes, and the Jacquard loom is thus a classic example of a macro-invention. The father of the idea of the modern computer, Charles Babbage, recognised Jacquard's breakthrough as a critical departure and owned a large portrait of Jacquard, appropriately made of woven silk.

Developments in the woollen industry were slower than in cotton. Woollen products were the largest industry in Britain before the industrial revolution and the largest component of exports and non-agricultural employment. Woollen cloth is made from the short-stapled, curly wool of merino sheep. The resistance of the fibre is such that the high-quality product required much preparation and finishing. The processes that prepared the raw wool for the spinning wheel were mechanised early, but although a primitive version of the jenny spread to some parts of the domestic industry, the mule was not adapted to spin woollen fibres until 1816. In weaving, similarly, mechanisation lagged behind the more versatile and flexible cotton yarns. The finishing processes of woollen cloth, on the other hand, lent themselves well to mechanisation. The hairy surface on the cloth (the 'nap') had to be raised and then trimmed off to ensure a glossy surface. A machine consisting of teasels in a revolving drum, known as the gig mill, and a shearing frame that replaced the workers who trimmed the finished cloth were introduced in the late eighteenth century. Steam engines in the finishing processes of wool appeared all over Yorkshire's West Riding, which became the centre of the industry.

In worsteds the order of technological change was reversed. Worsted fibres could easily be spun on mules. The combing of the wool which produced the lighter yarn that made worsteds special was hard to mechanise, however, and despite much experimentation, economically successful combing machines were not perfected until the middle of the nineteenth century. In the hosiery industry, too, change was unremarkable: the knitting frames, invented in the sixteenth century, remained the heart of the stocking manufacturers.

The history of linen, an ancient and venerable industry, and in many parts of Europe the leading textile industry, resembles that of the woollen rather than the cotton industry. Progress was slower and later than in cotton due to the physical properties of the fibre. A Frenchman, Philippe de Girard, discovered in 1810 that linen fibres could be spun mechanically if they were soaked in a hot alkaline solution before going to the spindles. De Girard's process was adopted (that is, pirated) in the big linen centres in Britain and Northern Ireland after 1825. Mechanical weaving was, however, slow to be adopted in linen, and hand-loom weavers remained dominant until the middle of the nineteenth century. The competition with cotton in the clothing market caused great grief to the industry, which ended up specialising in certain niches, particularly bedding and table-cloths.

To summarise, then, textiles show a complex and uneven pattern of progress. In the production of fibres and a number of activities in which the technical problems could be solved, there was rapid advance. In other stages, especially apparel making, progress came much later. The history of the industry illustrates that factories did not necessarily eliminate domestic industry immediately but could coexist with it, and at times closely cooperate with it. It is also quite obvious that technological advances could occur within the confines of the traditional sector. All the same, the overall trend is clearly one of mechanisation, of concentration and of growing productivity, producing cheaper, better and more versatile products. In the long run, the factory eliminated most of domestic production, though economic historians are not sure whether that was entirely the result of the new technology or whether other factors that favoured large-scale, concentrated enterprises played a role as well (Sabel and Zeitlin 1985). In this regard the textile industry is paradigmatic of the industrial revolution as a whole.

Energy utilisation

Energy comes to us in two forms: heat and work, also known as thermal and kinetic energy. Nineteenth-century physics has shown that the two are equivalent in certain respects and therefore can be converted into one another. The engineers of the eighteenth century did not understand this principle, yet it was they who made the first industrial application of the conversion of heat into work.

The first widespread use of devices that convert heat into work were firearms. The heat generated in the explosion causes the projectile to fly, and thus a gun is a one-cylinder combustion engine. No other applications of energy conversion were made until the discovery of atmospheric pressure in the seventeenth century. It then occurred to a number of people that, by heating a cylinder, one could create either a vacuum or a pressure chamber and then utilise the difference in pressure between the chamber and the environment to drive a piston in a cylinder; that is, an engine. A prototype was built by a Frenchman named Denis Papin in 1690, but the first operational steam engine was built by an Englishman, Thomas Newcomen, in 1712.

The Newcomen engine must be regarded as the first mechanical macro-invention to emanate from Britain since William Lee invented the stocking frame in 1589. It was important, not in its immediate economic impact (which was confined to pumping water from mines), but as a harbinger of things to come. Above all, it was radical in that it used a new physical principle. Steam engines, to be sure, had been used as toys in ancient Alexandria, but they had used the principle of the propulsive steam jet, not the force of pressure differentials which still propels our automobiles. Within a few decades, steam engines were pumping water out of mines in France, Germany, Spain and Hungary. By watching these machines at work, engineers and scientists came to realise the potential for the use of fossil fuels for work as well as for in heating, an idea that is still the cornerstone of our energy economy. Improvements in the Newcomen engine tried to curtail its voracious appetite for fuel but its low-energy efficiency confined it largely to coal mines.

What was needed were major design changes. One of them, the invention of the separate condenser by James Watt in 1765, is justly famous, to the point that Watt is often credited with the entire invention. The importance of Watt's idea was that Newcomen's original machine created steam and then condensed it by alternately heating and cooling a cylinder. Watt realised that if the main cylinder could be kept hot all the time, and condensation occurred in a separate cold vessel, the fuel savings could be huge (in fact, they increased fuel efficiency fourfold). Watt improved the steam engine in many other ways, including the all-important concept of double-acting expansion, automatic regulators known as 'governors', steam-jacketing and transmission gears (Dickinson 1958). In many ways, James Watt is a towering figure in the industrial revolution. He teamed up with a shrewd businessman, Matthew Boulton, thus relieving himself of the tedium of financial management. Yet he clearly understood the principle of *economic* efficiency (as distinguished from physical efficiency) and regarded reducing costs as a high priority. Steam engines were numerous in the late eighteenth century. It is now estimated that about 2,500 of them were built before 1800, of which Watt and Boulton accounted for about a third (Kanefsky and Robey 1980). Some steam engines were applied to textile machinery as early as 1784, but the importance of steam as a power source in manufacturing dates from the later 1790s.

Watt's engine had one dangerous competitor: the high-pressure engine. The idea of an engine that created a pressure chamber and thus utilised the difference between high pressure and the atmosphere (instead of that between the atmosphere and a vacuum) had been around for a long time, but Watt had resisted it. Because he held a wide-ranging patent, he succeeded in blocking its development for many years. In 1800, Watt's patent expired and the field of steam power was thrown wide open. Richard Trevithick built a successful prototype in 1802, and high-pressure engines were soon applied successfully in transportation and mining, whereas low-pressure engines like Watt's remained the prime form of steam power in manufacturing. The coexistence of low- and high-pressure engines are an instance of a phenomenon often observed in the history of technology, namely, that two similar technologies manage to work out a modus vivendi, dividing the market between them according to comparative advantage.

The same is true in some sense for the relation between steam power and water power. Water power played a central role in the power supply of the industrial revolution, more so at first than steam (von Tunzelmann 1978). This was not just because water power was a familiar and easy to control energy source, but primarily because despite its age, water-power technology showed an amazing agility and scope for improvement during this period (Reynolds 1983). John Smeaton, one of the most capable and versatile engineers of the period, perfected the breast wheel water mill, a revolutionary design which combined the advantages of the undershot and the overshot mills used since antiquity. The breast wheel takes its water neither from the summit of the wheel (as does the overshot mill) nor from the bottom (as does the undershot mill) but from a point in between, preventing spillage through a casing called the 'breast'. A number of micro-inventions followed, including the increasing use of metal parts, Rennie's sliding hatch and Poncelet's wheel using curved blades which reduced the cost and increased the reliability of water power. The growing efficiency of water power delayed in many areas the introduction of steam power.

The survival of water power demonstrates that sluggishness in the introduction of a certain new technique is by no means sufficient evidence of backwardness; as in textiles, many of the old techniques proved themselves amenable to transformation and survived. The developments in water power also demonstrate the fact that to view the industrial revolution as a switch from wood and animate energy to a coal-using economy is somewhat misleading. The consumption of coal increased enormously during the industrial revolution; yet in coal mining itself changes were relatively minor. The application of steam power to pump water from mines and haulage was clearly a step forward. Safety increased due to better ventilation and the Davy safety lamp. Yet the very core of the process remained the miner, working away with pick and shovel. The increase in coal consumption was clearly demand, not supply driven and the price of coal did not fall nearly as much as that of textiles. The progress of the coal industry was determined by technological developments outside the industry.

Metallurgy

Iron goes through two processes before it can be made into something useful. First, the raw ore is smelted in blast furnaces to produce pig-iron (the term is owed allegedly to the fact that the liquid metal flows out from different gates in the furnaces, forming little puddles of congealed iron that look a little bit like a sow nursing its piglets). The high-carbon pig-iron then has to be refined into wrought-iron by decarburisation.

The eighteenth century is famous for two major inventions in the processing of iron. One of these was the use of coke, a fuel derived from coal, instead of charcoal in smelting. Coke smelting was less of a breakthrough than might be imagined. The use of fossil fuels had been steadily increasing in Britain since the middle ages, and coke (refined coal, containing practically nothing but pure carbon) had been used in malting. In 1709, Abraham Darby succeeded in using coke in a blast furnace, in which iron ore was melted and turned into pig-iron, the basic raw material of the iron industry. The myth that the use of coke was brought about by a growing scarcity of wood in a classic response of technology to factor prices has been put to rest by Flinn (1959, 1978). The main advantage of coke was that it required less labour than charcoal. Yet coked iron was not at first of the quality of charcoal iron; subsequent experimentation showed that the main problem, that of silicone contamination, could be solved through remelting in a special foundry furnace that could produce very high temperatures. Better furnaces and stronger bellows (water-driven blowing cylinders were introduced by Smeaton in 1762) helped in bringing about the widespread use of coke smelting in the British iron industry after 1760 (Hyde 1977).

The produce of the blast furnace, pig-iron, was high in carbon and thus hard and brittle. For most industrial uses what was needed was wrought-(bar-) iron. Refining pig-iron was a difficult art, practised largely in small forges through repeated heating and hammering. After much experimentation, Henry Cort in 1784 suggested a path-breaking invention in which the pig-iron was first heated in a reverberatory furnace (in which the ceiling reflected heat) then puddled (stirred) to bring impurities to the surface, and then squeezed and pressed by cylinders in a rolling mill. Cort's method, after a few years of further improvement, turned out to be a spectacular success. The price of wrought-iron declined rapidly, and puddling furnaces and rolling mills supplied much of the raw materials used in the construction of the machinery associated with the industrial revolution. Output increased by about 500 per cent between 1788 and 1815 and the price of wrought-iron fell from £22 per ton to £14 per ton between 1801 and 1815 (Hyde 1977: 106). In 1829 James Neilson discovered that by using a blast furnace's own gases to preheat the air he could save on fuel costs and attain higher temperatures so that other fuels than coke could be used.

Steel, a form of iron intermediate between pig- and wrought-iron, combined the hardness of pig-iron with the versatility of wrought-iron. High-quality steel had been made since antiquity, especially after the perfection of the crucible or cast-steel technique by Benjamin Huntsman in 1740. The technique used a furnace employed by glassblowers and coke to heat the metal to hitherto unattainable temperatures that allowed it to be poured. But crucible steel was expensive and could only be made in small ingots. Wrought-iron, not steel, was the material of which the first industrial revolution was made. Despite repeated attempts by economists to relate technological progress to 'demand factors' it is clear that certain problems, such as cheap steel, faced a simple supply constraint; nobody knew how to solve the technological problem (Rosenberg 1976: 108–25, 260–79).

How do we assess the importance of the iron industry in the industrial revolution? The economist's test of the importance of any invention is its substitutability: if it had not been invented, would another technology have done? By that criterion, the steam engine and cotton look less of a strategic invention than the advances in iron. It is conceivable to imagine an industrial revolution based on water power and linen or wool – in fact in many places that is precisely what happened. There was no substitute for iron, however, in thousands of uses, from nails to engines. As its price fell, iron invaded terrains traditionally dominated by timber, such as bridges, ships and eventually buildings.

Other areas of progress

In addition to textiles, power and materials, the industrial revolution witnessed a host of changes in other industries. In chemicals, in part an ancillary industry to textiles, the most important breakthroughs were the development of chlorine bleaching, already mentioned above, and the invention of the soda-making process by Nicholas Leblanc in 1787. Soda was an important raw material, used in soap and detergent manufacturing as well as in gunpowder manufacturing.

The development of gas-lighting after 1798 is another case of an unsung macro-invention. Before the industrial revolution the technology of lighting had been static and confined to candles and primitive oil burners. The revolutionary nature of gas-lighting stemmed from the realisation that gas was something that could be burned in a controllable way (Holmyard 1958; Schivelbusch 1988). Gas-lighting, like chlorine bleaching, was first demonstrated in France, and then taken to Britain where William Murdock, who worked for Boulton and Watt, improved it by the use of coal gas instead of a gas derived from wood. By 1820 streets, factories, theatres and soon private homes were lit by gas. In terms of the novelty of the concept and its impact on daily life at home, the development of gas-lighting was not less revolutionary than the steam engine. Moreover, by setting up a central supply system to which customers were connected, gas-lighting became one of the first 'network' technologies, preparing the ground for similar systems (water, sewage, electric power, telephone) later in the nineteenth century.

The machine-tool industry was strategic to other industries. In order to produce their engines, Boulton and Watt, Trevithick, Stephenson and their colleagues required accurately constructed parts. Without the work-manship and materials to produce parts made according to specification, many of the best technological ideas of the period would have remained on the drawing board. It was precisely here that Britain had the biggest advantage. On the eve of the industrial revolution it could count on mechanics and instrument makers working in the shipping and mining industries; it had large-scale ironmasters whose fame was world wide (including the Scottish Carron works and the Welsh Cyfarthfa works) and small-scale metal goods makers known as the Birmingham toy trade; it also had one of the leading clock-making industries in Europe. From these traditions came an industry which was able to *build* machines, not just design them. Among the most important members of this trade were John Wilkinson, who bored the cylinders for Watt's steam engines; the machine tool makers Joseph Bramah (who also invented the water closet in 1778) and Henry Maudslay, a specialist in machine parts; instrument makers such as Jesse Ramsden; and engineers such as James Nasmyth, Bryan Donkin and Marc Isambard Brunel. Milling machines, planing machines, screw-cutting lathes, boring and sawing machines, and accurate measuring machines became the foundation of the machine industry. As Rosenberg (1976) has emphasised, the machine tool industry lies at the very foundation of mechanisation, and without accuracy and uniformity, modern mechanical technology could not exist.

In a few consumer goods, too, there was significant progress. The pottery industry is often cited as a good example of a progressive industry, despite the absence of great breakthroughs after John Astbury of Staffordshire produced the first salt-glazed earthenware in 1720. Josiah Wedgwood imaginatively applied the new technologies that became available in his time to his factory in Burslem, including steam power and chemicals. Above all, he adopted the rationalisation of production in the organisation of his factories, introducing a fine division of labour and quality control and at the same time skilfully adjusting to changes in demand. In glass making, the British adopted the French cast-plate process in window and mirror glass making. In paper, the Fourdrinier machine invented by the Frenchman Robert in 1798 and improved by the English mechanic Bryan Donkin changed the industry by converting it from the manufacture of single sheets to rolls of continuous paper. The same Donkin set up a food canning factory in 1810 and British sailors in the war of 1812 enjoyed canned soup and meat. In road construction, agricultural implements and sugar refining, the wave of innovations that swept Britain after 1760 was broad and wide.

All the same, large segments of the British economy were largely unaffected by technological innovation. It is incorrect to associate the industrial revolution in its early stages with the domination of factories or 'mills' as they were called: technological change penetrated into smaller workshops and domestic industry as well, and factories remained for a long time confined to a handful of industries. Much of the traditional industry remained just that. In construction, transportation, shipbuilding, retailing and many of the artisanal industries, from apparel makers to hardware forges to bakeries, the changes were slow. If the industrial revolution was like a gentle rain, writes McCloskey (1985: 58), the ground by 1860 was wet but not soaked even if a few puddles had gathered here and there. Yet, to continue the metaphor, after that came the deluge.

Gradual change is what one should expect: in a complex organism like an economy, 'revolutions' are by definition relatively drawn-out affairs. Technology changed single processes, sometimes industries. But for the economy *as a whole* to switch from manual techniques to a mechanised production required the ingenuity of hundreds of inventors, thousands of innovating entrepreneurs and tens of thousands of mechanics, technicians and dexterous rank and file workers. A self-organised system such as technology is inevitably dominated by inertia so that change spreads like an epidemic, emanating from a small number of starting points and gradually 'infecting' the economy as a whole. After the main waves of macro-inventions were completed in 1830, the economy needed at least four more decades during which the advances were consolidated and the new ideas spread to hitherto unaffected regions and industries.

Explanations

Any *single* explanation of the events described above is unlikely to persuade many readers. Clearly, Britain was fertile soil for technological ideas, and provided a relatively hospitable background to innovators. But a fertile soil without seeds will grow nothing but weeds. A sketch of the main institutional and economic factors that seem to have made progress possible is therefore necessary, followed by a discussion of the intellectual origins of technological progress.

Economics is a science of incentives, and innovation cannot be understood separately from its rewards. In eighteenth-century Britain, more perhaps than any other society before it, technological change was rewarded. Ancient prejudices, which regarded intellectual efforts devoted to production as something unfit for decent gentlemen, though not quite dead, no longer dominated British society. It was becoming socially acceptable to make money from industry, and therefore from innovation.

How did an inventor make money? First, Britain had a fully operational patent system in the eighteenth century, although some other countries had mechanisms which attempted to do the same. A patent was a fourteen-year monopoly awarded to the first one to think of a particular idea. Many of the inventors during the industrial revolution patented their inventions, though many others did not. Whether patents on the whole turned out to be a great benefit for inventors is much in doubt (Mokyr 1990a). Many patentors were ruined by endless court cases while suing competitors who had infringed on their patents, or lost their patent for some reason. What seems clear, however, is that people believed at the time that patents would guarantee a high return on their successful invention. Even if they were mistaken about this most of the time, the system enticed many would-be inventors to spend time, money and efforts in searching for a technological improvement (Dutton 1984). Second, society might reward the successful inventor through an official body awarding him a prize or a pension. In pre-revolutionary France this was the dominant mode of encouraging invention, but in Britain, too, some inventors, who for one reason or another failed to benefit from the patent system, received grants and pensions from Parliament in recognition of their contribution.

More than anything, however, the rewards of innovation were the profits earned by the innovating entrepreneur who could produce goods cheaper or better than his competitors. A patent may have been successful in keeping competitors out, thus giving the inventor a period in which he could relax and watch the money come in. Even without a patent, however, the profits earned during the period in which the competition had not fully caught up and driven the price down could be substantial; at times they were far more substantial than the monopolistic returns from a patent. Arkwright lost his legal battle for the patent right to his throstle, yet amassed an enormous fortune. These periods during which inventors earned quasi-rents could be extended by trying to keep some techniques secret, as Huntsman did for his crucible steel. Patenting demanded full disclosure of the technical details, so secrecy and application for a patent were often mutually exclusive. An inventor of a new machine could thus choose between three options: he could patent his machine and make his money selling licences to other users; he could make the machines himself under patent or secrecy protection and sell them; and he could make the machines and operate them himself, making his money by selling the final product. Watt chose the former routes, Arkwright the latter. In almost any industry we can find examples of these different cases, as well as combinations of them. To enhance the profitability of innovation, it was important to restrict the entry of potential competitors. Beside patenting and secrecy, innovative entrepreneurs used control of marketing channels, control of raw materials and parts and high capital costs.

Was the incentive system in Britain superior to that of other countries? MacLeod (1991) has cast serious doubt on the matter: the British patent system was ineffective, expensive and often provided little or no support for invention. France, her belated official patent law in 1791 notwithstanding, was enormously creative and its government followed an explicit if sometimes inconsistent policy of encouragement of inventions. A large number of the macro-inventions made during the industrial revolution indeed originated in France. Although their contributions to steam power and cotton spinning were not large, French inventors played a major role in all other industries in the British industrial revolution. What is surprising, then, is not that these inventions were made there at all but that they were usually exploited earlier and with greater success in Britain than in France, and that France was sluggish in returning the favour. A successful explanation of this fact would be a step towards answering the question of the secret of British success during the industrial revolution, assuming that what is true for France is true a fortiori for Germany and other parts of Europe.

A few hypotheses can be ruled out from the start. The notion that Britain provided a bigger market or that there was somehow a 'higher demand' there which led to the inventions that made the industrial revolution clearly is unsatisfactory by itself. France's population was three times bigger than Britain's, and while Britain probably had a better position in colonial markets, France had the edge in continental Europe. Moreover, the *overall* level of demand was not very relevant for individual innovators. Economic analysis suggests that, in an industry with many competitive firms, it is advantageous for a single firm to introduce a cost-saving innovation independent of the overall level of demand. The notion that 'necessity is the mother of invention' and that demand somehow generates a supply response in the form of inventions cannot be accepted without serious qualification.

To be sure, research and development – then and now – are stimulated by the expected payoff from a successful invention. The payoff is sometimes thought to be a function of the demand for a final good. Yet it is not clear precisley what is meant by that: an invention in a small market might create a 'niche' for an engaging entrepreneur. Economists raise a more serious objection: demand is itself a function of the changes in price and quality engendered by changing technology. In 1750, cotton was a small industry compared to wool; in 1850, the roles were reversed, but it is hard to believe that inventors such as Arkwright and Crompton could have foreseen that. Others have argued that the efforts devoted to new technology are believed to be a function of a technological disequilibrium or 'bottle-neck' created by technological advances in complementary processes (Landes 1969: 84–7). Thus the invention of the flying shuttle, which increased the productivity in weaving, raised the payoff of progress in spinning, bleaching and carding. Increased 'demand' for an invention should be seen as a 'focusing device' (Rosenberg 1976: 108–25): it directs the search into a particular trajectory.

Another way in which demand could be important is through economy-wide scale effects. A large market, as Adam Smith noted, encourages a fine division of labour. A high division of labour may be conducive to technological change. By breaking the production process into components, it mechanises it stage by stage. Integrated markets and a high level of demand would thus stimulate innovation (Szostak, 1991). Yet evidence on the connection between specialisation and innovation is still not conclusive, and on a priori grounds the reverse can be made just as plausible. Furthermore, invention and development involved substantial sunk costs, so that a certain minimum scale of sales would be necessary to cover these costs. Matthew Boulton wrote to Watt that 'it is not worth my while to manufacture [your engine] for three counties only, but I find it well worth my while to make it for all the world'. Yet regardless of whether Boulton was correct in this instance, the number of inventions for which the overhead cost was so large during that period was small. Moreover, if 'all the world' was the market, the *relative* advantage of Britain is far from clear. Indeed, successful continental manufacturers in 'small' economies such as the Belgian John Cockerill and the Swiss J. C. Fischer succeeded by expanding their businesses beyond their borders. Demand, then, was not the central factor, even if it had something to contribute.

Nor does it seem very plausible to argue that Britain's mineral deposits in and of themselves played a central role in giving it a technological edge. Much of the best iron was still imported from Spain and Sweden, and cotton production was entirely based on an imported raw material. Britain did have a large supply of coal, but by itself this did not lead to technological change any more than Saudi Arabia's oil has made it a leader in petrochemical engineering. Steam engines could – and did – run on anything that could burn, including peat and wood. It may be true, as Cardwell (1972: 74) has maintained, that the mining industry created technological problems whose solution had economy-wide repercussions. The steam engine, after all, started as an attempt to make a better pump. Yet if these advantages were in and of themselves of such importance, the slowness of technological progress in mining areas outside Britain and Belgium remains unexplained. Technological progress is as often linked to scarcity of resources as it is linked to their abundance. It has been argued that coal and iron technologies advanced under the pressure of resource and energy crises. There is some doubt whether this inference is historically valid. Von Tunzelmann (1993) suggests that what is needed is a general equilibrium model linking technology to relative prices. At this stage it is safe to say that natural resources, like demand, were at best something like a steering mechanism; yet it is the engine, not the steering wheel, that makes a car run.

Another argument, closely associated with the work of Habakkuk (1962), suggests that high wages stimulated labour-saving innovations, thus accounting for mechanisation. However, real wages were not rising during the industrial revolution, nor is there evidence that the regions in which technological progress was the fastest were high-wage areas. As was argued above, many of the critical innovations saved as much capital, time, fuel and raw material as they saved labour. In fact, high wages or low wages tend to be related to economic change in complex ways, depending on the determinants of wage levels. If wages were high because labour was skilled, motivated and productive, unit labour costs might have been lower (Mokyr 1991a).

One critical factor explaining Britain's advantage, which has so far not received much attention, was that between 1789 and 1815 France, and much of the rest of the Continent, had its attention directed elsewhere. The coincidence of the industrial revolution in Britain with the French Revolution and subsequent wars and upheavals in Europe helped determine the relative technological performance in both countries. It has been maintained that the war-effort stimulated technological progress, and a few instances can be cited that appear to confirm this (McNeil 1982). Cort's discovery of the puddling and rolling technique was clearly associated with military demand as Cort was a contractor for the admiralty. The military connection here, however, was largely accidental. The famous Portsmouth docks in which two of the best engineers of the period, Henry Maudslay and Marc Brunel, cooperated in a pioneering effort to mass-produce wooden gears and pulleys for ships on a basis of interchangeability and identical parts was a direct outcome of the war. Their efforts seem, however, to have produced no feedbacks to the civilian economy. In France, the enormous demand for ordnance, guns, uniforms, shoes and other military supplies had little positive effect on the technological level of industry, and the political and military shocks siphoned off the energy and attention of the French and German elites toward directions other than civilian technology. Talent and energy were wasted and at times destroyed. The great chemist Lavoisier, who spearheaded an effort to improve saltpetre production, was executed in 1794. Other inventors and engineers experienced disruptions during the French Revolution which halted their technological creativity (Mokyr 1990a: 253n). Moreover, the disruption of communications and trade between Britain and the Continent after 1793 slowed the diffusion of technology across the Channel (though it encouraged the creation of 'hothouse industries' benefiting from the protection provided by war). In short, the wars and political turbulence between 1793 and 1815 damaged the British economy, but damaged the Continent even more. They deepened and widened the chasm between Britain and the Continent, even if they did not create it.

A further difference that gave Britain an advantage relative to other countries is to be found in what may be called 'the political economy of technological change' (Mokyr 1992). Technological change almost inevitably ruffles feathers, because some economic agents have an interest in the existing technological state of affairs and would lose out if the new technology was widely adopted. This happens when people have assets, such as physical capital goods or skills, that are specific to the 'old' technology and cannot be readily converted to the new technology. In the terminology of economics, capital is specific and non-malleable. A profit-maximising agent, who is concerned with his or her own wealth (as economists believe people are), and not with that of society as a whole, will try to resist technological change if it will make him or her worse off. Resistance also occurs when new technology disrupts communities, threatens jobs, makes skills obsolete, alters labour relations and upsets customs and traditions. There are two avenues through which such resistance can take place: through the laws and institutions of the economy, and through illegal acts such as strikes, sabotage and violence.

Resistance against new machinery during the industrial revolution was well organised and energetic; in some cases and areas it slowed technological progress (Randall 1991). Parliament was inundated with petitions trying to enforce antiquated quality regulations and restrictions which would have retarded the adoption of new techniques. Time and again, groups and lobbies turned to Parliament to request the enforcement of old regulations or the introduction of new legislation that would hinder the machinery. Parliament refused. The old laws regulating the employment practices in the woollen industry were repealed in 1809, and the 250-year-old Statute of Artificers was repealed in 1814. When legal means failed, the vested interests took to rioting, culminating in the famous 'Luddite' riots in the northern midlands between 1811 and 1816. The identification of technophobic activity is not always easy because not all riots tagged as 'Luddite' were in fact aimed against the new technology as such (Thomis 1972). In some cases, machines provided an easy target for workers with other grudges.

Resistance to innovation failed in large part because the British government stood firm, and the Luddite riots and similar outbursts were suppressed, the leaders deported and the new machines given the protection they needed. The ruling establishment (mostly landed gentlemen) took this attitude because it fully realised that resistance to technological progress would only lead to its flight abroad, and thus benefit Britain's competitors and enemies. The ruling elites, however, also knew that they stood to gain privately from the new technologies, as land values around water-power sites, coal mines and urban areas soared. The social classes who stood to lose from the industrial revolution, the domestic weavers, the wool finishers, small artisans and merchants had little political influence. In the absence of guilds and strong professional associations, and in the face of a determined and well-organised government supporting the innovators, the losers were powerless to stop the relentless progress of mechanisation and technological change. When organisation was strong, as in the case of the Yorkshire wool-finishers, it was met head-on by the full power of the British government. Unlike the Continent, where resistance was at times strong and in some places highly effective, Britain's political economy was, at least for a while, ideally suited to technological progress.

In addition to institutional factors, the difference between Britain and other countries in their capability to produce and absorb technological progress depended upon the *individual* agents who were responsible for it: inventors, engineers and entrepreneurs. In other words, in addition to the incentive structure and the social constraints under which innovators worked, preferences and human capital were central to the understanding of technological success. New technology is new knowledge, and it is crucial to focus on the supply side, that is, how new knowledge was created and transmitted through the economy.

Modern scholarship seems to have reached two basic conclusions. First, the direct impact of science on the technological advances during the industrial revolution was relatively modest, but more subtle interactions between persons of learning and dexterous persons of enterprise did make a contribution. Second, there was a difference between the social and cultural nature of technical knowledge in Britain and the Continent. These differences were partially responsible for the technological gaps that emerged during the industrial revolution.

The notion that somehow British technological success was due to Britain having more advanced science is quite false. The premise itself is in dispute (Kuhn 1977: 43) but even if it were true, the technology developed during the British industrial revolution owed little to scientific knowledge. The inventions that set the British changes in motion were largely the result of mechanical intuition and dexterity, the product of technically brilliant but basically empirical tinkerers like Wilkinson, Smeaton, Trevithick and Stephenson. In a few cases, such as Berthollet's chlorine bleaching and Humphry Davy's safety lamp, inventions were made by scientists of note, but that correlation does not prove that science itself was of great importance. Leading scientists were not wholly specialised at this time, and dabbled in technology, as Galileo, Huygens, Hooke and Leibniz had a century earlier.

If science played a role in the industrial revolution, it was neither through the 'pure' foundation of technology on scientific understanding nor through the role of scientists in invention, but through the penetration of 'scientific method' into technological research: accurate measurement, controlled experiment, insistence on reproducibility and systematic reporting of materials and methods. Even more important, perhaps, is a scientific mentality, which taught engineers a rational faith in the orderliness and predictability of natural phenomena – even if the actual laws underlying chemistry and physics were not fully understood (Parker 1984: 27–8). The scientific revolution taught engineers the 'method of detail', analysing technical problems by breaking them into separate components that could be more easily analysed separately than as a whole (Pacey 1975: 137). Engineers such as Telford, Smeaton and Rennie moved effortlessly between experimental science and practical applications. George Stephenson, a prime example of this ability himself, wrote of the great Smeaton as having a 'truly Baconian mind' – a description that fits an entire class of British engineers active between 1760 and 1830.

In many cases science provided implicit theoretical underpinnings to what was done by empirically minded technicians, even if the complete scientific base had not been fully worked out. Thus the steam engine depended on the understanding of atmospheric pressure, discovered by continental scientists such as Torricelli and Guericke, which somehow must have filtered down to Newcomen despite the fact that his world was the local blacksmith's rather than the cosmopolitan academic scientist's. Chlorine bleaching depended on the discovery of chlorine by the Swedish chemist Carl Wilhelm Scheele in 1774. Phlogiston theory, the ruling physical paradigm of the eighteenth century, was eventually rejected in favour of the new chemistry of Lavoisier; but some of its insights (e.g. the Swede Tobern Bergman's contributions to metallurgy) were valuable even if their scientific basis was flawed. Cardwell (1972: 41–3) has shown that the idea of a measurable quantity of 'work' or 'energy' derives directly from Galileo's work on mechanics. The advances in water and steam power in the eighteenth century depended on this scientific base. More often, of course, bogus science produced bogus results, as in Jethro Tull's insistence that air was the best fertiliser. In the 'development' stage of the basic inventions, in which revolutionary insights were improved, modified and debugged to turn them into successful business propositions, science played essentially no role.

British science and scientists occupied a different position in society than elsewhere. As Kuhn states, the old cliché that British science was pragmatic and applied whereas French science was abstract, deductive and formal seems to have survived the test of time (1977: 137). The origins of this phenomenon may be traced to the intellectual bifurcation of the seventeenth century, when British science came under the influence of Bacon whereas in France more Cartesian ideals triumphed. Bacon argued that the purpose of science was to raise comforts and living standards, whereas the French traditions followed more lofty objectives. Bacon's science was empirical, experimental and pragmatic whereas French science was theoretical and abstract. Such generalisations are inevitably hazardous, but water power provides at least one persuasive example. In Britain research on water power was conducted by practical engineers such as Smeaton, John Banks, John Rennie and William Fairbairn, in search of a better water mill. On the Continent work on water power was largely theoretical and carried out by mathematicians such as Antoine Parent, Johann Euler and Jean Charles Borda (Reynolds 1983: 196–265).

Yet the roots of the differences go beyond that. Jacob (1988) has argued that in Britain scientists were part of the economic establishment, not of the opposition. They regarded it as a natural state of the world to cooperate with engineers and manufacturers to solve pragmatic technical problems. The interactions between them, as we have seen, were institutionalised in the various scientific and philosophical societies that provided the meeting places, and informal contacts further strengthened these ties. Even some members of the landowning elite displayed a strong interest in technology, in part for economic reasons but also out of sheer interest. The Earl of Dundonald, the Viscounts of Dudley and Ward, the Earl of Balcarres and others were deeply interested in the new technologies. Thus the communication between the scientists, the engineers and the entrepreneurs was strong, and they engaged in a common effort to recognise technical problems and solve them (Musson and Robinson 1969).

These special conditions of Britain's 'supply of technological knowledge' take us back to the earlier notion of the difference between macro-inventions and micro-inventions. Any period of successful technological creativity requires both fundamental breakthroughs and small, incremental, often anonymous improvements that take place *within* known techniques. The secret of British technological success was that it had a *comparative* advantage in *micro*-inventions. This may seem unorthodox to those who think of the milestones set by Trevithick, Arkwright and Cort, but it should be recalled that it is possible to have an absolute advantage in both areas yet a comparative advantage in one, although it is not altogether clear whether Britain had an *absolute* advantage in macro-invention. Apart from steam and cotton technology, most of the truly revolutionary inventions of the time originated in France – including the most spectacular of all inventions of the time, though at the time not of great economic importance: human flight through ballooning.

Evidence for the statement that the British comparative advantage was in improvement and not in originality comes in part from contemporary sources. In a widely cited comment, a Swiss calico printer remarked in 1766 that for a thing to be perfect it has to be invented in France and worked out in England (Wadsworth and Mann 1931: 413). In 1829, the engineer John Farey stated that the prevailing talent of English and Scottish people was to apply new ideas to use and to bring such applications to perfection, but they do not 'imagine' as much as foreigners (Musson 1975: 81). Continental Europeans felt frustrated, reflecting Leibniz's prophetic words, written in 1670: 'it is not laudable that we Germans were the first in the invention of mechanical, natural, and other arts and sciences, but are the last in their expansion and betterment' (cited in Clark 1991). A test of the theory of comparative advantage is in the establishment of net trade directions. Economies tend to specialise in the areas in which they have a comparative advantage. The British economy, to put it crudely, imported macro-inventions and exported micro-inventions and minor improvements. It took its major inventions where it could find them, but whatever it borrowed, it improved and refined.

The case of chlorine bleaching is revealing here: Scheele and Berthollet clearly produced the original breakthrough, but the commercial value of the idea was recognised by James Watt (whose father-in-law, James McGrigor, was a Glasgow bleacher) and a series of British chemists and entrepreneurs set to improve on the original invention (Musson and Robinson 1969: 251–337). The definitive improvement came when a Scottish bleacher, Charles Tennant, replaced potash with slaked lime as the solution in which chlorine was absorbed. Chemical bleaching, a continental macro-invention, was made into bleaching powder, a British improvement. Something similar is true for gas-lighting, which like bleaching originated on the Continent, but found its first successful applications in Britain. Similar patterns can be discerned in continuous-sheet paper making (where the Frenchman N. L. Robert made the crucial invention) and in food canning (invented by the Frenchman N. Appert, but first exploited on a commercial scale by English manufacturers). Philippe de Girard's revolutionary wet spinning process of flax was adopted successfully in Yorkshire and Scotland. The use of the binary coding of information, pioneered by the French Jacquard loom, was applied successfully to engineering by Richard Roberts (Mokyr 1991c). In short, ideas flowed from the Continent to Britain, whereas finished machines and working technologies – prohibitions on their export notwithstanding – flowed back to the Continent.

A similar pattern can be discerned in the movement of people. Inventors with major new ideas moved from the Continent to Britain. Among those of particular importance are Marc Isambard Brunel, a French engineer; J. G. Bodmer, a Swiss tool and instrument maker and a pioneer in interchangeable parts; Aimé Argand, inventor of the revolutionary Argand lamp; Friedrich Koenig, the inventor of cylindrical printing applied to newspaper and book printing. As Henderson (1954) argued, Britain repaid the Continent many times over with the export of a huge flow of technicians and engineers who helped export British technical knowledge. These British emigrants were rarely accomplished inventors, but in setting up textile, machinery and iron industries on the Continent, they had to make exactly those small improvements and adaptations to local conditions that account for most productivity gains. Names like Cockerill, Hodson, Ainsworth and Wilson are part and parcel of the industrial revolution in the Low Countries. In France there were the Manby family, John Holker, Job Dixon, Isaac Holden. In the Ruhr the Irishman W.T. Mulvany became a leading industrialist, while in Thüringen the textile industry was modernised by John Douglas. Similar influences can be documented in Switzerland and the Habsburg Empire. Moreover, hundreds of engineers and entrepreneurs from every country on the Continent travelled to Britain to observe and absorb the production technology they took back home.

If it is true that Britain had a comparative advantage in 'small' technology, how do we explain it? In part, it was a more tolerant environment to work in, as Karl Marx would be the first to agree. But an inventor needs more than a society willing to put up with rebels and deviants. In part, it was related to Britain's human capital. Inventions cannot be realised without subcontractors who can supply parts and materials according to specifications and skilled workers able to carry out plans from blueprints accurately not just once but over and over again. Britain's technological strength during the industrial revolution depended above all on the abundance and quality of its skilled mechanics and practical technicians who could turn great insights into productive applications. Britain had a large and impressive skilled labour force, but surely in this it was not unique in Europe. The difference was not in the level or spread of skills but in their nature.

How were these skilled workers trained? In pre-1750 Europe, most skilled artisans catered to basic consumer needs – bakers, millwrights, tailors, thatchers, shoemakers, carpenters – traditional craftsmen who carried out their trades in traditional Europe between the Vistula and the mountains of Donegal. Another class of skilled labourers, particularly developed on the Continent, specialised in luxury-good manufacturing. Draw-loom operators, perfume makers, porcelain makers, mirror and glass producers, wig makers, confectioners and arms makers catered to the rich and powerful.

In Britain, the specialised craftsmen were directed toward mechanical skills. One group was clock makers, many of whom emigrated to Britain from France after 1685 in large numbers and played an important role in eighteenth-century inventions (Landes 1983: 219). Another cluster of mechanics was created around Britain's ever-growing shipping industry; sawyers, shipwrights and makers of navigational instruments were protected by the Navigation Acts and buoyed by the rising level of commerce. Mining required specialised engineers, pumps and iron rails. Calico printing, glass-blowing, pottery, wool finishing and a number of other specialised industries also drew upon and contributed to the mechanical skills of Britain's labour force. These industries provided the kind of skills that came in handy during the industrial revolution: cutting and fitting of wooden and metal parts, manipulating chemicals, designing and constructing complex moving-parts machines, the handling of high-temperature reverberatory furnaces and so on (Mathias 1979: 33). Britain, of course, had no monopoly in these industries, but the large pool of mechanical skills, together with the direction provided by a society favourably inclined toward technological and material culture, gave it an advantage.

Unlike other European economies, the British government had virtually nothing to do with technical education. In France and in Germany the *grandes écoles* and the *technische Hochschüle*, many of which were founded during the industrial revolution or as a response to it, were central in providing technical education; in Britain technical training remained firmly entrenched in the venerable apprentice system. Formal education was of little help. The complaint of the author of an anonymous tract published in 1680 that 'our Youth never read any thing of Manufacture, Exportation, or Importation in *Homer* or *Virgil* or their Colledge Notes' was apt a century later as well (McCulloch 1954: 357). Though Britain was practically free of the rigid regulations of the medieval guilds, the only way to learn a trade was to learn it from somebody else, on the job. Father-and-son, or master-and-apprentice dynasties emerged even among Britain's best engineers. The Stephensons and the Brunels were the most famous father-and-son dynasties, and Bramah–Maudslay–Roberts the best-known master-and-apprentice dynasty.

For many years, this system of informal practical training supplied the British economy with the technical skills it needed. Gifted mechanics who were good with their hands relied on experience and intuition, not theory. Many of the important inventors in the industrial revolution were members of the middle class, who were apprenticed to skilled craftsmen (Landes 1969: 62). Moreover, on-the-job training turned out to be remarkably flexible. Apprentices often circulated between masters of different trades and were free to switch from one occupation to another, bringing the skills and insights from one speciality to bear on another. Indeed, it is striking how many of the important inventors in the industrial revolution received their training in somewhat different fields. Arkwright, trained as a wig maker, was an extreme case. John Kay, inventor of the flying shuttle, was a reed maker; his namesake (no relation) who helped Arkwright build the first water frame was a clock maker, as was Benjamin Huntsman. Smeaton and Watt were both instrument makers with diversified backgrounds. Donkin had been apprenticed to a millwright, Bramah to a cabinet maker. Flexibility and diversity in training were the taproot of British ingenuity.

The lack of formal scientific education seems to have worked well for Britain, where skilled mechanics and technicians provided the environment in which the macro-inventions could succeed. Even deep in the nineteenth century the great inventors such as Bessemer, Perkin and Gilchrist had limited technical training and their main discoveries were mostly due to inspired guesses, luck and persistent trial and error rather than anything they might have learned at school. This type of education was a normal part of society and did not suffer from social stigmas. Only with the advent of chemical engineering, electricity and internal combustion engines in the last third of the nineteenth century did Britain discover that the lack of formal technical education was an obstacle slowing down technical change.

To summarise, if Britain had a purely technical advantage that could account for its technological precocity, it was probably in the realm of mechanical skills, in the development and improvement stage rather than in the pure 'invention' stage. All the same, we need to know more about the timing of the industrial revolution. Although, as we have seen, not all the major breakthroughs occurred in the 'classical' period between 1765 and 1800, the concentration of successful inventions and development in these years compared with the previous and following years calls for some explanation of 'clustering' phenomena. Clustering is frequently observed in the cultural realm, yet rigorous explanations for it are not easy to find. In music, art, science and literature the sudden flourishing of certain 'schools' followed by subsequent shifts or declines are easily documented. The driving force in the industrial revolution was a similar clustering of a relatively small number of macro-inventions in a small corner of north-west Europe. These macro-inventions, by raising the rate of return on further improvement and development, unleashed waves of micro-inventions and 'learning by doing' phenomena, which jointly provided the technological basis of the industrial revolution. Yet for the question of *timing*, the original macro-inventions were crucial. The *annus mirabilis* as Cardwell (1972) has called it, 1769, observed the patenting of two of the central inventions of the industrial revolution, the separate condenser and the water frame. But in 1783, 1784, 1787, 1793, 1800, the experience of 1769 was repeated: each of those years witnessed more than one major breakthrough. Sullivan (1989), using patent statistics, has pointed to the later 1750s as the period in which the acceleration of technological change occurred.

Economists use 'critical mass' models to explain such phenomena, in which an economic change occurs only when a threshold has been reached. These models share what is known as 'positive feedback' or 'virtuous circle' mechanisms. The existence of increasing returns to scale, for instance, means that if output increases costs fall, which allows more output to be sold, causing costs to fall even further, and so on. There is typically a threshold level of output at which production becomes profitable.

A similar model of clustering postulates direct interaction between different agents (Schelling 1978). In these models economic agents do not take each other's actions as given, but respond positively to the level of activity of every other agent. Two basic types of interaction can be distinguished. One is a complementarity effect. A would-be inventor observes other agents making successful inventions. By creating technological disequilibria, this raises the expected payoff of any complementary activity (e.g. spinning and weaving). If the next invention overshoots its target, however, the process may go on and on once it gets started. The second is an imitation effect: successful inventors are observed by others who wish to follow in their footsteps. Learning occurred both laterally (from competitors and colleagues) and vertically (from masters and teachers). Whether they occurred through complementarities or learning effects, it seems true that invention breeds more invention once the critical mass is reached. The issue of exact timing is not so important because once the conditions are there, the beginning of the process could be set off by a relatively small event. That is not to say, of course, that the British industrial revolution was an accident, only that it seems less than pre-ordained that the changes in technology discussed here had to take place when they did and not fifty years earlier or later (Crafts 1977b, 1985a).

Conclusion

From a purely technological point of view, the industrial revolution remains a great discontinuity. Some writers have questioned whether the term industrial revolution remains apposite. Hartwell's recent conclusion expresses the view of those who find it less than helpful to jettison a term that communicates efficiently (Hartwell 1990; 575): 'of course there was an industrial revolution, as obviously as there was a French Revolution ... and it was British'. The finding that economic growth itself was 'slow' during the industrial revolution should come as a surprise only to those who associate the industrial revolution exclusively with growth of per capita income. One way of defending a term implying discontinuity is to argue with von Tunzelmann (1993) that 'change had become the norm' whereas before the industrial revolution it was the exception. For von Tunzelmann the changes were as much financial and organisational as they were technological, and the three interacted with each other.

All the same, Ashton's famed schoolboy's equation of the industrial revolution with a wave of gadgets has enough historical truth in it for us to venture to single out technological change as somehow different. A number of critical inventions constituted a fundamental discontinuity in humanity's struggle for material control of nature. The industrial revolution marked the solutions to the problems of converting thermal to mechanical energy, of refining pig-iron into wrought-iron quickly and cheaply, and of twisting yarn with a device that replaced the age-old human fingers technology. It witnessed human flight and discovered radical new ways of preserving food, lighting homes, making machines and coding information that controlled production processes. The great discontinuity thus consisted of a cluster of radical innovations or macro-inventions. The success of Britain was not so much in *generating* these ideas as in turning them into economically viable projects. Economic growth, rising living standards, the creation of an urban proletariat, and social and political reforms all followed, after assorted lags. Such lags have to be explored and analysed, but their existence does not warrant a failure to recognize how it all began.

3   The industrial revolution

Nick Crafts

Key aspects of structure and performance

Britain before the industrial revolution was already a rich economy by the standards of the time. Although the population was still predominantly rural, there was by now a substantial amount of urbanisation and industrial and commercial activity. While most people were indisputably poor, the economy had a considerable surplus above basic subsistence needs, although much of that surplus was concentrated in the hands of those in the top 10 per cent or so of the income distribution.

Tables 3.1 and 3.2 provide snapshots at discrete intervals of some important aspects of the socio-economic structure. These tables give a broad outline which is reasonably reliable (Wrigley 1985, 1987a), but it should be remembered that the quality of the underlying data is often quite imperfect and the information given here and elsewhere is generally in the nature of 'best guesses' rather than 'hard facts'. In particular, many families divided their labour time through the year between sectors and the industrial or agricultural proportion is not exactly known.

Table 3.1 reflects an increasing rate of industrialisation of the labour force. Indeed, by the second half of the eighteenth century, the agricultural employment share was already much below what might have been expected given prevailing income levels (Crafts 1984). It must be remembered, of course, that there was a change in the character of this employment over time as new factory-based activity displaced some of the earlier cottage and small-scale industry. Nevertheless, even in 1840, perhaps around 60 per cent of industrial employment was still in this traditional mode. If, as Mathias suggests, the most important feature of an 'Industrial Revolution' is the 'fundamental redeployment of resources away from agriculture' (1983: 2), then the remarkable change in Britain between 1760 and 1840 certainly qualifies for this description.

The eighteenth century also saw a gradual rise in the share of resources devoted to investment. The rise would probably have been somewhat greater but for the 'crowding out' effects of government military

44

Table 3.1. *Patterns of employment, income, expenditure and residence, 1700–1840 (%)*

	1700	1760	1800	1840
Male employment in agriculture	61·2	52·8	40·8	28·6
Male employment in industry	18·5	23·8	29·5	47·3
Income from agriculture	37·4	37·5	36·1	24·9
Income from industry	20·0	20·0	19·8	31·5
Consumption/income	92·8	73·6	76·3	80·1
Investment/income	4·0	6·8	8·5	10·8
Exports/income	8·4	14·6	15·7	14·3
Urban population	17·0	21·0	33·9	48·3

Sources: based on Crafts (1985a: Tables 3.6 and 6.6) amended to include revised investment estimates from Feinstein (1988) and urbanisation figures for England only for 1700 and 1760 based on Wrigley (1985).

expenditures, notably after 1793 (J. G. Williamson 1985). Investment before the industrial revolution was concentrated in agriculture, transport and housing; when a sectoral breakdown is first available in the 1760s these sectors accounted for 32 per cent, 19 per cent and 19 per cent respectively (Feinstein 1988: Table II). Only in the 1820s did investment in manufacturing at last exceed that in agriculture.

The urbanisation of the population in 1700 represents a considerable increase from a level of perhaps 5 per cent in the early sixteenth century, due in particular to the growth of London which by now comprised 11 per cent of the English population (Wrigley 1985). London was an expanding port and commercial centre which required food and fuel from elsewhere in the country. This was an important stimulus to the commercialisation of agriculture and to improvements in transport (Wrigley 1967). After 1750, London's share of total population fell slightly and by 1800 further urbanisation was starting to be based on the growth of new centres of manufacturing such as Leeds and Manchester.

The social tables in Table 3.2 are revised and improved from the original contemporary investigations by Gregory King for 1688, Joseph Massie for 1759 and Patrick Colquhoun for 1801/3 using burial records and wage data. Two points stand out from this table. First, and not surprisingly, it is clear that income was unequally distributed. Second, it is apparent that virtually all families, even in 1688, were involved in market-based activity rather than subsistence agriculture.

The pre-industrial revolution economy was experiencing a steady rate of economic growth, although that rate was modest by later standards.

Table 3.2. *Lindert and Williamson's social tables for England and Wales in 1688, 1759, 1801/3*

	Family numbers	% of total	£m incomes	% of total
1688				
1. High titles and gentlemen	19,626	1·4	8·81	16·2
2. Professions	42,960	3·1	4·46	8·2
3. Military and maritime	94,000	6·8	2·13	3·9
4. Commerce*a*	128,025	9·2	10·90	20·0
5. Industry and building	256,866	18·5	9·58	17·6
6. Agriculture*b*	227,440	16·4	12·21	22·4
7. Labourers*c*	284,997	20·5	4·27	7·8
8. Cottagers and paupers*d*	313,183	22·5	2·04	3·7
9. Vagrants	23,489	1·7	0·04	0·1
Total	1,390,586		54·44	
1759				
1. High titles and gentlemen	18,070	1·2	11·74	17·6
2. Professions	57,000	3·7	5·09	7·6
3. Military and maritime	86,000	5·6	2·13	3·2
4. Commerce*a*	200,500	13·0	14·01	21·0
5. Industry and building	366,252	23·8	11·72	17·5
6. Agriculture*b*	379,008	24·6	16·66	24·9
7. Labourers*c*	240,000	15·6	4·20	6·3
8. Cottagers and paupers*d*	178,892	11·6	1·25	1·9
9. Vagrants	13,418	0·9	0·04	0·1
Total	1,539,140		66·84	
1801/3				
1. High titles and gentlemen	27,203	1·2	27·54	13·9
2. Professions	74,840	3·4	17·31	8·7
3. Military and maritime	244,348	11·1	10·38	5·2
4. Commerce*a*	205,800	9·4	39·21	19·7
5. Industry and building	541,026	24·7	51·07	25·7
6. Agriculture*b*	320,000	14·6	38·00	19·1
7. Labourers*c*	340,000	15·5	10·54	5·3
8. Cottagers and paupers*d*	260,179	11·9	2·60	1·3
9. Vagrants	179,718	8·2	1·92	1·0
Total	2,193,114		198·58	

Notes: *a* Includes tradesmen, some of whom should be in 'industry and building'.
    b Excludes labourers; constituted of 'freeholders' and 'farmers'.
    c In 1801/3 'labouring people in husbandry' and labourers in industry counted in row 5; in earlier years 'labourers' is a term used without any clear sectoral demarcation and includes both agricultural and non-agricultural labourers.
    d Described just as 'paupers' in 1801/3.
Source: Lindert and Williamson (1982).

Table 3.3. *Output growth, 1700–1831 (% per year)*

	New estimates			Old estimates		
	GDP	Industry	Agri-culture	GDP	Industry	Agri-culture
1700–60	0·7	0·7	0·6	0·7	1·0	0·2
1760–80	0·6	1·3	0·1	0·6	0·5	0·5
1780–1801	1·4	2·0	0·8	2·1	3·4	0·6
1801–31	1·9	2·8	1·2	3·1	4·4	1·6

Note: the periodisation is based on the exigencies of the data sources rather than from an attempt to distinguish separate economic epochs. The revisions to the earlier estimates of Deane and Cole (1962), also reported in Table 3.3, come both from improved procedures to deal with index number problems and revised series for particular sub-sectors of the economy.

Sources: new estimates based on Crafts and Harley (1992) and Crafts (1985a), old estimates based on Deane and Cole (1962).

Income per head was rising at about 0.3 per cent per year in 1700–60. The later decades of the century saw an increase both in output and population growth, although the former is now generally accepted to have been rather less dramatic than was once thought. It is likely that the growth of income per head only moved significantly above the long-run pre-industrial average in the second quarter of the nineteenth century. Table 3.3 reports output growth estimates by Crafts and Harley (1992) updated from Crafts (1985a).

Imperfections of the available data are such that there will remain a margin of error around such figures. Industrial output is the most reliably measured but even here there are sectors which have left no quantitative record (Berg and Hudson 1992). Agricultural data leave much to be desired; although alternative methods of estimation give similar results over the long run, there is less congruence in the short run (Allen 1991a). The service and government sectors can only be traced by the use of somewhat doubtful proxy measures based mainly on employment and assumptions about productivity increase.

Future revisions are, nevertheless, highly unlikely to restore to favour among economic historians the picture of a rapid acceleration in growth after 1780 which was until recently conventional wisdom and a striking feature of Deane and Cole's estimates. Further work by Jackson (1992) has confirmed the findings of Harley (1982) and Crafts (1985a) that on the presently available evidence – mostly from trade and taxation records – industrial output growth was much less than used to be believed. Moreover, the sectors for which data on growth are still not available would have had to be implausibly large and to have grown unbelievably fast to resurrect Deane and Cole's estimate; if the unobserved sectors were as large as the observed sectors and grew at 4.8 per cent per year in 1780–1801 and 6.4 per cent per year in 1801–31, this would approximately reproduce Deane and Cole's estimates. For more general reviews of estimation difficulties and sensitivity analysis see Hoppit (1990) and Crafts and Harley (1992).

The growth of the pre-industrial economy was in considerable part based on processes which Adam Smith well understood at the time. Markets became better integrated as transport costs fell and new areas were added into Britain's international trading relations; the possibilities of greater specialisation along lines of comparative advantage were more fully exploited – the growth of London epitomises this. Given the large weight that agriculture still had in the economy, it is also important that it continued to accomplish increases in productivity which had been in progress since medieval times. By the eighteenth century productivity advance was coming notably from better crop rotations and from economies of scale due to the rising size of farms (Overton 1984; Allen 1988a).

Exports rose distinctly more quickly than GDP during 1700–60 (see Table 3.1) and accounted for about 37 per cent of purchases of increased industrial output during the eighteenth century (Crafts 1985a: 132). But this should be seen as the result of gains from specialisation in international trade particularly with the New World (Davis 1969) rather than as a net addition to aggregate demand and output. In general, it would seem that growth was determined by supply-side factors over the long run (Mokyr 1977).

The economy was characterised by quite considerable short-run fluctuations in output and employment which have been the subject of recent econometric research. The results confirm the traditional view that there was no regular business cycle in the eighteenth century and that these fluctuations were the effect of severe random shocks from variations in the harvest and from wars, which, of course, affected exports (Crafts *et al.* 1989). There also appears to have been a tendency, contrary to what was once thought, for changes in exports to lead rather than follow changes in imports, suggesting that external factors may have instigated many of these movements particularly in the second half of the century (Hatton *et al.* 1983).

Industrial growth in the first half of the eighteenth century was fairly equally spread across the main traditional sectors, notably textiles, the leather industries and building, which together may have accounted for close to two-thirds of industrial output. From the 1760s onward there was

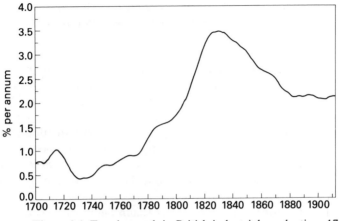

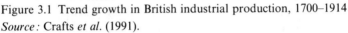

Figure 3.1 Trend growth in British industrial production, 1700–1914
Source: Crafts *et al.* (1991).

a spectacular acceleration in the growth of output of cotton textiles and also strong growth in iron, the most famous modernising industries of the industrial revolution period. It should be remembered, however, that these sectors were initially quite small relative to industry (together less than 10 per cent of output in 1770) and even more so relative to GDP. Proper recognition of this point has been fundamental to the downward revisions to estimates of late eighteenth- and early nineteenth-century growth rates (Harley 1982).

Modern econometric techniques provide improved insights into the timing of the acceleration in the underlying trend of overall industrial output growth during the later eighteenth century; in particular they remove the need arbitrarily to specify periodisation and they let 'the data speak for themselves', which is a major advantage given the severe disruptions during these years created by wars and the variability of the harvest. Figure 3.1 reports the results of an analysis of this kind based on the best available annual series which has been constructed as nearly as possible on the same basis as the estimates of Table 3.3. The notable feature of the estimated trend growth is that it increases steadily from the mid-eighteenth century all the way to the second quarter of the nineteenth century. The picture which emerges does not single out any particular short period, such as the much-touted 1780s as a decisive phase. Figure 3.1 also puts into perspective the growth rates of the industrial revolution as compared with those of Victorian Britain. Despite its increasing prowess the eighteenth-century economy was quite unable to match the industrial growth of the more mature economy of a century later.

Although the impact of technological change on overall growth in the early eighteenth century was still rather slight, it is important to note that there were signs of increasing inventive activity prior to the classic industrial revolution period (see Mokyr, ch. 2 above). Famous British inventions from these years include, in iron, Darby's coke smelting process (1709); in coal, Newcomen's steam pumping engine (1712); in power, Watt's steam engine (1763); in cotton textiles, Hargreaves' jenny (1768) and Arkwright's water frame (1769). A recent analysis of the data on patents suggests that there was a sharp acceleration in patenting dating from the late 1750s (Sullivan 1989). The implication is that the economy was starting to develop the capability for a new and faster rate of economic growth based on a considerably greater contribution from improvements in technology.

In 1776 as well informed an observer as Adam Smith was clearly quite unable to foresee the rapid industrialisation process of the next three-quarters of a century. If the metamorphosis of the economy to the 'workshop of the world' is seen as the outcome of the application of new types of energy and capital equipment (coal and iron replacing water and wood), the major transformation had still to come. Yet by 1780 a start had been made.

The sources of economic growth

Many of the central questions of eighteenth-century economic history revolve around issues of how and why increased economic growth came about. A provisional answer to the first of these can be obtained using the methodology of 'growth accounting': the growth rate of output depends on the growth rate of inputs on the one hand and the growth rate of the productivity of those inputs on the other hand.

In turn, the total growth of factor inputs is measured in terms of a weighted average of the growth rates of the factors of production, capital and labour. The weights must reflect the importance of the particular input in the productive process of which a convenient measure is the input's share in costs. For example, in making iron the spending on fuel to burn in the blast furnace is clearly more important than that on quill pens to write out invoices. Labour force growth is therefore weighted by the share of wages in national income and capital stock growth by the share of profits.

Thus we have the expression for the proportional change in output:

$$\Delta Y/Y = \alpha K/K + \beta L/L + r^* \tag{1}$$

where Y is output, K is capital, L is labour, α and β are the shares of profits and wages in national income respectively, while Δ represents 'the change

Table 3.4. *Sources of growth, 1700–1831*

	$\Delta Y/Y$	Due to $\Delta K/K$	Due to $\Delta L/L$	r^*
a. New estimates				
1700–60	0·7	$0·5 \times 0·7$	$0·5 \times 0·3$	0·2
1760–1801	1·0	$0·5 \times 1·0$	$0·5 \times 0·8$	0·1
1801–31	1·9	$0·5 \times 1·7$	$0·5 \times 1·4$	0·35
b. Old estimates				
1761–1800	1·1	$0·5 \times 1·0$	$0·5 \times 0·8$	0·2
1801–30	2·7	$0·5 \times 1·4$	$0·5 \times 1·4$	1·3
1831–60	2·5	$0·5 \times 2·0$	$0·5 \times 1·4$	0·8

Note: these measures of factor inputs are crude, especially that for labour. Crafts (1985a: 82) gives reasons why inputs of labour may have been growing a bit more quickly than indicated here.

in'. The growth rate of output per unit of all inputs together (total factor productivity) is r^*, which is found as a residual once information on the other variables in the equation has been collected; it can loosely be equated with improvements in the quality of men and machines. Equation (1) says, in words, that the rate of growth of output is the rate of growth of the capital stock times the share of profits in national income plus the rate of growth of the labour force times the share of wages in national income plus the rate of growth of total factor productivity. Table 3.4 reports estimates based on this growth accounting procedure.

Table 3.4 indicates that the acceleration of growth in the later eighteenth century was based on a faster growth of inputs rather than on faster total factor productivity growth which did, however, occur in the early nineteenth century. Even in 1801–31 only one eighth of the difference in growth of GDP from 1700–60 was, on these estimates, due to extra productivity growth. The payoff to the increase in inventiveness noted above did not bear its full fruit until the second quarter of the nineteenth century as the scope for application of the new technology widened and it diffused more widely. The impact of the technical progress on productivity growth in the later eighteenth century was too small to outweigh an apparent decline in agricultural productivity advance at this time.

Table 3.4 also shows that recent research has led to a considerable reassessment of the scale of productivity growth. The main reason for this has been the replacement of Deane and Cole's output growth estimates, which were discussed above, although Feinstein (1988) also provides better estimates for the growth of the capital stock. The new estimates themselves may be subject to errors, as Berg and Hudson (1992) have stressed, although the net effect of these could go either way. Aside from the problems of accurately measuring the growth rates of inputs and output, the weights attached to capital and labour have been questioned.

The theoretical conditions under which the shares of wages and profits would be exactly the right weights to be used in these calculations are unlikely to have been completely fulfilled. Fortunately, however, since capital and labour grew at relatively similar rates, in practice any bias from this source is likely to be very small. Crafts and Harley (1992) calculate that the *maximum* range for r^* in 1760–1801 is 0.1 plus or minus 0.04 and in 1801–31 0.35 plus or minus 0.18 while the 95 per cent confidence interval would be a great deal less. If the growth accounting estimates are in error, the main problems would lie in the output and, to a lesser extent, the input growth estimates.

This model is a way of accounting for *how* growth rates changed but it is, of course, far too simple to cope with the much harder but more intriguing questions as to *why* the rate of innovation or capital formation or population growth accelerated as the economy moved into the industrial revolution. To approach these issues it is necessary to allow for interactions between the variables of equation (1) and to cease to regard the right hand side variables as wholly exogenous (i.e. determined outside the economic system).

We may be able to throw further light on the circumstances which prompted the subsequent increase in the pace of growth and structural change by an investigation into the forces which might have restrained capital formation and innovation in the eighteenth-century economy. By modern standards the investment ratios reported in Table 3.1 are very low, especially in the early eighteenth century. Why was this so? A number of factors played a part and it is difficult to be sure of their relative importance.

Savings and investment

First, it is important to note that the economy had a considerable saving and investment potential as a result of its relatively high income and the highly skewed income distribution which is reflected in Table 3.2. That potential was rather little used at the start of our period but it is readily confirmed by the country's ability to finance extremely expensive wars. During the French Wars (1793–1815) the investment rate was maintained at a level twice that of 1700.

Second, there were institutional weaknesses relating to banking, finance and company legislation which must have had some inhibiting effects both on savers and on business investment. English banks were restricted to small-scale partnerships and thus to low levels of capitalisation by an Act of 1708. The Bubble Act of 1720 stood in the way of access to joint-stock company status and joint-stock companies with limited liability required special parliamentary dispensation until 1855. Asymmetries of information in the absence of modern forms of company regulation, auditing, etc., were a fundamental obstacle here. Nevertheless, research in the past twenty years has tended to suggest that to a large extent these problems could have been overcome by alternative arrangements, at least in the pre-railway age when in most activities scale was modest and overall capital requirements were still relatively limited (Mathias 1973). Thus, Cottrell (1980) stresses the use of the partnership form of organisation as a flexible basis for industrial production and Hudson (1986) shows that locally based sources of funds were available to growth industries in ways which minimised information problems.

Third, if, as seems likely in the light of these points, the supply of savings was relatively elastic, perhaps the main reasons for low investment are to be found in a paucity of attractive and profitable projects, i.e. a low marginal efficiency of investment. The chronology of parliamentary enclosure which entailed a major investment effort seems to confirm this with the timing much influenced by actual and expected agricultural prices (Crafts 1977b). From the late eighteenth century onward, this shortfall was remedied primarily by opportunities arising from technological progress (Mokyr 1990a and ch. 2 above). This interpretation is supported by the rising output to capital ratio of the early nineteenth century (see Table 3.4) which suggests that a rising payoff to investment rather than an independent increase in savings propensities may have underpinned the higher investment rate.

In terms of equation (1) a positive shock to r^* promoted a rise in $\Delta K/K$. Indeed there will be an automatic tendency for this to happen. $K = sY$; $K/Y = v$ where s is the propensity to save and v is the capital to output ratio. So $K = vY$ and $K/K = sY/vY = s/v$. The rise in r^* promotes a rise in Y relative to K and thus a fall in v. This implies a higher s/v and thus a higher K/K.

Invention and innovation

Accordingly, as we look for the emerging eighteenth-century origins of eventually faster growth in per capita income, our emphasis should be primarily on factors influencing the rate of innovation. Here too economic historians have generally argued that the acceleration in technological change should be thought of as largely endogenous rather than something happening quite independently of economic circumstances. The rationale for this view is that in eighteenth-century Britain: 'This is not a story of sophisticated inventions breaking through some technological barrier, and so creating the conditions for expansion. Developments that were technically so simple can only be responses to social and economic conditions' (Lilley 1973: 195).

This point of view can naturally be extended to suggest that in the eighteenth century the inducements to invention and innovation must have been stronger in Britain than in other leading European economies, and hence Britain was the first to enter the industrial revolution. Such an analysis was undertaken by Crouzet in a well-known article which concluded that 'The inventions were designed to make possible the replacement of relatively scarce and expensive resources, such as wood, water-power, and labour, by others which were relatively plentiful and cheap, such as coal, steam power and capital ... these shortages and bottlenecks, which in England exerted strong pressure in favour of innovation did not exist in France' (1966: 168).

It is certainly true that one of the major successes of the industrial revolution was a move to growth based on a mineral-based energy economy, as Wrigley (1988) in particular stresses; he points out that (1988: 77) a coal miner for 20 per cent of the food of a horse could deliver through the steam engine about four times the mechanical energy.

Nevertheless, it is much easier to find evidence of the role of economic factors in the subsequent take-up and diffusion of innovations than in their initial invention. Coke smelting illustrates this rather well: achieved in 1709 it was not generally taken up until charcoal prices rose in the 1760s and 1770s (Hyde 1977). Although the search for improvements was doubtless encouraged by prospects of profit, the success of such a search was highly uncertain. It may be wrong to look for something special about the mid-eighteenth-century economy which marked it out beforehand as more likely to embark on rapid industrialisation than the economy of, say, fifty years earlier – there was an element of randomness in the timing of particular inventions (Crafts 1977b). Indeed Crouzet (1990b) concluded that the factor scarcity hypothesis could not sustain the weight that he and others had put on it and that the search for the origins of the spurt in inventiveness had been inconclusive. Perhaps it is appropriate still to think of exogenous technological shocks raising the rates of return and economic growth.

While it may be unwise to rely too much on arguments that eighteenth-century growth led to the bidding up of prices of scarce factors of production and thus inexorably to a successful technological response, the long period of industrial growth in the centuries before the industrial revolution did lead to a build-up of expertise. At a time when improvements in productivity were often achieved by trial and error methods and through continuing incremental advances based on experience of using inventions, Britain had a major advantage in realising the potential gains when technological change materialised. In particular, this has been stressed in the case of coal-based technologies (Harris 1976) but Mokyr (1990a and ch. 2 above) argues that it applies also to engineering and machinery technologies generally.

Underlying mechanisms of growth and structural change

Population

Wrigley and Schofield's (1981) reconstruction of English demographic history allows us to apply a Malthusian-type analysis to the economy of the sixteenth to the mid-eighteenth centuries (see also Schofield in ch. 4 below). Two important points emerge.

Restraints on marriage and thus fertility acted to facilitate progress towards high income levels by the eighteenth century and averted the 'Malthusian Trap'. This is the proposition that a rising level of real income per head may generate sufficiently faster population growth to reverse the initial gains in living standards. Such a situation is more likely the greater is the response of birth and death rates to income levels in the way Malthus supposed (positively and negatively respectively) and the less the initial growth gives rise to additional investment or innovation. Wrigley and Schofield found that 'preventive checks' in the form of delayed or reduced incidence of marriage reflected in highly variable fertility levels were instrumental in slowing down excessive population growth. In the shorter run, however, the economy was very much prone to fluctuations in living standards as marriage behaviour changed relatively slowly and so the economy tended to experience quite big swings around a long-run, slow-growth equilibrium.

Second, during the eighteenth and early nineteenth centuries the economy developed a much greater ability to withstand demographic pressure as investment and innovation rates rose. In keeping with the long-swing pattern, the crude birth rate is estimated to have risen from a low point of 26.8 in 1661 in a period of falling population to 36.3 in 1776 and 41.9 in 1816 (Wrigley and Schofield 1981: 528–9), with population growth rising from −0.3 per cent to 0.9 per cent and finally to about 1.5 per cent per year. Wrigley and Schofield find that, in the two centuries before 1750, population growth of 0.5 per cent per year was the most that could be sustained without downward pressure on living standards. Seen against this background the impressive result of the industrial revolution period is the avoidance of a big decline in living standards in a Malthusian crisis.

Government

Although demographic restraint was important, the progress towards relatively high income levels was, as noted above, also predicated on the achievement of an increasingly efficient allocation of resources. In this regard, it is important to recognise the importance of economic and political institutions in creating adequate incentives and obviating market failures.

At the most general level Jones (E. L. 1988) has persuasively argued that impulses to growth which come from the pursuit of self-interest were always potentially to be found, provided that they were not swamped by institutions or governments who diverted energies into rent-seeking or stifled initiative with excessive taxation. Obviously well-defined and sustained property rights are essential for appropriate incentives and resource allocation. North and Weingast (1989) suggest that, particularly following the Glorious Revolution of 1688, the balance of power between the monarch and Parliament was more conducive to the elimination of the problems to which Jones refers. O'Brien (1988: 3 and ch. 9 below) calculates that between 1700 and 1780 taxes as a share of national income were always held within the range 8.7 to 11.7 per cent, while Beckett and Turner (1990: 386–7) point out that the main impact of taxation with its heavy reliance on customs and excise fell on consumption expenditures rather than savings and investment.

Parliamentary Acts were also directly of importance in achieving improvements in productivity via institutional innovation. Most obviously, the invention of the parliamentary enclosure act removed the sometimes intractable bargaining problems which could prevent the voluntary enclosure of land. The coming of parliamentary enclosure is a good example of the changed balance of power between the Crown and Parliament (McCloskey 1975: 133). Perhaps more important, however, were the Navigation Acts and the invention of the turnpike trust which led to significant investment and cost reductions in river and road transport and so improved the integration of markets.

Transport

Road transport is now regarded as much more important to the industrialising economy than was once thought; for example, London's carrying trade rose sixfold between 1715 and 1765 (Chartres and Turnbull 1983: 85). The first turnpike trust was established only in 1663 but by 1772 there were 519 trusts operating 14,000 miles of toll roads including all major trunk routes to London (Pawson 1977: 121). Such roads were generally kept in a much better state of repair, permitted heavier loads and considerably reduced journey times, perhaps reducing transport costs by as much as 30 per cent (Albert 1983: 54). Essentially the toll road was a (second best) solution to a well-recognised problem of market failure, the inadequate provision of 'public goods', otherwise known as the 'free-rider' problem, with which the previous 'parish repair' system had failed adequately to deal and which had led to sub-optimal provision of high-class roads.

By no means all such market failures were so well tackled. Although Municipal Improvement Acts, of which there were 125 between 1736 and 1799, led to the provision of better urban amenities through powers of property taxes (Jones and Falkus 1979), urban politics and taxation policies were generally such as to lead during the rapid urbanisation of the industrial revolution period to serious underinvestment in public health and housing (Williamson 1990a).

The shift from agriculture

The first section of this chapter explained rising income levels in the first half of the eighteenth century as based on better integration of markets and agricultural advance. It is important now to review the links between these developments and the structural changes which were involved in the fundamental redeployment of resources away from agriculture which is at the heart of the industrial revolution.

In an economy closed to international trade, the crux of the in-dustrialisation problem has been captured by models of the release of labour. Suppose agriculture is characterised by diminishing returns to labour and suppose also that food demand grows at the same rate as population. If the relative share of labour is to fall, it is necessary that the growth rate of the labour force in agriculture is less than the growth rate of population and the labour force overall. This appears to pose problems, for whilst the demand for food grows with population the food supply grows less rapidly, even if all the extra labour were to be used in agriculture (which would, of course, amount to deindustrialisation). Clearly, to feed all the extra population and also industrialise it is necessary to secure rising output per agricultural worker, which itself requires either innovation or investment in agriculture to permit the release of labour.

It is clear that between 1700 and 1760 the condition for release of labour was easily met by British agriculture. In fact, the sector could also cope with the additional demand for food associated with higher incomes per person (Crafts 1985a: 116–20). Indeed, productivity growth in agriculture was faster than elsewhere in the economy and over the period 1500–1800

Table 3.5. *Net exports of wheat and wheaten flour from Britain,*
1700–75 (000 of quarters)

1700	48·6
1725	158·2
1750	643·8
1775	− 149·4
1800	− 780·0
1825	− 587·8
1840	− 2,639·0

Source: Mitchell (1988: 220–1); figures are five-year averages centred on the year stated.

British agriculture was far more successful in achieving the conditions for labour release than was the case in other leading economies such as France (Wrigley 1985). By the mid-nineteenth century labour productivity in British agriculture was easily the highest in Europe.

In reality, Britain was heavily involved in international trade and the model just reviewed is therefore rather misleading as a result. Of itself, the very success of agriculture at home in raising productivity might have operated not to speed up but rather to slow down the industrialisation of the economy – or led to Britain becoming not the workshop but the granary of the world! There are even hints in the trade statistics of a tendency in this direction during the early eighteenth century with a growing surplus in trade in cereals, a position vastly different from that in the first half of the nineteenth century, as Table 3.5 reports.

The reason for the reversal of the early eighteenth-century trends in trade can be found in the idea of comparative advantage and was very clearly understood by Ricardo; as he put it in 1817:

a country possessing very considerable advantages in machinery and skill and which may therefore be enabled to manufacture commodities with much less labour than her neighbours, may in return for such commodities, import a portion of the corn required for its consumption, even if its land were more fertile, and corn could be grown with less labour than in the country from which it was imported. (1817; 1971 edn: 154)

Comparative advantage and the pattern of specialisation in trade depend on relative, not on absolute efficiencies, and during the later eighteenth and early nineteenth centuries Britain developed through technological change a productivity lead in exportable manufactures, notably cotton textiles, which outstripped that in agriculture (Crafts

1989a). Cotton textiles became a huge export and agricultural goods became importables.

Taken together with the argument above which suggested that there was a good case for regarding the timing of the famous inventions in cotton textiles as a random exogenous shock, this discussion leads to the implication that the rapid structural changes characteristic of the industrial revolution were not readily predictable in the mid-eighteenth century. In other words, technological change provoked a serious switch in direction from the course which was inherent in the type of growth experienced up to that time and the outcome can be regarded as truly revolutionary.

Conclusion

This survey has ranged selectively over many aspects of the eighteenth-century economy. In doing so it has presented both estimates of the magnitude of economic growth and structural change over time and an interpretation of the change in the nature of economic development which had materialised by the beginning of the nineteenth century. The macro-economic framework developed here provides a context into which can be placed the more detailed discussions of the chapters which follow while the exposition of the arguments offers a starting point for further discussion.

The issues raised here are of long-standing interest and will, of course, continue to be the subject of much debate. Eighteenth-century economic history is not the subject for those who wish for certainty but it is a field in which progress can be made. The current state of knowledge is already substantially different from that embodied in the textbooks of twenty or even ten years ago. In time, as more evidence comes to light and as more sophisticated modelling is possible, the estimates and, no doubt, some of the judgements made here may require amendment. It is as well, therefore, to regard the story told here as an interim rather than a final report.

4   British population change, 1700–1871

Roger Schofield

Introduction

At the beginning of the eighteenth century the economy of Britain, still predominantly agricultural, was subject to sharply diminishing returns to labour. Population increase at more than a modest pace would send real wages tumbling, as it had in the sixteenth and early seventeenth centuries, when a doubling of population had depressed real wages to about 40 per cent of their previous value (Phelps Brown and Hopkins 1956). By the early nineteenth century, however, British population was growing at an unprecedented rate, and the economy was able to absorb the expanding labour force with little change in living standards. Was this acceleration in both the population and in the demand for labour coincidental? Did the population grow in response to the demands of an expanding economy; or was the economy stimulated by the demands of an increasing population?

Many historians had a clear picture of the demographic regime they believed to have been typical of pre-industrial societies. Crude birth rates were imagined to have been high, if only because almost everyone married at an early age. And death rates were also high, with a 'remarkable tendency to recurrent, sudden dramatic peaks that reach[ed] levels as high as 150, 300 or even 500 per thousand ... The intensity and frequency of the peaks controlled the size of agricultural societies' (Cipolla 1965: 76–7).

In the conventional perspective, therefore, mortality, usually in the dramatic form of peaks, or 'crises', was seen as the dynamic variable in the relationship between population and the economy. This was true of all agricultural societies, at least before the demographic transitions which set in around 1870 with lower mortality which forced them to have lower fertility. As we shall see, the story of population change in Britain in the period before 1871 shows that every element in this description of a pre-transitional society was wrong.

Evidence

Part of the difficulty in addressing questions about population lies in the lack of direct evidence surviving from the countries that made up Britain. In none of them, for example, were collections made of the numbers of births, deaths or marriages before the Registrar General began to record these in the district registrar offices in 1837 (later in Scotland and Ireland). And in none of them were censuses made of the total number of people until 1801, unlike Sweden, for example, which began taking censuses along with counts of vital events in 1749 (Hofsten and Lundström 1976: 11). In the eighteenth century, therefore, there is a dearth of demographic information, while in the nineteenth it is plentiful only from 1837 onwards.

In the case of England, new evidence is now at hand assembled by the Cambridge Group for the History of Population and Social Structure, based on the church registers of good quality of 404 parishes (Wrigley and Schofield 1981). They record the demographic events of birth, marriage and death for about a sixteenth of the total population, occasionally for the whole period of observation from 1538 to 1840. These registers, therefore, give a direct view of the population history of England for our period, and with the addition of a new method of analysis, back projection, the registers can be used to derive censuses of the population.

In the case of Ireland and Wales, however, parish registers are usually of poor quality; nothing can be done for Wales, but in the case of Ireland, before the nineteenth century most estimates of a simple matter such as the size of the population are based on Hearth Taxes (Ó Gráda 1993). And in the case of Scotland, which has more registers of some quality, the population data are usually drawn from a comparison of the figures in Sinclair's *Analysis of the Statistical Account of Scotland* and the nineteenth-century figures (Anderson 1993). The general lack of any comparable demographic data for Scotland and for Ireland means that we shall proceed by discussing the English data first, and then draw what conclusions we can for the Celtic fringe. The lack of comparable data for Wales means that it cannot be included in the discussion.

England: the evidence

Each of the parish registers was first scanned for obvious gaps and registration deficiencies, and these were made good by interpolation. Then, because the parishes were just an 'availability sample' they were compared with a strictly drawn, but small, random sample (where every parish had the same chance of selection) to see whether they had a representative set of distributions across a number of standard social and economic characteristics. In fact, the parishes turned out to be representative of most of the characteristics – for example, they were in the same counties and they had the same proportions of the population employed in agriculture, manufacturing and commerce as defined in the 1831 census.

However, they were found to include too many parishes with large populations, and too few with small ones. In order to avoid any consequent bias from this source, the parishes were divided into a number of population size groups and the total numbers of vital events (i.e. baptisms, burials and marriages) were re-weighted to correct for the biassed size distributions of the parishes. The overall totals were then corrected for under-registration in two ways. First, the numbers of baptisms and burials that were missing because children died very young (in fact before they could be baptised) were estimated from special studies of infant mortality. Second, the numbers of events missing for other reasons, for example because of nonconformity or poor registration, were estimated for the early nineteenth century by adjusting the national totals of births, marriages and deaths by the age information contained in the early nineteenth-century censuses.

Thus the frequencies of baptisms, marriages and burials as originally recorded in the parish registers have passed through several stages of correction, each of which involves a risk of error in their conversion to totals of births, marriages and deaths. Nonetheless, the new estimates enable us to push our knowledge of population back on a continuous basis right to the middle of the sixteenth century. This can only be true if in the absence of a census, as indeed was the case before 1801, a way can be found to estimate the stock of individuals at risk (i.e. the size and age structure of the population) from the flows of events themselves. Some years ago Lee showed how this could be achieved in the case where migration was zero, or could be assumed to have been constant (1974). This assumption appeared too restrictive, given that emigration was far from negligible in England in the past. Accordingly, an alternative approach to the problem was devised, which was called back projection because it proceeded by successively back-dating and revising the known age structure of the 1871 census, thus deriving earlier 'censuses' at five-year intervals. This was achieved by taking into account the flows of previously occurring events. Our procedure followed Lee's 'inverse projection' in using model mortality schedules to allocate deaths by age, but it went further in finding a way to deduce the magnitude of the unrecorded flows of migrants of different ages from inconsistencies between the population age structures and the intervening flows of births and deaths.

Back projection was a complex system, and an example of a technique whose operation was made feasible only by the advent of high-speed computing. Potentially the harvest was very rich: on the basis of series of births and deaths alone quinquennial estimates were made of the size and age structure of the population, so deriving measures of population growth, net migration, fertility, nuptiality and mortality over a period of three centuries. Yet Lee has made some criticisms of back projection (1985), in which he could 'see no reason to alter any of the estimates', but claimed that they could not be held 'to provide independent evidence about the general level of population size and vital rates'. The grounds on which Lee bases his criticisms are complex and cannot be dealt with briefly (see Oeppen 1993). Oeppen, who designed back projection, has shown that both it and 'inverse projection' are variants of a more general class of problem in demographic estimation, and can be subsumed within a more inclusive system that he terms generalised inverse projection. It is reassuring that when generalised inverse projection is run down the English data, with the same age schedules of mortality and migration as in back projection, it produces estimates of population size and age structure, and of net migration, fertility, nuptiality and mortality, that are virtually indistinguishable from those based on back projection. It follows, therefore, that the results that are now to be reported are taken without amendment from *The Population History of England* (Wrigley and Schofield 1981).

England: population growth

To study population growth is rather like studying a flexible bath which expands and contracts according to the level of population within it. It is filled up through the water flowing in through the taps (fertility) and emptied out through the waste pipe (mortality). Fertility, the degree to which the taps are opened, is determined by the proportion of young people who get married, and the age at which they marry. It is also determined by the percentage of fertility which is illegitimate (i.e. supplied by the non-married), and by the presence of birth control within marriage. It is a rather curious bath because people can also leak in and out of it, through migration.

During the later seventeenth century, when our study begins, the population of England was at a standstill. Barely a century later, when it ends, it was growing faster than at any other period of English history. In 1656 the long period of growth which had lasted throughout the Tudor and Stuart period came to an end, with the population numbering 5.281 million. Thereafter it fell back substantially until in 1686 it was no more than 4.865 million.

Table 4.1. *Quinquennial English population totals, 1681–1871*

Year	Population	Compound annual percentage growth rate
1681	4,930,385	
1686	4,864,762	−0·27
1691	4,930,502	0·27
1696	4,961,692	0·13
1701	5,057,790	0·38
1706	5,182,007	0·49
1711	5,230,371	0·19
1716	5,275,978	0·17
1721	5,350,465	0·28
1726	5,449,957	0·37
1731	5,263,374	−0·69
1736	5,450,392	0·70
1741	5,576,197	0·46
1746	5,634,781	0·21
1751	5,772,415	0·48
1756	5,993,415	0·75
1761	6,146,857	0·51
1766	6,277,076	0·42
1771	6,447,813	0·54
1776	6,740,370	0·89
1781	7,042,140	0·88
1786	7,289,039	0·69
1791	7,739,889	1·21
1796	8,198,445	1·16
1801	8,664,490	1·11
1806	9,267,570	1·35
1811	9,885,690	1·30
1816	10,651,629	1·50
1821	11,491,850	1·53
1826	12,410,995	1·55
1831	13,283,882	1·37
1836	14,105,979	1·21
1841	14,970,372	1·20
1846	15,933,803	1·26
1851	16,736,084	0·99
1856	17,763,920	1·20
1861	18,937,536	1·29
1866	20,166,624	1·27
1871	21,500,720	1·29

Note: the totals refer to 30 June of each year indicated.
Source: Wrigley and Schofield (1981: 208–9).

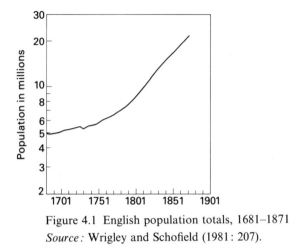

Figure 4.1 English population totals, 1681–1871
Source: Wrigley and Schofield (1981: 207).

The quinquennial population figures from 1681 to 1871 are given in Table 4.1 and Figure 4.1. They show that, although the population began to recover in the early eighteenth century, there was a further fall in the wake of the epidemics of the late 1720s, so that in 1731 the population total, at 5.263 million, was still below the level of the mid-seventeenth century. Years in which deaths had exceeded births, which had been fairly common in the later seventeenth century, were not quite over. Population declined for this reason in 1741 and 1746, but the figures in the second column of the table show that in the main the annual compound percentage rate of growth, which began in the 1730s, accelerated from 0.70 per cent in 1736–41 until it reached its peak rate of 1.55 in 1826–31. It then fell back to a stable 1.2 to 1.3 per cent until 1871. It was, therefore, only at the very end of the eighteenth century that the rates of population growth that were normal in the sixteenth century were equalled and then exceeded.

In the 140-year period from 1731 to 1871 the population of England no less than quadrupled from 5.263 to 21.501 million. From being a country with a population well below that of the major west European countries, England was rapidly approaching near parity with other large countries. With Scotland and Ireland added, it did achieve parity. Table 4.2 shows the populations of England, Scotland and Ireland and of five countries in west Europe (Germany, the Netherlands, France, Italy and Spain) in 1680, 1820 and 1900 (Wrigley 1983b). France continued to grow at its traditional slow pace, but in the nineteenth century it was exceeded in size by Germany, and by England, Scotland and Ireland. What is brought out especially clearly in this table is the percentage growth rate of England, Scotland and Ireland over the 'long' eighteenth century (at 154 per cent), and the very steep rate

Table 4.2. *Estimated population totals and percentage growth rates of selected European countries, 1680–1900*

	Population totals (millions)			Percentage growth rates	
	1680	1820	1900	1680/1820	1820/1870
England	4·9	11·5	30·5	133	166
Scotland	1·2	2·1	4·5	75	114
Ireland	2·0	7·0	4·5	350	−64
Total	8·1	20·6	39·5	154	92
Germany	12·0	18·1	43·6	51	142
Netherlands	1·9	2·0	5·1	8	149
France	21·9	30·5	38·5	39	26
Italy	12·0	18·4	32·5	53	77
Spain	8·5	14·0	18·6	64	33

Source: Wrigley (1983b: 122); for Scotland and Ireland see Table 4.7.

of growth of England alone (Ireland actually declined, see below) in the remainder of the nineteenth century. The change in population size in England was momentous, yet until late in the eighteenth century it was not greatly remarked by contemporaries. Not until the first census was held in 1801 was it clear beyond reasonable doubt that numbers were rising rapidly.

England: reasons for population growth

In accounting for this steep rate of population growth, we can first of all rule out immigration. In fact, there was net emigration throughout the period: to the Americas around 1700, and then to the many colonial territories overseas in the remainder of the period. Despite the very large numbers of Scots and Irish who did migrate into the country during the nineteenth century, there were even more English who migrated abroad. Migration being shown to have been a reason for population decline, rather than growth, the main constituents which played a role in determining the rates of population growth were the demographic ones of fertility and mortality.

Table 4.3 and Figure 4.2 set out the fertility and mortality findings of back projection. The figures represent not the birth rate and the death rate for any period, but the gross reproduction rate and the expectation of life at birth (e_0). The gross reproduction rate measures the average number of

Table 4.3. *Changes in English fertility and mortality, 1681–1871*

Year	Gross reproduction rate (GRR)	Expectation of life at birth (e_0)
1681	1·94	28·5
1686	2·17	31·8
1691	2·16	34·9
1696	2·18	34·1
1701	2·34	37·1
1706	2·25	36·4
1711	2·05	35·9
1716	2·25	37·1
1721	2·27	32·5
1726	2·21	32·4
1731	2·20	27·9
1736	2·37	35·6
1741	2·22	31·7
1746	2·27	35·3
1751	2·34	36·6
1756	2·32	37·3
1761	2·37	34·2
1766	2·39	35·0
1771	2·50	35·6
1776	2·53	38·2
1781	2·49	34·7
1786	2·62	35·9
1791	2·77	37·3
1796	2·76	36·8
1801	2·69	35·9
1806	2·93	38·7
1811	2·87	37·6
1816	3·06	37·9
1821	2·98	39·2
1826	2·86	39·9
1831	2·59	40·8
1836	2·53	40·2
1841	2·49	40·3
1846	2·37	39·6
1851	2·40	39·5
1856	2·44	40·4
1861	2·51	41·2
1866	2·55	40·3
1871	2·54	41·3

Source: Wrigley and Schofield (1981: 231).

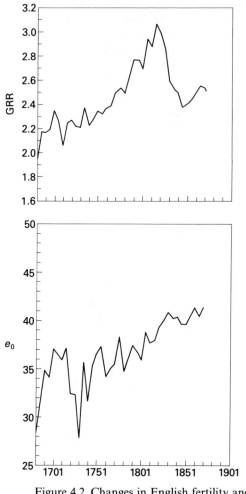

Figure 4.2 Changes in English fertility and mortality, 1681–1901
(quinquennial GRRs and e_0s)
Source: Wrigley and Schofield (1981: 231).

daughters that would be born to a woman during her lifetime, if she passed
through the childbearing ages experiencing the average age-specific fertility
pattern of that period. Expectation of life at birth is the average number of
additional years a person would live if the mortality conditions implied by
a particular life table applied (for an account of the methods used to
calculate the GRR and e_0 see Wrigley and Schofield 1981, appendix 15).
These measures of fertility and mortality are, in fact, superior to the crude
rates, as they take into account the age structure of the population.

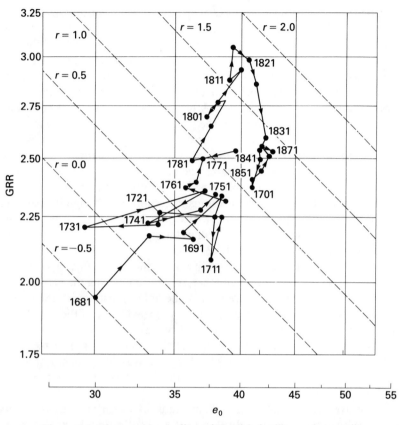

Figure 4.3 The combined effect of English fertility and mortality changes in determining intrinsic growth rates, 1681–1871 (quinquennial data)

Note: the years shown are the central years of the five-year periods to which each point relates.

Source: Wrigley and Schofield (1981: 242).

When our period opens at the end of the seventeenth century mortality was at a maximum, having passed from a mortality regime around 1600 that may have been unusually mild by the general standards of early modern Europe to one which was probably much closer to the norm. The last years of the seventeenth century and the early years of the eighteenth saw a considerable, but short-lived, improvement in mortality. The expectation of life at birth rose from 28.5 years in 1681 to 37.1 years in 1716 and then fell sharply to much lower levels in 1721 and 1726; while the level for 1731, at 27.9 years, was the lowest in our period. This five-year period saw one of the most severe attacks of epidemic disease since 1541, with 16.3 per cent of the 404 parishes being affected. After 1731 there was recovery and a steady improvement, though the early 1740s, the 1760s and the early 1780s were all periods of relapse from the rising trend in the expectation of life. Thereafter there was a decline in the scale of the fluctuations in the quinquennial levels of e_0, and between 1781 and 1821 the expectation of life improved from 34.7 to 39.2 years. After this the expectation of life at birth drifted upwards to 41.3 years in the final half century up to 1871.

This steady improvement in mortality was paralleled by a similar movement in fertility. The GRR was about 1.94 female children per woman, in 1681. It rose throughout the period until in 1816 it was 3.06. It fell to 2.37 by 1846, and then remained between 2.4 and 2.6 until 1871. The rise was remarkably free from serious interruptions, though it rose faster towards its ultimate peak in the 1810s than it had done so in the early decades of the period. In the first half of the eighteenth century, indeed, the trend was nearly flat at around 2.3.

Presentation of the main fertility and mortality findings of back projection, separately from each other, is less illuminating than considering them in conjunction. It is important to be able to distinguish the relative importance of each in affecting the intrinsic growth rate of the population, so that the question which has intrigued two generations of economic and demographic historians can be more conclusively answered. A rise in the GRR from 2.0 to 3.0, for example, does not look like much, but it does mean that the average woman had one-and-a-half as many children as she had before.

Is a movement of this size more important than a shift in the expectation of life at birth from thirty to thirty-nine years in affecting the growth rates? If the fertility and the mortality rates found for each quinquennium are plotted on Figure 4.3, we can see that changes in factors affecting fertility result in a vertical movement up and down the page, while changes in mortality lead to horizontal movement across the page. This is because the figure is constructed so that all the combinations of fertility and mortality which will yield the same intrinsic growth rate lie on a diagonal at 45 degrees to the origin (see Wrigley and Schofield 1981: 235–40).

It is clear from Figure 4.3 that, with the exception of the points for 1681 and 1731, the acceleration in growth rates in the eighteenth century owed far more to a rise in fertility than to a fall in mortality. The fertility (GRR) rises from 2.0, during the population stagnation of the late seventeenth century, to around 3.0 in 1821 and 2.5 in 1871; its vertical movement covers a greater distance on the graph than does the horizontal movement travelled by mortality, from an expectation of life at birth of about thirty-four to one of forty-two. It should be noted that all these data refer to the

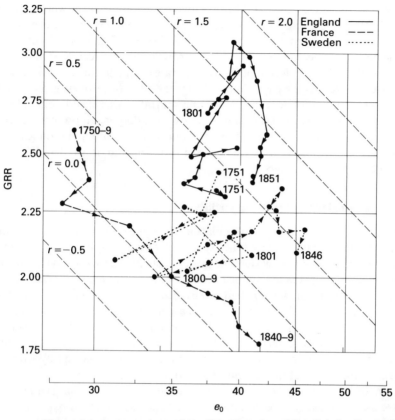

Figure 4.4 A comparison of English, French and Swedish fertility and mortality data, 1750–1850

Source: Wrigley and Schofield (1981: 246).

female population only; expectations of life for the sexes combined would be slightly lower. The points for 1681 and 1731 are much towards the left of the points for other years because the mortality of those years was considerably higher. With them excepted, the rise in the GRR accounted for the great bulk of the total change; it is in fact about three times the magnitude of the total horizontal movement assigned to mortality. It follows, therefore, that a satisfactory explanation of the remarkable rise in growth rates in the eighteenth and nineteenth centuries will turn largely upon attaining a fuller understanding of the fertility changes of the period.

Although English demographic trends, especially in the last half of our period, from 1751 onwards, were largely determined by fertility changes, it does not follow that the English experience was paralleled elsewhere in

Europe. Indeed, Sweden and France, two other countries for which details of GRR and expectation of life are available after 1751, neatly exemplify other possible demographic regimes, as is shown in Figure 4.4. In Sweden the bulk of the acceleration in intrinsic growth rates between 1751 and 1871 is attributable to declining mortality rates, which form a *horizontal* movement across the page. And in France, where the intrinsic growth rate was never far from zero, an improving mortality was exactly offset by a decline in fertility, so that France slid down the diagonal representing zero population growth, instead of moving out to a rate of population growth of 1 per cent per annum as was the case with England or Sweden (Wrigley and Schofield 1981: 246–8).

England: increases in fertility

To revert to the analogy of population growth as a bath, our immediate concern in the English case is to explain why the taps should have opened so markedly, while the waste pipe got only slightly narrower. An increase in general fertility could have occurred for one of three reasons: because the marital fertility of women had risen; because of an increase in extra-marital fertility; or because of an increase in the proportion of women of childbearing age who were married, i.e. of nuptiality. In all three cases it is the behaviour of women that is at issue: the behaviour of men is important, but changes in it are not essential as fertility is only produced by women aged between about fifteen and fifty years.

In order to study marital fertility (or fertility within marriage) it is necessary to perform yet another kind of analysis in which baptisms are linked to the marriage register entry of the mother. This is called family reconstitution, and it can only be done on really excellent registers. If it is done on those twenty-six parish registers which seem good enough for this kind of study, there is no evidence of a significant fluctuation in the level of marital fertility at any period before 1871. Within marriage, birth intervals were much the same, and the age at the birth of the last child remained close to thirty-nine years (Wrigley and Schofield 1981: 168–75). Thus regardless of whether general fertility was increasing (up to 1815) or decreasing (after that date), the pattern of marital fertility was constant. It should be noted that the present evidence is strongly against any practice of contraception within marriage. Up to 1871, married women seem to have had children with no interference from abstinence, or from condoms, or from any form of birth control.

This leaves changes in illegitimate fertility and in nuptiality to be considered. Of the two the former is clearly incapable of accounting for more than a fraction of the total rise in fertility since illegitimate births were never more than about a fifteenth of all births in England during the period in question (Laslett 1977b). Most of the increase in fertility must therefore be attributable to changes in the age at which women married, and in the proportions never marrying, which between them determine how many women of childbearing age will actually marry, and so be at risk to bear children.

England: increases in nuptiality

Table 4.4 shows the average age at first marriage of women, from the family reconstitution results for twenty-six parishes. The mean age at marriage went up just as our period began from 25.5 to 26.1 years (for the year ending in March 1990 it was 24.9 years in England). Then it dropped quite regularly until in the final period 1825–49 it was 23.2 years. In the 150 years after 1700, that is, the mean age of marriage for women fell by almost exactly three years. It is significant that the fall occurred with marked consistency in eight of the parishes that can be followed as far as 1849 (Ash, Banbury, Bottesford, Dawlish, Gedling, Morchard Bishop, Odiham and Shepshed). The second and third columns of Table 4.4 give the twenty-five-year period in which these parishes had their maximum and minimum ages at marriage. The maximum age for women fell either in the second or third periods: 5 in 1700–24, 3 in 1725–49. The minimum was almost always found in the penultimate period, or in the last period: 2 in 1800–24, 6 in 1825–49.

Since family reconstitution does not allow information about the numbers of women who failed to marry at all to be estimated, we have to supplement that form of analysis with data drawn from back projection. If we take from back projection the GRR figures, adjusted to allow for the change in mean age at maternity, and from family reconstitution the average age of marriage of women, we can calculate the proportion of women ever married at age forty to forty-four (Weir 1984). If we do this, we discover that in the sixteenth and seventeenth centuries, changes in celibacy emerge as very much more important than changes in the age at marriage in causing changing GRRs. This can be seen in Figure 4.5, where most of the points joined by a line fall around a vertical line, as the proportion never married varied (from 5 per cent in 1591 to 22 per cent in 1641), with little horizontal movement (about 1 year) for changing age at marriage (Schofield 1985: 11).

But with the eighteenth century onwards we come to a complete turn-round: from now on it is by changing the age at which women married that the number of children they brought into the world was determined. From 1716 towards 1816 the points lie almost on a straight line, as the mean age

Table 4.4. *Women's age at first marriage, 1675–1849 (means of twenty-six parishes)*

Year	Age	Of eight parishes up to 1825–49	
		Maximum	Minimum
1675–99	25·5	0	0
1700–24	26·1	5	0
1725–49	25·7	3	0
1750–74	24·6	0	0
1775–99	24·2	0	0
1800–24	23·6	0	2
1825–49	23·2	0	6

Source: reconstitutions from parish registers by the Cambridge Group.

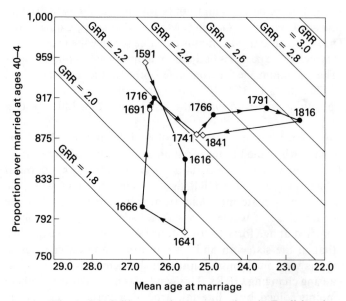

Figure 4.5 Celibacy and age at marriage in English cohort fertility, 1591–1841

Note: points refer to data for twenty-five-year marriage cohorts and are plotted against the mid-year of the cohort.
Source: Schofield (1985: 11).

of marriage fell from 26.4 to 22.6, while the percentage never marrying was almost static around 10 per cent. The great acceleration in population growth during the 'long' eighteenth century, therefore, was principally due to earlier marriage. In the nineteenth century, on the other hand, the average age at marriage of women began to rise once more, so that the value calculated for those who married in the twenty-five-year period grouped around 1841 was almost back at its early eighteenth-century level of 25.1 years. Not surprisingly the level of fertility (the GRR) was also falling fast during this period.

It might seem reasonable to expect that illegitimate births would be relatively common when marriage was long delayed, as around 1700, but less frequent in an era of early marriage as in 1816. Such an expectation accords well with French experience in the eighteenth century, but in England matters fell out otherwise. The very low illegitimacy which obtained at the end of the seventeenth century coincided with late marriage and frequent celibacy. Yet as the stock of unmarried women shrank steadily to reach a far lower level a century later, the illegitimacy ratio tripled, and it is clear that the illegitimacy rate must have increased much more sharply. At the start of the 'long' eighteenth century fewer than a tenth of all first births were illegitimate; before its end the proportion had risen to a quarter, and a further quarter of all first births were pre-nuptially conceived. So when nuptiality was low, and legitimate fertility was heavily constrained, the efficiency of the check on growth which this represented was not undermined by a large transfer of fertility from within marriage to outside it. On the other hand when nuptiality was high and most women entered marriage early in life, the degree to which the potential fertility of the population was impeded by delay or avoidance of marriage was in any case relatively slight (Wrigley 1981).

England: age structure of the population

Back projection also generates estimates of the numbers of people in each five-year age group every fifth year. The age structures emerging from back projection reflect changes in mortality and fertility, and changes in the estimated level and direction of migration. Figure 4.6 shows the percentage of the population found in each of the life-cycle stages: infancy (age 0–4), childhood (age 5–14), young adulthood (age 15–24) when most people were unmarried and many left home to go into service, adulthood (age 25–59) when most people were married and old age (age 60 and above). Indeed 1826 represents the point at which the population was at its youngest. Infants comprised 15.5 per cent of the population and children

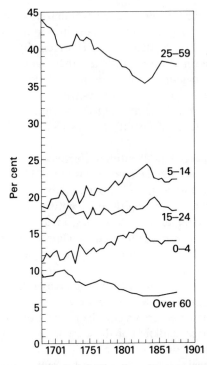

Figure 4.6 The changing age structure of the English population, 1681–1871 (percentages in five age groupings)

Source: Wrigley and Schofield (1981: 216).

a further 24.1 per cent, making 39.6 per cent of the population under age fifteen. Young adults made up 18.5 per cent of the population, adults 35.4 per cent and the elderly the final 6.5 per cent.

Tracking back through the eighteenth century the population becomes progressively older: the proportions of infants and children decline while those of adults and the elderly increase until in 1681 the age structure reaches its oldest configuration at any date before 1931. If the age structures in 1826 and 1681 are compared it is apparent that the greatest relative changes occurred in the smallest groups at either extreme of the age range. Thus the proportion of infants fell by almost a third from 15.5 to 11 per cent, while the proportion of the elderly rose by a third from 7 to 10 per cent. The proportion of children also fell, but by a quarter from 24 to 18 per cent, and that of adults rose by the same proportion from 35 to 44 per cent. The relatively old society that existed around 1700 is quite unlike the picture of a population weighed down with the very young and very old. Such a society, in which large numbers of dependants have to be supported by relatively few adults, is more typical of the developing world today, where the dependency ratio is largely controlled by the level of fertility, and where the proportion of the population under fifteen is usually over 40 per cent, as compared with the 28 to 31 per cent of the population in late seventeenth-century England. In England, we therefore have a relatively old population being made progressively younger as the level of fertility increased, until in 1826 it really looks like a population with a traditional heavy dependency burden.

There are, however, other aspects of the demand of different age groups which require attention. At its most basic, a population with a greater proportion of children has more people who produce relatively little, and consume more agricultural than non-agricultural goods. The rather low proportion of children at the beginning of our period allowed a higher proportion of consumption to be directed towards non-agricultural goods, producing a more favourable balance between production and consumption which in turn provided a greater potential for saving and investment. The mid-eighteenth century was a little less favourable in this respect, while during the late eighteenth and nineteenth centuries the increasing proportion of children in the population both reduced the relative surplus of production available for saving or investment and swung the direction of consumption back towards the agricultural sector. Industrialisation, therefore, occurred not only in the face of mounting population pressure, which for a time drove up agricultural prices and depressed real wages; it also occurred despite a changing age structure which, as it grew younger, became progressively less favourable to a surplus of production over consumption and to the generation of a demand for non-agricultural goods. In pre-industrial terms this aspect of the demographic background to industrialisation was far from propitious. The problems posed by an increased rate of population growth were aggravated by the changes in age structure that accompanied it.

England: the effects of population growth

The largest and most obvious effect of the sharp rise in population in the eighteenth century was on the national average wage of labour. Labour is one of the factors of production. When it grows in supply more rapidly than others, its relative price (the real wage) will fall, unless productivity change is sufficiently rapid. The pace of innovation and capital formation was apparently high enough in eighteenth-century England to allow a growth rate of 0.6 per cent per year with constant real wages (Lee 1986: 97). Slower growth than this (as in the first half of the century) allowed real wages to rise; faster growth (as in the second half) depressed them sharply.

The logic of this argument is reinforced by the truth of another of its implications. The increase in the labour force relative to agricultural land would have increased the value of land and increased rents. Prices of agricultural goods therefore would rise more than prices of manufactured goods, since agricultural production was relatively land intensive and manufacturing labour intensive. True to these predictions, in the first half of the century the ratio of industrial to agricultural prices rose and in the second half it fell. During the second half of the eighteenth century, then, population grew more rapidly and the evidence on wages, imperfect though it is, indicates a decline in the real wage of labour. At the same time, per capita income rose quite markedly (see ch. 3). On the face of it these opposite trends suggest a redistribution of income away from labourers and towards landowners and capitalists.

The effect on labour supply is one side; the effect on the demand for goods is the other. As the population grows, so does aggregate income and aggregate demand, creating a buoyant and less risky environment for investors and entrepreneurs, and stimulating the demand for investment goods. Population growth may therefore encourage economic growth more than might be expected from the growth in labour supply alone (Keynes 1937). However, population growth has an effect not only on the aggregate level of consumption but on the distribution between agricultural and industrial goods. The influence, unfortunately, operates in two opposite ways: through changes in income per head and through changes in relative prices. Poor people spend a high share of their incomes on food. As the income rises, the share falls: one says that the 'income elasticity' of expenditure on food is less than one – a proposition known as Engel's law. As the share of food declines, the share spent on industrial commodities rises. The demand for industrial goods therefore depends not only on total national income but also on the numbers of consumers, i.e. on how many poor people there are. While population growth does raise total income and demand, it typically reduces real wages or average income.

On the other hand, as we have seen, by depressing wages and raising land rents population growth made manufactured goods cheaper than agricultural goods. On this count, people would have substituted manufactured for agricultural consumption. In short, it can be shown that population growth alone increased the demand for 'manufactured' or non-agricultural goods by 14 per cent between 1751 and 1801, and by 29 per cent between 1801 and 1851. This is, however, less than 10 per cent of the total output growth for the first half of the nineteenth century, and probably even less for the period 1751–1801. Even if it is assumed that population growth was fully exogenous, its significance in generating the demand for increased industrial production was marginal (Mokyr 1985a: 101).

England: the effects of changing real wages

In the long run, according to the argument which Robert Malthus put forward towards the end of the eighteenth century, the population growth rate would inevitably outstrip the rate at which food could be produced (Malthus 1798). In such circumstances food prices would rise and, since with the population increasing, real wages would be likely to decline, the standard of living must fall. At the limit this would lead to progressive overcrowding, malnourishment, starvation and death: the 'positive check', which Malthus believed operated in populations of plants and animals. In human populations, however, and particularly in contemporary European societies, Malthus thought that this limit was short-circuited by the existence of another check, namely 'a foresight of the difficulties attending the rearing of a family'. This appreciation of a minimum viable standard of living, which obviously varied by social class, provided a 'preventive check [which] appears to operate in some degree through all the ranks of society in England'. Thus if population growth drove up food prices and the standard of living fell, more and more people would delay marriage, or never marry at all. This would reduce the level of fertility and so throttle back the rate of population growth to the point where it no longer exceeded the food supply. Indeed, it might overshoot the mark, reducing the population growth rate below the rate of increase in the food supply so that prices would fall and standards of living would begin to rise.

The link between the standard of living and marriage could therefore provide the means by which a population might keep in balance with its food supply, avoiding the runaway population growth and the terrible penalties of famine and catastrophic mortality that uncontrolled growth would ultimately entail. Malthus himself thought that the operation of the 'preventive' check through marriage would come into play very slowly, so that there would be long periods of population growth and declining standards of living (or of population decline and rising standards) before population and resources were brought back into balance again. Was Malthus right so far as England in the 'long' eighteenth and nineteenth centuries were concerned?

Figure 4.7 compares the change over time in the real wage index with the mortality history of England as measured by the expectation of life at birth. If the positive check were operating, there should be a positive association between movements in the two series: falling real wages should reduce the expectation of life and rising real wages increase it. It is not easy

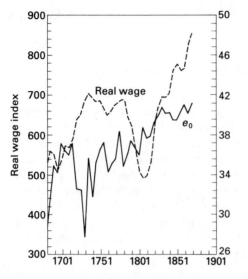

Figure 4.7 Quinquennial expectation of life at birth data compared with an eleven-year moving average of a real wage index, 1681–1871.

Note: the e_0 graph represents mortality in the five-year period centring on the years shown. The real wage graph is a twenty-five-year moving average centring on the years shown.

Source: Wrigley and Schofield (1981: 414), with revised estimates for the period 1716–86 including Gilboy's northern data (Wrigley and Schofield (1989: Fig. 1, xxii)).

to detect such a pattern in Figure 4.7. Between 1680 and 1740 mortality levels fluctuated rapidly while the real wage index continued to rise to a high peak. And the final period of mortality improvement took place against a background of falling real wages up to the second decade of the nineteenth century, and of rising real wages thereafter. The relationships between the two series are disorderly and frequently contrary to expectation. Figure 4.7 provides little evidence that long-term trends in scarcity or plenty, as captured by the real wage, caused marked differences in mortality levels.

If the positive check is difficult to discern in the English historical record, is the preventive check any more in evidence? Figure 4.8 plots the long-run movements in real wages against nuptiality measured by an estimated crude first-marriage rate. The general parallelism in the directions of movement of the two lines on the graph, suggests that secular changes in the standard of living were followed by secular changes in the intensity of marriage.

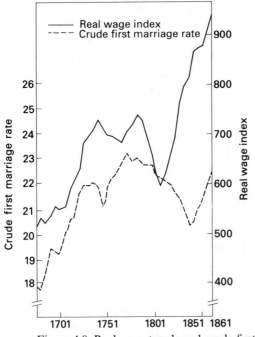

Figure 4.8 Real wage trends and crude first-marriage rates, 1681–1861 (both twenty-five-year moving averages centred on the dates shown)
Source: Wrigley and Schofield (1981: xxii).

The changes in the intensity of marriage involved shifts both in the age of marriage and the proportions ever marrying; when times were more difficult fewer married and they waited longer to do so. Since marital fertility rates varied little until the widespread adoption of family limitation toward the end of the nineteenth century, the movements in nuptiality were reflected, after a lag, by secular shifts in fertility. Moreover, as we have seen, in England rates of illegitimacy and pre-nuptial pregnancy moved in sympathy with nuptiality, reinforcing rather than offsetting its effects. Thus it was the intensity not only of marriage, but also of the sexual activity among the young in general that responded to the long-term trends in scarcity and plenty.

England: short-run fluctuations

However successful a pre-industrial society might have been in securing a long-run balance between demographic and economic change, it still had to cope with the substantial annual fluctuations in fortune caused by variations in harvest yields. In a world where the land was the source of all food and of most of the raw materials needed by industry, a harvest failure meant distress and depression, and abundant harvest an interlude of comparative plenty. These annual fluctuations of scarcity and plenty caused abrupt changes in the balance between a population and its economic resources which, if severe, could entail disaster rather than distress. Although England may have escaped the positive check in the long run, it may have been vulnerable in the short run. And if the preventive check operated in the short run, was nuptiality also sensitive to annual fluctuations in economic circumstances?

In answering such questions we usually make a calculation of the magnitude of the association between a fluctuation in one of the series (say food prices) and fluctuations in a second series (say mortality), not only in the year in which the fluctuation in the first series occurred; but also in the four subsequent years, so that lagged relationships between the series can also be examined. Since population size and age structure do not change much in the short run, fluctuations in death rates are essentially driven by fluctuations in the numbers of deaths, so a series of the latter can be used directly in the analysis without the need to calculate a mortality rate. This analysis takes account of fluctuations of all sizes both above and below trend, and so probes far deeper into the relationship between the series than is possible in a study based only on extreme fluctuations.

There are, however, some complications. For example, each series may carry within it echoes of previous fluctuations: for example, fewer people surviving to die in subsequent years. And the demographic series may be affected by fluctuations in other demographic series quite independent of prices: for example, a fluctuation in the birth series will change the proportion of infants in the population who have a higher than average risk of dying. Consequently, care needs to be taken to remove both internal echoes, and external contamination, when calculating the strength of the association between any pair of series. The latter, summed across fluctuations of all magnitudes in each direction, is usually reported as the percentage change in the second series (say mortality) that would be associated with a doubling of the current average value of the first series (say prices), net of the effects of earlier fluctuations in the series which are included in the analysis.

Lee has carried out a pioneering analysis of this kind on English data on vital events and prices during the period 1541 to 1834 (1981). He found that there was indeed a systematic relationship overall between fluctuations in wheat prices and mortality; but that it was weak. Only 16 per cent of the annual short-run variation in mortality was associated with price changes, and much of that was due to the effect of a small number of extreme upward fluctuations in prices. Mortality fluctuations, therefore, were overwhelmingly determined by other factors, such as the prevalence of epidemic disease. However, the pattern of the lag between fluctuations in prices and mortality was suggestive: only when prices were high did mortality rise in the same year, otherwise mortality fluctuated sympathetically after a delay of one or two years.

One interpretation of this result would be that it was only in years of exceptional shortage that the dislocation was such as to provoke life-threatening actions, such as recourse to contaminated food. Otherwise, the normal effect of harvest fluctuations would have been to vary the proportion of the population that could maintain its accustomed standard of living at home, driving the rest to seek food and work elsewhere, thereby more effectively spreading disease through the countryside. Furthermore, Lee also found that the sympathetic response to prices was followed by a compensating negative echo, so that the net effect of price fluctuations on mortality, cumulated over five years, was essentially zero. Nor did runs of consecutive years with high prices have any significant additional effects on mortality beyond the sum of the effects of the years involved. This suggests that most variations in scarcity or plenty merely advanced, or delayed, by a few years the normal pacing of deaths.

Similar analyses were carried out on the overall relationships between fluctuations in prices, on the one hand, and fluctuations in nuptiality and fertility on the other. In both cases the associations between fluctuations in the demographic series with fluctuations in prices were more pronounced: 41 per cent of the annual fluctuations in marriage, and 64 per cent of fluctuations in fertility, could be associated with annual variations in prices, compared with 16 per cent in the case of mortality. Moreover, in both cases the main effects occurred both in the same year as the price fluctuation and in the year after, and were followed by compensatory echoes.

Cumulated over five years the effects of price fluctuations were more substantial than in the case of mortality. A doubling of prices was associated with a 22 per cent loss of marriages and a 14 per cent loss in fertility. A more finely grained analysis also showed that the negative response of fertility to fluctuations in prices peaked after a lag of three to eighteen months. Thus variations in prices would seem to have affected foetal mortality during the first two trimesters of pregnancy, and to have influenced the number of conceptions that occurred during the following nine months. The latter may have been due to the effect of fluctuations in the level of nutrition on fecundity, or to the physiological or psychological effect of food shortage on the intensity of sexual activity.

Lee also estimated the strength of the short-run relationships for three sub-periods (1548–1640, 1641–1745 and 1746–1834) to examine how far they changed over time. The first period is too early for us and the results will be disregarded. Briefly, the cumulative five-year response of fertility and nuptiality to food price fluctuations showed no change; variation in the price of food had essentially the same negative effects on the number of both births and marriages recorded throughout the 'long' eighteenth century. But when a comparison is made of the results for the two sub-periods, the most dramatic decline was in the cumulative response of mortality to food price fluctuations. In the period 1641–1745 the cumulative response of mortality to prices fell to a third of its previous level, while from the mid-eighteenth century there was practically no response from mortality to the movement in prices.

Unfortunately, a later analysis of the same data by Galloway has somewhat upset this neat progression. If the second period is begun in 1675 rather than 1641, the response of mortality to price fluctuations remains close to the level it was during the period before this date. This result arises because there was an unexpected *negative* association between price and mortality fluctuations in the years 1641–74, which depressed the overall figure that Lee obtained for the second period when these years were included in it (Galloway 1988). Clearly there is some difficulty in this kind of analysis in dealing with periods in which relationships are temporarily inverted. Perhaps the safest conclusion to be drawn at present is that there was an association between fluctuations in prices and mortality in England up to the mid-eighteenth century, after which fluctuations in prices found no echo at all in movements in the death rate.

Analysis of the English data on the whole confirmed that food prices were not an important element in determining national fluctuations in mortality in England in the past, certainly not after 1745. But Lee's analysis also revealed many other aspects of the relationships between short-run changes in demographic behaviour and fluctuations in the environment. We have seen how both nuptiality and fertility were more affected in the short run by fluctuations in food prices than was the case with mortality. But fluctuations in fertility were also even more strongly affected by fluctuations in mortality, the cumulative negative effect after five years being more than twice as great as the response to price fluctuations. It would seem, therefore, that fluctuations in the prevalence of disease, in fact, had a double effect, increasing mortality and depressing fertility. Their combined demographic effect far outdistanced that caused by fluctuations in food prices.

England: population growth in the context of the eighteenth- and nineteenth-century economy

Malthus attributed the contrast between the relative affluence of European societies of his day and the economic misery of Asian populations to the presence or absence of the preventive check (1826). European living standards do indeed appear to have been high relative to those of other pre-industrial societies, and historically the European pattern of nuptiality was unusual in that it entailed for both sexes a relatively late, and far from universal, marriage. But within this broad distinctiveness of historical Europe, which sets it apart from most peasant societies, there were differences which have important implications for the operation of the preventive check and, more widely, for the nature of the interaction between demographic and economic processes.

One dimension of crucial importance is the degree to which the prevailing ideology of social relations was predicated on familistic, or individualistic, principles (Schofield 1989). Familistic ideologies tend to produce political and legal structures which favour stability, resisting change in the distribution of property, and constraining individual independence and mobility (Macfarlane 1978; Todd 1985). Thus familistic ideologies are likely to inhibit economic differentiation and the emergence of markets in labour and goods. In an undifferentiated economy of family farms and rural crafts and services, economic activity is largely a family affair in which labour is applied to capital in the family's control. Access to the means of production is mainly through inheritance (or by marriage to an heir); kinship plays an important role in marriage decisions and other property transactions; and support for the elderly is primarily a family responsibility. Consequently the population is relatively immobile.

At the other extreme stands the more differentiated pre-industrial economy, more typical of eighteenth- and nineteenth-century England, in which a significant proportion of the population sells its labour to be applied to capital over which it has no control. Although some individuals may acquire land or capital through inheritance, intergenerational links are weak: most children are expected to leave home, accumulate their own wealth, choose their own marriage partners and locate and occupy their own economic niche. Consequently the population is mobile. Since the generations no longer usually live in the same village children cannot easily care for their elderly parents. In pre-industrial conditions, therefore, an individualistic ideology needs to be complemented by a collective responsibility amongst neighbours for the support of the weak and elderly.

At the familistic, European, extreme the preventive check is likely to follow the simple replacement model, with nuptiality being linked to the mortality of the previous generation. In this kind of society, as in the case of societies subject to the positive check, children are valuable for their labour power and as a source of support in old age. At the non-familistic, or English, end of the spectrum, the preventive check is likely to operate through the more diffuse mechanisms of markets in goods and labour. For a substantial proportion of the population children have a negative, rather than a positive economic value; for support in old age and at difficult times their significant relations are not with their family, but with the community.

In many important respects the ideology of English social relations was non-familistic in its orientation. Apart from the celebrated lack of any family rights in property, which gave descendants no rights until the death of the property holder, in practice a substantial proportion of English children left home in their teens to work in a succession of other households scattered over several communities (Macfarlane 1978; Kussmaul 1981b, and ch. 1, above). In due course they chose their own spouses, and English registers significantly omit the long lists of relatives witnessing the marriage which are to be found in other countries. They lived after marriage in economically and physically separate households, in three out of four cases in a village other than the one in which they had been brought up and in which their parents still resided (Laslett and Wall 1972; Schofield 1970).

When we looked at the figure which showed the effect of changes in the mean age at marriage, and in the proportions ever married on fertility (Figure 4.5), it was evident that both aspects of nuptiality changed over time. Amongst those born before 1700 changes in the proportion ever marrying had a much greater impact on fertility than did changes in the age at marriage. On the other hand, for those born during the eighteenth or nineteenth centuries most of the changes in fertility were due to a sharp fall, then rise, in the age at marriage.

The first problem, then, is to explain why in England before 1700 the nuptiality valve operated through changes in the incidence, rather than the timing, of marriage. It only is a problem if we conceive of the acquisition of the material basis of marriage exclusively in terms of accumulating sufficient capital. If this were indeed the operative process, then changes in real wages should be reflected in changes in the age at marriage, which in fact was the case, but only to a limited extent in the period before 1700. The accumulation model may correctly capture one aspect of the economic dimension of marriage in the past; but it presupposes full employment after marriage. For labourers Malthus described the preventive check in terms of the degree of confidence they had in their ability to earn enough to support a *household* economy (1798).

That is, the critical issue would be their perception of the likely course of family earnings in the future. In sectors of the economy with structural underemployment, and no perceptible change in prospects during the critical years in early adulthood when marriage decisions were taken, the level of the demand for labour might well produce a dichotomous response in nuptiality, as individuals judged their future family earning prospects as constituting either a sufficient, or an insufficient, basis on which to enter into the reproductive state.

While a 'future earnings prospect' model of marriage for the poorest element in the population may make it easier to appreciate the operation of the preventive check before 1700, we still have to explain the shift to a dominance of changes in the age at marriage after that date. In tackling this question it is important not to exaggerate the phenomenon to be explained. Though the change is striking enough, it is important to remember both that age at marriage did vary before 1700, and that proportions ever marrying changed after that date. Furthermore, in the nineteenth century both components of nuptiality continued to change, though on a much reduced scale, and with age at marriage only slightly outdistancing proportions ever marrying in its impact on fertility. The problem to be explained is not a once-and-for-all nuptiality transition occurring in the eighteenth century, but rather a temporary interlude in which the age at marriage experienced a secular fluctuation of exceptional magnitude.

In searching for an explanation for the eighteenth-century shift in nuptiality patterns, one tempting possibility is to relate it to a major transformation in the structure of the economy, in which a society of peasants and craftsmen became urbanised and proletarianised. The temptation should be resisted. There is a problem of timing; long before 1700 England had acquired a substantial proletariat and a far from insignificant urban economy. It would be difficult to argue that there was a major transition from a subsistence and craft economy to a wage-labour economy in the early eighteenth century.

Nonetheless there may have been important changes in the structure of employment in the eighteenth century which so altered the evaluation of earnings prospects that those who at earlier dates would have foregone marriage altogether now married, and at progressively earlier ages. Levine has argued powerfully for the importance of the development of 'proto-industry' as providing a new and effective framework for family earnings (1987). Since the household was the unit of production, and since demand for the products often originated outside the immediate economic context, as for example with exports, individuals might well be inclined to take a more optimistic view of prospective family earnings than would be the case with general labouring. And the 'cottage economy' argument gathers more force from the observation that the main growth area in demand for labour in eighteenth- and nineteenth-century England lay outside agri-

Table 4.5. *Urban population, c. 1700–1801*

c. 1700	c. 1750	1801
London 575,000	London 675,000	London 959,000
Norwich 30,000	Bristol 50,000	Manchester 89,000
Bristol 21,000	Norwich 36,000	Liverpool 83,000
Newcastle 16,000	Newcastle 29,000	Birmingham 74,000
Exeter 14,000	Birmingham 24,000	Bristol 60,000
York 12,000	Liverpool 22,000	Leeds 53,000
Gt Yarmouth 10,000	Manchester 18,000	Sheffield 46,000
Birmingham ⎫	Exeter ⎫ 16,000	Plymouth 43,000
Chester ⎪	Leeds ⎭	Newcastle 42,000
Colchester ⎪	Plymouth 15,000	Norwich 36,000
Ipswich ⎬ 8–9,000	Chester ⎫ 13,000	Bath ⎫ 33,000
Manchester ⎪	Coventry ⎭	Portsmouth ⎭
Plymouth ⎪	Nottingham ⎫ 12,000	Hull 30,000
Worcester ⎭	Sheffield ⎭	Nottingham 29,000
Bury St Edmunds ⎫	York 11,000	Sunderland 26,000
Cambridge ⎪	Chatham ⎫	Chatham ⎫ 23,000
Canterbury ⎪	Gt Yarmouth ⎪	Stoke ⎭
Chatham ⎪	Portsmouth ⎬ 10,000	Wolverhampton 21,000
Coventry ⎪	Sunderland ⎪	Bolton ⎫
Gloucester ⎪	Worcester ⎭	Exeter ⎪
Hull ⎪		Gt Yarmouth ⎬ 17,000
King's Lynn ⎪		Leicester ⎪
Leeds ⎬ 5–7,000		Stockport ⎭
Leicester ⎪		Chester ⎫
Liverpool ⎪		Coventry ⎬ 16,000
Nottingham ⎪		York ⎭
Oxford ⎪		Shrewsbury 15,000
Portsmouth ⎪		
Salisbury ⎪		
Shrewsbury ⎪		
Sunderland ⎪		
Tiverton ⎭		

Source: Wrigley (1985: 160–1).

culture, in the manufacture of textile and metal goods, activities which were well suited to household production (Crafts 1985a).

England: the percentage urban

A consequence of the changing demand for labour can be seen in the percentage of urban populations in the economy. Table 4.5 gives the size of the towns with a population of 5,000 and above in *c.* 1700, *c.* 1750 and

Table 4.6. *Percentage distribution of the population and expectation of life at birth, 1811–71*

Category of place	Percentage of total population			Expectation of life at birth		
	1811	1841	1871	1811	1841	1871
London	11	12	14	30	33	39
Over 100,000	2	8	18	30	32	37
10,000–100,000	12	18	22	32	36	42
Rural	74	62	46	41	43	46
England and Wales	100	100	100	38	40	42

Source: Woods (1985: 650).

1801. London is at the head of the list, with 575,000 in *c.* 1700, a position it largely attained through phenomenal growth in the sixteenth and early seventeenth centuries. The seventeenth century had seen a notable acceleration of growth of an urban system of largely familiar names, as the other examples in the list make clear, but the eighteenth century brought a radical reordering of the urban hierarchy and further rapid urban growth. In the eighteenth century the list of towns contained Birmingham, Manchester and Leeds (actually from 1670) and Liverpool from 1700. London, though still vastly larger than any other city, no longer stood out for its rate of growth. In 1801 it comprised much the same proportion of the national proportion as 100 years earlier. Meanwhile, the share of other towns larger than 5,000 in population increased sensationally, rising from 5.5 to 16.5 per cent of the national total, and for the first time surpassing London.

For the period from 1811 to 1871, Table 4.6 divides the population up into London, large towns of over 100,000 inhabitants, small towns of 10,000–100,000 inhabitants and rural localities. While London's share of the population grew very little (from 11 to 14 per cent), the large towns increased their population dramatically (from 2 to 18 per cent). At the same time the small towns almost doubled their share (from 12 to 22 per cent), while the rural share was reduced to about 60 per cent of its 1811 value. Columns four to six of the table show estimates of the life expectancy at the same dates. The rural areas were always the healthiest place in which to live, followed by the towns in ascending order of size, but with London just more healthy than the large towns. Yet each category saw an improvement in life expectancy during this period. One of the consequences of the rush to the larger towns was, therefore, a reduction in life expectancy of between four and eleven years. It was not necessary for the urban environment to deteriorate for the overall mortality decline to be retarded; a rapid and substantial urbanisation was sufficient (Woods 1985; Williamson, ch. 13, below).

England: the demand for labour

To an increasing demand for labour outside agriculture, from both home and overseas markets, one might add significant changes in the structure of the demand for labour in the agricultural sector itself. The worsening ratio of food prices to nominal wage rates in the late eighteenth century was accompanied by a shift in farmers' preferences away from the traditional form of living-in labour on annual contract, which was becoming increasingly expensive to feed because of the rising relative cost of food, to labour that was living-out and hired by the day (Kussmaul 1981b). The progressive elimination of service in husbandry removed from the rural economy a structural demand for unmarried labour. Also in the later eighteenth century, under the pressure of population growth, jobs in agriculture became allocated preferentially to males, making it progressively more difficult to secure a dual-income household from labouring alone (Snell 1985).

Both the decline in service in husbandry, and the marginalisation of women from the agricultural labour force went much further in the arable zones of the south-east than in the pastoral regions of the north and west. We might, therefore, expect that nuptiality might be more depressed in the rural south-east, especially since the pastoral zones typically contained more opportunities for family-based household economies of a proto-industrial kind. However, unpublished research results of the ESRC Cambridge Group show that, with some exceptions, in the late eighteenth century age at marriage fell in villages full of agricultural labourers producing crops for the market as well as in those engaged in pastoral agriculture or in proto-industrial production. Interestingly, among the few places for which family reconstitution results are available, and which record little or no change in age at marriage, are Gainsborough and Banbury, two substantial market towns and regional service centres, each with a wide range of craft occupations. This may suggest that the large movements in age at marriage occurring in other communities in this period were produced, not by those in traditional occupations finding that economic circumstances enabled them to accumulate material wealth quicker and so marry earlier, but by those who sold their labour in a variety of sectoral markets finding that the structure of their employment now favoured early marriage.

To help explain how this could be the case even during periods when the prospects for earnings were deteriorating, we need to take into account the impact of contemporaneous changes in welfare policy. Towards the end of the eighteenth century welfare payments under the Poor Law not only took account of the size of the dependency burden in the family, but may also have come to be allocated preferentially to married males (Snell 1985: 348–52). If women, therefore, also experienced discrimination in the labour market, and it has been suggested that this occurred in the traditional urban craft sector as well as in the arable countryside, marriage may well have become a more attractive option to them. If more women found fewer viable economic alternatives to marriage as the eighteenth century progressed, the linking of welfare payments to prices and to the size of the family would have enabled both sexes to discount the economic consequences of reproduction, and to embark upon marriage at a young age. Changes in welfare policy would have removed the fear of the economic consequences of underemployment in the future, and so effectively disabled the traditional operation of the preventive check. Those who, at an earlier date, would not have married at all, could now do so at a young age (Boyer 1990: 172).

By the eighteenth century, therefore, a number of changes had occurred in the structure of the economy. These changes had produced a demand for labour that enabled a growing proportion of the population to become employed in activities in which, in the light of contemporary changes in the welfare support system, early marriage was not irrational. But in the early nineteenth century the age at marriage suddenly rose, in 1841 reaching a point on Figure 4.5 very close to where it had been in 1741. How can we explain the reversal? And does it not cast doubt on the validity of the explanations offered for the sharp fall in age at marriage in the eighteenth century? Yet the welfare system is the one factor that did change radically in the nineteenth century. In 1834 the provisions of the New Poor Law were framed with the express intention of reinstating a proper appreciation of the economic consequences of marriage, by abolishing child-related payments, and making financial assistance available only in an institutional context (Fraser 1976).

Thus one of the factors which in the eighteenth century provided individuals with economic support that enabled them to marry early in life was abruptly terminated in the nineteenth century. In this perspective the eighteenth century appears not so much as a decisive transition from one nuptiality regime to another, but as a temporary aberration in which major structural shifts in the economy combined with a particularly flexible operation of the welfare support system, to induce a 'perverse' movement in the age at marriage, of such a magnitude that it swamped the 'correct' movement in proportions ever marrying, and temporarily disabled the preventive check.

Scotland and Ireland

Scotland and Ireland largely lack a good parish register system during the period, so we are consequently reliant on converting the number of households mentioned in the Hearth Taxes into figures for the total population. Table 4.7 gives the population in millions for each country and for England, and also shows the compound annual growth rate attained by each population. During the eighteenth century, and the first part of the nineteenth, the Scottish growth rate was below that achieved by England, but not too far below. From 1830 population growth occurred strongly only in the urban and manufacturing communities in the centre of the country, with widespread decline appearing in part of the Highlands (Anderson 1993). The Scots seemed to have industrialised at about the same time as the English with the same tendency to go and live in large communities, where the death rate was markedly higher.

Recent research on Scotland has filled in some of the details lying behind this growth of population. For example, it has shown how the famine of 1696–9 caused a massive decline in population, so much so that the population in 1700 was probably less than in 1691, and the population in 1750 at almost the same level (Tyson 1992). Grain harvests continued to be poor in at least ten years between 1740 and 1816, and active intervention by government was vital in preventing mass hunger in 1740–1 when a poor harvest followed a winter in which trade was disrupted by frost and war. Government action was even more important in 1782–3 when, in some areas, three-quarters of the crop of oats was lost and bad weather ruined potato yields.

So far as it can be calculated from the mid-century population lists, Scotland had considerably higher mortality rates than was the case in England. By the 1790s the death rates had fallen somewhat. There does appear to be a major difference in the experience of the Scottish and English populations; it lies in the failure of the average age at marriage of Scottish women to fall in anything like so marked a way as it did in England. This, combined with the relatively high proportion celibate (in the 1790s it was as much as 15–20 per cent for the country as a whole), must have acted as a powerful check on Scottish fertility (Tyson 1992). As early as 1740, groups of families began to leave Scotland for the Americas, often led by the lesser gentry, while in the 1770s and 1780s social conditions encouraged a more general emigration. This continued during the war, and fluctuated upwards during each depression during the first half of the

Table 4.7. *Rates of population growth: Scotland, Ireland and England,
1691–1871*

Year	Scotland		Ireland		England	
	A	B	A	B	A	B
1691	1·2	—	2·0m	—	4·9m	—
1700	1·1m	−1·5	1·8–2·1m	−0·7 to 0·5	5·1m	0·4
1750	1·3m	0·3	2·2–2·6m	0·1 to 0·7	5·8m	0·3
1801	1·7m	0·5	5·0m	1·3 to 1·6	8·7m	0·8
1821	2·1m	1·2	6·8–7·2m	1·5 to 1·8	11·7m	1·5
1871	3·4m	0·9	5·2m	−0·5 to −0·7	21·5m	1·2

Notes: columns A – population; columns B – compound annual growth rate of
population; Ireland: 1687 (for 1691), 1800 (for 1801), 1881 (for 1871); England: 1701 (for
1700), 1751 (for 1750).
Sources: Scotland: Tyson (1992) and Flinn (1977: 302); Ireland: Ó Gráda 1993; England:
Wrigley and Schofield (1981: 208–9).

nineteenth century. From 1853, when more reliable figures are available,
significant emigration occurred every year; two-thirds of the emigrants
never returned (Anderson 1993).

The total Irish population figures in Table 4.7 show Ireland to have had
a similar rate of growth to England down to 1750, but a faster rate of
growth than anywhere else in western Europe between the 1750s and the
1820s (Ó Gráda 1993). On the eve of the Great Famine (1846–50) Irish
population growth was no longer exceptional by north-west European
standards; indeed a decline in population seems already to have been
under way in several areas. Unlike Scotland, Irish mortality seems to have
been relatively low for such a poor, and agricultural, country. Despite the
poverty the Irish tended to live relatively long lives with an early nineteenth-
century expectation of life in the high thirties, compared to one of about
forty years in England. Coupled with this is the evidence of higher age-
specific marital fertility in Ireland, both among Irish Quakers and among
the population at large in 1841 (Vann and Eversley 1992). Finally, it was
possible in Ireland to increase the number of rural holdings by an ever
smaller sub-division, as a result of a reclamation of the waste and a
growing dependence on the potato and the earnings from rural textile
industries. It was consequently relatively easy to acquire land and therefore
to marry at a young age.

Since nuptiality seems to have been unrestrained, there were clearly too
many people being produced in Ireland. Emigration played an important

and increasing part in the story, with 1.5 million leaving Ireland for good between 1800 and 1845. Of these about a half a million crossed into Scotland and England, but a million braved the Atlantic in ill-equipped ships to go to the States. While emigration was responsible for most of the slowing up of the population increase before the famine of 1847, there are signs too of some upwards adjustment in the age at marriage and in the proportions never marrying. But the adjustment was too little and too late: the standards of living of the Irish poor continued to decline (Ó Gráda 1993). When the potato famine struck in 1846, every region returned more deaths than normal, though the mortality was more severe in the west than in the east of the country. The excess mortality, at about one million deaths, occurred during a four-year period till 1850, and about 0.3 to 0.4 million births were averted. As a consequence emigration happened on a massive scale to the United States, as well as to England and Scotland, and Ireland continued to lose population until 1901.

Conclusion

The story that has emerged for Scotland and Ireland is very much less detailed than that for England. Yet in their very different attitudes to marriage the three countries placed very different emphases on various elements in the preventive check cycle. Ireland, in a sense, had the easiest task, in that it could multiply the number of 'holdings' suitable for a marriage, through reclamation or by planting potatoes, in a way that does not seem to have been possible for Scotland or for England. Such a strategy, though it seems successful in the short term, only works if emigration can progressively sweep away the disappointed surplus population. Though its economy may grow, per capita output is bound to fall, leading to a declining standard of living and an increase in poverty. To the problems posed by the preventive check cycle, it is no solution at all.

The Scottish tenants who found it difficult to obtain land, and who rarely grew potatoes, failed to marry at younger ages, and instead moved to the towns particularly in the west of the country, to England or to America. Yet they industrialised at much the same time as England, even if from a differing demographic background, and from a much lower standard of living. Without the escape route that emigration offered, one wonders whether the Scots would have read the signals aright and increased either the age at marriage or the proportion never marrying. In England, on the other hand, the preventive check cycle could be seen to have been operating through the real wage after a lag of fifteen to twenty years, and with only a backward glance towards emigration.

But here too, there is a final point to be made: there is no necessary connection between industrialisation and the increasingly rapid growth of population. The proportion of the population which had been caught up in the new ways of earning a living was quite small until the middle decades of the nineteenth century. In the 1831 census, for example, only 10 per cent of the adult male labour force was employed in manufactures, including 'proto-industry'; the other 90 per cent of adult males were earning a living from pursuits that had existed for centuries: farming, local service trades, handicraft manufacture for local markets, etc. Thus very little of the late eighteenth-century acceleration in population growth can be attributed to the direct effect of families becoming employed in 'new' jobs linked to the most conspicuous economic developments of the new economic age. As in the case of most of the demographic changes in our period, most of these too must have resulted from changed demographic characteristics in that part of the population which was still engaged in 'traditional' forms of employment.

5   Agriculture during the industrial revolution

Robert Allen

Introduction

British agriculture developed in a distinctive manner during the industrial revolution, and the sector made important contributions to economic growth. By the early nineteenth century, agricultural labour productivity was one third higher in England than in France, and each British farm worker produced over twice as much as his Russian counterpart (Bairoch 1965; Wrigley 1985; O'Brien and Keyder 1978; Allen 1988a). Although the yield per acre of grains was no higher in Britain than in other parts of north-western Europe, the region as a whole reaped yields twice those in most other parts of the world (Allen and Ó Gráda 1988; Allen 1992). Most accounts of British farming link the high level of efficiency to Britain's peculiar agrarian institutions. Unlike many parts of the European Continent, where traditional peasant farming was consolidated by the French Revolution, in Britain the open fields were enclosed, farm size increased and tenancy became general. While this transformation had been underway since the middle ages, it reached its culmination during the industrial revolution. Furthermore, it is often claimed that the agrarian transformation made important contributions to industrialisation by increasing output and supplying the industrial economy with labour and capital.

One of the most basic questions is the timing and nature of the agricultural revolution. Toynbee (1884), Mantoux (1905) and Ernle (1961) located the agricultural revolution in the eighteenth century, and their revolution comprised both institutional change and the modernisation of farm methods. Twentieth-century historians have emphasised that much productivity growth occurred before 1700 and have tended to decouple improvements in farming from enclosure and farm size increases. Certainly by 1700 crop yields were higher than in the middle ages, labour productivity had increased and output per worker in English farming was already 15 per cent higher than in France. The first half of the nineteenth century was also a time of sustained improvement, but a question mark hangs over the eighteenth century: some scholars see it as a period of stasis; others as a century of steady progress. The importance of enclosure and large-scale farming as bases for productivity growth is not independent of this issue since enclosure and farm amalgamation progressed so substantially during the eighteenth century. The relationships between productivity growth, rural social structure and agriculture's role in economic development remain fundamental questions of historical research.

The modernisation of agriculture took place in the context of fluctuating farm prices. They fell during the second quarter of the eighteenth century – the so-called agricultural depression – and then increased erratically until the 1790s. Corn prices doubled and tripled during the harvest years of 1795, 1799 and 1800, and the price level remained high and volatile until the end of the Napoleonic Wars. Then began a slide of prices that lasted until the middle of the nineteenth century. The pace of improvement of farm methods may have been an important determinant of the price history through its impact on agricultural supply. The fluctuations in the price level certainly affected the evolution of farming and rural society in general. Rising prices after 1750 and especially during the Napoleonic Wars accelerated enclosure; the high prices of the 1790s threatened the standard of living of the rural poor, gave rise to radicalism and brought on changes in poor relief like the Speenhamland system; landowners who had gained from the high prices of 1795–1815 sought to preserve their rent rolls during the succeeding deflation through the Corn Laws, which imposed substantial duties on imported grain (Hueckel 1981).

The rise of the great estate

In the mid-eighteenth century, 80 per cent of Britain's farm land lay in England and Wales, which produced 89 per cent of Britain's farm output (Feinstein 1978: 635 n. 55; cf. Solar 1983 and Table 5.1). While the agriculture of the Scottish Highlands was revolutionised by the clearances, the changes that affected the largest share of British agriculture occurred mainly in England and comprised the enclosure of the open fields, the growth in farm size and the consolidation of the great estate. Hence, discussion will focus on the English story. Many of the changes in farm methods and management affected Scottish agriculture as well.

Over half of the farm land in medieval England was organised in open fields and commons. Under this system, the land of the village was divided rigidly between arable and pasture. Holdings of arable consisted of strips scattered around the village. The strips were grouped into several large fields, which were also often units in a crop rotation. Three fields were common, in which case one was planted with wheat or rye, the second with

barley, oats, beans or peas and the third was fallow. Each year the fields
shifted to the next phase in the sequence. Every farmer had to follow this
communally agreed plan. The grass of the village included the meadow on
which hay was cut, and the commons where the sheep and cattle were
pastured in a village herd. In densely settled regions, the commons were
small, but in many parts of the kingdom there were great tracts of waste
used as common pasture for sheep. The herd was also turned on to the
fallow field as well as on to the other fields after they were harvested in
order that they should eat weeds and manure the land.

Enclosed farming was the antithesis of the open-field system. When land
was enclosed, the owners usually exchanged strips and divided commons,
so that each proprietor had large, consolidated blocks of property.
Communal rotations and grazing were abolished. Each owner acquired
exclusive control over his property, so every farmer could cultivate as he
pleased without reference to the rest of the community. In 1500, about 45
per cent of the farm land in England was already enclosed, and most of that
had probably never been open. The open fields in 1500 included much of
the grain-growing land in the country. In 1700, 29 per cent of England
remained open or common, and the proportion shrank to 5 per cent in
1914, where it remains today (Wordie 1983: 502). This phase of the
enclosure movement was particularly intense in the midlands where over
half of the farm land was enclosed in the eighteenth and nineteenth
centuries (Wordie 1983: 500). Most of the remaining open land is common
pasture.

In the eighteenth century, much of the enclosing was accomplished by
parliamentary act. In such an enclosure the principal landowners of the
village petitioned Parliament for a bill to enclose their village. Unanimity
of the owners was not required: in general the owners of 75 per cent to 80
per cent of the land had to be in favour in order for the bill to proceed.
Since landownership was highly concentrated, an enclosure could – and
often did – proceed with a majority of small proprietors opposed. In the
memorable phrase of the Hammonds (1924: 25), 'the suffrages were not
counted but weighed'. The bill named commissioners, who carried out the
enclosure, and endorsed their award in advance. The commissioners held
hearings in the village, identified the proprietors, appointed a surveyor
who mapped the village and valued each holding and finally reallocated the
land so that each proprietor (including those who opposed the enclosure)
received a grant of land in proportion to the value of his or her holdings in
the open fields; 3,093 Acts enclosed 4,487,079 acres of open field and
common pasture in this manner. A further 2,172 Acts were concerned
exclusively with the enclosure of an additional 2,307,350 acres of common
pasture and waste (Turner 1980: 26, 178).

A second major change was an increase in farm size. In the middle ages demesnes were already several hundred acres, but the farms of serfs were usually thirty acres or less (Kosminski 1956; Allen 1992). During the population decline in the fourteenth and fifteenth centuries, farm size increased. Estate surveys show that the average farm – including demesnes, copyholds and leased land – in northern England and in open-field villages in southern England was sixty-five acres in about 1700. Enclosed farms in the south were already larger, however. In the eighteenth century, small farms were amalgamated into large in both open fields and throughout the north. By 1800, 150 acres was the average across all types of farms in the south, and 100 acres was the average in the north (Wordie 1974; Allen 1988a).

The growth in farm size was accompanied by a revolution in land tenure. Many small farms in 1700 were either owned outright by their occupiers or were held on very long-term agreements such as copyholds for lives or beneficial leases. During the eighteenth century, small freeholds were bought up by great estates and manorial lords stopped renewing copyholds for lives and beneficial leases. The formerly yeomen lands passed into the hands of the gentry and aristocracy. The small farms were amalgamated into large and were then leased to large-scale farmers. The result was the consolidation of the great estate and the emergence of the three-tiered social structure of rich landlord, substantial tenant farmer and poor landless labourer.

Eighteenth-century agricultural improvers regarded enclosure and the creation of large farms as prerequisites for the modernisation of agriculture, and this view has become widespread among historians. Since enclosing began on a large scale in the late fifteenth century, its defenders have argued that it led to the adoption of modern methods. Quesnay, the French physiocrat, advanced the view that higher farm output required more investment, and that only large-scale farmers had access to the requisite capital. Arthur Young adopted this view and merged it with the claim that enclosure also led to modernisation. For Young (1774: 287–8), the large 'farmer, with a greater proportional wealth than the small occupier, is able to work great improvements in his business ... He also employs better cattle and uses better implements; he purchases more manures, and adopts more improvements.' Open fields inhibited this style of farming since they gave the small, backward farmers the power to check the initiative of the large-scale entrepreneur. Enclosure was essential to set free the process of investment and modernisation.

In the eighteenth century, there was a consensus that enclosure and large-scale farming raised output. There was, however, a deep difference of opinion about the impact of these changes on employment. One group of writers, whose origins ran back to the earliest critics of enclosure, argued that enclosures and large farms reduced employment in agriculture. By the seventeenth century, in an ironic twist, some advocates of this view were defending enclosures on the grounds that the expulsion of people from farming created a manufacturing workforce (Fortrey 1663). This, of course, became Marx's view on the subject. The other group argued that enclosures and large farms increased agricultural employment since they led to more intensive cultivation. Young endorsed this position, and argued that, nonetheless, large farms and enclosures stimulated manufacturing since they increased food production, which led to a larger population, most of whom were employed off the farm. The claims that enclosure raised employment and that the industrial workforce was the result of population growth (rather than the release of labour from agriculture) have become standard views since their restatement by Chambers (1953).

The role of enclosure and large farms in raising output, the impact of these changes on employment, the contribution that agricultural change made to manufacturing development – these issues remain central questions of English history. A first step in analysing them is to consider broad trends in agricultural outputs and inputs.

Outputs

It is only recently that historians have measured the increase in farm output between 1700 and 1850. Three different approaches have been taken.

The first approach was Deane and Cole's (1962: 62–75, 164–73). They recognised that the value of agricultural output equalled the sum of wages, profits and rents (value added) earned in farming. Hence, for 1800–50, they estimated agricultural output as the sum of those factor returns. Deflating value added by an index of agricultural product prices gives an index of real farm output. This index was extrapolated back to 1700 on the basis of population change with an adjustment for changes in the volume of corn imports and exports. This procedure assumes that per capita food consumption remained constant in the eighteenth century.

The second approach was proposed by Crafts (1976, 1985a: 38–44). He rejected Deane and Cole's assumption of constant per capita food consumption on the grounds that income rose and relative prices changed. He specified a demand equation and estimated a range of growth rates that depended on the income and price elasticities assumed. In the early eighteenth century, agricultural prices fell, which suggests that supply was growing faster than demand. Consequently, Crafts' procedure yields a

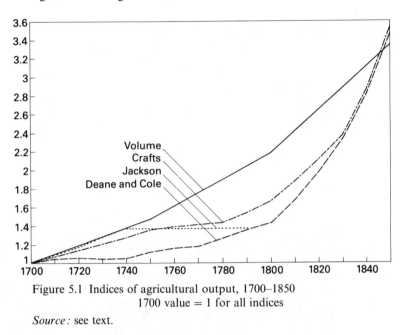

Figure 5.1 Indices of agricultural output, 1700–1850
1700 value = 1 for all indices

Source: see text.

faster growth of farm output than Deane and Cole's for 1700–50. The reverse is true later in the century as product prices rose: Deane and Cole's output index rose faster than Crafts'. Jackson (1985) has criticised details of Crafts' procedures and produced another set of estimates for the period 1660–1790. Jackson's calculation stretches Crafts' mid-century pause in output growth into stagnation lasting from 1740 to 1790. All three indices are shown in Figure 5.1.

The third approach is to estimate agricultural output directly from the details of farming. This approach is the most obvious but also the most difficult since there is considerable uncertainty about many elements of the calculation. Agricultural historians, however, have made great strides in assembling and assessing the necessary information (e.g. Chartres 1985 and Holderness 1989). Table 5.1 extends their work and presents estimates of the volume of output of the main farm products net of seed and the oats consumed by farm horses. (Unlike the other estimates, which pertain to Great Britain, these estimates apply only to England and Wales.) Aside from rye, whose production declined as wheat became the popular bread grain, the output of all products increased. The output of animal products increased more rapidly than the output of corn, beans and potatoes. The table shows the value of net farm output in 1815 prices, and it is plotted in Figure 5.1.

Table 5.1. *Output of principal commodities, 1700–1850*

	1700	1750	1800	1850
Part A Major commodities				
Corn (million bushels)	65	88	131	181
Meat (million lb)	370	665	888	1,356
Wool (million lb)	40	60	90	120
Cheese (million lb)	61	84	112	157
Part B Volume in 1815 prices (£m)				
Corn and potatoes	19	25	37	56
Animal products	21	34	51	79
Total	40	59	88	135

Note: corn includes wheat, rye, barley, oats, beans and peas, net of seed and oats consumed by livestock. Animal products include meat, wool, dairy products, cheese, hides and hay sold off the farm.

Sources: Corn, beans and potatoes: Chartres (1985: 444) and Holderness (1989: 145) except for the following: beans in 1700 taken to be the acreage in Table 5.6 multiplied by the yield in Table 5.7. Potatoes in 1700 estimated by multiplying an assumed acreage of 0·05 million acres by the yield used throughout by Holderness. For corn and beans, estimates of seed required were deducted from the gross production.

Meat and wool: quantities for 1750–1850 were taken from Holderness (1989: 155, 171–4). Quantities for 1700 taken from King (1696: 430).

Dairy products (fluid milk, cheese, butter, flet cheese): 1750–1850 taken from Holderness (1989: 169–70). 1700 quantities computed by reducing the 1750 quantities in proportion to the change in beef production.

Hides: 1750–1850: computed from Table 5.14 in Clarkson (1989: 470) by applying the coefficients detailed in n. 259. The estimates of hide output are about double those for leather production shown on p. 467, as they should be. 1700 quantity computed from King (1696: 430) using the procedure of Clarkson.

Hay for town horses: number of town horses taken from Feinstein (1978: 70). I applied an estimate of 0·2 million in 1760 to 1750 and assumed it also applied to 1700. I followed Thompson (1983a: 60) in assuming each town horse consumed 2·4 tons of hay.

Oats consumed by farm horses: I assumed that each horse of a farm consumed fifty-two bushels of oats per year. Number of horses as described in sources to Table 5.4. I subtracted the value of these oats from the value of gross output (less seed) to get net farm output.

Prices for aggregating commodities: most from John (1989). The price of hides from Clarkson (1989: 476). Hay price from *Gentleman's Magazine*, 1815, average of January and July prices at St James, Whitechapel and Smithfield.

The three methods imply similar estimates for output growth over the industrial revolution but differ in detail. From 1700 to 1851, output increased by a factor of 3.50 according to Deane and Cole, by 3.56 according to Crafts and by 3.37 according to the constant price index of net farm output. The disagreement between them is over when this growth occurred. As Figure 5.1 shows, the index of the volume of net output gives the most uniform rate of growth. Deane and Cole's and Crafts' series grow faster in the nineteenth century than in the eighteenth. Deane and Cole's series grows little from 1700 to 1750 when growth picks up for the rest of the eighteenth century. In contrast, Crafts' and Jackson's series show most of their eighteenth-century growth in the first half of the century. There is a pause in growth according to Crafts from 1760 to 1780. With Jackson's series, this pause is stretched to stagnation that lasts from 1740 to 1790.

There are arguments in favour of each series. The index of net farm output appears to be the most reliable since it is the most firmly based in farm practice. However, there are serious gaps in its component series and these are filled by extrapolation and interpolation. This procedure suppresses shorter-run fluctuations, creating an illusion of uniform growth. The series of Crafts and Jackson may give a more accurate indication of the rhythm of change since they avoid interpolation and bring other information (in particular price history) to bear on the problem. These considerations suggest that there probably was a pause or even stagnation in output growth in the last half of the eighteenth century, but the issue is open. Fortunately, the differences between these series over the long term are not substantial.

Inputs

Farm output went up for two reasons: the land, labour and capital used by agriculture increased, and those inputs generated more output due to improvements in farm methods and organisation. As with output, there is considerable uncertainty as to the exact magnitudes of the inputs. The figures discussed here relate to England and Wales rather Great Britain.

Land

The main sources that describe land use are contemporary estimates: as part of his social accounts for 1688, Gregory King estimated the acreage of arable, pasture, etc. W. T. Comber did the same in 1808, and his estimates agree in broad outline with B. P. Capper's figures for 1801. The noted agricultural writer James Caird produced further estimates for 1850–1. I have applied King's, Comber's and Caird's figures to 1700, 1800 and 1850, respectively (see Table 5.2). The most remarkable development was the growth in arable, pasture and meadow, which increased from 21 million acres *c.* 1700 to 29.1 million *c.* 1800 to 30.6 million *c.* 1850. In the eighteenth century, the growth was mainly in pasture and meadow; in the nineteenth century, it was the arable that expanded. These increases were

Table 5.2. *Utilisation of English and Welsh land, 1700–1850*
(*millions of acres*)

	c. 1700	c. 1800	c. 1850
Arable	11	11·6	14·6
Pasture and meadow	10	17·5	16·0
Woods and coppices	3	1·6	1·5
Forest, parks, commons	3	6·5	3·0
Waste	10		
Buildings, water, roads	1	1·3	2·2
Total	38	38·5	37·3
Total agricultural	34	35·6	33·6
Index of land input	1·00	1·35	1·37

Sources: c. 1700: King (1696: 428). He gives buildings, etc., as 2 million, which is manifestly too high. I have cut it to 1 million and the total accordingly.

   c. 1800: Comber's 1808 estimates summarised in Prince (1976: 103). Waste from Young (1799: 31–2).

   c. 1850: arable, pasture, meadow: English figures from Caird (1852: 521) with an allowance for Wales derived from tithe commutation reports summarised in Kain (1986: 431–56).

   Woods from *Agricultural Returns for Great Britain, 1872.*

   Waste equals rough pasture from later nineteenth-century statistics given in Stamp (1948: 481).

   Buildings, etc., as residual. This accords with later values, e.g. Stamp (1948: 197–8).

   Total agricultural land: sum of arable, pasture, meadow, forest, parks, commons and waste.

   Index of land input: the acreages of agricultural land were aggregated using their annual rental values as weights. Two calculations were done – one using King's (1696: 428) weights and one using Caird's (1852: 521). The indices agreed closely. The index reported here is a geometric average of the two.

accomplished by corresponding reductions in wood, common and waste. Some of this change was spurious: 'waste' has always been used to graze sheep, and thus has always been agricultural land. However, there was probably also a real improvement in the quality of the land – pastures were drained, fertilised and reseeded. Great tracts of land in northern and western England were developed into improved grazing in this way. In eastern England, arable was often the result. Young's (1813a: 2, 99, 100) account of Lincolnshire gives a flavour of the changes. He described the improvement of the heath near Lincoln 'which formerly was covered with heath, gorse, &c. and yielding, in fact, little or no produce, converted by enclosure, to profitable arable farms'. Much land had been improved, 'for these heaths extend near seventy miles'. On the coast, 'there spreads a great extent of lowland, much of which was once marsh and fen; but now become, by the gradual exertions of above 150 years, one of the richest tracts in the kingdom'.

Labour

The agricultural workforce is much more difficult to count than the acreage of farm land or even the volume of production. The subject is bedevilled by the problems of part-time work, unpaid family work, and by people dividing their time between farming and proto-industry. Perhaps for these reasons, King tallied much of the population as 'labourers' and 'cottagers' without assigning them to agriculture, commerce or manufacturing. Massie did the same with his social table for 1759 (Lindert and Williamson 1982). Estimates of the agricultural workforce must be erected on a basis other than contemporary estimates.

The oldest view about the size of the agricultural workforce – and one that appeals to common sense – is that it declined during the industrial revolution. This view is supported by the long-standing notion that enclosures were driving people off the land into the factories. Both of these positions have been called into question by historians. In particular, Deane and Cole (1962: 142–3) have used the occupational information in the nineteenth-century censuses to argue that farm employment in Great Britain increased from 1.7 million in 1801 to 2.1 million in 1851. Although they describe their 1801 employment estimates as 'little more than guesses', the idea that agricultural employment expanded during the industrial revolution (albeit at a slower rate than manufacturing employment) has become the standard view.

While the 1851 census does provide an acceptable basis for calculating the agricultural workforce at the end of the industrial revolution, the early censuses are not nearly so reliable, and, in any event, cannot be used to push the estimates back before 1800. Indirect methods are necessary. One procedure is to combine information from estate surveys with the returns collected by Arthur Young on his English tours (Allen 1988a). Young was a noted agricultural improver and prolific writer. He travelled through most English counties in the 1760s and reported the details of several hundred farms. Since the information includes the size and land use pattern of the farm as well as the number of regularly employed men, women and boys, equations can be estimated that correlate employment with variables like farm size. Applying those relationships to the distribution of farm sizes shown by estate surveys allows estimates of the agricultural labour force. The estimates encompass only those steadily employed: additional labour was hired during peak periods like the harvest. While important, the total number of hours worked by the additional labourers was small compared to the contribution of the regularly employed.

Table 5.3 shows that there was little long-run change in the English agricultural workforce. The total number employed fell between 1700 and 1800, then rebounded to 1851 when the total was still less than it had been in 1700. Weighting the employment of men, women and boys by the wage rates recorded by Young produces an index of the quantity of labour. It increased marginally over the period. Since the acreage of improved farm land was also rising, employment per acre (as measured by the ratio of the index of labour to the index of land) fell from a value of 1.00 in 1700 to 0.70 in 1800 and then returned to 0.85 in 1850. Even though farm employment was roughly constant, employment per acre declined, especially in the eighteenth century.

The composition of the agricultural workforce also changed significantly from 1700 to 1850. First, the share of adult males increased from 38 per cent of the workforce to 64 per cent. Second, more of these men were employees rather than farmers since the number of farms was probably falling. Third, most of the hired men in 1851 were day-labourers while in 1700 most had been servants hired by the year (Kussmaul 1981b). Fourth, while the servants in 1700 had been continuously employed over the year, about one third of the male labourers in 1851 were only employed in peak periods like the harvest. The contrast between 1700 and 1851 is far-reaching; in 1700, the agricultural workforce had been built around family labour supplemented by young adults in their late teens and early twenties hired on annual contracts as servants. These categories were still present in 1851, but the workforce had become much older, more male and more erratically employed.

Wrigley (1985, 1987a) has also analysed the agricultural labour force over the eighteenth and nineteenth centuries. He estimated that the 'agricultural population' was about 3 million people over the eighteenth century. This figure includes non-working children and retired people. Assuming that the average household had 4.5 members, 3 million people corresponds to 667,000 households – a figure close to the 595,000 and 628,000 thousand adult men shown in Table 5.3. An exact match is not expected since male servants did not head households and since some women did. Nevertheless, the correspondence confirms the order of magnitude of both calculations. Wrigley's procedure does not permit a separate examination of the employment histories of men, women and children, and so does not pick up the falls in the employment of women and boys.

Table 5.3. *Employment in English and Welsh agriculture, 1700–1851* (*thousands*)

	1700	1800	1851
Men	595	628	971
Women	505	426	409
Boys	453	351	144
Total	1,553	1,405	1,524
Index of labour input	1·00	0·95	1·16

Sources: 1700, 1800: the calculations are an elaboration of the method described in Allen (1988a). First, labour per acre was computed from farm size distributions. For 1700, three distributions were used: the distributions for open-field farms *c*. 1700 and enclosed farms *c*. 1800 given in Allen (1988a: 122), and the distribution of farms in 1714–20 summarised in Wordie (1974: 605). For 1800, two distributions were used: enclosed farms *c*. 1800 as given in Allen (1988a: 122), and farms in 1807–13 in Wordie (1974: 606). For the calculations involving Wordie's distributions, it was necessary to interpolate missing values to fill out the distribution of the acreage of land. For each distribution, labour per acre was computed as in Allen (1988a). Separate calculations were done for men, women and boys. Second, a weighted average of employment per acre was computed. Following Grigg (1963), I distinguished the north and west, a region of small farms, from the south and east, a region of large farms. Using Grigg's (1963: 273) map of 'large farm counties in 1851', I assigned counties to the two districts. According to the 1867 agricultural statistics, 49 per cent of the arable, pasture and meadow was in the large farm region and 51 per cent in the small farm region. I computed average labour per acre in 1800 as a weighted average of employment per acre from the Allen and Wordie distributions using these weights. For 1700, the same procedure was used except that labour per acre for the southern, large farm region was taken to be a weighted average of the 1700 open and 1800 enclosed distributions. The weights were 63 per cent for the first and 37 per cent for the second following the estimates for open and enclosed land *c*. 1700 in Allen (1992: ch. 2). Third, labour per acre was multiplied by the acreage of arable, pasture and meadow in Table 5.2 to compute total employment. Fourth, the procedures thus far assume that all farmers were men; that assumption is relaxed by estimating the number of women farmers in 1700 and 1800. Those estimates were made by multiplying the apparent number of farms in the country in 1700 and 1800 by the proportion of farmers who were women in 1851. The estimated number of women farmers was subtracted from the number of 'men' computed in step three and added to the number of 'women'. In the labour input index, female farmers are valued at the same wage as male farmers.

1851: computed from the 1851 census. I began with the occupational data. The labour force includes farmers, graziers, farmers' wives, sons and daughters, labourers, servants and shepherds. I include as male farmers the 22,982 'occupiers of land engaged in pursuits besides farming' (p. cclxxxv). Farmers' sons and daughters less than 15 years old were not tallied as working in agriculture, but many surely were. To form an estimate of their number, I assumed that the number of farmers' sons and daughters aged 0–14 working in agriculture equalled the corresponding numbers aged 15–19 that were recorded. I assumed people aged 65 and over were out of the labour force and not employed (see Allen 1991b). I assumed that farmers, their relatives, labourers, shepherds and servants under the age of 65 were employed. I took the employment of male labourers, shepherds and servants aged 15–64 to have been 665,651, the number enumerated as employed on the census day, and I estimated that female labourers and servants aged 15–64 employed equalled the numbers in those age categories multiplied by the unemployment rate of the corresponding men. 'Men' includes all males aged 15 and over; 'boys' includes males aged 14 and under; 'women' includes all females.

Wrigley (1987a) has also estimated the growth of the adult male agricultural labour force in the first half of the nineteenth century. He found it grew about 10 per cent from 1811 to 1851 when it equalled 1 million, a figure that includes men who only worked in peak periods as well as those steadily employed. Wrigley's estimate of the rate of growth is the right order of magnitude for the growth rate of the total, regularly employed agricultural labour force over the period. However, the number of steadily employed men grew more rapidly than Wrigley's estimate, as men displaced women and boys in farm labour.

Capital

The provision of capital was divided between landlords and tenants. Landlords financed most of the permanent improvements to the property – structures, roads, fences and enclosures. Tenants financed implements and livestock. Tenants also financed a few improvements to the soil such as marling or draining. Their benefits lasted a decade or two and were worthwhile from the tenants' point of view only if the tenant had adequate security. The tenants also had to pay wages, rent, taxes, etc., in advance of the sale of the crops. These expenses did not result in capital formation, strictly speaking, since they did not create assets that lasted longer than one year.

Landowners could finance their investments by mortgaging their property. Tenants obtained their capital in more diverse ways. At the outset, most farmers took over their parents' farms and secured their livestock and implements in that way. Thereafter, they bred their animals. Cash to pay wages and rents was saved from the sale of the previous year's output. Sometimes landlords provided their tenants with capital, for instance, when drains were installed. 'At Marston, much draining has been performed on a farm of Mr. Foster's, who pays all of the bushes [to line the drains], except what could be obtained from the farm, and the tenant is to allow interest for the money thus sunk by the landlord' (Batchelor 1808: 476). Money could be borrowed from relatives and other villagers (Holderness 1976). Corn merchants often bought the crop while it was still standing in the fields. According to Defoe (1727: II, part II, 36), 'These Corn-Factors in the Country ride about among the Farmers, and buy the Corn, even in the Barn before it is thresh'd, nay, sometimes they buy it in the Field standing, not only before it is reap'd but before it is ripe.' Whether or not the factors were 'cunningly taking advantage of the farmers by letting them have Money beforehand, which they, poor Men, often want', credit was being extended.

Feinstein (1978, 1988) and Holderness (1988) have estimated the growth

Table 5.4. *Capital in English and Welsh agriculture, 1700–1850*
(*£million in 1851–60 prices*)

	1700	1750	1800	1850
Landlords				
Structures, etc.	112	114	143	232
Tenants				
Implements	10	8	10	14
Farm horses	20	20	18	22
Other livestock	41	53	71	85
Total	183	195	242	353

Sources: Structures and implements were first estimated jointly from Feinstein (1988: 448) and then separated by subtracting Holderness' (1988: 31) estimates of implements from the total. Both Feinstein and Holderness estimated capital for Great Britain, and the first step was to reduce all of their figures by 20 per cent to eliminate Scotland. (Feinstein (1978: 635 n. 55) assumes Scotland contained 20 per cent of Great Britain's agricultural land. Applying Feinstein's livestock valuations to the 1867 agricultural census shows that Scottish livestock was 21 per cent of Great Britain's.) I applied Feinstein's estimate for 1760 to both 1750 and 1700. I applied Holderness' 1770 implement estimate to 1750 and interpolated the value for 1850. I assigned a large number to 1700 in view of the greater number of small farms. The figure for structures equals the total of structures and implements less implements.

Farm horses were valued at £20 each following Feinstein (1978: 20). Feinstein (1978: 70) and Holderness (1988: 32) both estimated the number of horses in British agriculture, but they do not agree. Feinstein's estimate for 1860 is much closer to the return in the 1870 agricultural statistics, and I follow his lead in adopting the value in that return (1·1 million) as the number of horses on farms in England and Wales in 1850. Between 1800 and 1850, the acreage of arable in England and Wales increased 26 per cent, and if the number of farm horses varied proportionately, there were 0·9 million in 1800. This is far closer to Holderness' estimate for that date than to Feinstein's. King (1696: 430) reported that there were 1·2 million horses in England and Wales in 1700. Feinstein (1978: 70) thought there were 0·2 million horses off the farm in 1760. Assuming the same number for 1700 implies there were 1 million farm horses then. It is plausible that there were more in 1700 than 1800 in view of the larger number of small farms. I take 1 million to have been the number of farm horses in 1700 and 0·95 million to have been the number in 1750.

The value of other livestock in 1700 were computed from King's (1696: 430) statement of the numbers using Feinstein's values and procedures. I reduced the 1851–60 prices by 25 per cent to allow for quality improvements between 1700 and 1851–60. For 1750–1850, I used Feinstein's (1978: 70) estimates, reducing them by 20 per cent to eliminate Scotland, applying the 1760 figure to 1750, and interpolating the 1850 value.

of capital supplied by farmers and landlords. Their results are shown in Table 5.4. Between 1700 and 1850, both components of capital approximately doubled. During the eighteenth century, capital grew at the same rate as improved farm land, so capital per acre remained constant. From 1800 to 1850, capital per acre rose 40 per cent. Capital was the fastest growing input.

Productivity growth

The history of output and inputs implies that productivity grew from 1700 to 1850. Over that period, land grew 37 per cent, labour 16 per cent, and capital 93 per cent. Giving equal weight to each input implies that inputs *in toto* grew by a factor of 1.45 from 1700 to 1850. Output grew more – between 3.37 and 3.56 times depending on which index is used. Total factor productivity increased by a factor of 2.32–2.46 from 1700 to 1850.

While the various output indices imply similar increases in productivity from 1700 to 1850, they imply different chronologies of productivity growth within the period since they disagree as to when output grew rapidly. Since the index of the volume of net farm output grows most uniformly, it implies the most uniform rates of productivity growth – 0.6 per cent per year in the eighteenth century and 0.5 per cent in the first half of the nineteenth (see Table 5.5). Since the other indices assign more of the output growth to the nineteenth century, they also identify the first half of that century as the time of rapid productivity growth. Crafts' index, for instance, implies that productivity grew at 0.4 per cent per year in the eighteenth century and 1.1 per cent in the nineteenth. A good deal hinges on the measurement of output: if the index of net farm output is correct, then farming methods improved continuously over the eighteenth and nineteenth centuries. If any of the other indices are correct, then the agricultural revolution – meaning a sustained rise in productivity – becomes a nineteenth-century affair.

One way to circumvent the difficulties in measuring the *quantities* of inputs and outputs is to infer productivity growth from the history of their *prices*. If productivity rises then a farmer can cut his price and still cover his costs. Hence, a fall in product prices with respect to input prices indicates productivity growth. Using this method, Allen (1992) found that the rate of productivity growth was negligible in the eighteenth century and accelerated to 1.7 per cent per year between 1800/24 and 1825/49. This pattern is closest to the output story of Deane and Cole or, indeed, Jackson for the eighteenth century. Using a similar method, McCloskey (1981b: 114, 126) computed a productivity rate of 0.5 per cent per year for the first half of the nineteenth century. This calculation suggests that production

Table 5.5. *Alternative measures of productivity growth, 1700–1850*
(*percentage annual rates of growth*)

	1700–1800			1800–50		
	Output	Inputs	TFP	Output	Inputs	TFP
Deane and Cole	0·4	0·2	0·2	1·8	0·4	1·4
Crafts	0·6	0·2	0·4	1·5	0·4	1·1
Jackson	0·3	0·2	0·1	—	—	—
Volume of output	0·8	0·2	0·6	0·9	0·4	0·5

grew along the lines of the index of net farm output. Some of the discrepancy between these calculations is due to differences in data and the details of the procedure, but there is an underlying theoretical problem. To measure productivity from the prices of outputs and inputs, the observed prices must equal marginal costs and the values of marginal products. This condition was probably not satisfied for many inputs, in particular land. Rents, for instance, were not adjusted annually and so could fall behind changes in land values (Allen 1982). In such cases price calculations can give spurious measures of productivity change. The measurement of both prices and quantities needs to be refined to pin down the chronology of the agricultural revolution.

Farm methods and productivity growth

The major reason that agricultural productivity rose was because output increased: the production of both corn and livestock products more than tripled from 1700 to 1850 (Table 5.1). No single innovation, nor even a short list of innovations, explains these increases. Many reinforcing changes were involved.

Corn output increased primarily because the yield per acre rose rather than because the sown area expanded. As Table 5.6 indicates, the acreage planted with corn and beans increased from 6.7 million acres in 1700 to 8.2 million in 1850, a gain of 22 per cent. At the same time, the net production of these crops increased 2.6 fold in constant prices. The gross yield per acre increased between 50 per cent and 75 per cent depending on the crop.

It is important to recognise that the rise in yields between 1700 and 1850 was the continuation of an earlier trend. On demesnes in southern England in the late middle ages, wheat, oats and beans typically yielded ten bushels per acre while barley yielded fifteen (Titow 1972: 121–35; Rogers 1866–1902: I, 38–45; *Victoria County History*, Cambridgeshire: II, 60–1).

Table 5.6. *Utilisation of the arable, 1700–1850 (millions of acres)*

	1700	1750	1800	1850
Wheat	1·4	1·8	2·5	3·6
Rye	0·9	0·5	0·3	0·1
Barley	1·9	1·4	1·3	1·5
Oats	1·2	2·0	2·0	2·0
Beans and peas	1·3	1·0	1·2	1·0
Turnips	0·4	1·0	1·3	2·0
Potatoes	0·1	0·2	0·3	0·4
Clover	0·5	1·0	1·2	2·2
Fallow	3·3	2·5	1·5	1·8
Total	11·0	11·4	11·6	14·6

Sources: 1700: wheat, rye, barley, oats from Chartres (1985: 444). Turnips, potatoes and clover are scaled down from the 1750 values. Fallow inferred from King (1696: 431). Beans and peas computed residually.
  1750–1850: all values except fallow and total from Holderness (1989: 145). Totals for 1800 and 1850 from Table 5.2. Total for 1750 interpolated, and fallow for that year computed residually.

Table 5.7. *Crop yields (following Chartres and Holderness), 1700–1850 (bushels per acre)*

	1700	1750	1800	1850
Wheat	16·0	18·0	21·5	28·0
Rye	17·0	18·0	26·0	28·0
Barley	23·0	25·0	30·0	36·5
Oats	24·0	28·0	35·0	40·0
Beans and peas	20·0	28·0	28·0	30·0

Sources: 1700: Chartres (1985: 444) except for beans and peas for which the yield is conjectured on the basis of Holderness (1989: 142).
  1750–1850: Holderness (1989: 145): gross yields.

The yields shown in Table 5.7 for 1700 already exceed these figures by 50 per cent for barley, 60 per cent for wheat, 100 per cent for beans and 140 per cent for oats.

The causes of the rise in corn yields are diffuse. First, there were improvements in seed. Farmers collected the seeds from the best plants and grew them separately to isolate high-yielding and disease-resistant strains. This practice, which began in the seventeenth century and was responsible for the pre-1700 advance of yields over medieval levels, was carried on by enterprising farmers through the eighteenth and probably into the nineteenth centuries (Plot 1677: 151; Marshall 1788: II, 4). Second, more manure was generated on the farm, and this fertilised the corn. The best indicator of the increase in manure availability is the rise in meat production since more meat required more fodder which resulted in more manure. Third, the cultivation of legumes (beans, peas, clover) increased during the eighteenth century. These crops fixed atmospheric nitrogen and thereby raised soil fertility (Chorley 1981). Fourth, soils were improved by marling and draining. During the Napoleonic Wars, the high price of corn relative to labour made it profitable to install bush drains on heavy clays. By the 1840s, the price of drain tiles fell enough to precipitate another round of drainage investment. Other investments that improved the quality of the soil included paring and burning and the application of lime. Fifth, the diffusion of seed drills and other improved farm machinery resulted in a better seed bed. Historians have not yet been able to pin down the relative importance of these factors, but together they were responsible for the rise in corn output.

Livestock output increased because the herds and flocks became more productive rather than because there were more animals. The number of cattle probably fell from about 4.5 million at the end of the seventeenth century to 3.9 million in the middle of the nineteenth, but the share of productive animals (i.e. dairy cows and those slaughtered) increased. Moreover, the weight of a carcase and the product of a cow rose. Likewise, the number of swine scarcely increased, so the main reason for the rise in pork output was a much greater rate of slaughtering and a very sharp rise in meat per carcase. In the case of sheep, the stock doubled between 1700 and 1850, but the weight of a fleece and the meat per carcase both increased (King 1696: 430; Holderness 1988: 32, 1989: 147–59, 169–70).

Meat per carcase increased for several reasons: improvements in the breed and increases in feed consumption were the main factors. A shift in tastes away from veal and young lamb toward the meat of older animals may have played a minor role as well (Holderness 1989: 155). Stock-breeders created new varieties of sheep, pigs and cattle in an effort to increase the rate of weight gain. The earliest and most famous break-through was the development of the New Leicester sheep by Robert Bakewell in the mid-eighteenth century. It reached a large size more rapidly than other breeds and it had a higher proportion of flesh to bone. Ellman's subsequent creation of the Southdown had a similar objective. Cattle breeds were also improved. Bakewell and Robert Fowler improved the Longhorn in the mid-eighteenth century, and it had a vogue for fifty years. After 1800 the Shorthorn gained popularity in the north and east as it was improved by Robert and Charles Colling, and by Thomas, John and

Richard Booth. In the first half of the nineteenth century, the Hereford emerged as an important fattening breed. Likewise, pigs were improved through the introduction of foreign, particularly Chinese, breeds. Rapid weight gain was the objective of most of these improvements.

The quantity of feed consumed by British livestock was increased by upgrading commons and waste into improved pasture and by cultivating animal feed in the arable rotations. Feed had always been grown by farmers. Much of the oat crop, for instance, was consumed by the farm horses, and peas and beans were often eaten by livestock. In the seventeenth century, the production of feed was increased with the cultivation of turnips and clover on a large scale. By the mid-eighteenth century, the classic Norfolk rotation (turnips–barley–clover–wheat) had emerged. The fallow was eliminated, and the clover and turnips provided winter fodder for animals. Other grasses like sainfoin and roots like Swedes and mangolds were also introduced into British rotations and fed to livestock. A major reason that sheep and cattle weighed more when they were slaughtered in 1850 than they had in 1750 was because they were eating better.

Farm size and productivity growth

The second reason why agricultural productivity increased during the industrial revolution was because labour per acre declined. The employment of women and boys fell. The employment of men grew but much less than the growth of improved land. The drop in labour per acre resulted from the growth in farm size.

Higher rent was the motive behind the creation of large farms. Big farms could afford to pay a higher rent since their costs were less – in particular, their labour costs. Large farms employed fewer boys per acre than small farms since boys were hard to supervise. The employment of women was also curtailed since their work was often tied to dairying and large mixed farms kept fewer cows per acre. There were also economies in the employment of men. Specialists replaced the ordinary labourer in tasks like tending hedges and caring for sheep. Activities like transporting grain and manure were carried out more efficiently when they were performed by groups of workers than when they were done by individuals. 'In harvest; two drivers, two loaders, two pitchers, two rakers, and the rest at the rick, or in the barn, will dispatch double the work that the same number of hands would do if divided into different gangs on different farms' (Arbuthnot 1773: 8). The growth in the average size of farms was the reason that the total employment of women and boys declined in the eighteenth century, and the employment of men remained constant even as the improved acreage expanded.

Enclosure and productivity growth

The most long-standing explanation for the rise in efficiency is enclosure. Eighteenth-century commentators regarded it as a prerequisite for improvement since the open-field system was supposed to have blocked advance. The rigid division of lands into arable and pasture precluded convertible husbandry, which involved alternating lands between the two uses. Collective management of the fields inhibited the adoption of new crops since a consensus was necessary among the farmers in order for change to occur. Pasturing the village livestock in a single herd led to overgrazing, the spread of animal diseases and the inability to control breeding. According to the critics, 'open-field farmers were impervious to new methods' (Ernle 1961: 199).

Enclosure is supposed to have rectified these problems by bringing land under exclusive private control. Communal controls were abolished, so that each owner – and thus each farmer – had exclusive control over his or her property. The scene was set for the enterprising farmers to take the lead in adopting new crops and improving the quality and care of their animals.

The case for the backwardness of the open fields and the modernity of the enclosures has rested mainly on eighteenth-century commentaries. In an extravagant phrase, for instance, Arthur Young (1813b: 35–6) contrasted 'the Goths and Vandals of open fields' with 'the civilization of enclosures'. There is some truth to this opinion, but enquiries by historians have shown that open fields were not nearly as backward as has been claimed. Havinden (1961) was one of the first to question the conventional indictment of open fields. He showed that such villages in Oxfordshire did, indeed, adopt new crops – in this case sainfoin. Yelling (1977: 146–232) strengthened the case with additional local comparisons, but remained unconvinced that open fields were really as flexible as enclosures. Allen (1989) has refined the assessment with a series of regional studies. These show that open-field villages adopted new crops and increased the share of grass when these innovations were profitable. However, enclosed villages always adopted the new methods more fully than did open-field villages.

Enclosure also led to greater output, but the increase was much less than the growth in production that occurred between 1700 and 1850. Chronology suggests this conclusion: much of the enclosure took place in the last half of the eighteenth century when Crafts and, especially, Jackson estimated the agricultural output growth stopped (Crafts 1985a: 42–3; Jackson 1985). Comparisons of corn yields in open and enclosed villages buttress the case. The data collected by Arthur Young on his tours of the 1760s show that yields of the main crops were 7 to 12 per cent higher in enclosed villages (Allen and Ó Gráda 1988: 98). Turner (1986: 691) found a larger increment – 11 to 23 per cent – in his sample drawn from the 1801 crop returns. A limitation common to both of these studies is that they did not standardise the comparisons by soil type. Allen (1989: 72) used data drawn mainly from Board of Agriculture county reports prepared between 1794 and 1816 and divided them into districts with relatively uniform environments. On the boulder clays of Cambridgeshire, Bedfordshire and Huntingdonshire, enclosure resulted in yield increases of 10 to 39 per cent for beans, barley and oats (but only 3 per cent for wheat) because the consolidation of property facilitated the installation of drains in the furrows that had formerly divided the open-field strips. In other regions, the yield increases were generally less than 10 per cent. Two important conclusions follow from these results: first, using medieval yields as a baseline for comparison, open-field villages had accomplished almost as much as had enclosed villages by the end of the eighteenth century. Second, the yield increases that followed enclosure were small compared to the yield increases that occurred between 1700 and 1850 (see Table 5.7). While enclosure did have some impact on yields, the boost was only a small part of the long-term advance.

Both Turner (1986) and Allen (1992) have combined their findings on yields with estimates of the impact of enclosure on cropping to measure the overall effect on output. Turner found that enclosure had little effect on total corn production, although declines were more frequent than advances. Allen found that enclosure increased corn production on the boulder clays where yields went up substantially, lowered output margin-ally on light soils where turnip cultivation was introduced and substantially reduced output where there was large-scale conversion of arable to pasture. Allen also included animal products in his comparison. He found that enclosure raised real farm output 12 per cent on the boulder clays in the east midlands and by 20 per cent on high-grade fattening pastures. Otherwise, eighteenth-century enclosures led to only minor increases or even reductions. As with the results on yields, the important finding is that the output increases which followed enclosure were very small compared to the more than doubling in output per acre which occurred in English and Welsh agriculture during the industrial revolution.

Enclosure affected the inputs in English agriculture as well as the output. The acreage of improved land increased substantially between 1700 and 1850. Enclosure was fundamental to this upgrading. In 1700, the waste that was later improved was legally common land. Only when it was enclosed and brought under individual control was it worthwhile for anyone to improve it.

Enclosure had a small impact on capital formation. The stock of fixed capital increased as landlords paid for the hedging, ditching, road building, etc., that accompanied enclosure. The capital supplied by farmers also increased as flocks were expanded and livestock upgraded to take advantage of the improved pastures and greater production of winter forage. However, Table 5.4 suggests that the total effect was not substantial during the eighteenth century – agricultural capital did not rise greatly before 1800.

The most hotly debated issue is the impact of enclosure on employment. In this regard, one must distinguish the charge that enclosure led to the expropriation of peasant lands from the impact of enclosure on labour demand per se. It is probable that many fifteenth-century enclosures did involve lords' usurping the land of small farmers and the destruction and depopulation of the villages concerned (Beresford 1954; Allen 1992). Such extreme results did not occur in the eighteenth and nineteenth centuries, since legal titles were protected in both parliamentary and non-parliamentary enclosures. There were still people at risk of losing property, however – principally cottagers who pastured stock on commons without a legal right to do so. They lost that privilege at enclosure. Moreover, even cottagers with legal common rights may have been worse off after enclosure since their land grants may not have generated as much income as their grazing right had previously. The losses were particularly serious for women (Humphries 1990; Neeson 1989).

There are strongly divergent views on the effect of enclosure on the demand for labour. Critics of enclosure have generally charged that people were put out of work, while defenders have claimed that enclosure created new jobs. In the modern literature, Chambers (1953) has championed the latter view and argued that the improved agriculture required more labour to hoe the turnips, thresh the additional corn, trim the hedges and scour the ditches. Recently, this view has been challenged. Snell (1985) has used Poor Law evidence to argue that enclosure led to increased seasonal unemployment rather than the greater stability in employment expected by Chambers. Allen (1988a) used Young's survey data to measure the impact of enclosure on employment. He found that enclosures had little effect on farm employment unless they led to the conversion of arable to pasture, in which case employment declined. In some regions, eighteenth-century enclosures did have this result. However, the total arable acreage increased slightly in this century (Table 5.2), so enclosure did not lead to a general decline in agricultural employment.

This review of the evidence about the impact of enclosure on agricultural outputs and inputs suggests that it had a positive but small effect on productivity. This conjecture is confirmed by measurements of total factor productivity. McCloskey (1972, 1975, 1989) suggested that the impact of enclosure on productivity could be inferred from the movement of rents.

Indeed, a rise in rent was the landlord's incentive to enclose, and, in the eighteenth century, the conventional expectation was a doubling from 10s to 20s per acre. (Allen (1988b) presents more refined comparisons of open and enclosed rents in various sub-divisions of the south midlands.) A stylised example shows how this increase might have arisen and its relationship to total factor productivity. In an eighteenth-century open-field village, output, as measured by farm revenue, was about £3.5 per acre. The cost of the labour, capital and materials applied to the land (including the opportunity cost of the labour and capital of the farmer and his family) was about £3.0 per acre. The difference, or Ricardian surplus, was £0.5 or 10s. If the market for farm tenancies were competitive, then rents would have been bid to equal this level. Suppose that enclosure involved no change in employment or capital per acre but resulted in an increase in output to £4 per acre. With costs the same, Ricardian surplus and rent would have risen to £1 (= £4−£3). In this example, the doubling of rent that followed enclosure was a consequence of the accompanying output increase.

While rents doubled, total factor productivity also increased but by a smaller proportion. Total factor productivity rises when output rises with respect to the 'bundle of inputs' used in production. In both the open and enclosed village in this example, the 'bundle' is the same – namely £3 of labour, capital and materials per acre of land. Output, however, increased from £3.5 to £4, i.e. by 14 per cent. That is the rise in total factor productivity.

The overall impact of the enclosure of open fields on the growth in productivity in English agriculture was less than 14 per cent for two reasons. First, the assumption that rental markets were always in competitive equilibrium so rents always equalled Ricardian surplus has been questioned – the rise in surplus may, in fact, have been less than the rise in rent (Allen 1982). Second, only 21 per cent of the farm land of England and Wales was enclosed between 1700 and 1850. Setting aside the first point, the enclosure of the open fields raised the total factor productivity of English and Welsh agriculture only 3 per cent (= 14 per cent × 0.21). This is an inconsequential amount compared to the more than doubling that took place over the period.

Enclosure did make another contribution to productivity growth in the same period – namely the reclamation of waste. This contribution can be analysed similarly using Gregory King's figures (1696). In the eighteenth century, about 3 million acres of 'forest, parks, and commons' were enclosed and improved as well as 3 million acres of waste. According to King the rental value of the first type of land was 3.5s per acre c. 1700 and the latter was worth 1s per acre. If the annual value of these lands was raised to 9s, the value of enclosed pasture, then the total value of English agricultural land increased from £8.75 million to £10.025 million – a gain of 23 per cent. Such a rent gain translates into a total factor productivity increase of about 7 per cent. This increase may well be an overstatement of the efficiency gains of the enclosure of waste since it values the improved land at a rent equal to the most productive land in King's account. Nevertheless, a 7 per cent gain in total factor productivity is still tiny compared to the 2.33 fold increase that occurred from 1700 to 1850. The overall conclusion must be that the enclosure movement made little contribution to agricultural productivity growth during the industrial revolution.

The only way to make the enclosure movement appear important in raising productivity is to confine the analysis to the eighteenth century and to use Jackson's index of the growth of farm output since it increases the least. With these figures, the total factor productivity of English and Welsh agriculture only grew by 14 per cent from 1700 to 1800, so the enclosure movement accounted for a large share. This, however, is a Pyrrhic victory since the choice of Jackson's output index implies that almost all the output growth – and, consequently, productivity growth – which occurred during the industrial revolution took place after 1800. Importance in the eighteenth century is of no consequence in the longer perspective.

Agrarian change and economic growth

Even if enclosure was not of great importance in boosting output or efficiency, it is possible that agricultural change *in toto* made an important contribution to economic development. The potential linkages include: providing a home market for manufactures; generating new capital by increasing the savings from the agricultural surplus; releasing capital by reducing the agricultural demand for investment; releasing labour by reducing the agricultural demand for workers; increasing output. Most of these functions were not performed by British agriculture.

A market for manufactures?

Agriculture did not provide a home market for manufactures. O'Brien (1985: 780) and Crafts (1985a: 133–4) independently estimated that the consumption of manufactures by agriculturalists increased about one third between 1700 and 1800 – a century when industrial production increased more than threefold (Crafts 1985a: 32). After 1800, the agricultural market became even less important. Exports and the urban economy, not agriculture, absorbed the manufacturing output.

A source of capital?

Industrial and commercial capital formation were not financed by tapping the agricultural surplus. Landlords received the bulk of the surplus – that is, the value of production less the consumption needs of farmers and labourers – in Britain as rent. While some landlords invested in urban and commercial activities, many borrowed instead. Crouzet (1972: 56) endorsed Postan's (1935: 2) 'view that "surprisingly little" of the wealth of rural England "found its way into the new industrial enterprises"'. Crafts (1985a: 122–5) has calculated that agricultural savings financed little non-agricultural investment.

The release of capital?

Agriculture did not release capital by reducing its demand for investment. Instead, as Table 5.4 indicates, agricultural capital increased. Any other result would be surprising in view of the eighteenth-century emphasis on rising investment as the source of rising agricultural output.

The release of labour?

One way in which British agriculture may have contributed to economic growth was through the release of labour. Here the conclusion depends on the definition adopted. The most straightforward meaning of 'labour release' is that farm employment declined. But male employment in agriculture was constant in the eighteenth century and rose in the first half of the nineteenth. The employment of women and children, however, declined throughout. If these 'freed' workers were reemployed in industry, then the resulting rise in manufacturing output would have been an indirect contribution of agrarian change to economic development. But this is a big 'if'. Most of the boys and women did not leave their villages. Only if employment were found in rural industry would it have been found at all. Throughout the industrial revolution, the employment prospects of women in the rural textile industries, their biggest employer, were declining in the face of mounting competition from factories. In 1724, Defoe wrote, 'The Farmers' Wives can get no Dairy-Maids ... truly the Wenches Answer, they won't go to Service at 12d. or 18d. a week, while they can get 7s. to 8s. a Week at Spinning' (Pinchbeck 1930: 140). By the 1830s, if not by 1800, these jobs had disappeared. Agricultural redundancies then resulted in structural unemployment rather than increased manufacturing output.

The problem of structural unemployment was greatest in southern England. Williamson (1990a: 178–218) has shown that southern urban wages were much higher than rural wages even allowing for the higher living costs and lower quality of life in the cities. There was no comparable disequilibrium in the north. Despite the fact that a large share of children born in rural England moved to cities when they reached adulthood, migration was not enough to equalise wages. This failure to allocate labour efficiently reduced the national income several percentage points, according to Williamson (1990a: 211). The fact that enclosures ceased to be depopulating during the industrial revolution may have meant – ironically – that agrarian change was less significant in raising the national income than traditional accounts suggest.

Crafts (1985b) has urged that declining farm employment is not the appropriate definition of labour release; instead, he proposes that a rise in output per worker that allows a decline of the fraction of the workforce in agriculture is a more revealing concept. In Crafts' terms, there is no doubt that labour was released from British agriculture during the industrial revolution. Output per worker tripled and the share of the workforce in agriculture declined significantly between 1700 and 1850.

Increasing output?

The greatest single contribution that British agriculture made to economic development was the increase in its output. Gross domestic product is the sum of value added in every sector. Since agriculture purchased little from other sectors, and since those purchases did not increase greatly, the rise in the value of agricultural output equals the rise in agricultural value added and, hence, the direct contribution of agrarian change to the growth in total output. In the eighteenth century, British GDP grew at an average rate of 0.82 per cent per year. In the first half of the nineteenth century, that rate accelerated to 2.10 per cent. If agricultural output had not grown at all while other sectors grew at their actual rates, then the rate of growth of GDP would have been reduced by one fifth to 0.68 per cent and 1.74 per cent per annum respectively. In the eighteenth century, this reduction would have been enough to reduce the positive growth in per capita income to almost nothing. If agricultural output grew according to the index of the volume of net farm output (rather than according to Crafts' estimates, which are assumed here), the contribution of agriculture was even greater in the eighteenth century and less in the nineteenth. Economic growth during the industrial revolution was broadly based and rapid in other sectors, but the contribution of agriculture was far from negligible.

From another perspective, the contribution of British agriculture was less impressive. Farm output did increase considerably during the industrial revolution, but the increased output did not keep pace with demand and the country became more dependent on imports. Further, the real price of food rose as supply grew less rapidly than demand. These increases began after the middle of the eighteenth century and were the counterparts to the pauses in output growth deduced by Crafts and Jackson. Prices rose substantially in the mid-1790s, and the standard of living of rural labourers was jeopardised. One result was the reorganisation of poor relief that is known as the Speenhamland system. Farmers were the immediate beneficiaries of the rise in prices, but ultimately landlords were the gainers as rents were raised upon the renewal of leases. Thus the fact that British agriculture increased its output less than the growth in demand contributed to rising inequality during the industrial revolution.

6   Factories, workshops and industrial organisation

Maxine Berg

Introduction

Current perspectives on the industrial revolution emphasise continuity rather than discontinuity; new estimates of the growth of industrial output and gross domestic product exhibit only gradual and intermittent increases between 1700 and 1830. To some degree these findings on the industrial revolution overall rely on new assessments of the industrial sector. In contrast to a long tradition of literature focussed on rapid changes in technology and work organisation – machinery, steam power and the factory system – the new perspectives point out the low productivity gains and traditionalism of most industries, apart from cotton and iron, between the eighteenth and early nineteenth centuries. Crafts has argued that one small and atypical sector, cotton, possibly accounted for half of all productivity gains in manufacturing: it was a modern sector floating in a sea of tradition. He draws the conclusion that 'not only was the triumph of ingenuity slow to come to fruition, but it does not seem appropriate to regard innovativeness as pervasive' (Crafts 1985a: 87).

Industrial performance during the first industrial revolution now seems unremarkable, and was characterised at the time by huge differences among industries, and an overall outcome of only gradual growth in output. But our understanding of why this was the case is, as yet, based only on aggregate estimates of value added for groups of industries. There has been little investigation recently into the factors which lie behind these estimates, and the extent to which they provide an adequate indicator of the nature of change taking place in the industrial sector. Two such factors are technical change and industrial organisation. The success or failure of the fundamental components of innovation to yield results within the accepted conventional period of the industrial revolution must be a subject for investigation rather than assumption.

The purpose of this chapter is to chart and to analyse the development of industrial organisation over the period. It will take industrial organisation beyond the well-known history of the transition to the factory system. After outlining the many different forms of organisational innovation in the period, the chapter will raise questions about currently accepted indicators of Britain's industrial performance during the industrial revolution.

Economic historians have certainly not been unaware of the significance of industrial organisation for the performance of individual industries. Recent examples include Lazonick (1986) and von Tunzelmann (1978: ch. 7). Among the leading interpreters of the industrial revolution as a whole, both Clapham (1926: chs. 5 and 6) and Landes (1969) put it at the forefront of their explanations. But even they did not attempt systematically to disentangle the components of organisation, the constraints on these and the efficiency gains which were meant to affect productivity growth. For the most part, recent economic historians have been even less inclined to seek out wider patterns of organisation and to generalise about their effects. Industrial organisation is not amenable to quantitative measurement, and consequently it has fallen between the concerns of business historians, historians of technology and social historians.

The components of industrial organisation and economic analysis

The first question we must answer is what precisely we mean by industrial organisation in an economy which has not yet industrialised. There is a tacit assumption among economists that discussions of industrial organisation only apply to the contemporary economy with its high levels of commercial and market development. But such issues apply just as significantly to the British pre-industrial and early industrial economy. Market relationships in this economy were widely developed, though frequently on a more regional than national basis.

Recent research in micro-economics and industrial economics has sought to gauge the effect of a number of aspects of industrial organisation upon output, efficiency and profitability. This research has considered the effects of differences in access to markets and degree of market power within an industry. It has also enquired into the institutional framework of an industry, that is to say, into its contractual arrangements and its means of saving on costs of information. Combining empirical research with theory, economists have also explored business structures. The questions to be asked concern the prevalence of family or large-scale firms, proprietorial or managerial capitalism, and whether an industry is structured around goals of mass production or of flexible specialisation. Other research enquires into what styles of work organisation and hierarchy prevail in firms – workshop production, putting-out arrangements or factories (Dosi 1988; Jacquemin 1987; Nelson and Winter 1982; O. Williamson 1985).

Many of these concerns, raised by modern industrial economists, are certainly also applicable to writing the history of industries in the eighteenth and nineteenth centuries. What is less easy to do is to reach any systematic quantitative estimation of the relationship between these aspects of industrial organisation and output, efficiency and profitability. Few records of any but the largest-scale firms remain: no surveys of manufacturing were conducted in the eighteenth century, and factory commissions and reports of the early nineteenth century were well known for their omission of smaller producers. Historians of British industry in this period are forced to rely on tax, probate and fire insurance records which rarely provide the detailed information on size of production units, capitalisation and employment structures which are needed by economists. Equally, data on rates of profit, wage and capital costs are available only from the records of a limited number of firms in an age of primitive accountancy techniques (Pollard 1965: ch. 6). But it is still possible to build up a picture, if a less systematically quantitative one than would be desirable, of the structure of British industry on the basis of those limited records mentioned, together with a wealth of contemporary qualitative descriptive accounts. With this evidence we can look at the size and scale of manufacturing units on the one hand, and at the extent of industrial concentration on the other.

Much research on the size of the firm and profitability follows the tradition of the 'Chandler thesis' of the drive to large-scale organisation, or what Chandler calls 'the logic of managerial enterprise'. Large-scale along with high-volume production, the so-called 'American system of manufactures', was combined with carefully defined managerial hierarchies. The results were economies of scale, but also of scope in keeping to core production technologies; both led to process and product innovation. The advantages went to those who made the first-mover investments to create a managerial enterprise. They gained competitive advantage even across nations, and took the laurels of the second industrial revolution (Chandler 1990b).

Do the lessons of the 'logic of managerial enterprise' also apply to the first industrial revolution? The Chandler thesis of the drive of competitive pressures to large-scale production lies behind many of the associations once supposed to have existed between the growth of productivity and the increasing capacity of mines, blast furnaces, mules and looms. But scale and scope also apply to the structures of enterprises.

Crouzet has argued that the industrialist proper only emerged at the end of the eighteenth century with the specialisation of investment to core production activities. The earlier versatility of businessmen and women and their absence of specialisation in investment were, in his view, archaic traits. Examples were the merchant-manufacturers with interests in many investments and in widespread activities.

Thomas Griggs, the mid-eighteenth-century Essex clothier, also kept up activities in the grocery trades, real estate, cattle fattening, malting and pawnbroking. John Glassford, the Glasgow tobacco lord, built up an enterprise which also included brewing, tanning, bleaching, dye and vitriol making, textile printing and hosiery (Crouzet 1985: 7). Very large-scale vertically integrated multi-plant enterprises such as the cotton mills owned by the Peels and the Arkwrights and the iron works owned by the Darbys and James Foster are described as more frequent in the early industrial revolution than later. By contrast, the cotton spinners who ran a single unit with one proprietor or two or three partners became the 'industrialists par excellence' of the Industrial Revolution (Crouzet 1985: 17). But as important as those enterprises which expanded in scale but simplified their scope were those like the classic textile merchant-manufacturers who controlled not only spinning mills but hundreds and thousands of dispersed hand-loom weavers. The historical route to 'scale and scope' in fact had many branches, and the 'Chandler thesis' cannot provide an exclusive model of the development of eighteenth- and nineteenth-century industry.

Together with the rise of the large-scale firm, economists have placed the drive to the increasing concentration of market power in fewer and fewer firms as the principal parameters of modern industrial organisation. Adam Smith saw the restriction of the market as a behavioural characteristic of the capitalist class; Marx and Engels saw increasing concentration and monopoly power as the inevitable outcome of the capitalist drive to increase profitability.

Industrial economists have seen the drive to increase market shares as an outcome of the increasing scale of production. But industrial organisation during the eighteenth and early nineteenth centuries did not follow these trends. Indeed, for many industries technological and organisational transformation brought about the disintegration of former monopolistic and oligopolistic structures. And for this period at least, while there were considerable pressures on small producers in many industries, market opportunity was such that there were few instances, for more than the very short term, of the other extreme of industrial concentration and monopoly power.

The hold of the Blackwell Hall factors on the woollen industry was broken in the course of the eighteenth century both through new competition from Yorkshire, and through the factors' own actions in extending credit to new entrants to the industry. The woollen companies in many towns lost their powers to enforce rules on entry and production standards. The small clothiers lost their former niche, but equally the large established producers now had to contend with new undercapitalised 'inferior' clothiers (Mann 1971: 98).

Mining, by the nature of its geological factors, lent itself to concentration in the hands of a few landowners, but ownership did not necessarily or even commonly go with proprietorship, for many mines were leased. In the earlier eighteenth century, and in the case of the Forest of Dean right up to the end of the century, mining technology and the scale of working allowed the proprietorship of working miners who leased smaller collieries. These were succeeded by large-scale enterprises built on partnerships of merchants, bankers, landowners and other industrialists. But the best-known instance of monopoly power in the industry belonged to the early, not the later, eighteenth century. This was the 'Grand Allies', a partnership of coal owners in the north-east formed over the period 1710 to 1726 for joint-stock mining and for restricting output and raising prices. Only the geographical shift of mining on Tyneside in the third quarter of the century broke its power (Flinn 1984: 38–42).

The iron industry provides yet another well-known instance of monopoly power in the eighteenth century. The Ironmasters' Associations go back to the mid-seventeenth century. At the local level they fixed selling prices and prices of raw materials and labour. But the scenario by the later eighteenth and early nineteenth centuries was one of failure of cooperation and fierce regional competition. The depression in the industry in the early nineteenth century was associated with competition and excess production (Birch 1967: 106–13; Hyde 1977).

For the period of the industrial revolution, therefore, industries did not fit into any 'logic of managerial enterprise' which associated scale, scope and market power. We may thus go on to ask what did dictate the behaviour of firms and its outcome in terms of industrial performance. We must now turn to the range of organisational structures which existed in the pre-industrial and early industrial period, and their social and regional backgrounds.

Organisational structures in the early industrial period

Clapham's view was that Britain abounded in ancient and transitional types of industrial organisation before 1830. But beside this we must put a considerable number of large-scale capitalist structures which dominated the public imagination of the day. Putting-out systems coexisted with artisan and cooperative forms of production, and many of these systems frequently interacted with some type of large-scale centralised production or proto-factory. The Kentish Weald in the sixteenth and seventeenth centuries had a rural textile industry organised on a putting-out system employing peasant labour, but it also had an important iron industry organised in centralised units around water-powered blast furnaces.

Even within a single industry, diverse forms of organisation prevailed at different stages of production. In eighteenth-century West Yorkshire, small artisan clothiers built and used their own cooperative mills for some of their preparatory processes. In eighteenth-century Lancashire, the Peels centralised their calico printing and spinning establishments, but ran extensive putting-out networks among weavers. In eighteenth-century Birmingham small artisans in the hardware trades gathered together to build a centralised processing unit which supplied their brass and copper, and they 'put out' the production of parts and pieces in much the same way as did the nineteenth-century watch makers of Coventry who relied on the outworkers of Warrington and Prescot. While putting-out prevailed in much of the Scottish linen industry, in Dundee the spinners dealt directly with the manufacturer. While the woollen industry of the West Country and the worsted industry of West Yorkshire were model examples of putting-out, the woollen industry of the West Riding was the seat of independent artisan production. The survival of the small independent clothiers was ensured well into the nineteenth century, when in the face of the advantages of machinery and concentration in some processes, these clothiers formed cooperative or company units (Clapham 1926; Hudson 1986). When large-scale factories were forming in Lancashire, Faucher wrote of Birmingham in 1830, 'whilst capitals tend to concentrate in Great Britain, they divide more and more in Birmingham' (Berg 1985: 86).

Recent debates on proto-industrialisation started from the assumption that gains in profitability in this pre-factory industry derived from the regional specialisation and division of labour in the organisational innovation of the putting-out system. But subsequent research demonstrated the coexistence and dynamism of both artisan-based and putting-out systems. Putting-out systems dominated by large-scale merchants might meet their match in the small-scale artisan. Artisan-organised production was the dynamic industrial structure of the urban villages, suburbs and unincorporated towns of eighteenth-century Britain in areas such as Birmingham and the London suburbs.

In addition to putting-out systems, artisan and cooperative manufacturing systems, there were those forms of industrial production which were centralised from the outset, as in mining and metal-processing, and in the proto-factories which existed in the silk industry, in calico printing, in pin making and in some of the factory colonies of the West Country woollen industry. But even among such centralised works, there were enormous differences of scale. In 1719 London had 123 calico printers, but of these only three had a large labour force, and large here meant 205, 121 and 49 employees respectively (Crouzet 1985: 30).

One industry, metal working, could contain classic large-scale capitalist works such as Crowley's iron works at Winlaton, and at the same time the extensive division of labour found in a putting-out framework as in Peter Stubs' Warrington file-making business. There was the Bristol wire-works producing pins in a proto-factory, or indeed Matthew Boulton's newly designed Soho works, side by side with dispersed and impoverished nail makers exploited in a highly developed putting-out system. Furthermore, the existence of centralised plants and processes did not prevent seasonal or even family divisions of labour between industry and agriculture in the time-honoured manner of the textile putting-out industries.

What is therefore striking is the pluralism of manufacturing structures in the pre-industrial and early industrial period. It is furthermore difficult to confine any one of these structures to a single formula, for no structure was static. They adapted to changing market conditions but also to institutional and social change with more or less success within their own individual industries and regions. The conditions for the emergence of specific industrial structures and the factors affecting how they changed lie not just in market forces and competitive pressures, for these cannot be pre-supposed. They lie fundamentally in institutions and social structures within industries and communities.

As we shall see, even with the industrial revolution, there was no linear development of organisational structures from small-scale to large-scale, proprietorial to managerial, or dispersed to centralised systems. The social values of domestic workers and artisans themselves are as significant to these issues as the social framework of the entrepreneurial class. The strength of artisan values reverberated in many industries and communities in the resistance to factories and to mechanisation, ultimately determining the location of much factory-based industry.

Explaining organisational choices

The story of the industrial revolution is frequently told in terms of the lead provided by the textile industries, and especially cotton. This is just as often set out as a series of transitions from artisan workshops to the putting-out system and thence to the modern factory system. Likewise in centralised industries such as mining and iron-working huge increases in scale and capitalisation are set alongside mechanisation. But in fact, features of all these types of work organisation, and various permutations on them,

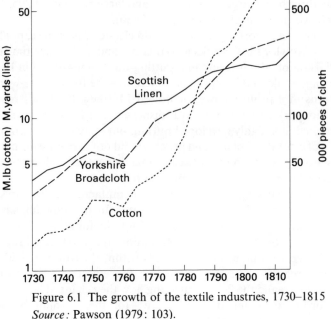

Figure 6.1 The growth of the textile industries, 1730–1815
Source: Pawson (1979: 103).

existed within and between the various textiles and metallurgical industries from before the eighteenth century. Let us turn first, then, to textiles.

The textile industries

The growth and transformation of the cotton industry was, to be sure, a unique one (Figure 6.1). But the other major textile industries – wool and worsted, stocking knitting, silk and linen – also grew, took on new forms of industrial and work organisation and developed new technologies. They were not unchanging 'traditional' industries. Why did such a variety of industrial organisation prevail across the textile industries?

Experiences across the textile industries reveal some patterns. There did seem sometimes to be a correlation between capitalist control, especially in the form of concentration or of high degrees of market power and the use of putting-out systems. Conversely, independent proprietorship and competitive structures coincided with artisan structures. But the great counter-example to this dualism was the cotton industry itself where the putting-out system developed in an industry with low levels of concentration.

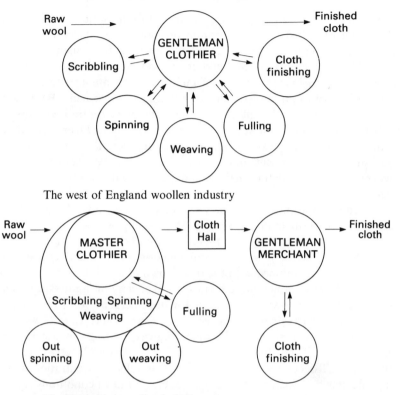

The west of England woollen industry

The Yorkshire woollen industry

Figure 6.2 The organisational structure of the west of England and Yorkshire woollen industries in the eighteenth century

Source: Randall (1989: 180–1).

Why different systems existed long before the industrial revolution can be explained only in part by the effects of costs of production and markets; social structures and institutions were even more fundamental. The woollen and worsted industries are good examples. Both industries developed contrasting structures in different regions – small independent clothiers dominated the Yorkshire woollen industry, but highly concentrated ownership, putting-out systems and proto-factories prevailed in the West Country (Figure 6.2). There were independent craftsmen in the Norfolk worsted industry, but large-scale merchant-manufacturers with putting-out systems in Yorkshire worsteds (Hudson 1986; Wilson 1973; Chapman 1973).

The subsequent decline of the worsted industry of Norfolk and the woollen industry of the West Country cannot be put down to the superiority of any single system of industrial organisation in Yorkshire. The extent of industrial concentration or competitive structures in each industry and region can to a large extent, however, be explained by local landholding structures which could create wide social divisions within a community, and by the heritage of guild or corporate structures which restricted entry to an industry or prevented aggrandisement (Berg 1985: ch. 9). These factors also affected the appearance of centralised units, or mills and factories in both wool and worsted. Mills existed from early times in the case of water-powered fulling mills, and were later developed for some other processes. But they were used for specific processes and were incorporated into existing artisan and putting-out structures (Hudson 1986).

The framework knitting industry started out as a trade of independent yeoman farmers in midland villages of middling wealth and relatively egalitarian social structures. But there were rapid changes in the market in the eighteenth century with the introduction of silk and cotton mix stockings. This, combined with the breakdown of landholding patterns in Nottingham into a much more divided rural society of landless squatters and large-scale landowners, accounts for the emergence of a new system marked by a sharp division between producers. There were large-scale hosiers with high entry thresholds operating vast putting-out systems and centralised units, and the knitters themselves who were largely degraded outworkers (Rogers 1981; Levine 1987). Capitalist concentration and a large, flexible and weakened labour force created ideal conditions for the proliferation of a mercantile putting-out system.

Silk, the country's primary luxury industry during the seventeenth and eighteenth centuries, contained both the best examples of the first factories – highly capitalist enterprises employing child labour – and one of the country's most highly skilled and traditionally organised artisan groups. These two systems confronted each other across the throwing and weaving branches of the industry. Factories, which were started in the throwing section of the industry in the first quarter of the eighteenth century, did not extend to weaving for another hundred years. The divide was furthermore one between province and metropolis, country and town. The strength of guild structures, the Spitalfields Acts and corporate structures as in Coventry reinforced the strength of the urban weavers, as against the suburban or rural outworkers who produced lower qualities or different goods and used different technologies.

The cotton and linen industries developed both putting-out structures and artisan industry, and soon the most widespread and rapid transition to factory production. It was cotton above all which seemed to present the unity between new industrial organisation and industrialisation in its road

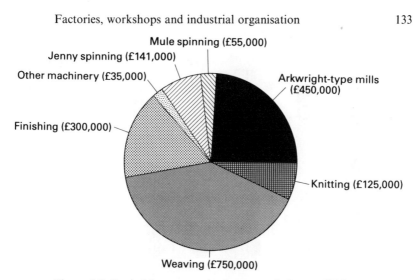

Figure 6.3 Capital investment in the cotton industry, 1788
Source: Chapman and Butt (1988: 109).

to the factory system. But this new organisation did not coincide with or require industrial concentration. A putting-out organisation existed from the earliest days in the form of middlemen, factors, chapmen or dealers, and in some cases merchants in linen, then fustians and cottons. But there was no market control by a small group; the small yeoman capitalist was the backbone of the system.

Pre-existing mercantile networks in linen and calico printing played the vital role in introducing cotton as a new product. Capitalist structures came with the new product, but the market opportunities created by a new product and the relatively open social structures of the cotton region encouraged dispersed ownership and the rise of the small- and medium-scale factory in addition to the well-known industrial giants (Figure 6.3). In 1780 Britain had no more than 15 or 20 cotton mills, but seven years later there were 145 Arkwright-type mills. Before the end of the eighteenth century there were 900 cotton-spinning factories. These ranged, however, from 300 Arkwright-type factories – purpose-built buildings of several storeys employing over fifty workers – through 600 'factories' using jennies and mules, some of which were little more than sheds or workshops employing some dozens of workers (Crouzet 1985: 32).

The social and institutional conditions giving rise to this plurality of capitalist structures across the textile industry produced a long heritage. Most of the early industrial structures so far described were not left behind with industrialisation, but intensified. Factories indeed became more widespread, but until the 1830s at least, they were to be found mainly in

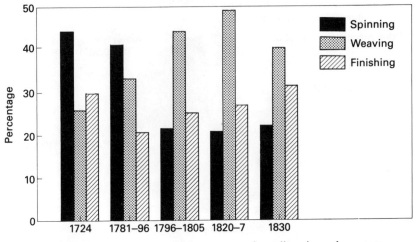

Figure 6.4 Percentage of labour costs of woollens in each process,
1724–1830

Source: Hudson (1986: 150).

industries where they already existed. It was still the case that decentralised,
workshop, artisan and putting-out systems were successful and profitable,
and indeed compatible with a substantial degree of technological change.
And as such they continued to develop over the eighteenth and nineteenth
centuries.

There was no single route to the factory system across the textile
industries, and the end result for each of them was a distinctive one. The
woollen and worsted industries in Yorkshire developed different factory
types, reflected in different degrees of concentration, size and labour forces.
In the 1780s the West Riding had 221 scribbling, carding and slubbing
mills in the woollen industry, while in 1800 there were still only 22 worsted
mills. By 1835 there were 1,333 woollen and worsted mills (Crouzet 1985:
33). But what kind of mills was another question (Figure 6.4).

The factory sector in the Yorkshire woollen industry developed out of
the 'company mills', centralised processes shared by artisan clothiers. It
remained closely connected to the artisan sector, and by the 1830s 75 per
cent of factory workers were men from artisan woollen backgrounds. The
Yorkshire woollen mills were small-scale ventures, and weaving was not
mechanised in the industry until the 1860s. The west of England, long
marked by extreme social division, had by the early nineteenth century,
turned over almost entirely to large factories supplying outworking
weavers. The Yorkshire worsted mills were altogether larger-scale concerns
than the woollen, owned by former putting-out merchants, and employing

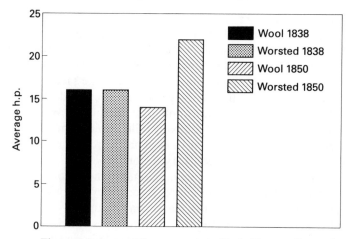

Figure 6.5 Average horse power in Yorkshire woollen and worsted mills, 1838 and 1850
Source: Hudson (1986: 40).

predominantly female and juvenile labour (Figure 6.5). The size of average mills varied considerably across the major textile industries – in the early 1830s linen mills employed an average of 93.3 persons; silk 125.3; cotton 175.5; and wool only 44.6 (Clapham 1926: 196).

Such differences within the factory sector were one matter. But other textile industries intensified their earlier decentralised organisation; where social division was already marked these were ideal conditions for the emergence of sweated outwork. 'Sweating' at this time involved extremely low-wage labour at highly sub-divided but dispersed manufacturing processes. Such production was generally organised under several levels of sub-contracting. This became the predominant form of manufacture in nineteenth-century framework knitting in Nottinghamshire, complemented by a number of large-scale factories. It also emerged in the silk industry with the decline of the Spitalfields silk weavers, and the social and gender divide between the silk ribbon weavers of Coventry and the women and children in the outlying rural parishes. In Spitalfields, the masters, on average large-scale entrepreneurs, dealt directly with the weavers. In Macclesfield and in Coventry a system of intermediaries, 'the undertaker system', prevailed from the eighteenth century until the 1820s, then went into decline to be succeeded by direct dealings between the manufacturer and the weavers.

The general effect of capitalist competition and technical change at the end of the eighteenth century was therefore to intensify existing differences in the manufacturing structures of the textile industries, rather than to endorse any single structure. Strongly based artisan systems in the wool and silk industries maintained their structures in the face of capitalist competition well into the industrial period. The Spitalfields weavers were sweated workers by the end of the Napoleonic Wars, but their counterparts in Coventry developed the compromise of the 'cottage factory', which sustained the artisan until the 1860s when new free trade legislation sacrificed the whole industry. The woollen sector of the West Riding developed its own cooperative or 'company mills' which remained viable until the 1850s and 1860s, when falling rates of profit brought restructuring and concentration in a large-scale factory sector.

Putting-out industries took the route in the end to the factory system or to sweating; the direction was determined, it seems, by the prior strength of the socio-economic base and the market in the industry concerned. Worsted, linen and cotton took the profit opportunities of a rising market, and of centralised processes in factories; framework knitting and some silk weaving followed cost-cutting manoeuvres into intensive sweating.

This diversity in the experience of textiles, the classic factory industry of the period, needs to be set beside that of the classic decentralised, workshop industries – the engineering and metal manufactures.

Workshop industries – metals and engineering

The engineering trades, the Birmingham hardware and Sheffield cutlery trades all conjure up images of a workshop culture with characteristics of high degrees of skill, a large predominance of urban manufacture and the endurance of small-scale production. They were the locus of the innovative capital goods sector which Rosenberg (1982) has credited with saving capital over the whole economy and with providing the prime mechanism for technological diffusion. Marx himself saw the paradox at the heart of industrial capitalism – the manufacture of the machines of large-scale factory industry was conducted by small-scale artisans; the source of the automatic power of the machine was lodged ultimately in the skill and craft of individual human effort.

And so these industries based in the manipulation of metals have provided historians with examples for other models of industrial organisation – thus we hear now of 'batch' production and of 'flexible specialisation'. This is production based on short runs, entailing constant changes in design, set up and product, and thus not amenable to the 'flow-line' processes of mass production. The 'craft economies' in these sectors, it is argued, found their own route to industrialisation on the basis of a highly innovative small-scale capitalism. Unlike the one-way drive to mass production which these models recognised, there were cases, most evident in current developments in micro-electronics, where the 'flexibility' of the manufacturing system in terms of variance of throughputs and variance of output outweighed the advantages of plant-related economies of scale.

They also found historical precedents for this new-found 'efficiency' of small-scale production. The British engineering trades, the Birmingham hardware trades and the Sheffield cutlery trades were thus no longer condemned to 'backwardness' for their failure to make the transition to the large-scale firm. Instead they offered 'flexible technologies', skill-intensive processes, external economies, interchangeability and product choice. Artisan production during the industrial revolution was not, therefore, part of a world which was already archaic, but had its own developing trajectory of industrial organisation.

The decentralised systems of the metal manufactures as much as the factory systems of the textile industries displayed a great variety of forms. There was the great Winlaton iron works established in 1691 by Sir Ambrose Crowley. By the 1720s it was a massive manufacturing complex with forges, mills, furnaces, warehouses and workshops (Levine and Wrightson 1991: 79). Hardware manufacture on the site was conducted in the manner of 'internal contracting' widely practised in factories a century and a half later. Clapham described the system thus:

In their separate shops at the works, the masters – they were so called – of 'Crowley's crew', who made nails, locks, chisels and all sorts of ironmongery – largely for export – got tools and materials from the works 'ironkeeper', employed their own hammermen and prentices, and were credited with the selling price of their goods less cost of material; in which, it must be assumed, would be included some overhead charges and profit for Crowley, now Sir Ambrose, 'ironmonger'.

(Clapham 1926: 176)

Such factories were not uncommon in the metal trades in the eighteenth century, and continued so into the nineteenth century. In these factories, the manufacturer owned the premises, the power source and some of the heavier machinery, but did not become deeply involved in the details of the manufacturing processes. Instead employees carried on the traditions of domestic manufacture by providing their own tools and paying for workspace and use of gas and power. In the brass manufacture, the head caster paid and supervised his own moulders and labourers; journeymen were employed on a payment-by-results system, and underhands were employed by journeymen at daywork rates. The journeyman in a large-scale brass finishing works was designer, supervisor, tool maker, tool setter and all-round workman (Kelley 1930: 43).

In the lighter 'toy' or ornamental and light hardware trades of Birmingham, women piecemasters ran groups of workers in button making, papier-mâché and lacquering shops within large-scale toy factories

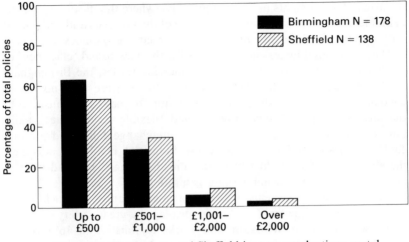

Figure 6.6 Birmingham and Sheffield insurance valuations, metal trades, 1777–87

Source: Berg (1991a: 192–3).

such as John Taylor's works, which in 1759 employed 600. Boulton employed between 800 and 1,000 at Soho by 1770, but the factory was arranged in a series of shops, each located according to a systematic order, but only one basic operation was performed within each shop, and payment was made through an elaborate system of piece rates. Maudslay's engineering works was another show-case factory of the eighteenth century, set up according to the principles of production organisation specified by Samuel Bentham; it was followed in the early nineteenth century by James Nasmyth's more advanced version. But in both the workman remained a semi-autonomous producer (Berg 1985: ch. 11).

The small-scale producer in the Birmingham and Sheffield trades as well as the engineering trades spanned the whole range between artisan workshop and sweated garret worker. In 1825 there were 400 to 500 engineering masters in the London area employing 10,000 men (Burgess 1969: 218, 221). And by 1851 Britain had 677 engineering firms. Yet two-thirds of these had fewer than ten employees and only fourteen had more than 350 (Crouzet 1985: 35).

Birmingham in the eighteenth century contained some large-scale and a substantial core of medium-scale metal-manufacturing firms deploying various forms of internal contracting and sub-contracting (Figure 6.6). There was gun making, for instance, where the gun maker owned a warehouse in the gun quarter, acquired semi-finished parts and gave these out to specialised craftsmen who undertook the assembly and finishing.

They in turn bought their parts from a range of independent manufacturers – barrel makers, lock makers, sight stampers, trigger makers, ramrod forgers, gun furniture makers and bayonet forgers. These levels of division of labour and specialisation prevailed across the hardware and toy trades, but skills were also sufficiently flexible that workers could turn their skills and expertise in the use of file and lathe to other trades if need be (Allen 1929: 17). The 'flexibility' of small-scale manufacturers in Birmingham, contracting and networking with a core of medium-scale manufacturers and a few dominant large-scale manufacturers, may be contrasted with the position of the small-scale nail and chain makers of the surrounding Black Country villages – here 40,000 sweated outworkers, substantial numbers of them women and children, lived tied by poverty, debt and dependency to the nail factors of the region.

In Sheffield the cutlery trades had developed a division of labour, going back to the seventeenth century, based on both product and process. By the eighteenth century, the knife- and scissor-making trades concentrated in the town were divided into forging and grinding. Forging was performed by one or two craftsmen in a small shop, while grinding was performed in separate departments of large works or in separate establishments. The actual building up or hafting of the knife was the craft of the cutler or individual artisan. By the nineteenth century, cost-cutting and rationalisation brought a restructuring of this 'decentralised' sector, but the result was a one-way road to concentration and large-scale units. The small producers remained, but were subordinated now to a few large firms.

In engineering there was indeed a trend after 1825 to larger, more heavily capitalised firms; with this the focus of the industry shifted from London to south Lancashire. In the hardware trades industrial dualism emerged. In 1843 there were 4,000 manufacturers in Birmingham and 1,344 cutlery warehouses in Sheffield (Crouzet 1985: 36). The substantial artisan workshops and medium-scale workshops gave way to a polarised production process. The size of the larger firms grew after the Napoleonic Wars, and large factories now dominated the industry; but there was also a proliferation of small garret masters, many of these subordinated to the large firms (Behagg 1990, ch. 2).

The post-Napoleonic recession was also a time for the multiplication of small units in Sheffield – 'the little masters'. These were either factors using the labour of outworkers, or small cutlers renting a room in a factory. By this time they were subject to a local group of merchant-capitalists who controlled the circulating capital of the trade and the distribution of the finished product; in reality they were little more than outworkers (Lloyd 1913; Smith 1982).

This polarisation was also a distinguishing feature of mechanical engineering, the industry responsible for the mechanisation of the rest of the industrial economy. As shown above, the industrial structure of most of the industry was way out of line with that of a few leading firms. The largest textile engineering firm, Platts of Oldham, employed 7,000 in 1875, and even at the beginning of the twentieth century produced as much as the whole American textile machinery industry (Saul 1970b: 144; Crouzet 1985: 249–50).

The later stages of the industrial revolution were not marked by the market expansion and opportunities for entry of the first phases. They were marked by falling rates of profit, cost-cutting, rationalisation and restructuring. The result for industrial organisation was a polarised structure between concentration on the one hand and dispersed sweating on the other. What effect did these phases of expansion and recession have on the giants of industry – the mines, the iron works, the large-scale brewers, paper makers and glass makers?

Centralised industries

The technical processes of the centralised industries, especially mining and iron working, required concentration of production at one site; they were nevertheless characterised, as were the textiles and metals manufactures, by a few giants among pygmies (Pollard 1965: 78–92 concentrates on the giants). The pits on Tyneside and the Wear were truly large for their time – those of the 1690s employed 72–90 people turning out 18,000 tons, and 260–325 people in the 1710s turning out 65,000 tons, but this size declined by the late 1750s to 68–85 people turning out 17,000 tons. This size of pit contrasted with the more common small outcrop in Lancashire employing a few hewers (Levine and Wrightson 1991: 214). By 1830 the forty-one working collieries on Tyneside produced c. 3,000,000 tons a year, and the average colliery there produced 60,000–70,000 tons with an average workforce of 300. But even as late as 1850, the average coal mine was said to employ no more than 'eighty men, women and boys under ground and above' (Clapham 1926: 186). The comparable tin and copper mines were altogether larger affairs – the Cornish mines in 1838 employed an average of 170 workers per mine.

Mine management also revealed these contrasts. In some areas of the country a few major landowners controlled a number of large-scale mines. In Scotland there were the Duke of Buccleuch and the Duke of Hamilton, in Lancashire the Earls of Crawford and Balcarres and the Duke of Bridgewater. In Yorkshire the Wentworth estate of the Fitzwilliams had four collieries around Barnsley in 1795 and six in 1828, while the Duke of Norfolk had several in the Sheffield area. The Lords Dudley had a number

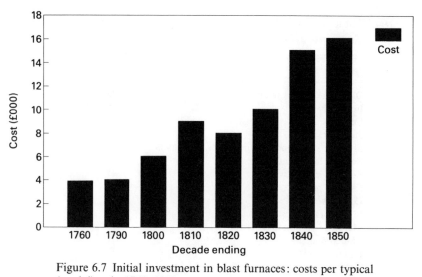

Figure 6.7 Initial investment in blast furnaces: costs per typical (modal) unit, 1760–1850

Source: Davies and Pollard (1988: 96).

of pits in the Black Country. Some of these mines were leased, as in the case of the Duke of Norfolk's Sheffield colliery leased in 1820 to a group of partners including a landowner, a merchant, a cutler and a collier (Flinn 1984: 37–8). Other mining ventures were integrated with iron companies, especially in Shropshire, Derbyshire, the Black Country and South Yorkshire. Whether owned or leased, such large-scale mines were directly managed by overlookers, overseers or managers.

Smaller collieries were, however, at least for the first half of the eighteenth century, frequently leased and run by working miners, as on the Derbyshire–Nottinghamshire border. There was also the celebrated case of the Free Miners of the Forest of Dean, where even as late as the 1780s 99 mines were worked by 442 free miners and boys (Flinn 1984: 42).

The contrast between the giant and the very small works was even more marked in iron working. In 1814, the Scottish Carron works employed 2,000, but the average Scottish foundry employed 20. After the Napoleonic Wars, the industry underwent massive restructuring in the face of overcapacity and technological change. The industry concentrated in South Wales, which now produced 40 per cent of total output, and the midlands. Works such as that of Samuel Walker and William Yates employed 700 men at one site. Average output per blast furnace grew in the early period from 300 tons in 1720 to 1,500 in 1805 and 2,600 in 1826 (Crouzet 1985: 34). In the 1830s and 1840s the introduction of the 'hot

Table 6.1. *Number of persons in the employ of the Dowlais Iron Company, 1 May 1866*

	No. of persons
Old works, forges and mills	1,429
Ifor works	775
Furnaces	802
Steel works	44
Fitting, pattern and smelting shops, carpenters	397
Engines, forges and blast	155
Engines, locomotives	21
Engines, pits	138
Collieries	2,023
Mine works, limestone quarries	1,709
Masons, roadmen and harries	310
Church building	31
Farms	32
Stables	84
Railway stations	4
Washhouse	4
Traffic	18
Weighers, croppers	52
Offices, library	48
Schools	55
Cardiff yard	64
Edge Hill mines	282
London houses	23
Total	8,500

Source: Birch (1967: 255).

blast' process spread fastest in Scotland, and the industry was then spread equally across three major regions – Scotland, South Wales and the Black Country (Riden 1986: 128).

Dowlais (Table 6.1) in 1866 had 18 blast furnaces, dozens of puddling furnaces and 6,000 employees (Crouzet 1985: 34). Concentration in large-scale units was also the norm in glass making; there were 116 'glass houses' in 1833 with one firm, Isaac Cookson, owning 9 of these (Clapham 1926: 190).

Apart from those industries lending themselves to centralised production in large-scale units, there were several others which managed to contain both a sector of large-scale producers reaping economies of scale and exercising managerial innovation, within a much larger sector of very small-scale producers producing for localised or specialised markets

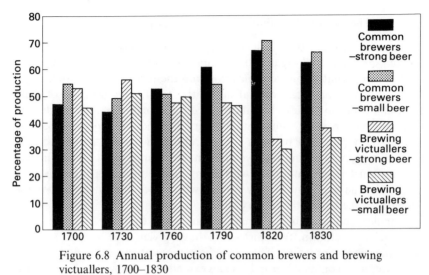

Figure 6.8 Annual production of common brewers and brewing victuallers, 1700–1830

Source: Mathias (1959: 542–3).

(Pollard 1965: 118–22). Brewing is the obvious example; in 1822 there were ninety-eight wholesale brewers in London – they were 6 per cent of the total number in England and Wales, but produced 43 per cent of strong beer (Weir 1980: 122) (Figure 6.8).

Josiah Wedgwood employed several hundreds at Etruria at the end of the eighteenth century, but he was uncharacteristic of an industry populated by all manner of small earthenware manufacturers and 'china men' making ordinary chinaware. By the 1830s there were seven other potteries employing over 500 workers, and a good number employing over 200 (Pollard 1965: 121–2). The itinerant paper makers of Kent held the stage in paper making until the beginning of the nineteenth century, when Foudrinier first successfully introduced into Britain the continuous paper-making machine previously invented in France by Nicholas Louis Robert (Mokyr 1990a: 106). Shipbuilding was another example – two shipbuilders on the Thames in 1825 employed 600 and 230 respectively. But the industry was still one of wood and sail, and was otherwise dispersed through a large number of very small yards between the Thames and the Bristol Channel and over most other rivers, especially the Mersey, the Clyde and the Humber (Slaven 1986: 132). And while shipbuilding may have been concentrated in these yards, the production process was basically a building process, combining the independent crafts of a large range of wood-working and metal-working as well as shipwrighting trades (Prothero 1979: 46–50, 163–71; Pollard and Robertson 1979).

The industrial revolution and the rise of the factory system

Across a wide range of British industry during the period of the industrial revolution, industrial organisation cannot be said to have been dominated either by concentration, centralisation and the factory system on the one hand, nor by small-scale capitalism on the other. The 'success' of great works was not so obvious that it drowned the efforts of smaller producers, but during the early nineteenth century production processes became increasingly polarised between concentration on the one hand and sub-contracting, outworking and sweating on the other. If part of the definition of the industrial revolution lies with changing organisations of production, especially the rise of the factory system, where does this outcome leave the debate on the rise of the factory system?

Smaller- and medium-scale manufacturers held the stage for much of the industrial revolution. Yet historians have given little weight to their experiences and practices. They have been more attracted to the few large factories with complex hierarchies and extended divisions of labour. For if these were not then the norm, they were gestures to the future domination of factory mass production.

Yet surprisingly enough there is no agreement among historians over a definition of the factory system. It is possible, for instance, to define the factory from a technological or an institutional perspective. For Andrew Ure, the great apostle of the factory system in the 1830s, technology provided the dictate for labour discipline. Factories meant physical concentration of plant around a centralised power source – they were in his view confined to textile mills. But factories have also been defined in terms of centralised and hierarchical management and labour discipline (Pollard 1965: ch. 5; Marglin 1974). Certainly in the eighteenth century they were associated in the public perception with congregations of unfree labour, workhouses and pauper apprentices (Pollard 1965: ch. 5). Contemporaries clearly distinguished between 'mills', which concentrated specific machinery around a power source, and 'manufactories', which concentrated labour and subjected this to hierarchical discipline and division of labour. Most historians since have defined the factory system with more or less emphasis on concentration of the workforce, division of labour, supervision, the use of machinery and a source of power to speed up the production process.

It is not surprising, then, that manufacturing organisation has thus far been analysed in the main in terms of scale of production. Larger scale has been associated with greater efficiency, lower relative costs and greater ability to develop and use new technology. Larger-scale firms were associated with the emergence of hierarchical forms of organisation, greater division of labour and a divide between supervisory and unskilled workers (Marglin 1974). Hierarchy and economy of skill were the significant advantages identified by Charles Babbage in 1831 in his Babbage Principle: the division of labour allowed tasks to be sub-divided according to skill requirements, so that only the requisite amount of skill was allocated to the needs of each task. Skilled as well as unskilled workers were thus arranged in a hierarchy, and masters could divide and rule them all.

Larger-scale firms were also more amenable to the diffusion of mechanised and powered technologies (Goldin and Sokoloff 1984). In Landes' view, the factories and the machines went hand in hand. There was a factory bias to technological change because (1) that was where the money was; (2) the saving in labour costs was higher because factory wages were higher; (3) the accumulation of small improvements was a function of the volume of investment – the new plant meant new and better equipment; (4) the factory environment was a more favourable environment for the perception of improvements. 'The logic of technology was moving towards ever wider mechanisation, toward doing more and faster, thereby enhancing the advantage of mass production and the factory system' (Landes 1986: 615).

The great technical innovation, the machine, had an internal logic pushing it in the direction of uniformity and standardisation (Landes 1987: 26). Scale economies associated with using certain types of machinery were greater than those due from the division of hand-performed tasks (Sokoloff 1984: 372). Indeed, adoption of the factory was a prerequisite to reaping economies of scale from 'indivisible' new technologies such as the steam engine (von Tunzelmann 1993) (Figure 6.9).

Large-scale production entailing the machine and the factory have thus appeared historically inevitable, and it has been the prevailing convention at least since the nineteenth century to put much of the progress of manufacture down to the economies of large-scale production. Yet much of the early textile machinery was originally planned for use within cottage manufacture or larger workshops which formed part of the putting-out system. And steam power had only limited uses in most manufacturing industry until the later years of the industrial revolution.

Recent work has drawn attention to the number and indeed the efficiency of organisational forms other than the factory, as outlined above in this chapter. These forms have not only endured; they have revived in recent trends to 'flexible specialisation', and the Japanese model of 'network capitalism'. Piore and Sabel have pointed out the disadvantages entailed in the bureaucratic structures of large-scale production: the indivisibilities, inflexibilities and rigidities (1984). Small-scale production,

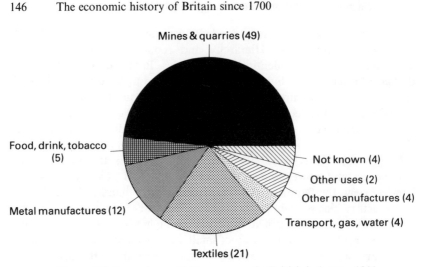

Figure 6.9 Percentages of steam power in British industry, 1800
Source: von Tunzelmann (1986: 78).

on the other hand, offered economic advantages of creativity, nimbleness and easy entry (Landes 1987). Small-scale firms could develop 'flexible technologies', skill-intensive processes and interchangeability, providing a range of product choices for localised and regional tastes (Sabel and Zeitlin 1985). Furthermore, in Marshall's view, the lack of a fundamental divide between idea and execution had great advantages. 'The master's eye is everywhere; there is no shirking by his foremen or workmen, no divided responsibility, no sending half-understood messages backwards and forwards from one department to another' (1890: 237). And the small-scale manufacturer could take advantage of external economies, especially in the form of trade knowledge, and in regional concentrations of skills, 'so great are the advantages which people following the same skilled trade get from near neighbourhood to one another. The mysteries of the trade become no mysteries; but are as it were in the air, and children learn many of them unconsciously' (1890: 237, 225).

The 'efficiency' of organisation was not always at issue; managerial control frequently was. Marglin saw the key advantage of the factory system not so much in its technical efficiency, but in its success in eliciting greater intensity of labour, and in giving maximum control over the production process and the direct producers. The division of labour allowed the concentration of knowledge in the hands of proprietors and their managers; hierarchical structures created systems of control and discipline over the labour force (1974, 1991).

Yet it was not just one or the other form of organisation which dictated the degree of control over labour. It was also the institutional setting of manufacture, notably the law. Masters had unequal advantage over labour before the law due to the existence of master-and-servant legislation, which made workmen and women liable to imprisonment for breach of contract of service. This legislation went back to the Statute of Labourers of 1349, and its worst injustices were not removed from the statute book until the Master and Servant Act of 1867 (Webbs 1902: 232–5). The legislation notably became the weapon of smaller employers and explains the widespread practice of long contracts and bonds of service.

Conviction was usual in cases which were brought to court because employers in the same trade would often sit as magistrates, and in areas such as the Black Country an employer-magistrate culture could develop (Haynes 1988: 245; Hay 1982: 152–8). Far more prosecutions were brought under this legislation than had ever been brought under the Combination Laws. A Parliamentary Return for 1863 showed that 10,337 cases of breach of contract of service came before the courts in a single year (Webbs 1902: 235).

Factories may have provided one way of controlling labour, but small producers and manufacturers using putting-out systems exerted control through the law and through extensive credit and debt bondage (Berg 1985: 280–2). Organisational innovation to increase efficiency, profitability or control over labour was thus available to manufacturers in many different forms.

The modern mechanised technologies of the large-scale factory hinged on a close dependency on 'traditional' artisan producers. As we have seen, cotton manufacturers typically combined steam-powered spinning in factories with extensive employment of dispersed domestic hand-loom weavers long after the availability of powered technology. This spread risks and deployed a cheap labour supply of women and children. The metal-working trades of Birmingham and Sheffield had both large and small firms primarily concerned with metal working diversifying into large-scale metal-processing ventures as a way of generating steady raw material supplies. The individual manufacturer might move simultaneously or in succession into 'large-scale mechanised production' and 'small-scale traditional' activities.

Innovation in organisational structures was also widespread within industries organised on a decentralised basis. New forms of putting-out, wholesaling, retailing, credit and debt and 'artisan cooperation' were devised as ways of retaining the essentials of older structures in the face of a new more competitive and innovative environment. Customary practices, organisational forms and 'traditional' technologies were themselves transformed partly in order to combat the spectre of large-scale factory production, and to find other ways of responding to the needs of more dynamic and market-orientated production. Research on proto-industrialisation has identified the significance of innovation in organisation in the form of elaborate putting-out networks, sub-contracting and artisanal cooperative and share ventures, as well as in marketing techniques, credit arrangements and product innovation. The interdependencies of small-scale and large-scale technical innovation tend to undermine the notion of a sharp divide in the capacities for and types of innovation developed within the different organisational forms.

In fact, as we have seen, most industries contained concentrated and decentralised firms, but what is striking is that most of the concentrated firms they did contain were not large-scale ventures at all. The leading factory industry, cotton, reveals an average primary processing firm in Manchester in 1840 of only 260 hands, with a quarter of all firms employing fewer than 100. The new cotton technologies were available at relatively low thresholds – small firms took advantage of small steam engines, and installed small numbers of spinning mules and power looms; they used traditional building methods and existing water-power resources (Chapman 1970; Gatrell 1977). Even when numbers of these small firms succumbed in the early nineteenth century to falling profit rates, recession and restructuring, their place was not taken by the cotton lords, but by larger but still moderately sized enterprises ranging between 150 and 500 employees (Lloyd-Jones and Le Roux 1980) (Figure 6.10).

Other industries could reap the gains of moderate and 'small-scale factories' for threshold sizes as low as six to fifteen employees. Even without mechanisation in these units, economies of scale could be derived from a division of hand-performed tasks within a firm, the use of simple tools, supervision and a more disciplined work regime. New organisation and the use of a new 'less skilled' or at least less restrictive workforce opened the way in the north-east of the United States in the early nineteenth century to substantial productivity gains. Much of this new workforce was made up of women and children (Goldin and Sokoloff 1982: 756, 1984: 480). These 'small-scale factories' were, furthermore, responsible for substantial inventive activity, prompted by the extension of the market with the growth of the canal economies and by the domestic competition which was ensured by the small scale of enterprise (Sokoloff 1988: 846; Sokoloff and Khan 1990: 377).

Evidence for the place of such 'small-scale factories', their internal structures and efficiency gains, is less systematic in Britain. Nevertheless, there is certainly a case to be made for an important place for this organisational form in British industry at a parallel stage of development, that is in the later eighteenth century and up to the end of the Napoleonic

Figure 6.10 The employment structure of Manchester cotton firms in 1815 and 1841

Source: Lloyd-Jones and Le Roux (1980: 75).

Wars. Market expansion, regional growth on the basis of the canal economies and a new departure in the use of child and female labour in textiles, potteries and the metal manufactures were parallel developments. The gains of these small-scale units could also be combined with a significant degree of mechanisation, notably the use of water and steam power. The extent of mechanisation in these units has been under-recorded because their small size precluded them from coverage under the Factory Acts (Kanefsky 1979: 363–9). After the first third of the nineteenth century, as outlined for several industries above, the pressures of falling profit rates and mechanisation as a form of cost-cutting brought trends to a polarisation of production processes into large-scale units on the one hand, and very small-scale dependent units on the other.

If the rise of the factory system was as much a question of regional, industrial and cyclical change as of organisational development, then there would appear to be no clear factors to identify it as a 'modern' organisational form. This is also the case within the factory sector itself. The modern trend to large-scale organisation on the lines identified by Chandler includes vertical and horizontal integration: economies of scale followed by economies of scope (1990a). Yet the British cotton industry remained vertically disintegrated throughout the nineteenth and into the twentieth centuries. The spinning and weaving sections of the industry remained separate, and marketing was controlled by separate groups of merchants. This is not to imply, however, that there was continuity rather than transformation of industrial organisation.

Instead, one-way routes to economies of scale and scope and to saving transactions costs were criss-crossed many times by most eighteenth- and early nineteenth-century industries. Industries developed within a plurality of organisational forms suitable to region, market and the economic cycle. Understanding the capacities within all these organisational forms for responding to market pressures and for using institutional environments should generate new analyses and measures of the performance of the industrial economy. Transformation, discontinuity and a rehabilitation of the industrial revolution may yet return to the historical agenda.

7 The finance of business during the industrial revolution

Larry Neal

Introduction

The finance of business during the industrial revolution in Britain presents an anomaly. On the one hand, a 'financial revolution' had clearly occurred in England well before any signs of an industrial revolution had appeared; on the other hand, the financial innovations produced from 1688 to 1750 appear to have been unheeded by the leading sectors of industrialisation (textiles, iron, coal, steam power) which emerged after mid-century. The elements of the financial revolution are now well understood (Dickson 1967; Neal 1990). They rested basically on the financial techniques developed in the Netherlands: the bill of exchange, both foreign and inland, which as a negotiable instrument became part of the medium of exchange; transferable shares in the permanent capital stock of corporations that were traded in an active secondary market; and perpetual annuities issued by a government which made them free of the risk of default. When transplanted wholesale to England by the Dutch advisers of William of Orange who ascended to the throne of England with the Glorious Revolution of 1688, they proved even more efficient in the new legal environment provided by English common and statutory law than they had been in the Netherlands. By the conclusion of the South Sea Bubble affair in 1723, when the South Sea Company was reorganised and carved up by the Whig government, all the elements of the financial revolution were firmly based in the London financial market and operated without further innovations in financial instruments or institutions until the disruptions caused by the Napoleonic Wars. Even then, the financial markets essentially expanded without changing their character until the technological and institutional changes which occurred after 1850.

On the industrial side, by contrast, the leading sectors of cotton, iron and steam power did not emerge as such until after 1760. And the internal structure of each sector changed rapidly, if convulsively, over the following century. By 1850 Britain had become the workshop of the world and later historians could agree that an industrial revolution had occurred, even if they could not agree on exactly when or how it occurred. Moreover, the industrial revolution had taken place, apparently, without any interaction with the preceding financial revolution.

The prevailing resolution of this anomaly is that the financial innovations were not needed by the new firms arising in the leading sectors. The costs of fixed capital required to embody the technological innovations which emerged at an accelerating pace after 1750 were typically quite small relative to the costs of circulating capital. The latter were the finance requirements of stockpiling raw materials, sustaining work in progress, maintaining inventories and awaiting final payment after delivery. Ploughback of the high profits to be earned in the new sectors enabled successful firms to expand their physical scale of production as rapidly as they wished without recourse to sources of finance outside their immediate circle of family, friends and close business colleagues. This resolution of the anomaly is the 'Postan–Pollard story'. Postan (1935) began the tale by arguing that although eighteenth-century Britain was the 'richest land in Christendom' there was no capital market to direct excess savings to the enterprises with excess investment demands. Pollard (1964) completed the story by demonstrating that, even with the coming of the factory system, fixed capital was a relatively small share of a firm's total assets. Only cotton-spinning mills by the 1830s had fixed capital as a major component of their assets and even for them the share was only a bit more than half.

In this story, the primary financial institution to make credit available to the early industrialists was the country bank, even if some London banks such as Glyn, Mills & Co. (Fulford 1953) and insurance companies (John 1953) did provide some finance for industrial firms outside the London area. The role of the country bank in most cases was limited to providing short-term financing to business firms when cash outlays on circulating capital were required in advance of cash receipts from final sales. In the case of 'company banks', of course, the capital of the bank could be used as an additional source of long-term financing for the parent firm. The primary role of short-term, commercial financing was important only insofar as it allowed firms to devote their net profits exclusively to building up their fixed capital – i.e., to facilitating the ploughback process of capital formation in the leading sectors. This part of the story can be called the 'Pressnell sub-plot' after Pressnell's description of the role played by country banks in the finance of industrial firms (1956).

The 'Postan–Pollard–Pressnell' story favours, then, separation of the financial revolution from the industrial revolution on the grounds that they really had very little to do with each other. It can then be serialised by telling the story of specific firms in terms peculiar to the personalities of each entrepreneur, a genre initiated by Unwin (1924) and his students and colleagues. These typically paid little attention to the means of finance used by the heroic textile entrepreneurs (although the early work of Heaton (1937) is an exception). This approach was sustained by each successive business biography. It encourages concentrating on the details specific to each industry, to each region and to each time period. As an inducement to a flourishing output of in-depth historical studies on the industrial development of Great Britain, it has served the entire profession of economic history very well. An unexpected consequence of this, however, has been the discovery of an increasing number of connections between industrial development and financial innovations – connections in which industry often determines what happens in the financial sector but frequently is directed by events in the financial markets. Examples include the work of Chapman (1970, 1972) for the textile industry in the 1970s, and more recently major works by Jenkins (1975) and Hudson (1986). A much more complex, but logically more compelling, story has been emerging that links the legal forms of business firms, specific financial instruments and various kinds of financial intermediaries with the entire spectrum of savers available to the British nation. It is too early to assign specific authorship to a story that is still being written and revised, but it is certainly high time to devise an analytical framework within which the various threads of the tale can be examined and pieced together.

Finance of the firm in the eighteenth century

The analytical framework to be used derives from the so-called loanable funds theory of investment behaviour. This comparative statics approach has the virtue of being simple and flexible enough to encompass all the issues. It concentrates on the financial activities of an individual firm, but assumes that they are taking place within the context of a set of inter-related financial markets in which the supply and demand of funds by the firm are relatively very small. The assumption of efficient financial markets (defined as markets in which all the information currently available to participants on both the demand and supply sides of the market is reflected in the current prices on the market, which are available to all potential participants) as the relevant environment in which the firm is making its financial decisions is very convenient when using the model.

It is true, these assumptions are controversial even when applying the model to today's business firms and they are much more so for the eighteenth century in Britain, when it is not clear that anything like a nation-wide capital market existed. For example, Ranald Michie (1985) argues that Scotland was a separate market until telegraph links with

London were established in the mid-nineteenth century. But Scottish bankers were sensitive to fluctuations in the Scottish balance of payments with London in the eighteenth century, particularly with respect to the fluctuations in the premium of the Edinburgh Exchange for money in London (Munn 1981; Checkland 1975). So Scottish separatism, even at this early date, must not be exaggerated.

It is a vital part of the argument of this chapter that an active and widespread, if amorphous, credit market, centred on London and radiating inland, operated throughout Britain during the entire eighteenth century. It conveyed accurate information on the current yields of government stocks traded on the London stock exchange throughout the kingdom, as well as throughout Europe. This meant that any firm in any sector had available to it the option of tapping into this market – albeit only on the market's terms, which would vary with its appraisal of the firm. This meant that local firms in diverse parts of the kingdom could borrow exclusively from local savers and yet all pay interest rates that moved in accord with those available in the London money market.

The finance needs of any firm can be divided into the two categories of working capital and investment capital. These are the financial counterparts of the concepts of circulating capital and fixed capital used above to distinguish two kinds of physical capital. The firm's demands for, and supplies of, working capital are determined by the mismatches that inevitably arise between the timing of accounts payable (its outlays) and the timing of accounts receivable (its revenues). It can solve the mismatch either by: (1) waiting for the accounts on the slower side of the ledger to catch up with those on the quicker side; or (2) financing the difference by borrowing short term when accounts receivable are slow to mature and lending short term if accounts payable are lagging. If the interest rate paid when borrowing is not too much higher than the interest rate received when lending, then the financing principle is surely the preferable one to follow. And if the interest rate paid when borrowing is actually less than that received when lending, then the firm should become a financial intermediary instead of remaining a trading or manufacturing enterprise. Even if the firm remains a non-financial enterprise, however, one of the options it has when it is lending is to lend to itself, i.e. to ploughback its earnings. There is a cost even to doing this, however, which, at a minimum, is the opportunity cost of the interest the firm forgoes by not investing in the safest, most liquid short-term financial asset available to it.

To summarise, the firm's supply of loanable funds for investment capital was determined first by its internal earnings – its net supply of working capital. The opportunity cost for this part of its supply curve was the yield available on the liquid, default-free government debt traded in London,

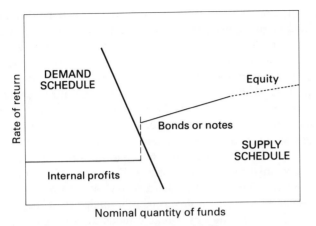

Figure 7.1 Sources of funds for the firm

which served as a convenient alternative short-run investment asset for private business from the end of the seventeenth century. The second source of loanable funds was debt, obtained first on collateral and from close associates familiar with the quality of the firm's assets and of its management, and then at higher interest charges without collateral and from more distant investors. The minimum interest payable for this source must be higher than the risk-free rate available on government stock, because any private firm has greater risk of default than a sovereign government, at least if that government is a constitutional monarchy or a parliamentary democracy.

The third source of external finance derives from the sale of additional equity – share capital in the case of joint-stock corporations, additional partners or co-partners in the case of partnerships. The cost of this may or may not be higher than acquiring debt – that really depends upon conditions in the capital markets and the appraisal made in these markets of the ability of the firm to service its existing stock of debt and equity. It does appear that the cost of equity for most firms was considered to be higher than the cost of debt for the entirety of the eighteenth century. Conditions may have changed with the increased pressures of government demands upon private savings during the French Revolutionary and Napoleonic Wars, 1793–1815.

The sources of loanable funds are shown in Figure 7.1 and a notional schedule of investment projects is sketched in to show how the optimal level of investment would be determined within this framework of analysis. More interesting than the equilibrium analysis, however, is how volatile the supply curve of loanable funds can be. The gap in the rate of interest charged implicitly on the use of internal funds and the rate paid explicitly to external lenders measures the degree of imperfection in the capital market available to the firm. Much, if not most, of this gap is due to asymmetric information – the firm is much better informed about its working capital situation and its internal capabilities than any external lender. As the firm becomes established and its reputation grows and spreads to a wider group of potential lenders the gap may diminish, but the ultimate asymmetry of information between borrower and lender ensures that it will not disappear. If the government's debt is widely available and still subject to price risk, then the entire schedule will shift up as prices of government debt instruments fall, and shift down when prices of government debt rise. The prices of Three Per Cent Consols, by far the largest component of the British government's funded debt, became the best barometer of the schedules of loanable funds for all activities in the British Isles by the Seven Years War (1756–63).

Trade crises and booms, which erupted with distressing frequency and apparently with increasing impact over the eighteenth century, also affected the supply schedule of loanable funds for the representative firm. Because they affect the speed of completion of accounts payable relative to accounts receivable, they shift the supply schedule laterally. During trade booms, accounts receivable are paid in faster than accounts payable are paid out, and the internal source of funds expands to the right. During trade crises, on the other hand, a liquidity crunch occurs so that the internal source of funds contracts to the left and may, in fact, become negative. This does not necessarily mean the firm fails. It may dilute its equity or appeal successfully to external lenders to lend at premium rates and without collateral. Continued recourse to these expedients, of course, increases the risk of bankruptcy.

Bankruptcy occurs when a firm in debt cannot make the payments required by its creditors. In the expansion of overseas trade that occurred in England in the late seventeenth century, temporary insolvency, as opposed to permanent insolvency, became more frequent and larger in scale when it occurred. In recognition of this fact of commercial life, the Act of Bankruptcy was first passed in 1706 and then made permanent in 1732 (see Hoppit 1987: ch. 3). Under its terms, a dissatisfied creditor of a firm could petition the Lord Chancellor to begin bankruptcy proceedings, putting up a £200 bond to discourage false charges. The Lord Chancellor would then appoint a Commission to investigate whether (a) the debtor was a trader, (b) he owed at least £100 to one creditor, £150 to two creditors or £200 to three or more creditors, and (c) he had evaded a reasonable demand for repayment. If they found he was bankrupt, the Commission appointed assignees to seize the debtor's estate, sell it off and divide the proceeds pro rata among all the creditors. If the bankrupt cooperated fully, he was granted a certificate of conformity which entitled him to keep 5 per cent of his estate, up to £200, freed him of any further liability up to the date of the bankruptcy and allowed him to start business again. The clear intent of this law was to provide a better means of dealing with temporary insolvency than had been available to creditors before. These alternatives were (a) informal compositions initiated by common agreement among all the creditors against a trader, (b) suit by individual creditors in small debt courts (Courts of Requests or Courts of Conscience) and (c) using the law of insolvent debtors, which basically limited the creditor to putting the debtor in prison. There the debtor could die miserably or, sometimes, live comfortably off his ill-gotten estate. In either case he left the creditor with his loss. So the law of 1706 was a more liberal law which helped facilitate the expansion of trade credit in Britain. This was the basic law that governed bankruptcy until the revisions that came after the unusually large number of bankruptcies occurring in 1826.

Most firms, however, remained solvent. The framework of loanable funds can be used to describe the means of payment available to them, the financial instruments that arose for provision of working capital, the debt instruments used for external finance and finally the techniques used for expansion of equity. Along the way, it is possible to assess the significance of different intermediaries who arose to provide finance for British business.

Forms of credit

The bill of exchange

The foreign bill of exchange took advantage of offsetting balances which merchants accumulated with each other in different ports, so that each merchant could use only local currency for local payments and not have to export coin or bullion for foreign payments. Instead, bills of exchange drawn against balances held abroad could be purchased locally and used for the foreign payments. The charges made by sellers of the bills of exchange would earn them a return on the balances they held abroad. So there are two ways to think of the bill of exchange: (1) as a means of payment for goods traded between distant markets; and (2) as an instrument of credit enabling holders of idle balances to earn a return on them.

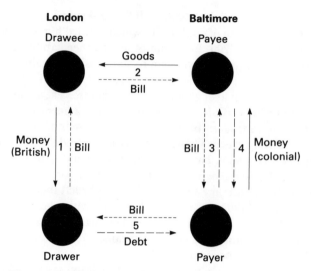

Figure 7.2a The foreign bill of exchange in trade

The bill of exchange as a means of payment

An example of the use of the foreign bill of exchange in the finance of foreign trade is illustrated in Figure 7.2a. Our example begins with a tobacconist in London importing several barrels of tobacco from a dealer in Baltimore. He has English pounds to pay for it, but the Baltimore dealer needs Maryland currency to pay his suppliers, the tobacco growers on the East Shore. So the tobacconist takes his English pounds to a merchant banker in London, buys a bill drawn on Baltimore, payable there in Maryland pounds (Step 1). He has become, in terms of Figure 7.2a, the buyer of a bill (drawee, or remitter) and he has purchased it from the drawer, a merchant holding balances abroad with his foreign correspondents, and has paid for it in local currency. He then remits it to Baltimore as payment for the imported tobacco (Step 2). In Baltimore, the bill drawn in Maryland currency is taken by the payee, the tobacco dealer who is exporting to the London tobacconist, to the merchant banker it is drawn against. If it is a valid bill, the Baltimore merchant banker accepts the bill by acknowledging on the bill that he will have the cash ready to pay out in return for the bill by a specific date, usually three months from the time he accepted it (Step 3). The payee in Baltimore now has a negotiable financial instrument in his possession. He can now use the accepted bill of exchange as a means of payment and it can then circulate until it is cashed in on its expiration date by the last holder (Step 4). In the final stage, the paid-off bill is 'extinguished' by the signature of the final holder of the bill and is sent back to the original drawer (Step 5) to show that the balances held abroad have now been drawn down by the amount of the paid-off bill. In other words, the bill of exchange has allowed payment for London imports to occur by an export of short-term capital from Baltimore to London.

The ability of the London importer to pay the Baltimore exporter in a bill of exchange depended, of course, on the willingness of the Baltimore merchant banker, who had to accept the bill, to extend credit to the London merchant banker. So there were typically four parties to the bill, shown in Figure 7.2a as the drawer and drawee on the London side, and the payer and payee on the Baltimore side, although the eighteenth-century usage was to refer to the drawee as the remitter of the bill, the payee as the possessor of the bill and the payer as the accepter (Postlethwayt 1774: s.v. 'Acceptances', 'Accepter', 'Bills of Exchange' and 'Drawer'). The payee could assign the bill to another party, but in so doing assumed responsibility for its eventual payment along with the drawer and accepter. Multiple assignments or endorsements therefore increased the security of this negotiable instrument and its liquidity.

This revolution in means of payment originated in Antwerp, where the negotiability of the long-established foreign bill of exchange was created by introducing serial endorsements. This innovation was transferred to Amsterdam with the Portuguese Jews and various Protestants expelled from Antwerp in 1585 and was perfected with the establishment of the Amsterdam Wisselbank in 1609. Using the Wisselbank, merchant bankers could transfer payments denominated in bank money (called banco) rapidly and securely among themselves without the delays and uncertainties caused when a bill was extinguished by sending it back to the original drawee. For example, the flow of new debt from the London merchant banker to the Baltimore merchant banker shown at the bottom of Figure 7.2a could occur by transfers from one account to another within the Wisselbank, as could the subsequent extinguishing of the bill. This actually improved the negotiability of the bill because the time delay in protesting bills refused by the designated accepter was then reduced, as was the risk to the accepter of default by the drawer. Moreover, it allowed so-called dry bills, or short-term lending by merchant bankers to local merchants, to become more efficient, reducing the rate of interest on short-term credit.

The bill of exchange as a means of credit

Under this variant, the flows shown in Figure 7.2a were reversed: the merchant banker bought a foreign bill from the local merchant as the basis for lending him money (Figure 7.2b, Step 1). In this credit transaction, note

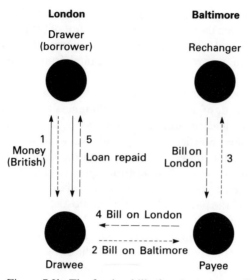

Figure 7.2b The foreign bill of exchange as credit

that the merchant banker now becomes the 'drawee' and the London importer becomes the 'drawer'. The merchant banker, as drawee, now sends the bill to his correspondent, who has it accepted by a colleague by promising immediate 'rechange' – purchase of a bill drawn on London with the proceeds of the bill drawn on Baltimore (Step 3). This bill then would be sent to the merchant banker in London (Step 4) and accepted by the local merchant there, who in paying it off two months later would also have repaid his original loan from the merchant banker, with an undisclosed amount of interest (Step 5) (Neal 1990: ch. 1).

The bill of exchange became the major source of credit for British merchants engaged in the growing trade with the North Atlantic colonies. Price (1980) has analysed in detail how the tobacco trade was financed. He sums up the amount of credit extended by British merchants to American planters in the American tobacco trade on the eve of the Revolution (1774) as around £4 million. Of this total credit extended by British firms, about £1 million can be accounted by the paid-in capital of the British firms – the equity of the proprietors and partners. Another £460,000 was borrowed on bond, £100,000 provided by banks and up to £440,000 by outside investors in the trade's ships and real estate. Another '£2 million is still left to be accounted for by commercial credit. For the entire North American–West Indian–West African trading complex in 1774, the figure may have been as high as £9 million' (Price 1980: 123).

Price's estimates of the relative magnitudes of the sources of loanable

funds indicate that the supply schedule of loanable funds for a representative firm, in terms of Figure 7.1, was one half internal and most of
the rest was unsecured debt, with relatively little coming from increasing
equity. But this picture compresses what in fact was a very complex
structure of firms engaged in production, marketing and shipping and the
composition of funding varied considerably at the various stages of
production. Price distinguishes five stages that were typical for firms
engaged in supplying the export commodities to the colonies – mainly
textiles and ironwares. These were (1) the cottage artisan; (2) the merchant-
manufacturer; (3) the factor in the marketing centre (London or a major
outport); (4) the warehouseman (wholesaler) and (5) the export (or
domestic) merchant. The strategic level in this hierarchy of production was
occupied by the warehousemen. As Price explains,

they mobilized capital partly by inheritance and marriage, partly by ploughing
back profits, and partly by borrowing on bond or note from those who wished a
higher rate of interest than was available (after Walpole's time) from government
securities or mortgages ... While the export merchant inevitably had most of his
effects (goods and credits) abroad, the factor and warehousemen usually held their
effects at home as stock on hand and as credit owing from persons in Great Britain.
Thus they probably appeared to be better risks than export merchants, and, other
things being equal, they had less trouble in attracting loans on bonds or notes:
hence their greater effectiveness as capital mobilizers. (Price 1980: 142)

Price notes that Ashton had emphasised the importance of the lower
interest rates on government stock during the mid-eighteenth century in
diverting savings toward investment in shares and mortgage bonds of
turnpike and canal companies. Price suggests that savings may also have
been diverted toward the higher yield of the commercial and industrial
sectors, as savers switched from government securities now offering lower
yields to the bonds offered by the warehousemen. This was an informal
market, but widespread and apparently very active. It is no coincidence,
according to Price, that many of the banks that arose in the latter half of
the eighteenth century originated as outgrowths of warehousemen who
found their skills as mobilisers of capital more remunerative. These
included Barclays and Paynes of London and Wilsons of Leeds (wholesale
linen drapers), Gurneys (dealers in woollen yarn) and Lloyds of Birmingham (wholesale ironmongers) (Price 1980: 142–3).

Although the warehousemen were the ultimate suppliers of credit in the
Atlantic export trades examined by Price, it is important to recall that they
were in close proximity to the central money market of London. It was in
London that the demands of the government and/or the large chartered
trading companies upon short-term funds were revealed in the price
movements of the stocks of the Bank of England, the East India Company

and the South Sea Company; the bonds of the East India Company; and of the perpetual annuities of the government. It was in London, therefore, that the ability of the warehousemen to provide cheap credit for the export trades of the country were determined. If they were competitive with one another, then the lowered yields on government securities after mid-century not only increased the supply of loanable funds available to them, as argued by Price, but also reduced the price at which the warehousemen could extend credit and still profit as financial intermediaries.

It is also necessary to recall that the warehousemen were at the apex of a vast network of trade credit relations among the hosts of intermediate suppliers and ultimate producers located throughout the kingdom. The network itself was linked together primarily by book credits, backed up when necessary by bills of exchange. While the export traders were linked by foreign bills of exchange, the domestic suppliers were linked by inland bills of exchange.

The inland bill of exchange

The importance of commercial credit in England was greatly reinforced by legislation in 1698 and again in 1705 that elevated the inland bill of exchange for amounts of £20 and above to the same status in law as the foreign bill of exchange. Under the terms of English law, the inland bill was an instrument of credit which was assignable and so negotiable. In England, it was not necessary to express on a bill that value had been given for the sum drawn; the law presumed that it had. Moreover, an inland bill could be drawn and made payable in the same place, so it could circulate in a local area where all the successive assignees were known to one another. After 1765, it could even be drawn payable to bearer. No wonder it constituted the bulk of the English money supply in this period (Cameron 1967). So the inland bill of exchange became the dominant form for the medium of exchange in England. In France, by contrast, value had to be expressed explicitly, because there a bill of exchange was only allowed as a contract of exchange, and it could only be payable to the order of a specified trader (Anderson 1970: 90). The volume of bills of exchange there was strictly determined by the conditions of trade, not of the financial markets.

The bill obligatory

The bill obligatory, or promissory note, was a standard form of credit used among businessmen for time out of mind and very likely in all places as well. It was in common use in England and, like the inland bill of exchange, was negotiable but, unlike the inland bill, was not readily assignable. That is, the original debtor on the bill was the only individual ultimately responsible for discharging it, whereas with an inland bill any possessor had equally valid claim on each previous possessor who had endorsed it. So the bill obligatory could only be used as a means of credit among a tight-knit circle of businessmen, who could monitor conveniently the ability of the original debtor to redeem the note. It could not become a medium of exchange outside this circle, much less as a means of long-term credit. Even knowledgeable investors found it preferable to lend on some tangible collateral if the loan was for any appreciable length of time.

The mortgage

Anderson (1969a) explains that the mortgage arose in the late seventeenth century with the widespread emergence of the strict settlement of land. Strict settlement made it more difficult to sell land for payment of debts so the mortgage offered the alternative of a loan raised on real security. One form of mortgage had the mortgagor convey his land outright in fee simple to the mortgagee with a covenant for reconveyance if the debt was repaid on time. The other had the mortgagor grant a lease to the mortgagee. Then he could either (1) grant a long lease, perhaps 500 years, to the mortgagee with a provision that he keep possession of the property himself unless he defaulted; or (2) grant a long lease and receive back a sub-lease from the mortgagee at a fixed rent, with a provision for the forfeiture of the sub-lease if he failed to make the rent payments. This became most popular in the early eighteenth century because it could be raised on both freehold and leasehold property. By the eighteenth century 'the mortgage was still a pledge in form but in practice it had become an "hypothecary trans-action", in which the entry into possession of the mortgagee was an extremely unusual step' (Anderson 1969a: 13). That is, the widespread use of mortgages led to more convenient forms of lending based on the possibility of a formal mortgage. One such was the 'conditional mortgage' in which a property was pledged as in a mortgage if the loan was not repaid within a year. Another was an 'equitable mortgage' in which the title documents would be deposited with a bank as security for a loan and in case of default the lender could foreclose. Mortgages were used well down the social scale and funds moved up and down the social ladder. They are found in the probate inventories of Lancashire individuals of all degrees of wealth and social status. Anderson argues from his analysis of these records that Lancashire savings went to 'building up an economic and social infrastructure' rather than 'the sterile pursuit of financing govern-ment borrowing' (1969a: 22). In other words, the bulk of the financial assets held by Lancashire individuals at time of death were mortgage bonds on local property rather than government securities registered in London. But this does not mean that their investing activities were independent of the London capital market or that the rates of interest they received on mortgages were independent of the yields on government debt.

Government debt

The large scale of their wars at the end of the seventeenth and beginning of the eighteenth centuries encumbered both France and England with their first major national debts (Hamilton 1947), mostly in the form of annuities at high rates of interest ranging from 8 per cent to 10 per cent. The rate of interest implicit in these annuities, issued during the wars and especially at their conclusion, was much higher than the rates of 5 per cent to 6 per cent that prevailed in the peaceful years of recovery that followed. Because of the awkwardness of transferring title on these securities from one owner to another, however, annuity holders could not easily realise their implied capital gains. Both governments, in making the annuities irredeemable at the time of issue and thereby guaranteeing potential investors that their annual payments would continue undisturbed for up to ninety-nine years, gave up the possibility of reducing their debt service after the wars by issuing replacement debt at lower, peacetime interest rates. The Mississippi Bubble and South Sea Bubble arose precisely from the competing efforts by France and England to convert fixed interest irredeemable debt into variable yield securities that could be more easily traded and retired. The premium paid by investors for the improved liquidity of these alternative financial assets translated into lower debt service for the government. Both the English and French governments seized on the weakened position of the once mighty Spanish Empire after the War of the Spanish Succession to convert their annuity debts into equity in large monopoly trading companies that would exploit the riches of the Spanish Empire – the Compagnie des Indes in France and the South Sea Company in England. In this endeavour they took inspiration from the success of the Dutch and English East India Companies in their successful exploitation of the riches of the Portuguese Empire in the Far East.

Placing the shares of these huge new companies on the relatively small stock markets of the time led to the famous bubbles of 1719 and 1720. In these episodes, the promises of financial gains from implementing proven innovations on a truly grand scale led to speculative excesses in which the prices of all shares rose quickly to unsustainable heights, collapsed, and left the markets in a disarray that invited political intervention and recriminations. Whereas those bubbles traditionally have been seen as disasters that effectively forestalled the rise of financial capitalism for over a century (Scott 1910: I, 436–8), they had an important effect in internationalising the European investment community of the eighteenth century to an unprecedented and irreversible extent. Dickson (1967: 311–12) makes this point for England, and it is made as well for Holland by Groeneveld (1940). Instead of equity in perpetual joint-stock companies or debt in the form of annuities, however, the new financial instrument became the perpetual and redeemable annuity: the 'Three Per Cent Bank Annuity' of 1726, the precursor of the 'Three Per Cent Consol', created in 1751. Financial investment activity thereafter focussed on this nearly ideal security, that essentially gave the holder an equity position in the financial fortunes of the state. But its attractiveness to the investing public depended on the relative ease by which it could be acquired and disposed of, the clear terms of the interest payments and the readily available information about its current price and the military and political events likely to affect its price.

The financial instruments just described – the bill obligatory, the mortgage bond, the foreign and inland bill of exchange, partnership and joint-stock equity and government stock – were the legal forms used by borrowers to create attractive assets for lenders to hold in place of the funds they loaned. They were varied, but each arose to serve a specific need for the provision of capital that had emerged by the early eighteenth century. Their relative usefulness for different purposes can be illustrated by examining the financial intermediaries that existed in England at the beginning of the eighteenth century.

The financial intermediaries

In the seventeenth century, there had arisen already three major classes of financial intermediaries – the goldsmiths, the scriveners and the attorneys. Each served a distinctly different clientele from the others and each operated within separate spheres of business activity. Each developed their function of financial intermediation as a natural spin-off of their original professional functions.

Goldsmiths

Goldsmiths were among the oldest and most prestigious of the organised guilds throughout medieval Europe. They worked all the precious metals – gold, silver, and copper – and from their familiarity with the qualities and varied uses of each metal they took on a wide variety of roles. Their prestige was high with respect both to Church and state. For the Church, they created precious settings for religious vessels, monstrances, reliquaries and the like – most works lost when the secularisation occurred. For the state, they monitored the quality of the metal at the mint; most mint-masters were pre-eminent goldsmiths. For the merchant guilds, they provided both means of payment and assessment of receipts of coins from foreign mints obtained in long-distance trade. And for local citizens, they provided not only secure investments in their precious wares, but also superior loan terms on the deposit in pawn of jewellery, plate or silverware.

Their significance for monetary history lies chiefly in the role they played as instruments of the extension of princely control over the economic activity of country and town in the late middle ages and the early modern period. The London guild was chartered in 1327 to maintain quality controls over the large amount of plate and coin then being brought into the country by foreign traders. In 1478 it obtained jurisdiction over all silver and gold wares produced in and around London. It assayed for a fixed fee samples of each at the Guildhall and stamped on the hallmark – a leopard crowned – if the gold were 18 carats fine and the silver of sterling quality. In 1509, its jurisdiction was extended to include the entire kingdom so they could test at will any object of silver or gold and confiscate it if it proved sub-standard and fine the maker. This power eventually led to a nation-wide network of goldsmiths centred on the London corporation. The London guild was constantly replenished by immigrants from the country and, increasingly with the growth of foreign trade, from abroad.

England's neutrality in the later years of the Thirty Years War (1618–48) then raging on the Continent diverted much of the carrying trade between Mediterranean and northern Europe through London. When Charles I seized in 1640 the stores of specie and bullion held by merchants at the Tower Mint, the plundered merchants relied thereafter upon well-known goldsmiths in London to hold their specie in security for them. The goldsmiths rapidly expanded from deposit banking into clearing and discount banking. Their network of correspondents in the provinces and abroad enabled them to discount both foreign and inland bills of exchange with minimal risk. When they began to give receipts for the value in pound sterling of the items, coins, bars and dust deposited rather than for the specific object, they quickly became banks of issue as well. Their receipts were negotiable instruments under English common law because such a receipt was then considered a note obligatory on collateral and so could be assigned to a third party and even carry a bearer's clause.

During the Civil War and the initial years of the Restoration, goldsmiths were also bankers to the various governments, discounting short-term public debt. This role was greatly damaged by the Stop of the Exchequer in 1672, when Charles II refused to meet payments due on the public debt.

But the goldsmith-bankers continued to influence the development of public finance until 1720. Their credits to the Exchequer on which payment had been stopped were successively funded into longer-term securities, first as Bankers' Annuities and Lottery Annuities issued under William and Mary, and then as shares in the South Sea Company's debt conversion of 1720. Even after 1688, they played a major role as agents collecting semi-annual payments for holders of the large quantities of annuities issued during the Wars of the League of Augsburg (1689–97) and Spanish Succession (1702–13). By the end of 1720, however, the note issue of the Bank of England far exceeded the total of all the goldsmith-bankers and their activities thereafter were concentrated on private deposit banking.

Scriveners

Scriveners wrote up the legal forms required for contracts of all kinds, especially those conveyancing titles to land. Their work required searching through previous conveyances to determine the details of the property in question such as its boundaries, its liens and its uses. Their knowledge of properties and their advantages in keeping records made them natural agents for potential lenders desiring to locate profitable mortgage opportunities. Melton (1986) even argues that funds deposited with them might be put to their own use until suitable mortgage investments were found for the depositors. Their clientele were primarily the landed gentry with residences in London, and their intermediation functions focussed on landed property, chiefly in agriculture. Due to the peculiarity of England that land titles were required to be registered in London, the scrivener-bankers concentrated there, at the centre of a web of agricultural credit that radiated out to all parts of the kingdom, save Lancashire and, in the eighteenth century, Yorkshire. They dealt with drafts and inland bills for remittances and with land mortgages as the assets eventually held by their depositor clients. Much of their expertise in title search and their specific knowledge of potential mortgage opportunities was shared, however, by attorneys.

Attorneys

By the eighteenth century, attorneys had acquired the role played by scriveners in the seventeenth century. They were especially important as financial intermediaries, not surprisingly, in Lancashire and later York-shire. Their role in Lancashire has been described by Anderson (1969a) and in Yorkshire by Hudson (1986). Attorneys were the legal representatives of others in matters of law, and for financial intermediation, their functions as estate stewards and as trustees of wills put them in the enviable position of representing both potential borrowers and potential lenders, and charging fees to both. The role of attorneys was especially important within a local region encompassed by the jurisdiction of the courts to which the attorney had access. They were not overshadowed by the rise of country banks until the last quarter of the eighteenth century in Lancashire and until the second quarter of the nineteenth in Yorkshire.

Country banks

The classic study of country banking in this period remains that of Pressnell (1956), who confirmed Edmund Burke's contemporary observation that such banks were virtually non-existent in 1750, numbering then perhaps a dozen in all of England and Wales. There were, in fact, many more private banks operating in London at that time, perhaps thirty in all. But it was country banks which grew most rapidly thereafter, rising in periodic bursts to approximately 100 in 1775, 370 in 1800 and 600 by the crisis year of 1825 (Cameron 1967: 33 n. 23).

They were typically small. Pressnell estimates that they averaged £10,000 in capital, and concentrated on (1) providing remittance facilities within the local area and from it to London; (2) keeping interest-paying deposits for local savers, which were used by the bank to buy up inland bills of exchange at a discount and to make short-term loans to local businesses, both merchants and manufacturers and (3) issuing notes which could be used as means of payment, at least locally. If they issued notes, and not all did, they were limited to being partnerships, with no more than six partners, by the law which had renewed the charter of the Bank of England in 1708. In sum, they provided a more general intermediation function in a local area between the savers (e.g. agricultural landlords) and investors (e.g. artisanal manufacturers) than could typically be provided by individuals with a limited range of contacts, such as scriveners and attorneys.

Oddly, they did not arise as rapidly in the cotton textile districts of Lancashire and the new woollen districts of Yorkshire as they did in the prosperous agricultural areas serving the London market or in the smallware manufacturing districts in the midlands. Their relative absence in Lancashire has been explained as the outcome of some early failures there of country banks, especially in 1788, and of the success of the attorneys as intermediaries and the inland bills of exchange as means of payment used in lieu of bank notes. The relative success of these older forms of intermediary and instrument in the case of Lancashire can, perhaps, be attributed to the dominance of the cotton trade there, compared to the more diverse range of products produced in the west midlands.

The growth of country banks was exceptionally rapid during the Napoleonic War period of 1800–10, and it rebounded from the crisis of that year very quickly. It was the rise of joint-stock banking after the Act of 1826, however, that characterised the most rapid period of their expansion and carried the number of country banks to their highest level in 1838 (over 1,100). By this time, their average size was increasing rapidly as well, and branch banking had begun to make its appearance, initiated by the larger joint-stock banks who concentrated on demand deposits rather than note issue (see vol. 2, ch. 1).

The rise of country banks in England was paralleled by the rise of provincial banks in Scotland, as chronicled by Munn (1981). These began outside Edinburgh to compensate for the lack of branches in Aberdeen and Glasgow by the two public banks, the Bank of Scotland (1695) and the Royal Bank of Scotland (1727), but their numbers grew from three to thirteen from 1761 until the crisis of 1772. Steady expansion followed the Act of 1765 and the salutary lessons of the crisis of 1772 when the Ayr Bank, which made short-term loans based on the landholdings of the major partners, failed and brought down several other banks. In 1793, a total of eighteen banks were scattered throughout Scotland, lending to merchants and to local manufacturers. Another twelve banks were formed during the war prosperity years of 1793–1810, despite the hostility they faced from the two public banks. More dangerous for their long-term survival than opposition of the Bank of Scotland and the Royal Bank of Scotland, however, was the founding of the Commercial Banking Company of Scotland, the first of the new joint-stock banks in Scotland that after 1825 were to replace the provincial banking companies, just as the joint-stock companies in England displaced the country banks there after 1825.

Merchant banks

It was the period of the Napoleonic Wars which also witnessed the initial upsurge of merchant banks, concentrated exclusively in London (Chapman 1984). Merchant banks combined the business of discounting and issuing foreign bills of exchange with underwriting new issues of government debt. This particular combination of functions seems to have been unique to Britain. Other countries generally separated commercial banking from investment banking and usually separated commercial banking into its domestic and foreign components as well.

Chapman (1984) argues that the expanding production of cotton goods in Lancashire and consumer goods in the midlands was financed during the last half of the eighteenth century by mercantile credit in London. Even after Liverpool's trade surpassed that of London early in the nineteenth century, it was financed through London. The finance of export trade to Europe had to be done through London rather than Amsterdam during the War for American Independence and it remained in London afterwards. The critical period 1780–1825 saw the leading industrialists taking increased marketing initiatives in the new export markets that were arising for British products. These were financed by mercantile houses in London or by representatives of continental houses who were sent to the provinces. (Nathan Rothschild was sent to Manchester by his Frankfurt family firm in 1799.) Only a very few large firms were successful in combining manufacturing and marketing abroad. After 1825 there was a rapid rise of accepting houses – London-based merchants who took on the financial risk of exporting. Especially successful were the London houses which had been created by the immigration of continental and American merchants during the Napoleonic Wars (Chapman 1984: 14–15).

The variety of financial institutions, intermediaries and instruments that arose in Britain over the course of the seventeenth and eighteenth centuries is remarkable among the countries of Europe at this time. The traditional explanation is that the monetary policy of the English government was unusually inept, forcing recourse to private substitutes for means of payment. But thanks to the flexibility of English law, created by the venality of English courts, these substitutes were more than adequate to sustain the payment streams required of a market economy. The mint was untrustworthy, as the episode with the rise of goldsmith-bankers indicates, but worse was its failure to maintain appropriate mint ratios between gold and silver from the time of Henry VIII until formal adoption of the gold standard in 1821. It was apparently inadvertence that in 1717 caused Isaac Newton as Master of the Mint (a position given him when his senility had become apparent to all) to undervalue silver and put England effectively on a gold standard. Unfortunately, it also meant that it had no small coinage until after the Napoleonic Wars. In Pressnell's memorable phrase, 'Thus the currency was in an unsatisfactory, even lamentable condition throughout the Industrial Revolution' (Pressnell 1956: 15). It is another of the ironies of history, reflecting the economic principle that there is an opportunity cost for every activity, that one of the most backward countries of Europe in terms of monetary developments should have been the leading innovator in financial matters.

The financial revolution in England

The achievement of financial innovation in English government securities took over thirty years from the first issue of government-backed annuities in 1693 and 1694. These turned out to be not as popular as prior experience with them in the Netherlands and France had led William III's advisers to expect. Indeed, rather than annuities, the most successful financial innovations proved to be the state lotteries, beginning with the Million Lottery of 1694. This built on the triumphs of private lotteries, in which prodigious numbers of tickets at relatively low prices had been made available from reasonably large numbers of outlets. For example, Thomas Neale's lottery of 1693 had £25,000 of 10s tickets available at eleven different goldsmiths, with 250 prizes at stake (Dickson 1967: 45). The success of the Million Lottery must be traced in large part to the low denominations in which the lottery tickets could be purchased, their ease of transfer, and the clear-cut (if uncertain and unfavourable) terms on which their returns were gained. They were sold in large numbers by ticket offices set up at major pubs.

All this stood in contrast to the restrictive conditions for purchasing, trading and receiving the income of the annuities. The transfer of annuities was entrusted to the Exchequer and remained very cumbersome until the process was taken over increasingly by the Bank of England through issuance of its own annuities after the South Sea Bubble. The subscriber to an annuity made his payment to the Exchequer and named the nominee whose life was being insured. In return, he received a tally of receipt and a paper 'Standing Order', that was assignable, for the future payment of the annuity (Dickson 1967: 76). At each semi-annual payment of the interest, the annuitant, his agent or his assignee had to present proof that the nominee was still living. This usually was an affidavit signed by the parish rector of the nominee, or, after 1694, simply a declaration by the annuitant notarised by a justice of the peace. But because the Standing Orders were liable to every imaginable vicissitude over the course of the term of the annuity, transfers were made very elaborate. Titles to annuities had to be examined as carefully as titles to land. As a consequence, transfers were much less frequent than were transfers of shares in the joint-stock companies (Dickson 1967: 458–9).

Transfers of these shares, though still cumbersome by modern standards, were effected much more quickly and inexpensively. The companies used a double-entry system with two sets of books, the transfer books equivalent to the journal or flow accounts of merchants of the time, and the ledger books equivalent to the ledger or balance sheets in mercantile accounting. Each proprietor's initial holding was recorded in the ledger book on the left-hand side under the 'Per' heading. Proprietors were arranged alphabetically and under each letter by size of holding. Additional shares purchased were entered on successive lines under the initial entry. New proprietors had entries created for them in rough alphabetical order at the end of the folios devoted to the original proprietors. Sales of stock by any proprietor were entered under a 'Contra' heading on the right-hand side. At the time of semi-annual dividend payments, the Per entries were totalled, and the Contra entries subtracted, and the balance was the basis for payment of the dividend. Each entry in the ledger book, Per and Contra, was initiated by a transfer-book entry. Here printed forms, three to a page, were filled out in sequence and numbered so that each ledger entry, Per for the buyer and Contra for the seller, could be identified by a uniquely numbered transfer. On the transfer forms were entered the folio numbers for the ledger accounts of the seller (top) and of the buyer (bottom) to complete the cross-referencing. The transfer form itself was filled in by a clerk, who also witnessed the transfer and gave, in order, the name, status and place of residence of the transferor, the date of the transaction, the nominal amount of shares in pounds sterling being transferred, and the name, status and place of residence of the transferee. The transfer was complete when signed by both parties, witnessed by the clerk and its margin embossed on payment of the required nominal transfer fee.

Transfers were easily and quickly done in whatever amount was mutually convenient to buyer and seller, title was secure and, moreover, current prices were made transparent by an active stock exchange with regularly published price lists. Indeed, from at least 1698, prices of all the major government securities as traded on the London stock exchange were printed twice-weekly and circulated widely throughout London, the provinces and to the Continent. The large stock of government debt and its ease of transfer provided English businessmen with the ideal short-term 'intervention' asset into which they could place idle balances and from which they could withdraw quickly the funds needed for transactions of any size. In other words, the government debt created by the financial revolution in England furnished a liquid asset for business as well as a relatively risk-free asset for women, orphans and timid investors.

The form of government debt most preferred by investors of all classes was the Three Per Cent Perpetual Annuity. This paid £3 annually on every £100 of the annuity purchased. The first annuities created on this basis were the annuities of the South Sea Company established in 1723 when it was reorganised under Bank of England supervision. In 1726, the Bank itself created its own Three Per Cent Annuity. Many more issues of this security were made during the War of the Austrian Succession, so many in fact that the last major issue after the war consolidated all the previous issues into the famous Three Per Cent Consols of 1752.

Although the Three Per Cent Consols were free of the risk of default, they were not free of the risk of price changes. In fact, their prices fluctuated frequently and violently on occasion due to the active trade in them among businessmen, brokers, rentiers and speculators. Because their nominal yield never varied, however, their price fluctuations reflect the changes in the interest rate faced by business people on the least risky financial asset available to them. If the Consols were selling at 110 per cent of par, for example, a buyer would be getting an actual yield of £3 for every £110 invested in them – 2.73 per cent. When they sold below par, 90 per cent for example, a buyer received an actual yield higher than the nominal yield of 3 per cent – 3.33 per cent in this case. Because the volume available of these securities was very large and transfers could be made almost every working day, they represented a viable investment opportunity for any merchant or manufacturer in London or anyone whose trade went through London, as purchases and sales could be made through an attorney.

Financial conditions for business in eighteenth-century England

The actual yields on Three Per Cent Perpetual Annuities issued by the government are shown in Figure 7.3 for the period 1700–99. These give the vertical movements in the entire supply schedule of loanable funds facing British business firms in those years, as well as indicators of when the horizontal shifts might have occurred in response to changes in the rate of return on government securities. The yields shown for the period 1700–18 are for shares in the Million Bank, basically a closed end mutual fund in long annuities sold during the War of the League of Augsburg before 1700. William Scott, in his magisterial study of joint-stock companies in the British Isles before 1720 (1910), remarked that the shares of the Million Bank in that period were the closest thing to a risk-free long-term investment. After 1720, their dividend was reduced, first to 3 per cent, then in 1724 to 2.5 per cent so their yields are well below those of the South Sea annuities, but the annual movements are similar.

The opening of the eighteenth century saw a decline in the risk-free yields until the effects of the War of the Spanish Succession took hold. After the establishment of the South Sea Company in 1711 and the consequent funding of the accumulated short-term debt of the government into the long-term debt it owed to that chartered joint-stock company, interest rates fell, sparking a stock market boom and the eventual excesses of the South Sea Bubble. Thereafter, the rate of interest was low, with a slight

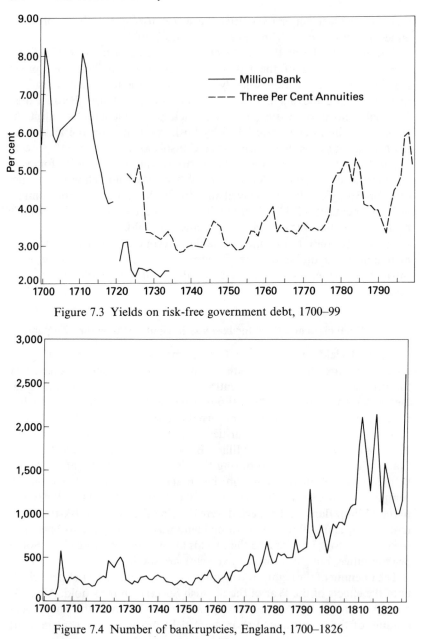

Figure 7.3 Yields on risk-free government debt, 1700–99

Figure 7.4 Number of bankruptcies, England, 1700–1826

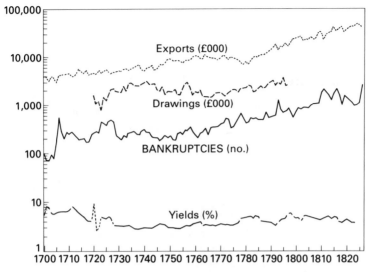

Figure 7.5 Bankruptcies and their determinants, 1700–1826

tendency to rise until the shocks of the American War and the French Revolutionary Wars in the last quarter of the century lifted it sharply upwards.

How did these long-term trends in the nominal rate of interest, and the episodic fluctuations in it associated with wartime demands, affect the course of business? It is interesting to examine the number of bankruptcies recorded in England over the course of the century, to see if these are associated with the movements in the rate of interest. Figure 7.4 shows the raw data on the number of bankruptcies reported in the *London Gazette* as extracted by Hoppit (1987). Figure 7.5 shows the course of bankruptcies and the main variables which, historians have thought, influenced the fluctuations in bankruptcies. The yields on Consols, or on prime government bonds in the period before the 1750s, reflect the risk-free interest rate, or opportunity cost of internal funds, for business firms throughout the period. Fluctuations in the yields generate vertical movements in the entire supply of funds schedule shown in Figure 7.1. The effect of a rise in the yields shown in Figure 7.3 upon the supply schedule of Figure 7.1 is illustrated in Figure 7.6a.

Higher yields, it seems intuitively obvious, reflect reduced supplies of credit to private firms to carry on the complex system of trade credit described above. Further reflection, however, should make it clear that vertical movements in the supply schedule may or may not be associated with reductions in the supply of internal funds available to firms. The

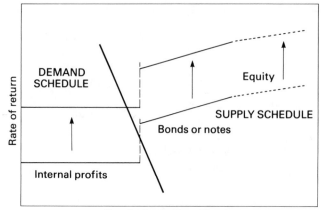

Figure 7.6a The effect of a rise of the yield on Consols

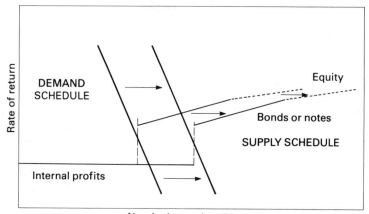

Figure 7.6b The effect of a rise in exports above trend

quantity of internal funds available depends rather upon trading conditions. These may improve in response, say, to wartime demands of military and naval suppliers and the same factors that improve trade opportunities may be driving up the yield on government debt. The effect of a rise in the level of exports above their previous trend, or an increase in wartime demands for supplies, is illustrated in Figure 7.6b, where the supply of internal funds increases, shifting the entire supply schedule outward.

Economic historians who have examined the determinants of bankruptcies (Duffy 1985; Hoppit 1987) have concluded, in fact, that yields on

Consols are not closely related to movements in the number of bankruptcies. Rather, they have found that fluctuations in exports seem to be the best indicator of trade conditions and the availability (and use) of trade credit. When export volumes turned down, the long line of trade credits analysed by Price for the Chesapeake trade was broken. With a lag of a year or more, the failure of credits to be repaid by export merchants reacted back to the wholesalers in London and bankruptcies rose. The rise in bankruptcies was greater, the greater the preceding rise in export volume.

Financial conditions obviously do have an effect on this relationship between exports and bankruptcies, but Duffy (1985) argues that it is the quantity of credit offered by the large private banks, ultimately coming back to the Bank of England, that is the critical factor affecting the number of bankruptcies, not the cost of credit. For the period 1795–1823, he analyses the figures on the volume of discounts made by the Bank of England (Silberling 1919: Table 11). For the earlier periods, Figure 7.5 shows the volume of 'drawing accounts' held in the Bank of England. These would be the resources available to make payments in London to exporters which were held at the Bank of England. These figures indicate whether fluctuations in export volumes were amplified or offset by financial responses.

Whatever relationship might have existed at any period of time surely did not hold over the entire eighteenth century. Even in the short period of 1795–1823 analysed by Duffy, a break in discounting policy by the Bank of England occurred, he argues, in response to the trade and credit crisis of 1810. This crisis was, he believes, exacerbated by very loose lending operations by the Bank to a large number of new clients created by the displacements of trade with the Continent and the vast new opportunities opened up in Spanish America and in the Dutch East Indies. Following the crisis, the Bank restricted its discounting facilities considerably, a feature of life that continued well after the Napoleonic Wars. In fact, the Bank's restrictiveness in offering discounts to London banks in the 1825 crisis probably exacerbated its effects and helped create an exceptional peak in bankruptcies in 1826.

Hoppit has argued that, during the previous century, a break occurred around 1760 when an upward trend in bankruptcies began. After that date, peaks in the number of bankruptcies were always associated with financial crises while before that date financial crises could occur in public finance and not affect bankruptcies, or there could be a crisis in the trading world and no effect on the public funds. The effects of a trade crisis, and of an increase in the drawing accounts available at the Bank of England upon the supply schedule of loanable funds available to businesses are illustrated in

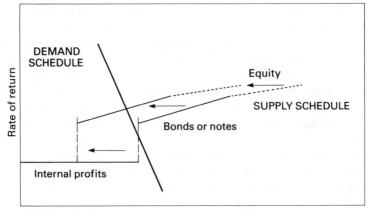

Figure 7.6c The effect of a trade crisis

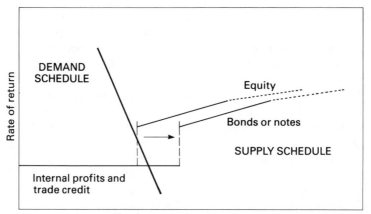

Figure 7.6d The effect of a rise in drawing accounts (or discounts)

Figures 7.6c and 7.6d, respectively. The trade crisis contracts the entire supply schedule by decreasing the availability of internal funds. An increase in drawing accounts shifts it back to the right.

To make a quantitative assessment of the possibilities presented in Figures 7.6a–d, it is useful to do some comparative regression analysis. Table 7.1 presents regressions in which the natural logarithm of the number of bankruptcies is taken as the dependent variable, and five independent variables are used to try to explain the variations in the number of bankruptcies – the natural log of the number of bankruptcies in the previous year, the natural log of the volume of exports (official values),

Table 7.1. *Regression results: bankruptcies on exports, Consol yields, drawings (or discounts), 1723–97 and 1798–1826*

A. 1723–97

Dependent variable	ln Bankruptcies			
Constant	−0·79			
Standard Error of *Y* Estimate	0·19			
R Squared	0·81			
No. of Observations	75			
Degrees of Freedom	68			

	lnBkrpts$_{-1}$	lnExports$_{-1}$	Yields	PctDevnExports
X-Coefficient(s)	0·64	0·28	0·11	−0·08
Std Err of Coef.	0·08	0·09	0·04	0·06
t-statistics	8·01	3·19	2·39	−1·32

B. 1798–1826

Dependent variable	ln Bankruptcies				
Constant	−7·61				
Root Mean Sq. Error	0·14				
R Squared	0·87				
No. of Observations	28				
Degrees of Freedom	22				

	lnBkrpts$_{-1}$	lnExports$_{-1}$	Yields	lnDisc'ts$_{-1}$	PctDvnExports
X-Coefficient(s)	0·35	0·87	0·14	0·29	0·19
Std Err of Coef.	0·11	0·18	0·08	0·07	0·07
t-statistics	3·09	4·95	1·87	4·43	2·85

Note: lnBkrpts = lognormal Bankruptcies
lnExports = lognormal Exports
Yields = yields on Consols or related securities
PctDevnExports = percentage deviation of exports from trend
lnDisc'ts = lognormal Discounts
$_{-1}$ indicates the use of the previous year's value of the variable.

the yields on Consols (or related securities), a dummy variable for wars (1 = wartime) and the natural log of the volume of drawing accounts (current £) or discounts (1798–1826).

The results seem to indicate that Duffy's analysis of the determinants of bankruptcies during the Napoleonic Wars holds up well for the entire eighteenth century. He argued that lagging exports and discounts by one period would give a positive effect on the number of current period bankruptcies, while wartime conditions had no particular effect. Both coefficients on Discounts and Exports are positive and significant, as he argued, while the coefficient on the War dummy (not shown in this table) was negative and insignificant. The same pattern shows up for the previous period 1723–97, when drawing accounts at the Bank of England are used in place of the volume of actual discounts.

However, in contradiction to the arguments both of Duffy and Hoppit, the Consol yields also had a positive, and significant, influence on the number of bankruptcies. It may still be, as Duffy argued, that the direction of causality was from the number of bankruptcies to the Consol yields. The mechanism that would generate this is straightforward. A sudden increase in bankruptcies would disrupt the normal lines of credit among a large network of traders, who would then seek alternative sources of liquidity. The immediate source available would be to dispose of holdings of government securities, driving down their price and increasing their yields to new purchasers. But examining the pattern of yields on Consols in the eighteenth century shown in Figure 7.3, it is clear that the periodic rises in yields were driven mostly by the increase in the supply of Consols immediately after the major wars, as the cumulated short-term debt was funded into long-term debt. So the causation is most likely to go from public finance to private finance.

The importance of the lagged bankruptcies shows up clearly in the regression analysis, but is easily explained by the interdependence of firms in the complicated web of credit that had grown up by the beginning of the eighteenth century and only became more complex as the century progressed. Any break in the web of credit, caused by the failure of a London firm at the hub, would continue to have repercussions for several years as the effects rippled out along one or more of the radiating strands of credit supported by the London house.

It is very interesting that the regression coefficients on the Consol yields are so similar for the two time periods, whose economic and financial characteristics are so different, as indicated by the marked changes in the coefficients on lagged bankruptcies and lagged exports. This suggests that the financial revolution in public finance, completed in England by 1725, had an enduring effect on the finance of business that was sustained right through the period of the industrial revolution (whenever it began!). The web of credit among merchants, manufacturers and bankers, however, had grown in terms of its radius, density and strength. By the end of our period, marked by the Banking Act of 1844, it extended into all the trading regions of the world as well as into every niche of the domestic economy. From 1723, when the pre-eminence of the Bank of England as the premier financial institution in England was assured and the state had developed the perpetual annuity as its primary form of long-term debt, this web of credit was anchored securely in the City of London. Without this anchor, it is very doubtful whether the British economy could have made the structural changes in techniques, products and markets that characterised its transformation from 1760 to 1850. The financial revolution was necessary, even if not sufficient, for the industrial revolution.

8   Mercantilism and overseas trade, 1700–1800

Stanley L. Engerman

Introduction

The role and importance of international trade – trade beyond the British Isles – has long been one of the most controversial topics in the study of eighteenth-century British economic history (see, e.g., Deane and Cole 1962; Davis 1962a; Crouzet 1980, as well as the general summary in O'Brien and Engerman 1991). It is of interest because the implications drawn from the analysis of the nature and magnitude of trade and other international flows are critical to some of the more politically charged debates concerning the period. Their resolution remains uncertain, however, because of the difficulties in agreeing upon the appropriate economic model with which to analyse these issues, disagreements based upon arguments concerning the empirical description of the economy of the period.

The relative importance of the home and the foreign markets in generating the demand for British production, particularly of manufactured goods, has long been debated (Eversley 1967; Engerman 1993; Lindert ch. 14 below). The pessimists in the standard of living debate, such as Hobsbawm, argue that foreign markets provided the major source of increased demand for British goods. In the absence of appropriate initial increases in British incomes, particularly among the large number of lower-income consumers, it is argued that an upsurge in foreign demands, from other countries or from overseas colonies, was needed to provide the markets for the new goods of the industrial era and to spur the process of growth.

By contrast, attention to increasing demands from the mass of the home population is more compatible with the views of the optimists in the standard of living debate, such as Hartwell, with the higher domestic incomes generating greater consumption demands (Shammas 1990). Another link between higher domestic incomes and increased demand for British goods was posited by Deane and Cole (1962), who argued that increased British incomes were used to import more goods from the colonies, who were thus enabled to purchase more British goods. It should be noted, however, that some arguments on the importance of the foreign sector seem to regard separately the two major components of trade. Following the earlier mercantilist logic, focus on the export demand for British production emphasises their effects in employment creation (Gomes 1987; Hutchison 1988). Attention to imports, mainly of food-stuffs and other raw materials throughout this period, emphasises the ability to acquire certain basic commodities at lower cost when purchased from other nations in exchange for domestically produced manufactures, thus mitigating the impact of diminishing returns in agricultural and mineral production.

Malthus (1836: 403) points to another expected gain from foreign trade: 'One of the greatest benefits which foreign commerce confers, and the reason why it has always appeared an almost necessary ingredient in the progress of wealth, is, its tendency to inspire new wants, to form new tastes, and to furnish fresh motives for industry.' (Mintz 1985; Austen and Smith 1990, on the importance of the taste for sugar in European colonial expansion.)

In addition to this overall debate on the relative importance of home and foreign markets, there are also discussions of the roles played by specific foreign areas in the onset of the industrial revolution. These debates often reflect divisions within the British colonial empire, and contain a strong moral as well as political tone. Eric Williams, later Prime Minister of Trinidad and Tobago, had presented most forcefully the argument that it was the slave trade from Africa to Britain's North American colonies, and the sale in Britain of slave-produced commodities from the New World, which provided much of the capital, as well as the demand, for the production of British manufactured goods. This suggested, to Williams and to some subsequent scholars, a necessary link between slavery and the industrial revolution, one that indicates not only the importance of the foreign sector to British development, but also the critical role of this one specific geographic area and type of trade (Williams 1944; Sheridan 1974; Solow 1985; Solow and Engerman 1987, 1991; Darity 1990). It is argued that, not only did this lead to growth in Britain but, because of the pernicious effects of the slave trade, it led also to the ensuing weakness of economic and political development within Africa (Rodney 1972).

Similarly, historians of India point to the relation between the presumed drain of capital out of India to Britain, as a result of the colonial relationship, and British economic development (Dutt 1901; Chaudhuri 1968; Barber 1975). Again, British growth is seen to rest on the contribution extracted from foreign sources, and, it is further argued, British growth meant the decline of the Indian economy. In regard to the

British colonies in North America, there is also some debate regarding the impact of the Navigation Acts regulating British trade with its colonies and other nations upon the income of the colonies as well as upon that of the metropolis (Harper 1942; Thomas 1965; McClelland 1969; Reid 1970; Walton 1971). The 'Burdens of the Navigation Acts' were debated at the time of the American Revolution, anticipating in many ways the British debates between free trade and mercantilistic controls which developed in the late eighteenth and early nineteenth centuries.

These arguments about colonial immiserisation with increased trade, whether due to adverse changes in the terms of trade, through too rapid expansions in the level of population, or through those production shifts against industry argued by dependency theory, do not describe the only possible outcomes, either theoretically or empirically. The more standard discussions of international trade point to the possibility of both partners experiencing some gains from the trade, total and per capita, based upon a set of economic conditions relating to the level of resource utilisation.

The question of the appropriate economic model with which to study the importance of foreign trade may seem conceptually rather straightforward; it is in finding agreement on empirical issues that the major problem arises. Most simply put, the question is whether or not there was an opportunity cost to using economic resources in a specific sector: were resources unemployed and unemployable in the absence of a particular demand source? If resources were basically fully employed, then a shift from home demand to foreign demand, which moved resources into production for the latter sector, would have had a much smaller impact upon measured income than if previously unutilised resources were placed into production as a result of an enhanced foreign demand. In the first set of circumstances there would have been a shift in the composition of output with little change in the total level of output (with the economic gain being less than the gross value of the output); in the other there would have been an increase in total output equal to (at the least, depending upon assumed multiplier effects) the value of the output.

Obviously, there will be considerable differences in the estimated magnitudes of the measured effects and of their implications for economic growth, depending upon which set of conditions is considered accurately to describe the state of the economy at that time. Even if there was 'full employment', however, it is possible that the differences between home and foreign demands for specific commodities could have generated differing long-term effects. If, for example, one of the demand sources was for a sector that permitted greater economies of scale, more useful flows of information in regard to production and distribution, more efficiency due to increased competition and reduced output variance, increased technical progress and more linkages with other sectors (with these characteristics), then growth prospects would not be independent of the demand source. Here, again, there are critical choices to be made in interpreting the nature of empirical differences. A further complication in examining foreign trade is the nation's need to equalise the net flows of goods and services, capital and specie, so that it is important to consider the endogenous balancing process as well as the exogenous initial changes in providing a full picture of the implications of changes in the foreign sector (Caves, Frankel and Jones 1990: part iv).

In the parlance of international trade theory, the full-employment model is usually referred to as Ricardian, after David Ricardo (1817), who formally analysed international trade using this set of assumptions. One variant of the unemployed (or underemployed) resource model, in its long-term variant, is called Smithian, after Adam Smith and his discussions of economic development on the basis of the vent-for-surplus in *The Wealth of Nations* (1776). The short-run variant of the unemployed resource model is referred to as Keynesian, with export sales providing for the use of resources that would otherwise have remained unemployed. The mercantilist arguments were often based on the assumption of some unemployment of labour as a long-term phenomenon. In both the Keynesian and mercantilist cases the society would be producing inside the production possibility curve, and production would be less than it would have been at full employment. Thus, any increases in demand for particular goods will lead to higher levels of total output, and not a shift from the production of other goods.

In the Smithian model there is a question not only about the nature and magnitude of the initial disturbance that generated foreign demand, but also about the properties of the economic responses within the nation. For growth to occur there must not only be an appropriate stimulus, but the workings of the economic system must also be such that they permit a favourable response to occur. The same stimulus can bring about different responses in different economies, depending upon the behaviour of the rest of the economy in adjusting to the stimulus. Thus, even if external factors play a critical role, it is necessary to consider the nature of the internal economy. Without the appropriate internal economic responses high ratios of external trade are unable to generate sustained economic growth, as the less-developed nations of the past and present have frequently demonstrated.

The evidence

Because of various political controls and revenue needs, goods crossing international borders have long been more frequently enumerated than goods traded internally. Thus we are able to describe, quantitatively and otherwise, aspects of international trade to a greater extent than most other economic variables. The foreign trade data presented by the government in the eighteenth century were prepared by evaluating the physical quantities of exports and imports each year, not by the prices current in that year, but by so-called official values. These official values were generally based on prices of the early eighteenth century (Clark 1938; Davis 1954, 1962a, 1979; Schumpeter 1960; Deane and Cole 1962; Mitchell and Deane 1962; Minchinton 1969). Therefore, these measures of exports and imports resemble time series prepared in constant pounds, and they can be used to describe changes in the volume of trade over time.

The basic data on overseas trade presented below are for England and Wales until the 1770s and for Great Britain thereafter. Trade with Ireland was regarded as international trade in this period, and is included with European trade below. Its magnitude, however, is such that any other definitions will not affect the general interpretations of trading patterns. These are for trade in goods and do not include invisibles such as insurance, banking and finance, and shipping earnings, nor do they include other items influenced by foreign trade, such as investment in ports and ships.

The easily available eighteenth-century trade statistics are for England and Wales, 1697–1791, for Great Britain after 1772 and for the United Kingdom after 1796 (Mitchell and Deane 1962). Scottish statistics were available in London after 1755, while separate data on Irish trade begin with 1698. The data in Tables 8.3 to 8.5 (from Davis 1962a and 1979) refer to 'real', not official, values. The computed 'real' values of exports and imports, based upon 'merchants' declarations' and 'current prices', increase at a more rapid rate than do the official values at the end of the eighteenth century (Davis 1979: 11, 79, 86).

The data are most complete for exports and imports of goods – the major omissions being for items smuggled (Cole 1958; Mui and Mui 1975). Statistics were not always collected for the so-called invisibles (services) – costs of shipping, insurance, finance, etc. – which are important in some periods, nor were data collected for international capital flows, flows of specie (gold and silver) and numbers of immigrants and emigrants. Thus more attention below will be given to flows of goods than to the other international flows.

The patterns of British overseas trade

Figure 8.1 presents the overall growth in the total of English foreign trade in goods over the course of the eighteenth century, indicating the general increase over the first seven decades of the century, the dip with the American Revolutionary War, and the very sharp rise from 1780 to the start of the nineteenth century. Table 8.1 presents the ratios of exports to gross national product for the British economy over the eighteenth century. There were swings in the importance of exports by this measure, rising from about 8.4 per cent in 1700 to 14.6 per cent in 1760, falling to 9.4 per cent in 1780 and then increasing to about 15.7 per cent in 1801. It is probable that the pre-1700 ratios of exports to income were below 8 per cent.

As often happens, the specific years for which data are presented had some atypical aspects, often being either years surrounded by, or in the middle of, major wars (D. W. Jones 1988 on 1700; Ashton 1959 on 1800). Thus there would be some differences in magnitudes, and in estimated shares of commodities and geographic destinations, as well as variations in the allowances for the movements of mercenaries and the financial problems due to war borrowing and capital flows, if alternative years were chosen; this would not, however, seriously influence the general conclusions. During the eighteenth century Britain was involved in a war in about half the years. The data in Tables 8.1 and 8.2, drawn from Crafts 1985a, refer to times of war, except for the first period. In Tables 8.3 through 8.5 the data shown are for the following years: 1699–1701 (peace), 1752–4 (peace) and 1794–6, 1804–6 (war). In Tables 8.6 and 8.7 the years are 1700–1 (peace), 1750–1 (peace), 1772–3 (peace) and 1797–8 (war).

These eighteenth-century changes in trade patterns were influenced by a variety of factors, including the frequent occurrence of wars. The particularly rapid growth of exports and of the ratio of exports to national output in the period 1780 to 1800 has featured extensively in debates on the industrial revolution (even though it is a period with the starting year in the middle of a major war). It is estimated that the increase in exports in this period accounted for over one fifth the growth in national output. The export share was higher in current dollars than in constant dollars in the early nineteenth century, but the share in constant (c. 1780) prices increased more rapidly over that period. It is not clear if such differences existed in the eighteenth century, even in the last decades of the century (Crouzet 1980: 79).

The peak British ratios of exports to gross national product were not reached, however, until the second half of the nineteenth century. Since, in the long term, allowing for flows of capital and specie and movements of

Table 8.1. *Exports and national output, 1700–1801*

Year	Ratio of exports to national output (current prices) (%)	Increase in exports as a proportion of increase in national output (%)
1700	8·4	30·4
1760	14·6	5·1
1780	9·4	21·0
1801	15·7	

Source: Crafts (1985a: 131).

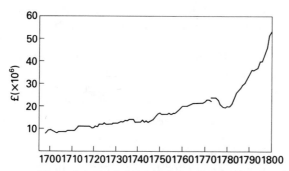

Figure 8.1 English foreign trade in the eighteenth century (net imports plus domestic exports; official values)

Notes and sources: (1) The statistics on which this figure is based are taken from Deane and Cole (1962: 48 and Appendix 1). (2) The statistics are for official values of imports and exports. They are, therefore, a rough approximation to a series of the volume of trade. (3) The statistics are for England, 1697–1774, and for Great Britain, 1772–1800. A three-year moving average has been computed from the original series.

invisibles, exports and imports tend to move in the same direction, these export ratios also reflect the general trend in imports. Given that most exports were of manufactured goods, the eighteenth-century shares of exports in industrial output were above the shares of exports in national output, rising from about one quarter at the start of the century to over one third at its end (Table 8.2).

Over the eighteenth century the bulk of British exports were – reflecting technical advantages in production – manufactured goods, primarily textiles (Tables 8.3 and 8.4). The share of agricultural commodities and

Table 8.2. *Exports and industrial output, 1700–1801*

Year	Gross industrial output (current prices) (£m)	Exports (£m)	Ratio of exports to gross industrial output (%)	Increase in exports as a proportion of increase in gross industrial output (%)
1700	15·6	3·8	24·4	56·3
1760	23·6	8·3	35·2	2·5
1780	39·9	8·7	21·8	46·2
1801	82·5	28·4	34·4	

Source: O'Brien and Engerman (1991: 188), based on Crafts (1985a: 132).

Table 8.3. *The composition of British exports, 1699–1800*

Year	Manufactures (%)	Food-stuffs (%)	Raw materials (%)
1699–1701	80·8	11·0	8·2
1752–4	75·4	16·8	7·7
1800*	87·2	7·7	5·0

* Based on average of 1794–6 and 1804–6.
Source: Davis (1962a: 302–3, 1979: 95–6).

raw materials in exports was below 25 per cent throughout the eighteenth century, being highest at mid-century before declining to about one half that level by the start of the nineteenth century (Davis 1962a, 1979; Ormrod 1985). There was, however, a dramatic change over the century in the composition of the textiles exported. Woollens, the major British export for centuries, had accounted for almost all textile exports (indeed, about 85 per cent of all manufactured exports) at the start of the century, and even as late as mid-century, they were still dominant. However, with the rapid expansion of cotton textiles in the last decade of the century, woollens amounted to only about one half of textile exports at the start of the nineteenth century, the share falling rapidly thereafter. The dramatic expansion of cotton textile exports, which began at the end of the eighteenth century, continued into the nineteenth century, and even while the woollen sector did not suffer an absolute decline, its proportionate decline persisted. The historians' perception of the role of foreign trade is

Table 8.4. *The composition of manufactured exports, 1699–1800*

	1699–1701 (%)	1752–4 (%)	1800* (%)
Woollens	85·0	61·9	22·1
Linens	—	3·3	2·9
Silks	2·2	2·5	2·0
Cottons, etc.	0·6	1·3	35·4
Metalwares	3·2	9·2	15·2
Rest	9·0	21·7	22·5

* Based on average of 1794–6 and 1804–6. If the 1800 data from Mitchell and Deane (1962: 281, 295) were used, cotton's share would have been about one quarter.
Source: Davis (1962a: 302–3, 1979: 95–6).

Table 8.5. *The composition of British imports, 1699–1800*

Year	Manufactures (%)	Food-stuffs (%)	Raw materials (%)
1699–1701	31·5	33·7	34·8
1752–4	22·2	41·4	36·3
1800*	8·4	45·1	46·5

* Based on average of 1794–6 and 1804–6.
Source: Davis (1962a: 300–1, 1979: 122–15). See Crafts (1985a: 143) for a breakdown of retained imports, based on these sources. While the trends are basically the same, the share of raw materials is larger, and those of food-stuffs and manufactures lower, reflecting the differences in shares of these commodities re-exported from England.

often influenced by a focus on cotton textiles rather than overall textiles in the period of rapid export growth, the last decades of the eighteenth century. The impact of different definitions of textile exports can be seen as follows: from 1784–6 to 1804–6, cotton textile exports grew at 16.4 per cent per annum; all textile exports at 7.5 per cent; and woollen and other textile exports grew at 2.9 per cent (Davis 1979: 15). The other major industrial source of exports, the metals industry, accounted for over 10 per cent of exports after mid-century.

There was a shift in the nature of imports over the century, with a decline in the share of manufactures, particularly textiles, and a rise in the share of food-stuffs, particularly sugar and tea (Table 8.5). The share of raw materials increased slightly through most of the century, and then more

Table 8.6. *The destination of English exports, 1700–98*

Year	Europe (%)	Americas (%)	Rest of world (%)
1700–1	85·3	10·3	4·4
1750–1	77·0	15·6	7·4
1772–3	49·2	37·3	13·5
1797–8	30·1	57·4	12·5

Source: Deane and Cole (1962: 87).

Table 8.7. *The source of English imports, 1700–98*

Year	Europe (%)	Americas (%)	Rest of world (%)
1700–1	66·4	19·9	13·7
1750–1	55·3	30·1	14·7
1772–3	45·1	36·4	18·5
1797–8	42·4	32·1	25·5

Source: Deane and Cole (1962: 87) for total imports.

sharply with the expansion in raw cotton imports at the end of the century. Most of the food-stuffs imported could be regarded as non-essentials, with basic food-stuffs such as rice, wheat and corn being only a small component. Throughout the first half of the century exports of grains exceeded imports, with this pattern reversing by the end of the century. There was also some increase in the total value of commodities re-exported. At times in the eighteenth century re-exports amounted to a sum equivalent to about one half of domestically produced exports. The re-exports were generally of colonially produced food-stuffs – tobacco, coffee, sugar, rice and tea – although various manufactured calicoes, linens and silks were also re-exported. The gains to Britain from such re-exports were basically the profits of carrying and selling, but whether the original producing areas gained from this arrangement is something that we shall return to when discussing the 'Burdens of the Navigation Acts'. In many instances the home country had imposed restrictions in regard to colonial products that precluded direct colonial trade with Europe.

There were also dramatic changes in the geographic destinations of British trade (Table 8.6). At the start of the century over four-fifths of exports were sent to Europe, the ratio falling to about 30 per cent at the end of the century. There were large increases in the shares going to the Americas, from 10 per cent to nearly 60 per cent, divided, at the end of the century, roughly 60:40 between the North American mainland (including Canada) and the British West Indian colonies and Latin America. At the start of the eighteenth century, imports were primarily from Europe, with the share falling over the century, while those of both the West Indies and the East Indies both rose (Table 8.7). Mainland North America was not an important source of imports for the British throughout most of the eighteenth century, before the great expansion in cotton. In general, therefore, British trade was primarily with the countries on the European Continent, with Ireland and with its colonies in the New World (and, after its achievement of independence, with the United States).

Exports to Africa represented a small component of trade, while those to India rose above 10 per cent only near the end of the century, although they did form an increasing share of total imports over the century, particularly after mid-century. Thus, after the middle of the eighteenth century about one half of British foreign trade was with its colonies (or, in the case of the United States, a former colony). Despite the attention given to the slave trade, trade with Africa accounted for a relatively small share of British exports and of its total trade, although the role of slave-produced commodities in the Americas accounted for a more substantial part of British imports and these areas also served as a market for British exports. It is this direct trade and the magnitude of slave-produced commodities re-exported from the colonies that became central to the arguments of Eric Williams linking slavery to the onset of the British industrial revolution. In general, however, there was rather limited British trade with the less-developed non-colonial areas of Asia, Africa and Latin America.

The geographic pattern of the trading links between Africa, the West Indies and Britain has been described as a 'triangular trade' (Minchinton 1979). While there were complex patterns of voyages for some trades and on some routes, the 'triangular trade' is the frequent depiction of the complex set of movements which saw the acquisition of slaves in Africa with British and empire-produced goods (particularly Indian textiles) to be shipped to the West Indies, and of slave-produced commodities grown in the West Indies to be shipped to Britain. While this reflects the balancing of goods and financing, the basic pattern of shipping differed somewhat (Inikori 1990). Although the ships that left England for Africa and then sailed to the West Indies did frequently return to England prior to their next sailing to Africa, this return leg was often in ballast – or at least carrying only limited amounts of sugar, rum and molasses. Those commodities were more frequently carried by ships engaged in a bilateral trade with Britain (Sheridan 1974). Thus while the image of the 'triangular trade' persists, it should be in a slightly modified form, not one regarding actual carrying trade as is frequently suggested, but rather focussing on the multilateral nature of trade and capital flows at the time.

Finally, as is suggested by the geographic breakdown of commodity flows, there were often regional imbalances in the amount of exports and imports of goods. In order to balance accounts there were compensating unbalanced trades in invisibles, movements of capital and movements of specie. There were, however, major contrasts in the nature of adjustments among colonies. The excess of British exports over imports from the continental America colonies was financed by trade in invisibles (mainly shipping) and by capital provided to the colonies, with only a limited persistent outflow of specie from the colonies (Shepherd and Walton 1972; Price 1980; McCusker and Menard 1985). The imbalance of imports over exports to India, however, principally because of the payments on invisibles to the British, the costs of imperial administration by the East India Company and the remittances of profits from the earnings of the British on their investments, is claimed to have been consistent with a flow of specie from India to Britain (Chaudhuri 1968, 1978).

The terms of trade is the ratio of the prices received from exports to the prices paid for imports. A favourable change in the terms of trade is defined as an increase in the ratio – a rise in export prices (compared with import prices) or a fall in import prices (compared with export prices). It should be noted that a decline in the terms of trade does not necessarily mean that the nation has been made worse off in comparison with an earlier period, only that if the relative price decline had not occurred (and all else did not change) it could have been made better off. If, for example, the price fall for exports were due to productivity improvements, the incomes of those producing the good could have increased even with a decline in the price received from sales of the good.

This, indeed, is what happened in the nineteenth century to the British, when there were increased cotton textile exports and a fall in their prices, due to rapid productivity improvement (Edwards 1967; Inikori 1989). Thus, in this export expansion, Britain was passing on some of the benefits of the increases in productivity in cotton textiles to the rest of the world. In general, however, in the eighteenth century it appears that there were fluctuations in the terms of trade, reflecting primarily the impact of wars upon import prices. Deane and Cole (1962: 83–4) indicate that whereas the gross barter terms of trade had moved, on the whole, against England between 1700 and 1745, between 1745 and the early 1780s the terms of trade were moving in England's favour, to be reversed again at the end of the century. Nevertheless, they point out that because of data difficulties it is not possible to be precise on the movements of the terms of trade, and thus such changes cannot be used to evaluate fully the gains to Britain from trade, as well as to measure those relative price variations needed to describe the changes in supply and demand conditions leading to the export expansions.

While there is a considerable discussion of the presumed importance of changes in exports of specific commodities or of the shifting geographic sources of demand for exports and supply of imports as providing critical – if not indispensable – contributions to British economic development, it is important to remember the specific requirements of any conclusive tests of these hypotheses. These include an understanding of what length of time has been permitted for evaluating the hypothetical reallocation of resources to other uses; statements as to the proposed alternative possibilities for technological change in different sectors; the causes of any 'exogenous' changes; the critical threshold size of any initial shift; and the mechanisms relating any initial shift to ensuing changes. The focus on those industries which experienced increased trade involvement by an expansion of exports ignores the offsets from other industries which were forced, directly or indirectly, to contract. The industries which grew, moreover, may have benefited from initial expansions within the home market before exports became dominant (Deane and Cole 1962: 185; Davis 1979: 65–6; Crouzet 1980). It may be that it is the scale of industrial output that is significant in explaining productivity change and technical advance, rather than the specific source of such demand. To point to complexity is not to deny the importance of the question, but rather to suggest the necessary directions that a complete analysis must take to provide a satisfactory answer.

Patterns of British overseas investment

There were significant international movements of factors of production in addition to the movements of goods and services. Over the course of the eighteenth century Britain shifted from being a net importer of capital, primarily from the Dutch, to being a net exporter of capital, primarily to the New World colonies and to the United States (Feinstein 1978; Price 1980; Neal 1990). While, after 1760 (with the exception of the era of the Napoleonic Wars), Britain was a net investor abroad, the sums and shares were small compared to those of the era of high imperialism in the second half of the nineteenth century when the share of foreign investment 'averaged around one-third' of British gross investment (Edelstein 1982: 25). At the end of the eighteenth century, by contrast, the shares of foreign investment were generally equal to about 10 per cent of total domestic investment. The accumulated investment by foreigners in Britain in 1760 was offset by British accumulation of coin and bullion, but even then the sum of foreign-owned assets was only about 1 per cent of British national wealth. By 1800, there was net British ownership of overseas assets, but only equal to about one half of 1 per cent of national wealth.

There have been two important discussions about the foreign investments of Britain over this period, both dealing with colonial problems. First, the investments in the colonies, particularly those in mainland North America, often took the form of short-term credits to meet imbalances between exports and imports in the different regions. There were periodic crises, however, when the creditors wished to receive payments on their outstanding loans, generating cyclical difficulties in the colonies. These credits did permit the colonies some short-run excess of imports over exports, without requiring further payments in specie, but such imbalances could not persist indefinitely (Ernst 1973; McCusker and Menard 1985).

Second, the capital investment in the West Indies led to the expansion of slave plantations and the highly profitable (at this time) sugar export trade (Sheridan 1974). Presumably much of the wealth in the West Indies reflected early investments, with continued expansion resulting from a reinvestment of earned profits (Pares 1937). Even then, the share of colonial wealth in total British wealth was relatively small and declining, helping, it is argued, to explain the subsequent British ability to end the slave trade and then slavery in the first half of the nineteenth century (Williams 1944; Eltis 1987). This political argument need not claim that slavery had grown less profitable or less important in absolute terms than previously, but only that it had now become less critical to the British economy because of the extensive domestic expansion (Solow and Engerman 1987; Drescher 1977).

Patterns of population movements

The British Isles were, during this period, the source of a net outflow of population, mainly to the North American mainland (Wrigley and Schofield 1981; Gemery 1984). The magnitudes varied over time, in part with British economic conditions, averaging about 50,000 per decade between 1700 and 1800, but with some decline over the last quarter of the eighteenth century. These amounts of outmigration were considerably below those of the preceding and subsequent centuries. In general, outmigration in the eighteenth century, including free migrants, indentured servants and convicts, never amounted to more than a small proportion of the total population. The outmigration, particularly of indentured servants, was disproportionately male (75 to 90 per cent, for servants – higher in the eighteenth than in the seventeenth century), and young adult (ages fifteen to twenty-five for servants). The indentured servants were obliged to work under contract after their arrival in America, generally for between four and seven years, depending on age, sex, literacy, skills and other factors, to repay the costs of transport, while the periods served by the convicts sent to the Americas were also limited. The indentured labourers represented over one half of white migration to the mainland, with a larger share for the southern colonies, although there, as in the Caribbean Islands, they were frequently replaced as the basis of plantation labour by African slaves (Galenson 1981, 1989a; Grubb 1992).

It was slave labour, imported from Africa, which became the basis of the population of the British West Indies, with relatively few whites arriving (and those suffering high rates of mortality) after the start of the eighteenth century. The West Indian slave population was, however, not self-reproducing in this period, and the numbers imported into the islands greatly exceeded the numbers surviving after the closing off of the British slave trade in 1808 – the same year that the international slave trade of the United States closed (Higman 1984). On the mainland, however, the slave population had a large excess of fertility above mortality and grew quite rapidly, even in the eighteenth century. Unlike the islands, however, many more whites continued to arrive and they, too, experienced a high rate of natural increase. Thus, even in the southern parts of the mainland colonies, the slave population did not represent anywhere near as large a share of the overall population and labour force as it did in the islands (Fogel 1989). There were few flows of population of any magnitude between Europe and Britain, and, at this time, only very limited flows within the British Isles, the large movement of Irish to England awaiting the next century.

The regulation of foreign trade

International relations, particularly in the age of mercantilism, obviously had strong political as well as economic dimensions (Brewer 1989; O'Brien 1988). Foreign trade was regulated with the intention of influencing relations with foreign countries, as well as affecting British revenues, its production structure and its overall wealth. The mercantilist policies, most generally, contained two different sets of measures, depending upon whether the foreign area was an independent nation (or the colony of an independent nation) or a colony of the British. In this period, tariffs on foreign-produced commodities provided the major source of governmental revenues (O'Brien 1988). In addition, the tariffs shifted the relative prices of foreign goods to make them more expensive in British markets. In regard to colonies, there were restrictions on their role in foreign trade, as well as various provisions that were intended to influence the development of the British and colonial shipping industries, and bounties were paid to colonial producers of several commodities to shift colonial production patterns, lowering the relative prices of these imports to British consumers and producers.

Mercantilist policies have been justified by policy makers and later by scholars on several different grounds. Some scholars have emphasised their purpose as having been the achievement of possibly different goals – of national plenty or of national power (Viner 1948). Others point to the policy makers' presumptions concerning the extent of unemployed domestic resources, and to the desirability of an increased demand for exports to generate employment. As to the possible conflict between national power and national plenty, it has been argued that, as with the infant-industry argument for tariffs, there were short-run economic costs to be borne that would be offset ultimately by economic gains in the long run. Thus power and plenty might be seen as congruent, not opposing, ends. Some argue, however, that even if the mercantilist rules were to be economically disadvantageous to Britain in the long run, such costs would have been acceptable insofar as there were other, non-economic, gains such as enhanced power or defence capabilities to meet national goals. Even as strong an anti-mercantilist as Adam Smith believed that there were some initial gains from the Navigation Acts; even their shipping regulations (and military actions) ultimately helped Britain to surpass the Dutch and 'defence is of much more importance than opulence'.

The mercantilist view stressed the rivalry among nations, and the 'zero-sum' nature of international power and wealth. The gains to one nation were seen as the loss to another, and policies aimed at national betterment thus served dual purposes. This concept, of course, remains a frequently argued one in policy debates even today, and at times the same presumptions as to the nature of unemployed resources are used. Some of the specific ends of mercantilist policies were to enhance domestic production, particularly of manufactures (thus increasing the nation's employment); to obtain control of international shipping; and to acquire more specie (to influence the domestic supply of money and lower the rate of interest). It is now appreciated that mercantilist opinion did not aim at the increased acquisition of bullion for its own sake, but rather regarded this as desirable as an indication of the trade balance (showing an excess of exports over imports), for its impact on the domestic money supply and interest rates and for use in clearing imbalances in trade with other nations, particularly in Asia. The broad outlines of mercantilist belief and policy held throughout Europe and even, after its independence, the United States, and the analysis of the effects of British mercantilist policies must consider that they were part of a world trading network in which the other participants followed a similar set of policies.

As part of the mercantilist beliefs, colonies were intended to provide economic benefits for the metropolis, with any possible gains to the colonies being only a secondary consideration. Colonies were not to compete with the home country in the provision of manufactured goods; were to serve as a basis for supplying needed raw materials; and, in the interests of providing specie and generating employment for the metropolis, were to sell most of their exports to other nations via Britain and to purchase most of their imports from Britain, and to do so in British (or colonial) shipping. The willingness of the British to meet most of the costs of the military expenditures to defend the parts of the empire did mean much lower taxes in the American colonies than in Britain (and elsewhere in Europe). This issue of taxation was, however, to play a critical role in the onset of the American Revolution, when Britain, after 1763, attempted to achieve some equalisation of tax burdens by imposing more taxes on the colonies.

The initial set of Navigation Acts, controlling relations with other nations as well as the colonial empire, were passed by Parliament in 1651, and systematically codified in 1660, although they drew upon some already existing pieces of legislation (Beer 1912; Harper 1939; Davis 1962b). They were intended to end Dutch commercial domination in the transatlantic trade as well as weaken the overall economic leadership of the Dutch. There were frequent legislative acts revising and updating the early provisions, until the Navigation Acts were finally ended two centuries later. Of particular importance were tariffs imposed on imports of foreign goods and the restriction of carrying exports and imports to British and colonial vessels, or to ships only from the primary country of destination or shipment. Thus a carrying trade by a trading nation, such as the Dutch had earlier thrived on, was now prohibited. The initial tariffs on imports, down to the last decade of the seventeenth century, were relatively low, but there was a sharp increase in the 1690s to raise more revenues to meet governmental needs, which also had the effect of increasing the restrictive impact on foreign trade (Davis 1966). The provisions of Acts did change over time, and the general level of tariffs tended to move upwards during this period.

The basic provisions of the Navigation Acts regarding the British colonies included several major components. Over the years, the laws did vary and specific inclusions changed, so it is necessary to turn to the specific details of legislation to learn what were the particular provisions at any one time. The major general categories were: (1) restrictions on imports – to come mainly from Britain and British colonies; (2) the 'enumeration' of certain colonial exports, in particular tobacco and sugar, that were to be sent directly to Britain prior to sale on the European Continent; for one other major colonial export, rice, after 1731 direct shipments were permitted to the Iberian Peninsula and southern Europe; and (3) restrictions of shipping to British and colonial vessels, with predominantly British and colonial crews. Other provisions included the prohibition of certain colonial exports (including fur hats and finished iron products) which would compete with British production; bounties paid to produce such raw materials as indigo and naval stores; and export taxes on certain commodities, including sugar. There were other Acts controlling colonial behaviour, such as restrictions against paper money and limitations on land settlement that, while not strictly part of the Navigation Acts, left a significant impact upon relations within the empire.

The 'Burdens of the Navigation Acts'

While the effect of the Navigation Acts upon the North American colonies was frequently discussed (at the time and subsequently), it is probably with the 1965 publication of an article by Thomas that the 'Burdens of the Navigation Acts' became a staple for economic historians. Thomas' study was the first systematic application of standard economic tools to the issue and, while specific assumptions and estimates have been criticised subsequently, the basic approach and general conclusion remain (Lee and Passell 1979; Thomas and McCloskey 1981).

Several possible impacts of the legislation had presumed burdens that, Thomas argued, were not important, for reasons that have broader applications to the study of economic policy even today. The restriction of manufactured imports to those produced in Britain had little, if any, effect since, based on pre- and post-Revolutionary War patterns, Britain was the major source of colonial (and then United States) imports of manufactured goods. Similarly, legislation to restrict colonial manufactures was believed to be of limited significance, given the great availability of land and the high productivity of the agricultural sector in the colonies.

To Thomas, and to his critics, the major component of economic costs to the colonies were imposed by the enumerated commodities, particularly tobacco, which had to be sent to Britain before being re-exported to continental consumers. The costs to the colonies arose if this roundabout shipment was not needed – if British merchants did not provide services to enhance saleability in Europe. (For the arguments that this degree of transhipment actually benefited colonial marketing in Europe, see Dickerson 1951. See also Davis 1962a, on the post-independence redirection of the American tobacco trade.) This would mean adding the costs of the indirect routing to the costs of colonial production to determine the full costs to European consumers. To the extent that these costs of indirect shipping exceed the 'true' costs of shipping direct from the colonies to European markets, the demand curve as seen by colonial producers would be lowered by that excess amount, leading to a decline in the quantity supplied (if the elasticity of colonial supply were greater than zero). Higher prices on the Continent, due to this indirect shipping, would have lowered the amount demanded in foreign markets, thus effecting the net prices received by the colonists, lowering them if the supply was less than perfectly elastic.

The magnitude of this decline in prices received varied with the elasticity of demand, while the costs to the colonists of such a demand reduction would also depend upon the alternatives open to tobacco producers – the elasticity of supply. (Note that the reduction in quantity available to European consumers means that higher prices will be paid there (Figure 8.2).) The supply elasticity varies with the opportunities for shifting production to other crops, either for sale in various markets or as part of a withdrawal into production for subsistence purposes. Thus the burden of the enumeration provisions would depend upon the elasticity of consumer demand in foreign markets and the elasticity of supply in colonial production, and the costs of indirect shipping – again, assuming that such indirect shipment would not have been required without the enumeration acts (Figure 8.2 and Thomas and McCloskey 1981).

Thomas argues that, for plausible estimates of elasticities and of the costs of reshipment, the overall burden of enumeration was relatively small as a proportion of colonial income; adding the various other components of possible gross burden did not increase the general order of magnitude. Subtracting colonial defence costs paid by the British leaves a very small net burden, under 1 per cent of estimated colonial income, too small by itself, Thomas argues, to serve as the basis for an argument for economic causation of the American Revolution. Basic criticisms have dealt less with the estimation of the magnitude of the burden than with its interpretation, and with the implications for the future of British–North American relations given the substantial rate of economic growth in the colonies (Ransom 1968; McClelland 1969; Reid 1970; Walton 1971).

It should be noted in relation to the enumeration acts that a burden to the colonies need not directly imply a benefit to the British. The costs to the colonies arising from the additional indirect shipping did require the use of actual ships and labour, and, in the absence of unemployed resources, would not have provided additional benefits to British merchants. And, to the extent that the costs of Dutch or other foreign shipping might still have been cheaper than those of British and colonial shipping, both the colonies and the British may have suffered some economic losses as a result of the legislated restrictions. To the extent that there were gains, they were to

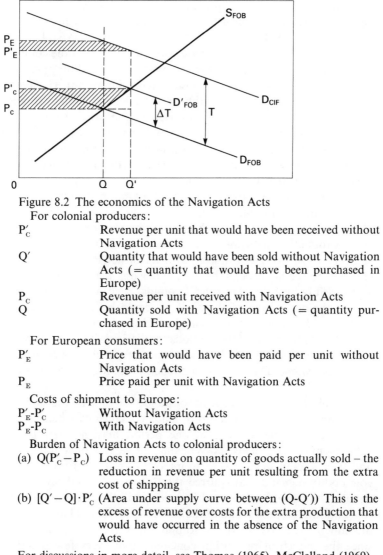

Figure 8.2 The economics of the Navigation Acts

For colonial producers:

P'_C Revenue per unit that would have been received without Navigation Acts

Q' Quantity that would have been sold without Navigation Acts (= quantity that would have been purchased in Europe)

P_C Revenue per unit received with Navigation Acts

Q Quantity sold with Navigation Acts (= quantity purchased in Europe)

For European consumers:

P'_E Price that would have been paid per unit without Navigation Acts

P_E Price paid per unit with Navigation Acts

Costs of shipment to Europe:

P'_E-P'_C Without Navigation Acts

P_E-P_C With Navigation Acts

Burden of Navigation Acts to colonial producers:

(a) $Q(P'_C - P_C)$ Loss in revenue on quantity of goods actually sold – the reduction in revenue per unit resulting from the extra cost of shipping

(b) $[Q' - Q] \cdot P'_C$ (Area under supply curve between $(Q-Q')$) This is the excess of revenue over costs for the extra production that would have occurred in the absence of the Navigation Acts.

For discussions in more detail, see Thomas (1965), McClelland (1969), Reid (1970), Lee and Passell (1979) and Thomas and McCloskey (1981).

British consumers, since more tobacco would be sold there as a result of the higher prices on the Continent. But these British gains were not necessarily equal to colonial losses, there being some dead-weight losses to the overall economy of the empire (Reid 1970).

Another examination of the impact of the Navigation Acts and of the gains or losses to the British empire in regard to colonies concerns the benefits and costs of the British West Indies (Sheridan 1965, 1968; Thomas 1968; Coelho 1973). Here there are two crucial costs of the colonies to the metropolis to be considered. First, there was the need for revenues to pay for defence and military purposes, items important given the great frequency of wars in the Caribbean (and elsewhere) in the eighteenth century. Second, there was the impact on the prices paid for sugar by British consumers resulting from restrictions on sugar imports from the French islands to protect the sugar production of the British West Indies. If French sugar was cheaper at this time, as frequently argued, then the net effect was that British sugar consumers paid a higher price and consumed less sugar, while the owners of slaves and land in the plantation colonies produced more and obtained higher incomes than they would have in the absence of the restrictions (Thomas 1968; Sheridan 1968). Thus while sugar production with the acquisition of slaves was profitable to those settlers – from Britain or descended from earlier British migrants – in the colonies, to the metropolis the economic gains were considerably smaller, and possibly negative. On other grounds, such as defence and national power, the acquisition of these islands could be, and was, justified, but colonies did have economic costs, in addition to benefits. Studies of the impact of empire for later periods similarly suggest that while some individuals and groups did benefit, on net there may have been costs to the nation as a whole (Davis and Huttenback 1986; Marx 1857; O'Brien 1982, 1990).

It is important to be precise as to the specific time period under study in analysing any of these questions, since conclusions which are possibly appropriate to the analysis in one period may not be applicable to subsequent developments. To Williams, the early profits of the slave trade and West Indian slavery were an important source of investment and of commodity demand that spurred the British industrial revolution. Most detailed studies of banking and finance within Britain stress, however, the role of domestic capital and of the London and inland banks as sources of investment. A study by W. D. Rubinstein of the very wealthy in Britain since the industrial revolution concludes that 'very few wealth-holders earned their fortunes in "immoral trades," such as slave-trading or plantation-owning based on slavery' (1981:113).

The success of the British West Indies was due, in part, to the integration with the North American mainland and its role as source of the food-stuffs needed to permit the high degree of specialisation in sugar on West Indian plantations (Shepherd and Walton 1972; Carrington 1988). After the American Revolution, however, British trade regulations limited West

Indian imports from the United States. This helped to start, according to Williams, the economic decline of the West Indies which, even despite the respite provided by the slave uprising in Saint Dominique, ultimately led to the ending of the British slave trade in 1808 and then slavery after 1834. Many aspects of the Williams arguments have been debated; the general magnitudes of profits or of trade seem too small to account for those significant initial effects on Britain that he claimed, and their changes insufficient to have later generated a British need for abolition. But his work has been important both in pointing to the role of the slave trade and slave-based colonies in British political and economic change in the seventeenth, eighteenth and nineteenth centuries, and in arguing for the political impact of the dramatic changes in economic fortunes throughout this period (Williams 1944; Drescher 1977; Solow and Engerman 1987).

The situation with the other major part of the empire, India, was somewhat different. India in this period experienced large surpluses of exports over imports, particularly with Britain, but neither added to its specie nor to its ownership of foreign capital. Part of this was because of purchases of invisibles, and part due to political transfers to Britain – the 'drain' – which, it is argued, helped lead to Indian backwardness, as well as serving as a major contributor to British economic change. While estimates of the so-called 'drain' are rather uncertain, the magnitudes relative to national incomes do not suggest that, alone, they could have had dramatic effects in the eighteenth-century period of British economic change, either on British or on Indian economic development (Chaudhuri 1968, 1978, 1983; Maddison 1971; Barber 1975; Neal 1990). Some debate remains, however, about the impact of the East India Company's trade policy upon the development of India's manufactures in the eighteenth (and nineteenth) centuries.

Conclusion

There are other aspects of international relations which are important, but are covered in more detail elsewhere in this volume or in other works dealing with such issues. These include the role of the foreign sector in the development of the power of the British state, and the nature of war as a factor in the expansion and preservation of the metropolis and of the empire. Much of this period was one of international conflict, with considerable costs in resources and manpower (Ashton 1959). No doubt a peaceful development of the empire and international trading relations was not possible in the eighteenth-century world, but it nevertheless remains useful to remember that empires, whatever their beneficial effects then and later, were not without their costs and difficulties. And, while the studies of the composition of trade flows and of their geographic patterns provide much important information about the patterns of economic change and of political and economic relationships, they cannot, by themselves, provide answers to questions about any possibly unique contributions of foreign trade to economic growth. For that, more information, as well as more use of analytical tools, will be required.

9   Central government and the economy, 1688–1815

Patrick O'Brien

The unity of the kingdom and the integration of the market

Between the Glorious Revolution of 1688 and the accession of George I in 1714 a new constitution emerged which resolved questions left over from the English Civil War, concerned with the locus of sovereignty and the form of parliamentary government. After union with Scotland in 1707 economic enterprise could be conducted both inside and beyond the boundaries of the Hanoverian kingdom within a political system which provided for first-class military defence; for effective regulation of international economic relations; tolerable standards of internal order and a usable framework of law, required to underpin the operation of commodity and factor markets.

Within a propitious political environment, private investors exercised responsibility for funding and promoting capital formation. Businessmen organised the nation's production, distribution and exchange. Both looked to the state primarily for external and internal security. They demanded insurance against risks emanating from warfare on British soil or in the islands' home waters. From the time of the Interregnum onwards, an economically important and influential minority (of merchants, shippers, shipowners, bankers, brokers, insurers, planters and inventors, engaged in international commerce) expected the state to protect their trades and assets located beyond the borders of the kingdom. They pressured the Hanoverian regime to use diplomacy and force to extend and protect opportunities for profitable enterprise overseas. Between 1688 and 1815, when conditions for participation in international commerce continued to be guaranteed through the overt exercise of military power, British governments responded to these demands by allocating the bulk of their revenue to sustain navies at sea and armies at home to defend the realm and its citizens' interests abroad.

Somehow a succession of ministries (overwhelmingly aristocratic in composition and ostensibly divorced from any direct involvement with trade and commerce) managed to create political conditions which turned

205

out over time to be conducive to British dominance of world trade in manufactures and international services. Yet the policies formulated by this 'patrician elite' usually had other objectives in view. Its actions should in no sense be interpreted as a 'strategy' for the long-term development of the British economy. Even though the great bulk of public expenditures between 1688 and 1815 can be classified as 'military', this does not imply that the kingdom's foreign and imperial policies can be represented as some well-conceived mercantilist drive for empire and the domination of world commerce. All the historical record shows is that Britain and not Portugal, Spain, Holland or even France eventually triumphed in the competition for world markets and for colonies in Asia and the Americas.

Within the kingdom businessmen possessed an obvious interest in the stability of central government, in the preservation of a free market and in the security of their persons and property, from economic losses during serious breakdowns in law and good order. In Tudor and Stuart times such events had all too often accompanied baronial insurrections against the Crown. As late as 1685 the last armed aristocratic challenge to a monarch launched on English soil by the Duke of Monmouth was quelled quickly and rather cheaply. Three years later Parliament deposed James II efficiently enough but his departure provoked considerable destruction of life and property in Scotland and Ireland and it took many years to incorporate the Celtic Provinces into a single realm (Speck 1988).

Even Scotland was not fully pacified until the second Jacobite rebellion of 1745 had been brutally put down by Hanoverian soldiers. Long before that, both governments protected their economies and restrained flows of commodities and capital across their borders. English mercantilist legislation treated Scotland as a foreign country; the Edinburgh Parliament imposed steep tariffs against the import of English manufactures (Keith 1910). During two long European conflicts between 1688 and 1713 the Scottish economy suffered from a trade war with England and from rising tariffs imposed by all European governments to fund their military expenditures. Impoverished aristocrats and anxious Scottish merchants looked to union with England and its expanding imperial markets as a solution for their own deprivation and their country's relative backwardness. In the early 1700s English statesmen worked for union in order to avoid the all too predictable threat of invasions from north of the border (Levack 1987: 138–68). To secure their aims they threatened major Scottish exports, of coal, cattle and linen, with exclusion from imperial markets. Sticks and carrots and a growing perception of the cost of maintaining independence persuaded Edinburgh's Parliament to vote for political and economic union in 1707 (Lenman 1977: 44–99).

In the short run the impact of union on Scotland may have been adverse as trade diversion exceeded trade creation. Agriculture, particularly animal farming, benefited more than industry. Despite concessions on the application of English customs and excise legislation to Scotland, her coal and salt industries suffered relative decline. In the longer run both economies presumably benefited from integration and Scottish historians have not yet developed counterfactual scenarios to support an argument for economic independence (Campbell 1974: 58–74). In any case their nation's record before 1707 did not augur well for separate development. Thereafter, Scotland obtained full access to imperial markets, stable rates of exchange and light burdens of imperial taxation. For sound political reasons the letter of Westminster's fiscal legislation was not seriously implemented north of the border and England's neighbour probably contributed a lot less than its 'due' share towards the mounting costs of national defence and imperial expansion.

Ironically, and despite all Parliament's efforts to buy 'loyalty' from Scotland, two rebellions erupted in the province, first in 1715 and again in 1745. Both, particularly the 'forty-five', represented more than trivial challenges to the constitutional settlements of 1688, 1707 and 1714. Jacobite troops controlled Scotland for several months in 1715 and Scotland plus large parts of northern England for ten months thirty years later. Jacobite sentiment in England failed to mature into military support for Charles Edward Stuart, but the Hanoverian regime took the challenge seriously and the revolt of 1745 was followed by brutal repression which included the expropriation of rebel estates and the abolition of seigneurial justice and military tenures throughout the Highlands. After mid-century Scotland remained peaceful and the unified market of 1707 suffered no further disruptions from across its 'northern frontier' (Lenman 1986).

The constitutional settlements of 1688 to 1714 also remained unacceptable to a not inconsiderable minority of English Tories. They engaged in serious attempts to restore the Stuarts with foreign assistance and the Hanoverian dynasty remained insecure as late as 1759. Businessmen of the day may not have taken political stability and the size of the home market for granted when they invested for the future. Although the Scottish Jacobites and their more timorous Tory sympathisers in England represented no real threat to established property rights as such, the 'panic' in London in 1745 suggested that holders of the national debt and corporate wealth in the City anticipated that something other than business as usual would follow from a change of regime. Such a change might well have led to a reorientation of foreign policy and some sharing of the gains from Asian and American trade with France (Cruickshanks and Black 1988).

Meanwhile, Ireland, a more significant component of the 'domestic home market', posed no further threat to stability for more than a century after William III 'pacified' that troublesome province. Irish troops fought at Culloden but their country remained relatively free from political disorders until the 1790s. William's victories at the Boyne and Limerick created conditions for the sullen acceptance of established property rights and internal peace guaranteed by a Protestant ascendancy, but the opportunity fully to incorporate the Irish economy into an enlarged United Kingdom was not taken before 1800. Both the London and the Dublin Parliaments continued to regulate trade between the two kingdoms in response to narrowly defined local and sectional interests.

This meant that the kingdom's 'Irish provinces' laboured under a body of legal disabilities in trying to work out their comparative advantages vis-à-vis their more economically advanced neighbour. For roughly a century after the Restoration mercantilist regulations (enacted largely to placate lobbies within the English Parliament) treated Irish exports of farm produce and manufactured goods to the mainland and imperial markets with the combative zeal normally reserved for trade with France. For example, the cattle acts of 1663 and 1667 first imposed heavy tariffs and then bans upon Irish live meat exports to Britain. Under statutes of 1698–9 which prohibited the export of finished woollens to England, Irish wool could only be sold within the realm. Further acts passed in 1721 prohibited exports of cottons, textiles and glassware. Although the linen industry received both subsidies and duty-free access to the British market most other manufactured imports from Ireland paid duties at foreign rates. Sail-cloth, tallow, soap and candles were taxed at prohibitive levels and the Navigation Acts prevented Irish shipping and mercantile enterprise from competing on equal terms with its English and Scottish rivals in imperial commerce (Cullen 1987).

Restraints on commerce could always be evaded but they survived down to the American War of Independence, when potential threats to political stability from within Ireland prompted North in 1779 and Shelborne in 1782–3 to liberalise the framework of legislation regulating Irish commerce with Britain and with the empire. Unfortunately Pitt's propositions of 1785 to move to complete free trade ran into a well-organised campaign of English manufacturers, anxious about competition from cheap Irish labour. Union with Ireland finally came in 1801, in the wake of the French Revolution and followed directly from the costly repression of the rebellion of United Irishmen of 1798. Full economic integration which had been on the cards and acceptable to Irish businessmen since the early seventeenth century had been successfully resisted by vested interests within England for nearly two centuries (Kelly 1987: 236–63).

As a politically unified home market the United Kingdom had taken a long time to emerge. Steps along the way occurred in order to secure stability for the regime rather than potential benefits from free trade. Scotland, and eventually Ireland, became steadily more integrated into an economically United Kingdom. Thereafter the persistence of fragmented markets owed less to political boundaries and more to inadequate communications, national antipathies and the narrow horizons of English and Celtic merchants.

Inside the kingdom's home market, at a time when the security of property from criminal expropriation, civil disorders, challenges to rights of ownership and to managerial authority left businessmen in an exposed position, the resources made available to the law enforcement agencies of central and local authorities attracted only a fraction of the public revenues allocated for such purposes in a modern capitalist society. The judicial framework required to promote the efficient operation of markets evolved at a faltering pace. Ancient laws continued to be enforced and new acts reached the statute book which hindered economic enterprise. Legal barriers to the extension of competitive factor and commodity markets persisted right down to the end of the Napoleonic Wars. Governments of the day often failed to provide private enterprise with the facilitating legislation it required to promote commerce and investment.

Although the Hanoverian state may still be held up as the closest approximation to a businessmen's government among the ancien regimes of Europe, what exactly did the Crown, Ministers and Parliaments do to carry the economy forward between 1688 and 1815? To analyse the potential impact of government policies on economic growth will be difficult enough. Their effects will be impossible to quantify, and to deal with omissions is to depart even further from controlled speculation. Thus the approach pursued here simply explores possible outcomes of state activity and by-passes the major concerns of historians with the motivations and perceptions of the political elite. This chapter will also attempt to appreciate policies from the viewpoint of those engaged in the management of agriculture, industry and commerce at the time. What did eighteenth-century businessmen want from their rulers? Because historians can rarely ascertain what their demands were, the question becomes: what might they have required from public authorities around them? How much assistance did governments extend to further the progress of the industrial revolution? Since the 'hands' of the state touched the economy at so many points, each and every contact cannot be covered. It is necessary to break down the topic under a few general headings and to deal with the period as a whole before some overall assessment can be attempted.

Perhaps the best way to begin is to ascertain how much money governments raised and spent between 1688 and 1815? Budgetary data does not encapsulate the economic role of the state because important functions are performed at very little cost. But runs of figures for public revenues and expenditures quantify changes in the scale of its 'fiscal impact' on the economy. They also expose major priorities into which the state poured most of the money appropriated as taxes and raised as loans.

The political economy of revenue and expenditure

The Glorious Revolution certainly led to a pronounced discontinuity in the burden of taxation. Before 1688 Stuart and Tudor monarchs collected and spent proportions of the national income that probably approached 6 per cent in wartime and fell back to 3–4 per cent in peacetime years. At the height of the first of eight wars that the new regime fought against France and her allies between 1689 and 1815 the revenues of the central government (taxes plus loans) jumped up to reach 12 per cent and in nearly all subsequent conflicts ranged from 15–20 per cent of gross national product. Most of the extra money required to fund wartime expenditures between 1689 and 1815 was borrowed on the London capital market and the government's interest bill increased rapidly. Transfers to holders of the public debt absorbed proportions of peacetime tax revenues which moved from a negligible share in the years just before the reign of William and Mary to something like 55 per cent of total taxes collected immediately after the long wars with France from 1793 to 1815 (O'Brien 1988: 1–33).

British industrialisation was accompanied by astonishing increases in taxation which went up sixteen times and at a far more rapid rate than the growth of national income between 1688 and 1815. This irresistible rise in taxation represents the fiscal expression of the strategic, diplomatic and imperial policies undertaken by the Hanoverian regime. In pursuit of these policies, successive British governments entered into armed conflict with France and her allies for no less than 65 of the 127 years between 1688 and 1815 and the nation's forces were on a war footing for an even longer period of time (Brewer 1989).

Military expenditures went up sharply during periods of armed conflict but they rarely fell back to previous peacetime levels between those wars. Taxes remained at ever higher levels, partly to sustain a permanently enlarged military establishment, but basically to service a national debt (which accumulated from a nominal capital of £2–3 million in the reign of James II to £821 million in the reign of George IV). That debt had been incurred to fund a continuous succession of conflicts with France, Spain and other nations which marked Britain's rise to the status of a great European and imperial power (Tilly 1990).

Two inter-related fiscal functions (debt servicing and allocations to the armed services) as well as the costs of civil administration are represented in budgetary data which expose the overwhelming proportion of public expenditure devoted to military purposes throughout the period. For example, during the interlude of peace from 1783 to 1793 the government allocated 56 per cent of taxes collected to servicing a debt incurred to pay for previous wars and a further 31 per cent for its enlarged military establishment. In wartime the Treasury continued to service debt and to fund a fully mobilised army and navy, largely on borrowed money. Given that never more than one fifth of its revenues were devoted to civil administration, in fiscal terms the Hanoverian state could be depicted as a military regime. That would be something of an exaggeration because the welfare aspects of government in the eighteenth century were organised and funded under the Poor Law at the local level and also because other economically important functions performed by governments could be undertaken at relatively small fiscal cost. But even if we add in the estimates by Innes of the sums spent by local government on the poor the picture would not change much (Innes 1985). 'Non-military' connections between government and the economy will, however, be analysed. Meanwhile I will deal very briefly with debates concerned with the economic consequences of raising and allocating ever-increasing amounts of tax revenues largely to fund policies designed to achieve external security, imperial expansion and hegemony at sea (O'Brien 1988 deals with these issues in detail).

Taxes

Since the time of Adam Smith, economists' perceptions of Hanoverian governments have been narrowly based upon analyses of the 'burdens' of taxes and loans collected in order to fund military expenditures. They assume that a large proportion of the fiscal costs of eighteenth-century government were avoidable, and that their expenditures cannot be connected in any positive way with the long-term growth of the economy. In short, Hanoverian governments have either been ignored or depicted as an incubus on an otherwise competitive economy (Ekelund and Tollison 1981). Some recognition has been accorded to a limited range of technological and organisational spin-offs for the civilian economy that accrued from military expenditures on weapons, ships and navigation, food-stuffs and transportation (John 1955: 329–44). And Anderson's suggestion that for long stretches of the eighteenth century the economy operated below full employment levels implies that augmented levels of government expenditure in wartime pushed the system towards a fuller utilisation of capacity. In that Keynesian sense military spending generated some unmeasured proportion of the extra income required to pay for the wars (Anderson 1972: 1–18). Anderson's perception can, moreover, be supported by numerous references from economists writing at the time (Hutchinson 1988). Thus the otherwise adverse effects that would inevitably flow from augmented levels of taxation and government borrowing cannot be measured by fiscal data.

Yet for the times Britain may well have been the most highly taxed society in Europe (Mathias and O'Brien 1976). The growth of the economy would certainly have been better served by lower levels of taxes, but their economic effects have proved to be very difficult to determine (Beckett and Turner 1990). Most of the extra revenue required came from indirect taxes levied upon goods and services; that fact and the more limited recourse to 'non-progressive' direct taxation seem almost designed to contain potentially adverse effects on incentives to save and invest. Although the basic necessities of the poor remained exempt from taxes, a majority of consumers found themselves paying higher prices for an ever-widening range of goods and services they purchased on the home market. The products and the materials of the most innovative sectors of industry continued to be lightly taxed but the ever-rising costs of government depressed domestic purchasing power and pushed businessmen to escape taxes by exporting their wares to imperial and foreign markets (O'Brien 1988).

Government debt

Nearly all the additional money required to wage war between 1688 and 1815 was, however, borrowed long term through the sale of irredeemable interest-bearing bonds on London's capital market. 'Irredeemable' meant the government was not required to repay the loans, only to meet annual interest bills. Yet the sums that Hanoverian governments managed to raise in this way astounded contemporaries and confounded their enemies who on numerous occasions confidently predicted the imminent collapse of one of Britain's most potent weapons of war, its so-called funding system (Dickson 1967). Indeed the sums raised do seem astonishing compared to expenditures on capital formation by private investors.

For example, over the long period from 1688 down to the final defeat of Napoleon in 1815 expenditures on manpower, goods and services purchased by the Army and Navy and Ordnance exceeded the allocation by private investors on the formation of capital, upon which the future growth of the economy depended, by roughly 45 per cent. Obviously gaps between military spending and expenditures to maintain and add to the stock of capital widened in time of war and narrowed during interludes of peace. O'Brien's table which juxtaposes the relevant data raises the question of how far did military expenditures in general and sharp upswings in government borrowing on the London capital market in wartime operate to crowd out potential additions to long-term capital formation (budgetary data are in O'Brien 1988). Obviously, a peaceful international order which obviated the need to accumulate public debt in order to wage war could have left more funds available for private investment. In the absence of eight conflicts with France and other powers, the economy might well have grown more rapidly between 1688 and 1815. Some private capital formation was surely crowded out by opportunities to lend more safely and profitably to British governments in wartime. The unanswerable question behind Williamson's counterfactual scenario which attempts to 'factor out' war from the industrial revolution is how much (Williamson 1984: 687–712).

Extreme versions of the crowding-out hypothesis which suggest that high shares of the money loaned to sustain Britain's military commitments between 1688 and 1815 would otherwise have been invested in productive assets are not, however, convincing. Historians know that down to the American War of Independence at least, Hanoverian governments managed to attract money from overseas, particularly from the Dutch but also from other foreigners who invested in the national debt. British interest rates went up in wartime, when London provided a safer haven for capital than any other financial centre in Europe. Funds could be readily repatriated once hostilities on the mainland ceased and the government's bonds increased in value when peace returned (Neal 1990). These attractive features of the paper assets marketed by the Treasury in wartime not only persuaded foreigners to transfer funds to London but induced British capitalists to save more and thereby increased the volume of investible funds available to the state and the private sector alike. Although certain lines of investment activity such as housing, mortgages on landed property and social overhead capital suffered from competition from successive waves of new loans floated on the London capital market, there seems to be no evidence that over the long run the overall rate of private investment was seriously depressed even during periods of rapid accumulation of the public debt in wartime. Markets for investible funds, especially local markets for industrial and commercial venture capital remained too segmented to experience the full force of countervailing pulls from the metropolis. Interest rates payable on government bonds rarely rose more than two percentage points above peacetime levels which does not suggest intensive competition between the public and private sectors for a fixed flow of household savings (Heim and Mirowski 1987).

On the contrary the monied elite, who invested in the national debt, recognised patriotic and prudential as well as profitable motives for supporting the war-effort. Their property values were both safeguarded and in time enhanced by the Hanoverian state's victories over Britain's enemies. They also appreciated that the real alternative to loans could be punitive taxation on incomes and wealth. At the time political commentators reported on the socially regressive effects of a budgetary process based upon the accumulation of debt obligations by the state in wartime which had led Hanoverian governments to collect more and more revenue from tax payers distributed across income bands in general in order to transfer interest to bondholders concentrated in higher income brackets. Economically that process operated to raise rates of saving and investment once peace returned.

Furthermore, the growth of the national debt and the institutions of the London capital market that developed to service the voracious needs of government for credit and loans carried benefits (externalities) in its train. Habits of impersonal investment, expertise in dealing in paper assets, improved financial intermediation and the evolution of correspondent banking and bill broking between Paris, Amsterdam, Frankfurt, Dublin, Edinburgh and English provincial towns on the one hand and the London capital market on the other can all be connected to the rise of the national debt. Such links constituted the components of a financial revolution which mobilised savings, and raised both opportunities and propensities to save (O'Brien 1989a: 335–83).

Alas, national accounts for the eighteenth century are simply not good enough to measure the macro-impact of wartime borrowing by the state, but the imperfect data we have for the period 1793 to 1815 suggest that consumption was more likely to have been depressed than either savings or investment (Crafts 1987: 245–66). Post-war fiscal redistribution operated to push savings and investments above previous peacetime rates (O'Brien 1989b). But it must not be argued that the rise of the national debt sustained higher rates of capital formation than would otherwise have been the case. The ever-increasing burden of taxation certainly had deleterious effects upon the growth of the economy. Furthermore, the rather severe constraints on raising and allocating tax revenues for other than military purposes meant that during the industrial revolution Hanoverian governments invested paltry sums of public revenue in social overhead capital, in the education and training of the workforce, improvements to the legal system, internal law and order and in the discovery and diffusion of new technologies (Colquhoun 1815: 205–32).

In Britain, compared to elsewhere in Europe, many of those important tasks of government were left entirely to private enterprise and crowded off the agenda by the Hanoverian state's overwhelming preoccupation with security and imperial expansion. Thus the very difficult question for economic historians to tackle is not so much the costs but rather the offsetting benefits that accrued to the economy from military expenditures. By any standards expenditures on armed force required to underpin the kingdom's foreign, strategic and commercial policies look massive. At the time opponents of the regime's stance in foreign affairs argued they were profligate and in large part avoidable. Waste certainly occurred. Numerous examples of ill-conceived and badly executed military campaigns litter the books on diplomatic and military history. Corruption remained endemic among military establishments throughout Europe and in any case might be perceived as a potentially productive leakage of cash back into the civilian economy.

Military expenditure and economic growth

In retrospect it can be argued that most of the money seems well spent because between 1688 and 1815 no invasions of the homeland wasted the domestic economy (O'Brien 1988 develops the argument). Before 1805 no great power emerged on the mainland of Europe capable of obstructing the kingdom's trade with the Continent. Foreign aggression against British commerce and territories overseas declined in significance. After the recognition of its independence in 1783 the United States was gradually 'reincorporated' into the Atlantic economy with Britain at its hub. Over the period diplomacy backed by military force compelled the rival empires of Portugal, Spain and Holland in the South Americas and Asia and the Mughals in India to concede entrée to British trade and ships. British privateering, together with blockades and assaults upon the mercantile marines of Holland, France and Spain by the Royal Navy (coupled with the vulnerability of Amsterdam and Frankfurt to invading armies on the Continent) formed 'military preconditions' for the City of London's domination of international services by the late eighteenth century.

Apart from the windfall associated with the loot from India (which flooded in after Plassey) gains for the national economy took nine wars and decades of diplomatic activity to achieve; even longer to mature into secure markets for exports and imports and into flows of private profits, rents, wages and jobs for the surplus population from the Celtic and other underemployed regions of the economy. During the eighteenth century mercantilist intellectuals and aristocratic politicians claimed that the security of the realm and the expansion of its empire and markets overseas represented sustainable returns for the ever-increasing burdens of funding offensive and defensive expenditures borne by British tax payers. Ignored for too long by the proclivity of liberal political economy to concentrate on the costs of military force they form the 'credit side' of an unconstructable balance sheet to offset against the costs of a slow pace of institutional reform, crowding out, rising and regressive taxation and the instabilities in economic activity associated with those unavoidable cycles of war and peace that accompanied Britain's industrial revolution.

During that long transition Hanoverian statesmen entertained no illusions about the international order their businessmen had to operate within (Baugh 1988: 1–88). For more than a century, when the British economy was on its way to maturity as the workshop of the world, its governments concentrated public expenditures on security, trade and empire. In a fruitful (if tacit and often uneasy) partnership with bourgeois merchants and industrialists they poured millions into strategic objectives which (with hindsight) we can see formed preconditions for the market economy and night-watchman state of Victorian England, as well as the liberal world order which flourished under British hegemony from 1846 to 1914 (Kennedy 1983). An analysis of expenditures as well as revenues must inform any long sweep or even short-term assessments of connections between government and the economy between 1688 and 1815.

The protection of persons and property

In a mature market economy the rights of businessmen, investors and innovators are not only guaranteed by law, but challenges to their autonomy are usually suppressed by political and judicial authorities. In such societies businessmen enjoy social approval and can count on the forces of law and order not merely to repress criminal activity directed against their persons and property, but to contain resistance from social groups defending their own traditional rights, perceived to be threatened by an 'encroaching capitalism'. In several important respects presumptions of such support from public authorities and the courts could not be entertained by merchants, industrialists, farmers, financiers, transporters and retailers operating between 1688 and 1815.

Crime

For example, Hanoverian businessmen conducted their affairs in a society in which crimes against property appear to have been on the rise (Beattie 1986: 200–32). Crime fluctuated upwards in times of dearth and recession and downwards in wartime when recruitment into the armed services both increased employment and removed potential criminals from civil society. Unfortunately the return of the brutalised young men to the community at the end of wars usually led to sharp upswings in theft (Hay 1982: 124). The industrialisation and imperial expansion of Britain may have been accompanied by an increasing amount of larceny, robbery, burglary, pilfering and fraud (Innes and Styles 1986: 380–435 disagree). But records of the numbers of prosecutions, convictions, by the courts for crimes against property, nor even a well-documented rise in the anxieties of the day, do not imply that criminals stole a rising share of the national income. Opportunities for theft expanded in line with income and wealth and with the increasing amount of moveable and vulnerable forms of private property.

Nevertheless, before the formation of urban and rural police forces after 1829, the range and quality of protection afforded by the Hanoverian state was widely recognised as inadequate. Most localities certainly found it easier to 'police themselves' than modern towns could possibly do today. But as urbanisation occurred community controls weakened and an increasing share of the population (who could not afford privately funded protection) became exposed to risks from theft and violence. Security developed into a problem for 'middling ranks' of British society, whose only redress was to spend their own money detecting criminals, gathering evidence, assembling witnesses and initiating prosecutions through the courts. By all accounts the numbers of victims, willing to bear the costs and uncertainties involved in private prosecutions, represented a tiny percentage of those burdened by crime (Emsley 1987).

Matters improved a bit after 1770 when middle-class groups formed associations to fund the apprehension of criminals. Freelance detective agencies also appeared to supply protection and deterrence. Peace-keeping forces at the disposal of local magistrates expanded slightly, and the authorities began to offer rewards and subsidies towards the cost of the private prosecution of persons committing criminal acts (Philips 1977). Basically Parliament's 'cheap' response to demands for protection was to widen the range of crimes against property that attracted the death penalty and the sentence of transportation. Statutes of the realm redefining felonies in terms of both the value and type of property stolen and the nature of the theft proliferated. For example, stealing sheep, cattle, horses and cloth from bleaching fields carried the death penalty, as did taking goods from houses while their owners were present. Thieves could be executed for purloining goods to the value of 5s from shops, workhouses and stables but could remove up to 40s worth of property from ships without risk of ending up on the gallows. Presumably transportation, branding and the 'bloody code' deterred (Hay 1975). At the end of the century it was regarded not simply as inhumane but ineffective. By the 1830s the Victorians started to shift to a more rational system of punishment coupled with more certain detection by properly constituted and publicly funded police forces (Gattrell 1980). Before that time England's patricians who ran law and order complacently relied upon deference, moral exhortations from the Anglican Church and an increasingly savage code of punishment.

Social disorder and protest

Apart from the 'encroachment' of crime, historians have also uncovered too many episodes of protest and active resistance to capitalism for students of the industrial revolution to assume that businessmen and property owners felt free to conduct their affairs in the kind of security enjoyed by their counterparts in the mid-Victorian period. On the contrary, collective intimidation occurred so frequently and in so many places that Porter has depicted Georgian England as 'pock-marked with disorder' (1982: 118). Again no way exists of quantifying either the scale or the severity of such intangible social constraints on managerial authority or of calculating the reactions of investors to disturbances to good order. Businessmen and investors knew, however, that they could not depend on the courts consistently to enforce the law in their favour. First because laws of the land supposedly available to restrain intimidation were by no means unambiguously on their side. Secondly, Hanoverian authorities lacked the means to secure law enforcement, and sometimes even connived at illegal behaviour in order to keep the peace.

That said, in the social history of organised forms of protest most episodes appear as geographically confined and of short duration. Local communities, combinations of workmen and disorderly crowds did not seriously challenge either the economic order or Britain's social hierarchy (Langford 1989). Only during periods of sharp upswings in food prices, recession and technological unemployment did breakdowns of order transcend village and town boundaries and turn into the kind of widespread disturbances to the peace likely to obstruct normal flows of economic activity. Nevertheless, landowners, farmers, millers, merchants, retailers, bankers, transporters and industrialists confronted threats to their authority frequently enough for economic historians to enquire how far the central government, its local representatives and its courts accorded effective protection against intimidation to businessmen who accumulated capital and managed the nation's stock of productive assets upon which the realm's long-term development depended?

For example, a legal framework and a quasi-judicial process for the enclosure of cultivable land and its consolidation into privately managed farms had been established long before 1688. Yet parliamentary enclosure continued to arouse rather violent protest throughout the 'long' eighteenth century (Sharman 1989: 45–70). Most examples of resistance to enclosure tend to be located in the uplands of Wales and Scotland, in forest country, the fens of Lincolnshire or Northamptonshire (Charlesworth 1983). Even on enclosed farm land the village poor continued to exercise ancient rights to glean and collect fuel well into the nineteenth century (King 1989: 116–50). It took increasingly savage penalties, imposed by local justices of the peace acting under the notorious game laws, to deter small farmers and rural labourers from 'stealing' wild birds, rabbits and fish from private estates of the gentry (Munche 1981). If the rights of property could not be enforced even in the countryside, respect for property located in towns could well have been more tenuous.

Turnpike trusts could also arouse strong opposition among local communities. Groups whose interests might be adversely affected by the authority accorded to trusts to charge tolls to those using the roads which they had constructed and repaired argued that traditional rights of way should be maintained out of taxes. When over-ridden by private Acts of Parliament their opposition sometimes spilled over into violence (Albert 1984: 57–68). This occurred when colliers and industrial workers in the West Country, Wales and the West Riding feared that outflows of food-stuffs along turnpike roads might raise local costs of living. In other cases local producers led the resistance when they perceived that turnpikes would intensify competition. In a number of cases the reactions of 'vested interests' led to riots and to the destruction of toll gates (Charlesworth 1983). In general the diffusion of improvements to rivers and the operation of canals and turnpikes could not for long be resisted by force (Pawson 1984: 57–65). Nevertheless the 'privatisation' of rights of way did not follow the ostensibly straightforward path prescribed for in the passage of private bills through the House of Commons. We have also yet to discover how many initiatives for improvements in transportation were not submitted to Parliament because they might have aroused resistance and 'unacceptable' levels of disorder among local communities (Pawson 1977).

Right down to the repeal of the Corn Laws in 1846 merchants, retailers, bakers, millers, farmers and others with an interest in the production and distribution of basic food-stuffs stand out as businessmen highly vulnerable to intimidation and collective violence. Their exposure to threats from below and pressure from the ruling authorities was bound to persist while the majority of the urban and industrial workforce spent very high proportions of their incomes on food, and at a time when fluctuations in grain prices caused genuine hardship to the population at large.

Throughout the period most people expected the Hanoverian authorities to ensure that their families did not suffer from malnutrition as a result of deficient harvests. Governments in Whitehall continued to take rather limited actions to contain abrupt rises in the prices of grain and bread. For example, when poor harvests arrived Ministers suspended bounties paid from tax revenues to exporters of grain under an act passed in 1688. In years of extremely bad harvests the king signed decrees which prohibited the export of grain entirely, closed distilleries and starch mills and suspended or lowered tariffs upon imported grain (Lipson 1934: II, 419–64). Such measures (often badly timed and incompetently enforced) usually failed to hold grain prices to a level that avoided acts of collective violence against millers and dealers in basic food-stuffs (Rose 1961: 277–92). Hanoverian governments then looked to local justices to protect the persons and property of those engaged in growing, processing and selling bread and grain. Confronted with hungry crowds who demanded immediate relief, admonitions from London to maintain good order could not easily be enforced, partly because the law itself afforded only ambiguous protection to those who traded in basic food-stuffs (Malcolmson 1981: 112–22). Statutes regulating internal trade in grain, meal, flour, bread and meat remained in place until 1772. Although laws against regrating and engrossing had been liberalised in 1663 middlemen remained liable to be prosecuted for forestalling grain and for charging 'unjust' prices under the common law as late as 1795 (Bohstedt 1983: 25–8). Indeed in times of dearth Ministers of the Crown continued to call upon magistrates to apply common law against those whose dealings in grain could be interpreted as operating to raise its price 'artificially'. Their pleas did not fall upon deaf ears. Local gentry, even judges of superior courts, sympathising with an older more 'moral economy', found it not uncongenial to prosecute parvenu middlemen, millers and others in 'trade'. In this way the anger of the crowds could be directed towards merchants, wholesalers, millers, bakers and other scapegoats who thereby carried the financial and personal costs of preserving order at times of subsistence crises (Shelton 1973).

Perhaps the Hanoverian way of handling periodic crises of subsistence can even be represented as politically adept. The law provided the authorities and consumers with some leverage over wholesale and retail margins embodied in the prices of basic food-stuffs. In this vital sphere, their actions taken in terms of an older 'moral economy' probably maintained more open and competitive markets in grain and other food-stuffs than might have been the case if farmers, millers, traders and other middlemen had been left free from all restraint. By focussing on food prices at points of processing, sale and transportation, the law, public authorities and the crowd implicitly diverted attention away from inadequate levels of money wages and from the rents and profits received by those who owned land and grew the nation's food. Industrialists, farmers and landowners gained security at the expense of millers, bakers and factors (Christie 1984). Wage rates and inequalities in the distribution of wealth could be maintained within a system of order which suffered no serious breakdown even at times of dearth (but see Thompson 1991; Wells 1976–7: 714–43).

Political authority and the control of the workforce

The labour market

Wages and the productivity of labour were certainly of greater significance than food prices for the long-term growth of the economy. In the critical area of labour relations merchants, industrialists, farmers and other 'masters' who employed the nation's workforce expected unequivocal support from the law when it came to exercising managerial authority over their 'servants'. Eighteenth-century terms like master and servant indicate that the Hanoverian labour market remained at some distance from the free, competitive and contractual systems depicted by economic theorists (Haines 1980: 262–96). Under Elizabethan and Stuart statutes the state retained very considerable powers (albeit held in abeyance) to determine wages and conditions of employment. Such powers appear onerous in relation to the tenuous rights of the majority of unskilled workers to negotiate over pay, to withdraw their services, to migrate in search of alternative employment, to refuse to obey orders and even to indulge in insubordinate behaviour. For example, the law maintained and strengthened a highly traditional and patriarchal-style authority over younger workers including apprentices and resident farm servants, hired by the year (Kussmaul 1981b; Lipson 1934: II, 280–92). Furthermore, and because a majority of eighteenth-century workers suffered regularly from seasonal and cyclical unemployment, their independence could be severely compromised and their servility (productivity) guaranteed by the authorities operating under the Old Poor Law. At such times a tiny minority drew on accumulated savings. Some managed to fall back on transfers from families and friends. Most applied for various forms of income supplement they were legally entitled to receive under the Elizabethan statute of 1601. Parish officials (overseers of the poor) could then exercise powers to compel able-bodied people of working age to take up jobs, to remain against their wishes in paid employment and to perform work they preferred not to undertake (Lipson 1934: III, 413–87; Innes 1985). Of course those without jobs retained the right to suffer from serious malnutrition. Otherwise the majority of the workforce vulnerable to unemployment became liable under the country's poor and vagrancy laws to be directed to return to their own parishes of settlement to claim relief. They could be confined to a workhouse or imprisoned in a house of correction for idle and disorderly behaviour. Some were stigmatised or whipped and in a few cases severely punished by transportation to the colonies (Innes 1987: 42–111). Although feudal servitude had disappeared from most English labour markets, in practice Tudor and Stuart statutes, which remained unreformed between 1688 and 1815, could be readily used to maintain vulnerable and wage-dependent workers in a position of subordination (Furniss 1920).

Combinations of skilled workmen

Such statutes and the common law (concerned basically with poverty, vagrancy, delinquency and order) strengthened the authority of employers and depressed wages but they did not, however, guarantee a subservient workforce. Their influence permeated agriculture and certainly affected the work loads extracted and wages paid to lowly paid labourers, juveniles and women. Both masters and the state found it more difficult, however, to bring skilled craftsmen, artisans and miners under the same kind of 'effective' control. Although the typology and extent of labour disputes with that active minority who constituted England's 'free' labour force from 1688 to 1815 is still being written, several pointers have emerged from recent research in labour history which illuminate the workings of the Hanoverian labour markets. For example, some industries (including woollens, silks, knitted stockings, tailoring and the mining and the transportation of coal) were 'strike prone'. Towns, especially London but also Newcastle, numerous centres for textile production in the south-west, East Anglia, the midlands and also the north-west witnessed prolonged and serious disorders over pay, apprenticeship and machinery (Dobson 1980). Workers in dispute could stay within the law by appealing to customs of the trade, to common law and where politic to Elizabethan and Stuart statutes in order to legalise and gain support for challenges to their masters. They appealed to tradition advisedly because combinations of workers formed to 'negotiate' with employers could be prosecuted for conspiracy under the common law and the courts (particularly under Lord Mansfield) did indict under these serious charges (Rule 1988). But recognising that the common law did not constitute a strong enough deterrent to collective action Hanoverian Parliaments enacted several statutes which outlawed combinations in specific trades and locations. By the end of the century about forty acts as well as the common law could be used by employers determined to assert their authority and protect their economic interests against demands from 'organised' labour (Holdsworth 1922–66: XI, 469–501).

Nevertheless, combinations continued to appear and in the 1790s when agitation increased Pitt's government (then at war with Revolutionary

France and over-concerned with any organised potential for sedition within the realm) legislated to ban unions altogether. From 1800 to their repeal in 1824 unions attempted to protect the interests of their members within the framework of wide-ranging and repressive Combination Acts – which effectively outlawed any effective form of collective bargaining on behalf of groups of workers (Orth 1987: 123–49).

Throughout the industrial revolution, when the law remained firmly on the side of employers, Parliament also rejected most petitions it received to protect the traditional rights of skilled workers (Dobson 1980; Rule 1986). Illegal combinations of craftsmen and artisans could sometimes, however, persuade local justices to arbitrate in ways that respected the 'customs' of their trades. If only to prevent peaceable disputes from degenerating into disorder, magistrates used powers granted by Elizabethan and Stuart statutes to arbitrate over wages and to regulate the employment of non-apprenticed labour. In general both central and local authorities preferred to intervene as little as possible in labour relations but normally did so in ways that strongly supported the authority of masters (Kelsall 1972: 109–25). This does not mean that eighteenth-century employers rapidly abandoned 'customary' methods of conducting industrial relations. Some masters undoubtedly ignored the expectations of local communities on how they should treat with their employees. In general paternalistic behaviour changed rather gradually. Ancient laws remained on the books. Aristocrats and gentry could overtly sympathise with the lower orders and (at no cost to themselves) remind masters of their duties towards those below them in a social hierarchy they worked assiduously to preserve (Christie 1984: 146–50; Bohstedt 1983). When such reminders from above failed to redress grievances, then, temporary associations or more permanent combinations of 'skilled' workers protected perceived traditional rights by violence, particularly at times of recession and rising food prices.

To intimidate masters they destroyed machinery, buildings and inventories. They attacked the houses of 'bad' employers as well as the persons of blacklegs and apprentices who cooperated with plans for infringing customs and traditions of trades. Not all workmen, journeymen and craftsmen conducted 'collective bargaining by riot' as frequently as colliers, keelmen, coalheavers, shearmen, crofters, weavers, combers, tailors and other occupational groups whose actions are mentioned so frequently in histories of labour and protest. Nevertheless the record of violent incidents is long enough to suggest that such collective action must have constrained the authority of employers in major industries, including all forms of textiles, coal mining and transportation, metal working and clothing (Rule 1981; Stevenson 1979).

For economic reasons at the head of the list must be placed the record of active resistance to the introduction of every kind of machinery, which seems to have been more serious than accounts of the triumph of industry has allowed. Neither inventors, nor industrialists and farmers, who diffused mechanised labour-saving techniques, could expect to be popular. Many famous innovators suffered violence to their persons and property. Their difficulties could be compounded by the failures of local magistrates to afford the full protection of law to innovations which created unemployment, increased poor rates and led to disturbances of the peace. Parliament reacted predictably to this social barrier to technical progress by transposing the destruction of new forms of industrial property into felonies, but enforcement of the law remained subject to eccentric interpretations by courts and local magistrates. Persistent attacks on machinery and industrial buildings (for example in several towns in the West Country in 1717, 1720, 1738, Leicester 1773, Blackburn 1779, Manchester 1792, as well as the widespread outbreaks of Luddism in the midlands, Lancashire and Yorkshire in 1811, 1812, 1817 and 1826) evoked a military response but not before serious damage had been done (Berg 1985, 1987). By no means all the attacks upon machinery reported for this period should be depicted as resistance by skilled workers to technological displacement. Indeed a majority probably represented the only effective way open to workers to negotiate the 'terms' and speed under which new machinery should be introduced (Randall 1982: 283–304).

Infringements of the Statute of Artificers and Apprentices of 1563 (not repealed until 1814) provided skilled workers in many trades with some pretence to legality when provoked to take action against masters who employed workers who had not served a full apprenticeship or who substituted cheap apprenticed labour for qualified journeymen. Many industries had remained exempt from the statute of 1563 and enforcement of the law clearly lapsed over the second half of the eighteenth century when combinations of skilled labour 'dealt directly' with non-apprenticed workers. Nevertheless, the statute was not a dead letter because, when campaigning for its repeal from 1809 to 1814, employers argued that the Elizabethan statute limited their autonomy to engage non-apprenticed labour and encouraged skilled men to believe they had the legal right to enforce closed shops. For their part artisans and craftsmen campaigned persistently for a redefinition and extension of apprenticeship in order to 'secure the regular bred artisan in future the exclusive enjoyment of the trade he has been brought up to' (Lipson 1934: III, 279–93).

Most breakdowns in labour relations involved pay, but perquisites attached by tradition to particular trades also became a potent source of friction between masters and men. During the long transition to factory-based manufacturing, with its regularised systems of money wages, a range of occupational groups continued to be partly remunerated in kind, either in the form of finished products or obtained a small share of the raw materials (yarn, cloth, iron, lead, brass, timber and building materials) which craftsmen worked up into saleable commodities. Provided these supplements to money wages could be confined to recognised allowances for 'wastage' they were tolerated by Hanoverian capitalists, who legally owned the raw materials, finished goods, even the machinery and tools temporarily under the control of their workers. In an age chronically short of coin and bank notes of small denomination masters also found it convenient to remunerate in kind. Smaller employers short of liquidity and capital for expansion found such payments a useful way of shifting the cost of marketing finished goods (or of borrowing money to meet wage bills) on to the shoulders of outworkers. Disputes arose when customary prerequisites degenerated into embezzlement and fraud; or when payments in kind, or rents charged for the hire of machinery or tools, were perceived to be exploitative. That usually occurred when both sides reacted to trade recessions by attempting to shift burdens of adjustment from profits to wages and vice versa. As usual Parliament came down on the side of profits and legislated in 1749, 1774, 1777 and 1779 against embezzlement in a variety of trades. Attempting to be impartial the House also outlawed truck and in the royal dockyards admiralty officials commuted established rights to wood 'chips' and other practices into cash payments. Other employers took both collaborative and individual actions in the courts to stamp out the purloining of raw materials and finished goods. Prosecutions became more frequent, penalties harsher and the law allowed more cases to be tried summarily and cheaply by local magistrates (Styles 1983: 173–205). Although the weight of law and authority certainly favoured masters against men, justices were not invariably disposed to sympathise with clothiers, undertakers, merchants, nailers and other industrialists, especially when their attempts to 'rationalise' wages and to protect their property against the 'extortion' of traditional customs led to disturbances to the peace (Rule 1986). Employers acted both within and outside the law to depress wage costs. Their outworkers protected living standards as best they could by embezzlement. For most of the period neither side enjoyed full support from the law. Over time Parliament shifted the legal definition of customary perquisites towards embezzlement and the attitudes of local justices to such crimes hardened (Emsley 1987: ch. 5).

Good order and good behaviour

Good order and support for the maintenance of authority over those they employed seem to be among the central political concerns of merchants, industrialists and farmers in Hanoverian Britain. Yet between 1688 and 1815 they found themselves exposed to increased risks from crime and embezzlement, challenges to property rights, food riots and above all to intimidation and lapses into violence from combinations of skilled workers. One interpretation of connections between government and the economy in the eighteenth century sees the Hanoverian regime as undermanned with the force required to cope with an ungovernable people and as leaving businessmen to manage their economic affairs as best they could. In this view politicians opted to preside over the early stages of transition to an urban industrial society without radically changing the framework for law and order within which free enterprise operated.

Police and policing certainly seem inadequate but on inspection several components of the regime for the maintenance of order and authority served the interests of businessmen rather well. For example, the institutions for dealing with poverty, unemployment and vagrancy maintained a repressive system of control over juvenile, female and unskilled male labour. For the lower orders who challenged the established hierarchy the punishment prescribed by Parliament for participation in riots, for attacks upon mills, factories, warehouses, barns, machinery and private houses; for idle and disorderly conduct; for embezzlement and even for insubordination became harsher. Mobs did disperse when confronted with troops aided by 'loyal' civilians, who could be indemnified under the riot act of 1715 for shooting rioters (Boyd 1787: 65). Presumably transportation and 'exemplary' hangings deterred all but the desperate from theft and organised attacks on property. Modern historians, less impressed than their Whig predecessors with Parliament's vaunted refusal to sanction a regular standing army in time of peace, are now aware that the actual numbers of troops in the kingdom seem to have been more than adequate for the tasks of restoring order when called out by the public authorities. Under the Mutiny Act the House of Commons voted year after year (in peacetime) to retain a regular army of approximately 17,000 troops in Britain and a further 12,000 in Ireland. Between 1688 and 1819 when the kingdom was in effect mobilised for war 60 per cent of the time considerably more soldiers, sailors, embodied militiamen and volunteers could be made available to quell local disturbances to the peace. Year after year it may not be obvious that, on a per capita basis, the political authorities of constitutional Britain commanded much less military force than those less than competent military 'despotisms' of continental Europe (Chisholm 1868: 1177–8).

Authorities in London displayed little reluctance to use regular or part-time troops when occasion demanded (Houlding 1981: 57–90). Between 1660 and 1740 local militias were also called out on numerous occasions to preserve the peace. Later in the eighteenth century when militia service became compulsory and unpopular, justices preferred to rely on dragoons or a yeomanry (of mounted farmers officered by gentry) to suppress urban demonstrations (Western 1965). Whenever 'property' came under serious attack from unemployed silk weavers, colliers, coalheavers, from the rampage of Wilksites or the followers of Lord George Gordon, governments of the day lacked neither the legal authority nor usually the military capacity to put down challenges to good order (Palmer 1978: 198–214). After the American rebellion of 1776 and still more in the wake of the war against Revolutionary France, organised threats to property invited rather effective retaliation from troops strategically located in barracks, constructed under Pitt's barrack-building programme of 1792. By 1808 the numbers of soldiers mobilised to combat Luddites in the midlands and north exceeded those under Wellington's command in the Peninsula (Emsley 1983: 10–21 and 96–110).

To sum up: through a judicious use of the apparatus of the Tudor Poor Law and repressive measures against vagrancy, by legislating for more punitive and exemplary punishments for crimes against property and by displays of military force, the Hanoverian state provided good order on the cheap for an economy on its way through an industrial revolution. Perhaps the social costs in both fiscal and in overall economic terms of maintaining that order may have been rather slight because respect for established property rights and hierarchy permeated all ranks of an increasingly cohesive nation (Clark 1987). Recent depictions of eighteenth-century society are inclined to emphasise religion, deference, virtual representation and other forces making for its polite and peaceable behaviour (Langford 1989; O'Gorman 1986: 1005–20). Furthermore when they occurred manifestations of disorder often emerged in the form of appeals to a traditional and passing social order. Belief in a 'moral economy' governed the actions and demands of English crowds and combinations of workmen for the enforcement of common laws and ancient statutes – which had supposedly regulated the grain trade, contracts of employment, wages, apprenticeships, quality controls, rights of access to land, roads, waterways, fuel, game and gleaning from the arable in a fair and acceptable way (Thompson 1991). Loyal to King and country, deferential towards birth, respectful to wealth and power the 'crowds' and the combinations of workmen of Hanoverian England rarely confronted their superiors with anything more challenging than a dereliction of duty. For reasons not yet fully understood by social historians they could be placated by rather minor concessions offered to uphold tradition and the common law (Colley 1986a: 359–79). As Shelburne observed: 'providence has so arranged the world that very little government is necessary' (Porter 1982: 121).

If this interpretation carries weight then the quality of order which prevailed during the industrial revolution rested ultimately upon wide-spread good behaviour. But the Hanoverian elite and its institutions also made for stability. Presiding as unchallenged arbiters in disputes between farmers and labourers, masters and men, industrialists and workers, merchants and customers stood the aristocracy, gentry, judges, magistrates and civil servants who made the personnel of the British state, and its local executives (Landau 1984). When confronted with threats to property and hierarchy they relied far more on armed force than Whig history has allowed. Fortunately for them and for the progress of the economy they did not confront a population prone to excessive acts of violence or persistent challenges to either political or managerial authority. Their status as the embodiment (or appointed representatives) of a hereditary ruling elite, enforcing traditional and widely accepted codes of conduct, helped to keep social tensions within bounds that did not seriously restrain progress towards a competitive market economy (Colley 1986b: 97–117). Their rewards for running the offices of state, Church, law and local government had long been secured as a charge on agricultural production. Their authority could be extended at minimal fiscal cost to include the additional tasks involved in preserving law and order during the transition to an industrial society. Happily for economic development, serious constitutional questions over the establishment of effective police forces could be deferred until the foundations of an industrial economy had been established. Britain's 'ancien regime' and its political and legal institutions proved to be secure and flexible enough to accommodate gradual but, by 1815, rather radical changes to the economy. The status and acceptance of aristocratic government helped to ensure that a potentially unproductive coincidence of population growth and rapid urbanisation on the one hand with serious challenges to established authority on the other did not occur. Unlike France, political disruption in Britain did not frustrate or even slow down the course of economic change until it became irreversible (Mathias 1985: 29–42).

Law, business transactions and the operation of markets for capital and credit

As markets widen and specialisation increases the costs of transacting business across time and space goes up. Well-defined and enforceable rules are required to promote patterns of cooperation and competition required to make impersonal exchange work efficiently. Insofar as rights to private property are already unambiguous and accepted then legislation and legal reform are not required. If personal codes of behaviour accepted by businessmen and their workforces contain impulses to cheat, renege on contracts, violate property rights and shirk on the job, then governments can allocate a smaller volume of resources to law enforcement in order to ensure that markets function properly. When businessmen monitor their own transactions with each other and deal honestly with their employees and customers police and judiciaries can confine their activities to preventing crime and disorder (North 1981).

After 1688 the English state assisted in the development of markets largely by repealing restrictive statutes or by encouraging the courts to neglect the enforcement of those areas of the common law which had hindered private exchanges and initiatives. Between 1688 and 1815 laissez-faire proved to be increasingly attractive as an ideology and as a political strategy for economic growth because a viable basis in law and behaviour for a market economy was already in place before the Restoration. By that juncture (indeed long before) private property rights in land, minerals, houses, transport facilities, agricultural, industrial and commercial capital, and in personal skills and labour power had already been established and accepted. Rules governing trade and exchanges had evolved into modes of conduct prudently adopted by most businessmen. Equally important conventions promoting well-understood relations between employers and their workers also existed to provide for reasonably cooperative labour relations.

After the Glorious Revolution markets for commodities and factors of production continued to operate within a framework of laws and codes of conduct that had taken centuries to mature. Thus in their relations with the economy, eighteenth-century Parliaments and the courts can be perceived to be engaged in a process of rescinding, amending, interpreting and enforcing a traditional body of law; and to be adding new laws at the margin. Furthermore, a considerable area of their functions consisted in arbitrating between local interests through the medium of private bill legislation in order to change the infrastructure for economic activity (Lambert 1971; Lieberman 1989). But statutes of the realm or codifications of the common law available in printed form are a seductive source for understanding the legal framework for economic enterprise because laws might be obeyed, ignored or applied more or less rigorously by the rather incompetent executive machinery available to the authorities for their enforcement (Chitty 1820). Interpretations of particular laws by the courts are not nearly as accessible, and knowledge of how eighteenth-century laws actually worked are pretty much confined to dramatic cases of serious crimes (Sugarman and Rubin 1984).

In noting the small amounts of public money allocated by central and local governments to the courts and to law-enforcement agencies we might be tempted to conclude that again standards of personal behaviour precluded the need for more purposeful regulation of private transactions by governments and the judiciary. But by looking more closely at particular areas of law we will suggest that economic growth was in some degree constrained because in at least three important areas of economic activity the Hanoverian state failed to provide proper legal conditions ('public goods') conducive to (a) the operation of efficient markets for the exchange of commodities; (b) for raising long-term capital and (c) for the regulation of credit supplies.

Contracts and insolvency

For example, in their dealings with each other firms could turn to the King's courts to safeguard and indemnify them from risks of fraud, bankruptcy, bad debts and any breach of contract. For the vast majority of transactions legal disputes could be avoided because most businessmen abided by well-established codes of conduct backed by sanctions which rested upon mutual interdependence, and the preservation of local reputation (Sugarman 1983b: 213–66). No doubt the Anglican Church (and especially nonconformist churches) which demanded exemplary conduct from men of wealth and social standing reinforced some sense of honour in the market place. The common law also purveyed its own ideology for proper behaviour. Hanoverian businessmen preferred not to use the King's courts to prosecute for fraud, collect debts or sue for breach of contract. In general they resorted to their own informal, cheaper and more speedy systems of arbitration conducted by trade associations, guilds, chambers of commerce and other peer groups who applied commercial rules to disputes. Alternatively businessmen had recourse to specialised courts adjudicating in terms of local variations on the common law. Apparently English common law did not establish a national hegemony over economic matters until rather late in the nineteenth century. Before that time the King's courts attracted only a fraction of the adjudication in breakdowns arising from transactions in commerce and industry. When it was required, arbitration seems to have been conducted in many places under pluralistic systems or rules which survived presumably because the common law, as interpreted by the established courts, did not supply those cheap services required to promote the expansion of markets (Arthurs 1984: 380–404; Baker and Milsom 1986: 341–68).

For example, the law of contract continued to offer an unpredictable safeguard against risk of default or failure to deliver. Modern contract law is founded upon expressed and implied mutual agreements. Today the courts award damages in relation to expectations or anticipated returns. In the eighteenth century and guided by 'equity' and by 'consideration' for the parties involved, justices could set aside 'unfair' contracts (Atiyah 1979: ch. 6). Juries could award damages in terms of 'a sound price for a sound commodity' and they regarded futures contracts as 'wagering'. Not until Mansfield's tenure as Lord Chief Justice did the courts begin to accord primacy to promises and intentions (Lieberman 1989: 102–21). Although the law guaranteed freedom to contract, on the face of it contracts remained far too problematical and expensive for businessmen to enforce in established courts. When it came to dealing with debts arising out of losses incurred in the normal course of transacting on credit or in taking risks with borrowed money, businessmen again had to find ways of circumventing England's highly constricting laws dealing with insolvency and bankruptcy (Hoppit 1987). On paper the laws of the land treated debtors with such severity that all forms of borrowing or risk taking must have been commensurately discouraged. Under the law creditors could exercise power to imprison debtors until they paid up. That harsh threat (mitigated only by sporadic acts of clemency by Parliament which from time to time released hundreds of debtors from gaol) seems to have been sufficient to secure 'settlements' of outstanding debts in a majority of cases. The law also provided some relief from imprisonment for 'traders and merchants' who accepted the stigma of bankruptcy and distributed all their assets equally among their creditors. Bankruptcy remained legally available only to persons who earned their living by 'buying and selling' for merchants and traders but not producers, farmers and professional men. This arbitrary distinction became somewhat more flexible with time but full liability (up to and including imprisonment) was the penalty prescribed by law for the majority of businessmen who could not settle their debts until late into the nineteenth century (Innes 1980: 153–72). English law continued to be based on an assumption, spelled out in preambles to the statutes, that insolvency and bankruptcy were caused 'not so much by reasons of losses and unavoidable misfortunes' but rather by an 'intent to defraud and hinder creditors of their just debts and duties to them due and owing'. In other words a body of law, which existed to protect against fraud, restrained the extension of a network of debt, credit and risk taking upon which economic growth depended (Cohen 1982: 153–65).

Business organisation

Similar impediments, and for comparable reasons, operated in relation to the institutions of the market for long-term capital which continued to evolve within a traditional framework of inefficient legal rules and precedents suffused with morality. Businessmen who required capital to start or to expand their enterprises could either operate with their own funds or form partnerships or associate together as corporate enterprises. Personal or family proprietorships raised few if any problems for Parliament and the courts. Partnerships as well as incorporated and unincorporated forms of economic associations certainly did. Yet the advantages of legally constituted forms of corporate enterprise had long been apparent. The form allowed firms to raise capital through the sale of reassignable stocks and shares; to operate through time as a unit which could sue and be sued in the courts and to limit the powers and financial liabilities of investors in strict proportion to the value of individual shares in the total capital of the firm (Cottrell 1980: 40–2).

Incorporation by Act of Parliament can be traced back to the sixteenth century, and that useful form of organisation started to account for a growing proportion of the nation's stock of reproducible capital in the late seventeenth and early eighteenth centuries (Holdsworth 1922–66: VIII, 192–222). This 'efficient' institutional development promised to increase rates of capital formation. It permitted individuals to diversify their portfolios, and to allocate investible funds more efficiently across sectors and regions. It helped firms to realise economies of scale and associated new money and talent with commerce and industry. All these potential advantages were, however, cut off by the Bubble Act of 1720. Thirteen years later Barnard's Act placed severe legal difficulties in the way of the evolution of a market in stocks and shares (Dubois 1971: 1–25).

A Parliament of landowners (antipathetic to forms of ownership that were not proprietorial or family based) reacted to familiar abuses associated with incorporated forms of business organisation, by making it difficult and expensive to secure corporate status under the law. Some company promoters, stock jobbers and politicians had behaved fraudulently particularly in the booms of the 1690s and notoriously during the 'bubble' of 1710–20 (Carswell 1960). Investors' funds were misappropriated and used for undisclosed and risky purposes by promoters and managers of corporations. No doubt the accountability of top executives remained difficult to secure and the rules and purposes prescribed by company charters were too frequently violated. Associations of business-men without any legal authority to do anything appeared and pretended to act as if they had secured a charter of incorporation and issued assignable shares (Shannon 1954: 361–5). Instead of designing a legal framework which both protected shareholders and secured the advantages of incorporation, Parliament reacted to episodes of speculation and political corruption by erecting legislative barriers to the evolution of corporate forms of enterprise and to limited liability. Under the Bubble Act incorporation could only be secured by Act of Parliament and the House displayed a reluctance to grant charters to firms above a certain size. Incorporated companies tended to emerge only in certain sectors of economic activity, including public utilities, transportation and insurance. For reasons, difficult to understand, that privilege was not available to bankers or to marine insurers, which contributed to the instability of financial intermediaries and to the diffusion of deflationary crises through bank failures in the downswings of trade cycles.

Parliament's antipathy to corporate forms of organisation did not stop businessmen and investors from forming associations outside the law. Acting as corporate firms they somehow managed to solve most disputes that arose with other firms, with customers, with employees and even with public authorities by informal systems of arbitration (Dubois 1971). They often survived because the Crown made few attempts to prosecute firms who behaved as if they had secured legal incorporation. But the majority of businessmen who required proper legal security conducted their affairs in association with others within the laws of trusteeship and partnership or by retaining traditional family and proprietorial forms of organisation (Shannon 1954: 361–5).

A priori, the disadvantage of the eighteenth-century legal framework seems obvious. After 1720 few firms managed to secure the privilege of incorporation and then only for specified purposes. Parliament made no attempt to regulate their activities to ensure shareholders against fraud and mismanagement by prescribing either for the publication of accounts or for regular audit. Before 1825 the interests of most investors (and of capital formation as a whole) could only be secured through associations in the form of partnerships or under deeds of trust which allowed for some measure of limited liability.

Even so the laws affecting partnerships (which permitted associations of not more than six partners) were also unsatisfactory. Bogus or recalcitrant partners could easily ruin a business. Partners enjoyed no limitation on their liabilities for the debts or actions of those with whom they may have been only nominally associated (Holdsworth 1922–66: VIII, 191–220).

Furthermore, partnerships could only be transferred with the full agree-ment of all other partners and partners could not sue as an association, unless empowered to do so by private Act of Parliament (Shannon 1954: 361–4). Over time the courts (again under Mansfield in the 1770s) began to formulate rules affecting the liabilities of partners and relations between business colleagues. But the whole system of business organisation rested upon a mound of case law which was not tidied up until the very end of the nineteenth century (Stebbings 1984: 152–62).

Some historians have suggested that, because the industrial revolution proceeded without benefit from an efficient framework of company law and did without a properly regulated market for dealings in stocks and shares, this implies that businessmen found ways of circumventing the patent inadequacies of common and statute law. Supposedly enough capital was mobilised to dismiss the legal obstacles as minor or irrelevant (Crouzet 1972: 185–8). But were rates of capital formation impressive and the allocation of investable funds efficient enough to exonerate Parliament and the courts for their conservatism towards business organisation (Crafts 1985a)? Was the structure and scale of firms optimal for the longer-term needs of the economy? Was the rather ineptly self-regulated market for dealings in stocks and shares good enough to encourage the evolution towards more corporate forms of industry (Powell 1914)? Did the law not operate to sustain proprietorial and family forms of business organisation for too long? Certainly that traditional structure did not change fast enough to meet the requirements of the second industrial revolution. (Kennedy 1987).

Metallic money and paper credit

Meanwhile industrial and commercial firms, landowners, farmers and individual proprietors obtained the funds used for the expansion of their enterprises from personal resources, from ploughed-back profits and from forms of association which (at some cost) circumvented legal obstacles to the evolution of a more satisfactory market for long-term capital. But Hanoverian businessmen had a greater need for credit and for a convenient means of payment in order to support production and trade on a day-to-day basis. As markets widened across space, and production and sales became more roundabout and protracted through time, their demands for short-term loans and for ready cash multiplied. For transactions purposes they made increasing use of paper instruments (bills of exchange, promissory and bank notes and cheques) as well as the services of specialised financial intermediaries (banks, billbrokers, attorneys, etc.). Paper instruments are essentially signed promises to pay on demand, or at some specified date in the future, in an acceptable medium of exchange. Various paper instruments had been used by European merchants as a means of payment and for granting credit (time to pay and deliver) for centuries before the industrial revolution. Conventions and rules surrounding their use, first in trade and then in production, were widely understood in many spheres of economic activity (Neal 1990). In England the legal security required for business transactions using paper instruments developed rather slowly. Paper money and credit evolved as 'customs and practices' of merchants, only gradually incorporated into common law. Compared to the Continent English courts proved tardy in recognising negotiability. The legal problem was how safely to convert a promise to pay between two businessmen into an assignable liability in order that bills of exchange, promissory and bank notes could circulate freely as cash.

For a long time the common law remained hostile to this commercially convenient practice. Issues of where liability resided in cases of default constituted serious problems for lawyers to solve. They took their time but by the late seventeenth century the law related to bills of exchange had become part of the common law which recognised their assignability among individuals. Even then it remained costly to sue for assigned debts and in 1704 it took a special act of Parliament to overthrow a judgement against the negotiability of promissory notes (Atiyah 1979: 134–40). The acceptability and legal status of bank notes preoccupied the courts well into the nineteenth century.

Parliament did not, however, legislate (except by default) to provide the economy with a framework of law within which financial intermediaries could develop. This significant example of negligence seems all the more serious because successive governments also failed to mint sufficient supplies of metallic money to underpin the growth of trade and production. After all the Revolution of 1688 shifted responsibility for the minting of silver, gold and copper coins to Parliament. That constitutional change certainly put an end to the danger of arbitrary debasements of the currency as a technique for securing extra revenues for the King, but Parliament's responsibility was exercised with visible incompetence (Craig 1953).

At no time during the industrial revolution did the mint supply either the volume or the denominations of coins required to support the ever-expanding needs of trade and payments. Complaints about shortages of coin particularly for retail trade and wage payments are a constant theme of eighteenth-century writings on money (Feavearyear 1963). And the mint's failure did not occur because of a persistent deficit on the income account of the balance of payments. On the contrary, the expansion of Britain's commodity trade and increasing sales of services overseas probably provided the economy with sufficient bullion reserves to meet domestic demands for an adequate supply of coin (O'Brien and Engerman 1991: 177–209). Short-term balance-of-payments crises (associated with war, military remittances overseas and downswings in the trade cycle) could occasion rather serious deflationary pressures from time to time (Ashton 1959). On the whole the government's imperial and mercantilist policies (designed to secure a favourable balance on income account and circumvent the deflationary effects on activity associated with outflows of the economy's monetary reserves, silver and gold) worked. Furthermore the country was fortunate because such deflationary pressures could be more easily avoided after imports of Brazilian gold and Mexican silver flowed freely once again into Iberia, from the late seventeenth century onwards (Gomes 1987).

There seems to be little excuse for the government's lack of response to the needs of internal trade for increased supplies of coins. Ministerial decisions regulating the prices of silver, gold and copper offered to the mint for coinage and the inept selection of the bimetallic price ratio between gold and silver even exacerbated the shortage of coins. This occurred because the quantity of gold purchasable with a fixed weight of silver remained persistently higher on the Continent, and considerably higher in India, China and Japan, than the officially stipulated ratio (the mint price) offered in England. 'Undervalued' silver bullion was, therefore, not offered to the mint for coinage and (along with melted-down silver coins) was instead exported to countries where its command over gold was greater. As a result between 1663 and 1800 silver coins (crowns, half crowns, even shillings and sixpences) almost disappeared from circulation. They were not replaced by comparable gold coins which continued to be minted in large units of a guinea and a half guinea (Ashton 1959: 188–96).

Both silver and to a lesser extent gold coins issued by the mint suffered from undervaluation in relation to the international purchasing power of the quantities of metal they contained. Predictably the persistence of a premium between the mint and international market prices prompted speculators in London and other ports to melt down and export English coins in order to realise the greater command over commodities that silver and gold bullion possessed overseas. That differential also encouraged counterfeiters to 'sweat' and 'clip' coins not merely to pass sub-standard money into circulation within the kingdom but to export metals overseas. Counterfeiters, who reduced the intrinsic metallic content of coins of a designated nominal or face value, attracted the heaviest of penalties from the law where they were apprehended, but their fraudulent activities helped to mitigate what were remedial shortages of official coins (Styles 1980: 177–240).

The mint's prices for bullion (and for copper) might have been maintained in line with market prices. More careful attention could have been paid to bimetallic price ratios if the government wished to retain silver coins in circulation. There was no particular virtue in adhering rigidly to fixed mint prices regardless of conditions in international markets for gold, silver and copper. After 1663 when the law allowed for the export of bullion and foreign coins (and the state recognised it was powerless to prevent the illegal export of melted-down coins of the realm) the very real problems connected with the volume, state and structure of the coinage could surely have been dealt with in more sensible ways? Instead, Ministers stuck to established mint prices and parities and then dealt with the debasement and depreciation of the coinage by two widely dispersed and expensive acts of recoinage in 1696 and 1774 (Craig 1953). Meanwhile for long stretches of the eighteenth century domestic economic activity was not only frustrated by shortages of coin but the majority of coins in circulation lost the convenience they possessed, when first minted, of being widely accepted as an invariable standard of value. Transactions simply became more and more difficult to negotiate with the defective coins of the Hanoverian realm (Styles 1980).

Private enterprise found ways of alleviating this example of negligence by the state. Counterfeiting has been mentioned, but another initiative, the issue of private bank notes of small denominations was also repeatedly proscribed by law. Fortunately, the issue of copper tokens by merchants and industrialists which attracted political opprobrium was not stamped out and provided a useful supplement to the coinage until the mint eventually supplied enough small change in the 1820s (Feavearyear 1963: 147–64; Pressnell 1956: 15–24).

Bank money made all the difference, and a variety of paper instruments emerged to replace all but smaller denominations of coin. Banks evolved to promote the use of paper instruments and credit in business transactions. A rising share of the total value of national expenditure came to be conducted with paper money – bills of exchange, bank notes and eventually cheques (Coppieters 1955). The state 'facilitated' this functional development basically by allowing it to happen untrammelled by regulation. Already in the early eighteenth century bills of exchange could circulate from hand to hand by assignment. Such bills enjoyed an increasing degree of legal security under the common law. Banks could be established by anyone. Bankers could attract deposits, issue notes (above a prescribed denomination), create overdrafts and carry on their business almost without reference to a single statute, except common laws related to contract and insolvency (Gregory 1936: 1–36). Thus between 1688 and the Bank Charter Act of 1844 the economy enjoyed (some historians have argued suffered under) a regime of 'free banking'. Presumably even their critics would recognise that private banks together with mercantile bills supplied the credit and paper instruments required to service an expanding economy but would point to the misallocation and waste of investible resources involved in leaving control of money and credit to unregulated private financial intermediaries (Pressnell 1956).

Banks did indeed extend credit to support projects and firms which sometimes failed. The downswings of business cycles were all too often accompanied and exacerbated by the collapse of London and country banks. To some degree the vulnerability of banks to cyclical fluctuations in the economy can, however, be imputed to another example of parliamentary myopia, namely the failure to accord them the privilege of incorporation. Between 1697 and 1826 only the Bank of England was allowed corporate status. Outside Scotland (where more banks secured charters of incorporation) the vast majority of banks combined the capital at the disposal of no more than six partners allowed under law. Most banks tended to be small-scale undercapitalised firms and vulnerable to downswings in the trade cycle, wars and bad debts. At moments of liquidity crises they called on too little capital to meet their liabilities – however prudentially or recklessly incurred. Too many collapsed frequently carrying other firms and depositors in their train (Pressnell 1956: 448–51).

Incorporation, as the Scottish experience suggests, and Parliament eventually accepted for Ireland in 1821 and for England five years later, imparted a greater degree of stability to banks (Cameron 1967: 20–7). Apart from this obvious and long-delayed amendment to the law, it is not certain how a regulated financial system could have avoided bank failures and their contingent effects during downswings in economic activity entirely – except perhaps at the cost of slower rates of economic growth. Contemporary critics of English banking (especially the classical economists) seem unduly worried by the risks taken by firms operating on borrowed money and unduly suspicious of the successes of venturesome entrepreneurs operating with bank credit. There can be no presumption that a banking regime under the earlier, firmer and supposedly prudential control of the Bank of England (ultimately answerable through its Charter to Parliament) could have effected the difficult transition to paper currency and credit more efficiently (White 1984).

Even if Hanoverian Parliaments had legislated to place private banks under the control of the Bank of England, the Bank's Governors still needed time to forge policies and instruments to make centralised direction effective. Meanwhile the use of bank rate to regulate the cost of loans and discounts was hampered by the maintenance of defunct usury laws – which prohibited interest charges above 5 per cent. Furthermore, the principles and theories which could also guide the Bank on how the money supply could be regulated on behalf of the nation also took decades to evolve into an acceptable orthodoxy. Even when 'principles' for efficient and sound monetary management finally emerged after 1844 those principles are no longer accepted (either by modern economists or by historians) as a sound basis for providing economic growth with monetary stability (Fetter 1965; Collins 1988). With all its deficiencies to allow a regime of free banking to develop was perhaps the only sensible course for governments of the day to have pursued.

Neither Ministers of the Crown nor Governors of the Bank of England ever pretended to 'control' the nation's money supply. Nevertheless, the fiscal and financial policies pursued by governments, particularly in wartime when the state borrowed large sums of money to fund its military expenditures, did affect the availability and terms upon which the private sector obtained access to bank credit and longer-term loans (Clapham 1944). With the exception of the years 1797–1819, the previous succession of eighteenth-century wars were fought without change to the rules or obligations accepted by the Bank of England and the rest of the banking system to convert bank notes and other paper instruments into silver and gold on demand. This flexibly administered commitment to convertibility imposed a degree of prudence on the extension of bank credit. In wartime, when the state's demands for finance increased rapidly, businessmen found it more expensive than difficult to secure the accommodation they required. Their needs could in some degree be crowded out by the more urgent and enforceable priorities of the state. Unlike their successors in 1914–18 and 1939–45 eighteenth-century governments abided by the dictates of convertibility (loosely interpreted by the Bank of England and the banks) and did not fund wars by inflating the money supply. Their restraint meant that the wars which accompanied the industrial revolution were not marked by serious inflation. Post-war adjustments to cuts in government expenditures tended to be achieved and without longer-term dislocation to private investment. Higher interest rates, and curbs upon fixed capital formation, tended to occur in wartime and were kept to a minimum by the flexible and pragmatic way the banking system operated in relation to its reserves of specie (Barro 1987: 221–487).

In 1797 during the most costly and protracted war against Revolutionary and Napoleonic France 1793–1815, Pitt's government suspended convertibility in order to avoid a drastic and sudden curtailment of bank credit to the state and to the private sector. This first and unavoidable suspension of specie payments allowed the banking system to accommodate both government and private demands thereafter. For twenty-two years the economy operated quite successfully with an inconvertible paper currency.

New rules for the regulation of the money supply did not, however, appear even though the experiment was accompanied by a modest rate of inflation, exchange rate depreciation and an unusually painful adjustment to convertibility from 1816 to 1821. While suspension carried the economy through difficult times and kept the industrial revolution on course, neither the Treasury nor the Bank of England displayed any wish to assume long-term responsibility for controlling the money supply. During the war day-to-day policy was left to 'the good sense' of the Bank's Directors and to the 'prudence' of the Treasury. After the war Lord Liverpool's government returned the monetary regime to the status quo ante bellum – to full convertibility, at the old parity (O'Brien 1989a, 1989b).

This left bankers relatively free for another three decades to run their own affairs and to extend or refuse credit as they thought best, restrained only by the dictates of convertibility. Their detractors continued to point to a lack of prudence, foresight and responsibility. Contemporary economists used the dubious evidence of bankruptcy statistics and pointed to a succession of speculative booms supposedly fuelled by bank credit to reinforce their calls for central control. Fortunately, the monetary system escaped the strait-jacket of a Bank Charter Act until 1844. During the industrial revolution, neither central governments nor its Bank were ready to assume responsibility for the regulation of the money supply and wisely left well alone (Collins 1988; Wood 1939).

Conclusions

Hanoverian governments formulated no plans for the long-term de-velopment of the British economy. Nevertheless, their policies, actions and failures to remedy flaws in the legal framework within which private enterprise operated certainly influenced the rate of long-term growth achieved between 1688 and 1815. For example, as a politically unified common market, the United Kingdom of England, Wales, Scotland and Ireland did not finally emerge until as late as 1801. Inside that market and at some immeasurable cost businessmen continued to manage production and internal trade in ways designed to circumvent the unsatisfactory body of common and statute law for the regulation of contracts, debts, bankruptcy, money and credit, corporate organisation and other rules which hindered the efficient operation of commodity and factor markets within the kingdom.

Their persons and property were not it seems effectively protected from the risks of crime. Their authority and autonomy over production and trade within the realm were not properly secured against the resistance and violence of those who perceived that their interests would be harmed by the operation of free markets. Although Hanoverian authorities (central and local) certainly stood prepared to repress all challenges to good order and social stability from the working classes, the acceptance and safety of private enterprise may have depended more upon traditions of behaviour and deference than upon the political and legal system.

After 1688 Parliament became more sympathetic and accessible to the aspirations of merchants, masters and manufacturers, farmers and landowners. When requested the House usually facilitated locally formulated plans for roads, river improvements, canals, docks, harbours, bridges, enclosed farms, etc., through private bill legislation (Holdsworth 1922–66: XI, 625–31). For the rest Hanoverian governments preferred to regulate the economy as little as possible and refrained from spending tax payers' money on social overhead capital, research and development, the education and training of the workforce or upon any of the functions of central government, assumed at that time by other European states. Instead, the Exchequer's revenues (taxes and loans) which increased extremely rapidly over this period were reserved almost exclusively to fund the armed forces of the Crown. That massive rise in military expenditure which followed the Glorious Revolution of 1688 exceeded the allocations made for gross domestic capital formation by the private investors by a substantial margin. To analyse and evaluate the political economy of revenue and expenditure it will be necessary to escape from the preoccupations of liberal economists since the time of Adam Smith with the opportunity costs of taxes and the crowding out effects of loans and ask how much of the military expenditures incurred by Hanoverian governments were avoidable and wasteful. Meanwhile the case that the conjoined strategic, imperial and commercial policies pursued by the Hanoverian governments contributed positively (even significantly) to the long-term progress of the economy has been argued in this chapter.

Donald McCloskey

Introduction

The heart of the matter is twelve. Twelve is the factor by which real income per head nowadays exceeds that around 1780, in Britain and in other countries that have experienced modern economic growth (for the international comparisons Maddison 1991; for Britain itself Feinstein 1978, 1988 and Crafts 1985a).

Such statistics are of course not perfect. What is measured by 'real income per head' does not measure all of human happiness and does not measure what it measures perfectly well. The techniques of national income were not designed for such remote comparisons: goods and services unimaginable in 1780 now crowd our lives, from air conditioning to anaesthesia; and on the other side, less weighty, the forests primaeval and the hosts of golden daffodils are rarer, if more cheaply reached. Nor is the income per head divided out perfectly fairly, then or now. But the factor of increase could be nine or fifteen or thirty, rather than twelve, and the distribution of income now less equal than it actually is, and leave the heart of the matter – the logic of the argument – undisturbed. Most conservatively measured, the average person has about twelve times more bread, books, transport and innocent amusement than the average person had two centuries ago. No previous episode of enrichment approaches modern economic growth – not China or Egypt in their primes, not the glory of Greece or the grandeur of Rome.

Observations and predictions

Britain was of course first. And Britain was also first in the study of economics, from the political arithmeticians of the seventeenth century through David Hume, Adam Smith, T. R. Malthus, David Ricardo, John Stuart Mill to the modern masters, Marshall, Keynes and Hicks. Economics was for long a British, even disproportionately a Scottish, subject. What is odd is that the British economists did not recognise the factor of twelve as it was happening. The economists' theories took useful account of little changes – a 5 per cent rise of income when cotton textiles grew or a 10 per cent fall when Napoleon ruled the Continent. But they did not notice that the change to be explained, 1780 to 1860, was not 10 per cent but 100 per cent, on its way to 1,100 per cent. Only recently has the enquiry into the nature and causes of the wealth of nations begun to recognise this astonishing oversight.

Between 1780 and 1860, dates covering the classic 'industrial revolution' (a dispute breaks out from time to time about the drama in the term, but it survives in use), British national income per head doubled – this even though population also more than doubled. A much larger nation was much richer per head, the beginning of the factor of twelve.

In his *Essay on the Principle of Population* (1798) the economist T. Robert (as he preferred to be called) Malthus predicted the opposite. Malthus told a great truth about earlier history. In medieval England a rising population had become poorer and in Shakespearean England the impoverishment happened again. But in late Georgian and early Victorian England a rising population became richer, much richer. The fact was contrary to every prediction of the economists, those 'dismal scientists', in Carlyle's phrase, who saw nothing in prospect *c.* 1830 but misery for the working man and riches for the rentier.

The economists, in other words, did not notice that something entirely new was happening 1780–1860. As the demographer Wrigley put it recently to the economic historian Cameron, 'the classical economists were not merely unconscious of changes going on about them that many now term an industrial revolution: they were in effect committed to a view of the nature of economics development that ruled it out as a possibility' (personal correspondence, quoted in Cameron forthcoming). At the moment that Adam Smith and John Stuart Mill came to understand an economy in equilibrium the economy grew away from their equilibrium. It was as though an engineer had satisfied himself of the statics that kept a jumbo jet from collapsing as it sat humming on the tarmac, but did not notice when the whole thing proceeded to launch into dynamic flight.

An historian like Thomas Babington Macaulay, respectful of the economics of his day but with a longer view, could see the event better than could most of the economists. He wrote in 1830:

If we were to prophesy that in the year 1930 a population of fifty million, better fed, clad, and lodged than the English of our time, will cover these islands, that Sussex and Huntingdonshire will be wealthier than the wealthiest parts of the West Riding of Yorkshire now are, ... that machines constructed on principles yet undiscovered will be in every house, ... many people would think us insane. (1830: I, ii, 185)

It has been customary to deprecate such optimism, and to characterise Macaulay in particular as hopelessly Whiggish and pro-capitalist in his sentiments. That he was, a bourgeois to the core. But Whiggish and pro-capitalist or not he was correct, down to his estimate of British population in 1930 (if one includes the recently separated Irish Republic, he was off by less than 2 per cent). The pessimists of his times – both economists and anti-economists – were wrong.

In the suggestive jargon of statistics, the startling rise of income 1780 to the present can be called the 'first moment', the *average* change. There is little historical disagreement about the first moment, at least in its order of magnitude. Macaulay was correct in prospect and so are the dozens of economic statisticians who have confirmed it in retrospect. Few doubt that by the third decade of Victoria's rule the ordinary subject was better off than eighty years before, and was about to become still better off (Lindert and Williamson 1983a).

The *second* moment is the variability of the change, its pattern of acceleration and deceleration. Second moments are more difficult to measure. You can know the average height of British women more exactly than you can know its variability. As Kuznets, the economist who pioneered the historical study of national income, once said, perhaps too gloomily, during our period 'the data are not adequate for testing hypotheses concerning the time patterns of growth rates' (1971: 41–2). An error of plus or minus 20 per cent in measuring income c. 1800 may not matter much for the 1,100 percentage points of change down to the present, but will matter a great deal in deciding whether working people paid for the French Wars (see ch. 13).

The second moment, in other words, is the detail of the factor of twelve, and around it the debates of British economic history gather. Has Britain done well since 1980? Did mass unemployment during the 1920s and 1930s check its growth? Did late Victorian Britain fail? And for present purposes, when exactly did the factor of twelve begin? Kuznets wrote early in the research, and we have found new sources and methods since he wrote, but the violence of controversy about such second-moment questions tends to confirm his view.

In the growth of British industry there was at least a before and after, if not a sharp discontinuity. Various emblematic dates have been proposed, down to the famous day and year: 9 March 1776, when Adam Smith's *The Nature and Causes of the Wealth of Nations* provided an ideology for the age; the five months in 1769 when Watt took out a patent on the separate condenser in his steam engine and Arkwright took out a patent on the water frame for spinning cotton; or 1 January 1760, when the furnaces at Carron Ironworks, Stirlingshire, were lit.

It sometimes seems that each economic historian has a favourite date, and a story to correspond. Carus-Wilson spoke of 'an industrial revolution of the thirteenth century': she found that the fulling mill was 'due to scientific discoveries and changes in technique' and 'was destined to alter the face of medieval England' (1941:41). Bridbury found in the late middle ages 'a country travelling slowly along the road ... that [it] travelled so very much more quickly in Adam Smith's day' (1975:xix–xx). In the eyes of Marxist writers the sixteenth was the century of discontinuity, when capitalism set off into the world to seek its fortune. Nef, no Marxist, believed he saw an industrial revolution in the same century, depending on coal (1932), though admittedly it slowed in the seventeenth century. A student of the seventeenth century itself, such as Coleman (1977), finds glimmerings of economic growth even in that disordered age.

Wider perspectives are possible, encouraging the observer to see continuity instead. Looking at the matter from 1907, the American historian Adams could see a 'movement from unity into multiplicity, between 1200 and 1900, ... unbroken in sequence, and rapid in acceleration' (1907: 498). Jones and Mokyr have taken a similar long view of European exceptionalism (Jones 1981, 1988; Mokyr 1990a). The principal modern student of the age of industrialisation, Hartwell, appealed against the jostling throng of dates (1965: 78): 'Do we need an *explanation* of the industrial revolution? Could it not be the culmination of a most unspectacular process, the consequence of a long period of economic growth?' Cameron has thrown up his hands in the face of such confusion, arguing that the very idea of an industrial revolution – so named early in the nineteenth century in explicit imitation of the upheavals of the French Revolution – is an obstacle to thought (1990 and forthcoming).

The most widely accepted period for It, whatever exactly It was that led to the factor of twelve, is the late eighteenth century, within which some emphasise the 1760s and 1770s (Mantoux 1928; Landes 1969), others later. Rostow (1960) placed the 'takeoff into self-sustained growth' in the last two decades of the eighteenth century. The dating held through the great work of Deane and Cole (1962; and the parallel project, Mitchell and Deane 1962), which first undertook comprehensive measurement. Deane and Cole, however, for all their excellences, had to build on existing evidence, especially the evidence on foreign trade and on Hoffmann's pioneering index of industrial output. The main statistical finding after their work, in the 1980s, was that the sharpness of the take-off in Britain was exaggerated by the pioneering generation of quantifiers. True, growth could be faster for the late comers. Italy and Switzerland could adopt what Britain and Belgium had invented. But the first industrial nation, rather unsurprisingly, was slow in coming. A hard coming we had of it.

The slowness is documented in the important work of Crafts (1985a) and Harley (1982). They discovered that the indexes of industrial growth put too much weight on the fastest-growing sectors. In particular, Harley noted that in Hoffmann's index the cotton textile industry, growing explosively in the 1780s and 1790s, is given more weight than its size warrants. The overweighting of cotton, Harley argues, makes an interesting sector into an important sector before its time. The bias imparted to the figures is similar to the bias from non-quantitative sources. Without some way of measuring the importance of an industry a qualitative narrative will naturally focus on its early heroes, overweighting the importance of the industry because of its later prominence. The heroism of the cotton industry came when it was devoted chiefly to producing muslin shawls for ladies of fashion. Similarly, an index like Hoffmann's overweights the early years of cotton, during which the cotton grew heroically fast, but when, after all, the industry was nothing like as important in the life of the nation as it later became.

Still, the larger change must start somewhere, and the individual industry is the place to start. As the great student of European industrialisation, Alexander Gerschenkron, once remarked,

If the seat of the great spurt lies in the area of manufacturing, it would be inept to try to locate the discontinuity by scrutinizing data on large aggregate magnitudes such as national income ... By the time industry has become bulky enough to affect the larger aggregate, the exciting period of the great spurt may well be over. (1962b: 34–5)

In a footnote he remarks that 'Walt Rostow's failure to appreciate this point has detracted greatly from his concept of the take-off.'

In other words, small beginnings (exciting as they are, perhaps over-exciting) will be hidden by the mass until well after they have become routine. Mokyr has put it as a matter of arithmetic: if the older sector of an economy is growing at a slow 1 per cent per annum, and starts with 90 per cent of output, then by mere arithmetic the modern sector, growing at 4 per cent per annum, will take three-quarters of a century to account for as much as half of output (1985c: 5). We may call it the Weighting Theorem (or the Waiting Theorem, for the wait is long when the weight is small to begin with).

Gerschenkron was hoist by his own petard. For Italian industrial output he placed his 'big spurt' in the period 1896–1908, and wished to explain it with big banks founded in the 1890s. Stefano Fenoaltea, briefly his student, applied the Weighting Theorem to the case. Surely, Fenoaltea reasoned, the components of the industrial index – the steel output and the chemical output – are the 'real' units of economic analysis. If the components started accelerating *before* the new banks appeared, becoming bulky only later, then the new banks could not have been the initiating force. The components did just this, spoiling Gerschenkron's bank-led story: the components accelerated not in the 90s but in the 80s, not after but before the banks.

Crafts (1977b) has pointed out that the detailed timing of the beginnings of modern economic growth should not anyway be the thing to be studied, because small beginnings do not come labelled with their probabilities of developing into factors of twelve. He is identifying a pitfall in storytelling. If the onset of modern economic growth fed on itself, then its start could be a trivial accident. Yet one might wonder why then it did not happen before. 'Sensitive dependence on initial conditions' is the technical term for some 'nonlinear' models – a piece of so-called 'chaos theory'. But history under such circumstances becomes untellable (McCloskey 1991).

Mokyr identifies another pitfall in storytelling (1985c: 44): rummaging among the possible acorns from which the great oak of the industrial revolution grew 'is a bit like studying the history of Jewish dissenters between 50 BC and 50 AD. What we are looking at is the inception of something which was at first insignificant and even bizarre', though 'destined to change the life of every man and woman in the West'. What is destined or not destined to change our lives will look rather different to each of us. Mokyr pointed out later (1993) that the destiny was not unified, and is therefore not well explained by a dice throw: the industrial revolution was not one event but a set of loosely related events, a trick in steam engines here, a new dock there. Something more widespread than mere chance was going on.

The slow-growth findings from Harley and Crafts do not mean that British income was low absolutely, or in any way disgraceful, merely that it grew at a stately pace. British economic development – like British population growth in the recent revisions (ch. 4) above – is therefore spread back into the early eighteenth century. The revision, again, affects the second moment, the pattern of industrial development over time, not its size in total. The factor of twelve remains; what is in dispute is whether much of it happened in a few decades in the late eighteenth century, as once believed. Again we see the difficulties with getting exact measures of the second as distinct from the first moment.

Economic and industrial structure

In any case the historians have long known that Britain was no factory in 1860. Mokyr's Weighting Theorem asserts itself: even cotton textiles, growing apace, could not absorb all the many workers in agriculture and other trades less immediately affected by the machine age. Clapham made the point in 1926, observing that still in 1850 half the population was in employment untouched by 'the first industrial revolution'. Musson's figures imply, as Cameron notes (forthcoming), that steam power in Britain increased by a factor of fully ten from 1870 to 1907, long after the dark satanic mills first enter British consciousness (Musson 1978: 8, 61, 167–8). Clapham, indeed, eschewed the very phrase 'industrial revolution', although he would not have denied that something portentous happened 1780–1860. The statistical revisionists of the 1980s, Harley and Crafts, constitute so to speak a Claphamite sect.

The Claphamite view, in summary, is that industrial change was a slow turning, no revolution if that means short and sharp. Perhaps, to get back to the puzzle, that is why it was largely invisible to economists and some others watching it – though not to many possessed of common sense and eyes to see. Macaulay wrote in 1830, 'A single breaker may recede; but the tide is evidently coming in' (1830: 185). It was not 'evident' to many classical economists, who were predicting when Macaulay wrote that landlords would take all the increase, leaving the workers in precisely the condition they began. The first edition of this book (1981) called it 'The Quiet Revolution'. By now in the thinking of economic historians the revolution is still quieter, but longer and more impressive:

> For while the tired waves, vainly breaking,
>   Seem here no painful inch to gain,
> Far back, through creeks and inlets making,
>   Comes silent, flooding in, the main.

The new estimates by Feinstein and Pollard (1988), Crafts and Harley imply a growth in what people got for their effort of a trifle over half a per cent per year, a little faster in the late eighteenth century, a little slower in the early nineteenth. (The deceleration after 1800 – the second moment again – is not surprising, considering the acceleration of population growth and an expensive war against the French.) The British people also saved and added to their equipment. All told their income per head rose at about 1 per cent per year. It takes something growing at 1 per cent a year seventy-two years to double.

It took a long time, then, at the slow rates of growth that characterised British industrialisation, to transform the economy. The fact does not make the old and new sectors into what is known in development economics as a 'dual economy'. Though Britain did come at last to have many factories, there is nothing intrinsically unprogressive about non-manufacturing sectors. For example, Karl Marx sneered at the 'idiocy of rural life,' but Britain's rural life at the time was notably unidiotic, economically speaking, at least by comparison with agriculture on the Continent. In later Victorian times it was to become technologically sophisticated, by any standard (vol. 2, ch. 6). Similarly the French physiocrats, a century before Marx, had asserted that services are somehow less genuinely productive than the making of things in factories (and that factories after all merely transform the Fundamental Goods: agricultural goods). The notion that agriculture for one reason and services for another are by nature less progressive or important has had a long life, surviving into present politics. But it is false economically, and false when applied to western European industrialisation (vol. 2, ch. 5). Danish industrialisation was led by butter, for example, Norway's by shipping services, Sweden's by timber. It just happened that Britain's was led by manufacturing.

As Berg (ch. 6 and 1985) and Hudson (1986, 1989) have noted, some technologically stagnant sectors (building, say) saw large expansion, some progressive sectors little or none (paper); some industries working in large-scale units did little to change their techniques (naval shipyards early in the period), some in tiny firms were brilliant innovators (the metal trades). Big factories in the famous sectors were not the whole of the factor of twelve.

Productivity change

The wider point notwithstanding, productivity change was fast in sectors like cotton textiles, 1780–1860. We do not have industrial censuses in Britain until well after the event (1907), and so it would appear impossible to measure productivity industry-by-industry. We can know roughly what the aggregate equipment of the nation was and how it grew (vol. 3, ch. 4; Feinstein 1978; Feinstein and Pollard, 1988). But we do not know for most industries – coal mining, for example, or pottery – how output or employment grew until well into the nineteenth century. Knowing productivity change by industry therefore would appear to be out of reach. It appears that Kuznets' gloom is justified: 'the data are not adequate for testing hypotheses concerning the time patterns of growth rates'.

But wait. We can some day, if not at present, know the details of productivity change sector-by-sector during the period, though the knowledge will require more archival research. We do not know annual quantities of china plates and steam coal, admittedly, and probably never can. On the other hand, we know practically anything we choose about the *price*. Britain was in 1800 (as in truth it had been since the danegeld) a thoroughly monetised society, with prices for everything, many of which have survived in the records of Eton, All Souls College and a hundred other archives. The technique is to measure physical productivity change

Table 10.1. *The fall in the real cost of cotton cloth, 1780–1860*

	Real cost index	Annual percentage growth of productivity
c. 1780	100	
c. 1812–15	32	3·4
c. 1860	13	2·0

by the changes in prices. The two measures, physical and price-based, are connected by definition, because the value of output must be the same as the value of inputs. Productivity can therefore be measured either on the physical side (output per unit of physical input) or on the value side (real costs).

To illustrate: a piece of cotton cloth that was sold in the 1780s for 70 or 80s was by the 1850s selling for around 5s. In the process cotton cloth moved from fashionable to commonplace, in the manner a century and a half later of nylon (first called 'artificial silk') and other synthetics. A little of the decline in the price of finished cotton cloth was attributable to declines in the prices of raw cotton itself after the introduction of the cotton gin (invented in 1793) and the resulting expansion of cotton plantations in America. But in other ways the price of inputs rose: by 1860, for example, wages of cotton workers had risen markedly. Why then did the price of manufactured cloth fall? It fell because organisation and machinery were massively improved in cotton textiles, 1780 to 1860. The degree to which the price of the cloth fell relative to the price of the inputs is therefore a measure of productivity change. *Quod erat demonstrandum.*

The real costs of cotton cloth, after allowing for the changing prices of inputs, are shown in Table 10.1. In other words, cotton cloth was made with 13 per cent of the real resources in 1860 that it had been made with in 1780. Or, to put it in physical terms, productivity had increased by a factor of $100/13 = 7.7$ times. (The expression and the idea of 'real cost' are the invention of the first modern historical economist, a student of Clapham's named G. T. Jones. Jones invented what is now known as 'total factor productivity measurement' a quarter century before it was reinvented, in ignorance of Jones, by Moses Abramowitz and Robert Solow. For a demonstration that Jones' measures are precisely the 'price dual' of the measures of productivity change see McCloskey 1973: 103n.)

The case is typical in showing more about the second moment than one might at first think knowable. It shows for example that productivity growth slowed in cotton, because power weaving – which came late – was apparently less important than power carding of the raw wool and power spinning of the wool into yarn. And it shows that invention is not the same thing as innovation (ch. eleven; cf. Chapman and Butt 1988). The heroic age of invention ended by the late 1780s, by which time Hargreaves, Arkwright, Kay, Crompton and Cartwright had flourished. But the inventions saw steady improvement later – one of the main findings of quantitative economic history is that the pattern is typical, invention being only the first step (the same is true, for example, of railways, which improved in scores of small ways down to the twentieth century, with large falls in real costs). The real cost of cotton textiles had halved by the end of the eighteenth century. But it was to halve twice more down to 1860.

Few sectors were as progressive as cotton textiles. Productivity in iron grew a half to a third as fast. Productivity is not the same as production. The production of iron increased enormously in Britain 1780 to 1860 – by a factor of 56, in fact, or at 5.5 per cent per year (Davies and Pollard 1988; 'small' growth rates, as you might think 5.5 is, make for big factors if allowed to run on: 5.5 per cent is explosive industrial growth by historical standards, a doubling every $72/5.5 = 13.2$ years). The expanding British industry crowded out the iron imported from Sweden and proceeded to make Britain the world's forge. But the point is that it did so mainly by applying a somewhat improved technology (puddling) to a much wider field, not by the spectacular and continuous falls in cost that cotton witnessed. The cost of inputs to iron (mainly coal) changed little from 1780 to 1860; during the same span the price of the output (wrought-iron) fell from £20 a ton to £8 a ton. The fall in real costs, again, is a measure of productivity change. So productivity in wrought-iron making increased by a factor of about 2.5, an admirable factor of change. Yet over the same years the productivity in cotton textiles, we have seen, increased by a factor of 7.7.

Other textiles imitated the innovations in cotton (Hudson 1986), significantly cheapening their products, though less rapidly than the master industry of the age: as against cotton's 2.6 per cent productivity growth per year, worsteds (wool cloth spun into a thin yarn and woven flat, with no nap to the cloth) experienced 1.8 per cent and woollens 0.9 per cent (McCloskey 1981b: 114). Coastal and foreign shipping experienced rates of productivity growth similar to those in cotton textiles (some 2.3 per cent per year as compared with 2.6 in cotton). The figure is derived from North's estimates for transatlantic shipping during the period, rising to 3.3 per cent per year 1814–60 (1968). Again the 'low' percentage is in fact large in its cumulative effects: freights and passenger fares fell like a stone, from an index of around 200 after the Napoleonic Wars to 40 in the 1850s. Canals and railways experienced productivity growth of about 1.3 per cent

(Hawke 1970). Transportation was therefore among the more notably progressive parts of the economy.

But many other sectors, like iron as we have seen, experienced slower productivity growth. In agriculture the productivity change was slower still (ch. 5), dragging down the productivity of the economy as a whole; taking one year with another 1780–1860, agriculture was still nearly a third of national income. Productivity change varied radically from one part of the economy to the other, as it has continued to do down to the present, one sector taking the lead in driving up the national productivity while another settles into a routine of fixed technique. Agriculture itself, for example, came to have rapid productivity change in the age of the reaper and the steam tractor (vol. 2, ch. 5), and still more in the age of genetic engineering in the twentieth century. But from 1780 to 1860 textiles and transport were the leaders.

Such methods of analysis might be applied more widely, and would discipline thinking about when and where the quickening of industrial growth happened. For instance: iron machinery doubtless made possible the faster running speeds of the second and third generations of textile machines, and so iron was important in the nineteenth century as an input (ch. 11); but the industry producing the iron was not especially important. The value of iron's output relative to national income 1780–1860 was only 2 per cent.

The archival materials for seeing how productivity grew industry-by-industry are ample: prices are among the most abundant of historical statistics; an historian of ancient Mesopotamia will complain to his colleague in economic history that the cuneiform tablets are '90 per cent prices'. The collection of price statistics has been a low priority, mainly because economic historians think of the prices as useful only for calculating the standard of living. The price measure of productivity allows the prices to be used to see how the living was obtained in detail. Lindert and Williamson have done well in exploiting governmental sources (ch. 14; Lindert and Williamson 1983a; Williamson 1985), finding the wages for a range of service workers from porters to doctors (though again in aid of calculations of the standard of living). They 'urge other scholars to harvest additional wage series from the archives' (Mokyr 1985b: 183), a suggestion which can be seconded. It is a trifle scandalous that the wage estimates marching and countermarching in impossible intellectual campaigns are as old as Gilboy's (1934) for the eighteenth century and Wood's (1910) and Bowley's (1900) for the nineteenth. The price statistics are almost as old. Again Lindert and Williamson have recently improved them, by adding rents (from which one could calculate productivity change in housing per year; Jones in 1933 calculated it for housing construction) – although, as they remark, the evidential basis is slim. The collection of prices should be a high priority, in Tycho Brahean quantities. To write the history of the period without detailed prices of inputs and outputs is like studying astronomy without detailed descriptions of stars.

Some economic historians, incidentally, have formed the impression that using prices to measure productivity requires additional, and dubious, assumptions. The impression is mistaken. Physical productivity change can come from economies of scale or from monopoly. So can change in the price measure. If the price measure is misleading, so is the physical measure, and for the same reasons. In accounting the two are not merely correlated with each other; they are identical. The stars can be observed with a refracting telescope or a reflecting telescope, but are the same stars.

For the edification of the mathematical reader, a simple demonstration can be given for the case of one output and one input. (It can be generalised easily.) With one input, I, costing P_i per unit the total cost is just IP_i. The revenue from output Q at the price P_q is, similarly, QP_q. The two are equal if the accounting for inputs and outputs is complete. And so $IP_i = QP_q$. So of course $P_i/P_q = Q/I$. So the rate of change of physical productivity (which is the rate of change of Q/I) will be the same as the rate of change of the price-measured productivity (which is the rate of change of P_i/P_q). It is no chancy theorem. It is an accounting identity.

The causes of growth

Even without the requisite star maps, though, we now know enough about the second moments of growth to say some things about its causes, 1780–1860. We have learned in the past twenty years of research into the era, to put the findings in a nutshell, that reallocation was not the cause. To put the findings another way, we have learned many Nots: that industrialisation was not a matter of foreign trade, not a matter of internal reallocation, not of transport innovation, not investment in factories, not education, not science. The task of the next twenty years will be to untie the Nots.

Foreign trade

Consider foreign trade. An old tradition carried forward by Rostow and by Deane and Cole puts much emphasis on Britain's foreign and colonial trade as an engine of growth. What the recent research has discovered is that the existence of the rest of the world mattered for the British economy, but not in the way suggested by the metaphor of an 'engine of growth' (O'Brien and Engerman 1991 demur).

What has become increasingly clear from the work of Williamson and Neal (ch. 7; Williamson 1985, 1987, 1990b; Neal 1990) among others is that Britain functioned in an international market for many goods and for investment funds. More exactly, the fact has been rediscovered – it was a commonplace of economic discussion by Ricardo and the rest at the time (it became obscured in economics by the barriers to trade erected during the European Civil War, 1914–45, and aftermath just ended).

By 1780 the capital market of Europe, for example, centred in Holland and England, was sophisticated and integrated, capital flowing with ease from French to Scottish projects. True, the market dealt mainly in government debt. The old finding of Pollard (1964) and others survives: industrial growth was financed locally, out of retained earnings, out of commercial credit for inventories and out of investors marshalled by the local solicitor (Richardson 1989; ch. 7). But 'the' interest rate relevant to local projects was determined by what was happening in wider capital markets, as is plain for example in the sharp rises and falls of enclosure in the countryside with each fall and rise in the rate on Consols (ch. 5). The interest rate in the late eighteenth century also determined booms and busts in canal building. And the interest rate in turn was determined as much by Amsterdam as by London.

The same had long been true of the market in grain and other goods, as David Ricardo assumed in his models of trade c. 1817 as though it were obvious. The disruptions of war and blockade masked the convergence from time to time, and regulations – such as the Corn Law (ch. 12) – could sometimes stop it from working. But the European world had a unified market in wheat by the eighteenth century, as is becoming clear. Already in 1967 Braudel and Spooner had shown in their astonishing charts of prices that the percentage by which the European minimum was exceeded by the maximum price fell from 570 per cent in 1440 to a mere 88 per cent in 1760 (1967: 470). Prices continued to converge, a benefit of the rapid growth of productivity already noted in shipping and railways. The same could be said of prices of iron, cloth, wood, coal, skins and the rest of the materials useful to life around 1800. They were beginning to cost roughly the same in St Petersburg as in New York.

The reason the convergence is important is this: an economic history that imagines the British economy in isolation is wrong. If the economy of Europe is determining the price of food, for example, it makes little sense to treat the British food market as though it could set its own prices (except, of course, by protective tariffs: which until the 1840s it imposed). Purely domestic assumptions, such as those around which the controversy over agriculture's role in industrialisation have raged (Ippolito 1975), will stop making sense. The supply and demand for grain in Europe, or indeed the world, not the supply and demand in the British portion of Europe, was setting the prices faced by British farmers in 1780. Likewise for interest rates or the wages of seamen. Centuries earlier the price of gold and silver had become international.

The intrusion of the world market can become so strong that the domestic story breaks down entirely. One can tell a domestic story in the eighteenth century of how much was saved, but not a domestic story of what interest rate it was saved at. One can tell a domestic story in the early nineteenth century of the supply of labour from a slowly growing agricultural sector, but not a domestic story of the entire supply of labour to Liverpool, Glasgow and Manchester, if Ireland is not included. Nots.

Pollard, again, has argued persuasively that for many questions what is needed is a European approach, or at least a north-western European regional approach (Pollard 1973, 1981a; within Britain cf. Hudson 1989 and Crafts 1989a). He wrote in 1973 (Mokyr 1985b: 175), 'the study of industrialization in any given European country will remain incomplete unless it incorporates a European dimension: any model of a closed economy would lack some of its basic and essential characteristics'. The political analogue is that it would be bootless to write a history of political developments in Britain or Italy or Ireland 1789 to 1815 without reference to the French Revolution. Politics became international – not merely because French armies conquered most of Europe but because French political ideas became part of political thinking, whether in sympathy or in reaction. Likewise in economic matters. The world economy from the eighteenth century (and probably before) provided Britain with its framework of relative values, wheat against iron, interest rates against wages.

The point is crucial, to return again to the puzzle, for understanding why the classical economists were so wrong in their dismal predictions. Landlords, they said, would engorge the national product, because land was the limiting factor of production. But the limits on land seen by the classical economists proved unimportant, because north-west Europe gained in the nineteenth century an immense hinterland, from Chicago and Melbourne to Cape Town and Odessa. The remarkable improvement of ocean shipping tied Britain to the world like Gulliver to the ground, by a hundred tiny threads. Grain production in Ukraine and in the American Midwest could by the 1850s begin to feed the cities of an industrial Britain; but the price of wheat in Britain was constrained even earlier.

Trade, then, was important as a context for British growth. Yet it was not an engine of growth (chs. 8 and 12). For the period in question Mokyr makes the clearest case (Mokyr 1985b: 22–3 and works cited there). The underlying argument is that domestic demand could have taken the place of foreign demand (Mokyr earlier (1977) had shown likewise that the shuffling of domestic demand was no more promising). To be sure, Britons could not have worn the amount of cotton textiles produced by Lancashire at its most productive: cotton dhotis for the working people of Calcutta would not have become fashionable at the High Street Marks and Spencer. But in that case the Lancastrians would have done something else. The exporting of cotton cloth is not sheer gain. It comes at the cost of something else that its makers could have done, such as building more houses in Cheshire or making more wool cloth in Yorkshire.

In other words, the primitive conviction most people have that foreign trade is the source of wealth is wrong. Nations, or villages, do not have to trade to live. (The power of the conviction is shown nowadays by the role of fish exports in the political economy of Iceland or of exports generally in that of Japan.) Exports are not the same thing as new income. They are new markets, not new income. They are a shift of attention, not consciousness itself. Not.

The trade, of course, benefits the traders. Although not all the income earned in trade is a net gain, nonetheless there is such a gain. But – here is the nub – the gain can be shown in static terms to be small. One of the chief findings of the 'new' economic history, with its conspicuous use of economic models, is that static gains are small. Fogel's calculation of the social savings from American railways is the leading case (1984, replicated by Hawke in 1970 for Britain with broadly similar results). However essential one may be inclined to think railways were, or how crucial foreign trade to British prosperity, or how necessary the cotton mill to industrial change, the calculations lead to small figures, far below the factor of twelve.

The finding that foreign trade is a case in point, with small static gains, can stand up to a good deal of shaking of the details. Its robustness is a consequence of what is known informally among economists as Harberger's Law (after A. C. Harberger, an economist famous for such calculations). That is, if one calculates a gain amounting to some fraction from a sector that amounts to again a fraction of the national economy one is in effect multiplying a fraction by a fraction. Suppose X per cent of gain comes from a sector with Y per cent of national income. The resulting fraction, X times Y, is smaller than either of its terms. For most sectors and most events – here is the crucial point – the outcome is a small fraction when set beside the 1,100 percentage points of growth to be explained 1780 to the present, or even beside the 100 percentage points of growth to be explained 1780 to 1860.

To take foreign trade as the example, in 1841 the United Kingdom exported some 13 per cent of its national product. From 1698 to 1803 the range up and down of the three-year moving averages of the gross barter terms of trade is a ratio of 1.96, highest divided by lowest (Deane and Cole 1962; Mitchell and Deane 1962: 330); Imlah's net barter terms range over a ratio of 2.32, highest divided by lowest (1958). So the variation of the terms on which Britain traded was about 100 per cent over century-long spans like these. Only 13 per cent of any change in income, then, can be explained by foreign trade, statically speaking: $100 \times 0.13 = 13$. Another Not.

Faced with such an argument the non-economists, and some of the economists, are likely to claim that 'dynamic' effects will retrieve trade as an engine of growth. The word 'dynamic' has a magical quality. Waving it about, however, does not in itself suffice to prove one's economic and historical wisdom. One has to show that the proffered 'dynamic' effect is quantitatively strong.

For example, one might claim that the industries like cotton textiles encouraged by British trade were able to exploit economies of scale, in perhaps the making of textile machinery or the training of master designers. There: a dynamic effect that makes trade have a larger effect than the mere static gain of efficiency. Not Not.

It may be true. And in fact a smaller cotton textile industry would have been less able to take advantage of technological change nationally. After all, cotton was unusually progressive. But is the dynamic effect large?

One can answer the question by a thought experiment. If the cotton textile industry were cut in half by an absence of foreign markets 1780–1860 the importance of cotton in national productivity would have fallen from 0.07 to 0.035. Resources would have had to find other employment. Suppose that the released resources would have experienced productivity growth of 0.5 per cent per year (on the low end of the available possibilities) instead of the princely 2.6 per cent they in fact experienced in cotton. The cotton industry in the actual event contributed a large amount – namely, (0.07) (2.6 per cent) = 0.18 per cent per year – to the growth of national income; this one giant contributed some 18 per cent of the total growth of income per person nationally 1780–1860. With the hypothetical cut-off of trade the resources would contribute instead (0.035) (2.6 per cent) + (0.035) (0.5 per cent) = 0.11 percentage points a year. The fall in national productivity change can be inferred from the difference between the actual 0.18 per cent attributable to cotton and the hypothetical 0.11 per cent attributable to a half-sized cotton industry and the industries its resources went to. The difference is about a 7 per cent fall in the national rate of productivity change, that is, a fall from (notionally) 1.00 per cent a year to 0.93 per cent a year. In the eighty years 1780–1860 such a lag would cumulate, however, to merely 9 per cent of national income. Remember that a 100 per cent change is to be explained. The dynamic effect sounds promising, but in quantitative terms does not amount to much. Another Not.

A 'dynamic' argument has a problem as an all-purpose intellectual strategy. If someone claims that foreign trade made possible, say, unique economies of scale in cotton textiles or shipping services, she owes it to her readers to tell why the gains on the swings were not lost on the roundabouts. Why do not the industries made *smaller* by the large extension of British foreign trade end up on the losing side? The domestic roads in Shropshire and the factories unbuilt in Greater London because of Britain's increasing specialisation in cotton textiles may themselves have had economies of scale, untapped. (The argument applies later to the worries over 'excessive' British specialisation in foreign investment, insurance and shipping; see vol. 2, chs. 7 and 8).

All this Not-saying is not to say that foreign trade was literally a nullity. Trivially, of course, some goods – the banana for the Englishman's breakfast table was the popular instance late in the nineteenth century, raw cotton the most important instance throughout – simply cannot be had in England's clime. Trade is a conduit of ideas and competitive pressures, as is best shown by the opening of Japan after 1868. And trade insures against famine, as the Raj knew in building the railways of India. A literal closing of trade is not what is contemplated: the question is, was trade a stimulus to growth in the simple, mercantilist way usually contemplated in the literature? Not.

To put the wider Not finding in a sentence: we have not discovered any single factor essential to British industrialisation. Gerschenkron a long time ago argued that the notion of essential prerequisites for economic growth is a poor one (1962a). He gave examples from industrialisation in Russia, Italy, Germany and Bulgaria that showed substitutes for the alleged prerequisites. Big banks in Germany and state enterprises in Russia, for instance, substituted for entrepreneurial ability. The British case provided the backdrop for comparison with other industrialisations. But Gerschenkron's economic metaphor that one thing can 'substitute' for another applies to Britain itself as much as to the other countries. Economists believe, with good reason, that there is more than one way to skin a cat. If foreign trade or entrepreneurship or saving had been lacking, the economist's argument goes, other impulses to growth – with some loss – could conceivably have taken their place. A vigorous domestic trade or a single-minded government or a forced saving from the taxation of agriculture could take the place of the British ideal of merchant-adventurers left alone by government to reinvest their profits in a cotton factory.

Transport

Transportation, for example, is often cast in the hero's role. The static drama is most easily criticised. Canals carrying coal and wheat at a lower price than cartage, better public roads bringing coaching times down to a mere day from London to York, and then the railway steaming into every market town were of course Good Things. But land transportation is never more than 10 per cent of national income – it was something like 6 per cent 1780–1860. Britain was well supplied with coastwise transportation and its rivers flowed gently like sweet Afton when large enough for traffic at all. Even unimproved by river dredging and stone-built harbours, Mother Nature had given Britain a low cost of transportation. The further lowering of cost by canals and railways would be, say, 50 per cent (a figure easily justified by looking at freight rates and price differentials) on the half of traffic not carried on unimproved water – say another 50 per cent. By Harberger's Law, 50 per cent of 50 per cent of 10 per cent will save a mere 2.5 per cent of national income. One would welcome 2.5 per cent of national income as one's personal income; and even spread among the population it is not to be sneezed at. But it is not by itself the stuff of 'revolution'.

Yet did not transportation above all have 'dynamic' effects? It seems not, though historians and economists have quarrelled over the matter and it would be premature to claim that the case is settled (for the pro-transport side see Szostak 1991). A number of points can be made against the dynamic effects. For one thing the attribution of dynamism sometimes turns out to be double counting of the static effect. Historians will sometimes observe with an air of showing the great effects of transport that the canals or the railways increased the value of coal lands or that they made possible larger factories – dynamic effects (the word is protean). But the coal lands and factories are more valuable simply because the cost of transporting their outputs is lower. The higher rents or the larger markets are alternative means of measuring what is the same thing, the fall in the cost of transporting coal or pottery or beer.

For another, some of the dynamic effects would themselves depend on the size of the static, 2.5 per cent effect. For example, if the 'dynamic' effect is that new income is saved, to be reinvested, pushing incomes up still further, the trouble is that the additional income in the first round is small.

For still another, as has already been stressed, the truly dynamic effects may arise from expensive as much as from cheap transportation. Forcing more industry into London in the early nineteenth century, for example, might have achieved economies of scale which were in the event dissipated by the country locations chosen under the regime of low transport costs.

The balance of swings and roundabouts has to be calculated, not merely asserted.

Enclosure

Sector by sector the older heroes have fallen before the march of Notting economists and historians. Marx put great emphasis for instance on the enclosure of open fields, which he claimed enriched the propertied classes and drove workers into the hands of industrialists. By now several generations of agricultural historians have argued, contrary to a Fabian theme first articulated eighty years ago, that eighteenth-century enclosures were equitable and did not drive people out of the villages. True, Parliament became in the eighteenth century an executive committee of the landed classes, and proceeded to make the overturning of the old forms of agriculture easier than it had been. Oliver Goldsmith lamenting The Deserted Village wrote in 1770 that 'Those fenceless fields the sons of wealth divide,/ And even the bare-worn common is denied.' But contrary to the romance of the poem, which reflects poetic traditions back to Horace more than evidence from the English countryside, the commons was usually purchased rather than stolen from the goose.

The result of enclosure was a somewhat more efficient agriculture. But was enclosure therefore the hero of the new industrial age? By no means. The productivity changes were small (McCloskey 1972; Allen 1992; ch. 5), perhaps a 10 per cent advantage of an enclosed village over an open village. Agriculture was a large fraction of national income (shrunk perhaps to a third by 1800), but the share of land to be enclosed was only half (McCloskey 1975; Wordie 1983). Harberger's Law asserts itself again: $(1/3)(1/2)(10 \text{ per cent}) = 1.6$ per cent of national income was to be gained from the enclosure of open fields. Improved road surfaces around and about the enclosing villages (straightening and resurfacing of roads went along with enclosure, but is seldom stressed) might have been more important than the enclosure itself.

Specialisation and the division of labour

Nor was Adam Smith correct that the wealth of the nation depended on the division of labour. To be sure, the economy specialised. Kussmaul's work on rural specialisation shows it happening from the sixteenth century onward (ch. 1). Berg and Hudson (ch. 6; Hudson 1989) have emphasised that modern factories need not have been large, yet the factories nonetheless were closely divided in their labour. Most enterprises were tiny, and accomplished the division of labour through the market, as Smith averred. It has long been known that metal working in Birmingham and the Black Country was broken down into hundreds of tiny firms, anticipating by two centuries the 'Japanese' techniques of just-in-time inventory and thorough sub-contracting. Division of labour certainly did happen, widely.

That is to say, the proper dividing of labour was, like transport and enclosure, efficient. Gains were to be had, which suggests why they were seized. But a new technique of specialisation can be profitable to adopt yet lead to only a small effect on productivity nationally – look again at the modest, if by no means unimportant, productivity changes from the puddling and rolling of iron. The gains were modest in the absence of dynamic effects, because the static gains from more complete specialisation are limited by Harberger's Law.

A similar thought experiment shows the force of the argument. Specialisation in the absence of technological change can be viewed as the undoing of bad locations for production. Some of the heavy clay soil of the midlands was put down to grazing, which suited it better than wheat. Or the labour of the Highlands was ripped off the land, to find better employment – higher wages, if less Gaelic spoken – in Glasgow or New York. The size of the reallocation effect can be calculated. Suppose a quarter of the labour of the country were misallocated. And suppose the misallocation were bad enough to leave, say, a 50 per cent wage gap between the old sector and the new. This would be a large misallocation. Now imagine the labour moves to its proper industry, closing the gap. As the gap in wages closes the gain shrinks, finally to zero. So the gain from closing it is so to speak a triangle (called in economics, naturally, a Harberger Triangle), whose area is half the rectangle of the wage gap multiplied by the amount of labour involved. So again: $(1/2)(1/4)(50$ per cent$) = 6.25$ per cent of labour's share of national income, which might be half, leaving a 3 per cent gain to the whole. The gain, as usual, is worth having, but is not itself the stuff of revolutions. The division of labour: Not.

Natural resources

Geography is still another Not. Some economic historians (e.g. Wrigley 1988) continue to put weight on Britain's unusual gifts from Nature. It must be admitted that coal correlates with early industrialisation: the coal-bearing swath of Europe from Midlothian to the Ruhr started early on industrial growth. But economically speaking the coal theory, or any other geographical theory, has an appointment with Harberger. Coal is important, blackening the Black Country, running the engines, heating the homes. But it does not seem, at least on static grounds, to be important enough for the factor of twelve. The calculations would be worth doing, but one suspects they would turn out like the others.

Classical models of economic growth

The claim is that the economists' static model does not explain the factor of twelve. It can tell why it did *Not* happen, a series of Nots, useful Nots, correctives to popular fable and sharpeners of serious hypotheses. But the kind of growth contemplated in the classical models, embedded now deep within modern economics as a system of thought, was not the kind of growth that overtook Britain and the world in the late eighteenth and nineteenth centuries.

One might reply that many small effects, static and dynamic, could add up to the doubling of income per head to be explained: trade, coal, education, canals, peace, investment, reallocation. No, Not. One trouble is that doubling – 100 per cent – is not enough, since in time modern economic growth was not a factor of two but a factor of twelve – not 100 per cent but 1,100 per cent. Another is that many of the effects, whether in the first or the second century of modern economic growth, were available for the taking in earlier centuries. If canals, say, are to explain part of the growth of income it must be explained why a technology available since ancient times was suddenly so useful. If teaching many more people to read was good for the economy it must be explained why Greek potters signing their amphora *c.* 600 BC did not come to use water power to run their wheels and thence to ride on railways to Delphi behind puffing locomotives. If coal is the key it must be explained why north China, rich in coal, had until the twentieth century no industrial growth. The mystery inside the enigma of modern economic growth is why it is modern.

The classical model from Smith to Mill was one of reaching existing standards of efficiency and equipment. To put it in a name: of reaching Holland. Holland was to the eighteenth century what America is to the twentieth, a standard for the wealth of nations.

The province of Holland [wrote Adam Smith in 1776] ... in proportion to the extent of its territory and the number of its people, is a richer country than England. The government there borrows at two per cent., and private people of good credit at three. The wages of labour are said to be higher in Holland than in England, and the Dutch ... trade upon lower profit than any people in Europe. (1776: I.ix.10: 108)

The emphasis on profit at the margin is characteristic of the classical school. The classical economists thought of economic growth as a set of investments, which would, of course, decline in profit as the limit was reached. Smith speaks a few pages later of 'a country which had acquired that full complement of riches which the nature of its soil and climate, and its situation with respect to other countries allowed it to acquire' (1776: I.ix.14: 111). He opines that China 'neglects or despises foreign commerce' and 'the owners of large capitals [there] enjoy a good deal of security, [but] the poor or the owners of small capitals ... are liable, under the pretense of justice, to be pillaged and plundered at any time by the inferior mandarines' (1776: I.ix.15: 112; cf. 1776: I.viii.24: 89). In consequence the rate of interest in China, he claims, is 12 rather than 2 per cent (Smith, incidentally, was off in his facts here). Not all the undertakings profitable in a better ordered country are in fact undertaken, says Smith, which explains why China is poor. Smith and his followers sought to explain why China and Russia were poorer than Britain and Holland, not why Britain and Holland were to become in the century after Smith so very much more rich. The revolution of spinning machines and locomotive machines and sewing machines and reaping machines that was about to overtake north-west Europe was not what Smith had in mind. He had in mind that every country, backward China and Russia, say, and the Highlands of Scotland might soon achieve what the thrifty and orderly Dutch had achieved. He did not have in mind the factor of twelve that was about to occur even in the places in 1776 with a 'full complement of riches'.

Smith, of course, does mention machinery, in his famous discussion of the division of labour: 'Men are much more likely to discover easier and readier methods of attaining any object, when the whole attention of their minds is directed towards the single object' (1776: I.i.8: 20). But what is striking in his and subsequent discussions is how much weight is placed on mere reallocations. The reallocations, mere efficiencies, we have found, are too small to explain what is to be explained.

In a deep sense the economist's model of allocation does not explain the factor of twelve. If allocation were all that was at stake then previous centuries and other places would have experienced what Britain experienced 1780–1860. Macaulay says, in a Smithian way, 'We know of no country which, at the end of fifty years of peace, and tolerably good government, has been less prosperous than at the beginning of that period' (1830: 183). Yes. But 100 per cent better off, on the way to 1,100 per cent better off? Not.

To put it another way, economics in the style of Adam Smith, which is the mainstream of economic thinking, is about scarcity and saving and other puritanical notions. In the sweat of thy face shalt thou eat bread. We cannot have more of everything. We must abstain puritanically from consumption today if we are to eat adequately tomorrow. Or in the modern catch-phrase: there's no such thing as a free lunch.

The chief fact of the quickening of industrial growth 1780–1860 and its aftermath, however, is that scarcity was relaxed – relaxed, not banished or overcome by an 'affluent society', since whatever the size of income at any one time more of it is scarce. Modern economic growth is a massive free lunch.

In 1871, a century after Smith and at the other end of the period (but not the end of modern economic growth) John Stuart Mill's last edition of *Principles of Political Economy* marks the perfection of classical economics. Listen to Mill:

Much as the collective industry of the earth is likely to be increased in efficiency by the extension of science and of the industrial arts, a still more active source of increased cheapness of production will be found, probably, for some time to come, in the gradual unfolding consequences of Free Trade, and in the increasing scale on which Emigration and Colonization will be carried on. (1871: Bk IV, ch. ii.1: 62)

Mill was wrong. The gains from trade, though statically commendable, were trivial beside the extension of industrial arts ('science' means here 'systematic thinking', not, as it came to mean shortly afterwards, the natural sciences alone). The passage exhibits Mill's classical obsession with the principle of population, namely, that the only way to prevent impoverishment of the working people is to restrict population. His anxieties on this score find modern echo in the environmental and family-limitation movements. Whatever their wisdom today, the Malthusian ideas told next to nothing about the century to follow 1871. British population doubled again, yet income per head increased by nearly a factor of four. Nor did Mill's classical model, as we have seen, give a reasonable account of the century before 1871.

Mill again: 'It is only in the backward countries of the world that increased production is still an important object: in those most advanced, what is economically needed is a better distribution, of which one indispensable means is a stricter restraint on population' (1871: Bk IV, ch. vi.2: 114). Still more wrong, in light of what in fact happened during the century before and the century after. Mill is unaware of the larger pie to come – unaware, so strong was the grip of classical economic ideas on his mind, even in 1871, after a lifetime watching it grow larger. He says elsewhere, 'Hitherto it is questionable if all the mechanical inventions yet made have lightened the day's toil of any human being' (1871: Bk IV, ch. vi.2: 116), a strange assertion to carry into the 1871 edition, with child labour falling, education increasing, the harvest mechanising and even the work week reducing.

Mill was too good a classical economist, in short, to recognise a phenomenon inconsistent with classical economics. That the national income per head might quadruple in a century in the teeth of rising population is not a classical possibility, and so the classicals from Smith to Mill put their faith in greater efficiency by way of Harberger Triangles and a more equitable distribution of income by way of improvements in the Poor Law. It should be noted that Mill anticipated social democracy in many of his later opinions, that is, the view that the pie is after all relatively fixed and that we must therefore attend especially to distribution. That the growth of the pie would dwarf the Harberger Triangles available from efficiency, or the Tawney Slices available for redistribution, did not comport with a classical theory of political economy. Macaulay's optimism of 1830 turned out to be the correct historical point: 'We cannot absolutely prove that those are in error who tell us that society has reached a turning point, that we have seen our best days. But so said all who came before us, and with just as much apparent reason' (1830: 186). The pessimistic and puritanical classical economists, with the pessimistic and puritanical romantic opponents of industrialisation, were wrong.

Expanding the models

To account for the startling growth of income before 1860 and the still more startling growth to come it would seem that we must let our economic models expand. That economists have not explained modern economic growth is indeed something of a scientific scandal, although economists are not the only ones to blame: a hundred times more funds, perhaps a thousand times more, are spent on mapping distant galaxies or mapping the genes of E. coli than explaining the economic event that made the telescopes and the microscopes for the mappings possible. Some economists have recently turned back to questions of economic growth, questions neglected for some decades by most non-historical economists. They have tried on the blackboard to modify the economic models to fit what is by now two centuries of growth, building especially on the speculations in the 1920s by the American economist Allyn Young about economies of scale. But the new growth economists have not read more than a page or two of economic history or the history of economic thought, and so repeat the mistakes of earlier generations of economists, though exhibiting greater mathematical imagination.

Science

Turn then to less material causes, looking for some way of supplementing a materialist but unsuccessful theory in economics. Pure thought, perhaps: Science, in sense 5b in the Oxford English Dictionary, now 'the dominant sense in ordinary use', lab-coated and concerned with distant galaxies and

E. coli. Science by this modern definition, however, is another Not (Musson and Robinson 1969; Musson 1972). A powerful myth of moderns is that Science Did It, making us rich. Scientists believe it themselves, and have managed to convince the public. The finding of Not is again relatively recent. Simon Kuznets (1966) and Walt Rostow (1960) both believed that science had much to do with modern economic growth, but it is increasingly plain that they were mistaken (chs. 2 and 11). The Victorians when in an optimistic mood tended to combine technology and science together in a vision of Progress. They were mistaken as well. Workshop ingenuity, not academic science, made better machines. Chemistry made no contribution to the making of steel until the twentieth century, the reactions of a blast furnace being too complex in their details. Sciences mechanical and otherwise had little or nothing to do with inventions in textiles, which depended instead on a craft tradition of machine makers. The same could be said for the other mechanical inventions of the nineteenth century. Steam might be thought to have had a theoretical base, for it was necessary to know that an atmosphere existed before an atmospheric engine would have seemed plausible. But it is notorious among historians of physics that the steam engine affected thermodynamics, not (until very much later) the other way around (von Tunzelmann 1978). Few parts of the economy used much in the way of applied science in other than an ornamental fashion until well into the twentieth century. In short, most of the industrial change was accomplished with no help from academic science.

Literacy

Literacy, too, is a Not, though more of a Not-But than is science. Literacy was not essential for modern industry, as is apparent in its *fall* during periods of intense industrialisation (Mitch 1992; West 1978). But a mute, inglorious Watt would lie undiscovered in an illiterate nation, and doubtless did in Russia and Spain. Britain, especially north Britain, with northern Europe (and the United States), was more literate than other countries in the eighteenth century (Japan, with a more difficult form of writing, had at the time similar attainments in literacy; it appeared ready for economic growth, which was only with difficulty killed by its government).

Culture

So we have more Nots in the world of the mind. 'Cultural factors' more or less mental are promising and much studied. We have learned from Richard Roehl and Patrick O'Brien a good deal about the French/British comparison, learning for example that French agriculture was not backward, despite an old British presumption that Frenchmen simply cannot get it right. On the technological front it is notable that Frenchmen invented in the eighteenth century what Englishmen applied (ch. 2). Something was different in England that encouraged more application. Yet looked at from a distance it seems wrong to separate France from England. It was north-west Europe as a whole that developed fast, as Pollard points out. Southern France lagged, but so, after all, did southern England: Macaulay promised in 1830 that backward Sussex could some day hope to equal the West Riding. Belgian industrialisation was almost as early and vigorous as Yorkshire's and Lancashire's.

Technology and invention

Suppose then we look at the problem from a chronological distance. 'Give me a lever and a place to stand on', said boasting Archimedes, 'and I shall move the world.' What is odd about his world of the classical Mediterranean is that for all its genius it did not apply the lever, or anything much else, to practical uses. Applied technology, argue Jones (1981) and Mokyr (1990a), was a northern European accomplishment. The 'Dark Ages' contributed more to our physical well being than did the glittering ages of Pericles or Augustus. From classical times we got toy steam engines and erroneous principles of motion. From the ninth and tenth centuries alone we got the horse collar, the stirrup, and the mould-board plough.

Then from an explosion of ingenuity down to 1500 we got in addition the blast furnace, cake of soap, cam, canal lock, carrack ship, cast-iron pot, chimney, coal-fuelled fire, cog boat, compass, crank, cross-staff, eyeglass, flywheel, glass window, grindstone, hops in beer, marine chart, nailed horseshoe, overshoot water wheel, printing press, ribbed ship, shingle, ski, spinning wheel, suction pump, spring watch, treadle loom, water-driven bellows, weight-driven clock, whisky, wheelbarrow, whippletree (see 'The Wonderful One-Hoss Shay') and the windmill. Down to 1750 the pace merely slackened, without stopping: note that the pace of invention *decelerated* on the eve of the sharpest industrial change. And then came 'The Years of Miracles', as Mokyr (1990a) calls them, from 1750 to 1900.

Why? Can one give an economic account that does not run afoul of the Nots and the Harbergers?

The economist, Kirzner, has argued recently that profit is a reward for what he calls 'alertness' (1989). Sheer – or as we say 'dumb' – luck is one extreme. Hard work is the other. Alertness falls in between, being neither luck nor routine work. Pure profit, says Kirzner, earned by pure entrepreneurs, is justifed by alertness.

The story of European, and British, ingenuity can be told in Kirzner's metaphors, improving both the story and the metaphor. As many economists have emphasised – relying once again on their conviction that there is No Free Lunch – the systematic search for inventions can be expected in the end to earn only as much as its cost. The routine inventor is an honest workman, but is worthy therefore only of his hire, not worthy of supernormal profit. The cost of routine improvements in the steam engine eats up the profit. It had better, or else the improvement is not routine. Routine invention is not the free lunch experienced since the eighteenth century. Rationalisation of invention has limits, as Joseph Schumpeter and Max Weber did not appreciate. The great research laboratories can produce inventions, but in equilibrium they must spend in proportion to the value invented – or else more research laboratories will be opened until, in the way of routine investment (see Smith on Holland above), the cost rises to exhaust the value.

If hard work in invention was not the cause of the factor of twelve, is the explanation to be found at the other extreme of Kirzner's spectrum, sheer, dumb luck? No, it would seem not. After all, it happened in more than one place (in Belgium and New England as well as in Britain, for instance; in cotton as well as in pottery) but spread selectively (to northern but not southern Italy; to Japan and then Korea but not China – though time will tell). Modern economic growth seems to select countries and sectors by some characteristic.

Well, then, is it Kirzner's metaphor of 'alertness' that explains the European peculiarity? Perhaps it is. Mokyr makes a distinction between micro-inventions (such as the telephone and the light bulb), which responded to the routine forces of research and development (both the telephone and the light bulb were sought methodically by competing inventors), and macro-inventions (such as the printing press and the gravity-driven clock), which did not (Mokyr 1990a). He stresses that both play a part in the story. Yet he is more intrigued by the macro-inventions, which seem less methodical and, one might say, less economic, less subject to the grim necessities of paying for lunch. Guttenberg just did it, says Mokyr, and created a galaxy. Macro-inventions such as these come to the alert, not to the lucky or the hard working, and macro-inventions seem to lie at the heart of the modern miracle. In short, as Mokyr says, from the technological point of view the quickening of industrial change was 'a cluster of macroinventions': the steam engine, the spinning jenny, and so to a factor of twelve.

But there is something missing in the metaphor and the story, needed to complete the theory. From an economic point of view, alertness by itself is highly academic, in both the good and the bad sense. It is both intellectual and ineffectual, the occupation of the spectator, as Addison put it, who is 'very well versed in the theory of a husband or a father, and can discern the errors of the economy, business, and diversion of others better than those engaged in them'.

Persuasion

If his alert observation of error is to be effectual the spectator has to persuade a banker. Even if he is himself the banker he has to persuade himself, in the councils of his mind. What is missing, then, from the theory of technological change is power. (Those outside the mainstream of bourgeois economic thinking will here find something to agree with.) Between the conception and the creation, between the invention and the innovation, falls the shadow. Power runs between the two. An idea without financing is just an idea. In order for an invention to become an innovation the inventor must persuade someone with the financial means or some other ability to put it into effect.

What matters, to put the point another way, are the conditions of persuasion. Europe's fragmented polity, perhaps, made for pluralistic audiences, by contrast with intelligent but stagnant China. An inventor persecuted by the Inquisition in Naples could move to Holland. The Jews of Spain, expelled in 1492, invigorated the economic life of hundreds of towns on the Mediterranean, such as far Salonika in northern Greece.

Early in his book Mokyr asserts that there is no necessary connection between capitalism and technology: 'Technological progress predated capitalism and credit by many centuries, and may well outlive capitalism by at least as long' (1990a). In the era of the factor of twelve one doubts it, and even before one might wonder, so close bound are gain, persuasion, and ingenuity. Capitalism was not, contrary to Marx's story – which still dominates the modern mind – a modern invention. As the medieval historian Herlihy put it long ago, 'research has all but wiped from the ledgers the supposed gulf, once thought fundamental, between a medieval manorial economy and the capitalism of the modern period'. And any idea requires capitalism and credit in order to become an innovation. The Yorkshireman who invested in a windmill *c.* 1185 was putting his money where his mouth was, or else putting someone else's money. In either case he had to persuade.

What makes alertness work, and gets it power, is persuasion. At the root of technological progress, one might argue, is a rhetorical environment that makes it possible for inventors to be heard. If such a hypothesis were true – and its truth is untried, and may at last end up itself on the pile of weary Nots – it would also be pleasing, for it would suggest that free speech and an openness to persuasion leads to riches. Europeans tortured, beheaded and burnt people they disagreed with in alarming numbers, to be sure, but it may be argued that their fragmented polity let new thinkers escape more often than in China or the Islamic world at about the same time. And when the Europeans, or at any rate some of them, stopped torturing, beheading and burning each other, the economy grew. No wonder that the nations where speech was free by contemporary standards were the first to grow rich: Holland, Scotland, England, Belgium and the United States.

Conclusion

The conclusion, then, is that Harberger Triangles – which is to say the gains from efficiency at the margin – cannot explain the factor of twelve. This is lamentable, because economics is much more confident about static arguments than about dynamic arguments. And yet the conclusion is not that static arguments have no role. On the contrary, they give us the means to measure what needs to be explained on other grounds. A static model of costs and revenues, for example, allows one to measure productivity change with the abundant material on prices. One can find out with static models how widespread was the ingenuity set to work in the eighteenth and nineteenth centuries. A static model of international trade allows one to see the wider context for the British economy, to see that political boundaries do not cut economies at their joints.

But going beyond the usual models, static or dynamic, appears to be necessary. In particular we need to consider the role of persuasive talk in the economy (in modern economies it is a quarter of national income). Adam Smith wrote at the beginning of the period that '[The division of labour is a] consequence of a certain propensity ... to truck, barter, and exchange ... [He could not pause to discuss] whether this propensity be one of those original principles in human nature ... or whether, as seems more probable, it be the necessary consequence of the faculties of reason *and speech*' (1776: 17). 'The faculty of reason' has been much studied by economists since then, resulting in their splendid, useful static models. But they have not taken up his phrase, 'and speech'. In his other book, *The Theory of Moral Sentiments*, he gave it prominence: 'The desire of being believed, the desire of persuading, of leading and directing other people, seems to be one of the strongest of all our natural desires. It is, perhaps, the instinct on which is founded the faculty of speech, the characteristic faculty of human nature' (1790: VII.iv.25: 336). We need an account of the age of industrialisation that admits into the tale the characteristic faculty of human nature, which is to say a combination of reason and of speech, the economic historian's calculations and the social historian's sensibilities.

11 Technology in the early nineteenth century

Nick von Tunzelmann

Introduction

The distinction between macro- and micro-inventions has been shown in chapter 2 above to help in understanding the classical period of the industrial revolution but, as chapter 2 makes clear, the distinction is difficult to draw. Sometimes it is only with hindsight that particular technological changes can be seen as radical, that is as macro-inventions; the case of the hot-air balloon is an example. Conversely, macro-inventions are often the culmination of a cluster of micro-inventions, and it is not at all easy to define exactly when the breakthrough comes about.

In discussing the years following the 'wave of gadgets' which is often regarded as characterising the industrial revolution, both of these problems arise. At least two of the macro-inventions (in the broadest sense – that is, in the sense that they ultimately gave rise to new industries) were not to achieve any great impact for many years to come. One was the electric telegraph – a foundation of the telecommunications industry, but one which in this period remained largely tied to railway signalling and messaging. A second was the calculating engine of Charles Babbage – regarded by most present-day scholars as the foundation of the computer, but which got little beyond the design and planning stage in the period that we are describing.

A macro-innovation which, on the contrary, did have a dramatic impact in this period was the railway itself. An economic evaluation of the impact of the railway is contained in Hawke (1970, 1981). From a technological standpoint, the railway is one of those advances where there are many contenders for the honour of the moment of breakthrough: its origins lay in the gradual evolution from tracks and waggons used for transporting coal over land to the waiting ships.

In manufacturing, with which this present chapter is mainly concerned, the innovations were therefore generally not of the kind that forged whole new industries. In manufacturing at least, most of the innovations of the day were micro-inventions. Some indeed displayed outstanding technical skill: for example, the self-acting version of the cotton mule (by Richard Roberts in 1825 and 1830), the screw gill for preparation of flax and wool fibres (by Horace Hall and others from 1815) and the nip principle in wool-combing machinery (by Josué Heilmann and others from 1841), to name but three. But technical complexity itself, as we shall see, was one reason why the diffusion of such advances was more laboured than in the earlier days of the industrial revolution.

Yet this was indeed an age of economic growth – chapters 3 and 10 show that this was a period in which total factor productivity (TFP) began to grow at appreciably higher rates. Since TFP is often regarded as a crude proxy for the rate of technical progress (plus other related changes), we are left with the puzzle of trying to explain how TFP should have accelerated when, seemingly, the drive to macro-inventions was slowing down. Moreover, Crafts' data (ch. 3: Figure 3.1) indicate that growth rates of industrial production were, over the period 1800–60, at their highest until the modern era. The main task of this chapter is to attempt to resolve this puzzle.

One obvious answer is that the potential impact of a particular innovation increased with the size of the industry to which it related. An advance that lowered costs by 1 per cent in an industry contributing 5 per cent to the GNP would be as significant in its immediate cost-reducing effect as one that lowered costs 50 per cent in an industry contributing only 0.1 per cent to GNP, the size of such 'sunrise' industries as cotton textiles and iron in the mid-eighteenth century. This is part of the story, but only part of the story, because there were obviously as many losers as winners in terms of industry shares in GNP.

The more important issue that must be faced is therefore why growth, and technological progress specifically, became so pervasive in manufacturing in this era. McCloskey has reminded us that, 'The industrial revolution was not the Age of Cotton or of Railways or even of Steam entirely; it was an age of improvement' (Floud and McCloskey 1981: 118). However, chapter 2 above indicates that in the early years invention was largely concentrated in a small number of sectors. In the subsequent years a much larger proportion of sectors was affected by technological change, and the economy approached the broad-based notion of an age of improvement which Briggs (1959) intended in his book with that title – Briggs aimed to speak of economy and society as a whole, and not just technical progress in particular.

Analysis of the procedures and underlying causes for this permeation of change and improvement requires an explanatory framework. Many have been devised but few have found general support. Orthodox economic analysis is only a limited guide through such territory: it approaches technological change through the neoclassical concept of the production function, relating certain inputs (traditionally labour, capital and land) to output. Technological change is then interpreted as the change in the ratio of output to inputs over time. For historians this eliminates many of the important questions. How does the production function come to be as it is, at any point in time? How does it change? Technological change needs to be made endogenous to the analysis rather than being left as exogenous 'manna from heaven' for any degree of historical understanding.

A more anthropological approach is to see technology as a set of artifacts – as tools and machines which are modified in different environments in a technically logical manner (Basalla 1988; cf. Mokyr 1990a). This, however, is of little practical use unless we can know how the environments were themselves modified, and the circumstances in which this would bring about a new range of artifacts. Still less does it help in modern societies where there is a massive proliferation of artifacts. Unless we bring in the role of knowledge we are unlikely to be able to understand how change comes about – technology is not just a matter of techniques; it is also one of knowledge (Fores 1981).

Again, economics is of limited use in analysing knowledge. Knowledge is usually equated with information, but the two differ fundamentally in that information is (potentially) tradable – the messages can potentially be priced in a market, although it may be difficult or even impossible to agree on a fair price (Arrow 1962b). Knowledge, however, is not tradable, as it rests on the ability of individuals or institutions – including firms – to accumulate understanding both from their own experience and from filtering externally provided information (Pereira Mendes 1991). Knowledge is thus cumulative and generally tacit: individuals may find it difficult to express and communicate exactly what they 'know', as modern attempts to develop practical programmes of 'artificial intelligence' have demonstrated. Moreover knowledge is likely to be unique – each individual's or firm's knowledge will probably differ from that of any other (Pavitt and Soete 1982).

In this chapter we shall consider first the process of accumulation of knowledge in our period, then at greater length examine the economic and historical stimuli which helped to direct the accumulation of knowledge along particular paths. The terminology of 'search' and 'selection' follows that of the evolutionary approach to the economics of technical change pioneered by Nelson and Winter (1982; see also Crafts 1977b; Elster 1983; Dosi et al. 1988); although the distinctions drawn here may differ from those of such authors.

Search mechanisms

Economic theorising about innovation has usually and implicitly reflected a 'linear model' of knowledge acquisition. In the linear model, science makes exogenous discoveries, which through invention become translated into technology; the inventions then become commercially viable innovations, and the innovations are duly diffused throughout industry. In more recent times, this linear model has heavily influenced government policy in areas like research and development (R&D), defence and higher education.

Yet students of the R&D process have shown repeatedly that the linear model is a poor description of a vastly more confused reality. In particular, in the real world there exists a profusion of 'feedback loops' in which diffusion generates innovations, innovations generate science and so on. To add to the complications, the process of technological change is powerfully influenced by – as well as powerfully influencing – organisational change, capital formation (and its determinants), demand changes and the like (von Tunzelmann 1989). For the period considered in this chapter, Rosenberg (1982: ch. 2) shows that a similar complex view of technology emerges from the dialectical method of Karl Marx. As has been pointed out, it is not necessary to subscribe to Marx's politics in order to accept the broad validity of his views concerning the interactions of technological change (the 'forces of production') and organisational change (the 'relations of production') (Lazonick and Brush 1985). Hence the present chapter needs to be read in conjunction with chapter 6 above.

The clues to a more adequate economic approach can be traced within the writings of economists back even further than Marx, to the celebrated opening pages of Adam Smith's *Wealth of Nations*. While discussing the division of labour, Smith succinctly expressed the three categories of learning (i.e. acquisition of knowledge) to be used here:

All the improvements in machinery, however, have by no means been the invention of those who had occasion to use the machines. Many improvements have been made by the ingenuity of the makers of the machines, when to make them became the business of a peculiar trade; and some by that of those who are called philosophers [scientists] or men of speculation, whose trade it is not to do any thing, but to observe every thing. (1776: 21)

Despite such promising beginnings, the firm and its technology have remained, in Rosenberg's phrase, a 'black box' for the subject of economics since Smith's day.

Learning by doing

Strictly speaking, Arrow's concept of 'learning by doing' applies to knowledge acquisition in capital goods industries – Adam Smith's 'makers of the machines' – arising out of accumulated experience in practical production (Arrow 1962a). But it can also be applied to the role of practical inventors – some of them well known, most of them not – in the workshop activities described in chapter 6.

Even if attention is restricted to a short list of the most famous inventors, there are examples to support virtually every source of inspiration for invention: some were external to the industry of their invention, others internal; some were businessmen, some professional engineers, etc., some skilled workers. Coleman (1973: 13) was provocatively putting only one side of the story in remarking that textiles were 'a national industry that had to rely on one parson to invent the stocking frame; on another one two centuries later to invent the power-loom, and on a barber to develop a spinning machine invented by a carpenter'. The greater detachment of external contributors sometimes enabled them to suggest a radical departure from previous ways, but unless they were prepared to enter the industry and had entrepreneurial flair to match, they were unlikely to see their inventions approach the status of commercial success (compare the commercial failure of Cartwright's power loom and combing machine with the success of Arkwright's water frame). By the early nineteenth century, the more celebrated names were predominantly internal to their industries, thus indicating the growing importance of experience. Dutton (1984) has, however, drawn attention to a class of professional inventors who continued to patent profusely in diverse fields. Scrutiny of the patent lists certainly reveals their numerical significance, but few of them achieved any notable breakthrough in the form of a major innovation; of those who did, such as Joseph Bramah, it was generally within their own industry.

Skills which were developed by workers in the increasingly intricate tasks that characterised the expanding industries could spill over into both process and product innovations (to use the categories introduced in chapter 2). However, the time required to acquire sufficient skill to be able to improve machinery could differ by an order of magnitude from that needed for day-to-day operation. Dr H. J. Catling, himself consecutively a mule spinner, textile engineer, then historian of the mule, estimated that the time taken to train a spinner to work a hand mule or self-acting mule – one of the most skilled jobs of its day – was about three months for anyone brought up in a mill. To learn how to maintain the mule took a minimum of three years, and for the self-actor (where the operating skills were less) about seven years was required (Jeremy 1981: 30). As explained in chapter 2, the acquisition of operating skills generally came through formal or informal apprenticeship. The skilled workers passed on 'information' to the apprentices, but the extent to which this information became 'knowledge' for the latter depended on their own abilities to interpret and build upon such information. Knowledge concerning the improving of machinery, as opposed to just operating it, could continue throughout a worker's life.

There was an obvious disincentive to developing inventions that might ultimately lose the worker his or her job; for such reasons the bulk of the advances towards mechanisation and automation (self-acting machinery), that is process innovations, did not come from the workers. Introducing product innovations, however, might allow skilled workers to protect or even advance their careers. Consequently one finds that in industries such as the various branches of metals, the role of skilled workers is particularly powerful (Berg 1985: ch. 11). Rewards in the pay packet as well as the job could come from designing and making new types of nail, or brassware or knife, etc. With wages paid by the piece, that is in proportion to output rather than to time, there was a greater incentive for employees to speed up operations or to improve product quality; hence the advocacy of piece rates by Taylorist 'scientific management' in later times. But the nineteenth century as a whole saw a drift from piece to time rates, and this shifted the incentive for improvements from employees to employers (or their agents). If employers were paying the same wages to their workers regardless of how much the latter produced, the onus fell on the former to see that as much could be produced as cheaply as possible in a certain time.

The shift of responsibility towards managers was associated with their rising public profile. Chandler (1977) describes the emergence of the 'visible hand' of management, and believes that it evolved further and faster in the US than in Britain from the middle of the nineteenth century. Nevertheless, in the workshop activities for which learning-by-doing was relevant, the prominent employers were often major innovators – people such as Peter Fairbairn, Sir William Fairbairn, Sir Henry Bessemer and Sir George Armstrong were the stuff of success stories that populated the biographies of Samuel Smiles (although Smiles' story is darker than often supposed).

A significant aspect of this story was the shift in emphasis within machine making from division of labour based on handicrafts, to a more capital-intensive structure based on machine tools; this was associated with a shift in location from the textile areas to London, and the rise of men such as Bramah and Maudslay. The machine tools foreshadowed the rise of interchangeable parts (Floud 1976).

The role of the professional agent was increasingly important, either within the firm or as consultant. Engineering developed as a local response to technology 'imported' from another locality, and was initially carried out by millwrights and smiths (Berg 1985: ch. 3). As its identity coalesced, engineering became associated, by way of both cause and effect, with the emergence of professional societies along the lines of the scientific societies noted in chapter 2. It was also associated with the dissemination of literature which combined the professional and the popular such as the *Mechanics' Magazine* (1823–72). The contract of an engineer like Richard Roberts enabled him to work on behalf of the employers to develop the self-acting cotton mule for the immediate objective of disrupting possible strikes of skilled workers.

For all the growing professional advice, the accumulation of knowledge in capital goods was generally a tortuous process. Henry Cort's famous puddling process for wrought-iron was long in gestation and long commercially unsuccessful, even after royalties had been slashed to try to encourage take-up. 'Both entrepreneurs and workers had to go through a learning period, making many mistakes that often resulted in low outputs of uneven quality' (Hyde 1977: 92). This extended process of trial and error is sometimes known as 'learning by failing'.

Learning by using

What seems clear is that the operation of learning by doing in capital goods industries like machine making could not operate in a vacuum without feedbacks from the using ('downstream') industries. Rosenberg's concept of 'learning by using' focuses on this type of improvement activity, especially in the consumer goods industries (Rosenberg 1982: ch. 6). Economics distinguishes 'embodied' from 'disembodied' technical changes; in the former, new techniques are made available in the form of new types of capital equipment, so that the technological advance is 'embodied' in new fixed capital formation; 'disembodied' changes, on the other hand, are envisaged as new knowledge that can be grafted on to existing machinery and processes. Experience in use permitted both embodied changes, re-designing the equipment, and disembodied changes such as operating the equipment over longer lifetimes. As in the previous section, learning is here thought of as the process of acquiring knowledge; for the user of machinery it depends crucially on the capabilities of the particular individual (or firm) as well as on information obtained from elsewhere – such as that embodied in the machines being purchased. One common repercussion of such learning via use of machinery in our period was increased control over product quality, and the attainment of higher quality standards.

Such changes were often quite simple; for example, the historian of Marshalls, the Leeds-based flax-spinning firm of the early nineteenth century, states that John Marshall 'had no flair for fundamental invention and simply aimed at some modifications bearing on quality and costs' (Rimmer 1960: 49). This was nevertheless sufficient to make the firm one of the largest in any branch of consumer goods production in its time. Initially Marshall left the more sophisticated advances in the highly capable hands of the engineer, Matthew Murray. However, lack of sustained contact with best practice in the middle of the century allowed dominance in the use of flax-spinning machinery to shift from Leeds to Belfast (Rimmer 1960: 259). The general conclusion of recent investigation has been that very few entrepreneurs of the period were heroic in their innovatory achievements, but many of the more successful were good imitators (Payne 1974; Crouzet 1985).

There were attempts to institutionalise the improvement of products and processes, such as the schools of design in the woollen industry around 1850, about which contemporaries like Edward Baines Jr were effusive (Baines 1875: 129). Of particular importance were the major exhibitions and their 'juries', beginning with that at Crystal Palace in 1851. Little study has been made of such developments, but what there is suggests little practical effect until the 1870s, at least in the woollen and worsted industries (Sigsworth 1958: 57–8). Competence in improving products remained largely specific to firms and to skilled workers. There has been considerable debate among historians of art and design about whether the industrial revolution and Victorian era saw a rise or fall in standards of design (Klingender 1968; Leavitt 1972; Kusamitsu 1981; H. Clark 1984). Did the introduction of machinery elevate or debase product design and quality? Much obviously depends on individual taste, but it seems conceivable that average standards rose at the same time as standards for fine qualities declined. There also appears to be a consensus that the French continued to lead in industrial design in areas like textiles, even if (or because) they lagged in mechanisation.

It was the interaction of learning by doing and learning by using that promoted success. The historian of the wool-combing machine used in the worsted industry expressed it in this way:

No one of the great combing machines of to-day [1889] can be said to have been entirely created by one man. The leading principle may represent a single creative effort, but the successive developments which have led to the complete practicable machine have only been reached, stage by stage, by constant experiment, and by a grouping as it were from time to time of the hints, deductions, and suggestions of others than the inventors-in-chief in the application of some decided improvement. (Burnley 1889: 406)

Burnley went on to stress again the role of 'learning by failing': 'The history of the wool-combing machine is a record of gradual progress built up of failures as well as successes. The former have pointed the way to the latter' (1889: 414).

The lesson is that the productive system as a whole mattered in fostering technical progress. Mutual interaction of producers and users widened the pool of talent available, and deepened the competitive strength. This was most obviously exerted in those regions, often quite small in geographical size, which were associated with the most dynamic developments in particular industries. The complexity of interactions and accumulated skills restricted the degree to which such knowledge could be portable to new regions although, as the Belfast flax-spinning example shows, it could sometimes occur. In general, even the migration of skilled workers and mechanics, although often a necessary condition for the geographical spread of industry, was not a sufficient condition, as exemplified by the role of British emigrants in the relatively unsuccessful Norwegian textile industry (Bruland 1989).

Still less was the export of machinery any such guarantee, as demonstrated by the early attempts to ship cotton-spinning machinery to the United States; the machines were soon dismantled and returned (Jeremy 1981: 76). Such geographical diffusion as took place emphasises the distinction between information and knowledge; equally, the rise of foreign competition rested on developing competences in such quarters. A deputation of Bradford worsted manufacturers to France in 1855 was

unable to find out the causes of this undeniable superiority [of the French in high-quality goods, and] were obliged to ascribe it to the well-known truth that a trade once established in a certain locality cannot be carried on with the same success at another place, though the latter may, to all appearances, possess even superior advantages. (James 1857: 526n)

This was at a time when Bradford was nicknamed 'Worstedopolis' and was the world's leading centre of worsted production.

Technological imitation

'Imitation' in this section is not intended to mean straight copying, as it is often regarded in the literature on technological diffusion. Instead it means the imitation of particular principles observed in earlier technologies, sometimes in the same kind of process but sometimes not. These principles, which represent 'information', are incorporated into the innovator's own knowledge of his or her activity to bring about a technical improvement.

The period from the Napoleonic Wars until the 1860s or so is often seen as a period of relative technological quietness in manufacturing, even though the technological sophistication of some of the developments was high. Typical changes of the second and third quarters of the nineteenth century were, for example, the better control of colour flow in textile printing (Chapman and Chassagne 1981: 43–4), greater ductility, etc., of metals (Berg 1985: ch. 10) and wet puddling in iron refining (Hyde 1977: chs. 7, 8, 11). Many were the outcome of 'scaling' (Sahal 1981) – that is, taking an earlier innovation and enlarging it one step further. Often the novelty required was small, as in the steadily higher blast temperatures and furnace sizes in iron smelting; but sometimes breakthroughs were needed in related areas to ensure success.

An important aspect of such technological imitation was the growing vertical separation between machine-making and machine-using activities. For the American machine-tool industry, Rosenberg (1963) showed the critical significance of two kinds of organisational change: the vertical disintegration between machine making and machine using was accompanied by a horizontal technological convergence. Since the number of kinds of activity that machine tools had to carry out was relatively limited (boring, grinding, cutting, etc.), it paid for a producer to develop tools to work in the whole range of user industries. Such technological 'fusion' then further fuelled the vertical distinction between tool makers and tool users. The capacity for learning by doing in machine making was increased, but so also was the need for learning by using in order to adapt the tools and machines to a wide range of uses. These organisational changes were not limited to machine tools, as the rise of the mechanical engineering sector from the second quarter of the nineteenth century more broadly demonstrates.

The previous century had witnessed cases of more radical technological imitation, such as the copying of roller drafting in iron by textile spinning, of roller printing of books by textile finishing, of precision boring in cannon by steam-engine builders, etc. However, the organisational changes of the mid-nineteenth century, like the rise of mechanical engineering, helped foster the process to which Rosenberg had drawn attention and put it on a more consistent basis (Floud 1976).

Formal learning

The description above of informal learning processes assumes that advances stem more or less spontaneously from experience in production and use (Bell and Scott-Kemmis 1990). Chapter 2 above also considers the role of exogenous advances in science and technology. A link running directly from the 'scientific revolution' from the mid-seventeenth century to the industrial revolution a century or so later would support the 'linear model' of progression of knowledge and has been supported by some distinguished economic historians (Kuznets 1966: 9; Rostow 1975: 2). Chapter 2 shows, however, that the links were less frequent than is often supposed; when they did occur, they sometimes ran in the opposite direction to that predicted by the 'linear model'; and they were more inclined to be demonstrations of method (how to go about establishing findings, using experiments) than of precise results.

By the early nineteenth century, some examples of information cross-flow were becoming more evident. Marx noted the recent occurrence of such contributions, which for him came long after the rise of capitalism, and stressed that a technological capacity was already required to develop the scientific response (Rosenberg 1976: ch. 7). Thus scientific work on electricity and magnetism was being extended by technological developments in telegraphy by the late 1830s and commercial success in such a field led to widened scientific and technological interest by the early 1850s. In the past there had been much longer lags between scientific and technological advances. The chemistry that was utilised by industry remained highly empiricist until well into the nineteenth century, working on the 'hit and miss' principle of learning by failing, for example in calico printing, until science was used more formally in developing manganese compounds from the 1820s (Baines 1835: 274–8). One outstanding case of information flowing between science and technology was the link between the high-pressure steam engine and the rise of the subject of thermo-dynamics, but this too was initially an example of reverse causation, from technology back to science (Cardwell 1971; von Tunzelmann 1978).

In addition to the use of scientific experimentation in industry, it was also possible to adopt the instruments used to conduct those experiments (Price 1984). Regular use of instruments became the norm in industries like brewing (hygrometer, thermometer, saccharometer, etc. (Mathias 1959)) and pottery (the pyrometric bead). The significance of increasing stan-dardisation of weights and measures has been studied by Pollard (1983).

Working in such ways and with such new instruments and equipment called for increased skills among the workforce as well among the inventors, for example the use of the stamp and press in the Birmingham metals trades (Berg 1985: ch. 12). This spurred the rise of popular science movements from the 1830s (Berg 1980). In such ways, formal learning became integrated with the informal types of learning-by-doing and learning-by-using discussed above. Formal learning could convey in-formation, often in parrot fashion as ridiculed by Charles Dickens in *Hard Times*. But it could also be justified as increasing the capabilities of individuals to acquire information on their own initiative, that is to expand their knowledge. However, formal learning of such kinds is not a by-product of production experience as are the informal types, but involves economic decisions to allocate resources and invest in the potential for technical change, through providing education both at higher levels of science and at vocational or training levels. This argument for what economists would call 'externalities' became intertwined with 'social control' arguments for educating the working classes, and led to the classical economists, supposedly wedded to the free market, uniting behind the case for state intervention in education.

The conclusion of this study of 'search' processes which underlay technological change for the bulk of the nineteenth century is that, while it is necessary to examine each category of learning in detail and in isolation, a satisfactory picture requires reintegrating all of these into some conception of the industrial system as a whole. The complexity of this procedure no doubt explains why no satisfactory general account of the causes of technical progress has yet emerged.

Selection characteristics

The simplest answer to the question of what determined selection was the market (Nelson and Winter 1982; Eatwell 1982). Some see the rise of the market as the very core of the 'great transformation' associated with industrialisation (Polanyi 1944), though others believe that some markets (at least) operated efficiently for many centuries before. The view that markets emerged or were extended at this time is consistent with the argument that, in the late eighteenth and early nineteenth centuries, there was a fundamental shift in society, as well as in the economy, from a 'moral economy' based on rights and obligations to a market economy ruled by prices, although this view too has been contested (E. P. Thompson 1963; Williams 1984).

The difficulty with providing information as a free good, as required for the operation of a perfect market, is that it left no financial incentive for invention – known as the problem of 'appropriation', or of 'intellectual property rights'. Hence Arrow (1962b) argued for the superiority of a 'socially managed economy' – possibly some form of moral economy – over a pure market economy, since the former could award prizes to inventors while still facilitating the free flow of information. As noted in chapter 2, to cope with this problem the British had imitated the Italians in issuing patents from the early seventeenth century; at first mostly for imitation and importation of foreign technology, later for originality (MacLeod 1988). In addition, professional societies for both agriculture and industry awarded prizes for solving perceived problems, especially in the mid-eighteenth century (though few of these ended up going to the most deserving). Finally, Parliament on occasion granted financial rewards for lifetime achievements, for example to Samuel Crompton.

But the problem to which Arrow and others drew attention became increasingly contested from the time of Watt's first patent in 1769; this was accused first of patenting knowledge (a principle) rather than an artifact, secondly of having been too generous to the inventor (especially in how long it was eventually allowed to endure). Judges awarding patents tightened up in the early nineteenth century, but from the 1830s were granting a much higher proportion of patent applications (Dutton 1984). The swing in favour of the inventors rather than users was embodied in the Patent Law Amendment Act of 1852. The most notorious example in the nineteenth century of the use of patents as a device to consolidate a monopoly and thereby impede the workings of a perfect market was by Lister with the combing machine (Burnley 1889; Sigsworth 1958). This included the granting of defensive patents for inventions which he had little intention of pursuing himself in order to anticipate every possible challenge (James 1857: 569), buying up rights to earlier important patents and allegedly applying for patents in the names of his workmen.

The main task here, however, will not be to debate the importance of the market, but to analyse the ways in which market forces, in the form of prices and especially costs, imparted particular directions to the trajectories pursued by technology. This means looking less at selection mechanisms than at selection characteristics: why did the market select certain types of innovations but not others? Or, in certain cases, what urged innovators to search for particular types of advance rather than randomly in every direction?

Product and process innovation

The eighteenth-century phase of industrialisation is traditionally associated with process innovations, especially those in textiles, replacing the emphasis on product innovation (for example the so-called 'New Draperies', which were new cloth mixtures) of preceding centuries. The search procedures surveyed above for the early nineteenth century are mostly concerned with process innovation.

There are, however, some indications that product innovations were becoming increasingly important by the middle of the nineteenth century, for example the use of new materials like alpaca and mohair in the 'worsted' industry. Product innovation was said to be hindered by the lack of patent protection of the kind that process innovation might expect. Those developing new products, for instance twilled cloth, could resort to patenting only some minor tools rather than the products themselves, in an attempt to protect their own innovations (Ponting 1971: 62). The Great Exhibition of 1851, and the prizes awarded by its juries, was the first in a series of major international exhibitions which aimed to restore incentives to product innovators.

The practical problems with distinguishing the two sorts of innovation are twofold. In the first place, much of the product innovation in this period required supporting changes in machinery, that is in processes, although in many cases these were relatively minor such as deeper combs and improved gills for spinning alpaca and mohair, the cap for throstles spinning fine worsteds, extra harnesses for looms, and so on. Indeed, without associated process innovation (mechanisation), mere product innovation, in developing finer qualities, could be simply a step on the road to industrial decline, as was said of the East Anglian worsted industry (James 1857: 437). This argument cuts both ways, with process changes sometimes hinging on product developments, as in the famous case of the substitution of coke for charcoal in iron smelting, which suited Darby's production of thin-walled castings (Hyde 1977: ch. 2), or later in areas like calico printing. Secondly, product changes in the 'upstream' industries which supplied the materials, capital goods, etc., became process innovations when installed in 'downstream' uses; for example the proliferation of varieties of steam engine represented product innovation for the suppliers and process innovation for the users. The interdependence of system changes is again underlined by this kind of vertical interaction.

The gain from splitting innovations into product and process categories is primarily one of pinning down the selection factors involved. It is a rough-and-ready, but sometimes useful, distinction to contrast the role of prices in dictating product innovation with that of costs for process innovation. An interesting – though appropriately cautious – application is by Mitchell (1984: 96) to the coal industry in the later nineteenth century, comparing the slow introduction of mechanisation with the more rapid diffusion of coal preparation (washing, etc.). A possible explanation for the slower advance of the process innovation (mechanisation) was the continuing low level of costs, which left little incentive to cut them much further; whereas the low level of prices encouraged product innovations such as coal washing.

The precise link between levels of prices and costs and innovative effort is, however, in urgent need of attention from historians, as there is no agreement among economists on this matter. High costs may well be a stimulus to innovate, but equally costs may be so high as to discourage any such effort. Little is known, even for the present day, about the circumstances in which costs may be an incentive or a disincentive. Still more is this the case with the links to prices: in neoclassical models high

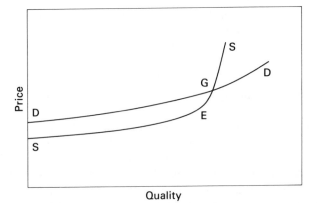

Figure 11.1 Demand and supply curves in relation to quality
Source: based on Swann (1986).

prices relative to costs imply high profits, and are consistent with a positive incentive in which innovation is seen as a type of investment activity. In some evolutionary models, however, low prices, as in a cyclical depression, are seen as the motivation (Nelson and Winter 1973), because they encourage search efforts. The problem is further complicated by the feedback effects of successful innovation on lowering costs and prices.

More persuasive could be the analytical work of Swann (1986) on 'quality innovation'. Quality innovation can be thought of as similar to scaling effects in process technology. Swann shows that one can draw demand and supply curves with quality rather than quantity on the horizontal axis. This is illustrated in Figure 11.1. The demand curve for higher qualities – say of cotton clothing – slopes upward to the right, as customers are willing to pay more for the higher grades (curve DD). Costs of production also rise as quality increases, reflecting the greater effort and time involved. So the supply curve relative to quality also slopes upward to the right (curve SS). Initially we can suppose that the quality-related supply curve lies below the demand curve, so that some profits are earned in producing low qualities. But at some point the supply curve is likely to steepen markedly, as production becomes too awkward for existing machinery. Beyond the point called G in Figure 11.1, consumers are not willing to pay the greatly increased costs. The point at which the supply price begins to turn sharply upwards (point E in Figure 11.1) is an obvious focus for innovative activity. Looking at price trends, we observe a much more rapid decline in price of cotton yarn of the fine count of 100 as compared with medium counts of 40 or low counts below 20. It is less clear how much of this is due to the process changes (for example the mule in cotton or the gill frame in flax) and how much to access to cheaper raw materials (for example, Sea Island cotton).

According to Crouzet (1985), the British, in contrast to the French, specialised in medium-quality products for middle-class consumption. However, by comparison with the United States, Britain failed to develop a mass market in certain products; for example, in guns and gun-stocks the British obsession with elegant sporting pieces for country gentlemen (encouraged by the game laws) restricted the diffusion of the 'American system' of interchangeable parts, which in the USA was to lead on to mass production (Fries 1975; Rosenberg 1969a, 1972; Hounshell 1984). This demonstrates the importance of factors such as income distribution for the demand side of the Swann model. It also reflects, in the implied supply curve, the differing skills in the various countries, and especially the role of machinery in advancing British competitive strength in the earlier years of the nineteenth century. Most machinery was first introduced for low qualities, for the cheaper yarns, fabrics, etc., and was steadily scaled upwards to high qualities through focussing innovative effort in the manner reflected in Figure 11.1. The competition with the older hand methods became most acute in producing finer and fancier goods. There is some dispute about exactly the level of quality below which the cost of cloth from the power loom undercut that from the hand loom at particular points of time (von Tunzelmann 1978: ch. 7; Lyons 1987), stemming from different assumptions made about the extent of labour saved, but none about the steady erosion of the hand-loom weaver who tried vainly to survive by retreating to the fine or fancy grades.

Savings in natural resources

Both product and process innovations will normally be associated with reduced costs for a particular quantity or quality of output. In the case of completely new products such savings may be purely hypothetical, but for the more incremental quality innovation of the kind just referred to it may be possible to detect savings in materials or labour.

Two of Landes' three categories of innovation during the industrial revolution fall under the sub-heading of natural resources:

the substitution of inanimate for animate sources of power, in particular, the introduction of engines for converting heat into work, thereby opening to man a new and almost unlimited supply of energy; the use of new and far more abundant raw materials, in particular, the substitution of mineral for vegetable or animal substances. (Landes 1969: 41 (the first category was machinery))

The substitution of coal or coke for timber or charcoal meant adopting a fuel source that was, for a time, more elastic in short-run supply, as the sinking time for new coal pits was considerably shorter than the growing time for new trees. In the longer run timber was more obviously renewable than coal, but as demand increased in the early years of industrialisation, timber supplies were unable to match demand (Hammersley 1973), and coal/coke substitution became the norm.

In the nineteenth century, the general trend ran the other way. Now that coal was the basis of the nation's fuel supply, the object became one of economising on coal use. The most obvious way of doing so was by improving the fuel economy of the steam engine, a process which Smeaton and Watt had fostered in the eighteenth century, and which was now advanced by the likes of Trevithick and Woolf for the high-pressure and compound engines, together with a host of post-innovation improvements in their efforts to adapt such engines to factory, steamship, railway and other uses. The earlier stages of these developments were to be found in areas where coal costs were rather high but not unaffordable, such as in the copper and tin mines of south-west England where Trevithick, Woolf and others worked (von Tunzelmann 1978). Best practice in the second half of the nineteenth century progressed less rapidly, but the diffusion of better practices (more thermodynamically efficient steam engines) continued. The radical change in this trajectory came with Parsons' steam turbine in the 1890s. An alternative route was to use the coal indirectly, e.g. for generating gas or in association with compressed air. The culmination of this process was the advent of coal-fired electricity generation, again late in the nineteenth century.

There were, similarly, trends in economising on the use of coal or coke as a feedstock, especially in the iron industry. The amount of coal required to produce just one ton of pig-iron fell from about 9.5 tons in the late eighteenth century to under two tons by the end of the nineteenth (Jeans 1885). Neilson's hot blast of 1828 permitted the use of coal rather than coke, and in terms of cost savings its advantages lay in the coal rather than the iron ore (Hyde 1977: ch. 9). Use of iron in buildings, machinery, etc., in turn helped to economise upon wood, particularly because of the greater durability of iron.

Over the longer run, the difficulty of mining coal that was less accessible because it lay at greater depths or in thinner seams might have been expected to generate diminishing returns and rising costs for users. The threat on this score was first drawn to the attention of the public at large by the economist W. S. Jevons (1865). However, through a combination of extensive growth (finding new sources) and especially intensive growth (technical and organisational changes in coal mining), the price of coal in real terms actually fell a little until the last quarter of the nineteenth century (Flinn 1984; Church 1986; von Tunzelmann 1992a). Thus technical change was sufficient to meet the challenge of diminishing returns, notwithstanding an unwavering rate of growth in coal production. In similar fashion, the stationary steam engine did not greatly lower the cost of power in the first half of the nineteenth century, but did prevent it from rising as would no doubt have happened if the country had had to depend on older energy sources (von Tunzelmann 1978).

Similar comments could be made about land and other natural resources. In the case of land, the biological advances (rotational systems, etc.) of the eighteenth century, together with high farming in the nineteenth, did not physically increase the land available to any extent, but did make that land productive on a more continuous basis. However, the diminishing returns to land feared by the classical economists were more readily met in the nineteenth century by extensive growth through overseas trade and colonisation, giving access to American cotton and wheat, Australian wool, the minerals of many countries and so forth (Wilkinson 1973; Jones 1981).

Saving labour and capital

In contrast to the effort that went into saving natural resources, that directed at saving labour appears less sustained. Habakkuk (1962) showed that there was a much more profound and persistent bias towards saving labour in the nineteenth-century USA than in the UK. Care must be taken to specify what concept of labour-saving is being used. Two are perhaps relevant here. The first is to look at what inventors and innovators of the time believed they were achieving in their work; the second is the relative measure emphasised by economists for analysing induced innovation.

The latter defines an innovation as being 'labour-saving' only when it saves labour to a greater degree than it saves capital (or other defined inputs); similarly an innovation is 'capital-saving' when it saves a greater proportion of capital than of labour. This relative measure has been criticised as an arbitrary construct since the worker rendered unemployed through a particular technical change feels the same whether that change is seen by economists as relatively labour-saving or relatively capital-saving (Berg 1985: ch. 10), but this consideration – important as it is – is more relevant to the appraisal below of the consequences of technological change. The basic problem is that many (successful) technical changes saved at least two if not three of Adam Smith's 'holy trinity' of factors of production, namely 'land' (natural resources), labour and capital. The first concept – that of the intentions of the inventor – seems most immediately relevant to the study of causation being attempted here, and probably relates more closely to relative than absolute measures of factor-saving, precisely because radical changes are likely to reduce most or all inputs per unit of output.

MacLeod (1988: ch. 9) analyses the declarations made in applications for patents from 1660 to 1800. Of the 42 per cent of patents which gave an explanation of their intentions, she finds that only 4.2 per cent aimed to save labour (partly offset by 1.9 per cent aiming to create employment), while no less than 30.8 per cent aimed to save capital, another 5.2 per cent to save time, 29.3 per cent to improve quality, etc. A generous extension to include patents that were 'effectively labour-saving' even if not specified as such raises the labour-saving percentage to 21.6 per cent (MacLeod 1988: 170). Comparison with macro-economic trends underpins the view (Floud and McCloskey 1981: ch. 11) that until about 1830 there was no strong tendency towards a relative saving of labour, apart from a period during the Napoleonic Wars.

Figure 11.2 gives some macro-economic data on ratios of capital to labour, based on decadal averages from 1761/70 to 1851/60. There are considerable problems in using these data, not least in the heroic assumptions required to assemble the capital and population aggregates, as the authors responsible would be first to admit (Feinstein 1978; Feinstein and Pollard 1988; Wrigley and Schofield 1981). In addition, the capital figures relate to Great Britain, and the population data to England less Monmouth; there are, moreover, lags between population growth and labour force growth. As the capital and labour data were, however, compiled independently, and as we are looking at ratios and growth rates rather than totals, there is no obvious reason why the general impressions conveyed should be very misleading.

Figure 11.2a shows that the ratio of net capital stock to population increased slowly until the 1830s, but that this was followed by a marked rise in trend growth rates thereafter (the logarithmic scale means that a straight line connotes a certain rate of growth – the steeper the line, the higher the growth rate). Figure 11.2b instead compares indications of changes, by looking at net capital formation and rates of population growth. It too shows a pronounced divergence in the second quarter of the nineteenth century. This is paralleled by the shift of discourse from 'division of labour' to 'capital formation' at that same time (Berg 1980). There are indications of the phenomenon sometimes known in development economics as the 'big push' (akin to Rostow's 'take-off') in the second quarter of the nineteenth century, in which capital formation rises to levels characteristic of an industrialised economy. After that, once the capital goods sector is in place, the scope for capital-saving re-emerges, as learning processes thereafter permit the evolution of more and more efficient capital goods (Rosenberg 1969b).

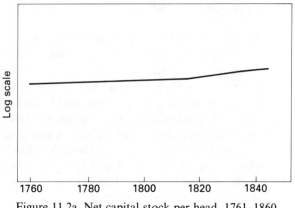

Figure 11.2a Net capital stock per head, 1761–1860

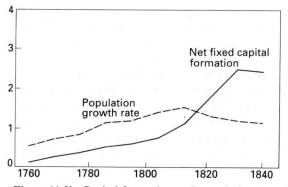

Figure 11.2b Capital formation and population growth rates,
1761–1860

Note: population levels are calculated as decadal means of annual
levels. Population growth rates are the equivalent annual increase over
the preceding decadal mean.

Sources: population from Wrigley and Schofield (1981: 533–5); capital
stock and capital formation from Feinstein and Pollard (1988: 441).
Author's own calculations from these data.

The most obvious manifestation of a shift towards more labour-saving
technology after 1830 was the installation of machinery. However,
machinery, even if aiming to save labour, was often intended to save
particular kinds of labour – usually groups of highly skilled adult males,
who were seen as not only relatively expensive but potentially threatening;
this was noted above for the case of the self-acting mule, and occurred
again in the late 1840s for the wool-combing machine. The temptation to

use machinery to 'de-skill' labour by substituting cheap and docile women and children for fractious or expensive males is assessed below. There seems little doubt that in areas like Lancashire, the technological unemployment created by mechanisation was felt most severely by adult males. Yet the continuing labour surplus of males acted to dampen the drive to further savings of labour.

Saving time

That inventions save time as well as labour is a matter of everyday language, but economists, before the advent of the information technology revolution of the twentieth century, have devoted vastly more attention to the saving of labour than of time (Oda 1990). Although economists generally suppose that saving time can be thought of as an aspect of saving capital, there are some good reasons for distinguishing time-saving from capital-saving (von Tunzelmann 1992b). One is the pragmatic one, that time-saving changes will often save labour (in absolute terms) as well as capital – indeed MacLeod's extended definition of 'effectively labour-saving' patents, quoted above, includes time-saving under labour-saving. A more important reason is that the motivation for saving time may differ from that for saving (fixed) capital. The rise of the factory – the most important organisational change of the industrial revolution – achieved a saving in time over domestic forms of organisation (putting-out production was typically spread over a number of months or even longer) but only through increased expenditure on fixed capital.

Contemporary studies of industrialisation were in fact replete with references to time-saving incentives or outcomes, which can arise in a number of different ways. An important source of time-saving is the reduction of 'downtime', that is periods in which the machinery is not in operation. The rising proportion of capital that was fixed rather than circulating exerted pressure to spread overhead costs by working as near to full capacity as possible. One form this took in our period was by using factories, with their high fixed and low operating costs, to provide the average level of output demanded, and to resort to outworkers as and when demand conditions required (Matthews 1954 shows this for the cotton industry). With hours of work increasingly restricted by legislation, firms were encouraged to work multiple shifts ('relays', etc.). For the same reason, it was economical to run the more elaborate machines now in place for as long as possible. The power loom was not able to compete with hand-loom weavers in the finest fabrics; and the basic explanation was that it broke the yarn too frequently, hence increasing 'downtime' – consequently there could be little saving of labour as the ends had to be laboriously mended. A similar problem limited the diffusion of mechanically similar operations from spinning and weaving the relatively tensile material of cotton to other fabrics, which were either finer (for example, silk) or less easy to stretch (for example, wool and flax).

The rise of fixed capital in the form of plant and equipment in itself caused delays, as the new plant took longer to construct and install. This problem of lengthening gestation lags was met in the short run, as just noted, by resorting to the more elastic supplies of outworkers. So long as demand was expanding, it is hardly surprising that the transition to factory industry was rather long-drawn-out. At the other end of the production chain, in distribution, speed to market was fostered by major advances in transportation and communications. For the economy as a whole, there may have been little economic advantage in faster transportation because average distances were still so short (Hawke 1970, 1981); but for individual firms, towns or regions, the advantages of speed to market ('lead time') were frequently decisive – naturally at the expense of other firms.

In a similar vein, new techniques which increased the reliability of time spent in various operations might benefit particular firms. Steamships may have been little faster or cheaper than sailing ships over coastal routes for many years, but the much stronger guarantee of arrival on time with raw materials or marketed goods was a notable reason for preferring them. The same happened with energy sources – wind and water were roughly competitive in cost with steam until well into the nineteenth century. However, the dependence on natural causes (floods, freezes, etc., in the case of water) meant that water-power users might have to make up time at night. When legislation stipulated reductions in night working, they were compelled to look to steam, at least as an auxiliary form of power supply at times of difficulty (Marvel 1977; von Tunzelmann 1978: ch. 6).

The most obvious and important form of time-saving, however, was by way of increasing the rate of throughput, the speed at which the production process took place. In this lay the origins of mass production (Chandler 1977; Hounshell 1984). The major 'gadgets' associated with the industrial revolution were in themselves more rapid than the methods they supplanted. Subsequently, through the post-innovation improvements, they were steadily speeded up (Lyons 1987 for the power loom). Whether or not the faster technique was more profitable depended on the structure of prices and costs – for example, the US cotton industry shifted to the continuous process of ring spinning, while in the UK the discontinuous process of the mule was long seen as preferable on the finer yarns spun in this country (Sandberg 1969; see also Field 1983 for a more general comparison of Britain and America). Instead, self-acting mules were stretched out and speeded up (Lazonick 1981). Not only did such higher speeds involve secondary innovations in the equipment, sometimes of considerable complexity, but they may also have required changes in the wider productive system. The speed-up of the spinning mule and power loom in cotton and other textiles depended partly on the availability of cheaper sources of power (von Tunzelmann 1978: chs. 7–8).

Speeding up particular operations could place strains on other levels of the production chain. The most famous example was the interaction between the speed-up of weaving and of spinning in cotton textiles in the eighteenth century. While this is a clear enough example of what Rosenberg (1969b) calls a 'compulsive sequence', the direction which it took also reflected the particular supply or cost problems involved; when weaving became faster, a shortage of yarn arose which in turn was caused by a shortage of female spinners, so the jenny aimed to increase yarn output per female spinner. This helps to underline the point that time-saving cannot be considered separately from its context of factor inputs. One of the most dramatic savings in time during the industrial revolution period was the development of chemical methods for bleaching cloth, reducing a process which had previously taken six to eight months to a matter of days or even hours; here the principal saving was in the land previously required for bleaching fields. Furthermore, the older methods were often speeded up in the face of competition from the newer, for example the water wheel when steam engines were worked faster (leading to the turbine), the power loom when the automatic loom threatened, and so on.

The most obvious incentive to time-saving change came from the pressure of increased demand in the face of factor supplies that were not infinitely elastic. As the rate of output grew, total costs would rise even faster, unless unit costs could be cut by saving time. As explained above, employees had incentives to increase output per unit of time so long as they were being paid piece rates; but they often lacked the confidence that, when bad times returned, their piece rates would not be cut accordingly. Hence trade unions in the mid-nineteenth century tended to favour time rates as being easier to standardise. Employers found time rates increased their control over the work process, and the incentive to save time thus switched to them (obtaining more output for a given time wage).

In summary, the motives that focussed the intentions of inventors and innovators in particular directions have to be studied as a system. Objectives of saving (limited) natural resources and saving (limited) time were perhaps most pronounced, but even they interacted with savings in labour and capital – it was through savings in land, labour and capital that speed-up became transformed into reductions of cost. Both the demand side and the supply side come into the story, the more so as we turn back to the question of product as well as process innovations. Finally, the question of technology needs to be integrated with other constraints faced by firms, like organisation and finance which are dealt with in other chapters.

Consequences

Just as the selection of successful innovations was found to interact with the search mechanisms for locating them, so the assessment of the contribution of the advance of technology cannot be made independently of the above assessment of its causes; there was a dynamic interaction between cause and effect. It is true that modern innovation theory pays some attention to the unintended consequences of particular actions (Dosi et al. 1988); and there is some evidence for these in the historical record – for instance Samuel Crompton designed his mule to permit hand spinners to compete with factories, whereas the outcome was that the mule became the main technological foundation of British cotton-spinning factories. For the most part, however, we know little of the intended consequences, and are compelled to deduce them from outcomes. For this reason, many of the consequences of technical change have already been covered.

There is, however, an important way in which the relevant concepts differ when considering effects rather than causes. In studying the selection characteristics, relative measures of factor-saving were thought to be more useful. For the consequences, absolute measures are more significant.

Capital

The rise of machine technology and of a distinct machine-making (capital goods) sector evidently helped to sponsor the growing capital formation discussed in chapters 3 and 10. Improved technology could raise the rate of return on investment and encourage capital formation; in turn that capital formation fed into the overall rate of economic growth and, as a result of higher aggregate demand, stimulated further innovation of the kinds discussed above. Machines naturally represented 'embodied' capital, and thus were part of the rising trend towards fixed rather than working capital. However, the extent of embodiment required for many of the minor developments that were cumulatively so important in this period did not have to be large – there was no close relationship in every case between the technological success and the additional capital required. Many improvements, if not totally 'disembodied' (though some were), stood part-way between the economist's two categories. Moreover, machinery remained only a small fraction of total fixed capital formation (Field 1985 and ch. 10).

As a counterpart to the changes in labour process described next, the 'capital process' shifted from one-off and small-batch production to something more like continuous-flow production. With the time-saving characteristics of many advances already discussed, there was certainly a substantial rise in throughput. This created difficulties of controlling the workplace so as to have it running as smoothly and efficiently as possible. Later in the nineteenth century this question of control, linked to speed-up, became the central problem of management (Beniger 1986). In the United States, resolving the problem came from mass production and big business (Chandler 1977), but in Britain it is widely believed that the issue was evaded (see vol. 2, ch. 4). The typical response in Britain was to leave day-to-day running of the workplace to 'gangs' of labourers, headed by a skilled worker.

Labour

The speeding-up of industrial processes also lay near to the heart of the problems of industrialisation for labour. As Marx argued in *Capital* (1887: I), there were three main ways of 'exploiting' labour: (1) through increased employment of women and children; (2) through longer working hours; (3) through 'intensification' of work coming from speeded-up machinery. There is some statistical debate over whether either of the two former actually affected the economy as a whole during the industrial revolution, but there would seem to be evidence that, for a time, both rose within the industrialised sector.

The discussion of labour-saving tendencies above noted that technology often abetted the replacement of skilled by unskilled labour. The Luddite riots of 1811/12 are often supposed to be mindless acts of violence against new technology, but in actuality many were responses to 'labour dilution', that is to the replacement of adult male labour by women and children, often on very old machinery. Textile machinery in areas like Lancashire continued to be biassed against adult males, and the retreat of unemployed males into hand-loom weaving was one of the most harrowing aspects of industrialisation. In the factories proper, wages were not reduced other than through labour dilution, and the general trend of real wages was upward after about 1820; the savage wage and income declines instead occurred in the pre-industrial sectors like hand-loom weaving, as their productivity was increasingly outdistanced by the speeding up of machinery. However not all machinery was 'de-skilling', and in a number of cases new grades of skills were created, as with the cotton mule (Lazonick 1979). The real struggle was not over whether or not to introduce machinery, but about who was to control it – the employer (or agent) or the skilled worker. As we have just seen, in many cases the latter prevailed. Although some groups of workers became unemployed as a result of machinery, more benefited than lost; and there is evidence that most hostility was not to the machinery itself but rather to the capitalistic environment in which it was introduced (Berg 1985). This continues to be a basic issue in industrial relations up to the present day.

The problem with exploiting labour in either of the two former ways indicated by Marx is that legislation, along with social norms, was placing increasing obstacles on such exploitation. Legislation for coal mines restricted employment for women and children, while that for factories limited hours of work, initially for children only, but effectively for all in a factory system. Possibly the most decisive event was the agitation for Ten Hours in the late 1840s (to reduce standard hours of work from twelve per day). This brought renewed zeal among employers for installing technology which would intensify labour according to Marx's third principle, that is by working the machines – and thus the employees – faster. The speeding-up of factory operations in turn accentuated the need for employers to exert greater control over the labour process in their factories. In the cotton industry, the steady enlarging and speeding-up of the machinery became the focus for wage bargaining and nascent trade-union activity: if the employees obtained the full benefit in terms of their wages rising proportionately with output, the employers would have little incentive to improve; while if the employers kept all the proceeds to themselves, the workers would go on strike, and this was indeed an important cause of strikes (Boyson 1970: 108, 143, 148, 153).

Factory discipline meant 'time-thrift', to use the phrase of Pollard (1963, 1965), and was associated with a shift from 'natural' work rhythms to 'clock time' (Thompson 1967). Control over the pace of work passed out of the hands of the labourers, as employers and their machines and steam engines paced the work process (Braverman 1974). Thus, while certain groups of labourers became unemployed as a result of mech-anisation and technological progress, the main effect for most was of a change in the conditions of work.

Output

Ideally one would have available, at the micro level, dozens of calculations of 'social savings' with which to assess the contributions of innovation to output and growth (Hawke 1970, 1981; von Tunzelmann 1978). Outside the well-publicised field of transportation, however, these do not exist for our period. This is not simply lack of effort by historians, as major problems with applying such methodology remain. With the approach used in this chapter, it is not appropriate to single out an innovation and relate its contribution a number of years later to the original innovation (David 1969; Ayres 1990; von Tunzelmann 1990). The processes of learning-by-doing and learning-by-using are by definition dependent on that resulting growth of output, which in turn would have been different without them. Social savings calculations to date have been a significant contribution to historical analysis of particular times and places, but an overall assessment of the role of technological progress is more complicated. We are forced to compromise with more macro-level reckonings of the growth contribution, although it should be recognised that this is a way of concealing rather than facing the difficulties.

The picture that emerges from steadily improving statistics on the growth of national income and productivity in the nineteenth century is one of accelerating growth from around 1820 (ch. 10). The intensifying contribution of capital formation to this growth is partly offset by a falling rate of growth of labour, so that much of growth appears to come from a rising TFP (total factor productivity) growth rate. This may seem surprising, in view of the common belief noted above that the period under discussion saw less radical innovation than its predecessor. Many authors have stressed the limitations on identifying TFP with the contribution of technology, since by its residual nature it includes a variety of other things. The implication of the approach of this chapter also raises a more fundamental difficulty – that technology is not simply exogenous, but much of it is produced through the workings of the economy.

Since we have seen that rising demand as well as supply factors helped induce innovation, it follows that to some degree innovation was a result of economic growth (that is of increased levels of aggregate demand), and not simply a cause. There are, indeed, a number of problems attached to the orthodox attribution of growth to technical change for our period. For example, the establishment of industries in regions that were to dominate industrialisation in their fields mostly pre-dated the age of mechanisation, as was the case with Yorkshire in the woollen and worsted industries (Heaton 1920: 281). Again it seems better to see the early phase of innovation as coming about as a result of still earlier industrial growth – the localisation of skills bred learning by doing and using in the ways described above. Moreover, in terms of international comparisons, the French seemed to have attained comparable rates of growth without comparable levels of inventiveness (Crouzet 1985). It should be admitted that there are severe problems with measuring rates of economic growth in a context of product innovation; but it is highly unlikely that the kinds of problems just noted can simply be dismissed as errors of measurement.

The most likely solution to the puzzle is that, while economic growth may have been the major stimulus to innovation, the diffusion of those innovations in turn underpinned continued economic growth. In this sense a dynamic framework emerges: from demand to supply to additional demand. In addition to this toing-and-froing between demand and supply – which itself is something of a caricature – there were dynamic inter-actions within the supply side itself. The most significant factor here was the lack of separation in practice between innovation and diffusion, whatever the theoretical literature might argue. The rate of diffusion responded to the relative 'profitability' of the newer technique over the older, and where such advantage was low – as in the cases of the self-acting mule (as compared with hand mule) on fine cotton yarns, or the power loom (as compared with hand loom) on fancy fabrics, the diffusion could be quite slow, regardless of the technical superiority of the newer technique. But 'profitability' here is simply the economist's shorthand to cover the range of economic and technical circumstances in which diffusion was taking place. Thus secondary innovation arose out of diffusion, as machines developed originally for a certain variety or quality of textile were extended to other varieties and qualities, etc. These secondary advances deepened the cost advantage of the new methods and widened the scope for their application. Herein therefore lay some of the feedback loops described in the early part of this chapter.

Conclusion

As compared with the sharp peaks of invention in the eighteenth century, the micro-inventions of the early nineteenth century were more like foothills. However these foothills rolled on endlessly, each giving way to its successor. The period did not witness the creation of major new industries, like the iron, or engineering, or branches of chemicals and textiles, seen in the early industrial revolution. Nor was there any counterpart to the rise of newer sectors still, like the electricity, steel, automotive and new chemicals activities of the later nineteenth century. For all that, productivity for the first time grew at the kind of rate associated with an industrialising economy. The cumulative impact of these multifarious small changes was therefore considerable.

This chapter has aimed to give some understanding of how innovation became the norm rather than the exception. The mechanisms involved in 'search' for new processes and new products were described as 'learning' procedures, although most of the learning was in the form of insights obtained from the accumulation of experience rather than from formal rote learning. The 'selection' mechanisms of firms and markets weeded out successful from unsuccessful innovations. The successful were likely to be characterised by cost savings in natural resources or in time – savings in labour and capital costs were less frequently the objectives, although all interacted. This increasingly potent capability for sustaining growth led ultimately to rising employment, rising capital formation and rising industrial output.

12   Foreign trade: comparative advantage and performance

Knick Harley

The dimensions of trade

Britain in the mid-eighteenth century was already the world's greatest trading nation. Textile and hardware manufacturers exported much of their output, rich London and Bristol merchants imported tropical goods and more modest provincial merchants dealt in Baltic timber and grain. In 1913 Britain remained the greatest trading nation in a world transformed by demography, policy and technology. Population grew steadily and, although British agricultural technology remained the best in the world, half her citizens' food now came from distant overseas farms. Policy and technology changed episodically, and defined recognisable epochs. Eighteenth-century mercantilism – a tradition of trade policy protecting domestic interests – gave way in the 1840s to a policy of free trade.

Two distinct episodes of technological change also marked the period. First, the industrial revolution provided British cotton and iron firms with technological leadership. In the decades after the Napoleonic Wars, they could sell more cheaply than rivals even on the latter's doorsteps. Second, after mid-century cheap railroads and steamships revolutionised long-distance trade. Great unsettled plains of America and Asia attracted farmers and investors. Speculators, adventurers, settlers and investors quickly built a truly international economy with an industrial centre and a raw material-producing periphery. British lending overseas and the expansion of Britain's role as carrier, banker and insurer to the world added new dimensions to Britain's international accounts. As never before the world was tied together in one great market place, with Britain as its centre. Multilateral settlements became commonplace: American imports of tea from India (say) were financed by exports of cotton to Britain, financed in turn by earnings of British ships and exports of British rails to India. By the early twentieth century 'frontiers had closed'. Trade began to assume a more twentieth-century character with the exchange of manufactured goods among advanced countries growing most rapidly.

300

Trade and growth

British trade and British growth flourished together. The usual understanding of these events divides neatly at 1870. Before 1870 the questions
asked by the historian of British trade are variants of 'How did foreign
trade make us rich?' In the years to 1914 they are variants of 'How did
foreign trade make us poor?' Contemporaries and historians viewed trade
as the engine of economic growth while the export-oriented cotton textile
industry grew by selling world-wide and as Britain consolidated industrial
leadership during the mid-Victorian boom of the 1850s and 1860s. After
1870 exports grew more slowly and trade became viewed as a brake.

Whether engine or brake, trade is often viewed now as the activity on
which the nation 'depended', just as it was by many contemporaries.
Wherever one looks in recent summaries by economic historians of the
issue of British trade and growth, the nineteenth century speaks. Richard
Cobden and John Bright would find little with which to disagree in the
assertions of Deane and Cole that 'from the beginning to the end of this
story... the British people have depended for their standard of living
largely on their ability to sell their products in the overseas markets'
(Deane and Cole 1962: 39). Peel could have used Ashworth's formulation
of the case in proposing free trade to the House of Commons – 'Britain's
livelihood depended on international trade and the performance of
international services' – just as Gladstone or Asquith might have used
Court's defence of it from later critics – 'In a century in which economic
growth depended very much on international commerce, no country's
development had benefited more from world trade' (Ashworth 1960: 256,
cf. 138; Court 1965: 181–2).

The correlation between British exports and British incomes lends an air
of verisimilitude to this tale of dependence. Britain's place as 'workshop of
the world' rested on the great export industries. As the rate of growth of
exports declined after 1870 so too did the rate of growth of incomes.
Exports of commodities per head grew 4.4 per cent per year from 1821 to
1873, almost four times as fast as the growth of income per head; but from
1873 to 1913 they grew at only 0.93 per cent per year, rather slower than
income per head, which now compared unsatisfactorily with German or
American growth. Little wonder, then, that economists of all sorts have
assigned a causal role to British foreign trade (Robertson 1938: 501;
Haberler 1959: 6; Cairncross 1961: 243; Meier and Baldwin 1957: 228,
257; Matthews *et al.* 1982: chs. 14 and 15).

Other statistics appear to confirm the impression that trade was
important (Crouzet 1980; Saul 1965). After a doubling of its share during
the second third of the century, for example, imports equalled 25 to 30 per

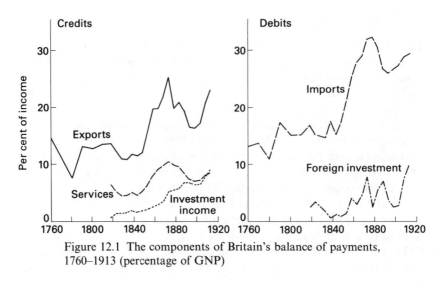

Figure 12.1 The components of Britain's balance of payments,
1760–1913 (percentage of GNP)

cent of national income (see Figure 12.1): at minimum £1 out of every £4
spent by Britons at the end of Victoria's reign was spent abroad, a higher
share than in France or Germany, and much higher than in the United
States. Some three-quarters of all imports were foods and raw materials,
frequently the only or the major source of British supply (see Table 12.1).
On the other side of the ledger, British exports consisted in the main of the
products of a few major industries. Textiles of cotton, wool and linen,
which had contributed nearly three-quarters of the value of exports at the
beginning of the century, still contributed nearly 40 per cent by its end.
Cotton alone, the prototypical industry of the industrial revolution, still
accounted for 25 per cent of all British commodity exports; iron and steel
for 15 per cent and machinery another 7 per cent, smaller figures perhaps
than one would expect from the metaphor of Britain as a nation of steam
and steel, but nonetheless large. Coal became a major export during the
century because industry and transport demanded fuel as they had not
before, and Britain was well placed to supply it, earning thereby 10 per cent
of all her exports. These 'old' industries of the industrial revolution –
textiles, iron and steel, and coal – earned two-thirds of the revenue from
the exports of commodities, and themselves squarely faced the outside
world. Foreigners purchased 80 per cent of the cotton textiles made in
Britain, about half the iron and steel, and a third of the coal. With such
exports of manufacturing commodities, not forgetting the growing exports
of services, Britain was fed. Of the £530 million worth of domestic
commodity exports in 1913, nearly 80 per cent were, in the language of the
Trade and Navigation Accounts, 'Articles Wholly or Mainly Manu-

Table 12.1. *Approximate proportions of imports in domestic consumption of food and raw materials, 1913 (%)*

Food	
Wheat	80
Meat	45
Dairy products	45
Raw materials	
Raw cotton	100
Raw wool	80
Iron ore	60
Tin	90
Lead	90
Copper	100

factures'. Of the £660 million worth of retained commodity imports, only 25 per cent were manufactured articles that Britain did not make as well as others did, 33 per cent were raw materials to make manufactures and the rest, fully 42 per cent, were food. By means of foreign trade, in other words, Britain produced far more manufactures than it consumed and consumed far more food than it produced. As Clapham put it, 'The countries which fed, or nearly fed, themselves all had a much more even balance of agriculture with manufactures and commerce. A balance – or lack of balance – such as that in Britain had not been known before in the record of great nations' (Clapham 1938: 2).

Furthermore, Britain bulked so large in the trade of the world that events in Britain affecting her trade, such as the move to free trade in the middle decades of the century or the alleged failure of entrepreneurship at its end, might be expected to react on the British economy for good or evil with special force. That Britain was the pivot of international trade in the nineteenth century is apparent in the statistics of world trade in manufactures. In the decade 1876–85, the earliest dates for which usable statistics on the matter are available, Britain's exports of manufactured goods were about 38 per cent of the world's total, and in earlier years the share had no doubt been larger (Hilgerdt 1945: 157–8). By 1899 her share had fallen, but was still about 33 per cent of the exports of manufactured goods from the industrial countries (western Europe, Canada, the United States and Japan) and India (Maizels 1963: 430–1). This position of dominance was unique in modern economic history, approached but not equalled only by the United States whose share in the manufactured exports of the industrial countries and India in the seven years of Maizels' statistics (1899, 1913, 1929, 1937, 1950, 1955 and 1957) reached its peak –

only 27 per cent – in 1950. Only after the First World War did the United States exceed Britain in exports of all kinds (with American wheat and British coal included in the accounting) and only after the Second World War in total exports of manufactures (Maizels 1963; and pp. 10–11 in his 'Corrections').

Why Britain did not 'depend' on trade

Britain and the world, then, appear to have been mutually dependent. But 'dependent' suggests that removing foreign trade would have impoverished Britain. In particular, statistics of 'dependence' suggest that removing trade would have cut national income by 25 or 30 per cent and would have cut British wheat consumption (for example) by 80 per cent – after all, these were the shares of foreign supplies in national income and in wheat consumption. The volume of a trade, however, is a poor guide to how much the economy's prosperity depends on it. You may hire a professional house painter to paint your house, but were you denied his services you would not lose all their value. You would paint your house yourself, or instead of having a painted house spend the resources on an alternate project. A Britain denied imports of wheat, similarly, would grow its own, albeit at greater expense than wheat from the fertile plains of Illinois or the Ukraine, or would shift resources to other, home-grown foods. The loss to British happiness would not be the whole value of the wheat imported.

The reasoning here is characteristically economic, focussing as it does on the alternatives to acquiring imports by trade (McCloskey 1981a: ch. 7). The more usual reasoning is non-economic, making exports, not imports, the things-to-be-desired. One hears it said, for example, that Britain had to import corn and timber and wine in order to give foreigners the wherewithal to buy British. A person or nation fully employed, however, yearns to acquire goods, not to get rid of them. Exports are an unfortunate sacrifice that people or nations must make to acquire imports for consumption. As Adam Smith remarked in his attack on the mercantilist doctrine that an excess of exports over imports should be the goal of policy, 'Consumption is the sole end of and purpose of all production ... The maxim is so perfectly self-evident, that it would be absurd to attempt to prove it' (Smith 1776: 625). If Britain's foreign trade can (as it must) be viewed as a way of acquiring imports, then the question of the extent of British dependence on trade reduces to a question of how well Britain would have done had this way to imports been blocked.

The answer has little significance in itself, for no historical issue turns on the literal abandonment of British foreign trade. Finding it, however, is

Table 12.2. *The terms of trade, 1820–1910* (*1860 = 100*)

1820	170
1840	130
1860	100
1880	110
1900	130
1910	130

useful as background to more modest experiments in counterfactuals and as a check on exaggerated opinions of Britain's dependence on trade. The answer proceeds as follows. Foreign trade can be viewed as an industry producing imports, say wheat, in exchange for sacrifices of exports, say cotton cloth. The 'productivity' of this industry is the rate at which quarters of wheat exchange for yards of cloth, i.e. the 'terms of trade'. The price of Britain's exports of cotton cloth, iron, coal, shipping services and so forth divided by the price of imports of wheat, lumber, tobacco, raw cotton and so forth is the terms of trade, and has the same relevance for British welfare as does a person's real wages. The money wage for an hour of work (exports) divided by the price of what is consumed (imports) is the real wage, i.e. the physical amounts of consumable goods that an hour of work buys. The terms of trade show the amount of imports a unit of exports can buy. The effect on national income of a change in the productivity of Britain's foreign trade (the terms of trade) depends on the importance of the foreign trade 'industry' relative to other, domestic industries. That is, it depends on the ratio of exports (or imports) to national income, which rose from about 0.12 early in the century to about 0.30 by its end. If the terms of trade rose by 10 per cent, therefore, national income would rise on this account by ((10 per cent) × (0.12)), or 1.2 per cent.

This matter of concept settled, the remaining question is the counter-factual one of how much in fact the terms of trade would have moved had Britain insisted on growing all its own wheat, and by the same token consuming all its own cotton cloth. Clearly the price of now-abundant exportables like cloth would have fallen relative to the price of now-scarce importables like wheat. In other words, the terms of trade would have deteriorated. How much? Since no such event occurred we cannot answer this question precisely but the actual course of the terms of trade over the nineteenth century, shown in Table 12.2, gives some guidance. The massive fall from 170 in 1820 to 100 in 1860 was a consequence of Britain's own ingenuity in making exported cotton cloth cheaper and of the push of population in Europe against supplies of grain. The (smaller) rise thereafter was a consequence of the full application of steam and steel to the making and especially to the shipping of imports to Britain. In view of these 70 or 30 per cent rises and falls in the terms of trade we might suppose that the change in the terms of trade for self-sufficiency in say, 1860, was not much lower or higher.

But where exactly is difficult to say. Not much of a rise in the price of German toys relative to British clocks, perhaps 10 per cent, would have been necessary to stop shipments of either into or out of Britain. But quite a large rise would have been necessary to stop wheat and raw cotton coming in or textiles going out, so powerful in these goods were the forces of specialisation. A tariff of fully 40 per cent was necessary to stop foreign corn from entering Britain in years of good harvest under the Corn Laws. A doubling of the price of cotton cloth exports during the cotton famine caused by the American Civil War abated demand by only a third, although the experiment is inconclusive because the prices of Britain's competitors in this market went up as well. As an illustration we may consider that a prohibition of trade might have reduced the price of exportables relative to importables by, say, 50 per cent. The share of imports in income to multiply the 50 per cent would be half the way from zero, under the prohibition, to the 25 per cent that actually occurred in 1860. Self-sufficiency in 1860, then, would have cost Britain only $((50 \text{ per cent}) \times (0.125))$, or about 6 per cent of national income.

This figure of 6 per cent of national income – or even, if the terms of trade effect were twice as great, 12 per cent – looks small beside the bold metaphor of Britain's 'dependence' on foreign trade. Indeed, the calculation is worthwhile only to loosen the grip of the metaphor (for other attempts see Kravis 1970, 1973; Crafts 1973). The gains from trade increased as British population grew and limited agricultural resources strengthened the comparative disadvantage in food production but the conclusion remains that even on the absurd premise of no foreign trade at all Britain would have survived. True, had Britain suddenly been denied all trade by strike or edict, the immediate effects would have been larger (Crouzet 1958 and 1964; Olson 1963). The experiment relevant to all the history of this period except times of war and blockade, however, is not a sudden denial of trade but a failure of it to grow over the long term, because it is precisely the steady and rapid growth over the long peace of 1815 to 1914 that has led people to attribute to foreign trade great powers for good.

Circumstances can be imagined that would have increased trade power for good even in the long run, but the empirical impact of these possibilities was probably small. Both traditional historical narratives and some modern analytical models have placed considerable emphasis on learning-by-doing as an important source of technological change and hence growth (Helpman and Krugman 1985; ch. 11 above). However, trade implies not only that some industries grow relative to the size they would have been without trade but also that some become smaller. Therefore a net gain in technological progress requires that the gains from learning in the expanding industries exceed the losses from failing to learn in the industries from which resources are drawn. British exporting industries would have been large even if they had not captured export markets and there is no evidence that the expansion from trade contributed learning that would not have occurred in somewhat smaller industries. Expanding trade could also have increased growth if by chance the people enriched by the extension of foreign trade, such as coal owners and cotton manufacturers, saved or invested more than the people impoverished by the trade, such as timber owners and silk manufacturers. But there is no persuasive evidence that the chances especially favoured saving. Britain was left with, say, its 6 per cent – no trivial sum, to be sure, but, measured against the whole rise in output per worker of roughly 80 per cent from 1855 to 1913, only one thirteenth of the story.

Industrial revolution and trade

A visitor approaching Manchester in 1842 – 'the lowest ebb' of trade depression – to hear the anti-Corn Law agitators might be excused for failing to appreciate the subtleties of the economists' argument about alternatives and opportunity costs. Here before him, beneath clouds of smoke from factory chimneys, lay a phenomenon – threatening or promising depending on his beliefs – that had not existed when he was a boy: the great industrial city, much smaller than London, to be sure, but of quite different character with factories and proletariat and the absence of traditional establishments. Manchester was home to new industry, created by foreign trade and the technology of Arkwright, Crompton and Watt. Nearly two of every three pounds of yarn and yards of cloth which left the factory doors were destined for export; all the raw cotton came off ships in Liverpool. This city, so dependent on trade (and Liverpool, Glasgow and Birmingham like it) shook the foundations of Britain's aristocratic society. Its factory-owning middle class, with growing economic power, had already forced reform on Parliament, and now agitated for free trade; their employees, the new 'proletariat', raised more radical demands in the People's Charter – manhood suffrage, secret ballot, equal electoral districts, abolition of property qualifications for MPs, payment for MPs and annual Parliaments. Trade might not have greatly increased per capita income but it had created the cities and classes that challenged the aristocratic establishment that had ruled from time immemorial.

The British industrial revolution was not a widespread transformation of industrial technology but one of great innovations in a few industries. Cotton, iron and engineering's spectacular growth affected too little of Britain's economic activity to accelerate overall growth greatly, but technological advance gave these industries tremendous international comparative advantage (Crafts 1989a). Arkwright's, Hargreaves' and Crompton's inventions revolutionised the spinning of cotton; in 1812 medium-grade cotton yarn (40 count) could be spun for a sixth of what it had cost in 1779, despite wartime inflation that had doubled prices generally. British cotton spinners rapidly exploited export opportunities. They could sell to foreigners at low cost and they could attract labour to expand. Spinning mills, freed from rural water power by Watt's engine and concentrated in favoured locations, brought workers to new tasks and their families to new homes. The concentrations of cotton factories grew rapidly as exports expanded and weaving joined spinning in the factories. The factories created industrial urbanisation in Lancashire and in the western Scottish Lowlands (Ellison 1886: 55–60).

During the first decades of Victoria's reign, British firms dominated the world's modern industry and many contemporaries, and historians after them, talked of a British monopoly. Bairoch (1982: 288–97) has calculated that in the middle third of the nineteenth century Britain produced some two-thirds of the world's output of 'new technology' products. But despite Britain's dominance there was no monopoly. Firms entered the British cotton industry easily and had to sell in competitive markets; they were unable to prevent price from falling to the cost of production. The benefits of technological change passed to consumers in lower prices; the foreign two-thirds of cotton textile customers shared the benefits. The competitive structure of the cotton textile industry meant that the British – but not the world – gained little from the rapidly growing exports of British cloth. Had the British industry been able to act as a monopolist in its foreign sales and to sell at a higher price, Britain would have benefited more.

Britain exported cottons to obtain raw materials and food-stuffs. In the twenty-five years after the Napoleonic Wars, technological change nearly halved the expenses of capital and labour needed to spin and weave a piece of cotton cloth in Lancashire. Competitive pressure drove textile prices down; in 1840 an exported piece of cloth could purchase only half the foreign food it had commanded at war's end (Imlah 1958). The technological change that caused British industry to grow also caused deterioration in its terms of trade. Because price changes transferred the benefits of technological change to foreign consumers, conventional

Table 12.3. *Cotton textile production and consumption: the effects of the terms of trade, 1815–41*

	Index of quantities produced (textile production 1815 = 100)		Index of prices (1815 = 1·0)	
	1815	1841	1815	1841
Output	100	520	1·0	0·5
Raw cotton	25	160		
Consumption:				
Cotton	40	210	1·0	0·5
Imports	35	75	1·0	1·0
Aggregate consumption (output 1815 = 100):			Index of consumption (consumption 1815 = 100):	
1815 prices	75	285	100	378
1841 prices	55	180	100	324

aggregation of national income overstates the benefits to Britain of the cotton industry's growth.

Calculations in Table 12.3 illustrate the orders of magnitude involved. In 1841 Britain produced 5.2 times the amount of cotton textiles it had produced in 1815. About 60 per cent of output was exported in both years. Think of these exports as first paying for the industry's imported raw cotton and the remaining revenue purchasing other imports for consumption. In 1815, the raw cotton imports cost about a quarter of the total industry output; in 1841 the proportion was somewhat higher at 31 per cent. About 35 per cent (60 per cent minus 25) of the output in 1815 was exported for foreign consumption goods. In 1841 about 29 per cent of output was exchanged for such consumption goods – 4.3 times as many textiles as in 1815. But a given piece of cotton cloth could now purchase only half as many imports. The quantity of cotton produced increased over fivefold, but the consumption (British consumed cotton goods and imports) it provided increased less than fourfold. The growth of exports increased the industry's size and social impact but had a modest impact on national income.

Repeal of the Corn Laws

The British political consensus shifted radically in the middle of the nineteenth century from supporting a trade policy designed to protect vital interests – particularly the landed interest – to a commitment to free trade.

On 26 June 1846, Parliament repealed the Corn Laws. Repeal of the Corn Laws presents something of a paradox. British tariffs were lowered only slightly and the ratio of tariff revenue to the value of imports remained higher than it did in France until the 1870s (Nye, 1991: 25–31). More importantly, however, the politics of repeal completely changed the politics of tariffs in Britain. 'Free trade' – which meant forswearing the use of tariffs to protect domestic interests although retaining revenue tariffs – took on a nearly constitutional status that removed the possibility of imposing protective tariffs from usual political discussion. Britain's leaders changed policy in response to various forces: industrialisation and urbanisation altered British society; growing population, both in Britain and elsewhere, changed the economics of the grain market (Fairlie 1965, 1969); the Reform Act of 1832 altered the politics; agitation outside of Parliament became more effective; economic crises demanded action from the administration.

The late eighteenth-century tariff was an almost incomprehensible amalgam of statutes from an age in which 'the British parliament seems rarely to rise to the dignity of a general proposition' (Maitland 1910/11: IX, 605). Two separate principles motivated the various customs duties, bounties and prohibitions; either they protected domestic interests or they provided revenue for the state, and occasionally they achieved both. Agriculture – the great interest of the aristocratic classes that ran the state – received aid through export bounties at times of low domestic price and duties that protected from cheap imports. The customs protected British textile manufacturers from Irish linen and Indian cotton, iron masters from cheap Swedish iron and much else. But not all customs duties were prohibitive; duties had long been the principal source of government revenue. Duties on spirits, tobacco, tea and sugar complemented similar excise taxes to finance government operation. The move to free trade is no exception to the historiographical rule that examination of the roots of great events smooths historical discontinuities. Ideological preparation for free trade can be traced back at least to the appearance of *The Wealth of Nations*. Administrators in the 1780s tentatively began simplifying and rationalising the customs without changing its basic philosophy.

The Napoleonic Wars interrupted these stirrings of rational tariff policy. To fight the French, the government taxed and retaxed every commodity and transaction within reach, from dogs and attorneys to incomes and imports. The income tax – 'the oppressive and inquisitorial tax' to contemporaries – was repealed with the peace. Other war taxes remained to pay the debt incurred in financing the war (over half the budget down to the 1850s). In 1820, Sydney Smith could write, after five years of peace, that 'the dying Englishman, pouring his medicine, which has paid 7 per cent, into a spoon that has paid 15 per cent, flings himself back upon his chintz bed which has paid 22 per cent, and expires in the arms of an apothecary who has paid a license of a hundred pounds for the privilege of putting him to death' (Smith 1820).

Protection of interests as well as revenue continued to shape tariff policy. Parliament reacted to sharp declines in grain prices following the Napoleonic Wars with new protective Corn Laws. High wartime duties on timber had both raised revenue and, through strong discrimination in favour of Empire timber, promoted a Canadian timber industry which now became a new interest to be protected. Policies to protect established interests generally recommended themselves to Britain's aristocratic political elite; they had been badly frightened by revolution in France.

Rationalisation of the tariff structure resumed in Huskisson's budgets of 1824 and 1825: obsolete duties on imports of manufactures such as cotton textiles and iron (in which Britain had now established crushing comparative advantage) were repealed; some duties on raw materials were reduced; many export bounties were abolished; and most prohibitions, except those on certain agricultural products, were abolished. The goal was Benthamite rationalisation rather than reduction – who could quarrel with removal of contradictory or inoperative duties? Tariff revenue could be collected more efficiently even without a fundamental change in commercial policy. Even this modest programme was far from complete in 1840 (Clapham 1910); on the eve of the move to free trade the tariff remained complex and consciously protective of British interests. The tariff contained prohibitions on imports of live or dead meat, duties on 'slave-grown' sugar two or more times higher than those on sugar from British colonies, drawbacks on timber for use in the mines of Cornwall or in churches, eighty-odd different specifications of skins – from badger to weasel – with associated duties, export duties on coal and wool, and over 2,000 import duties on items ranging from agates to zebra wood. As sources of revenue many duties were superfluous; 17 of 721 articles in the tariff schedule produced 94.5 per cent of the tariff revenue (Great Britain Parliamentary Papers 1840: 102).

Despite its bewildering detail, the tariff had two clear aims: it raised revenue and it protected land-intensive products, these being in any case the dominant products of importation. In other words, the categories of the simple theory of trade – importables, exportables and non-traded goods – corresponded well in Victorian Britain to agriculture (including some mining), manufacturing and the residual sector, services. A few manufacturing industries, notably silk, still received substantial protection but for most protection would have been superfluous. Indeed, by 1840 manufacturing received a slightly negative rate of effective protection. As free traders pointed out, Britain's exports of manufactures contained raw materials made more expensive by tariff, whether for revenue on warm-climate raw materials such as raw cotton, for the good of the empire and its landowners on cold-climate materials such as timber, or for the protection of British rents on metals such as copper and tin ore. The British tariff in the early 1840s raised the price of land-intensive raw materials and food relative to manufactures and services. A tariff designed by committees of landlords in Parliament and imposed on the imports of a nation which required little but raw materials and food from the rest of the world could hardly be expected to be otherwise.

Political and economic events brought the tariff to the forefront of parliamentary concern in the early 1840s. Severe economic recession in the late 1830s created extensive distress in the manufacturing districts and, by curtailing revenue from customs and excises, brought a crisis in government finance. The years of distress bred powerful political challenges, mainly outside Parliament, to the Corn Laws which were characterised as a particularly iniquitous tax for the benefit of the rich on the food of the poor. Anti-Corn Law agitation by lower-class Chartists and the middle-class Anti-Corn Law League threatened the existing order. When the Whig government failed to master the situation in 1842 and fell, the electorate returned a Tory administration headed by Sir Robert Peel. In his first budget in 1842 Peel acted decisively to strengthen government finance and unexpectedly reintroduced the income tax. Revenue from the income tax permitted tariff reform; the Corn Laws and the timber duties were modified. Return of prosperity increased revenue and Peel undertook further tariff reform in 1845 – including the removal of the import tax on raw cotton and the reduction of the sugar duties.

Peel was already moving toward the removal of agricultural protection. Distress among the manufacturing workers in the early 1840s had convinced him personally that protection of the agricultural interests with tariffs on food was both morally wrong and politically unsustainable in the long run; the majority of his Tory party, however, remained committed to protection. In the autumn of 1845 bad weather, which seriously damaged the grain harvest and spread potato blight throughout northern Europe, forced action on Peel's government. It became apparent that the potato blight would bring famine to Ireland in the new year. Customary response to famine was temporary suspension of the Corn Laws, but the Cabinet agreed that the situation in the country would make subsequent restoration of the Corn Laws impossible. The government, with Peel and most of his closest associates advocating immediate repeal but unable to convince their fellows, split and resigned, only to resume office when the opposition Whigs failed to form a government. Peel then brought repeal before

Parliament in the face of opposition from most of his party, securing its passage with the support of the Opposition (Gash 1986: chs. 9, 10, 15, 16).

Peel, having split his party, was defeated in the Commons on the night repeal passed the Lords, but the political climate had decisively changed. Gash, Peel's recent biographer, sums up the great political impact of repeal (1986: 714):

It is easy now to see how contemporary opinion exaggerated the effects, both baneful and beneficial, of the repeal of the Corn Laws. But the significance of the action taken by Peel in 1846 was symbolic; and as a symbol it was rivalled only by the Reform Act of 1832 as the decisive event in domestic politics in the first half of the nineteenth century. The Reform Act had been a gesture of deference to public opinion and the enhanced stature of new political classes. After 1832 the aristocracy continued to govern the country but it governed on trust. In that situation there were two dangers that might have destroyed the good effects of reform. One was that the aristocracy might be unable to carry out its trust for lack of internal cohesion; the other that it would fail to recognise the terms of its trusteeship. By 1845 the Corn Laws had been elevated in the public mind into a test of governmental integrity. Peel's response and the sacrifice it entailed did more than anything else to heal the social breach and restore public confidence in the good faith of a system which was still essentially oligarchic.

As early as 1849 Benjamin Disraeli, who emerged as the Commons leader of the protectionist majority of the Tory party that had split from Peel, recognised that the reimposition of protection would subject the established order – the Tory's overwhelming concern – to savage and perhaps fatal popular attack (Blake 1966: 278–84). On the other side of the House, Whigs, Radicals and Peelites, despite their many differences, unitedly opposed protectionism.

Repeal did not completely end protection. The British government continued to raise a large portion of its revenue from import duties on consumption goods. Nonetheless, the principle of removing protective tariffs had been achieved and only consolidation remained. The Navigation Acts were repealed in 1849. In 1853, William Gladstone – a leading Peelite, now Chancellor of the Exchequer in a Whig–Peelite government – continued the income tax, but with the intention of eliminating it in 1860, introduced a succession duty and further reformed the customs. Most protection had now been removed. When war against Russia in the Crimea loomed the following year – with financial requirements that might have provided an excuse for the reimposition of protection – Gladstone doubled the income tax and increased the excise and duties on malt and spirits, but did not consider protectionist duties. Gladstone's 1860 budget, and the associated Cobden–Chevalier Treaty with France, removed the last vestiges of the protective system – duties on some 400 articles, but only

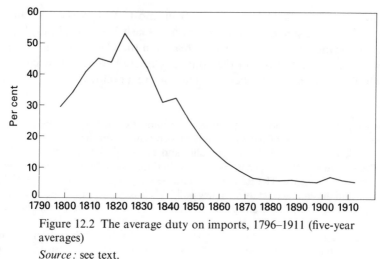

Figure 12.2 The average duty on imports, 1796–1911 (five-year averages)

Source: see text.

those on silk manufacture, and leather boots and gloves were of much significance. Although small 'registration duties' remained on grain imports, the British customs had been transformed from its Byzantine eighteenth-century structure to revenue duties on a little more than a dozen imports. Tariffs on sugar (complicated by West Indian interests and Brazilian slavery and finally removed in 1874), tea and coffee, spirits, wine and tobacco remained – important in a tax system that included comparable excise taxes on domestic production. These duties, as the French in particular pointed out particularly with respect to wine, continued to distort trade and protect some British interests (Nye 1991), but return to old-style protection was politically precluded in Britain for two generations.

The tariff in the early 1840s had bulked large in British economic and political life. Duties were high and imports were substantial in relation to national income. Tariff revenues financed much of government. The height of the tariff and its changes may be measured by the ratio of tariff revenues to the value of imports (see Figure 12.2). In 1841, import duties equalled 35 per cent of the value of imports; in 1881 duties had fallen to only 6 per cent of the value of imports. The change in political direction under Peel contributed only modestly to this decline. Most revenue before 1846 came from the duties on sugar, spirits and wine, tea and coffee, and tobacco (in 1840 these items accounted for three-quarters of tariff revenue) which remained in the tariff structure after repeal ('that the labouring classes should bear their share of the burden in a form in which it will be palpable and intelligible to them', as Gladstone said in presenting his 1860 budget).

Much of the decline in tariffs between 1841 and 1881 occurred because government expenditure declined from 9 per cent of income to 6 per cent of income and imports rose from 12 per cent of income to 30 per cent of income (in part due to falling tariffs). Import duties could have fallen to about 9 per cent of imports and still have provided the same share of government revenue. New tax sources – primarily the income tax and the estate duties – provided a bit over a fifth of revenue and a shift of tax burden from customs duties to excise taxes lowered customs duties to 6 per cent of the value of imports (McCloskey 1980: 309–13).

The first effect of free trade is obvious in view of the weight of protection which the tariff gave to land-intensive goods. By abandoning high tariffs British landlords lost income relative to their countrymen. Political argument at the time took it as axiomatic that what landlords lost the workers would gain, because protection of British corn producers was a tax on the mainstay of the workers' diet. In the event the real wages of workers did rise sharply after the 1840s but real rents of landlords did not fall until a generation or more later. Neither event is strictly relevant, for history was not a controlled experiment in which all factors except tariffs were held constant. It is unlikely that a controlled experiment would have produced the symmetry which contemporaries expected between the incomes of landlords and workers, because they were not in fact symmetrically located in the British economy.

Removal of tariffs affected both the prices of goods and the incomes of labourers, capitalists and landlords. Landlords were located, of course, in agriculture and their incomes would fall. But workers were located everywhere: in the very agriculture made worse off by the fall of protection, in manufacturing made better off, and what is most important in the vast sector of goods and (especially) services that did not cross Britain's borders on their way from producer to consumer. Workers were not committed to one vulnerable sector. Most of the distributional consequences of the fall of protection were to shift income from wealthy landlords committed to agriculture to wealthy capitalists committed to manufacturing, and even this was no dramatic amount.

Contemporary critics of the Corn Laws, and later historians, viewed agricultural protection as a tax on food and saw its impact working not primarily through incomes but through the cost of living (Williamson 1990b). Certainly the Corn Laws were intended to keep the price of grain high. Since the poorest classes spent a much larger proportion of their income on bread than did the richer classes this had a considerable distributional impact. The poorest two-fifths of society spent nearly half their income on grain-based food, the next two-fifths of the income distribution spent only about half that proportion while the very rich spent only a negligible portion of their income on grain. Williamson estimated the extent of the income redistribution that this entailed; the higher prices of corn around 1830 probably decreased real wages of unskilled workers by between 12 (if allowance is made for a deterioration of Britain's terms of trade as a result of tariff reduction – see below) and 24 per cent (Williamson 1990b: 143). These calculations are uncertain; in particular, Williamson probably overestimated the extent to which grain prices would have declined with removal of the Corn Laws by not perceiving that grain prices in the Baltic export ports would have had to rise to attract grain from more distant areas in Byelorussia and the Ukraine. But the distributional impact of the tax on food remains considerable.

The tariff also affected the size of national income. Even the direction of this effect, however, is in doubt, although free traders past and present have had no doubts whatever. Surely a man is made worse off if he artificially restricts his dealings with the rest of the world. So too, they argued for the nation. British landlords may be made better off by a tariff on corn, but because the nation as a whole must be worse off with less access to corn the worsening of the rest of the nation is necessarily larger. The argument implies that every extension of British trade, and therefore every reduction in tariffs, was good for Britain (Habakkuk 1940). The argument is flawed. Just as a monopolist can raise his income by withholding some of what he sells from the market, so can a country. As we have seen, Britain attained technological leadership in cotton textiles, iron and machinery during the industrial revolution. Competition among small firms ensured that the benefits of technology lowered the prices that consumers (many of whom were foreigners) paid rather than increasing the profits of the firms. The tariffs of the early nineteenth century provided some monopoly advantage because they in effect restricted British willingness to accept foreign goods for new industrial goods. Since Britain was the dominant source of supply of these goods and the main buyer of many foreigners' exports, foreigners faced with the tariff received less cloth and iron for their exports. British terms of trade were better than they would have been without tariffs. Britain had a unique position of monopoly at mid-century, which by abandoning protection it magnanimously scorned to exploit. Paradoxically, it was only at the end of the century when monopoly was gone forever that protection began to recover its political appeal. In the time of greatest enthusiasm for free trade the usual argument is probably the reverse of the truth. The move toward free trade in the 1840s and 1850s may have hurt Britain.

The hurt was not large. At the extreme Britain's monopoly was so powerful that the tariff of 1841 pushed the world price of British exports relative to British imports up by the full extent of the tariff. That is, a tariff of 29 per cent on the free trade price of wheat could at most lower the world price of wheat by 29 per cent (29 per cent is the difference between the actual tariffs in 1841 and 1881), which is to say it could have raised the relative price of British exports by 29 per cent. By a familiar line of reasoning, then, the hurt could have been at most this reduction multiplied by the share of imports in national income, which was 30 per cent at most. The hurt was at most, then, 29 per cent multiplied by 30 per cent, or about 9 per cent (McCloskey 1980). As recent calculations show this is a gross exaggeration and the small gift to the rest of the world could easily have been offset by the positive effects which the British repeal of the Corn Laws had on freeing trade elsewhere (Irwin 1988). Free trade may also have had offsetting benefits, such as the reaping of economies of scale in export industries, the employment of pools of unemployed labour or a raise in the savings rate consequent on redistribution. That none of these left clear evidence in the historical record is merely testimony to the small size, whether positive or negative, of the effects of free trade on income (cf. Church 1975a: 59–65). The exact effect of the move to free trade is uncertain but we must conclude that accumulation and productivity at home, not free trade, were the key to mid-Victorian prosperity.

Although repeal had a modest impact on the growth of British national income, Britain's political commitment to free trade conditioned the evolution of the international economy for more than half a century. Disraeli and the Conservatives – representatives of the protectionist landowning interests – accepted Peel's premise that free trade was necessary to protect their primary interest in the established aristocratic order. Gladstone and the Liberals found free trade ideologically attractive and suited to the interests of their supporters. Free trade remained unchallenged until Joseph Chamberlain launched his campaign for Tariff Reform in 1903, only to be decisively rejected by the electorate in 1906. Britain's commitment was unusual; the United States remained highly protectionist. On the European Continent, the Dutch were committed to free trade earlier than Britain and remained staunchly so but elsewhere a brief period of free trade which was adopted in a period of enthusiasm that began with the 1860 Cobden–Chevalier Treaty between Britain and France soon gave way to renewed protection in the late 1870s when imports threatened domestic interests (Bairoch, 1989).

Britain's unwavering free trade supported expansion of world trade for over half a century. New regions on the periphery of the European economy, made attractive by transportation developments and drawing settlement, could depend on open access to the world's greatest import market. The assured market increased the attractiveness of these regions to European capital and labour. In addition, Britain's forswearing of the use of tariffs to protect domestic interests probably aided the relatively smooth working of the late nineteenth-century gold standard. In contrast to the 1930s when governments rushed to protect domestic interests with tariffs and accelerated the descent into the Great Depression, the British steadfastly allowed markets to work, with apparent success.

Exports as an engine of decline

Britain's growth to international prominence in the industrial revolution did not depend on foreign trade and it is equally hard to blame Britain's relative decline after 1870 on foreign trade. Yet the belief is widespread. The rate of growth of industrial production and of income in Britain declined about the same time as the growth of exports declined; Britain's growth on all scores was slower than that of her 'rivals' (as Germany and the United States came increasingly to be called). These two observations have led many to suggest that the one decline in exports caused the other decline in income and industry. In the 1890s especially the editorial pages and parliamentary debates spoke of 'defeat' in a German commercial 'invasion', or of the 'conquest' by Americans of another 'outpost' of British exports (Hoffman 1933). The military metaphors have proved to be irresistible to later students of the matter, the more so as the less colourful testimony of the statistics of foreign trade seem to agree. Suggestive though it is, that growth at home followed exports abroad does not mean that exports caused growth (nor, as we shall see in the next section, that growth caused exports). The brute fact is not enough.

The seemingly common sense notion that demand caused growth has been reinforced by the theoretical notion of simple Keynesian income analysis that the level of demand determines the level of national income. The Keynesian interpretation of the facts depends on the British economy not being fully employed at the successive peaks of boom and bust in the late nineteenth century. In a fully employed economy an increase in demand for, say, exported cloth does increase the output of cloth, but only by reducing the output of another, domestic commodity. In the language of economics, in such an economy there are opportunity costs, or colloquially, there is no such thing as a free lunch. An increase in demand for exports can cause little increase in total output, merely a reallocation of resources and a restructuring of output. Under such a constraint, as we have seen repeatedly, events in the international sector have modest influence on the size of national income. The present case is no exception. If the late Victorian economy was fully employed it is no trick at all to show that the 'defeat' at the hands of Germans and Americans in export markets was a trivial cause of slower British growth (McCloskey 1970–1).

If the economy was not fully employed, however, an increase in export demand would have increased the nation's income not only directly, by setting men and machines to work in making ships and coal and machinery for export, but also indirectly, by setting men and machines to work making steel for the shipyards and pit props for the collieries and machine tools for the machine shops, as well as food, housing, transport and so forth for the men now earning and spending incomes. Buoyant export demand gave the economy a free lunch; sagging export demand took it away. The assumption of less than full employment is well suited to the understanding of an economy coming out of bust and moving into a boom, for it is plain in such a case that new workers are indeed being drawn out of involuntary idleness as the economy expands. It is doubtful that the assumption helps to understand growth between peaks of the cycle of boom and bust (Matthews 1954: 74).

Doubts on this score have not deterred students of the late Victorian economy, especially economists (Rostow 1948; Coppock 1961), from trying it on. Meyer (1955), for example, noted the sequence of the deceleration of exports and of industrial production, and asked whether maintaining the mid-Victorian growth rate of exports would have maintained the growth rate of industry in late Victorian Britain. Generalising the notion that ships for exports require steel, which requires coal, which requires pit props, and so forth, in a gradually diminishing ripple throughout the economy, Meyer constructed a so-called 'input–output table' from the First (1907) British Census of Production to measure the indirect effects of greater exports. He found them to be large. But the conclusion is unacceptable, on several minor technical matters that need not detain us, and on one major substantive matter. The substantive matter is that the Meyer exercise, like others less explicit in their assumptions, assumes without evidence that the economy was not fully employed. As McCloskey argued (1970) the evidence suggests otherwise; there were simply no large reserves of unemployed resources that could have been set to work if exports had been larger. The limits on the late Victorian economy, in other words, were limits of supply.

The argument linking export deceleration with late Victorian decline has not depended exclusively on the existence of unemployed resources. More promising theoretical connections between exports and growth lead to an exploration of ways in which Britain's international transactions may have limited the capacity of the domestic economy. Some have argued that sluggish markets for exports reduced the scope for investment in export industries at home and drove British savings (already low by international standards) overseas, to Indian railways or Brazilian plantations. It is said that the private returns from such reallocation of resources were satisfactory, but the social return was not (Coppock 1956: 2; Kennedy, 1987). Even if this last is true, however, it does not follow that the effects of misallocating savings were large. In the article critical of Meyer, McCloskey also examined these alternative links in the chain from exports to economic growth in Britain and found them weak. His arguments have been criticised by Kennedy (1974, 1987: chs. 2 and 3), who contends that he underestimated the effect of reallocating savings and the labour force in response to more buoyant export demand, and by Crafts (1979), who contends that he underestimated the effect on capital formation of bringing savings home. Kennedy, however, based his argument on an untenable calculation of the gains from reallocating British production (McCloskey 1981a: 119–25; Harley 1989) while Crafts assumed that relatively low-risk foreign investment if invested at home would earn the return to riskier domestic investments (McCloskey 1980).

In an important study of British long-term growth, Matthews, Feinstein and Odling-Smee presented a demand-influenced view of growth that included an opinion that slower export growth seriously hurt late nineteenth-century growth (1982: 445–65). They concluded that, although unemployment did not increase, the slower growth of exports depressed British activity, encouraging disguised unemployment and, most importantly, slowing growth of total factor productivity. They presented no direct evidence for this conclusion but appealed to a supposition (the 'Verdoorn Law') that total factor productivity growth is caused by output growth in manufacturing.

The conclusion, however, can hardly be regarded as established. The Verdoorn proposition is by no means generally accepted and the slowdown in exports and manufacturing growth which Matthews et al. document occurred almost exclusively in textiles, where they felt there was little scope for total factor productivity growth. The counterfactual of faster growth of manufacturing exports and a continuing increase in the share of British income in manufacturing seems improbable. Britain's share of world manufacturing at the middle of the nineteenth century was uniquely high and could only have been expected to decline. Britain's manufacturing sector already employed modern proportions of the economy's resources by the mid-nineteenth century and continued increase in its share was improbable. Modern economic growth inevitably involves readjustment of the output mix in response to changing technology and demand; and the late nineteenth century seems little different from other periods. While it is conceivable that particular adjustments hampered growth, a simple connection of exports to income is untenable. In short, 'it is implausible ... to draw the lines of causation in late Victorian England from export demand to the output of the economy' (McCloskey 1970: 459).

Foreign trade: evidence of decline or response to opportunities?

Foreign trade, then, does not appear to have been an engine of growth and decline. It was, nonetheless, an important fact about the British economy, a large sector among a few illustrating the economy's strengths and weaknesses in plain form. The illustrative role of foreign trade in writings on British history is largest at the end of the nineteenth century, when its share in national income was largest.

In every year after 1822 the value of Britain's commodity imports exceeded the value of commodity exports. Both contemporaries and historians became aware that the growing deficit in commodity trade was more than covered by receipts from the international sale of shipping, commercial and financial services, and by the interest and dividends from foreign assets (see Figure 12.1). In fact there was a substantial overall surplus from these receipts to finance foreign lending.

Many, however, have seen the slow growth of commodity exports and the rapid growth of imports after mid-century as evidence of a competitive failure in Britain. Many studies of British industries have focussed on the emergence of a foreign challenge in the late nineteenth century and the inability to maintain competitive positions in export markets. Mathias (1983: 289) summarised the prevailing view:

> The conclusion to be drawn from Britain's accounts with the rest of the world in 1913 is to see to what a great extent the economy was being protected, or cushioned from the failure of exports to pay for imports, by the £4,000 million of capital invested abroad ... Even quite a marked degree of failure in the competitive standards of some British export industries might be tolerated without much strain, as long as the £200 million came in interest each year.

It is inappropriate to ignore in this way the spectacular successes in exporting services (the deficit of £130 million on British commodity trade in 1913, for example, was more than made up by a £190 million surplus on service trade) and interest and dividends as returns to past lending, but the fixation on commodity trade and its failure is usual.

The impression of weakness in Britain's export performance and by inference its industrial performance is enhanced by the market and commodity structure of British exports. Britain's exports throughout the nineteenth century, as we have noted, were heavily concentrated in a few basic industries which had been at the forefront of the industrial revolution. Exports remained concentrated in these industries up to the war, with textiles, iron and steel, and coal – the 'old' industries – contributing two-thirds of commodity export earnings. To look at it in another way, these few exporting industries were heavily oriented toward export markets. The dependence of export earnings on a few industries whose technology had been set during the industrial revolution and whose prosperity was dependent on export markets has been seen as a weakness in the British economy of the early twentieth century (Aldcroft 1968). 'Overcommitment', it is said, produced vulnerability to change in international conditions, for newly industrialising countries were protecting and attempting to stimulate domestically these very industries. Their predominance in Britain made more difficult adjustment of the economy toward the newer light engineering industries, emerging around 1900 as technological leaders (Richardson 1965).

The British economy apparently maintained its traditional industries instead of taking advantage of the new technologies. When tariffs and domestic industrialisation severely curtailed sales to traditional markets in Europe and the United States, new export markets were found elsewhere. In the 1850s customers in western and central Europe and the United States had purchased over 40 per cent of Britain's exports. In 1870 these customers still took nearly 40 per cent of British exports, but by 1910 the proportion had declined to well under 30 per cent. In contrast, British exporters found customers in empire markets and in areas of Latin America and Asia where less formal but still important ties bound primary-producing areas to Britain. British specialisation in less sophisticated markets worried observers. Nor were foreign markets the only problem. By the early twentieth century, foreign manufactured goods were becoming increasingly evident in Britain. Shipbuilders and other users of steel were buying from German firms. American engineering products were finding British markets. Surely something had gone wrong. Many began to believe that the British entrepreneur had failed, or that the policy of free trade was a mistake.

The exploration of the belief in British failure is the task of chapters 1 and 3 of volume 2. Here the point is that these conclusions do not necessarily follow from the observed patterns of trade. It seems more likely, in fact, that the late nineteenth-century trade pattern emerged from a dynamic period of trade growth that affected Britain's trade and that of her trading partners and rivals. Falling transportation costs and growing European population stimulated new staple exports from Asia and the Americas. Expansion of production in these areas revolutionised the supply of primary products to Europe, and European trade patterns adjusted. These growing staple-producing areas drew large amounts of British capital which, in turn, generated large return flows of interest and dividends; and the export of staple products required British shipping, financial and commercial services.

In this and similar cases conclusions about economic performance cannot be easily drawn from patterns of trade. Trade arises from comparative advantage, not absolute advantage. Britain exported the things it could produce cheaply relative to the other things it could produce – cheap coal, cotton goods, insurance, shipping relative to food, timber and in the end steel – not necessarily the things that it could produce with less labour or capital than could other nations. So efficient was British agriculture, for example, that Britain could have produced food using fewer resources than were used to produce it in Argentina or Illinois. But it would have been foolish to do so in 1900, as Britain's continued adherence to free trade recognised. A better use for British resources was the making of machinery and insurance policies. The 'failure' of Britain to export food, the 'decline' in the size of agriculture (cf. Olson and Harris 1958; and vol. 2, ch. 6) and the 'invasion' of British markets by imports was no sign of technological inferiority in agriculture. So too elsewhere in the economy.

In the second half of the nineteenth century world markets became increasingly integrated. Understandably Britain with wealth, well-developed markets, sophisticated mercantile and financial services, a long tradition of overseas trade, and a recent political commitment to free trade, became the centre of international expansion. Other industrial economies were initially preoccupied by domestic industrialisation and, after 1880, unlike Britain, insulated themselves from international forces with tariffs on both manufactured goods and agricultural imports to protect domestic interests (Bairoch 1989).

International trade grew for several reasons after mid-century. Britain's trade expanded rapidly early in the century because British firms had improved technology in textiles, iron and machinery, and were able to attract foreign customers with low prices. Although British firms retained technological leadership in these industries for many more years, their technological change slowed. Technological improvement in other industries quickened, but British firms now shared technological leadership with American and continental European rivals. Settlement of raw material-exporting regions, initially encouraged by Britain's repeal of protection but sustained by falling transport costs, replaced technological leadership as the primary engine of trade growth. The economic world became characterised by an industrialised core – western Europe and the eastern United States – that traded manufactured goods for raw materials of a primary-producing periphery.

Europe remained the centre, importing from the periphery; the frontier – where new settlement occurred in response to opportunities to export food – which stood first in the American Midwest, then moved into the steppes of southern Russia and the high plains of North America and eventually into the southern hemisphere. Two underlying forces made the world a single market, even for bulk commodities. First, steam power and improved metallurgy revolutionised long-distance transportation; new railroads and steamships dramatically cheapened shipment. Second, population grew rapidly in Europe and older settled areas of the United States. Population growth put upward pressure on European food prices and falling transportation costs meant that a given Liverpool price produced a higher local price in remote areas of the world. As local prices rose, production of staple food-stuffs and raw materials became profitable in areas that had previously been unattractive (Harley 1979, 1985, 1992; but see Olson 1974).

Before mid-century, two integrated trading economies, largely separated by high transportation costs, had existed. One was centred on the industrial areas of north-western Europe and extended into a Baltic hinterland for agricultural supply; a second was centred on the north-eastern United States and extended into the American Midwest. As transportation costs fell, these trading blocks integrated and extended their influence beyond the Black Sea in one direction and beyond the Mississippi in the other, finally to encompass the entire globe.

For approximately a generation between 1860 and 1890 the cost of shipment by rail and ship fell rapidly and revolutionised international trade. The interior of North America, the Ukraine and central Asia, South America and Australasia and even significant portions of South Asia entered a Europe-centred food economy. The general outlines of the developments of railroads and steamships are well known, but the extent of the change is often underestimated. Spatial relationships were revolutionised; primary product prices rose in the frontier regions while they fell in Europe, despite an approximate doubling of European population. The contrasting trends of grain and meat prices in the American Midwest and Britain are illustrated in Figure 12.3. British prices fell dramatically but the cost of shipment from Chicago to Liverpool also fell (from equalling the Chicago price to insignificance in a half century), so much so that prices rose gently in Chicago and more rapidly in exporting regions farther west.

European agriculture came under tremendous pressure (see vol. 2, ch. 6). Trade had seldom before forced down the price of well-established activities on such a scale (although British textile's impact on foreign competitors earlier in the century provided some parallel). During the previous century, trade had increased dramatically as new products – sugar, tobacco and cotton – not produced in the importing region became international staples. Britain's timber imports had grown dramatically, but in response to domestic depletion and rising prices. The great late nineteenth-century expansion of trade in agricultural commodities, in contrast, generated dramatic declines in the price of food in the consuming

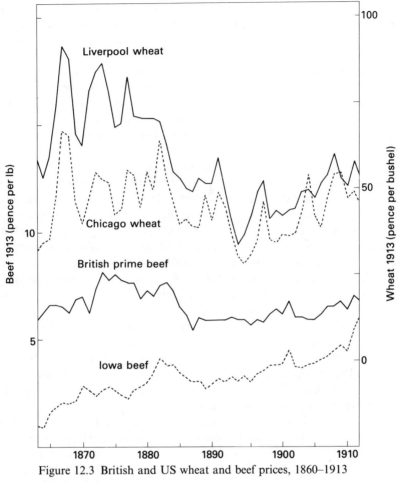

Figure 12.3 British and US wheat and beef prices, 1860–1913
Source: see text.

regions. The decline in British agricultural interests, which had been prevented after the Napoleonic Wars by the Corn Laws, been feared after the repeal of the Corn Laws but prevented by growing population, finally came in the 1880s as a result of transportation improvements.

Britain's commitment to free trade remained unshaken while, in contrast, continental governments quickly moved to protect their agricultural interests; the growth of trade, adjustment of prices and relocation of production was allowed to continue. The adjustment was quick and decisive; British food prices began to fall in the 1880s and downward pressure continued until the end of the century. Then the unique era of transportation improvement ended and prices slowly rose. Soon after the First World War, geographical expansion of agriculture was complete. Agricultural output eventually resumed its growth but that growth was now based on biotechnology instead of on geographic expansion while protective policies discouraged international trade in food-stuffs. By the First World War, the era of expanding trade based on the exchange of agricultural commodities for manufactured goods was ending. Already, particularly in Europe, the more modern pattern of trade, dominated by the exchange of manufactured goods among advanced economies, was emerging.

The spread of specialised agriculture and raw material production into distant areas involved the movement of people and the construction of transportation and distribution networks. Because the investment required to build railroads and cities to serve frontiers in the plains of North and South America far exceeded the resources available there, most of the capital was drawn from older areas. British investors found the securities issued by overseas railroads and governments attractive investments and bought them in large amounts. Nearly 70 per cent of the foreign securities issued in London in the late nineteenth century were to finance railroads and other forms of overhead capital (see vol. 2, ch. 7). The staple products had to be marketed, financed, insured and transported. British firms already had experience in these fields and the large investments of British capital in the development of exporting regions further directed business toward British firms. Because British-owned ships made up about half the world's merchant marine the increase in demand for shipping also generated business for British firms.

It is worthwhile to underline the conclusion. The pattern of British trade in the late nineteenth century reflected more the world which Britain dealt with than any peculiar development in British economic character. The increase in the supply of food and raw materials came from distant, often frontier, areas. Britons migrated to these areas, and British firms and investors aided the construction of transport and urban infrastructure needed to support new production. Not surprisingly, British firms traded actively with these regions, providing the consumer and investment goods which the pioneers demanded. These regions needed textiles and railroad iron and other heavy investment goods which Britain had long produced with such skill; they had only modest demands for new industrial goods.

The commodity composition and the markets of British exports and the bilateral payments patterns at the end of the nineteenth century need to be seen within the context of the development of new areas of staple supply. Figure 12.4 presents the pattern of multilateral trade balances around 1910. Britain's trade possessed the features that have been ascribed to

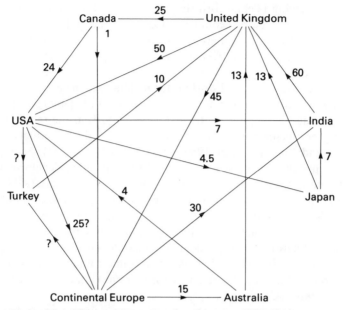

Figure 12.4 The world pattern of settlements, 1910 (£m)

Note: the arrows point to the country of each pair having a surplus with the other, indicating, therefore, the direction of the flow of settlement. Thus the United Kingdom had a surplus of £60m in trade and payments with India.

Source: Saul (160: 58).

weakness. Britain imported much more, including manufactured goods, from Europe and America than she sold to these countries. British exporters sold large amounts of manufactured goods to the staple-exporting areas – including, importantly, India – and generated surpluses there that had their counterpart in the import surpluses which Europe incurred with all the primary exporters and which the United States incurred with the tropics (Saul 1960: chs. 3, 4; Hilgerdt 1942). Britain's large overall commodity deficit, equalling more than a third of imports, was paid for, along with a large surplus to invest abroad, by interest and dividends and by foreign purchases of British services (see Figure 12.1).

Britain's deficits with the industrial economies and surpluses with the primary-producing economies occurred within a world settlement pattern. Other industrial economies balanced deficits with the primary-producing areas by running surpluses with Britain. Interpretation of this pattern is not obvious, for it could have emerged and been maintained in more than one way. Those who see weakness in the British economy see the trade pattern emerging because British firms had lost the ability to compete in the markets of developed countries. Ties of formal and informal empire, it is said, allowed increasingly non-competitive British firms to sell in primary-producing countries. Imperialism supported the sale of non-competitive exports.

Those who have studied world trade in detail see the pattern differently. '[The] world-wide interconnecting network of trade [emerged] in the last three decades of the nineteenth century mainly from the rapid growth of primary producing countries and the demand for their products arising in Europe and America' (Saul 1960: 62; Hilgerdt 1942, 1943). As imports of primary products increased, continental Europe had to develop exports to finance new imports. Since the means for effective multilateral settlement existed, these countries exploited comparative advantage multilaterally rather than bilaterally. Germany's and America's competitive advantage lay not in the products demanded by the primary producers, but in the products of new industries in demand in developed economies. Exports to the unprotected British market, where consumers and investors demanded new products, proved the best way for Germany and America to finance primary imports.

Foreign investment and international services were a natural feature of the international economy, as we have seen, and provided over a third of British international earnings. British firms and investors were paid for important contributions to the international economy. The earnings were no artificial cushion but they did affect Britain's commodity trade. To the extent that the British were unwilling to invest amounts equal to these earnings outside Britain, the surpluses on the investment income and service accounts had to be balanced by import surpluses in commodity trade. International prices adjusted to support this surplus; Britons' actions to spend foreign earnings adjusted prices until the trade deficit equalled the service surplus. Service and investment earnings retarded British export growth just as exports of Dutch natural gas exports in the 1960s hurt Holland's export industries – what economists came to call 'the Dutch disease' (Matthews et al. 1982: 455–6, 526; Crafts 1985a: 163).

The commodity and market composition of British exports reflected the multilateral world economy. Britain continued to export the products of the old industries of the industrial revolution and sold outside the industrial nations while Germany and America gained markets with new industrial products that found buyers primarily in richer industrialised countries. This pattern emerged from three characteristics of the late nineteenth century. First, tariffs on industrial products inhibited British manu-facturing exports to the other industrial countries. Second, many areas of primary production had expanded with the aid of British capital and commercial expertise. The import trades of these areas were naturally oriented towards Britain. Third, when British industries were compared with their German and American counterparts it was clear that Britain's competitive position was strongest in certain old industries – textiles, shipbuilding, heavy engineering and even some branches of ferrous metal production. This advantage appears to have been based on the skills that the labour force had developed over a century of industrial experience. Though British firms appeared old-fashioned in their use of skilled labour and comparative shunning of new machine processes, they produced at lower cost than they could have with more mechanised methods, or than was achieved elsewhere.

In newer branches of industry Britain did not enjoy the advantages of existing skills. Here mechanised production was the rule in Britain, as elsewhere, and Britain lacked advantage (Harley 1974). In short, because it industrialised first Britain's comparative advantage lay in the old industries while its rivals' comparative advantage lay in the newer industries. And notice again that this finding about comparative advantage provides no insight into the relative technological or economic efficiency of production in the various countries. Investigation of that issue requires detailed study of the technological choices that industries faced (see chs. 2 and 11 above and vol. 2, ch. 3). The multilateral settlement pattern, then, reflected the process of economic expansion outside Europe and the accidents of precedence in industrial growth.

Britain's concentration on exporting products of the old industries to primary-producing countries emerged from the working of the international economy. The concentration in a few industries was the legacy of the lead that Britain had achieved in the industrial revolution. Technological precocity led British industries to supply a substantial portion of world industrial demand in historical circumstances where demand was highly concentrated in a few commodities. The legacy of early leadership continued to shape British trade into the twentieth century; but were there not costs of 'overcommitment'? Learning by doing appears to generate much of technological change and Britain's productivity growth may have suffered because trading opportunities concentrated resources in old industries where technological opportunities were meagre at the expense of new industries with potential for technological advance. Certainly British productivity growth appears to have slowed in the years before the First World War (Matthews *et al.* 1982: 229).

Recent research by Crafts and Thomas (1986; Crafts 1985a: ch. 8) suggests that education also suffered. Britain's comparative advantage, historically derived, lay in industries that required low skill; in contrast the advantage of German and American firms lay in new industries that used human capital. British human capital formation may have lagged in consequence; an efficient response to Britain's position as the first industrialised country, perhaps, but a restraint on future growth. Britain's lead in the industrial revolution, in 1870, and perhaps even in 1913, rested on industries that did not require skills imparted by formal education. So the British economy provided less basic education to their general labour force and directed educational reform toward clerical skills, demanded by Britain's internationally dominant service sectors, rather than toward scientific skills. This legacy left Britain relatively poorly placed to take advantage of the new technology of the so-called 'second industrial revolution' in fine chemicals, industrial equipment, electricals, and cars and aircraft. This was a legacy that was to cause twentieth-century difficulties.

With the benefit of hindsight we can also see that twentieth-century Britain paid a considerably more direct price for the industrial concentration caused by large exports of a few commodities to a few markets by the eve of the First World War. Unemployment in the inter-war economy occurred mainly in these old industries, because labour drawn to these industries in the pre-war period could not be moved without cost to other employments. The loss to the economy was enormous. Still this does not imply that the industrial structure prior to the war was necessarily wrong. Even if we leave aside the issue of the management of the international value of the British pound in the inter-war period – perhaps no small leaving aside – it is not clear that hindsight is appropriate for historical judgement. To be sure, adjustment would have had to occur even without the trauma of the war and the associated disruption of the international system in which Britain was so involved; but it would have been a slower adjustment. The British economy began to adjust long before the war. Traditional industries were declining as a proportion of national income and of foreign earnings. It is of course unfortunate that much of the shift went into international services which depended on a stable international economic environment that was so shaken by the war and by its aftermath. And it is an irony of history that the interests of these service industries heavily influenced the suicidal exchange rate policy of the inter-war years.

Perhaps an appropriate question to ask is: Would an omniscient, but not prescient, planner have made a different choice than the British economy actually made through the workings of atomistic markets? That question is hard but does not obviously demand an affirmative answer. Britain's international specialisation conformed to her comparative advantage: there were gains from trade that would have been lost by some other structure. The newer industries which expanded slowly in Britain were the wave of the future and were industries where technological change was developing most rapidly. Perhaps dynamic gains in learning by doing and human capital formation were overlooked, but those are hard to identify even now. Future advantage does not imply that the economy should have shifted to its future structure more rapidly. The concentration of export markets and the concentration in industries certainly increased the risk to the economy – as the inter-war period dramatically revealed – and a cautious planner might have chosen to forego present gains from trade to reduce this risk. But it turns most of the historical literature on its head to suggest that the structure of the British economy before the First World War was inappropriate, not because of excess caution being exhibited through the market decisions, but instead paucity of caution.

13   Coping with city growth

Jeffrey Williamson

Looking backward from the present

The past four decades have witnessed economic progress in the Third
World which is unprecedented by the standards of the first industrial
revolution. Economic success of that magnitude has always created
problems of dislocation and structural adjustment. City growth is one such
problem and, given the unprecedented progress in the Third World, their
problems of city growth seem, at least to those who ignore history,
unprecedented as well. Rates of Third World city growth have bordered on
the spectacular, averaging between 4 and 5 per cent per annum.

Analysts and policy makers are sharply divided on the wisdom of these
city-growth trends. Pessimists stress the Third World's inability to cope
with the social overhead requirements of rapid urban growth and high
urban densities, citing ugly squatter settlements, poverty, pollution and
environmental decay as evidence of their inability to cope. Third World
city growth is viewed by the pessimists as another example of the tragedy
of the commons, a classic example of overuse of a collective resource. In
contrast, optimists view city growth as a central force raising average living
standards. They view urbanisation as the natural outcome, indeed a
carrier, of economic development. Debate over public options remains
intense, the optimists favouring an open-city approach and the pessimists
searching for ways to close the cities down to new immigrants.

Economic success breeds problems of adjustment and they certainly
seem severe in Third World cities. Development economists have spent
three decades debating urban unemployment, underemployment and the
alleged failure to absorb the flood of rural emigrants into city labour
markets; the persistent influx of newcomers makes it extremely difficult for
municipal planners to improve the quality of social overhead; the migrants
crowd into densely packed urban slums, jammed into primitive dwellings
with little or no social services; and the rising density and size of the city
augments pollution while lowering the quality of the city environment.

None of this would sound unfamiliar to Victorians coping with city growth in the middle third of the nineteenth century. They too were overwhelmed by the same 'success', and they did not have World Bank loans and foreign technologies to help them cope. They too took innumerable surveys, held countless parliamentary hearings, published one official document after another, searched for scapegoats and struggled with reform. Thus, the debate between optimist and pessimist is hardly new, and can be found in the British Parliamentary Papers as early as the 1830s, in treatises by political economists and in the British press.

Britain's city growth in comparative perspective

During the reform debates of the 1830s and 1840s, the conventional wisdom had it that Britain was undergoing unusually rapid city growth. This characterisation is embedded in the historiography even today. To offer one example, Flinn's sublime introduction to Chadwick's *Report on the Sanitary Condition of the Labouring Population* cites census data to show that some nineteenth century towns grew at rates 'that would bring cold sweat to the brows of 20th century housing committees' (Flinn 1965: 4). Thus, Glasgow grew at 3.2 per cent per annum in the 1830s, Manchester and Salford at 3.9 per cent in the 1820s, Bradford at 5.9 per cent in the 1830s, and Dukinfield nearly trebled in the 1820s. These were fast-growing cities and towns in the industrialising north, of course, and, as it turns out, these were the decades of most rapid growth. The average British city grew at a slower 2.5 per cent per annum in the 1820s, and this rate was almost half of those for the Third World in the 1960s (Table 13.1).

But contemporary observers who lived during the first industrial revolution had reason to view their city growth as unusually fast. After all, they had no previous industrialised country with which to compare their own. They had only the evidence that city growth was far faster in the early nineteenth century than it had been in the previous one. Modern historians do not suffer the same disadvantage. So, was Britain's city growth rapid by the standards of the typical European industrial revolution? As Table 13.1 shows, there was little that was unusual about Britain's city growth during her industrial revolution, except, of course, that it was first. The rest of Europe reached its peak rate of city growth much later in the nineteenth century. Yet, the rate of city growth at their respective maxima were almost identical: 2.5 per cent per annum for England in the 1820s versus a little less than 2.6 per cent per annum for the rest of Europe between 1880 and 1900.

The level of urbanisation is quite a different story. Because urbanisation is highly correlated with per capita income, it is useful to compare levels of urbanisation between countries of comparable incomes. At roughly the

Table 13.1. *A comparative assessment of city-growth performance since 1800*

Country	Date maximum city growth reached			Maximum rate of city growth per annum (%)
	Early 1800–50	Middle 1850–1900	Late post-1900	
England and Wales	1821–31			2·50
France	1830–50			1·58
Germany	1830–50			3·43
Austria		1800–1900		2·10
Belgium		1880–1900		1·95
Denmark		1880–1900		3·22
Finland		1880–1900		4·00
Italy		1880–1900		1·86
Norway		1850–70		2·94
Sweden		1850–1900		2·91
Netherlands			1900–10	1·93
Spain			1900–10	1·82
Switzerland			1900–10	3·22
Europe (excluding England and Wales)		1880–1900		2·58
Third World (excluding China)			1960–70	4·21

Source: Williamson (1990a: Table 1.1, 3).

same per capita income, England in 1840 had a much higher share of her population urban, about 48 per cent, than did the rest of Europe in the mid-late nineteenth century or the contemporary Third World, about 26 per cent. Yet this comparison tells us far more about British comparative advantage and eighteenth-century preconditions than it does about its alleged unusual city growth in the early nineteenth century, while it is the latter which is at issue in this chapter.

Birth, death, and local labour supplies in city and countryside

Understanding the demographic dimensions of what has come to be called the urban transition should help to improve our understanding of the first industrial revolution. Certainly it is essential in searching for answers to any of the following questions. Did English cities grow more by natural increase than by migration? Did city immigration rates rise as industrialisation accelerated? Did rural emigration respond vigorously to the employment demands of rapid city growth, or were rural English men and

Table 13.2. *Crude birth rates (CBR), crude death rates (CDR) and crude rates of natural increase (CRNI) in various regions of England and Wales, 1841–66*

Region	1841			1856			1866		
	CBR	CDR	CRNI	CBR	CDR	CRNI	CBR	CDR	CRNI
England and Wales									
Total	36·24	22·29	13·95	35·73	22·17	13·56	36·22	22·42	13·80
Urban	37·86	25·96	11·90	37·22	24·82	12·40	37·58	25·10	12·48
Rural	35·41	20·39	15·02	34·86	20·62	14·24	35·39	20·77	14·62
Urban detail									
London	34·75	25·86	8·89	35·10	23·63	11·47	36·42	24·31	12·11
4 largest cities	36·55	27·34	9·21	36·12	25·17	10·95	37·06	26·00	11·06
Cities > 100,000	37·50	27·16	10·34	36·70	25·42	11·28	37·71	26·20	11·51
Cities < 100,000	38·35	24·30	14·05	37·93	24·00	13·93	37·39	23·64	13·75
Southern cities	34·39	25·23	9·16	34·58	23·36	11·22	35·87	23·82	12·05
Northern cities	41·12	26·64	14·48	39·79	26·25	13·54	39·23	26·33	12·90
All cities	37·86	25·96	11·90	37·22	24·82	12·40	37·58	25·10	12·48

Source: Williamson (1990a: Table 2.1, 12).

women more attached to their villages than has been true of other industrial revolutions since? What role did push and pull forces play in rural and urban labour markets? These questions have always been at centre stage, or at least lurking in the wings, in debates about the first industrial revolution. The answers hinge on an assessment of those forces which created and displaced jobs in the two labour markets, as well as on the migration thought to link them, assessments which can be made far better with the prior demographic information summarised in this section, which is an introduction to the demographic and economic links underlying city growth.

Table 13.2 supplies estimates of crude birth rates, crude death rates, and crude rates of natural increase across the middle third of the nineteenth century. It is important to emphasise some of the facts that emerge from the table, especially given that mid-nineteenth-century England exhibits vital rates which are in sharp contrast to those in the contemporary Third World. That is, rural birth rates exceed urban in the Third World: the opposite was true of England. Rural death rates exceed urban death rates in the Third World: the opposite was true of England. Rural rates of natural increase never exceed urban rates by much in the Third World: they exceeded urban rates by a lot in England.

The demographic dimensions of English experience a century and a half ago were thus very different from those in the Third World today, and this fact had very important implications for city immigration, rural emigration and labour market behaviour during the first industrial revolution. The higher rates of natural increase in the countryside must have placed even greater stress on rural–urban labour markets in Britain compared with the Third World, as booming labour demands in her cities were distant from booming labour supplies in the countryside. Although Third World economies have certainly grown faster than did Britain, they never had to cope with Britain's poor demographic match between excess city labour demands and excess rural labour supplies. Perhaps this is one reason why, as we shall see, city immigration and rural emigration rates were so high in England even though the rate of industrialisation was fairly modest compared with the Third World. And perhaps this is one reason why, as we shall also see, wage gaps between city and countryside were so large in England compared with the Third World. England was characterised by a demographic mismatch between city and countryside which placed an unusually heavy burden on labour market adjustment.

The key explanation for the demographic mismatch is that crude death rates were much higher in the cities. They were highest in large cities (although London was an important exception), somewhat lower in small cities, but lowest in rural areas. These death rate differentials between city and countryside declined some time after 1841 but they were still pronounced in 1866. They continued to decline during the remainder of the nineteenth century, but the switch to a regime of relatively benign city mortality environments did not take place until around the First World War.

Thus, the role of public health and sanitation reform in making the city a relatively benign mortality environment is a twentieth-century phenomenon. In nineteenth-century Britain, the cities were killers, a very important fact in understanding the operation of urban labour markets during the first industrial revolution.

Much of this differential between city and countryside in crude birth and death rates may be due to differences in age distributions between the two. Both economists and demographers have long understood that fast-growing areas which absorb immigrants tend to have large proportions of young adults since it is the young adults who migrate in large numbers; Britain in the mid-nineteenth century was no different in that regard. Thus, to the extent that the cities tended to have a higher proportion of young adults, the crude death rate differentials between city and countryside understate the true mortality experience by age, a prediction borne out, for example, by infant mortality rates. Similarly, the higher crude birth rates in the cities may be attributable in large part to the fact that young adults comprised a high proportion of urban populations.

Leaving the village to go to the city: augmenting local labour supplies

Although some cities grow without industry and some industries grow outside cities, modern industrialisation tends to be city-based. As a result, industrial revolutionary events tend to augment the demand for labour and capital in the city far more rapidly than in the countryside. Labour and capital supplies, on the other hand, tend to be abundant in rural areas, a result of centuries of gradual agrarian-based pre-industrial development. One of the fundamental problems created by industrial revolutions is, therefore, to reconcile excess factor demands in the cities with excess factor supplies in the countryside. How do labour and capital markets cope with the disequilibrium?

Rural emigration is documented in Table 13.3. With the exception of the war-induced good times for English agriculture between 1801 and 1806, rural emigration took place at every time between 1776 and 1871. Furthermore, the rate of emigration more than doubled over the period. That rural emigration rates rose while urban immigration rates fell may seem odd, but the arithmetic is almost inevitable. After all, these rates are calculated as the ratio of migration flows to a population base, and because the urban population base enjoyed fast growth (augmented by the immigrants) while the rural population base did not (depleted by the emigrants), city immigration and rural emigration rates would have moved in opposite directions solely because of the demographic arithmetic.

These measured rates of rural emigration are inconsistent with the conventional wisdom that English farm labourers were reluctant to move, and that the agricultural counties were full of 'a vast, inert mass of redundant labour' who were 'immobile' (Redford 1926: 84 and 94). On the contrary, these are quite impressive emigration rates by almost any standard. Indeed, after the 1820s they were higher than they have been in the Third World recently, and by the 1860s they were twice as large. The comparison suggests that rural English men and women were no more reluctant to leave their village parishes than were rural populations in the Third World, although that judgement should await evidence on the size of the earnings differentials between city and countryside which were necessary to induce the emigration.

Did England's cities grow more by immigration or by natural increase? This question is motivated in part by a debate over contemporary Third World experience, where city growth has been spectacular. Modern

Table 13.3. *Urban immigration and rural emigration, England and Wales, 1776–1871*

Years	Urban annual rates (%)			Urban population increase due to immigration (%)	Rural emigration rate (%)
	Population increase	Natural increase	City immigration		
1776–81	2·08	0·87	1·26	59·49	0·86
1781–6	1·81	0·21	1·62	88·99	0·50
1786–91	2·20	0·89	1·37	61·08	0·56
1791–6	2·17	1·04	1·20	53·69	0·79
1796–1801	2·08	1·03	1·10	51·87	0·83
1801–6	2·15	0·27	1·91	88·18	−0·18
1806–11	2·07	1·52	0·59	27·53	1·07
1811–16	2·40	1·10	1·37	55·55	0·59
1816–21	2·39	1·40	1·06	42·82	0·87
1821–6	2·61	1·57	1·12	41·35	1·19
1826–31	2·33	1·34	1·06	43·95	1·14
1831–6	2·08	1·10	1·04	48·66	1·01
1836–41	2·04	1·26	0·83	39·50	1·20
1841–6	2·41	1·25	1·23	49·68	1·57
1846–51	2·05	1·13	0·97	45·89	1·73
1851–6	2·06	1·34	0·77	36·39	1·54
1856–61	2·08	1·52	0·60	27·92	1·60
1861–6	2·35	1·36	1·06	43·67	2·10
1866–71	2·29	1·21	1·15	48·63	2·05

Source: Williamson (1990a: Table 2.5, 26).

demographers have shown that the answer depends where in the urban transition the assessment is made: at some intermediate point in the urban transition most countries tend to switch from migration-driven to urban-natural-increase-driven city growth. English experience during the first industrial revolution is similar. Immigration accounted for about 60 per cent of city growth 1776–1811 but for about 40 per cent 1846–71. The cross-over point – where the contribution of natural increase began to exceed immigration – appeared in the 1810s and 1820s. In any case, immigration accounted for a far higher share of city growth in England between 1776 and 1871 than it has in the Third World. Those high nineteenth-century city death rates and low rates of natural increase account for the difference.

Cities were prime movers during the industrial revolution, but how much of that dynamism was attributable to the fact that they were full of young adults, a demographic fact which had advantageous economic

Table 13.4. *Population distribution by age, immigrants and non-immigrants: Britain's cities in 1851 (%)*

Group	Less than 20	Greater than or equal to 20
Irish immigrants	25·6	74·4
Other immigrants	23·0	77·0
Non-immigrants	58·9	41·1
Total	42·8	57·2

Source: Williamson (1990a: Table 2.11, 41).

consequences? If so, was it caused by a migrant-selectivity bias, young adults favouring the cities and shunning the countryside? It turns out that cities had a significantly larger share of people in their twenties and thirties than the countryside in 1861 (33 versus 28 per cent). The opposite was true of the tails of the age distribution: the countryside had more old people and children. Furthermore, the young-adult bias during the first industrial revolution was stronger than it is today in the Third World. And since Britain's cities were full of young adults in 1861, it is not surprising to find that they had been even more full of young adults a few decades earlier. After all, the cities were absorbing immigrants at a more rapid rate in the late eighteenth century than they were in the mid-nineteenth century, and immigrants tended to be young adults.

Migrants incur costs when they move and these were sufficiently large in nineteenth-century Britain that significant returns over a number of years were necessary to motivate even short-distance moves. Older people with shorter expected productive lifetimes and bigger village commitments must have found the migration costs too high and the returns too low. Thus, migration selected young adults, those who had the greatest chance for immediate employment and who could recoup their migration costs over a longer lifetime (including the emotional pain of leaving the village). It follows that the greater the influence of urban job pull, the greater the young-adult selectivity bias. The greater the influence of rural push, the more likely migration would be a family affair.

The influence of the young-adult selectivity bias can be seen in two ways, in the stock of city immigrants enumerated in any given census and in the flow of city immigrants between any two censuses. The census figures for 1851 in Table 13.4 should be enough to illustrate the point. About 41 per cent of the non-immigrants in Britain's cities were adults, while the figures for the Irish and other immigrants (primarily from the British countryside) were almost twice that figure, about 74 and 77 per cent. The adult-selectivity bias mattered a lot in the cities.

The cities had lower dependency rates and an abundance of young adults. Partly as a result of this favourable demographic feature, the cities had higher per capita incomes than the countryside. This favourable demographic feature also helps explain why the cities had lower relief burdens than the countryside. Many historians have explored the sources and impact of the Old Poor Laws in England; all stress the fact that the Speenhamland system was an agricultural relief scheme. Yet, how much of that fact was due simply to demography – young adults selecting the cities and shunning the countryside, leaving behind dependants who were more vulnerable to pauperism? At least in 1851, the incidence of pauperism was higher in the villages than in the cities and most of the difference is explained by the young-adult bias. Furthermore, this fact may help to explain why the cities seem to have higher saving and accumulation rates than the countryside. This inference follows directly from what development economists call the dependency hypothesis: more children and elderly people per productive adult increases consumption requirements at the expense of saving. This dependency rate effect may have been manifested by a direct influence on the household saving behaviour of common labour. But it seems more likely to have had its impact indirectly, first on poor relief, then on the local tax burden and thus finally on disposable incomes of potential savers paying the taxes (who were certainly not common labourers). In any case, the inference is that the young adult bias must have favoured saving in the cities where the accumulation requirements were highest, and it did so when the city immigration rates were highest (in the late eighteenth and early nineteenth centuries), and when financial capital markets were most poorly equipped to cope with the problems of capital transfer from village to city.

The young adult bias had another favourable influence on British industrialisation. As the demand for labour boomed in the cities, village immigrants were needed to fill the new jobs. But the immigrants who arrived in large numbers were young adults who had two attributes: they were in the age groups least vulnerable to the high mortality environment, and they were in the age groups with the highest fertility rates. Thus the first generation of new immigrants generated a bigger increase in the local labour force in the next generation than would have been the case without the young-adult bias. The next generation of city growth, therefore, required less immigrants to satisfy those booming labour demands. These demographic responses would have tended to ease the pressure on labour markets linking city with countryside had not industrialisation quickened after the Napoleonic Wars, augmenting those city labour demands even more. Alternatively, without the demographic accommodation, city immigration would have been even higher in the post-Napoleonic era, and so too would have been the pressure on labour markets linking city to countryside.

City labour demand and migrant absorption

Where were the jobs that absorbed the farm exodus? Was it rapid job creation in manufacturing that pulled the farm emigrant to the city, or was it the threat of agricultural unemployment that pushed the farm emigrant into low-wage jobs in the city service sector? These are very old questions which concerned Marx and Mayhew in the nineteenth century just as much as they concern the International Labour Organisation and the World Bank now.

Table 13.5 disaggregates non-agricultural employment growth into three sectors. Panel A makes it clear that manufacturing was hardly the leading sector driving non-agricultural employment growth during the French Wars. On the contrary, employment growth in manufacturing was a bit below that of services and far below that of mining. Rapid employment growth in a small sector may not create very many jobs, of course, so Panel B shows the share of the non-agricultural employment increase which was attributable to each sector. Panel B shows that between 1755 and 1811, manufacturing and mining job creation were about of equal importance, and services were more than twice as important as both. The service sector, not manufacturing, was the main source of new urban jobs up to 1811. Conditions changed somewhat after the wars because new jobs in manufacturing increased as a share of total new non-agricultural jobs. Even so, at least between 1841 and 1861, the service sector maintained its position as the main source of new urban jobs. City growth across the British industrial revolution cannot be understood by looking at booming labour demand in manufacturing alone; mining and the heterogeneous service sector were equally or even more important.

Figure 13.1 offers a simple characterisation of the city labour market which helps to organise the discussion for the remainder of this section. Total city employment appears on the horizontal axis and grew at 1.75 per cent per year between 1821 and 1861 (or, at least, non-agricultural employment did). The real wage facing city firms (not to be confused with workers' living standards) is on the vertical axis and grew at 0.91 per cent per year over roughly the same period. Figure 13.1 supposes that all city immigration was attributable to the combined effects of the pull of wages and employment conditions in the cities as well as to the push of conditions in Irish and British agriculture. Thus, the labour supply curves are taken to

Table 13.5. *The sources of civilian employment growth in non-agriculture, 1755–1861*

Period	Manufacturing	Mining	Services	Non-agricultural
A Percentage per annum				
1755–1811	0·70	4·31	0·79	0·92
1821–61	n.a.	n.a.	n.a.	1·56
1841–61	1·45	4·69	1·88	1·82
B Percentage of non-agricultural employment increase due to				
1755–1811	23·8	22·4	53·8	
1841–61	34·6	11·5	53·8	

Source: Williamson (1990a: Table 4.2, 85).

be very elastic, reflecting a powerful response of potential immigrants to rising city wages. Labour supply shifts rightward in response to the forces of natural increase which underlay the demographic behaviour of the resident labour force, as well as conditions in British and Irish agriculture which pushed labour into the cities. In equilibrium, the incremental labour supply matching the boom in labour demand comes from two sources, the natural increase in the resident labour force and immigration.

This figure makes it clear that there were four forces at work that influenced immigrant absorption and wages in this labour market. First, there was the shift in labour supplies generated by the combined effects of demographic forces in the city and by all the push forces in Ireland (like the famine) and in British agriculture (like enclosures). There is a second force at work in Figure 13.1, namely the elasticity of city labour supply which was conditioned primarily by potential farm emigrants' response to the more favourable employment conditions in the city, a force which will be considered later. The more elastic the labour supply, the cheaper will be city labour, the bigger will be city employment growth, and the smaller will be wage gaps between city and countryside. If these two forces are big enough, a glut in city labour supply can force wages down and blight otherwise dynamic urban growth with poverty. Those city demographic forces were discussed in the previous section, and immigration from the British countryside will be discussed at greater length below. What about the Irish?

To add to all the other social problems which Britain's cities had to face during the first industrial revolution, they also had to absorb the Irish. Rapid growth after the French Wars made the absorption easier, but the Irish immigrants still serve to complicate any assessment of Britain's

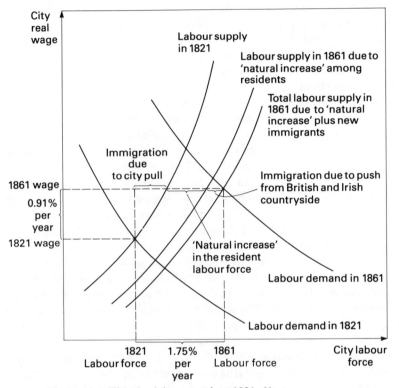

Figure 13.1 The city labour market, 1821–61
Sources: see text.

economic performance up to the 1850s. Would the cities have been able to cope with growth far more easily in their absence? Would common labour's wages and living standards in the city have risen much more rapidly? Was rural emigration from the British countryside strongly suppressed by Irish competition in the cities? Did British industrialisation receive a powerful boost from an elastic supply of cheap Irish labour? That immigration lowers the wages of comparably skilled native-born, and serves to 'crowd out' the native-born from city jobs, is obvious. What is not so obvious, however, is whether the Irish had a significant quantitative impact. Are they important to any fundamental understanding of British city growth in the four decades after 1820? Like other immigrants, the Irish were, of course, unskilled, urban and young adults, but were they really a big part of labour supplies to the cities? With the possible exception of the famine-driven 1840s, they were not: they were never more than about 8 per cent of the British labour force. In any case, when we pose the counterfactual 'What would Britain's economy have been like in the absence of Irish immigrations after 1820?', the answers are: Yes, the Irish immigrations did tend to inhibit rural emigration from the British countryside. No, they did not play a significant role in accounting for the behaviour of real wages in Britain. No, they did not foster industrialisation. (Williamson 1990a: ch. 6).

There are two other forces at work in Figure 13.1. There is the shift in city labour demand over time as technological and accumulation events associated with the industrial revolution unfolds over time. Finally, there is the elasticity of city labour demand, an issue over which opinions abound but on which evidence is slight. Debates in development economics would suggest that this fourth issue needs more of our attention.

Development economists have always stressed a technological asymmetry between modern and traditional sectors. They view the modern sector (typically manufacturing) as capital intensive in a technology where the elasticity of substitution between capital and labour is low. In contrast, they view the traditional sector (typically agriculture) as labour intensive where the elasticity of substitution is high. These conditions imply that the elasticity of demand for labour in the city is low, conditions that make the absorption of immigrant labour difficult because it takes a big drop in wages to encourage firms to expand employment very much. The elasticity of city labour demand will be even lower if the price elasticity of product demand is low, a condition typical of many Third World economies which, by hiding behind protective tariff policies, are relatively closed to trade.

So much for development economists and so much for the contemporary Third World. What about Britain during the first industrial revolution? Here there may be reason to have a more optimistic view of those labour demand elasticities. After all, real wages did rise sharply after the French Wars, and especially in the cities, so there is little evidence suggesting that British cities had unusual difficulties absorbing the immigrants.

What about the shifts in labour demand in Britain during the first industrial revolution? There are four forces that underlay that boom in city labour demand.

First, there were output price movements. If world market conditions tended to raise the relative price of manufactures (or to lower the price of raw material inputs), manufacturing should have boomed on that account, the derived demand for city labour should have shifted outward to the right, and immigrants would have been absorbed by this rapid rate of job creation. Between 1821 and 1861, however, just the opposite took place. Instead, the terms of trade moved against manufacturing. In cotton textiles, for example, the terms of trade fell by more than 30 per cent over the three decades following 1821. It has long been argued that a good share of that fall in the terms of trade was due to rapid technological advance which lowered costs in British textiles. A plausible argument can be made, however, that other world market conditions were also helping to drive down the relative price of British manufactures after the French Wars. There is the rapid expansion of competitive foreign supplies to consider. Between 1820 and 1860, Britain's share in trade between France, Germany, Italy, the United States and Britain itself declined from 27 to 25 per cent, and Britain's share in industrial production also declined, from 24 to 21 per cent. This extraordinary expansion of industrial production among Britain's competitors served to glut world markets and to drive down the relative price of manufactures. Second, the rise in protectionism on the Continent also must have weakened Britain's terms of trade. Thus, to the extent that some of those price trends were attributable to world market conditions, then they must have held back rightward shifts in city labour demand.

Second, there is capital accumulation to consider. Capital accumulation in manufacturing clearly served to augment capacity, to create jobs and to shift labour demand to the right. Although the rate of capital deepening (an increase in capital per worker) was very slow during the first industrial revolution, the rate of capital widening (an increase in employment at fixed capital per worker) was much more impressive. Indeed, the non-agricultural capital stock grew at 2.65 per cent per year between 1830 and 1860.

Third, productivity advance in manufacturing augmented labour demand there. For an economy so dependent on trade, where output demands were fairly price elastic and where manufactures could be vented on to foreign markets, rapid productivity advance in British manufacturing surely played an important role in fostering the expansion of that sector, thus causing the demand for labour to shift out to the right. Marx made the claim that capitalist development is uneven, and that unbalanced technological advance tends to breed an increasing concentration of production and employment in industrial activities. The limited evidence on sectoral rates of total factor productivity growth seems to confirm the premise that industry leads agriculture. It is certainly consistent with nineteenth-century United States evidence, and it seems to be consistent with Third World experience as well. McCloskey (1981b: Table 6.2) has argued that the evidence, such as it is, supports the view for Britain between 1780 and 1860: productivity growth rates are estimated to have been 1.8 per cent per year in industry and transport, much higher than in agriculture at 0.45 per cent per year. Lack of hard evidence, however, has kept the debate alive.

Fourth, there is the possibility of labour-saving to consider. Ever since Marx started us thinking about labour displacement and the reserve army, labour-saving has become entrenched in the lexicon of growth theorists, economic historians and development economists. Yet surprisingly little has been done to isolate its impact on the derived demand for labour during the British industrial revolution. Certainly there have been many anecdotal accounts of how certain craftsmen were displaced by modern technology (e.g. the hand-loom weavers), but a comprehensive assessment of the impact of these disequilibrating technological forces has yet to be made. Von Tunzelmann (1981: 158), however, finds no evidence to support the labour-saving hypothesis. If he is correct, then Britain would have contrasted sharply with America after 1820 and certainly with the Third World where labour-saving is generally agreed to have been pronounced. The jury is still out on labour-saving during the first industrial revolution.

There is one more influence to consider, the so-called urban bias. While it dominates the Third World, it played no role in Britain. The urban bias refers to those policies which favour city growth at the expense of the countryside. There is no shortage of policies which have that effect in the Third World: the domestic terms of trade are twisted against agriculture, thus encouraging more rapid rural emigration to the city than would have been true in the absence of such policies; tariffs and exchange-rate management also serve to protect urban industry, fostering its expansion at agriculture's expense; financial markets are manipulated by government policy to create cheap capital for favoured urban industries; and social overhead capital is allocated disproportionately to the cities (schools, health facilities, roads, water supplies and electricity), all offered at less than user cost, and all financed from general tax revenues rather than from urban land taxes.

Given the dominance of this view (Lipton 1976), it is important to stress that the urban bias played no role in Britain between 1780 and 1860, although it certainly did for post-Civil War America and the Soviet economy under Stalin. Indeed, it could be argued that a rural bias motivated British policy. The policy that mattered, of course, was the Corn Laws. At least until the repeal in 1846, tariffs favoured rural agriculture and penalised city industry. Certainly the debates from 1815 to 1846 posed the issue that way. Cobden and the Anti-Corn Law League made it absolutely clear who gained and who lost. Landlords gained from high rents and the urban working man suffered from the 'bread tax'. Manufacturers rightly complained that they had to pay higher nominal wages, that the export trade was repressed and that their profits were choked off. In short, city growth would have been faster in the absence of the Corn Laws (Williamson 1990b). Whether the great Victorian trading boom following the late 1840s was due mainly to repeal and free trade has, of course, been debated at length (ch. 12 above), but that event did not herald the replacement of a rural bias with an urban bias, but rather it implied a policy switch from rural bias to neutrality.

Debate over Third World urbanisation generates the same gloomy pessimism that characterised Britain in the early nineteenth century. Even the rhetoric is the same, Victorian and modern critics both citing urban unemployment, primitive housing, inadequate public services and poverty. Many modern analysts think the Third World has 'overurbanised', and many Victorian urban reformers thought the same was true of Britain. According to this view, the cities are too large and too many, and they got that way in part through some perverse migration behaviour. Pushed off the land by technological and institutional events in agriculture, by harvest failure and by Malthusian pressure, rural emigrants flood the cities in far greater numbers than good jobs can be created for them. Attracted by some irrational optimism that they will be selected for those scarce high-wage city jobs, the rural immigrants keep coming. Lacking high-wage jobs in the growing industrial sectors, the glut of rural immigrants spills over into low-wage service sectors, manifested by unemployment and pauperism, while their families crowd into inadequate housing.

Many contemporary economic historians have used this Third World paradigm in thinking about British cities during the first industrial revolution (Pollard 1981b, Williamson 1981), and many point to low-wage casual labour on the docks and in the building trades to illustrate the point. Certainly Mayhew made much of what now would be called London's informal services, and low-wage casual labour, sweat-shops and street vending have all played an important part in nineteenth-century labour histories since. Whether one adopts the view that the urban service sector was a vast holding area for the reserve army of immigrants who were pulled into the city in anticipation of getting those high-wage industrial jobs, or whether one shares Mayhew's view that London street people were pushed into those low-wage jobs, both predict the following: while the earnings of new city immigrants may have caught up eventually with those of previous residents, newcomers faced poor job prospects early on since the cities had problems absorbing them when they first arrived. Thus, if Victorian cities really had serious absorption problems, immigrants must have had lower earnings than non-immigrants.

The limited information in the 1851 census (Williamson 1990a: ch. 5) provides little evidence to support this view. Unemployment and poverty certainly blighted Britain's cities in the mid-nineteenth century, but the same was true of the countryside. There is nothing inconsistent between the well-known finding of poverty in Britain's cities during the industrial revolution and a relatively efficient city labour market that absorbed the migrants quickly into the labour force. And quick absorption it was. With the significant exception of the Irish, male immigrants into Britain's cities did not exhibit lower earnings than non-immigrants. Nor did they suffer higher unemployment rates. The evidence seems to be inconsistent with the view that migrants entered the city in response to inflated expectations of future earnings possibilities, suffering unemployment or underemployment in traditional low-wage service sector jobs while they waited for better jobs. Rather, they were motivated by current job prospects, and those prospects were confirmed. This is not to say that migrants were never unemployed or that they could not be found in large numbers in the low-wage service sectors. The evidence from the 1851 census simply confirms that city immigrants had the same earnings experience as non-immigrants.

Leaving the village to go to the city: a second look

Did farm labourers respond quickly to economic opportunities in the cities? Or, did inelastic migrant labour supplies to the city create urban–rural wage gaps and drive up the cost of city labour, thus choking off the rate of industrialisation?

Table 13.6 shows that an index of the gap between the average nominal earnings of unskilled city and farm labour (1797 = 100) rose sharply across the first half of the nineteenth century. The rise in farm wages lagged far behind the rise in city wages. The table suggests that the nominal wage gap did not begin to rise until well after the French Wars. Indeed, the index implies that wartime conditions served to erode the gap. Because the conflict caused a contraction in foreign trade (cutting back the import supply of grains and choking off the foreign export demand for manufactures), the relative price of grains rose, and domestic agriculture was favoured. It is hardly surprising, therefore, that the wage gap collapsed since wartime labour demands were unusually strong in the countryside. With the end of the wars, however, the pace of British industrialisation accelerated and agriculture resumed its long-run relative demise. Labour demand in the cities far outstripped local labour supplies. Rising wage gaps between farm and city need not imply that rural emigration was small (Table 13.3). Rather, they imply only that it was not big enough, so the relative cost of labour rose in the cities as a consequence. By the 1830s, nominal city wages were 73 per cent higher than farm wages.

Have other countries repeated the British experience? The absence of comparable data makes it impossible to say for sure, but one thing is certain: wage gaps of this magnitude have been commonly observed in the middle of industrial revolutions ever since Britain experienced the first. City wages are about 41 per cent higher than farm wages in the contemporary Third World, and they were about 51 per cent higher among

Table 13.6. *Trends in the British nominal wage gap, 1797–51*
(1797 = 100)

Year	Index
1797	100·0
1805	86·0
1810	96·7
1815	105·1
1819	99·7
1827	132·4
1835	134·7
1851	148·3

Source: Williamson (1990a: Table 7.1, 182). The gap is calculated as the difference between the unskilled earnings rate of urban labour and the farm-earnings rate, divided by the farm-earnings rate. Thus, it is the percentage differential by which city unskilled wages exceeded farm wages, the common measure used in the development literature.

late nineteenth-century industrialisers. Nor were things much different in the New World: wage gaps were about 50 per cent in America in the mid-1890s at the end of three decades of fast industrialisation after the Civil War.

Why were English farm labourers in the 1830s willing to accept much lower wages than those available in city and town? Perhaps these nominal wage gaps fail to measure the better quality of village life compared with the city. After all, these nominal wage gaps fail to take account of the fact that the cities were expensive places in which to live, that the cities were ugly places in which to live, that there were relief schemes in the countryside to ease the burden of seasonal unemployment, and that farmers made some payments in kind. While these attributes do help to explain that 73 per cent wage gap in the 1830s, an equally interesting question is whether they can help account for the rise in the wage gap after the French Wars. There are reasons to think so, especially those related to the rising cost and falling quality of city life, events which city employers must have been forced to offset with higher nominal wages if they were to attract rural workers in large numbers.

One price which increases sharply during industrial revolutions is city rents. There are three reasons for this. First, housing construction is labour intensive and per unit labour costs do rise during industrial revolutions. Second, urban housing is space intensive, and rising urban land scarcity is a fact of life during all industrial revolutions. Third, the rate of productivity advance in the building trades is slower than that of commodity production. All of these factors should serve to raise the cost of urban housing as industrialisation unfolds. It is manifested by a rise in rents, and it is manifested by families saving on rising dwelling costs by moving into smaller dwellings and by the dwellings themselves packing in closer together, events which serve to raise mortality and morbidity, while lowering the quality of city life.

The facts support this view. From the 1790s to the 1840s, real rents (nominal rents relative to the cost of living) in Leeds, Black Country towns and an industrial village in Staffordshire rose by 2.5 per cent per year, for a whopping 30 per cent per decade. Since rents accounted for about 20 per cent of the urban labourer's budget, this explosion raised the rate of city cost of living growth by perhaps as much as 0.5 per cent per year. A good share of the increase in the nominal wage gap between city and farm may simply reflect these forces.

Furthermore, what about the poor quality of urban life? Did urban employers have to pay a premium to attract potential rural emigrants to locations of poorer environmental quality, manifested most vividly by the much higher mortality and morbidity in nineteenth-century cities, so much so that Frederick Engels called it 'social murder'? The next section will discuss at greater length how to estimate the value of these ghastly urban disamenities. It turns out that the premium may have been as high as 24 per cent in England as a whole.

After adjusting for the fact that cities were expensive, that cities were environmentally unattractive and required some compensation for the 'bads' prevailing there, and that poor relief was used to augment workers' incomes in the countryside during slack seasons, the nominal wage gap drops to a true wage gap of about 33 per cent. The central fact remains: although they left their villages in large numbers, farm emigrants were slow to take advantage of better city jobs.

Did these wage gaps matter? Contemporary development economists think that they do, and they have been central to debates over development strategy since the Second World War. By appealing to sluggish migration and resulting distortions which make wages 'too high' in the city, development economists have used this evidence to support arguments for protection. Since Britain did not protect city industries with tariffs, did wage gaps in the 1830s lower rates of industrialisation well below what they should have been? If farm labour had responded to city employment opportunities robustly enough to erase the wage gap, would industrialisation have taken place even more rapidly than it did up to the 1860s? It can be shown that it would have. Indeed, one estimate has it that industrial employment growth might have been something like 2.7 per cent per year without those wage gaps, instead of the 2 per cent actually achieved, and manufacturing output might have grown at 3.9 per cent per year, not the 3.1 per cent it actually achieved (Williamson 1990a: ch. 7).

As Sir Arthur Lewis pointed out some time ago, the urban transition can be slowed down or choked off if inelastic urban labour supplies drive up the nominal cost of labour facing urban firms. Based on the first industrial revolution, Sir Arthur is right: the wage gaps between farm and city did indeed choke off British city growth and industrialisation between the 1820s and the 1860s.

Housing, disamenities and death

The quality of urban life has always played a key role in debates over the British industrial revolution. It certainly attracted the attention of Chadwick, Kay and other social reformers in the 1830s and 1840s, but for hot rhetoric it is hard to beat Frederick Engels, who, as we have seen, viewed the migration of rural labour to British cities as 'social murder'. High density, crowding and resulting environmental decay all contributed to high city mortality and morbidity, and immigrants entered that environment at their peril. The early Victorian perception persists in academic debates even today, and the 'pessimists' in the standard of living debate have made much of the issue. Although even the most ardent pessimist would acknowledge the dreary environment of rural England at this time, urban disamenities have, nonetheless, been viewed as seriously lowering working-class living standards up to the 1840s and beyond. Not only was this true of old residents – whose cities, it was alleged, deteriorated in quality over time – but it was true of new urban immigrants, who left more benign rural environments for employment in the ugliest districts of Bradford, Salford, Leeds, Manchester, east London and elsewhere.

What did the rural emigrant forego by leaving his village for some ugly urban district during the first industrial revolution? The answer can be found by applying methods suggested by recent research on twentieth-century urbanisation. Application of these methods to assess the perils of city life in the early nineteenth century is especially attractive because it makes it possible for the workers themselves to reveal their preferences. For more than a century, our perceptions have been coloured by the more verbal Victorian middle-class observer who wrote books and pamphlets which, as it turns out, reveal far stronger preferences for urban amenities than did the workers themselves who placed higher priority on better-paying jobs.

That there was wide variance in crude mortality rates across cities, towns and villages in nineteenth-century England cannot be denied (Table 13.2). But the best indicator of environmental quality is the infant mortality rate, and the Registrar General started to publish comprehensive evidence on it back as early as 1841. Not only was infant mortality higher in the 1840s than in the 1900s, but the cities had much higher rates than the countryside. Furthermore, the difference between city and countryside was far bigger in the 1840s than in the 1900s. These differentials had disappeared by the 1920s, but for nineteenth-century England, the cities were indeed the killers advertised by Engels' rhetoric.

What role did density, crowding, city size and industrialisation play in accounting for the wide variance in infant mortality rates in the 1830s? It turns out that city density and size both play a positive role, confirming the conventional wisdom that urbanisation bred high mortality. Municipal social overhead and housing simply could not or did not keep up with the requirements that were generated by population size and density, thus implying a deterioration in the mortality environment. In contrast, the industrial orientation of the city, or lack of it, played no role. It was not industrialisation that generated the disamenities associated with the high infant mortality rates, but rather urbanisation. The south of England and Wales were regions of very high quality of life, even after controlling for regional urban and industrial attributes. In summary, a very large share of the infant mortality variance across England in the 1830s can be explained by two forces: crowding within dwellings, and the density of the urban environments within which those dwellings were located.

Increasing land scarcity, rising labour costs, lagging productivity advance, more expensive resource-intensive building materials and fore-gone dwelling investment during the French Wars all served to generate the spectacular increase in city rents from the 1790s to the 1840s. Workers responded by economising on dwelling space and quality. Crowding resulted. Perhaps for some of the same reasons, municipal planners found it difficult to maintain the necessary social overhead capital to serve the environmental needs of a rapidly expanding city population. City environments deteriorated as a result. Both of these forces kept disamenity levels, mortality and morbidity high in the cities.

Did workers demand a premium (above the lower village wages) for that city life? It turns out that they did. The premium was higher in the north of England where the towns were environmentally worse (ranging between 12 and 30 per cent) than in the south of England (ranging between 8 and 20 per cent), and ranged between 10 and 24 per cent for England as a whole (Williamson 1990a: ch. 9). These premia were not big enough to erase the wage gains from moving from village to city. Nor were they large enough to erase the wage gains for the average Englishman between the 1800s and the 1860s. But they were large enough to confirm the views of Victorian reformers that the cities were an environmental mess which needed to be cleaned up by more active policy intervention.

Did Britain underinvest in cities?

By the standards of the contemporary Third World and the late nineteenth century, Britain recorded very modest investment shares in national income and very modest rates of accumulation. That fact has generated a long and active debate centred around the question: was the investment share low because investment requirements were modest, or was the investment share low because of a savings constraint? The first argues that investment demand in the private sector was the critical force which drove accumulation during Britain's industrial revolution, low rates of technical progress and the absence of a capital-using bias both serving to minimise private sector investment requirements. The second argues that Britain's growth was savings-constrained. Until very recently, the first view dominated the literature.

This dominant view sees early nineteenth-century Britain as so labour intensive and innovations so capital-saving that investment requirements to equip new workers could easily be fulfilled by modest amounts of domestic savings, so easily in fact that domestic savings had to look for outlets overseas. There are some odd omissions from this view. First, rarely is there any mention of housing, infrastructure and social overhead. This is a puzzling omission because there is another strand of historical literature which stresses crowding in the cities, a deteriorating urban environment and lack of public investment in infrastructure (sewers, water supplies, street paving, lighting, refuse removal and so on). It is also puzzling because such investments loom very large in typical industrial revolutions, the Third World included. Indeed, many development economists and historians have argued that such investments are essential complements to the plant and equipment set in place in modern industry. Without them, rates of return in the modern private sector may sag and industrialisation can be choked off. Dirty and unhealthy cities can serve to drive up the effective price of labour to urban firms either by producing sick workers or by requiring large nominal wage bribes to get reluctant workers to enter dirty cities. Both would serve to raise the effective cost of labour and choke off industrial profits. Thus, low rates of accumulation in industry may be induced, in part, by low rates of investment in complementary public infrastructure and private housing.

Second, discussion on this subject may have confused what actually was with what should have been. It may be a mistake to conclude that Britain's labour-intensive growth strategy was a good thing. Those modest investment requirements may reflect an attempt to achieve an industrial revolution on the cheap. If so, the strategy may have turned out to be more expensive in the longer run.

If investment requirements were really modest at the margin during the first industrial revolution, this should have been reflected in declining average capital–output ratios (ACORs) between, say, 1800 and 1860. Decline they did: Britain's economy-wide ACOR underwent a spectacular drop from about 5.2 in 1800 to about 3.6 in 1860, the biggest fall by far taking place in the first three decades of the nineteenth century. The fall is a little less spectacular outside agriculture, but big nonetheless: from 4.9 in 1800 to 3.5 in 1860. At the margin, therefore, Britain's investment requirements during the industrial revolution were far below eighteenth-century averages. Yet, one of the key reasons why investment requirements were so modest, and why the ACOR drops so steeply, is that Britain failed to commit resources to those urban infrastructure investments that, to paraphrase Sir Arthur Lewis, makes city growth in the contemporary Third World so capital intensive and thus so expensive. Investment in housing and public works simply failed to keep pace with the rest of the economy in the first half of the nineteenth century. One can see this very clearly when the ACOR outside agriculture is calculated to exclude housing and public works: then the ACOR rises over those six critical decades. One can also see it by looking at per capita growth in social overhead capital stock (residential housing plus public works and public buildings). These growth rates were negative from 1760 to 1800, and they were far below those of the rest of the economy between 1800 and 1860. Indeed, these estimates suggest that dwelling stocks per capita were lower in 1860 than they had been in 1760!

Investment requirements during the late eighteenth century were kept modest by allowing the stock of social overhead per capita to fall, contributing to a deterioration in the quality of urban life. This growth regime continued for the first three decades of the nineteenth century, although not with quite the same intensity. By 1830, therefore, Britain had accumulated an enormous deficit in her social overhead capital stocks by pursuing seventy years of industrialisation on the cheap. It cost her dearly, as the social reformers were about to point out. Between 1830 and 1860, there is some evidence of catching up in public works, in part a response to the goading of the social reformers, but the gap in growth rates between dwelling stocks and all other fixed capital per capita increased. In short, while actual investment requirements may have been modest during the first industrial revolution, they would not have been so modest had investment in social overhead kept pace. It had its price: the cities became ugly, crowded and polluted, breeding high mortality and morbidity. The reformers were moved to political agitation.

In early July 1842, during a summer of high unemployment and social protest in the cities, Edwin Chadwick, secretary to the Poor Law Commission, presented to the House of Lords his 'Report on the Sanitary Condition of the Labouring Population of Great Britain'; it has been viewed as a turning point in sanitary reform ever since. Part of a flood of public documents which were directed toward social reform in the 1830s and 1840s, Chadwick's Report is far and away the best. As a piece of pure legislative and social protest rhetoric, it is superb. The Report also contains an extraordinary amount of empirical documentation about the economic condition of the urban labour force – disease, mortality, morbidity, housing and, most important, the state of city sanitation or what we would now call the quality of public health infrastructure. It also offers engineering and cost details on sewage and water systems. The Report even goes so far as to compute benefit/cost assessments of various projects. It also contains explicit administrative and legislative proposals on how the sanitary reform could be best implemented. Although an outstanding social document, the Report also represented a turning point in another way. It reflected the fact that the public health movement now had a leader in Chadwick, who gave the reformers a well-defined legislative focus.

It is said that the Sanitary Report awakened middle-class and upper-class sensibilities to the ghastly environment of Britain's urban poor, an environment which most non-poor Victorians failed to comprehend. Most Victorians with political influence were located at a safe distance from the worst part of that environment, and their pride in Britain's economic success was based on the manifest evidence of booming industrialisation, accumulation and world trade. The Report informed them of the ugly underside of urbanisation, and it appealed to their humanitarian and economic instincts to make an investment in cleaning up the cities and thus to improve the sanitary and economic condition of the labouring poor.

Yet it is easy to make too much of the 1842 Sanitary Report. Remarkable as the document and Chadwick may have been, the fact remains that the Report was preceded by at least a century of accumulated understanding and public health experimentation. If we fail to appreciate that fact, then we will be left with the mistaken impression that a far greater commitment to cleaner cities through social overhead investment was technologically out of reach prior to 1842. We will also make the far greater error of assuming that a major commitment of public resources to sanitation and housing reform took place in the decades immediately following. In truth, Britain was well into the late nineteenth century before she made significant progress towards cleaning up her cities.

A final remark

It is appropriate to leave this chapter on coping with city growth during Britain's industrial revolution with this central policy debate, and with a question: Was Britain's environmental ugliness the most efficient path to industrialisation?

Because the British tax system was highly regressive at this time, certainly prior to Peel's tax reforms of 1842, the working class would have borne most of the cost of cleaning up the cities and improving housing earlier in the nineteenth century. To the extent that the incidence would have fallen on the working class through indirect taxation of necessities and through rising rents on now-greater-taxed urban property, then their real consumption levels might well have been eroded. Efforts to legislate higher residential health standards and lower levels of tenement crowding would also have inflated rents. So too would have space-intensive municipal urban renewal schemes. If the contrary is believed, that urban landlords, merchants and capitalists would have absorbed the tax burden, how would they have responded? Surely they would have responded in part by diminished saving as their disposable incomes contracted through the rise in taxes. If some industrial accumulation and capacity creation had been foregone as a consequence, some future urban jobs would also have been foregone. Fewer urban jobs imply a lower absorption of low-wage rural workers into high-wage urban employment. Thus workers' nominal incomes would have diminished on that score too.

The trade-off between commodities and environment was very real and the reform debates much more subtle than first meets the eye. Did the unfortunate environmental ugliness of Britain's cities reflect, nonetheless, an efficient path to industrialisation? We simply do not know.

14   Unequal living standards

Peter H. Lindert

Caring about inequality

The battleground

Beliefs about the proper role of government in the economy are still shaped by perceptions over how industrialisation and the private market economy treated people 200 years ago. Support for central control and the welfare state still draws on the belief that the gaps between rich and poor widen, and workers are often impoverished, if government does not intervene. Support for privatisation and the market place rests on the opposing belief, that the invisible hand gives workers a fair shake, raising their absolute living standards and perhaps even reducing inequality between rich and poor. Both sides are convinced that their beliefs are well rooted in historical facts. The paradigmatic history is still, for both sides, a story about how the workers of England fared between 1750 and 1850.

Two debates have been inevitably intertwined. One concerns absolute living standards: Did material life get absolutely worse for much or all of the working classes between 1750 and 1850? The other concerns inequality, or relative living standards: Whatever the trends in absolute material comfort, was the gap between the highest and lowest incomes widening or narrowing? This chapter interprets the state of both debates, and adds an overview of England's famous poor relief policies between 1750 and 1850.

The great economists, like members of Parliament, participated in both debates. Most of the economists writing in the late eighteenth and early nineteenth centuries thought that workers' absolute living standards were not improving. In 1776 Adam Smith thought that workers' real wages had gone down in the last decade, though they had increased over the previous century (Smith 1776: 66, 69–70). Malthus also cited the history of workers' real wages to support the pessimism that is still attached to his name. He found that the workers' ability to buy food, and to a lesser extent their overall living standard, had fallen between 1400 and 1800. In the early nineteenth century pessimism continued to prevail among economists, as among other writers. Workers were getting no better off, and possibly worse off, according to Ricardo, John Stuart Mill, McCulloch and of course Marx and Engels. True, there were exceptions, even among those writers who laboured hardest to describe poverty. Eden, in *The State of the Poor* (1795), challenged Malthus and others on the alleged drop in real wages. Even Chadwick, the intrepid investigator of the horrors which life held for the urban working classes, thought in the depression of 1842 that workers were still better off than in decades past. While the debate was unresolved, the pessimists (those believing in a downtrend) seem to have commanded a bare majority, at least among writers of political economy.

From about 1850 on, as signs of advance in absolute living standards became clearer, attention was increasingly turned to the debate over inequality: Were the workers falling further behind the wealthier and more propertied? Here the opposing allegations covered the whole sweep of modern British history, not just the classic century 1750–1850. A cornerstone of modern socialism is that the gaps between England's rich and poor widened, both in the industrial revolution and since. George Bernard Shaw even drew on economic history to *define* socialism: 'It is in this phase of capitalistic development, attained in Great Britain in the nineteenth century, that Socialism arises as a revolt against a distribution of wealth that has lost all its moral plausibility ... The inequalities [have] become monstrous' (Shaw 1929: 896).

This view was rebutted by many, of course, including such economists as Porter, Giffen and Marshall, each of whom asserted that the gap between the propertied and working classes was in fact narrowing across the nineteenth century.

Both debates have continued ever since, fed by the social importance of the subject and by the paucity of convincing data. People of goodwill differed then, as now, not only because their values differed but also because it was truly hard to know what had happened to different large social groups.

Solving the mystery of what happened to living standards and inequality demands keen sleuthwork. The clues are scattered and often deceptive. To gather them takes alertness, to weigh them takes care. Hope can be drawn from the imaginative way in which Clapham once studied the rag trade for clues about living standards in the statistical darkness before the First World War:

There was some evidence, in the years 1901–14, of a slight deterioration in [German] living standards ... English specialists noted, in the ten years before the war, that German rags were not quite so good as they used to be. This was a sure test; for prosperous nations and classes throw away their clothes early. The best rags on the market are American and Canadian; the worst Italian and Greek. (Clapham 1928: 406–7)

Yet it is possible to go beyond just emulating his imagination. Better information is now at hand, even for an earlier era in which almost everybody was too poor to throw away any rags. Information about a past era does not just fade away. It does so for the first three generations, as those who lived in that era die and those whom they told forget. Later, though, the historical record about life in a given year starts expanding again. Geologists dig further, archivists preserve and collate more materials and scholars supplement their reading with photocopying and the computer.

While comprehensive data will always be elusive, a myriad of partial and indirect clues now support these broad conclusions.

(1) It now appears that workers' living standards showed no clear progress before 1820, but definitely improved from 1820 to 1850. The era of definite improvement is the one for which improvement has been debated most, and doubted most.

(2) Incomes and wealth were as unequally distributed in Victorian England as in any other advanced country before the First World War.

(3) Income and wealth inequality may have risen in the late eighteenth century and the early nineteenth, though by less than it dropped in the twentieth.

(4) British government redistributed a greater share of national product to the poor in the era 1780–1834 than at any other time before the First World War, and a greater share than in other countries.

The first task is to agree on generalities about what indicators of unequal 'living standards' should be sought.

Inequality of what?

In the end, most of us read the phrase 'living standards' as a direct translation of the material side of happiness. It is hard to measure happiness for any group at any point in time, and there is even evidence that societies change their standards so as to express about the same level of happiness at very different levels of comfort. Still, it is not hard to fix on some indicators that should make one historical setting better than another in the eyes of almost anybody. Some are indicators of health (life expectancy, suicide mortality, sickness, height). Others are direct or indirect clues about the material inputs that people had available for improving their health and happiness. In general, the pursuit of health and happiness depends on these three inputs from the material world: first, ones enjoyment of ones own time, a key input into everything; second, ones enjoyment of commodities, ones purchasing power for a given sacrifice of time for work; and third, the quality of ones material environment.

Each of these lends itself to useful indirect measurements from economic history. For example, clues can stem from people's enjoyment of their time by following data on the number of years they spent at work, and the number of hours they worked each year. To judge people's command over commodities, it is possible to measure their lifetime income either by its uses or by its sources:

Uses	Sources
Consumption + saving	= wages + property income − net taxes
	= disposable income
	= purchasing power over commodities.

Sometimes history measures whole incomes, as in some famous English social tables estimating the whole income distribution. Sometimes there are separate estimates about parts of income, such as data on real wage differentials or property income (wealth) differentials, or data on the part of income that is consumed in a given year. All these indirect clues can be used – carefully. One preliminary caution: it is necessary to think hard about what measures of income mean when they differ because people worked different amounts. Did people's work and earnings differ because some were unable to find the extra work, or because they preferred more free time? It will make a difference to some interpretations of the clues history has left.

Inequality among whom?

Who were the human units whose unequal living standards we are discussing? Individuals alive at a moment in time? Individuals born in a certain span of time? Families? Classes? Regions? And who are the 'workers' whose living standards have been the subject of so much debate?

Vague humanism generally settles on a concern about the inequality of lifetime resources available to individuals born in a certain time span, abstracting from the distribution of incomes across families, classes or regions. Yet this forces compromises with the available facts. For a start, information never exists about the material resources enjoyed by individuals over entire lifetimes. Rather, we must settle for indicators dated by year, such as average earnings of common labourers in the harvest season of 1843. Often, too, the census and other documents leave records of the fortunes of families or occupational classes, not individuals.

In order to minimise the dangers of compositional shift while using grouped data, one should stick as closely as possible to fixed quantile-group definitions. In what follows, the 'working class' will be defined as the lower 50 per cent of individual income earners. Such a definition honours the spirit of two original definitions of working class: the half of society whose individual labours bought the least, and those whose livelihood depended on selling the fruits of their labour, not their non-human property (as was always true of the lower-income 50 per cent at any time before the Second World War). When viewing trends on income and wealth inequality, it is possible to afford the slight luxury of switching back and forth between such a lower-half focus and viewing trends in the shares going to finer quantile groups, such as the richest 5 per cent or the poorest 20 per cent.

Workers' absolute living standards

To explore all the revealing indicators of workers' well being or suffering, many different kinds of clues must be used. First, some obviously fundamental indicators, such as how long Britons lived, how many hours they worked and how much they consumed on the average, will help; then, for clearer results about long-run trends, measures that refer more specifically to workers, such as their real wage rates and their implicit valuations of environmental quality.

Survival and health

Length of life is a good indicator of people's state of health while living, as well as a direct measure of time at their disposal. A natural starting point is therefore to ask how long workers lived if they were born in 1750, or in 1800 or in 1850.

In 1850, mortality rates were still deplorable by any twentieth-century standard, and were deplored by parliamentary enquiries at the time. Someone born in England at that time faced an average life expectancy of less than forty years, versus forty-six or forty-seven years in Chad or Ethiopia or seventy-five years in Britain today. At the mortality rates then prevailing, one baby in seven failed to survive until a first birthday. The infant mortality ratio was more like one in five babies in England's cities, where crowding and high rents added to the squalor and pestilence. Medical knowledge was still crude, with smallpox vaccination being one of the few tangible advances.

Were the life chances always so grim, or were the people of 1850 destined to die younger than their great grandparents' generation? Crude death

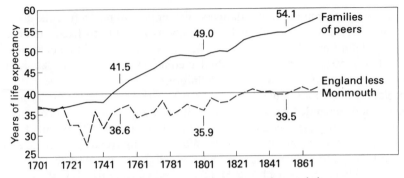

Figure 14.1 Life expectancy at birth, the nation and the peerage, 1701–1871

Sources: five-year averages for England less Monmouth are from Wrigley and Schofield (1981: 528–9). Those for the British peerage families are period rates (not birth-cohort rates) calculated from Hollingsworth (1977: 326–8). Both series are averages for both sexes.

rates for counties and cities, and infant mortality rates for a few cities, are known back into the eighteenth century, thanks largely to the leadership of census taker John Rickman. These local series do not show that mortality worsened between 1750 and 1850. On the contrary, crude death rates suggest that mortality was nearly constant in fast-growing Manchester and Liverpool, while infant mortality rates fell in London and rural areas. Signs of improvement were spread over both the late eighteenth century and the early nineteenth, but especially after 1811 (Marshall 1832; Flinn 1970; Cherry 1980; Jones 1980; Wrigley and Schofield 1981; Wrigley 1983b; Woods 1985). The life-expectancy trend was also probably positive for Scotland, though more recent studies imply a different timing from that suggested by Flinn's earlier work (Flinn 1977; Tyson 1992).

So far, the average of available local studies seems to suggest a gain in English life expectancy between 1750 and 1850, especially after Waterloo. Yet averages by locality could misrepresent trends in working-class mortality, for two reasons. First, the true national average apparently improved less than a fixed-weight average of all regions, because population was shifting from the healthier rural areas to the more deadly urban centres (Woods 1985). Second, even the true national average is not a working-class average.

To infer trends in mortality in working-class families, we need to combine two other series on life expectancy. Figure 14.1 plots two life expectancies at birth: that for the whole population and that for the peerage families. To see what they suggest about the hidden history of working-class mortality, let us start with the average life expectancy for all of England (less Monmouth). According to the Wrigley and Schofield (1981) estimates, the deplorable life expectancy of only 39.5 years as of 1850 was slightly better than any experienced between 1701 and 1816. Back in the 1720s and 1730s death struck at very young ages, especially in London, where more than a third of all babies apparently died before their first birthday. (This statement is based on calculations starting with figures on deaths of infants before their second birthday as recorded in the London bills of mortality from 1729 onwards (Marshall 1832). The share of these dying before their first birthday was estimated by applying the third English life table and under-registration ratios from Wrigley and Schofield.) The infant mortality rate had dropped considerably by mid-century. There may have been no improvement in the second half of the eighteenth century, but life may have lengthened slightly between about 1816 and 1831, with no peacetime relapse thereafter.

The national average is not the working classes, however. Perhaps, behind that average, the better-off were living much longer around 1850 than their wealthy counterparts in 1750, while workers could not stay alive as long in 1850 as in 1750. The answer requires mortality data giving the occupations of the deceased or, for infants and children, their parents. While such data are generally lacking, there is one indirect clue. For one small class at the top of the economic and social ranks, namely peers and their families, Hollingsworth's (1977) research permits estimation of life expectancy in peerage families for each quinquennium of history. As shown in Figure 14.1, life chances improved dramatically for peers and their extended families after 1740. While they had lived no longer than the national average at the start of the eighteenth century, by the 1850s they lived fully fifteen years longer than average.

No large social group was likely to have had better life expectancy than the peerage families, at least after 1750. This likelihood puts bounds on what could have happened to average life expectancy in the working classes. Define the working class as the lower-income 50 per cent of the population, a group whose life expectancy would not have exceeded the national average plotted in Figure 14.1. Presumably, the best life chance that English workers' families could have experienced was just that national average for England less Monmouth, which improved slightly to 39.5 by 1850. So the national average was a ceiling on workers' average life chances, one that did not rise very fast until the twentieth century. Their worst life chance at any given date, as far as we can tell, would have occurred if the whole upper half of English society lived as long as the peerage families. In this opposite and extreme case, life expectancy in the working-class half of the population would have been as far below the national average as peerage life expectancy was above it. That is, workers' life expectancy in 1850 might have been as low as 24.9 years (i.e. as far below 39.5 as the peers' 54.1 was above it). This figure seems implausibly low, given the sustained rapid population growth of the time, but it gives a warning needed here: in a long historical period for which the national average life chances improved only slightly or not at all, the dramatic improvement in upper-class life expectancy means that some ranks of the population suffered a decline in length of life. Workers' lives may have shortened over the generations. This warning is strongest for the latter half of the eighteenth century, for which the national average shows no gain. It is possible that the national average life expectancy failed to improve over the latter half of the eighteenth century despite the improvements documented for several regions and cities. Indeed, the national average could have remained the same even if *all* areas showed separate improvements, because population kept shifting toward the cities, where mortality was greater. For the early nineteenth century, especially after 1816, workers' average life expectancy may have improved somewhat, though there is room for doubt.

Since health and happiness depend not only on the length of life, but also on being well during life, we should also seek information on sickness and incapacity. A quantitative history of sickness has already begun to be written (Riley 1991). Like the mortality evidence, it suggests little or no progress, though also no deterioration, before 1850. Another health indicator is height by age. Societies differ in the timing and extent of the teenage growth spurt, and the patterns suggest that the heights attained by adulthood depend on nutritional status, a concept correlated with overall healthiness during childhood. If we knew how tall people became, we would have another clue as to the health they enjoyed, or suffered, in infancy and childhood. Recent studies have followed exactly that lead, measuring the heights of over 100,000 males inducted into the Army, the Marines, the Royal Military Academy, and the Marine Society (Floud *et al.* 1990), and of convicts sent to Australia (Nicholas and Steckel 1991).

The height studies agree that the pace of health improvement before 1850 was gradual, though the trends within the century 1750–1850 remain uncertain. There is disagreement as to whether the English became shorter or taller across the (birth cohorts of) the late eighteenth century. From around 1820 to around 1840, the height of boys and men rose a bit, like their life expectancy. Yet heights, unlike measurements of life expectancy, then fell back around mid-century (Floud *et al.* 1990). Where the height studies and the mortality studies agree most strongly is that the progress before 1850 could not have been as fast as twentieth-century progress.

Own time versus work time

Over the whole century 1750–1850 the average amount of time away from work enjoyed by succeeding generations of English workers may have stayed about the same. If the average length of life showed no clear trend between 1750 and 1816, and then maybe a slight increase between 1816 and 1850, the same may be true of the amount of time spent at work, leaving a constant average amount of own time (time away from work).

This no-change conjecture is the net result of weighing a variety of inadequate clues. Little is known about the life-cycle patterns of time use in those days, and fresh data are badly needed. Yet thanks to the efforts of several scholars (Pinchbeck 1930; Bienefeld 1972; Tranter 1981), there are some very rough ideas of trend in time spent at work, to supplement our information on the average life span.

The share of life spent at work is the product of three measures: working hours per day, working days per year, and working years per life. Working hours per day did not rise as much as one would infer from classic portrayals of the march from farm life to the sweated textile mills. While arduous fourteen-hour days were indeed common in the new textile factories, the net shift toward either textiles or factories was only a small share of the labour force before 1850. While this could have brought a rise in average working hours in industry in the early nineteenth century, the ten-hour day that was common in industry by the end of the eighteenth century fell short of the twelve-hour industrial work day that was more prevalent in the sixteenth and seventeenth centuries (Bienefeld 1972: 11–89). Furthermore, the rise of long-hour factory employment probably reduced the daily working hours of women and children in such home handicrafts as spinning. On balance, there was no trend in daily working hours in the latter half of the eighteenth century and only a slight hint of a longer average work day in the first half of the nineteenth.

Working days per year may have expanded gradually, both in agriculture and in industry. Within agriculture, work may have increased slightly in the slack winter and mid-summer seasons, due to changes in crop rotation and the slight shift toward dairy and meat products, with their fuller-year labour demands. Within industry, work on Saturday became more common. The typical industrial work year may have risen from 2,500 hours to anywhere between that figure and 3,000 hours by 1850.

The number of years spent at work probably did not change significantly. The famous fact that children were sent to work in factories at earlier ages suggests lost years of home time. Yet children in the pre-industrial setting also began work very early, so that being sent to factories meant only more odious and regimented work, not more work years. The age at which work

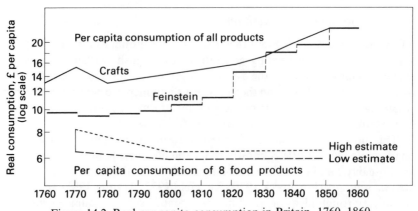

Figure 14.2 Real per capita consumption in Britain, 1760–1860

Sources: Feinstein (1981), Crafts (1985a: Table 15.1). Estimates of total consumption are for Great Britain in prices of 1851–60, while those of the eight food products are for England and Wales in prices of 1850.

ended may not have changed much at all, given hints that people retired around ages sixty to sixty-five in the late nineteenth century, much as they do today (Tranter 1981: 221–2). Thus with a steady number of work years, steady or slightly rising daily hours and gradually rising work days per year, the average English person probably spent any extra length of life at work, with no gain in own time before 1850.

Consumption

Even if there was no change in the hours of own time enjoyed by the average person between 1750 and 1850, living standards could have changed if people's ability to consume or save commodities changed. For Britain as a whole, that did happen. Not only did Britons save more and more real wealth per capita over these decades (Feinstein 1988), but they apparently consumed more as well, as shown in Figure 14.2. While any estimates of total consumption must remain rough and tentative, a pattern emerges from the decadal averages of Feinstein (1981: 136) and the benchmark estimates of Crafts (1985a: 95). Between 1760 and 1820, any gain in real consumption per capita was slight, yet between 1810–20 and 1850–60 the average consumption standard rose markedly, and may even have doubled.

Yet national averages may have trends opposite to those experienced by workers' families, as already noted in connection with mortality. Unfortunately, glimpses into working-class households before 1850 are confined to

Table 14.1. *Availability of food products in England and Wales, 1770–1850: a range of estimates (£m at 1850 prices)*

	1700	1800	1850
Wheat	1·1–2·1	0·9–1·5	1·6–2·0
Barley	0·7–1·5	0·3–0·6	0·4–0·5
Oats	0·7	0·7–1·1	0·5–0·6
Rye	0·0–0·1	0·1	0·0
Beans and peas	0·7	0·8	0·4
Potatoes	0·2	0·3	0·4
Grains, etc.	3·5–5·2	3·5–4·0	3·5–4·0
Meat	2·7	2·2	2·1
Sugar	0·2	0·3	0·4
Sub-total	6·4–8·1	5·9–6·4	6·0–6·5
Milk	n.a.	0·6	1·0
Butter	n.a.	0·2	0·2
Cheese	n.a.	0·4	0·3
Total	n.a.	7·1–7·7	7·5–8·0

Notes: each pairing of figures shows a range of plausible estimates by different scholars, while each solo figure is a scholarly best guess subject to an unstated range of error. Details may not add up to totals, both because of rounding and because not all low estimates (or all high estimates) were simultaneously ventured by any one author. Estimates of production for England and Wales have been combined with net imports for Great Britain by assuming that England and Wales received its population share of Great Britain's food imports.

Sources: Beveridge (1939); Salaman (1949); Mitchell and Deane (1962); Fairlie (1969); Davis (1979); Holderness (1988, 1989).

a few hundred families at different income levels, hardly enough for a judgement of consumption trends across the generations. Movements in aggregate consumption tell most about working-class living standards for those commodities that take a bigger budget share in working-class households than in others. To look at a kind of consumption tied more closely to workers' income fortunes, one needs to turn to changes in the English diet.

Estimates of food consumption are as difficult as they are central to a view of the whole working of the British economy in this famous century. Britain's imports and exports of food items are measured well enough, but estimates of Britain's own production are disturbingly weak, as noted in chapter 5. Figure 14.2 and Table 14.1 gather high and low estimates for consumption per capita in England and Wales at three benchmark dates.

Clearly, different stories can be told. Food consumption may have dropped by 27 per cent between 1770 and 1800, if one believes Arthur Young's controversial optimistic figures for 1770 and Susan Fairlie's pessimistic figures on grain marketings around 1800. Or average food consumption may not have dropped at all over these thirty years. Over the first half of the nineteenth century, average food consumption may have remained the same, or it may have risen by 13 per cent. Or more: if one accepts the Deane–Cole estimates of agricultural incomes and the Rousseaux price index for agricultural products, Great Britain's real agricultural income (and consumption) per capita rose more than 30 per cent over this half century, mainly after 1820.

If per capita food consumption did not rise greatly in the first half of the nineteenth century while the average consumption of all goods rose, a possibility Figure 14.1 admits, what were people buying more of in 1850 than in 1800 or 1820? Were they things that workers could have afforded? Some were not: coffee, for example, was still a middle-class luxury in 1850 (Mokyr 1988: 77–9). Yet workers could afford some of the rapidly expanding non-food items: tea, clothing, fuel, bricks, iron goods, bottles, simple furniture, hard soap. Both for the nation and for the working classes, puzzles linger: Does it make sense that consumption increases should have been so tilted toward non-food items? If the data are at fault, are the bigger errors in the food data or in the total-consumption data? For the present, these puzzles remain unsolved. Workers' incomes could have been either stagnant or declining between 1770 and 1800, and either stagnant or rising in the first half of the nineteenth century.

Real wage trends

For more direct indicators that really do refer to workers, and not to the whole population, one needs to turn to evidence on what happened to sources of income. It is wise to start with the most abundant kind of evidence, wage rates for adult males, before tackling the tougher task of measuring income losses from unemployment and the lower earning power of women and children.

Like Smith, Malthus and Marx before them, twentieth-century scholars have invested heavily in finding records of what workers were paid in the past, and what prices they had to pay for consumer goods. A sampling of the real-wage literature commenting on national trends over at least a half century of the 1750–1850 period includes Phelps Brown and Hopkins (1956), Flinn (1974), von Tunzelmann (1979), Lindert and Williamson (1983a, 1985a), Crafts (1985a, 1985b, 1989b), Schwartz (1985, 1990), and Botham and Hunt (1987). While gatherers of fresh data can still add much to our knowledge, a rough picture of real-wage trends for adult males has recently begun to emerge. There are broad national patterns, though variations by region and occupation are an essential part of the history of what happened to workers between 1750 and 1850.

The broad national trends are sketched in Figure 14.3. To appreciate these trends, and the most striking departures from them, one should divide that whole hundred years into periods before, during and after the French Wars of 1793–1815.

Between 1750 and 1790, real wages showed no clear sign of progress over the nation as a whole, as Figure 14.3 suggests. Behind the trendless national average, workers' fortunes declined seriously in London and the rural south and improved noticeably in the midlands and the north of England. In the south, one of the best of times for purchasing power was that period of dreadful mortality, the second quarter of the eighteenth century. From 1750 to 1790 (and especially on to 1815), an hour of a man's labour bought less and less in the south (Gilboy 1934, 1936; Tucker 1936; Phelps Brown and Hopkins 1956; Flinn 1974; Schwartz 1985, 1990).

The opposite trend held in the industrial midlands and industrial north. Eccleston (1976) found advances in real wages in the midlands, especially for skilled trades. Botham and Hunt (1987) found a rise of about 18 per cent in the real wage of north Staffordshire labourers, carpenters, and bricklayers, and better increases for potters and coal miners, between 1750 and 1790. Similar results are described by Gilboy (1934, 1936) and Armstrong (1989: 699–702). There was an historic shift: sometime between 1760 and 1790, the industrial north replaced the south as the high-wage region, a pattern that was to hold until the First World War, after which labour demand favoured the south again. For the nation as a whole, however, wages stagnated in the period 1750–90.

The stagnation in men's real wages continued beyond 1790, and through the whole French War era 1793–1815. Again purchasing power deteriorated in the south (Richardson 1977; Flinn 1974; Schwartz 1985) but not in the midlands and north. While the grand averages may not have changed much over the war years, it was in fact a stormy time in which workers' fortunes fluctuated widely. Around 1795, harvest failures and disruptions in the flow of grain from the Continent brought back local famines on a scale not seen for a century. It was also an era of increased rioting over food supplies, price hikes, mechanisation, and other perceived injustices to workers.

Not until after 1810 or 1815 did men's purchasing power seem to improve. On this delayed improvement, Figure 14.3 is explicit, showing that real wages rose, along with per capita consumption and national life expectancy, between Waterloo and mid-century. If the figures are to be

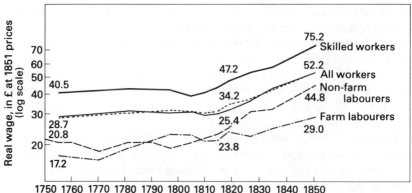

Figure 14.3 Real wages per year for adult male workers at normal employment rates, 1750–1851

Source:

Most data and procedures are from Lindert and Williamson (1983b, 1985b). The benchmark years are 1750, 1755, 1760, 1770, 1781, 1790, 1797, 1805, 1810, 1815, 1819, 1827, 1835 and 1851. Each figure divides an estimate of nominal annual earnings by a 'best guess' cost-of-living index based on 1851. Each is a rough national average mixing together data from different regions of England and (less faithfully) Wales.

The occupational categories are defined as follows:

Farm labourers = adult male agricultural labourers, averaging their harvest, winter and other wage rates. Earnings for fifty-two weeks in 1851 = £29.04.

Non-farm labourers = those outside of agriculture called just 'labourers' in the census or other records; in this case the wage series refer mainly to building labourers. Earnings for forty-six weeks in 1851 = £44.83.

All non-farm unskilled workers not defined in the caption above. Earnings for forty-six weeks in 1851 = £51.87.

Non-farm skilled = skilled production workers in shipbuilding, engineering, printing and building. Earnings for forty-six weeks in 1851 = £75.21.

Some minor revisions are introduced here. First, the cost-of-living indices are extended from the 1781–1851 period to cover 1750–90, using a simple average of the northern index of Botham and Hunt (1987) and Crafts' (1989b) 'best guess' southern index. Second, the wage series for farm and building labourers are extended to more eighteenth-century dates using Schwartz (1990) and Young–Bowley average farm wages for 1770. Third, the hand-loom weavers' wages and employment are incorporated by a special aggregation of them with the non-farm labourers from whose ranks they came in 1780–1800 and whose ranks they joined in large numbers in 1825–50. The trusted, the average working man in 1851 earned 72 per cent more than in 1810, or 66 per cent more than in 1815, or 53 per cent more than in 1819.

Note that even farm workers shared in the net gains, both for the whole century and for the post-war era 1815–50. Their wage gains contradict the traditional emphasis on their being pushed out of villages and into mills by enclosures and other upheavals. If the 'push' of declining rural opportunity had driven as many migrants from agriculture to industry as the 'pull' of rising opportunities in industry and the cities, a clear decline in the real wage in agriculture would be expected. The figures imply otherwise (see also ch. 13).

Can the figures be trusted? How could working men in 1851 have been much better off than their grandfathers, as Figure 14.3 implies? There are many reasons to wonder. After all, the period 1815–50 was the era of greatest outcry against the impoverishment of the workers. Public sympathies and outrage were stirred by parliamentary revelations of harsh treatment and appalling living conditions for factory workers, by Chartist agitation and by Charles Dickens. English working-class consciousness emerged unmistakably (E. P. Thompson 1963). This was also the era which produced Engels' *The Condition of the Working Class in England in 1844* and the *Communist Manifesto*. And was it not in the first half of the nineteenth century that the livelihood of the hand-loom weavers was destroyed? Beyond such suspicions, Figure 14.3 omits quantitative evidence needed to reach the conclusion that workers' living standards improved in the early nineteenth century. We need to know what happened to unemployment, to earnings by women and children and to the quality of life.

The most direct conflict is between Figure 14.3's upswing and the infamous demise of the hand-loom weavers. By 1811, perhaps 3–4 per cent of the British labour force consisted of persons working significant hours weaving cloth in homes or small shops, most of them in or near Lancashire. Their numbers had grown rapidly after 1780, as improvements in factory-spinning technology created an abundant supply of yarn to be woven.

---

earnings series for non-farm labourers and hand-loom weavers is a weighted average of earnings for the two sub-groups, the weights shifting over time. For 1750–90 the aggregation does not matter if we accept the plausible assumption that the two sub-groups had the same average earnings. For 1797–1851, the combined earnings are first dragged down by the disastrous fall in hand-loom weavers' wages, but after 1827 the fall of weavers' piece rates is more than offset by the fact that those left weaving to hire out as labourers experienced a pay increase.

While it is difficult to say what income they earned per week or year, because they were typically paid by the piece of cloth, not by the hour, an adult male in the decade 1806–15 could earn about the same amount weaving at home as an unskilled non-farm labourer would be paid for working the same number of hours. The weavers' earning power was then destroyed, however, first by the post-war slump in textile prices and later, after 1822, by new competition from the power looms of the factories. Real earnings for an adult male hand-loom weaver, in pence per week at 1850 consumer prices, were 144 in 1806, 103 in 1810/16, 88 in 1818/20, 70 in 1823/26, 66 in 1836, 41 in 1839/41 and 58 in 1849/50 (Brown 1990: 610). The figures from the mid-1820s on have been raised 30 per cent to reflect a likely increase in the average number of weekly hours. Throughout the period, 50–60 per cent of the hand-loom weavers were adult males, the share rising slightly as the hand-loom sector shrank. For a fuller economic history of England's hand-loom weavers see Bythell (1969), Fleischman (1985) and Lyons (1989), and the sources they cite. Scotland's hand-loom weavers suffered a similar fate, though with different timing. Their real wage was cut in half more slowly, over the period 1790–1840, and the number of weavers did not fall until the 1840s, when it dropped about 70 per cent (Murray 1978: 23, 40–75, 114–16).

If hand-loom weaving brought only an unskilled labourer's wage in its 1806–15 heyday, how could the hand-loom weavers subsist on less than half that income from the 1820s through the 1850s? They did not. Between 1825 and 1840, the number of hand-loom weavers dropped by half, and by 1851 they represented only about 0.5 per cent of the British labour force. In the second quarter of the nineteenth century perhaps 200,000 weavers left their looms rather than work for so little. As far as we know, they did not die earlier than those around them (in Lancashire at that time, death came early regardless of occupation). Rather, most of them sought and took up other work. Many hand-loom weavers shunned factory textile jobs out of distaste for its harsh discipline. In all likelihood, most hired out as common labourers – a low wage, but a higher one than weaving brought after 1820. The result seems to be that by 1850, most of the former hand-loom weavers, like the weavers of 1806–15, were earning about what ordinary hired labourers earned. Accordingly, including them in the overall average real-wage calculation has had little effect on the trends shown in Figure 14.3 above, even allowing for the abysmally low pay received by the small number of hand-loom weavers still at their looms.

Unemployment

Trends in workers' living standards have long been obscured by the absence of data on unemployment for any year before 1856. It is hard to know what to make of the trends in real wages for the fully employed if it is not known how many could not find full-time jobs. In fact, however, it is possible to estimate how serious unemployment might have been, and our limited knowledge suffices to clarify the timing and extent of the rise in workers' real incomes.

First, what is known about the post-war depression around 1817–20 suggests that the rise of workers' incomes may not have begun until 1820. There are strong hints that post-war unemployment could have been bad enough to cancel the real wage gain from £30.4 in 1810 to £34.2 in 1819 shown for all workers in Figure 14.3 above. In those early post-war years, prices dropped severely in agriculture and in textiles. Accounts from the time suggest considerable underemployment of farm labour and of hand-loom weavers. Since it would take only a rise in unemployment of 12 per cent of the labour force to cancel the measured real-wage gain, it is unwise to date the start of the upward income trend any time before 1820.

Second, the sheer magnitude of the subsequent real-wage gains for those at work limits the relevance of any likely movements in the unemployment rate. For employed workers, the 'all workers' series in Figure 14.3 plots a rise from £34.2 in 1819 to £52.2 in 1851, a gain of 52.6 per cent. For any year, workers' average earnings are equal to $w(1-u)$, where w is the measured wage rate for those at work and u is the share of workers unemployed. If w advanced by 52.6 per cent, imagine how much unemployment would have had to rise between 1819 and 1851 to cancel the net gain. If, contrary to fact, we believed unemployment were *zero* in 1819, unemployment in 1851 would have to be *more than 34 per cent* of the labour force for average earnings to have been below the £34.2 figure experienced three decades earlier (i.e. for $(1-u)$ times £52.2 to be below £34.2). That could not have been true. By all indications, the worst unemployment in British history was in the early 1930s, and that rate was not above 25 per cent. Back in the era studied here, the worst unemployment came either at the *c*. 1820 starting date (reinforcing the impression of subsequent improvement) or in the early 1840s. Yet other clues about the 'hungry forties' say it is unlikely that more than 10 per cent of the labour force was unable to find work (Lindert and Williamson 1983a: 12–16). There must have been a substantial rise in the real earnings of working men between 1820 and 1850, even allowing for unemployment.

Work by women and children

Working-class families derived much of their income from the work of women and children. Just how much is hard to say, since historical records tend to follow adult male work and wages more closely than the less regular work and pay of women and children. Estimates of how many women and children worked for pay, and for how many hours, are less scarce than estimates of the wage rates they were paid. Unfortunately, data on women's and children's paid work time tell little about their well being. For example, if we find that over a given decade women worked more, is it a sign of improving welfare (more earnings) or of declining welfare (more need to supplement inadequate male incomes, less free time)? Does a drop in their work show improvement (more free time, less need) or impoverishment (thrown out of work)?

A better indicator is the wage rate a woman or child could earn in a fixed number of hours. The wage rate helps to attach a value not only to their paid-work time but also to the time they spend on other things. For those persons who juggled time freely between paid work and other activities, the wage shows how they valued any hour of their time, in or out of work. In other cases, the wage rate may overstate or understate the value they put on their time. Despite such cases, the most direct clues to the earning power of women and children are the wage rates they earned. This is despite the fact that the wage is too low a value for the home time of a person who refuses to work at all at that wage. Such a person clearly values home time more highly than the wage. On the other hand, many a woman or child probably felt that time at home was worth less than the wage rate, yet was kept from paid work by a disapproving patriarch or by social norms.

The best initial working hypothesis is that, because women and children were concentrated in low-paid trades in competition with unskilled males, their wage rates shared the same trends with those paid adult male common labourers. Comparisons of eighteenth- and nineteenth-century earnings suggest that the woman/man and child/man wage ratios could have been steady over the whole century surveyed here (Lindert and Williamson 1983a: 17–19).

While an average working child's wage rate may have been a steady share of that for adult male common labour, there are hints that the relative wage of adult women did not fully keep pace before the 1820s. In the late eighteenth century, the mechanisation of spinning displaced many women (and girls) from one of their main sources of earnings (Pinchbeck 1930: 129–55). By the end of the century many women, like many men, had become hand-loom weavers; after 1815, however, that trade declined severely, as we have seen. Women's earning power in agriculture was

Table 14.2. *Real annual earnings, 1823–7 to 1848–52* (*in £ of 1851*)

	General servants	Cooks	Female industrial workers (forty-six weeks)
1823–7	18·5	22·3	12·3
1828–32	19·8	22·2	12·0
1833–7	20·9	23·0	13·5
1838–42	20·6	22·7	12·5
1843–7	23·3	25·8	14·0
1848–52	23·8	25·9	17·3

compromised to an unknown degree, first by wartime enclosures that denied women the ability to keep livestock on the commons (Humphries 1990) and then by the agricultural depression of the decade after 1815. Thus, up to the 1820s, the demise of female-intensive sectors of the economy suggests that women's wage rates may not have kept pace.

From the 1820s onwards, some very rough numbers imply that between 1825 and 1850 real wage rates rose 28 per cent for servants, 16 per cent for cooks and 38 per cent for female factory workers.

The underlying estimates are Higgs' (1986: 138) collations of figures previously presented by Wood, Layton and Horn. Higgs warns that the data are shaky. Adjusting servants' cash wages for the cost of living, adding in food and lodging worth £13 a year at mid-century prices, and assuming that women in industry worked forty-six weeks a year yields the results in Table 14.2. Such gains approach those for men in the same quarter century: 30 per cent for adult male labourers on farms, 42 per cent for non-farm adult male labourers, 41 per cent for all working men.

So far, the scarce and fragile data suggest that (a) from the 1750s to the 1820s, children's wages may have been a steady percentage of men's wages, while women's real wage rates may have either stagnated or declined; and (b) women's real-wage rates advanced, though perhaps less rapidly than men's common-labour wages, between the 1820s and the 1850s.

Changes in the quality of life

Much of what matters in life is missed by numbers on income or consumption. To many observers, the most disturbing features of material life in the eighteenth and nineteenth centuries were qualitative: the indignity of having to submit to the harsh discipline of factory masters; the monotony of the work; the crowded squalor, pollution and disease of the new towns and cities; and the disruption of traditional family roles. The debate over trends in workers' well being has long been frustrated by an inability to weigh the quality of life against quantifiable trends in income and consumption. It need not be so.

To weigh seemingly immeasurable qualities of life against the purchasing power of income or consumption, the key is to use the values of the people whose welfare is being weighed. It is not for twentieth-century scholars, or even the Victorian upper classes, to say how much more clothing should have been taken from a worker's back to clean up the street in front of the worker's tenement, nor how many chairs and pans the worker should have given up to avoid long hours in the satanic mill. Nobody can better judge what cloths, filth, chairs, pans or the horrors of the mills meant to workers in 1750 or 1850 than those workers. How can we hear their voices after so many years? They were not allowed to vote. Most remained silent on these issues, while an articulate minority spoke out, often in protest. Yet it is dangerous to infer workers' values from either the silence or the outcries. A better approach is to find situations in which workers themselves actually chose between conditions more prevalent in 1850 and conditions more prevalent in, say, 1780. If incomes seemed to rise, as we found, yet the quality of life might have deteriorated, how much income did choosing workers seem to forego in order to avoid the lower quality of life?

Workers made their key choices when deciding whether to migrate to industry and the cities (see also ch. 13). However grim the choices, they faced a market of sorts. Industry and the cities offered more pay, along with living conditions that today we would consider appalling. Some workers refused the bribe, others took it. As with other markets, we can value the extra quality of life by the amount the marginal person, here the marginal non-migrant, gave up to keep it. Once we learn workers' price for better living conditions, we should use that price to value three parts of the historical change in the quality of life: first, the change that took place within the rising urban or industrial sector; second, the change that took place within the declining rural or non-industrial sector; and third, the deterioration experienced by the population share that lived in the rising sector in 1850 but whose counterpart had lived in the declining sector back in the eighteenth century.

Such a calculation sheds considerable light. Workers' behaviour reveals that they resisted industrial and urban conditions, yet the value they put on better living conditions implies little about *trends* in their well being because there was in fact so *little* industrialisation and urbanisation in an era famous for these changes.

Statistical tests suggest how much higher a city's unskilled wage had to be to offset each percentage rise in infant mortality, or crowding, or other disamenities (Williamson 1990a: 255–6; Brown 1990). In the 1830s, that compensating wage premium was perhaps 12–30 per cent in northern England and perhaps 8–20 per cent in the south. To err on the side of overstatement, however, let us imagine that industrial and urban conditions were so abhorrent to workers that the most extreme English wage differential for unskilled workers was nothing but a compensation needed to offset the odium of working in industry and living in cities. In 1838 that extreme differential was 65 per cent, the extra annual income a labouring man earned in Manchester factories over the farm wages in distant and bucolic Norfolk. The differential reflected the cost of moving plus the cost of living in Manchester plus some labour-market disequilibrium (see ch. 13) as well as compensation for industrial–urban disamenity, but imagine that it was all just a disamenity premium. That is a large potential loss for the people who switched from bucolic England to satanic mills and urban squalor.

Yet only a small share of the English population made such a shift. Between 1780 and 1850, the rise of industrial jobs (mining and manufacturing) was only about 10 per cent of the labour force. The rise of the share of the population living in cities was only 14.89 per cent. Here again we meet a basic truth brought out by other chapters: very little of the nation's historic transformation happened in the 'industrial revolution' century, 1750–1850. So the 65 per cent wage-revealed cost of urban/industrial disamenities multiplied by only 10–15 per cent equals only a 6.5–10 per cent loss in the average worker's well being due to the third change above, the shift to industry and cities. That certainly does not erase wage gains like the 72 per cent gain for 1810–50 or the 53 per cent for 1819–50, and even the 6.5–10 per cent figure is an overstatement.

As for changes in the quality of life, first within the urban/industrial sector and, second within the rural/non-industrial sector, the little evidence which exists suggests no net deterioration within either sector. While health was poorer and life shorter in the expanding cities, the trend in health and mortality within cities or within the countryside was either flat or slightly improving. As noted already, for example, infant mortality fell in London, and there was no clear mortality trend either in cities like Manchester and Liverpool or in the countryside (but see ch. 13). And despite the frequent mention of urban crowding in the nineteenth century, even in infamous urban Lancashire the local increases in persons per house had stopped by 1811. 'Conditions in Lancashire and Manchester did not deteriorate during the Industrial Revolution; they were simply pretty dreadful to begin with' (Fleischman 1985: 303–17).

Thus combining real-wage data with data on unemployment, migration and workers' valuation of externalities makes clear what trends in consumption and life expectancy could only suggest: after seventy years of stagnation, workers' absolute living standards improved from 1820 to 1850.

Inequality movements

The Victorian extremes

The other debate, about inequality between rich and middle and poor rather than about trends in workers' absolute well being, was rightly heated in the nineteenth century. We now know that in Victorian Britain the incomes and wealth of the richest 5 per cent were as far above the national average as in any other industrialising country for which we have good data before the First World War. More specifically, the income share of the top 5 per cent of households in the United Kingdom in 1867 was about 41 per cent. That exceeded the top 5 per cent shares of income for similar years in Germany, Denmark or the United States. As for wealth, the shares held by the richest 5 per cent in England and Wales in 1875 exceeded those for the Scandinavian countries, France and the United States at similar dates (Rubinstein 1981; Lindert and Williamson 1983b; Lindert 1986; Phelps Brown 1988).

The extreme inequality of Victorian income and wealth was rooted in the special economic and political dominance of the English landed aristocracy. Buttressed by disproportionate voting power, laws to keep large estates intact and an insulating class culture, the landed interest clustered at the top of the income and wealth structure (E. P. Thompson 1963; Mingay 1976; Cannadine 1980; Stone and Stone 1984; Beckett 1986). The share of landed wealth controlled by the English landed elite was extreme among industrialising countries, and even rivalled the control of Latin American *latifundistos*, both for rural land and for all land. In England and Wales in 1873, the most landed 5 per cent held 79 per cent of all real-estate value. Of the countries for which we have comparable early data on landownership, only Mexico in 1923 yielded figures showing such concentration. Landownership was more concentrated in England and Wales than in pre-war Bulgaria, China, Denmark, Egypt, Finland, Japan and the United States. No other countryside, apparently, was worked more by tenants and less by owners than Great Britain, according to pre-war data on Belgium, Brazil, Canada, Croatia, China, Denmark, France, Germany, Holland, Hungary, Japan, New Zealand, Transylvania and the United States (League of Nations 1927; Lindert 1987). And in no other country, perhaps, has land in booming cities been so concentrated in the hands of a few aristocrats, such as London's Duke of Marlborough (Grosvenor, as in West End) and Duke of Bedford (Russell, as in

Bloomsbury and Covent Garden). The same concentration of land-ownership was evident in Birmingham, Edgbaston and other cities in the nineteenth century (Cannadine 1980: 81–135, 229–3; Lindert 1987). Little wonder, then, that England's classical economists talked of the factor of production called 'land' as if it were owned only by the top income class.

Since the First World War, much has changed. Today over half of all British households own some real estate, usually their homes, whereas only one household in seven owned any in the 1870s. Correspondingly, the distributions of income and wealth have also become more equal, the main change being the narrowing of the gap between top and middle ranks (Atkinson and Harrison 1978: 138–70; Phelps Brown 1988: 305–24, 362–93). While market forces deserve some of the credit for the levelling, high tax rates also decimated top fortunes, both in the Lloyd George era and across the 1940s. Tax pressure caused some estates to be sold even during the First World War, and by the 1970s the Duke of Bedford had turned the grounds of Woburn Abbey into an imitation Disneyland to meet his tax bills.

When did the English become so unequal?

If the English (and British) were outstandingly unequal in income and wealth around 1870, compared with Britain today or with other countries back then, had it always been so? The origins, and legitimacy, of English inequality were questioned at least as early as the fourteenth century. One wonders whether the Victorian extremes of inequality go all the way back to the Dark Ages, or whether they arose during, say, the industrial revolution. In theory, income and wealth gaps should have been narrowed by the Black Death but widened by Tudor population pressure and the transfer of church lands to friends of Henry VIII. The data needed to test such ideas are lacking. Still, for the era from the late seventeenth century on, new evidence on the incomes and wealth of all classes (Lindert and Williamson 1983b; Lindert 1986,1987) hint at some tentative conclusions about trends for England and Wales.

Movements in average income or wealth by *socio-economic class* suggest a dramatic widening of the gaps between rich and poor from the middle of the eighteenth century to the middle of the nineteenth. Average incomes by socio-occupational class suggest a widening after 1760. Landlords and the richest (long-distance, wholesale) merchants gained ground on the middle and lower classes. In the early nineteenth century these class income gaps continued to widen, as did the wage gap between industry and agriculture and possibly (as we have seen) the wage gap between male and female workers. Average personal wealth shows a similar widening between classes, with landlords and merchants growing richer faster than other groups.

The true inequality trends between *percentile ranks*, however, seem to have been more subtle. Figure 14.4 graphs top-decile shares for income and wealth over 300 years. The income measures (lower curve) seem to say that inequality rose between the late seventeenth century and the late nineteenth. But the increases in income inequality were less dramatic than the class averages would have suggested, and one cannot say with certainty that there was any rise at all. For wealth, the top curve shows no trend at all before 1875, despite the fact that the average wealth of the richest classes shot up faster than that of any less wealthy class.

There is no logical contradiction here. Inequality between the percentile ranks, as portrayed in Figure 14.4, did not change as dramatically as did the class-average gaps because the richest classes were shrinking in their population share. Both the landed aristocracy and even the major-merchant class shrank as a share of the population. What was happening in that top decile was that while its shrinking landed classes and merchants prospered faster than the nation, its ranks were increasingly filled by less wealthy professionals and other less prosperous socio-occupational groups. While many observers rightly sensed that the rich *classes*, on the average, were getting richer faster, they were also becoming less relevant. One leveller at work was the decline of agriculture, which reduced the economic relevance of land and landlords.

It is still too early, however, to conclude that the English were just as unequal in 1688 as they were two centuries later. Two demographic subtleties suggest a rise in true inequality not captured in Figure 14.4. One is that the best available numbers follow the distribution of income and wealth among households, whereas the focus here is more about the inequalities among individuals. In the late seventeenth century, the richest households had more members than the average. By the end of the nineteenth century, household size was inversely related to income, stretching the measured incomes of poorer households out over more persons. This historic switch in the correlation of household size and affluence means that the trend in resources available per person was more toward inequality than is shown in Figure 14.4.

Another whole dimension of rising inequality is the gap in life expectancy between rich and poor. As Figure 14.1 shows, the life expectancy of peerage family members rose much faster than that of the whole population. If later research finds that there was a more general widening of life-expectancy gaps between rich and poor groups, then their real *lifetime* resources could have diverged more dramatically than the income and wealth figures have yet revealed. While firm conclusions are not yet

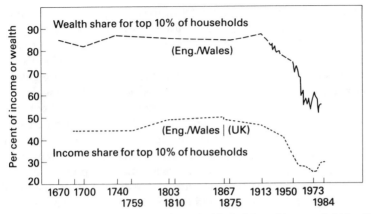

Figure 14.4 Shares of all household wealth and income held by the top
10 per cent of households, England/Wales and the UK, 1670–1984

Sources: those cited in Lindert (1986: 1145–9), except for revisions to
convert the 1867 and 1913 data from distributions among individuals
to distributions among households, and extensions to 1982 (wealth)
and 1984 (income) using official series.

possible, the best tentative guess is that lifetime resources became
somewhat more unequally distributed, most likely between 1750 and 1815.
The present view of inequality trends from the late seventeenth century to
the early twentieth is close to those of Lindert and Williamson (1983b,
1985b), J. G. Williamson (1985), Rubinstein (1986: 44–106) and Phelps
Brown (1988: 305–21, 372–84), but now with emphasis on a likely rise in
inequality in 1750–1815 instead of a rise and fall peaking around 1870. The
null hypothesis of no change at all until the twentieth century was
presented earlier by Soltow (1968).

The level of poor relief

To deal with the poorest victims of her economic inequalities, England
became the workhouse of the world long before she became its workshop.
By the late eighteenth century she had developed a complex national
network of parish institutions for 'indoor' (workhouse) and 'outdoor' (in-
home) poor relief. The original Elizabethan Poor Law of 1597 and 1601
laid out the eternal twin tasks of helping the deserving disabled poor and
forcing the able-bodied poor ('vagabonds', 'rogues', gypsies, the lazy,
etc.) to seek work. Parish workhouses offered shelter and sustenance to the
first group and a punishing regime to the second. The idea of making the
workhouse pay for itself by exploiting the labour of inmates failed in the

eighteenth century, having proved inferior to both slavery and free labour. Poor relief thus remained a financial burden on parish rate payers.

The history of English (and British) poor relief up to 1870 remains a rich source of puzzles, despite repeated scholarly attention. England's poor relief probably became the most generous in the world in the late eighteenth century and early nineteenth, even though a majority of those with power and voice continued to view the poor with condescension and contempt. While Dutch poor relief may have approached the English in generosity as of the 1820s, other countries gave less, especially the Americans, who gave only negligible amounts of 'welfare payments' until the 1930s. Why did the dominant classes relent and allow so much 'outdoor' poor relief in the eighteenth century and early nineteenth? Why did they then try to take away that support in 1834? Why did the generosity of relief vary so much across regions within England? This chapter can only frame these questions more clearly, leaving answers to readers, with the help of chapter 9's description of the larger fiscal regime and the discussion of poor relief after 1860 in volume 2, chapter 11 and volume 3, chapter 10.

The ebb and flow of English poor relief is sketched in Figure 14.5, which shows what share of the nation's income was redistributed from tax payers to the poor. Clearly, there was a rise in the late eighteenth century to a plateau of about 2 per cent of national product, followed by a sharp drop after the Poor Law Reform of 1834. Poor relief, then, cost tax payers less until this century, when it has soared. For a discussion of the remarkable twentieth-century rise of the welfare state, again see the chapters in volumes 2 and 3. Note also a few patterns from Figure 14.5. The three greatest jumps were around the two world wars and in the 1980s. Their nature differed. The jump in the decade of the First World War was more the result of covering more unemployed than of more generosity toward each person relieved. The jump across the Second World War, with the arrival of the welfare state in 1945, was a true jump in generosity toward poor persons of given condition. The pinnacle of non-pension welfare spending under Thatcher was due to a rise in the number of unemployed qualifying for relief, rather than a rise in generosity toward persons in given economic situations. The steady post-war rise of pensions was due more to repeated political decisions to favour the elderly than to a rise in the elderly share of the population.

As a first step toward understanding these historic movements, one should combine the expenditure shares of Figure 14.5 with what little is known about the share of the population receiving aid. Between 1688 and 1750, the share of the population called poor may have dropped from about 16 per cent to about 10 per cent, but the generosity with which each pauper was supported apparently remained unchanged. Across the second

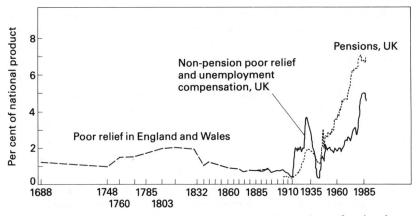

Figure 14.5 Poor relief and pension spending as a share of national product, England/Wales and the UK, 1688–1987

Sources and notes:
The national-product denominators for England and Wales, 1688–1811 are from Lindert and Williamson (1983b) and O'Brien (1988). Those for 1830 on are based on the estimates of Deane, Feinstein and the Central Statistical Office. The national product of England and Wales for 1830–1936 was assumed to be 0·813 times that of the United Kingdom, a ratio implied by Baxter for 1867. (This may be too low for the inter-war period, after the separation of southern Ireland.)

The poor relief expenditures for 1688–1803 are from King, Davies and the official returns. Later figures for England and Wales are from Williams (1981: 145–234). All expenditures for the United Kingdom are from the Central Statistical Office. Pension expenditures include all public sector pension programmes as well as social insurance pensions, and include both contributory and non-contributory pensions. Non-pension poor relief in the twentieth century includes employment insurance, family allowances and supplemental benefits.

half of the eighteenth century, every relief ratio rose: those called poor and those getting aid both rose as a share of the national population, aid rose as a share of national product, and the share of recipients given the less onerous 'outdoor' relief rose to exceed 90 per cent by 1803. The Reform of 1834 did not cut the generosity to those still entitled to relief so much as it forced able-bodied adults off the rolls. Actual practice was less harsh than the intent of the Reform itself, which removed control from the parish overseers, who had more direct human contact with the poor, and set up regional parish unions at greater distance from the poor. Tough as the Reform tried to be, the less onerous outdoor relief continued to account for about three-quarters of the relieved paupers and half the expenditures.

The timing of the early rise and retreat of English poor relief had something to do with need. Food became increasingly scarce across the second half of the eighteenth century and real unskilled wages may have fallen in southern England. Part of the food scarcity was due to wartime trade disruptions and harvest failures after 1793. Part was also due to the attempt of the poor relief officials themselves after 1795 to give the poor more money when the price of bread rose, causing a further rise in the demand for, and price of, food. However, another policy also contributed to the hardship and food scarcity before and after the French Wars. England's Corn Laws were designed to make food and land expensive, as they increasingly did from 1765 to 1793. The wars of 1793–1815 so exacerbated the crisis of food scarcity and poverty that Parliament wisely suspended the Corn Laws, perhaps with an eye to revolutionary events across the Channel. After Waterloo, however, the Corn Laws were reapplied, holding up the price of food for another quarter century (Lindert 1992), while the pendulum also swung against outdoor poor relief. Thus, the political system seemed willing to tax the poor only up to a point, and shifted to more food supply and poor relief when the threat of destitution was greatest.

Among the many complexities of the Old (pre-1834) Poor Law was a striking spatial pattern in English poor relief. The generosity of rural relief ranked regions as follows: south-east > south-west > north-east > north-west. In fact, the poor relief map of England resembled one drawn by Caird to portray agricultural zones in 1850. Broadly speaking, poor relief seemed negatively related to agricultural wage rates (more relief in the east, less in the west), and positively related to the seasonal imbalance in the demand for farm hands (more relief in the southern arable zone with its harvest peaks, less relief in the northern pastoral zone) (Armstrong and Huzel 1989: 762–6; Boyer 1990). Relief was also, as a rule, more generous in the countryside than in the cities. Why?

The spatial pattern, like the temporal one, may be explained partly by variations in need. Poor relief was inversely related to wages and the demand for labour, both among rural regions and between the countryside and the cities. Perhaps the system was simply a paternalistic provider of social insurance, responding where and when the need was greatest (Mandler 1987), though as we have seen paternalistic benevolence does not fit the vigorous application of the Corn Laws before and after the French Wars.

An alternative idea seems to have more predictive power. The spatial pattern of poor relief appears to have fit differences in local dominance by labour-hiring landlords, as Boyer (1990) has shown at length. The dominant landlords were also the dominant hirers of rural labour

(Armstrong 1989: 673) and dominant in politics, especially in the heyday of poor relief and the Corn Laws.

Why would it be in the interests of large landlords to raise tax-supported poor relief, especially in the south-east? On the benefits side, more generous rural poor relief, given mainly in the winter off-season, would help prevent emigration or malnutrition of labourers needed at harvest time. The need for support in the off-season was acute in the highly seasonal arable agriculture of the south-east. By contrast, employers in pastoral, industrial and urban areas with their steadier yearly rhythm of labour demand, had less self-interest in supporting people out of work. On the cost side, hiring landlords did not in fact bear the full tax burden used to keep the poor labourers around. A large share of the rates fell on the less landed family farmers who hired little or no labour, a point about which the yeomanry increasingly complained. Yet under the voting rules of local government in effect between 1782 and 1834, voting power was weighted in favour of those who occupied a greater value of land, giving them (the more landed, who hired more non-family labour) a greater potential, say, in local tax rates and poor relief.

Overview

The absolute living standards of English workers stagnated between 1750 and 1820, but then began rising substantially after 1820. Curiously, the period of clear gains began near the birth date of Marx (1818) and the emergence of intense parliamentary debate over the conditions workers were enduring. The last era in which succeeding generations of workers lived no better than their ancestors on the average was that earlier period, 1750–1820. Attention is turning toward an earlier era in the standard-of-living debate, as is our view of when England industrialised.

Concern about inequality between rich and poor turns out to have been appropriately centred in Britain. While all early data are rough on this subject, it now appears that the English, and more so the British, were as unequal in their economic fortunes as the population of any industrialising country before the First World War. It may have been so for centuries. The extreme inequalities now evident during Victoria's reign were not entirely new. There was *probably* an earlier rise of inequality, especially in the era 1750–1815. The rise is still debatable, however, and was surely less dramatic than the twentieth-century decline of inequality. No generation of Britons in the 250 years up to the First World War had income or wealth as evenly distributed as they have been since the Second World War.

England's policy response to poverty was also distinctive in the era covered here. In the late eighteenth century the share of national product given to the poor rose to about 2 per cent, as great a share as was given by any country's government. The support remained at that level until the Poor Law Reform of 1834. From then until the First World War, poor relief was only about half as great a share (1 per cent) of national product. Complex as the Old Poor Law was, it showed a remarkable spatial pattern: relief was more generous in the countryside than in the growing cities, and rural relief was more generous in the south and east. Both the temporal rise and fall and the spatial pattern hint at an underlying responsiveness to the danger that the local poor would exit, through mortality or emigration or revolt. Whenever and wherever that danger was small, as in most of the period covered and as in the rising industrial and urban centres, poor relief was meagre. Indeed, in such times of less imminent social danger (before 1793 and after 1815), policy charged the poor more for food, through the Corn Laws. Yet when and where the danger of exit was greatest, the government moved to relieve extreme destitution. So it was in the rural south-east more than in the rest of England. And so it was in one of the worst of times for the poor, the French War era 1793–1815.

Chronology

Wade E. Shilts
The University of Iowa

1650–99

ECONOMIC AND SOCIAL CONDITIONS

Average family income, England and Wales (1688): £39.
Population of England (excluding Monmouthshire, 1688): 4·9 million.

1663	Law allows for export of bullion, foreign coins.
1665	Final major outbreak of the Great Plague.
1688	Responsibility for minting coin shifted to Parliament.
1693–4	First issue of government-backed annuities. Founding of the Bank of England (1694).
1698, 1705	Inland bills of exchange given same legal status as foreign bills of exchange.

TECHNOLOGY AND IDEAS

1662	Founding of Royal Society.
1667	Publication of Bunyan's *Pilgrim's Progress*.
1689	Publication of Locke's *Two Treatises on Government*.
1691	Ambrose Crowley establishes Winlaton iron works.
1696	Publication of King's *Natural and Political Observations and Conclusions Upon the State and Condition of England*.

POLITICS, LAW AND PUBLIC POLICY

1651	Passage of initial Navigation Acts.
1660	Restoration of Charles II. First systematic codification of Navigation Acts.
1663	First turnpike trust established.
1688	Glorious Revolution; accession of William of Orange.
1689	Bill of Rights settles succession to throne.
1690s	Sharp increase of tariffs on imported goods.

INTERNATIONAL EVENTS

1664–83	Colbert's economic reforms in France.
1689–97	War of the League of Augsburg.

1700–24

ECONOMIC AND SOCIAL CONDITIONS

Agriculture in 1700: land remaining open or common: 29 per cent. Agricultural output (in 1815 prices): £40 million.

Exports in 1700 as per cent of national output: 8·4.

Populations of England (excluding Monmouthshire, 1701): 5·1 million.

1717	Britain goes on gold standard.
1720	Note issue by Bank of England exceeds total of all goldsmith bankers.
1720	Crowley's iron works in Winlaton a massive manufacturing complex.
1721–3	South Sea Bubble Affair.

TECHNOLOGY AND IDEAS

1700s	Development of seed drill (Tull).
1709	Use of coke in iron smelting (Darby).
1712	First working model of Newcomen's steam engine.
1717	Thomas Lombe establishes silk-throwing works in Derby.
1720	First salt-glaze earthenware (Astbury).

POLITICS, LAW AND PUBLIC POLICY

1701	Act of Settlement settles royal succession on House of Hanover.
1706	Passage of Act of Bankruptcy.
1707	Union of England and Scotland.
1708	English banks limited to small-scale partnerships.
1714	Accession of George I.
1715	First Jacobite rebellion; Riot Act.
1716	Septennial Act sets maximum duration of Parliament at seven years.
1720	Bubble Act.

INTERNATIONAL EVENTS

1702–13	War of the Spanish Succession.
1715	Death of Louis XIV of France.

1725–49

ECONOMIC AND SOCIAL CONDITIONS

Population of England (excluding Monmouthshire, 1731): 5·3 million.

Life expectancy at birth (1731): 27·9 years.

TECHNOLOGY AND IDEAS

1730	Dutch plough patented.

1733	John Kay invents flying shuttle.
1738	'Conversion' of John Wesley and start of Methodism.
1740	Development of crucible technique for cast steel (Huntsman).
1748	Publication of Montesquieu's *Spirit of the Laws* (France).

POLITICS, LAW AND PUBLIC POLICY

1732	Act of bankruptcy made permanent.
1734	Barnard's Act prohibits dealing in options and forward contracts by stockbrokers on London Exchange.
1736–99	125 Municipal Improvement Acts passed.
1745	Second Jacobite rebellion ('Bonnie Prince Charlie').

INTERNATIONAL EVENTS

| 1740 | Frederick the Great becomes King of Prussia. |
| 1740–8 | War of the Austrian Succession. |

1750s

ECONOMIC AND SOCIAL CONDITIONS

Average family income, England and Wales (1759): £43.
Agricultural output (1750, in 1815 prices): £59 million.
Manufactures as per cent of exports (1752–54): 75·4.

| 1751 | Creation of Three Per Cent Consols. |

TECHNOLOGY AND IDEAS

1750s	Introduction of breast water wheel (Smeaton).
1752	Adoption of Gregorian calendar.
1754	Founding of Society of Arts.

INTERNATIONAL EVENTS

| 1756–63 | Seven Years War. |
| 1757 | British victory over Bengal at Plassey. |

1760s

ECONOMIC AND SOCIAL CONDITIONS

Exports as per cent of GNP (1760): 14·6.
Population of England (excluding Monmouthshire, 1761): 6·1 million.

TECHNOLOGY AND IDEAS

| 1760 | Furnaces lit at Carron iron works in Stirlingshire. |
| 1761 | Duke of Bridgewater's canal opens. |

1760s	Use of coke in blast furnaces widespread.
1764	Invention of spinning jenny (Hargreaves).
1769	Patents on high-pressure steam engine (Watt) and cotton-spinning water frame (Arkwright).

POLITICS, LAW AND PUBLIC POLICY

1760	Accession of George III.
1763	Issuance of general warrants against John Wilkes.
1765	American Stamp Act (repealed 1766).

INTERNATIONAL EVENTS

| 1763 | Peace of Paris ends Seven Years War. |

1770s

ECONOMIC AND SOCIAL CONDITIONS

| 1770s | Canal links between major rivers begin to be established. |

TECHNOLOGY AND IDEAS

1775	Invention of carding machine (Arkwright).
1776	Publication of Smith's *Wealth of Nations*.
1778	Invention of water closet (Bramah).
1779	Invention of spinning mule (Crompton).

POLITICS, LAW AND PUBLIC POLICY

1772	Over 500 turnpike trusts established; removal of statutes regulating internal trade in meat, grain and grain products.
1774	Quebec Act allows French residents of Canada to live under French civil law.
1779	Spitalfield Acts.

INTERNATIONAL EVENTS

| 1776 | United States of America declares independence. |

1780s

ECONOMIC AND SOCIAL CONDITIONS

Exports as per cent of GNP (1780): 9·4.
Population of England (excluding Monmouthshire, 1781): 7·1 million.
Life expectancy at birth (1781): 34·7 years.

TECHNOLOGY AND IDEAS

| 1780–7 | Number of cotton mills increases eightfold. |

1783	Invention of cylinder printing (Bell).
1784	Invention of puddling and rolling process for wrought-iron (Cort); discovery of bleaching properties of chlorine (Berthollet, France).
1785	First design of power loom (Cartwright).
1787	Invention of soda-making process (Leblanc, France).

POLITICS, LAW AND PUBLIC POLICY

1780	Gordon Riots.
1783	Recognition of American independence.
1784	East India Act establishes government board of control.

INTERNATIONAL EVENTS

1789–1815	French Revolutionary and Napoleonic Wars.

1790s

ECONOMIC AND SOCIAL CONDITIONS

1797	Britain goes off gold standard.

TECHNOLOGY AND IDEAS

1790s	Number of hours to spin 100 lb of cotton falls to 300. Approximately 2,500 steam engines in production. Development of gas lighting.
1793	Invention of cotton gin (Whitney).
1796	Introduction of vaccination for smallpox.
1798	Publication of Malthus' *Essay on Population*.

POLITICS, LAW AND PUBLIC POLICY

1795	Speenhamland system of poor relief.
1798	Introduction of income tax.
1799–1800	Combination Acts suppressing trade unions.

INTERNATIONAL EVENTS

1792–9	First French Republic.
1793	Abolition of slavery in French colonies.

1800s

ECONOMIC AND SOCIAL CONDITIONS

Average family income, England and Wales (1801–3): £92.
Agriculture: land in arable, pasture or meadow *c.* 1800: 29·1 million acres.
Agricultural output in 1800 (1815 prices): £88 million.

Exports as per cent of GNP (1801): 15·7.
Manufactures as per cent of exports (1800): 87·2.
Population of Great Britain (1801): 10·5 million.

TECHNOLOGY AND IDEAS

1800	Expiration of Watt's steam engine patent.
1801	Invention of Jacquard loom (Jacquard, France).
1802	Invention of successful high-pressure steam engine (Trevithick).

POLITICS, LAW AND PUBLIC POLICY

1801	Union with Ireland.
1801	First census of population.
1802	Peel introduces first factory legislation.
1807	Abolition of slave trade.
1809	Repeal of laws regulating employment practices in woollen industry.

INTERNATIONAL EVENTS

1804	Issuance of Napoleonic Code.
1804	Haiti gains independence from France.
1804–24	Latin America gains independence from European governments.
1806	Napoleon establishes continental system prohibiting all trade with England.

1810s

ECONOMIC AND SOCIAL CONDITIONS

1811–16	Luddite riots in Midlands.

TECHNOLOGY AND IDEAS

1815	Use of screw gill for preparation of flax/wool fibres. Invention of mining safety lamp (Davy).
1816	Mule adapted to spinning of wool.
1817	Publication of Ricardo's *Principles of Political Economy*.

POLITICS, LAW AND PUBLIC POLICY

1814	Repeal of 1563 Statute of Artificers and Apprentices.
1815	Passage of Corn Laws.
1819	Peterloo massacre. Passage of Six Acts.

INTERNATIONAL EVENTS

1812–14	Anglo-American War.

| 1814 | Restoration of Bourbon monarchy in France. |
| 1815 | End of Napoleonic Wars. Congress of Vienna. |

1820s

ECONOMIC AND SOCIAL CONDITIONS

National product of Great Britain (1821, at 1865/85 prices): £218 million.
City growth: Britain reaches highest rate of city growth (2·5 per cent per annum over the decade).
Population of Great Britain (1821): 14·1 million.
Life expectancy at birth (1821): 39·2 years.

1821	Formal resumption of gold standard.
1822–on	Britain runs commodity trade deficit.
1825	Banking crisis.

TECHNOLOGY AND IDEAS

1820s	Beginning of adoption of power loom. Introduction of wet-spinning process for linen. Widespread use of gas lighting. Widespread use of Leblanc's soda-making process.
1825 (1830)	Invention of self-acting cotton mule (Roberts).
1825	Stockton and Darlington railway opens.
1829	Invention of hot-blast smelting process (Neilson).

POLITICS, LAW AND PUBLIC POLICY

1824, 1825	Huskisson's budgets provide for 'rationalisation' of tariff structure.
1825	Legalisation of trade unions.
1826	Joint-stock banking allowed outside of London.
1829	Catholic emancipation. Establishment of Metropolitan Police.

INTERNATIONAL EVENTS

1821	Greek revolution. Mexico and Peru declare independence.
1822	Brazil becomes independent from Portugal.
1823	Monroe Doctrine.
1825	Decembrist revolt in Russia.

1830s

ECONOMIC AND SOCIAL CONDITIONS

1830–2	First major cholera epidemic.
1831	'Swing' riots against mechanisation of agriculture.
1834	Robert Owen founds Grand National Consolidated Trade Union.
Late 1830s	Severe recession.

TECHNOLOGY AND IDEAS

1830	Liverpool and Manchester Railway opens.
1831	Invention of dynamo (Faraday).
1838	Founding of Royal Agricultural Society.

POLITICS, LAW AND PUBLIC POLICY

1832	First Great Reform Act.
1833	Factory Act limiting child labour. Abolition of slavery in British colonies.
1834	New Poor Law.
1837	Accession of Queen Victoria. Vital registration (births, deaths, marriages) begins in English district offices.
1838	Founding of Anti-Corn Law League. London Workingmen's Association issues People's Charter.

INTERNATIONAL EVENTS

1830	Revolutions in France, Belgium and Poland. Louis Philippe becomes King of the French; Belgium gains independence from Holland; Poland suppressed by Nicholas I.
1834	Formation of *Zollverein*.

1840s

ECONOMIC AND SOCIAL CONDITIONS

National product of Great Britain (1841, at 1865/85 prices): £394 million.
Population of Great Britain (1841): 18·5 million.

1842	Lowest ebb of Manchester trade depression.
1844–5	Railway mania.
1845–7	Potato famine in Ireland.

TECHNOLOGY AND IDEAS

1842	Publication of Chadwick's *Report on the Sanitary Condition of the Labouring Population*.
1844	Publication of Engels' *Condition of the Working Class in England*.
1848	Publication of Marx' and Engels' *Communist Manifesto*, Mill's *Principles of Political Economy*.

POLITICS, LAW AND PUBLIC POLICY

1840	Institution of penny post.
1842	Peel becomes Prime Minister, reintroduces income tax.
1844	Bank Charter Act.
1846	Repeal of the Corn Laws.

| 1848 | Public Health Act. |
| 1849 | Repeal of Navigation Acts. |

INTERNATIONAL EVENTS

| 1848 | Revolutions in France, Austria and Prussia. Hungarian Diet abolishes serfdom. |
| 1848–51 | Second French Republic. |

1850s

ECONOMIC AND SOCIAL CONDITIONS

Output growth rate (constant factor cost, 1856–73): 2·3 per cent per annum.
Agriculture: land in arable, pasture, or meadow *c.* 1850: 30·6 million acres.
Agricultural output (1850, in 1815 prices): £135 million. Up by factor of 3·5 from 1700.
City growth: urban population reaches 50 per cent of total.

| 1850 | Founding of Amalgamated Society of Engineers. |
| 1850s–1860s | Growth of New Model Unions. |

TECHNOLOGY AND IDEAS

1850s	Widespread adoption of power loom. Ship construction begins shift to iron hulls.
1851	Great Exhibition.
1857	Invention of Bessemer process for making steel.
1859	Publication of Darwin's *Origin of Species*, Mill's *On Liberty*.

POLITICS, LAW AND PUBLIC POLICY

1852	Patent Law Amendment Act makes it easier for inventors to get patents.
1855	Palmerston becomes Prime Minister.
1856	Joint-Stock Companies Act provides for general limited liability.

INTERNATIONAL EVENTS

1851	Louis Napoleon becomes Napoleon III in France.
1854–6	Crimean War.
1857	Indian Mutiny.
1859–70	Unification of Italy.

NOTE ON SOURCES

Economic and demographic statistics found under 'Economic and social conditions' above were taken from the following sources:
Income/output. Average family income, 1688–1801: Lindert and Williamson

(1982: 385–408, Tables 2–4, as corrected in 1983b: 329–330). National product, 1821–81: Deane and Cole (1962: 282). Rate of growth, 1856–1973: Feinstein (1972: 11, 19), as updated in Matthews *et al.* (1982: 28).

Agriculture. 1700–1851: ch. 5.

Exports. 1700–1801: ch. 8.

Population. 1688–1781: Wrigley and Schofield (1981: Table A3.3). 1801–1981: Mitchell (1988: 9).

Life expectancy. 1731–1821: ch. 4.

City growth: ch. 13.

Bibliography

Place of publication is London unless otherwise stated. All references to the *Economic History Review* are to the Second Series, unless otherwise stated.

Adams, H. 1907. *The Education of Henry Adams*. New York.
Albert, W. 1972. *The Turnpike Road System in England*, 1663–1840. Cambridge.
   1983. The turnpike trusts. In Aldcroft and Freeman 1983.
   1984. Popular opposition to turnpike trusts and its significance. *Journal of Transport History*, 3rd Ser., 5: 66–72.
Aldcroft, D. H., ed. 1968. *The Development of British Industry and Foreign Competition*, 1875–1914.
Aldcroft, D. H., and Freeman, M., eds. 1983. *Transport in the Industrial Revolution*. Manchester.
Allen, G. C. 1929. *The Industrial History of Birmingham and the Black Country, 1860–1927*.
Allen, R. C. 1982. The efficiency and distributional consequences of eighteenth century enclosures. *Economic Journal* 92: 937–53.
   1988a. The growth of labour productivity in early modern English agriculture. *Explorations in Economic History* 25: 117–46.
   1988b. The price of freehold land and the interest rate in the seventeenth and eighteenth centuries. *Economic History Review* 41: 3350.
   1989. Enclosure, farming methods, and the growth of productivity in the south midlands. *Research in Economic History*, Supplement 5, Part A: 69–88.
   1991a. *Agriculture during the Industrial Revolution, 1700–1850*. University of British Columbia, Mimeo.
   1991b. Labor productivity and farm size in English agriculture before mechanization: reply to Clark. *Explorations in Economic History* 28: 478–492.
   1992. *Enclosure and the Yeoman: The Agricultural Development of the South Midlands, 1450–1850*. Oxford.
Allen, R. C., and Ó Gráda, C. 1988. On the road again with Arthur Young: English, Irish, and French agriculture during the industrial revolution. *Journal of Economic History* 48: 93–116.
Anderson, B. L. 1969a. The attorney and the early capital market in Lancashire. In Harris 1969 and Crouzet 1972.
   1969b. Provincial aspects of the financial revolution in the eighteenth century. *Business History* 11: 11–22.

1970. Money and the structure of credit in the eighteenth century. *Business History* 12: 85–101.

Anderson, J. 1972. Aspects of the effect on the British economy of the war against France, 1790–1815. *Australian Economic History Review* 12: 1–20.

Anderson, M. 1993. The British Isles: Scotland. In Bardet and Dupâquier 1993.

Appleby, J. O. 1978. *Economic Thought and Ideology in Seventeenth-Century England*. Princeton.

Arbuthnot, J. 1773. *An Inquiry into the Connection between the Present Price of Provisions and the Size of Farms*.

Armstrong, W. A. 1989. Labour I: rural population growth, systems of employment, and incomes. In Thirsk 1989.

Armstrong, W. A., and Huzel, J. P. 1989. Labour II: food, shelter, and self-help, the poor law and the position of the labourer in rural society. In Thirsk 1989.

Arrow, K. J. 1962a. The economic implications of learning by doing. *Review of Economic Studies* 29: 155–73.

1962b. Economic welfare and the allocation of resources for invention. In Arrow 1962c.

1962c. *The Rate and Direction of Inventive Activity*. Princeton.

Arthurs, H. W. 1984. Special courts, special law: legal pluralism in nineteenth century England. In Rubin and Sugarman 1984.

Ashton, T. S. 1948. *The Industrial Revolution, 1760–1830*.

1955. *An Economic History of England: The Eighteenth Century*.

1959. *Economic Fluctuations in England 1700–1800*. Oxford.

Ashworth, W. 1960. *An Economic History of England, 1870–1939*.

Atiyah, P. S. 1979. *The Rise and Fall of Freedom of Contract*. Oxford.

Atkinson, A. B., and Harrison, A. J. 1978. *Distribution of Personal Wealth in Britain*. Cambridge.

Austen, R. A., and Smith, W. D. 1990. Private tooth decay as public economic virtue: the slave-sugar triangle, consumerism, and European industrialization. *Social Science History* 14: 95–115.

Ayres, R. U. 1990. Technological transformations and long waves, Part I. *Technological Forecasting and Social Change* 37: 1–39.

Baines, B. W. 1980. English labour laws and the separation from contract. *Journal of Legal History* 1: 262–97.

Baines, E. 1835. *History of the Cotton Manufacture in Great Britain*. Ed. W. H. Chaloner, 1966.

1875. *The Woollen Manufacture of England*. Ed. K. G. Ponting, Newton Abbot, 1970.

Bairoch, P. 1965. Niveau de développement économique de 1810 à 1910. *Annales: Economies, Sociétés, Civilisations* 20: 1091–117.

1982. International industrialization levels from 1750 to 1980. *Journal of European Economic History* 11: 269–333.

1989. European trade policy, 1815–1914. In Mathias and Pollard 1989.

Baker, A. R. H., and Gregory, D., eds. 1984. *Explorations in Historical Geography*. Cambridge.

Baker, J. H., and Milsom, S. F. C. 1986. *Sources of English Legal History: Private Law to 1750*.

Barber, W. J. 1975. *British Economic Thought and India, 1600–1858*. Oxford.

Bardet, J.-P., and Dupâquier, J., eds. 1993. *History of the Population of Europe, vol. II: Times of Change: The Demographic Transition (18th–19th centuries)*. Paris.

Barro, R. J. 1987. Government spending, interest rates, prices and budget deficits in the United Kingdom. *Journal of Monetary Economics* 20: 221–48.

Basalla, G. 1988. *The Evolution of Technology*. Cambridge.

Batchelor, T. 1808. *General View of the Agriculture of the County of Bedford*.

Baugh, D. A. 1988. Great Britain's blue water policy, 1689–1815. *International History Review* 10: 1–58.

Beattie, J. M. 1986. *Crime and the Courts in England*. Cambridge.

Beckett, J. V. 1986. *The Aristocracy in England, 1660–1914*. Oxford.

Beckett, J. V., and Turner, M. E. 1990. Taxation and economic growth in eighteenth century England. *Economic History Review* 43: 377–403.

Beer, G. L. 1912. *The Old Colonial System, 1660–1754*. 2 vols. New York.

Behagg, C. 1990. *Politics and Production in the Early Nineteenth Century*.

Bell, R. M., and Scott-Kemmis, D. 1990. *The Mythology of Learning-by-Doing in World War II Airframe and Ship Production*. Science Policy Research Unit, University of Sussex, Mimeo.

Beniger, J. R. 1986. *The Control Revolution: Technological and Economic Origins of the Information Society*. Cambridge, Mass.

Beresford, M. 1954. *The Lost Villages of England*.

Berg, M. 1980. *The Machinery Question and the Making of Political Economy, 1815–1848*. Cambridge.

   1985. *The Age of Manufactures: Industry, Innovation and Work in Britain 1700–1820*. Oxford.

   1987. Women's work, mechanization and the early phases of industrialization in England. In Joyce 1987.

   1991a. Commerce and creativity in eighteenth century Birmingham. In Berg 1991b.

   ed. 1991b. *Markets and Manufacture in Early Industrial Europe*.

Berg, M., and Hudson, P. 1992. Rehabilitating the industrial revolution. *Economic History Review* 45: 24–50.

Berg, M., Hudson, P., and Sonenscher, M., eds. 1983. *Manufacture in Town and Country before the Factory*.

Beveridge, W. H. 1939. *Prices and Wages in England from the Twelfth to the Nineteenth Century*. Reprinted 1966.

Bienefeld, M. A. 1972. *Working Hours in British Industry: An Economic History*.

Birch, A. 1967. *The Economic History of the British Iron and Steel Industry, 1784–1879*.

Blake, R. 1966. *Disraeli*.

Bohstedt, J. 1983. *Riots and Community Politics in England and Wales, 1790–1810*.

Bonfield, L., Smith, R. M., and Wrightson, K., eds. 1986. *The World We Have Gained: Histories of Population and Social Structure*. Oxford.

Botham, F. W., and Hunt, E. H. 1987. Wages in Britain during the industrial revolution. *Economic History Review* 40: 380–99.

Bowley, A. L. 1900. *Wages in the United Kingdom in the Nineteenth Century*. Cambridge.

Boyd, R. 1787. *The Office, Power and Jurisdiction of His Majesty's Justices of the Peace*. Edinburgh.

Boyer, G. R. 1990. *An Economic History of the English Poor Law, 1750–1850*. Cambridge.

Boyson, R. 1970. *The Ashworth Cotton Enterprise: The Rise and Fall of a Family Firm, 1818–1880*. Oxford.

Brack, O. M., ed. 1985. *Studies in Eighteenth Century Culture*. Madison, Wis.

Braudel, F., and Spooner, F. 1967. Prices in Europe from 1450 to 1750. In Rich and Wilson 1967.

Braverman, H. 1974. *Labor and Monopoly Capital*. New York.

Brewer, J. 1989. *The Sinews of Power: War, Money and the English State, 1688–1783*.

Brewer, J., and Styles, J., eds. 1980. *An Ungovernable People? The English and their Law in the Seventeenth and Eighteenth Centuries*.

Bridbury, A. R. 1975. *Economic Growth: England in the Later Middle Ages*. Brighton.

Briggs, A. 1959. *The Age of Improvement*.

Broadberry, S., and Crafts, N. F. R., eds. 1992. *Britain in the World Economy, 1870–1913*. Cambridge.

Brown, J. C. 1990. The condition of England and the standard of living: cotton textiles in the northwest, 1806–1850. *Journal of Economic History* 50: 591–614.

Bruland, K. 1989. *British Technology and European Industrialization: The Norwegian Textile Industry in the Mid-Nineteenth Century*. Cambridge.

Bruland, T. 1982. Industrial conflict as a source of technical innovation: three cases. *Economy and Society* 11: 91–121.

Brundage, A. 1978. *The Making of the New Poor Law, 1832–39*.

Buchanan, B. J. 1986. The evolution of the English turnpike trusts: lessons from a case study. *Economic History Review* 39: 223–43.

Burgess, K. 1969. Technological change and the 1852 lockout in the British engineering industry. *International Review of Social History* 14: 215–37.

Burnley, J. 1889. *The History of Wool and Wool-Combing*. London.

Bythell, D. 1969. *The Handloom Weavers: A Study of the English Cotton Industry during the Industrial Revolution*. Cambridge.

Caird, J. 1852. *English Agriculture in 1850–1*. Ed. by G. E. Mingay, 1967.

Cairncross, A. K. 1961. International trade and economic development. *Economica* 28: 235–51.

Cameron, R., ed. 1967. *Banking in the Early Stages of Industrialization: A Study of Comparative Economic History*. Oxford.

   1990. La révolution industrielle manquée. *Social Science History* 14: 559–65.

   Forthcoming. Misunderstanding the industrial revolution. In a Festschrift for Eric Lampard.

Campbell, R. H. 1974. The union and economic growth. In Rae 1974.

Cannadine, D. 1980. *Lands and Landlords: The Aristocracy in Towns, 1774–1967*. Leicester.

Cardwell, D. S. L. 1971. *From Watt to Clausius: The Rise of Thermodynamics in the Early Industrial Age*.

   1972. *Turning Points in Western Technology*. New York.

Carlsson, B. 1989. *Industrial Dynamics: Technological, Organizational and Structural Changes in Industries and Firms*. Boston, Mass.

Carrington, S. H. H. 1988. *The British West Indies during the American Revolution*. Dordrecht.

Carswell, J. P. 1960. *The South Sea Bubble*.

Carus-Wilson, E. M. 1941. An industrial revolution of the thirteenth century. *Economic History Review* 11: 39–60. Reprinted in Carus-Wilson 1954.

ed. 1954. *Essays in Economic History*.

Caves, R. E., Frankel, J. A., and Jones, R. W. 1990. *World Trade and Payments*. 5th edn, Glenview.

Chadwick, E. 1842. *Report on the Sanitary Condition of the Labouring Population of Great Britain, 1842*. Ed. M. W. Flinn, Edinburgh.

Chalmers, G. 1802. *An Estimate of the Comparative Strength of Great Britain*.

Chambers, J. D. 1953. Enclosure and labour supply in the industrial revolution. *Economic History Review* 5: 319–43.

Chandler, A. D. 1977. *The Visible Hand: The Managerial Revolution in American Business*. Cambridge, Mass.

1990a. The enduring logic of industrial success. *Harvard Business Review* 68: 130–41.

1990b. *Scale and Scope*. Cambridge, Mass.

Chapman, S. D. 1970. Fixed capital formation in the British cotton industry, 1770–1815. *Economic History Review* 23: 235–66.

1972. *The Cotton Industry in the Industrial Revolution*.

1973. Industrial capital before the industrial revolution, 1730–1750. In Harte and Ponting 1973.

1984. *The Rise of Merchant Banking*.

Chapman, S. D., and Butt, J. 1988. The cotton industry, 1775–1856. In Feinstein and Pollard 1988.

Chapman, S. D., and Chassagne, S. 1981. *European Textile Printers in the Eighteenth Century: A Study of Peel and Oberkampf*.

Charlesworth, A., ed. 1983. *An Atlas of Rural Protest, 1549–1900*.

Chartres, J. A. 1977. Road-carrying in England in the seventeenth century, myth and reality. *Economic History Review* 30: 73–94.

1985. The marketing of agricultural produce. In Thirsk 1985.

Chartres, J. A., and Turnbull, G. 1983. Road transport. In Aldcroft and Freeman 1983.

Chaudhuri, K. N. 1968. India's international economy in the nineteenth century: an historical study. *Modern Asian Studies* 2: 31–50

1978. *The Trading World of Asia and the English East India Company, 1660–1760*. Cambridge.

1983. Foreign trade and balance of payments (1757–1947). In Kumar 1983.

Chaytor, M. 1980. Household and kinship: Ryton in the late 16th and early 17th centuries. *History Workshop* 10: 25–60.

Checkland, S. G. 1975. *Scottish Banking: A History 1695–1973*. Glasgow.

Cherry, S. 1980. The hospitals and population growth: Part 1. Eighteenth and nineteenth centuries. *Population Studies* 34: 251–66.

Chisholm, J. 1868. *Accounts of Public Income and Expenditure 1688–1869*, PP 1868–9, xxxv.

Chitty, J. 1820. *A Treatise on the Laws of Commerce and Manufactures and the Contracts Relating Thereto*. 4 vols.

Chorley, P. 1981. The agricultural revolution in northern Europe, 1750–1880, nitrogen, legumes, and crop productivity. *Economic History Review* 34: 71–93.

Christie, I. R. 1984. *Stress and Stability in Late Eighteenth Century Britain: Reflections on the British Avoidance of Revolution.* Oxford.

Church, R. A. 1975. *The Great Victorian Boom, 1850–1973.*

ed. 1980. *The Dynamics of Victorian Business: Problems and Perspectives to the 1870s.*

1986. *The History of the British Coal Industry, vol. III: 1830–1913: Victorian Pre-Eminence.* Oxford.

Cipolla, C. 1965. *The Economic History of World Population.* Harmondsworth.

ed. 1973. *The Fontana Economic History of Europe,* vol. III.

Clapham, J. H. 1910. The last years of the Navigation Acts. *English Historical Review* 25: 480–501 and 687–707. Reprinted in Carus-Wilson 1954.

1926. *An Economic History of Modern Britain: The Early Railway Age, 1820–1850.* Cambridge.

1928. *The Economic Development of France and Germany, 1815–1914.* 3rd edn, Cambridge.

1938. *An Economic History of Modern Britain, vol. III: Machines and National Rivalries, 1887–1914.* Cambridge.

1944. *The Bank of England. A History.* 2 vols. Cambridge.

Clark, G. N. 1938. *Guide to English Commercial Statistics, 1696–1782.*

Clark, H. 1984. The design and designing of Lancashire printed calicoes during the first half of the nineteenth century. *Textile History* 15: 101–18.

Clark, J. C. D. 1987. *English Society 1688–1832: Ideology, Social Structure and Political Practice during the Ancien Regime.* Cambridge.

Clark, P., ed. 1984. *The Transformation of English Provincial Towns, 1600–1800.*

Clark, P., and Souden, D., eds. 1987. *Migration and Society in Early Modern England.*

Clark, W. 1991. The scientific revolution in the German nations. In Porter and Teich 1991.

Clarkson, L. A. 1989. The manufacture of leather. In Mingay 1989.

Coelho, P. R. P. 1973. The profitability of imperialism: the British experience in the West Indies, 1768–72. *Explorations in Economic History* 10: 253–80.

Cohen, J. 1982. The history of imprisonment for debt and its relation to the development of discharge in bankruptcy. *Journal of Legal History* 3: 153–72.

Cole, W. A. 1958. Trends in eighteenth-century smuggling. *Economic History Review* 10: 395–410.

Coleman, D. C. 1973. Textile growth. In Harte and Ponting 1973.

1977. *The Economy of England 1450–1750.* Oxford.

Colley, L. 1986a. The politics of eighteenth century British history. *Journal of British Studies* 25: 359-79.

1986b. Whose nation? Class and national consciousness in Britain 1750–1830. *Past and Present* 113: 97–117.

Collins, M. 1988. *Money and Banking in the U.K.: A History.*

Colquhoun, P. 1815. *Treatise on the Wealth, Power and Resources of the British Empire in Every Quarter of the World.*

Connolly, S., Houston, R. A., and Morris, R. J., eds. 1992. *Conflict, Identity and Economic Change in Ireland and Scotland.* Edinburgh.

Conrad, A. H., and Meyer, J. R. 1955. *The Economics of Slavery and other Studies in Econometric History*. Chicago.

Cope, S. R. 1983. *Walter Boyd, a Merchant Banker in the Age of Napoleon*.

Coppieters, E. 1955. *English Banknote Circulation 1694–1954*.

Coppock, D. J. 1956. The climacteric of the 1890s: a critical note. *Manchester School of Economic and Social Studies* 24: 1–31.

1961. The causes of the great depression, 1873–1896. *Manchester School of Economic and Social Studies* 29: 205–32

Cottrell, P. L. 1980. *Industrial Finance, 1830–1914*.

Court, W. H. B. 1965. *British Economic History 1870–1914: Commentary and Documents*. Cambridge.

Crafts, N. F. R. 1973. Trade as a handmaiden of growth: an alternative view. *Economic Journal* 83: 875–84.

1976. English economic growth in the eighteenth century: a re-examination of Deane and Cole's estimates. *Economic History Review* 29: 226–35.

1977a. Determinants of the rate of parliamentary enclosure. *Explorations in Economic History* 14: 227–49.

1977b. Industrial revolution in England and France: some thoughts on the question, Why was England first? *Economic History Review* 30: 429–41.

1979. Victorian Britain did fail. *Economic History Review* 32: 533–7.

1984. Patterns of development in nineteenth century Europe. *Oxford Economic Papers* 36: 438–58.

1985a. *British Economic Growth during the Industrial Revolution*. Oxford.

1985b. English workers' living standards during the industrial revolution: some remaining problems. *Journal of Economic History* 45: 139–44.

1985c. Income elasticities of demand and the release of labor by agriculture during the British industrial revolution: a further appraisal. In Mokyr 1985b.

1987. British economic growth 1700–1850: some difficulties of interpretation. *Explorations in Economic History* 24: 245–68.

1989a. British industrialization in an international context. *Journal of Interdisciplinary History* 19: 415–28.

1989b. Real wages, inequality and economic growth in Britain, 1750–1850: a review of recent research. In Scholliers 1989.

Crafts, N. F. R., and Harley, C. K. 1992. Output growth and the British industrial revolution: a restatement of the Crafts–Harley view. *Economic History Review* 45: 703–30.

Crafts, N. F. R., and Thomas, M. 1986. Comparative advantage in UK manufacturing trade 1910–1935. *Economic Journal* 96: 629–45.

Crafts, N. F. R., Leybourne, S. J., and Mills, T. C. 1989. Trends and cycles in British industrial production, 1700–1913. *Journal of the Royal Statistical Society*, Series A, 152: 43–60.

1991. Britain. In Sylla and Toniolo 1991.

Craig, J. 1953. *The Mint. A History of the London Mint from* A. D. *286 to 1948*. Cambridge.

Crouzet, F. 1958. *L'Economie britannique et le blocus continental, 1806–13*. Paris.

1964. Wars, blockade and economic change in Europe, 1792–1815. *Journal of Economic History* 24: 567–88.

1967. England and France in the eighteenth century: a comparative analysis of two economic growths. In Hartwell 1967.

ed. 1972. *Capital Formation in the Industrial Revolution.*

1980. Toward an export economy: British exports during the industrial revolution. *Explorations in Economic History* 17: 48–93.

1985. *The First Industrialists: The Problem of Origins.* Cambridge.

1990a. *Britain Ascendant: Comparative Studies in Franco-British Economic History.* Cambridge.

1990b. Criticisms and self-criticisms of a comparison. In Crouzet 1990a.

Cruickshanks, E. G., and Black, J. B. eds. 1988. *The Jacobite Challenge.* Edinburgh.

Cullen, L. M. 1987. *An Economic History of Ireland since 1660.*

Darby, H. C. 1976a. The age of the improver: 1600–1800. In Darby 1976b.

ed. 1976b. *A New Historical Geography of England after 1600.* Cambridge.

Darity, W., Jr. 1990. British industry and the West Indies plantations. *Social Science History* 14: 117–49.

David, P. A. 1969. Transport innovation and economic growth: Professor Fogel on and off the rails. *Economic History Review* 22: 506–25.

Davies, R. S. W., and Pollard, S. 1988. The iron industry, 1750–1850. In Feinstein and Pollard 1988.

Davis, L. E., and Huttenback, R. A. 1986. *Mammon and the Pursuit of Empire.* Cambridge.

Davis, R. 1954. English foreign trade, 1660–1700. *Economic History Review* 7: 150–66.

1962a. English foreign trade, 1700–1774. *Economic History Review* 15: 285–303.

1962b. *The Rise of the English Shipping Industry in the Seventeenth and Eighteenth Centuries.*

1966. The rise of protection in England, 1689–1786. *Economic History Review* 19: 306–17.

1969. English overseas trade, 1700–1774. In Minchinton 1969.

1979. *The Industrial Revolution and British Overseas Trade.* Leicester.

Deane, P. 1957. The output of the British wool industry in the eighteenth century. *Journal of Economic History* 17: 207–23.

Deane, P., and Cole, W. A. 1962. *British Economic Growth, 1688–1959.* Cambridge.

1967. *British Economic Growth, 1688–1959.* 2nd edn. Cambridge.

Defoe, D. 1727. *The Complete English Tradesman in Familiar Letters.*

Devine, T. M., and Dickson, D., eds. 1983. *Ireland and Scotland: 1600–1850.* Edinburgh.

Dickerson, O. M. 1951. *The Navigation Acts and the American Revolution.* Philadelphia.

Dickinson, H. T., ed. 1989. *Britain and the French Revolution, 1789–1815.*

Dickinson, H. W. 1958. The steam engine to 1830. In Singer *et al.* 1958.

Dickson, P. G. M. 1967. *The Financial Revolution in England: A Study in the Development of Public Credit, 1688–1756.*

Digby, A. 1975. The labour market and the continuity of social policy after 1834: the case of the eastern counties. *Economic History Review* 28: 69–83.

Dobson, C. R. 1980. *Masters and Journeymen. A Prehistory of Industrial Relations.*

Dosi, G. 1988. Sources, procedures, and microeconomic effects of innovation. *Journal of Economic Literature* 26: 1120–71.

Dosi, G., Freeman, C., Nelson, R., Silverberg, G., and Soete, L., eds. 1988. *Technical Change and Economic Theory*.

Drescher, S. 1977. *Econocide*. Pittsburgh.

Dubois, A. B. 1971. *The English Business Company after the Bubble Act*. New York.

Duffy, I. P. H. 1982. The discount policy of the Bank of England during the suspension of cash payments, 1797–1821. *Economic History Review* 35: 81.

  1985. *Bankruptcy and Insolvency in London during the Industrial Revolution*. New York.

Dutt, R. 1901. *The Economic History of India under Early British Rule*.

Dutton, H. I. 1984. *The Patent System and Inventive Activity during the Industrial Revolution, 1750–1852*. Manchester.

Eatwell, J. 1982. *Whatever Happened to Britain?: The Economics of Decline*.

Eccleston, B. 1976. A survey of wage rates in five Midland counties, 1750–1834. Unpublished PhD thesis, University of Leicester.

Edelstein, M. 1982. *Overseas Investment in the Age of High Imperialism*. New York.

Edwards, M. M. 1967. *The Growth of the British Cotton Trade, 1790–1815*. Manchester.

Ekelund, R. B., and Tollison, R. D. 1981. *Mercantilism as a Rent Seeking Society*. College Station, Texas.

Ellison, T. 1886. *The Cotton Trade of Great Britain*. Reprinted 1968.

Elster, J. 1983. *Explaining Technical Change: A Case Study in the Philosophy of Science*. Cambridge.

Eltis, D. 1987. *Economic Growth and the Ending of the Transatlantic Slave Trade*. New York.

Emsley, C. 1983. The military and popular disorder in England 1790–1801. *Journal of the Society for Army Historical Research* 61: 10–21 and 96–112.

  1987. *Crime and Society in England 1750–1900*.

Engels, F. 1845. *The Condition of the Working Class in England*. New edn, St Albans, 1974.

Engerman, S. L. 1993. Reflections on 'the standard of living debate': new arguments and new evidence. In James and Thomas 1993.

English, H. 1827. *A Complete View of the Joint Stock Companies Formed during 1824 and 1825*.

English, W. 1958. The textile industry: silk production and manufacture, 1750–1900. In Singer *et al.* 1958.

Ernle, Lord. 1961. *English Farming: Past and Present*.

Ernst, J. A. 1973. *Money and Politics in America, 1755–1775*. Chapel Hill.

Eversley, D. E. C. 1967. The home market and economic growth in England, 1750–80. In Jones and Mingay 1967.

Fairlie, S. 1965. The nineteenth century Corn Law reconsidered. *Economic History Review* 18: 562–75.

  1969. The Corn Laws and British wheat production, 1829–1876. *Economic History Review* 22: 88–116.

Feavearyear, A. 1963. *The Pound Sterling. A History of English Money*. Oxford.

Feinstein, C. H. 1972. *National Income, Expenditure and Output of the United Kingdom, 1855–1965*. Cambridge.

1978. Capital accumulation and economic growth. In Mathias and Postan 1978.

1981. Capital accumulation and the industrial revolution. In Floud and McCloskey 1981.

1988. National statistics, 1760–1920. In Feinstein and Pollard 1988.

Feinstein, C. H., and Pollard, S., eds. 1988. *Studies in Capital Formation in the United Kingdom, 1750–1920*. Oxford.

Fetter, F. W. 1965. *Development of British Monetary Orthodoxy 1797–1875*. Cambridge, Mass.

Field, A. J. 1983. Land abundance, interest–profit rates, and nineteenth-century American and British technology. *Journal of Economic History* 43: 405–31.

1985. On the unimportance of machinery. *Explorations in Economic History* 22: 402–16.

Firot, J. W., and Jacobsen, J., eds. 1992. *Humans and the Environment*. Boulder, Colo.

Fischer, W., McInnis, R. M., and Schneider, J., eds. 1985. *The Emergence of a World Economy, 1500–1914, vol. II: 1850–1914*.

Fleischman, R. 1985. *Life among the Cotton Workers of Southeastern Lancashire, 1780–1850*. New York.

Flinn, M. W. 1959. Timber and the advance of technology: a reconsideration. *Annals of Science* 15: 109–20.

1965. Introduction to Chadwick 1842.

1970. *English Population Growth, 1700–1850*.

1974. Trends in real wages, 1750–1850. *Economic History Review* 27: 395–411.

1977. *Scottish Population History from the Seventeenth Century to the 1930s*. Cambridge.

1978. Technical change as an escape from resource scarcity: England in the seventeenth and eighteenth centuries. In Parker and Macsak 1978.

1984. *The History of the British Coal Industry, vol. II, 1700–1830: The Industrial Revolution*. Oxford.

Floud, R. C. 1976. *The British Machine Tool Industry, 1850–1914*. Cambridge.

Floud, R. C., and McCloskey, D. N., eds. 1981. *The Economic History of Britain since 1700, vol. I: 1700–1860*. 1st edn, Cambridge.

Floud, R. C., Wachter, K. W., and Gregory, A. 1990. *Health, Height and History: Nutritional Status in the United Kingdom, 1750–1980*. Cambridge.

Fogel, R. W. 1984. *Railroads and American Economic Growth: Essays in Econometric History*. Baltimore.

1989. *Without Consent or Contract*. New York.

Fores, M. 1981. The myth of a British industrial revolution. *History* 66: 181–98.

Fortrey, S. 1663. *Englands Interest and Improvement*. Cambridge.

Fraser, D. 1976. *The New Poor Law in the Nineteenth Century*.

Fries, R. I. 1975. British response to the American system: the case of the small-arms industry. *Technology and Culture* 16: 377–403.

Fulford, R. 1953. *Glyn's*.

Furniss, E. S. 1920. *The Position of the Labourer in a System of Nationalism*. New York.

Galenson, D. W. 1981. *White Servitude in Colonial America*. Cambridge.

1989a. Labour market behaviour in colonial America: servitude, slavery, and free labour. In Galenson 1989b.

ed. 1989b. *Markets in History: Economic Studies of the Past.* Cambridge.

Galloway, P. R. 1988. Basic patterns in annual variations in fertility, nuptiality, mortality and prices in pre-industrial Europe. *Population Studies* 42: 487–505.

Gash, N. 1986. *Sir Robert Peel: The Life of Sir Robert Peel after 1830.* 2nd edn.

Gattrell, V. A. C. 1977. Labour, power and the size of firms. *Economic History Review* 30: 95–140.

1980. The decline of theft and violence in Victorian and Edwardian England. In Gatrell *et al.* 1980.

Gattrell, V. A. C., *et al.*, eds. 1980. *Crime and the Law.*

Gayer, A. D., Rostow, W. W., and Schwartz, Anna J. 1975. *The Growth and Fluctuation of the British Economy 1790–1850*, 2 vols. (repr. of 1953 edn). New York.

Gemery, H. A. 1984. European emigration to North America, 1700–1820: numbers and quasi-numbers. *Perspectives in American History*, New Series, 1: 283–342.

Gemery, H. A., and Hogendorn, J. S., eds. 1979. *The Uncommon Market.* New York.

Gerschenkron, A. 1962a. *Economic Backwardness in Historical Perspective.* Cambridge, Mass.

1962b. On the concept of continuity in history. *Proceedings of the American Philosophical Society* (June). Reprinted in Gerschenkron 1968.

1968. *Continuity in History and Other Essays.* Cambridge, Mass.

Giersch, H., ed. 1982. *Emerging Technologies: Consequences for Economic Growth, Structural Change and Employment.* Tübingen.

Gilboy, E. W. 1934. *Wages in 18th Century England.* Cambridge, Mass.

1936. The cost of living and real wages in eighteenth-century England. *Review of Economics and Statistics* 18: 134–43.

Goldin, C., and Sokoloff, K. 1982. Women, children and industrialisation in the early republic: evidence from the manufacturing censuses. *Journal of Economic History* 42: 721–74.

1984. The relative productivity hypothesis and industrialisation: the American case, 1820–1850. *Quarterly Journal of Economics* 99: 461–87.

Gomes, L. 1987. *Foreign Trade and the National Economy.*

Grantham, G., and Leonard, C. S., eds. 1989. Agrarian organization in the century of industrialization: Europe, Russia, and North America. *Research in Economic History* Supplement 5, Part A: 89–120.

Great Britain Parliamentary Papers 1833. V. 6, *Select Committee on Commerce, Manufacturing and Shipping.*

1840. V. 99, Paper 601, *Select Committee on Import Duties.* Report and evidence.

1845. V. 47, *Return of All Joint Stock Companies Registered as having been in Existence before the Passing of 7 & 8 Vict. c. 110.*

Gregory, T. E. 1936. *The Westminster Bank through a Century*, vol. I.

Grigg, D. B. 1963. Small and large farms in England and Wales, their size and distribution. *Geography* 48: 268–79.

Groeneveld, E. J. 1940. *Economische Crisis van het jaar 1720.* Groningen.

Grubb, F. 1992. The long-run trend in the value of European immigrant servants,

1654–1831: new measurements and interpretations. *Economic History* 14: 167–240.

Gustafsson, B., ed. 1991. *Power and Economic Institutions*. Aldershot.

Habakkuk, H. J. 1940. Free trade and commercial expansion, 1853–1870. In Rose, Newton and Benians 1940.

1962. *American and British Technology in the Nineteenth Century: The Search for Labour-Saving Inventions*. Cambridge.

Haberler, G. 1959. *International Trade and Economic Development*. Cairo.

Haines, B. W. 1980. English labour laws and the separation from contract. *Journal of Legal History* 1: 262–96.

Hamilton, E. J. 1947. Origin and growth of the national debt in western Europe. *American Economic Review* 37: 118–30.

Hammersley, G. 1973. The charcoal iron industry and its fuel, 1540–1750. *Economic History Review* 26: 593–613.

Hammond, J. L., and B. 1924. *The Village Labourer, 1760–1832*.

Harley, C. K. 1974. Skilled labour and the choice of technique in Edwardian industry. *Explorations in Economic History* 11: 391–414.

1980. Transportation, the world wheat trade and the Kuznets cycle, 1850–1913. *Explorations in Economic History* 17: 218–50.

1982. British industrialization before 1841: evidence of slower growth during the industrial revolution. *Journal of Economic History* 42: 267–89.

1985. Late nineteenth century transportation, trade and settlement. In Fischer, McInnis and Schneider 1985.

1989. Review of W. P. Kennedy, Industrial structure, capital markets, and the origins of British economic decline. *American Historical Review* 94: 1380.

1992. The world food economy and Argentina. In Broadberry and Crafts 1992.

Harper, L. A. 1939. *The English Navigation Acts*. New York.

1942. Mercantilism and the American Revolution. *Canadian Historical Review* 23: 1–15.

Harris, J. R., ed. 1969. *Liverpool and Merseyside: Essays in the Economic and Social History of the Port and its Hinterland*. New York.

1976. Skills, coal and British industry in the eighteenth century. *History* 61: 167–82.

Harte, N. B., and Ponting, K., eds. 1973. *Textile History and Economic History: Essays in Honour of Miss Julia de Lacy Mann*.

Hartwell, R. M. 1965. The causes of the industrial revolution: an essay in methodology. *Economic History Review* 18: 164–82. Reprinted in Hartwell 1967.

ed. 1967. *The Causes of the Industrial Revolution in England*.

1990. Was there an industrial revolution? *Social Science History* 14: 567–76.

Hatton, T. J., Lyons, J. S., and Satchell, S. E. 1983. Eighteenth century British trade: homespun or empire made? *Explorations in Economic History* 20: 163–82.

Havinden, M. A. 1961. Agricultural progress in open field Oxfordshire. *Agricultural History Review* 9: 73–83.

Hawke, G. R. 1970. *Railways and Economic Growth in England and Wales 1840–1870*. Oxford.

1981. Transport and Social Overhead Capital. In Floud and McCloskey 1981.

Hay, D. 1975. Property authority and the criminal law. In Hay *et al.* 1975.

  1982. War dearth and theft in the eighteenth century. *Past and Present* 95: 117–60.

Hay, D., *et al.*, eds. 1975 *Albion's Fatal Tree.*

Haynes, M. 1988. Employers and trade unions 1824–1850. In Rule 1988.

Heaton, H. 1920. *The Yorkshire Woollen and Worsted Industries.* Oxford.

  1937. Financing the industrial revolution. *Bulletin of the Business Historical Society* 11: 1–10. Reprinted in Crouzet 1972.

Heim, C. E., and Mirowski, P. 1987. Interest rates and crowding-out during Britain's industrial revolution. *Journal of Economic History* 47: 117–39.

Helpman, E., and Krugman, P. D. 1985. *Market Structure and Foreign Trade.* Cambridge, Mass.

Henderson, W. O. 1954. *Britain and Industrial Europe, 1750–1870.*

Hidy, R. 1949. *The House of Baring in American Trade and Finance: English Merchant Bankers at Work, 1763–1861.* Cambridge, Mass.

Higgs, E. 1986. Domestic service and household production. In John 1986.

Higman, B. W. 1984. *Slave Populations of the British Caribbean, 1807–1834.* Baltimore.

Higonnet, P., Landes, D., and Rosovsky, H., eds. 1991. *Favorites of Fortune: Technology, Growth and Economic Development since the Industrial Revolution.* Cambridge, Mass.

Hilgerdt, F. 1942. *The Network of Trade.* Geneva.

  1943. The case for multilateral trade. *American Economic Review* 33, Papers and Proceedings: 393–407.

  1945. *Industrialisation and Foreign Trade.* Geneva.

Hills, R. L. 1979. Hargreaves, Arkwright, and Crompton: why three separate inventors? *Textile History* 10: 114–26.

Hobsbawm, E., and Rudé, G. 1968. *Captain Swing.* New York.

Hoffman, R. J. S. 1933. *Great Britain and the German Trade Rivalry, 1875–1914.*

Hofsten, E., and Lundström, H. 1976. Swedish population history. Main trends from 1750 to 1970. *Urval* 8.

Hohenberg, P. M., and Lees, L. H. 1985. *The Making of Urban Europe 1000–1950.* Cambridge, Mass.

Holderness, B. A. 1976. Credit in English rural society before the nineteenth century, with special reference to the period 1650–1720. *Agricultural History* 24: 97–109.

  1988. Agriculture, 1770–1860. In Feinstein and Pollard 1988.

  1989. Prices, productivity, and output. In Thirsk 1989.

Holdsworth, W. S. 1922–66. *A History of English Law.* 3rd edn, 16 vols.

Hollingsworth, T. H. 1977. Mortality in the British peerage families since 1600. *Population* 32: 323–52.

Holmyard, E. J. 1958. The chemical industry: developments in chemical theory and practice. In Singer *et al.* 1958.

Hoppit, J. 1986a. Financial crises in eighteenth-century England. *Economic History Review* 39: 39–58.

  1986b. The use and abuse of credit in eighteenth-century England. In McKendrick and Outhwaite 1986.

  1987. *Risk and failure in English business 1700–1800.* Cambridge.

1990. Counting the industrial revolution. *Economic History Review* 43: 173–93.

Houlding, J. A. 1981. *Fit for Service. The Training of the British Army 1715–1795.*

Hounshell, D. A. 1984. *From the American System to Mass Production, 1800–1932: The Development of Manufacturing Technology in the US.* Baltimore and London.

Houston, R. A. 1988. *Literacy in Early Modern Europe: Culture and Education, 1500–1800.*

Hudson, P. 1986. *The Genesis of Industrial Capital: A Study of the West Riding Wool Textile Industry c.1750–1850.* Cambridge.

  ed. 1989. *Regions and Industries.* Cambridge.

Hueckel, G. 1981. Agriculture during industrialisation. In Floud and McCloskey 1981.

Humphries, J. 1987. '...The most free from objection...' the sexual division of labor and women's work in nineteenth century England. *Journal of Economic History* 47: 929–50.

  1990. Enclosures, common right, and women: the proletarianization of families in the late eighteenth and early nineteenth centuries. *Journal of Economic History* 50: 17–42.

Hunt, B. C. 1936. *The Development of the Business Corporation in England 1800–1867.* Cambridge, Mass.

Hutchison, T. 1988. *Before Adam Smith: The Emergence of Political Economy 1662–1776.* Oxford.

Hyde, C. K. 1977. *Technological Change and the British Iron Industry.* Princeton, N. J.

Imlah, J. A. H. 1958. *Economic Elements in the Pax Britannica: Studies in British Foreign Trade in the Nineteenth Century.* Cambridge, Mass.

Inikori, J. E. 1989. Slavery and the revolution in cotton textile production in England. *Social Science History* 13: 343–79.

  1990. The credit needs of the African trade and the development of the credit economy in England. *Explorations in Economic History.* 27: 197–231.

Inikori, J. E., and Engerman, S. L., eds. 1992. *The Atlantic Slave Trade.* Durham.

Innes, J. M. 1980. The king's bench prison in the later eighteenth century: law, authority and order in a London debtors' prison. In Brewer and Styles 1980.

  1985. Social problems, poverty and marginality in 18th century England. Somerville College, Oxford, unpublished paper.

  1987. Prisons for the poor: English Bridewells 1555–1800. In Snyder and Hay 1987.

Innes, J. M., and Styles, J. 1986. The crime wave in recent writings on crime and criminal law. *Journal of British Studies* 25: 380–435.

Ippolito, R. A. 1975. The effect of the agricultural depression on industrial demand in England: 1730–1750. *Economica* 2: 298–312.

Irwin, D. A. 1988. Welfare effects of British free trade: debate and evidence from the 1840s. *Journal of Political Economy* 91: 1142–64.

Jackson, R. V. 1985. Growth and deceleration in English agriculture, 1660–1790. *Economic History Review* 36: 333–51.

  1992. Rates of industrial growth during the industrial revolution. *Economic History Review* 45: 1–23.

Jacob, M. C. 1988. *The Cultural Meaning of the Scientific Revolution.* New York.

Jacquemin, A. 1987. *The New Industrial Organization*. Oxford.

James, J. 1857. *History of the Worsted Manufacture in England*. Reprinted 1968.

James, J. 1988. Personal wealth distribution in late eighteenth-century Britain. *Economic History Review* 41: 543–65.

James, J., and Thomas, M., eds. 1993. *Capitalism in Context: Essays in Honor of R. M. Hartwell*. Chicago.

Jeans, J. S. 1885. *England's Supremacy: Its Sources, Economics and Dangers*.

Jenkins, D. T. 1975. *The West Riding Wool Textile Industry, 1770–1815: A Study of Fixed Capital Formation*. Edington, Wilts.

Jeremy, D. J. 1981. *Transatlantic Industrial Revolution: The Diffusion of Textile Technologies between Britain and America, 1790–1830s*. Oxford.

Jevons, W. S. 1865. *The Coal Question* 3rd edn, ed. A. W. Flux, 1906.

John, A., ed. 1986. *Unequal Opportunities: Women's Employment in England 1800–1918*. Oxford.

John, A. H. 1953. Insurance investment in the eighteenth century. *Economica* 20: 137–58.

1955. War and the English economy. *Economic History Review* 7: 329–44.

1989. Statistical appendix. In Mingay 1989.

Jones, D. W. 1988. *War and Economy*. Oxford.

Jones, E. L. 1981. *The European Miracle: Environments, Economics and Geopolitics in the History of Europe and Asia*. Cambridge.

1988. *Growth Recurring*. Oxford.

Jones, E. L., and Falkus, M. E. 1979. Urban improvement and the English economy in the seventeenth and eighteenth centuries, *Research in Economic History* 4: 193–233.

Jones, E. L., and Mingay, G. E., eds. 1967. *Land, Labour, and Population in the Industrial Revolution*.

Jones, G. T. 1933. *Increasing Returns*. Cambridge.

Jones, R. E. 1980. Further evidence on the decline in infant mortality in pre-industrial England: rural north Shropshire, 1561–1810. *Population Studies* 34: 239–50.

Joslin, D. M. 1954. The London private bankers, 1720–1785. *Economic History Review* 7: 167–86.

Joyce, P. J., ed. 1987. *The Historical Meanings of Work*.

Kain, Roger J. P. 1986. *An Atlas and Index of the Tithe Files of Mid-Nineteenth Century England and Wales*. Cambridge.

Kanefsky, J. W. 1979. Motive power in British industry and the accuracy of the 1870 Factory Return. *Economic History Review* 32: 360–76.

Kanefsky, J. W., and Robey, J. 1980. Steam engines in eighteenth century Britain: a quantitative assessment. *Technology and Culture* 21: 161–86.

Keith, T. 1910. *Commercial Relations of England and Scotland, 1603–1707*. Cambridge.

Kelley, T. 1930. Wages and labour organization in the brass trades of Birmingham and district. Unpublished PhD thesis, Birmingham University.

Kelly, J. 1987. The origins of the Act of Union: an examination of Unionist opinion in Britain and Ireland 1650–1800. *Irish Historical Studies* 25: 236–63.

Kelsall, R. K. 1972. Wage regulation under the state. In Minchinton 1972.

Kennedy, P. M. 1983. *The Rise and Fall of British Naval Mastery*.

Kennedy, W. P. 1974. Foreign investment, trade and growth in the United Kingdom, 1870–1913. *Explorations in Economic History* 11: 415–43.

1987. *Industrial Structure, Capital Markets and the Origins of British Economic Decline.* Cambridge.

Keynes, J. M. 1937. Some economic consequences of a declining population. *Eugenics Review* 29: 13–17.

Kindleberger, C. P. 1984. *A Financial History of Western Europe.*

King, G. 1696. Natural and political observations and conclusions upon the state and condition of England. In Chalmers 1802.

King, P. 1989. Gleaners, farmers and the failure of legal sanctions in England, 1750–1850. *Past and Present* 125: 116–56.

Kirzner, I. 1989. *Discovery, Capitalism, and Distributive Justice.* Oxford.

Klingender, F. D. 1968. *Art and the Industrial Revolution.* Bath (1st edn 1947).

Kosminski, E. A. 1956. *Studies in the Agrarian History of England in the Thirteenth Century.* Translated by Ruth Kisch, ed. R. H. Hilton, Oxford.

Kravis, I. B. 1970. Trade as a handmaiden of growth; similarities between the nineteenth and twentieth centuries. *Economic Journal* 80: 850–72.

1973. A reply to Mr Crafts' note. *Economic Journal* 83: 885–9.

Kuhn, T. S. 1977. *The Essential Tension: Selected Studies in Scientific Tradition and Change.* Chicago.

Kumar, D., ed. 1983, *The Cambridge Economic History of India, vol. II: c. 1757 – c. 1970.* Cambridge.

Kusamitsu, T. 1981. British industrialization and design before the Great Exhibition. *Textile History* 12: 77–95.

Kussmaul, A. 1981a. The ambiguous mobility of farm servants. *Economic History Review* 33: 222–35.

1981b. *Servants in Husbandry in Early Modern England.* Cambridge.

1986. *The Autobiography of Joseph Mayett of Quainton (1783–1839).* Buckingham.

1990. *A General View of the Rural Economy of England, 1538–1840.* Cambridge.

Kuznets, S. S. 1966. *Modern Economic Growth: Rate, Structure and Spread.* New Haven.

Lambert, S. 1971. *Bills and Acts: Legislative Procedure in Eighteenth Century England.*

Landau, N. 1984. *The Justices of the Peace 1679–1760.* Berkeley.

Landes, D. S. 1969. *The Unbound Prometheus: Technological Change and Industrial Development in Western Europe from 1750 to the Present.* Cambridge.

1983. *Revolution in Time.* Cambridge, Mass.

1986. What do bosses really do? *Journal of Economic History* 46: 585–623.

1987. Small is beautiful. Small is beautiful? Fondazione ASSE, Instituto per la Storia dell Umbria Contemporanea. In *Piccola e grande impresa: un problema storico,* Milan.

Langford, P. 1989. *A Polite and Commercial People: England, 1727–83.* Oxford.

Langton, J., and Morris, R. J., eds. 1986. *Atlas of Industrializing Britain* 1780–1914.

Laslett, P. 1965. *The World We Have Lost.*

ed. 1977a. *Family Life and Illicit Love in Earlier Generations.* Cambridge.

1977b. Long-term trends in bastardy in England. In Laslett 1977a.

Laslett, P., and Wall, R. 1972. *Household and Family in Past Time.* Cambridge.

Lawes, J. B., and Gilbert, J. H. 1868. On the home produce, imports, and consumption of wheat. *Journal of the Royal Agricultural Society of England* 4: 359–96.

Lazonick, W. 1979. Industrial relations and technical change: the case of the self-acting mule. *Cambridge Journal of Economics* 3: 231–62.

1981. Production relations, labor productivity and choice of technique: British and US cotton spinning. *Journal of Economic History* 41: 491–516.

1986. Social organisation and productivity growth in Britain and the U.S., 1820–1913. In O'Brien 1986.

Lazonick, W. H., and Brush, T. 1985. The 'Horndal Effect' in early U.S. manufacturing. *Explorations in Economic History* 22: 53–96.

League of Nations, International Economic Conference. 1927. *Agricultural Problems in their International Aspect*. Rome.

Leavitt, T. W. 1972. Fashion, commerce and technology in the nineteenth century: the shawl trade. *Textile History* 3: 51–63.

Lee, C. H. 1972. *A Cotton Enterprise, 1795–1840: A History of McConnel and Kennedy, Fine Spinners*. Manchester.

Lee, R. D. 1974. Estimating series of vital rates and age structures from baptisms and burials: a new technique, with applications to pre-industrial England. *Population Studies* 28: 495–512.

1981. Short-term variation: vital rates, prices, and weather. In Wrigley and Schofield 1981.

1985. Inverse projection and back projection: a critical appraisal and comparative results for England, 1539–1871. *Population Studies* 39: 233–48.

1986. Population homeostasis and English demographic history. In Rotberg and Rabb 1986.

Lee, S. P., and Passell, P. 1979. *A New Economic View of American History*. New York.

Lenman, B. P. 1977. *An Economic History of Modern Scotland, 1660–1976*.

1986. *The Jacobite Cause*. Glasgow.

Levack, B. P. 1987. *The Formation of the British State. England, Scotland and the Union, 1603–1707*. Oxford.

Levine, D. 1977. *Family Formation in an Age of Nascent Capitalism*.

1983. Protoindustrialization and demographic upheaval. In Moch and Stark 1983.

1987. *Reproducing Families: The Political Economy of English Population History*. Cambridge.

Levine, D., and Wrightson, K. 1991. *The Making of an Industrial Society, Whickham 1560–1765*. Oxford.

Lieberman, D. 1989. *The Province of Legislation Determined: Legal Theory in Eighteenth Century Britain*. Cambridge.

Lilley, S. 1973. Technological progress and the industrial revolution, 1700–1914. In Cipolla 1973.

Lindert, P. H. 1980. English occupations, 1670–1811. *Journal of Economic History* 40: 685–712.

1986. Unequal English wealth since 1670. *Journal of Political Economy* 94: 1127–62.

1987. Who owned Victorian England? The debate over landed wealth and inequality. *Agricultural History* 61 : 25–51.

1992. Historical patterns in agricultural policy. In Timmer 1992.

Lindert, P. H., and Williamson, J. G. 1982. Revising England's social tables, 1688–1812. *Explorations in Economic History* 19: 385–408.

1983a. English workers' living standards during the industrial revolution: a new look. *Economic History Review* 36: 1–25.

1983b. Reinterpreting Britain's social tables, 1688–1913. *Explorations in Economic History*. 20: 94–109.

1985a. English Workers' real wages: a reply to Crafts. *Journal of Economic History* 45: 145–53.

1985b. Growth, equality and history. *Explorations in Economic History* 22: 341–77.

Lipson, E. 1934. *The Economic History of England: The Age of Mercantilism*, vols. II and III.

Lipton, M. 1976. *Why Poor People Stay Poor: Urban Bias in World Development*. Cambridge.

Livesey, H. 1989. Entrepreneurial dominance in business large and small, past and present. *Business History Review* 63: 1–21.

Lloyd, G. I. H. 1913. *The Cutlery Trades*.

Lloyd-Jones, R., and Le Roux, A. A. 1980. The size of firms in the cotton industry, Manchester, 1815–41. *Economic History Review* 33: 72–83.

Lyons, J. S. 1987. Powerloom profitability and steam power costs: Britain in the 1830s. *Explorations in Economic History* 24: 392–408.

1989. Family response to economic decline: handloom weavers in early nineteenth-century Lancashire. *Research in Economic History* 12: 45–91.

Macaulay, T. B. 1830. *Southey's Colloquies on Society*. In *Macaulay's Essays* (1860 edn), vol. I.

McClelland, P. D. 1969. The cost to America of British imperial policy. *American Economic Review*. Papers and Proceedings 59: 370–81.

McCloskey, D. N. 1970. Did Victorian Britain fail? *Economic History Review* 23: 446–59.

1970–1. Britain's loss from foreign industrialisation: a provisional estimate. *Explorations in Economic History* 8: 141–52.

1972. The enclosure of open fields: preface to a study of its impact on the efficiency of English agriculture in the eighteenth century. *Journal of Economic History* 32: 15–35.

1973. *Economic Maturity and Entrepreneurial Decline: British Iron and Steel, 1870–1913*. Cambridge, Mass.

1975. The economics of enclosure: a market analysis. In Parker and Jones 1975.

1980. Magnanimous Albion: free trade and British national income, 1841/1881. *Explorations in Economic History* 17: 303–20.

1981a. *Enterprise and Trade in Victorian Britain: Essays in Historical Economics*.

1981b. The industrial revolution: a survey. In Floud and McCloskey 1981.

1985. The industrial revolution 1780–1860: a survey. In Mokyr 1985b.

1989. The open fields of England: rent, risk, and the rate of interest, 1300–1815. In Galenson 1989b.

1991. History, nonlinear differential equations, and the problem of narration. *History and Theory* 30: 21–36.

McCulloch, J. R. 1854. *A Descriptive and Statistical Account of the British Empire*. ed. 1954. *Early English Tracts on Commerce*. Cambridge. Originally published 1856.

McCusker, J. J., and Menard, R. R. 1985. *The Economy of British America, 1607–1789*. Chapel Hill.

Macfarlane A. 1978. *The Origins of English Individualism: The Family, Property, and Social Transition*. Oxford.

McKendrick, N., and Outhwaite, R. B., eds. 1986. *Business Life and Public Policy*. Cambridge.

McKendrick, N., Brewer, J., and Plumb, J. H. 1982. *The Birth of Consumer Society: The Commercialization of Eighteenth Century England*.

MacLeod, C. 1988. *Inventing the Industrial Revolution: The English Patent System, 1660–1800*. Cambridge.

1991. The paradoxes of patenting: invention and its diffusion in 18th and 19th century Britain, France and North America. *Technology and Culture* 32: 885–910.

McNeil, W. H. 1982. *The Pursuit of Power*. Chicago.

Maddison, A. 1971. *Class Structure and Economic Growth*. New York.

1991. *Dynamic Forces in Capitalist Development*. Oxford.

Maitland, F. W. 1910/11. English law (history). In *Encyclopaedia Britannica*. 11th edn.

Maizels, A. 1963. *Industrial Growth and World Trade*. Cambridge. And his corrections, 1969.

Malcolmson, R. W. 1981. *Life and Labour in England*.

Malthus, T. R. 1798. *An Essay on the Principle of Population*. Reprinted in Wrigley and Souden 1986.

1826. *An Essay on the Principle of Population*. 6th edn, reprinted in Wrigley and Souden 1986.

1836. *Principles of Political Economy*. 2nd edn.

Mandler, P. 1987. The making of the new poor law redivivus. *Past and Present* 117: 131–57.

Mann, J. de Lacy 1971. *The Cloth Industry in the West of England from 1640 to 1880*. Oxford.

Mantoux, P. 1905. *La Révolution industrielle au xviiie siècle*. Paris.

1928. *The Industrial Revolution in the Eighteenth Century*. 2nd edn, New York, 1961.

Marglin, S. 1974. What do bosses do? The origins and functions of hierarchy in capitalist production. *Review of Radical Political Economy* 6: 33–60.

1991. Understanding capitalism: control versus efficiency. In Gustafsson 1991.

Marshall, A. 1890. *Principles of Economics*. 8th edn, 1949.

Marshall, J. 1832. *Mortality of the Metropolis*.

Marshall, W. 1788. *The Rural Economy of Yorkshire*.

Marvel, H. P. 1977. Factory regulation: a reinterpretation of early English experience. *Journal of Law and Economics* 20: 379–402.

Marx, K. 1857. British incomes in India. Reprinted in Marx and Engels 1972.

1887. *Capital*. trans. S. Moore and E. Aveling, ed. F. Engels.

Marx, K., and Engels, F., eds. 1972. *On Colonialism.* (First published 1857.) New York.

Mathias, P. 1959. *The Brewing Industry in England, 1700–1830.* Cambridge.

1973. Capital, credit and enterprise in the industrial revolution. *Journal of European Economic History* 2: 121–43.

1979. *The Transformation of England.* New York.

1983. *The First Industrial Nation.* 2nd edn.

1985. Concepts of revolution in England and France in the eighteenth century. In Brack 1985.

Mathias, P., and O'Brien, P. K. 1976. Taxation in England and France 1715–1810. *Journal of European Economic History* 5: 601–50.

Mathias, P., and Pollard, S., eds. 1989. *The Cambridge Economic History of Europe, vol. III: The Industrial Economies: The Development of Economic and Social Policies.* Cambridge.

Mathias, P., and Postan, M. M., eds. 1978. *The Cambridge Economic History of Europe, vol. VII: The Industrial Economies: Capital, Labour, and Enterprise, part 1, Britain, France, Germany, and Scandinavia.* Cambridge.

Matthews, R. C. O. 1954. *A Study in Trade-Cycle History: Economic Fluctuations in Great Britain, 1833–42.* Cambridge.

Matthews, R. C. O., Feinstein, C. H., and Odling-Smee, J. C. 1982. *British Economic Growth, 1856–1973.* Stanford, Calif.

Mayr, O., and Post, R., eds. 1975. *Great Britain and her World: Essays in Honor of W. O. Henderson.* Washington, DC.

Meier, G. M., and Baldwin, R. E. 1957. *Economic Development: Theory, History, Policy.* New York.

Melton, F. 1986. *Sir Robert Clayton and the Origins of English Deposit Banking, 1658–1685.* Cambridge.

Meyer, J. R. 1955. An input–output approach to evaluating British industrial production in the late nineteenth century. Reprinted in Conrad and Meyer 1955.

Michie, R. C. 1978. Transfer of shares in Scotland, 1700–1820. *Business History* 20: 153–64.

1985. The London stock exchange and the British securities market, 1850–1914. *Economic History Review* 38: 61–82.

Miles, M. 1981. The money market in the early industrial revolution: the evidence from West Riding attorneys, c. 1750–1800. *Business History* 23: 127–46.

Mill, J. S. 1871. *Principles of Political Economy, with Some of their Applications to Social Philosophy* (1st edn 1848).

Minchinton, W. E., ed. 1969. *The Growth of English Overseas Trade in the Seventeenth and Eighteenth Centuries.*

ed. 1972. *Wage Regulation in Pre-Industrial England.*

1979. The triangular trade revisited. In Gemery and Hogendorn 1979.

Mingay, G. E. 1976. *The Gentry.* London.

ed. 1989. *The Agrarian History of England and Wales, vol. VI: 1750–1850* Cambridge.

Mintz, S. W. 1985. *Sweetness and Power.* New York.

Mitch, D. 1992. *Education and Economic Development in England.* Princeton, N. J.

Mitchell, B. R. 1984. *Economic Development of the British Coal Industry, 1800–1914*. Cambridge.

1988. *British Historical Statistics*. Cambridge.

Mitchell, B., and Deane, P. 1962. *Abstract of British Historical Statistics*. Cambridge.

Moch, L. P., and Stark, G. D., eds. 1983. *Essays on the Family and Historical Change*. College Station, Texas.

Mokyr, J. 1977. Demand vs supply in the industrial revolution. *Journal of Economic History* 37: 981–1008.

1985a. Demand vs supply in the industrial revolution. In Mokyr 1985b.

ed. 1985b. *The Economics of the Industrial Revolution*. Totowa, N. J..

1985c. The industrial revolution and the new economic history. In Mokyr 1985b.

1988. Is there still life in the pessimist case? Consumption during the industrial revolution, 1790–1850. *Journal of Economic History* 48: 69–92.

1990a. *The Lever of Riches: Technological Creativity and Economic Progress*. New York and Oxford.

1990b. Punctuated equilibria and technological progress. *American Economic Review* 80: 350–4.

1991a. Dear labour, cheap labour, and the industrial revolution. In Higonnet, Landes and Rosovsky 1991.

ed. 1991b. *The Vital One: Essays Presented to Jonathan R. T. Hughes*. Greenwich, Conn.

1991c. Was there a British industrial evolution? In Mokyr 1991b.

1993. Progress and inertia in technological change. In James and Thomas 1993.

Morgan, E. V., and Thomas, W. A. 1962. *The Stock Exchange, its History and Functions*.

Mui, H., and L. H. 1975. 'Trends in eighteenth century smuggling' reconsidered. *Economic History Review* 28: 28–43.

Munche, P. B. 1981. *Gentlemen and Poachers. The English Game Laws 1671–1831*. Cambridge.

Munn, C. W. 1981. *The Scottish Provincial Banking Companies, 1747–1864*. Edinburgh.

Murray, N. 1978. *The Scottish Hand Loom Weavers 1790–1850: A Social History*. Edinburgh.

Musson, A. E. 1972. *Science, Technology and Economic Growth in the Eighteenth Century*.

1975. Continental influences on the industrial revolution in Great Britain. In Mayr and Post 1975.

1978. *The Growth of British Industry*. New York.

Musson, A. E., and Robinson, E. 1969. *Science and Technology in the Industrial Revolution*. Manchester.

Neal, L. 1990. *The Rise of Financial Capitalism: International Capital Markets in the Age of Reason*. Cambridge.

Neeson, J. M. 1989. Parliamentary enclosure and the disappearance of the English peasantry, revisited. In Grantham and Leonard 1989.

Nef, J. U. 1932. *The Rise of the British Coal Industry*. 2 vols.

Nelson, R. R., and Winter, S. G. 1973. Towards an evolutionary theory of economic capabilities. *American Economic Review*, Papers and Proceedings, 63: 441–9.

1982. *An Evolutionary Theory of Economic Change*. Cambridge, Mass.

Nicholas, S., and Steckel, R. 1991. Heights and living standards of English workers during the early years of industrialisation, 1770–1815. *Journal of Economic History* 51: 937–57.

North, D. C. 1968. Sources of productivity change in ocean shipping, 1600–1850. *Journal of Political Economy* 76: 953–70.

1981. *Structure and Change in Economic History*.

North, D. C., and Weingast, B. R. 1989. Constitutions and commitment: the evolution of institutions governing public choice in seventeenth century England. *Journal of Economic History* 49: 803–32.

Nye, J. V. 1991. The myth of free-trade Britain and fortress France: tariffs and trade in the nineteenth century. *Journal of Economic History* 51: 23–46.

O'Brien, P. K. 1982. European economic development: the contribution of the periphery. *Economic History Review* 35: 1–18.

1985. Agriculture and the home market for English industry, 1660–1820. *English Historical Review* 100: 773–800.

ed. 1986. International productivity comparisons and problems of measurement, 1750–1939. *Ninth Congress of the International Economic History Association*. Berne.

1988. The political economy of British taxation, 1600–1815. *Economic History Review* 41: 1–32.

1989a. The impact of the revolutionary and Napoleonic wars, 1793–1815 on the long run growth of the British economy. *Review of Fernand Braudel Center* 12: 335–83.

1989b. Public finance in the wars with France, 1793–1815. In Dickinson 1989.

1990. European industrialisation: from the voyages of discovery to the industrial revolution. In Pohl 1990.

1993. Political preconditions for the first industrial revolution. In O'Brien and Quinault 1993.

O'Brien, P. K., and Engerman, S. L. 1991. Exports and the growth of the British economy from the Glorious Revolution to the Peace of Amiens. In Solow and Engerman 1991.

O'Brien, P. K., and Keyder, C. 1978. *Economic Growth in Britain and France, 1780–1914: Two Paths to the Twentieth Century*.

O'Brien, P. K., and Quinault, R. E., eds. 1993. *The Industrial Revolution and British Society*.

O'Gorman, F. 1986. The recent historiography of the Hanoverian regime. *Historical Journal* 29: 1005–20.

Ó Gráda, C. 1993. The British Isles: Ireland. In Bardet and Dupâquier 1993.

Oda, S. H. 1990. The application of Pasinetti's vertical hyper-integration to time-saving technical progress and the input–output table. *Cambridge Journal of Economics* 14: 241–6.

Oeppen, J. E. 1993. Back-projection and inverse projection: members of a wider class of constrained projection models. *Population Studies*, forthcoming.

Ojala, E. M. 1952. *Agriculture and Economic Progress*. Oxford.

Olson, M. 1963. *The Economics of the Wartime Shortage. A History of British Food Supplies in the Napoleonic Wars and in World Wars I and II*. Durham, N. C.

1974. The United Kingdom and the world market in wheat and other primary products, 1870–1914. *Explorations in Economic History* 11: 325–55.

Olson, M., and Harris, C. C. 1958. Free trade in 'corn': a statistical study of the prices and production of wheat in Great Britain from 1873 to 1914. *Quarterly Journal of Economics* 73: 145–68.

Ormrod, D. 1985. *English Grain Exports and the Structure of Agrarian Capitalism, 1700–1760*. Hull.

Orth, J. 1987. The English combination laws reconsidered. In Snyder and Hay 1987.

Outhwaite, R. B., ed. 1981. *Marriage and Society: Studies in the Social History of Marriage*.

Overton, M. 1984. Agricultural revolution? Development of the agrarian economy in early modern England. In Baker and Gregory 1984.

Pacey, A. 1975. *The Maze of Ingenuity: Ideas and Idealism in the Development of Technology*. New York.

1990. *Technology in World Civilization: A Thousand-Year History*. Cambridge, Mass.

Palmer, S. H. 1978. Calling out the troops: the military, the law and public order in England, 1650–1950. *Journal of the Society for Army Historical Research* 56: 198–214.

Pares, R. 1937. The economic factors in the history of empire. *Economic History Review* 7: 119–44.

Parker, W. 1984. *Europe, America, and the Wider World*. Cambridge.

Parker, W. N. 1971. From old to new in economic history. *Journal of Economic History* 31: 3–14.

Parker, W. N., and Jones, E. L., eds. 1975. *European Peasants and their Markets: Essays in Agrarian History*. Princeton, N. J.

Parker, W. N., and Macsak, A., eds. 1978. *Natural Resources in European History*. Washington, D.C.

Pavitt, K., and Soete, L. 1982. International differences in economic growth and the international location of innovation. In Giersch 1982.

Pawson, E. 1977. *Transport and the Economy: The Turnpike Roads of Eighteenth Century England*.

1979. *The Early Industrial Revolution. Britain in the Eighteenth Century*. New York.

1984. Popular opposition to turnpike trusts. *Journal of Transport History*, 3rd Series, 5: 58–65.

Payne, P. L. 1974. *British Entrepreneurship in the Nineteenth Century*.

Pereira Mendes, V. 1991. R&D, technical change and tangible investment. Unpublished MPhil thesis, Science Policy Research Unit, University of Sussex.

Perkin, H. J. 1969. *The Origins of Modern English Society. 1780–1880*.

Phelps Brown, E. H. 1988. *Egalitarianism and the Generation of Inequality*. Oxford.

Phelps Brown, E. H., and Hopkins, Sheila V. 1956. Seven centuries of the prices of consumables, compared with builders' wage-rates. *Economica*, New Series, 23: 296–314.

Philips, D. 1977. *Crime and Authority in Victorian England.*

Pinchbeck, I. 1930. *Women Workers and the Industrial Revolution, 1750–1850.* Reprinted. 1969.

Piore, M., and Sabel, C. 1984. *The Second Industrial Divide.* New York.

Plot, R. 1677. *The Natural History of Oxfordshire.* Oxford.

Pohl, H., ed. 1990. *The European Discovery of the World and its Economic Effects on Pre-Industrial Society.*

Polanyi, K. 1944. *The Great Transformation.* New York and Toronto.

Pollard, S. 1963. Factory discipline in the industrial revolution. *Economic History Review* 16: 254–71.

   1964. Fixed capital in the industrial revolution. *Journal of Economic History* 24: 299–314.

   1965. *The Genesis of Modern Management: A Study of the Industrial Revolution in Great Britain.*

   1969. Capital accounting in the industrial revolution. *Yorkshire Bulletin of Economic and Social Research* 15: 75–91.

   1973. Industrialization and the European Economy. *Economic History Review* 26: 636–48. Reprinted in Mokyr 1985b.

   1978. Labour in Great Britain. In Mathias and Postan 1978.

   1981a. *Peaceful Conquest: The Industrialization of Europe, 1760–1970.* Oxford.

   1981b. Sheffield and sweet auburn – amenities and living standards in the British industrial revolution: a comment. *Journal of Economic History* 41: 902–4.

   1983. Capitalism and rationality: a study of measurements in British coal mining, ca 1750–1850. *Explorations in Economic History* 20: 110–29.

Pollard, S., and Robertson, P. 1979. *The British Shipbuilding Industry 1870–1914.* Cambridge.

Ponting, K. G. 1971. *The Woollen Industry of South-West England.* Bath.

Porter, R. 1982. *English Society in the Eighteenth Century.*

Porter, R., and Teich, M., eds. 1991. *The Scientific Revolution in National Context.* Cambridge.

Postan, M. M. 1935. Recent trends in the accumulation of capital. *Economic History Review* 1st Series, 6: 1–12.

Postlethwayt, M. 1774. *The Universal Dictionary of Trade and Commerce.* Reprinted 1971.

Powell, E. T. 1914. *Evolution of the London Money Market.*

Pressnell, L. S. 1956. *Country Banking in the Industrial Revolution.* Oxford.

   ed. 1960. *Studies in the Industrial Revolution.*

Price, D. de S. 1984. The science/technology relationship, the craft of experimental science, and policy for the improvement of high-technology innovation. *Research Policy* 13: 3–20.

Price, J. M. 1980. *Capital and Credit in British Overseas Trade: The View from the Chesapeake, 1700–1776.* Cambridge, Mass.

   1989. What did merchants do? Reflections on British overseas trade, 1660–1760. *Journal of Economic History* 49: 267–84.

Prince, H. C. 1976. England circa 1800. In Darby 1976b.

Prothero, I. 1979. *Artisans and Politics in Early Nineteenth Century* London. Folkestone.

Rae, T., ed. 1974. *The Union of 1707. Its Impact on Scotland.* Glasgow.

Randall, A. J. 1982. The shearmen and the Wiltshire outrage of 1802: trade unionism and industrial violence. *Social History* 7: 28–34.

1989. Work, culture and resistance to machinery in the west of England woollen industry. In Hudson 1989.

1991. *Before the Luddites*. Cambridge.

Ransom, R. L. 1968. British policy and colonial growth: some implications of the burden from the Navigation Acts. *Journal of Economic History* 28: 427–35.

Redford, A. 1926. *Labour Migration in England, 1800–1850*. Manchester.

Reid, J. D. 1970. On navigating the Navigation Acts with Peter D. McClelland: comment. *American Economic Review* 60: 949–55

Reynolds, T. S. 1983. *Stronger than a Hundred Men: A History of the Vertical Water Wheel*. Baltimore.

Ricardo, D. 1817. *Principles of Political Economy and Taxation*.

Rich, E. E., and Wilson, C. H., eds. 1967. *The Cambridge Economic History of Europe, vol. IV: The Economy of Expanding Europe in the Sixteenth and Seventeenth Centuries*. Cambridge.

Richardson, H. W. 1965. Overcommitment in Britain since 1930. *Oxford Economic Papers* 17: 237–62.

Richardson, P. 1989. The structure of capital during the industrial revolution revisited: two case studies from the cotton textile industry. *Economic History Review* 42: 484–503.

Richardson, T. L. 1977. The standard of living controversy, 1790–1840. Unpublished PhD dissertation, University of Hull.

Riden, P. 1986. Iron and steel. In Langton and Morris 1986.

Riley, J. 1991. Working health time: a comparison of pre-industrial, industrial, and post-industrial experience in life and health. *Explorations in Economic History* 28: 169–91.

Rimmer, W. G. 1960. *Marshalls of Leeds: Flax-Spinners, 1788–1886*. Cambridge.

Robertson, D. H. 1938. The future of international trade. *Economic Journal* 48: 1–14.

Rodney, W. 1972. *How Europe Underdeveloped Africa*.

Rogers, A. 1981. Rural industrial and social structure: the framework knitting industry of South Nottinghamshire 1670–1840. *Textile History* 12: 8–17.

Rogers, J. E. T. 1866–1902. *A History of Agriculture and Prices in England*. Oxford.

Rose, J. H., Newton, A. P., and Benians, E. A., eds. 1940. *The Cambridge History of the British Empire*, vol. II. Cambridge.

Rose, R. B. 1961. Eighteenth century price riots and public policy in England. *International Review of Social History* 6: 277–92.

Rosenberg, N. 1963. Technological change in the machine tool industry, 1840–1910. *Journal of Economic History* 23: 414–46.

ed. 1969a. *The American System of Manufactures: The Report of the Committee on the Machinery of the United States 1855 and the Special Reports of George Wallis and Joseph Whitworth*. 1854. Edinburgh.

1969b. The direction of technological change: inducement mechanisms and focusing devices. *Economic Development and Cultural Change* 18: 1–24.

1972. *Technology and American Economic Growth*. New York.

1976. *Perspectives on Technology*. Cambridge.

1982. *Inside the Black Box: Technology and Economics*. Cambridge.

Rostow, W. W. 1948. *The British Economy of the Nineteenth Century: Essays*. Oxford.

　1960. *The Stages of Economic Growth*. Cambridge.

　1975. *How It All Began: The Origins of the Modern Economy*. London.

Rotberg, R. I., and Rabb, T. K., eds. 1986. *Population and Economy: Population and History from the Traditional to the Modern World*.

Rowlands, M. B. 1989. Continuity and change in an industrializing society: the case of the west midlands industries. In Hudson 1989.

Rubin, G., and Sugarman, D., eds. 1984. *Law, Economy and Society*. Abingdon.

Rubinstein, W. D. 1981. *Men of Property*. New Brunswick, N.J.

　1986. *Wealth and Inequality in Britain*.

Rule, J. G. 1981. *The Experience of Labour in Eighteenth Century Industry*.

　1986. *The Labouring Classes in Early Industrial England 1750–1950*.

　1987. *Exploitation and Embezzlement*.

　ed. 1988. *British Trade Unionism 1750–1850: The Formative Years*.

Sabel, C., and Zeitlin, J. 1985. Historical alternatives to mass production: politics, markets, and technology in nineteenth-century industrialization. *Past and Present* 108: 133–76.

Sahal, D. 1981. *Patterns of Technological Innovation*. Reading, Mass.

Salaman, R. N. 1949. *The History and Social Influence of the Potato*. Cambridge.

Sandberg, L. G. 1969. American rings and English mules: the role of economic rationality. *Quarterly Journal of Economics* 83: 25–43.

Saul, S. B. 1960. *Studies in British Overseas Trade. 1870–1914*. Liverpool.

　1965. The export economy, 1870–1914. *Yorkshire Bulletin of Economic and Social Research* 17: 5–18.

　1970a. The market and the development of the mechanical engineering industries in Britain, 1860–1914. In Saul 1970b.

　ed. 1970b. *Technological Change: The United States and Britain in the Nineteenth Century*.

Schelling, T. 1978. *Micromotives and Macrobehavior*. New York.

Schivelbusch, W. 1988. *Disenchanted Night: The Industrialization of Light in the Nineteenth Century*. Trans. Angela Davies, Berkeley, Calif.

Schofield, R. S. 1970. Age-specific mobility in an eighteenth century rural English parish. *Annales de Démographie Historique* 1970: 261–74. Reprinted in Clark and Souden 1987.

　1985. English marriage patterns revisited. *Journal of Family History* 10: 2–120.

　1989. Family structure, demographic behaviour, and economic growth. In Walter and Schofield 1989.

Scholliers, P., ed. 1989. *Real Wages in Nineteenth and Twentieth Century Europe*. New York.

Schumpeter, E. B. 1960. *English Overseas Trade Statistics, 1697–1808*. Oxford.

Schwartz, L. D. 1985. The standard of living in the long run: London, 1700–1860. *Economic History Review* 38: 24–41.

　1990. Trends in real wages, 1750–1790: a reply to Botham and Hunt. *Economic History Review* 43: 90–8.

Scott, W. R. 1910. *The Constitution and Finance of English, Scottish and Irish Joint-Stock Companies to 1720*. 3 vols. Cambridge.

Shammas, C. 1990. *The Pre-Industrial Consumer in England and America*. Oxford.

Shannon, H. A. 1954. The coming of general limited liability. In Carus-Wilson 1954.

Shapiro, S. 1967. *Capital and the Cotton Industry in the Industrial Revolution*. New York.

Sharman, F. A. 1989. An introduction to the Enclosure Acts. *Journal of Legal History* 10: 45–70.

Shaw, G. B. 1929. Socialism: principles and outlook. In *Encyclopaedia Britannica*, 14th edn, 20: 895–7.

Shelton, W. J. 1973. *English Hunger and Industrial Disorder. A Study of Social Conflict during the First Decade of George III's Reign*. Toronto.

Shepherd, J. F., and Walton, G. M. 1972. *Shipping, Maritime Trade, and the Economic Development of Colonial North America*. Cambridge.

Sheridan, R. B. 1965. The wealth of Jamaica in the eighteenth century. *Economic History Review* 18: 292–311.

1968. The wealth of Jamaica in the 18th century: a rejoinder. *Economic History Review* 21: 46–61

1974. *Sugar and Slavery*. Aylesbury.

Sigsworth, E. M. 1958. *Black Dyke Mills: A History*. Liverpool.

Silberling, N. J. 1919. British financial experience, 1790–1830. *Review of Economics and Statistics* 1: 282–97.

Singer, C., et al., eds. 1958. *A History of Technology, vol. IV: The Industrial Revolution, 1750–1850*. New York and London.

Slaven, A. 1986. Shipbuilding. In Langton and Morris 1986.

Slaven, A., and Aldcroft, D. H., eds. 1982. *Business, Banking, and Urban History; Essays in Honour of S. G. Checkland*. Edinburgh.

Smith, A. 1776. *An Inquiry into the Nature and Causes of the Wealth of Nations*. Ed. R. H. Campbell, A. S. Skinner and W. B. Todd, 1976. Oxford.

1790. *The Theory of Moral Sentiments*. Glasgow Edition. Ed. D. D. Raphael and A. L. Macfie, Indianapolis, 1982.

1820. Article. *The Edinburgh Review* 19 January 1820.

Smith, D. 1982. *Conflict and Compromise. Class Formation in English Society, 1830–1914: A Comparative Study of Birmingham and Sheffield*.

Snell, K. D. M. 1985. *Annals of the Labouring Poor: Social Change and Agrarian England 1660–1900*. Cambridge.

Snyder, F. G., and Hay, D., eds. 1987. *Labour, Law and Crime*.

Sokoloff, K. 1984. Was the transition from the artisanal shop to the non-mechanised factory associated with gains in efficiency? *Explorations in Economic History*. 21: 351–82.

1988. Inventive activity in early industrial America: evidence from patent records, 1790–1846. *Journal of Economic History* 48: 813–50.

Sokoloff, K., and Khan, B. Z. 1990. The democratization of invention during early industrialization: evidence from the United States, 1790–1846. *Journal of Economic History* 50: 363–78.

Solar, P. 1983. Agricultural productivity and economic development in Ireland and Scotland in the early nineteenth century. In Devine and Dickson 1983.

Solow, B. L. 1985. Caribbean slavery and British growth: the Eric Williams hypothesis. *Journal of Development Economics* 17: 99–115.

Solow, B. L., and Engerman, S. L., eds. 1987. *British Capitalism and Caribbean Slavery*. Cambridge.

eds. 1991. *Slavery and the Rise of the Atlantic System*. Cambridge.

Soltow, L. 1968. Long-run changes in British income inequality. *Economic History Review* 21: 17–29.

Souden, D. 1984. Migrants and the population structure of later seventeenth-century provincial cities and market towns. In P. Clark 1984.

Speck, W. A. 1988. *Reluctant Revolutionaries*. Oxford.

Spufford, M. 1984. *The Great Reclothing of Rural England: Petty Chapmen and their Wares in the Seventeenth Century*.

Stamp, L. D. 1948. *The Land of Britain: Its Use and Misuse*.

Stebbings, C. 1984. Jus accrescendi inter mercatores locum non habet. *Journal of Legal History* 5: 152–62.

Stevenson, J. 1979. *Popular Disturbances in England 1700–1870*.

Stone, L., and Stone, J. C. F. 1984. *An Open Elite? England 1540–1880*. Oxford.

Styles, J. 1980. Our traitorous money makers: the Yorkshire coiners and the law 1760–83. In Brewer and Styles 1980.

1983. Embezzlement and the law. In Berg *et al.* 1983.

Sugarman, D. 1983a. Introduction and overview. In Sugarman 1983b.

ed. 1983b. *Legality, Ideology and the State*.

Sugarman, D., and Rubin, G., eds. 1984. *Law, Economy and Society*. Abingdon.

Sullivan, R. 1989. England's 'age of invention': the acceleration of patents and patentable invention during the industrial revolution. *Explorations in Economic History* 26: 424–52.

Swann, G. M. P. 1986. *Quality Innovation: An Economic Analysis of Rapid Improvements in Microelectronic Components*. London.

Sylla, R., and Toniolo, G., eds. 1991. *Patterns of European Industrialization*.

Szostak, R. 1991. *The Role of Transportation in the Industrial Revolution*. Montreal.

Szreter, S. R. S. 1986. The first scientific social structure of modern Britain 1875–1883. In Bonfield, Smith and Wrightson 1986.

Thick, M. 1985. Market gardening in England and Wales. In Thirsk 1985.

Thirsk, J. 1978. *Economic Policy and Projects: The Development of a Consumer Society in Early Modern England*. Oxford.

ed. 1985. *The Agrarian History of England and Wales*, vol. V. Cambridge.

ed. 1989. *The Agrarian History of England and Wales*, vol. VI. Cambridge.

Thomas, R. P. 1965. A quantitative approach to the study of the effects of British imperial policy upon colonial welfare: some preliminary findings. *Journal of Economic History* 25: 615–38.

1968. The sugar colonies of the old empire: profit or loss for Great Britain? *Economic History Review* 21: 30–45.

Thomas, R. P., and McCloskey, D. N. 1981. Overseas trade and empire, 1700–1860. In Floud and McCloskey 1981.

Thomis, M. 1972. *The Luddites*. New York.

Thompson, E. P. 1963. *The Making of the English Working Class*.

1967. Time, work-discipline and industrial capitalism. *Past and Present* 38: 56–97.

1991. *Customs in Common*.

Thompson, F. M. L. 1963. *English Landed Society in the Nineteenth Century*.

Wood, G. H. 1910. *The History of Wages in the Cotton Trade during the Past Hundred Years.*

Woods, R. 1985. The effects of population redistribution on the level of mortality in nineteenth-century England and Wales. *Journal of Economic History*, 45: 645–51.

Wordie, J. R. 1974. Social change on the Leveson–Gower Estates, 1714–1832. *Economic History Review* 27: 593–609.

1983. The chronology of English enclosure, 1500–1914. *Economic History Review* 36: 483–505.

Wrigley, E. A. 1967. A simple model of London's importance in changing English society and economy, 1600–1750. *Past and Present* 37: 44–70.

1981. Marriage, fertility and population growth in eighteenth-century England. In Outhwaite 1981.

1983a. English population history from family reconstitution: summary results, 1600–1799. *Population Studies* 37: 157–84.

1983b. The growth of population in eighteenth-century England: a conundrum resolved. *Past and Present* 98: 123–50.

1985. Urban growth and agricultural change: England and the continent in the early modern period. *Journal of Interdisciplinary History* 15: 683–728. Reprinted in Wrigley 1987b.

1987a. Men on the land and men in the countryside: employment in agriculture in early nineteenth century England. In Bonfield, Smith and Wrightson 1986.

1987b. *People, Cities and Wealth.*

1988. *Continuity, Chance and Change: The Character of the Industrial Revolution in England.* Cambridge.

Wrigley, E. A., and Schofield, R. S. 1981. *The Population History of England 1541–1871.*

Wrigley, E. A., and Souden, D. C., eds. 1986. *The Works of Thomas Robert Malthus.*

Yelling, J. A. 1977. *Common Field and Enclosure in England, 1450–1850.* Hamden, Conn.

Young, A. 1774. *Political Arithmetic.*

1799. Waste lands, *Annals of Agriculture* 33: 12–59.

1813a. *General View of the Agriculture of Lincolnshire.*

1813b. *General View of the Agriculture of Oxfordshire.*

List of British Isles cities, towns, villages, parishes, counties, regions and other geographic landmarks cited

Note: in 1974 county boundaries in Britain were redrawn; many were consolidated and renamed. Post-1974 county names and descriptions have been given *only* in those instances where they were cited in the text; otherwise all county references are to the pre-1974 counties and boundaries. Not all counties are included.

MAJOR DIVISIONS AND COUNTRIES

England
   The southern portion (excluding Wales) of Great Britain; roughly 50,875 square miles; London is its capital.
Great Britain
   England, Wales and Scotland.
Ireland (Eire)
   Western island of the British Isles; by a new constitution effective 29 December 1937, Ireland declared itself a 'sovereign, independent, democratic state'; full independence from the British Commonwealth was achieved with the Republic of Ireland Act in 1948; 27,137 square miles; Dublin is the capital.
Northern Ireland
   A self-governing state established in 1920 with the Government of Ireland Acts; made up of the former counties of Antrim, Armagh, Down, Londonderry, Tyrone and Ulster; area of 5,238 square miles; a focal point of social, economic and political unrest between Protestants and Catholics; Belfast is the seat of government.
Scotland
   The northern part of Great Britain; 29,796 square miles in area; the border with England extends from roughly the Solway Firth to the Cheviot Hills to the river Tweed; composed of the Southern Uplands, the Central Lowlands (frequently referred to in combination as 'the Lowlands'), the Northern and Western Highlands ('the Highlands'), the Hebrides or Western Isles and the Orkney and Shetland Isles; Edinburgh is Scotland's capital.
United Kingdom of Great Britain *and Ireland*
   Political union established 1 January 1801; comprised of England and Wales, Scotland and Ireland; superseded by the United Kingdom of Great Britain *and Northern Ireland* on 6 December 1921; the Irish Free State recognised as a free member of the British Commonwealth (until 1937 when Ireland declared its independence).
Wales (Cymru)
   Principality in the SW of Great Britain; area of some 8,000 square miles;

429

commonly divided according to 'North Wales' and 'South Wales'; the Welsh capital is Cardiff.

CITIES, TOWNS AND VILLAGES

Aberdeen
Seaport city and county town of Aberdeenshire, Scotland; $130\frac{1}{2}$ miles N of Edinburgh and 524 miles N of London.

Ayr
Seaport and county town of Ayrshire, Scotland, on river Ayr; $41\frac{1}{2}$ miles SW of Glasgow and $87\frac{1}{2}$ miles WSW of Edinburgh.

Balcarres (House)
In E Fifeshire, Scotland; $\frac{3}{4}$ miles NW of Colinsburgh.

Banbury
Town in Oxfordshire; 22 miles N of Oxford.

Barnsley
Town in Yorkshire (West Riding); 16 miles N of Sheffield, on river Dearne.

Bedford
County town of Bedfordshire, straddles river Ouse; $49\frac{3}{4}$ miles NW of London.

Belfast
Principal town of county Ulster in Northern Ireland; 113 miles N of Dublin, across the Irish Sea from Glasgow (135 miles) and from Liverpool (156 miles); site of Queens University.

Billingham
Urban district in SE Durham; $2\frac{1}{2}$ miles NE of Stockton-on-Tees.

Birmingham
City in Warwickshire; 113 miles NW of London; located roughly in the centre of England on the edge of a major coal and iron district; metal manufactures were central to Birmingham's industrial development.

Blackpool
Town in N Lancashire; $16\frac{1}{2}$ miles NW of Preston and 227 miles NW of London by rail.

Blackwell Hall
Seat in S Durham, on river Tees; $1\frac{1}{2}$ miles SW of Darlington.

Bradford
City in Yorkshire (West Riding); 9 miles W of Leeds, 35 miles SW of York and 192 miles from London by rail; England's primary seat for woollens and worsteds manufacture; nicknamed 'Worstedopolis'.

Bristol
Seaport city in Gloucestershire (and Somerset); port 26 miles from Cardiff, Wales, and 71 miles from Swansea, Wales; $117\frac{1}{2}$ miles W of London.

Cambridge
County seat of Cambridgeshire; 57 miles NE of London by rail; most notably the site of Cambridge University and its related colleges.

Cardiff
Seaport and county town of Glamorgan, Wales; 152 miles W of London; voluminous exports of coal and iron fromi nearby Taff and Rhymney Valleys made through the port; industries also included iron foundries, tinplate manufactures and iron shipbuilding.

Carnarvon
County town of Carnarvonshire, Wales; 246 miles NW of London by rail.

Carron
Village in Stirlingshire, Scotland; near river Carron; ironworks established there in 1760.

Coventry
City of Warwickshire; 19 miles SE of Birmingham and 94 miles NW of London by rail; manufactures included cycles, motors, ribbons, silk, watches, woollens, carpets, cotton, metalwork and iron founding.

Crook
Village in S Durham.

Derby (där'bē)
County town of Derbyshire; 42½ miles NE of Birmingham, 60 miles SE of Manchester and 129 miles NW of London by rail.

Dublin
Metropolis of Eire (Ireland); port 60 miles from Holyhead, Carnarvonshire, Wales, 196 miles from Glasgow.

Dudley (and Ward)
Town in Worcestershire; 8 miles NW of Birmingham; 121½ miles NW of London.

Dundee
Seaport city on the Tay in Angus, Scotland; 59½ miles N of Edinburgh, 84 miles NE of Glasgow, and 452¾ miles NW of London by rail; principal manufactures included jute and linen, shipbuilding, engineering, foundries and brewing.

Dundonald
Village in Ayrshire, Scotland.

Dunkinfield
Municipal borough in Cheshire.

Edinburgh
Capital of Scotland and county town of Midlothian, on the Firth of Forth; 392½ miles N of London; seaport section known as 'Leith'; principal industries included printing, bookbinding, machine-making, rubber and brewing.

Edgbaston
Parliamentary division of Birmingham.

Etruria
Village near Stoke-upon-Trent, N Staffordshire; site of Josiah Wedgwood's earthenware manufactures.

Gainsborough
Town in Lincolnshire; 15 miles NW of Lincoln and 145 miles NW of London; a sub-port of Grimsby.

Gateshead
Town in N Durham on river Tyne, opposite Newcastle; industrial composition mimicked that of Newcastle.

Glasgow
City on the river Clyde in Lanarkshire, Scotland; 47½ miles W of Edinburgh and 401½ miles NW of Euston Station in London by rail; principal industries were textiles, printing, iron manufacture, engineering; regarded as the seat of the Scottish iron trade.

Gleneagles
Place in Perthshire, Scotland; site of grand hotel with golf course and tennis grounds.

Hereford
County town of Herefordshire on river Wye; 144 miles NW of London by rail.

Hull
City at the confluence of the river Hull and the estuary the Humber; $55\frac{1}{2}$ miles SE of Leeds and $173\frac{1}{2}$ miles N from London; one of England's largest ports; also known as 'Kingston-upon-Hull'.

Huntingdon
County town of Huntingdonshire on river Ouse; 59 miles N of London.

Inverness
County town of Inverness-shire, Scotland, at NE end of Caledonian Canal; 192 miles from Edinburgh, 585 miles from London; principal industries included railway repair, shipbuilding, iron founding and woollen cloth.

Keighley (kēth'lē)
Town in Yorkshire (West Riding); 9 miles NW of Bradford; connected to Hull by the Leeds & Liverpool Canal.

Leeds
City on river Aire in Yorkshire (West Riding); 25 miles SW of York, 43 miles NE of Manchester and 186 miles NW of London by rail; site of most major industrial undertakings.

Leicester (les'ter)
Capital city of Leicestershire on river Soar; 99 miles by rail NNW of London; principal centre for a large agricultural market, including wool-producing districts.

Lincoln
County town of Lincolnshire; 120 miles NW of London.

Liverpool
Seaport city in Lancashire on the river Mersey; 31 miles W of Manchester by rail, 201 miles NW of London; chief port for Britain's transatlantic trade.

London
Capital city of England; seat of government for Great Britain; on the Thames; principal financial and commercial centre for Britain; the financial centre is sometimes simply referred to as 'the City'.

Macclesfield
Town in Cheshire; $17\frac{1}{2}$ miles S of Manchester, 166 miles NW of London by rail; adjacent to the Macclesfield Canal.

Manchester
City in Lancashire, separated from Salford by river Irwell; connected to the sea $35\frac{1}{2}$ miles away by the Manchester Ship Canal; 183 miles NW of London.

Marston
Village in Cheshire on river Trent and on Mersey Canal.

Meriden
Village in Warwickshire; $5\frac{1}{2}$ miles NW of Coventry.

Monmouth
County town of Monmouthshire, England; 19 miles S of Hereford.

Newbury
Town in Berkshire on river Kennet; 17 miles SW of Reading, 53 miles WSW of London by rail.

Newcastle-upon-Tyne
City in Northumberland on river Tyne; $268\frac{1}{2}$ miles N of London; being the port

nearest one of the largest coalfields in England, immense quantities of coal were exported from there; played a central role in the coal trade.

Northampton

Capital of Northamptonshire on river Nene; $65\frac{3}{4}$ miles NW of London; principal seat of boot and shoe manufactures; also host to the Pytchley Hunt in March and November.

Nottingham

Capital of Nottinghamshire; $123\frac{1}{2}$ miles by rail NW of London's St Pancras Station; important industries were lace making and cotton hosiery manufacture.

Oldham

Town in SE Lancashire on river Medlock; 6 miles NE of Manchester.

Oxford

County town of Oxfordshire between rivers Cherwell and Thames; 63 miles from London by rail; principally an educational centre, site of Oxford University.

Prescott

Town in SW Lancashire; $7\frac{1}{2}$ miles E of Liverpool; site of Liverpool Corporation's water supply reservoirs.

Preston

Port and manufacturing town in Lancashire; on the Lancaster Canal near the head of river Ribble's estuary; 28 miles NE of Liverpool and 31 miles NW of Manchester.

Salford

City in Lancashire, W of Manchester; 'it forms practically a part of Manchester'.

Sheffield

City in Yorkshire; $42\frac{1}{2}$ miles SE of Manchester, $158\frac{1}{2}$ miles NW of London; long recognised for its cutlery industry, but had almost every other manufacturing industry, too.

Southampton

Seaport in Hampshire; 79 miles SW of London; one of Britain's major port centres, particularly for passengers.

Southend-on-Sea

Town in Essex on the Thames; 42 miles E of London by rail.

Stirling

County town of Stirlingshire, Scotland on river Forth; $20\frac{1}{2}$ miles NE of Glasgow and $36\frac{1}{2}$ miles NW of Edinburgh by rail.

Turnberry

Place on Ayrshire coast on Turnberry Bay; 56 miles SW of Glasgow by rail.

Warrington

Town in Lancashire; 16 miles WSW of Manchester.

Warwick

County town of Warwickshire on river Avon; 108 miles NW of London.

York

County town of Yorkshire; 188 miles NW of London.

COUNTIES

Ayrshire

Maritime co. in SW of Scotland; mineral deposits included coal, iron, limestone and sandstone – all extensively worked; had manufactures of woollens, cotton, iron and earthenware; also dairying.

Bedfordshire
    Inland co. N of London; primarily agricultural, with some manufactures related to agricultural implements; some mineral extraction.
Berkshire (Bark'shir)
    Inland co. W of London; agriculture included dairying and crop cultivation; manufactures of agricultural implements and malt making; Reading had a large biscuit enterprise.
Berwickshire
    Maritime co. in SE of Scotland; mineral deposits of limestone, coal and copper; coastal location supported an important fishing industry; agriculture limited to a fertile area called 'the Merse'.
Borders
    (Post-1974) co. in SE of Scotland; encompasses the former counties of Berwickshire, Roxburghshire, Selkirkshire, Peebles-shire and parts of Midlothian.
Buckinghamshire
    Inland co. adjacent NW to London; agriculture centred around grazing in the south and cultivation of wheat, beans, etc., to the north.
Cambridgeshire
    Inland co. N of London; large fens and marshlands drained for agriculture.
Cheshire
    Maritime co. S of Lancashire; serviced by the Manchester Ship Canal; mineral deposits of salt, coal and ironstone; railway rolling-stock manufacture was an important industry.
Cornwall
    Maritime co. at the extreme SW of England; tin and copper mining and manufacture were dominant industries.
Derbyshire
    Inland co. in N central England; pasture and crop lands as well as endowments of coal, iron ore, lead, limestone and marble; manufactures included paper making, silk, lace, cotton, brewing and iron founding.
Devon
    Maritime co. in SW of England; like Cornwall, tin and copper mines and manufactures, as well as lead, iron and various clays; industries were coarse woollens, linens, lace, paper, and gloves and shoes.
Durham
    Maritime co. in N of England; some of England's most important coalfields located here; many various industries, including chemicals, glass, shipbuilding, paper, woollens & worsteds, large ironworks and machine making.
Essex
    Maritime co. adjacent NE to London; primarily agricultural with few industries not related to local supply of agricultural implements.
Glamorgan
    Maritime co. in S of Wales; commercially the most important Welsh county due to its endowment of coal and iron ore and its convenient seaboard location; home to some of the world's largest ironworks of the time.
Gloucestershire
    Co. in W of England; two large coalfields in the west; industries included silk, woollens and cotton, gloves, glass and dairying.
Hampshire
    Maritime co. in S of England; also called 'Hants'; rolling countryside supported

sheep and pigs; main industry located at the ports – shipbuilding and shipping services.

Hertfordshire
Inland co. N of London; economy dominated by agriculture: animal husbandry, grains, hay, fruit and vegetable gardens for urban markets; very few manufactures.

Humberside
(Post-1974) co. on the NE English coast; composed the former counties of East Riding, Yorkshire, parts of West Riding, Yorkshire and the Lindsey division of Lincolnshire; 'Humberside North' is that part of the co. N of the Humber, previously East Riding.

Huntingdonshire
Inland co. in E of England; primarily agricutural with market gardens and dairying; manufactures essentially limited to the local supply of implements.

Kent
Maritime co. in SE of England; largely agricultural, producing more hops than the rest of the country; manufactures centred around paper, gunpowder and pottery; late exploitation of a coal measure on the eastern coast.

Lancashire
Maritime co. in the NW of England on the Irish Sea; major industrial area: coal and iron, shipbuilding and immense cotton and textile manufactures.

Limerick
County in Munster province, Ireland; rolling plain considered quite productive; chief manufactures were woollens, paper and milled grains; also town on river Shannon, W Ireland.

Lincolnshire
Maritime co. in E of England; divided into divisions of Holland, Kesteven and Lindsey; primarily agricultural with a few heavy industries of shipbuilding and machine making.

Midlothian
Co. in SE of Scotland on Firth of Forth; formerly Edinburghshire; mineral deposits of coal, shale, ironstone and limestone; principal industries were brewing, paper manufacture and brick and tile making.

Monmouthshire
Maritime co. in W of England, adjacent to border with Wales; some agricultural production (wheat, rye, barley and oats); best known for its large industries centred around iron and coal; occasionally included as part of the 'South Wales' region.

Norfolk
Maritime co. in the E of England; principal industries were fishing and agriculture: livestock – including cart horses and poultry.

Northamptonshire
Inland co.; hilly district with large deposits of iron; dominant industry centred around iron, but also had boot and shoe industries; colloquially 'Northants'.

Northumberland
Most northerly co. in England; coalfields and lead deposits dominated economy; major industrial area with ironworks, shipbuilding and chemicals manufacture.

Nottinghamshire
N central co. in England; several coal mines, but primarily agricultural; hosiery, cycles, woollens and cotton, and iron foundries among the industries.

Oxfordshire
   Central inland co.; primarily engaged in agriculture.
Ross and Cromarty
   Co. in extreme NW of Scotland; encompassed some mainland areas and islands
   of the Outer Hebrides and Lewis (except Harris); lowlands cultivated and
   industry limited to the distillation of whiskey.
Shropshire
   Inland co. in W central England; famous for its breed of sheep; cattle and
   dairying; deposits of coal and ironstone – only heavy industries related to iron.
Staffordshire
   Co. in NW central England; two major coalfields; heavy industry drawn to
   nearby coal; 'the Black Country' well known for all branches of iron and
   related industries.
Strathclyde
   (Post-1974) co. in W Scotland; formerly counties of Argyllshire, Ayrshire,
   Lanarkshire, Dunbartonshire and parts of Stirlingshire.
Suffolk
   Maritime co. in E England; produced agricultural crops of wheat, barley, peas
   and beans, butter, sheep and cart-horses; manufactures limited to agricultural
   implements.
Surrey
   Inland co. adjacent S to London; some industries: pharmaceuticals, tobacco,
   calicoes and woollen goods.
Sussex
   Maritime co. in SE England; administratively divided into East and West
   Sussex; coastal lowlands cultivated with grains and hay; primary sheep pastures;
   manufactures included woollens, paper, gunpowder and brick and tile making.
Sutherland
   Maritime co. in extreme N of Scotland; economy dominated by fishing and
   sheep-grazing.
Western Isles
   (Post-1974) co. in far NW Scotland; formerly parts of Ross and Cromarty and
   Inverness-shire.
Wiltshire
   Inland co. W of London; woollens, carpets, cutlery and steel goods, and iron-
   founding traditional industries; a unique industry was training dogs for truffle-
   hunting.
Yorkshire
   Large co. on NE coast; major deposits of limestone and coal; divided into three
   Ridings: North, East and West.
      North Riding, in N of co.; endowments of limestone, lead, and ironstone;
      industries related to iron smelting.
      East Riding, in SE of co.; primarily agriculture-related industry; included
      major seaport of Hull.
      West Riding, in W and SW of co.; centre of Yorkshire's industry;
      encompassed the major Yorkshire coalfield in an area 45 miles × 20 miles;
      industrial centres in West Riding included Barnsley, Bradford, Dewsbury,
      Halifax, Huddersfield, Leeds and Sheffield.

REGIONS

arable zone
Counties of Yorkshire (East Riding), Lincolnshire, Nottinghamshire, Rutland, Huntingdonshire, Warwickshire, Leicestershire, Northamptonshire, Cambridgeshire, Norfolk, Suffolk, Bedfordshire, Buckinghamshire, Oxfordshire, Berkshire, Hampshire, Hertfordshire, Essex, Middlesex, Surrey, Kent and Sussex.

Black Country
A term used to designate the manufacturing district south of Staffordshire, occupies radius about 10 miles round West Bromwich.

Cyfartha
In northern vicinity of Merthyr Tydfil, Glamorgan, Wales; seat of iron works.

East Anglia
Counties of Huntingdonshire, Cambridgeshire, Norfolk and Suffolk.

east midlands
Counties of Derbyshire, Nottinghamshire, Lincolnshire (Kesteven & Holland divisions), Leicestershire, Rutland and Northamptonshire.

Forest of Dean
WNW in Gloucestershire; forest supplied wood needed for charcoal in early iron making; largely deforested by 1800.

Highlands
General region of Scotland beyond the Grampians; population primarily of Celtic heritage.

Home Counties
Counties of Essex, Kent, London, Middlesex and Surrey; sometimes referred to as 'the Six Home Counties' including Hertfordshire with those above.

Lothians
District on the south side of the Firth of Forth; included the Scottish counties of East Lothian, Midlothian and West Lothian.

midlands
Counties of Derbyshire, Herefordshire, Leicestershire, South Lancashire, Northamptonshire, Nottinghamshire, Rutland, Shropshire, Staffordshire, Warwickshire, Worcestershire; divided into the east midlands and the west midlands.

north-east
Counties of Northumberland, Durham and Yorkshire (North Riding).

North Wales
Counties of Anglesey, Carnarvonshire, Denbighshire, Flintshire, Merioneth and Montgomeryshire.

north-west
Counties of Cumberland, Westmorland and Lancashire (perhaps also including Cheshire).

pastoral zone
Counties of Northumberland, Cumberland, Durham, Yorkshire (North & West Ridings), Westmorland, Lancashire, Cheshire, Derbyshire, Staffordshire, Shropshire, Worcestershire, Herefordshire, Monmouthshire (Wales), Gloucestershire, Wiltshire, Dorsetshire, Somersetshire, Devonshire and Cornwall.

Scottish Lowlands
The Scottish mainland not included in the Highlands; generally applied to the counties south of the Firths of Clyde and Tay; 'eastern': East Lothian,

Midlothian, West Lothian, Peebles-shire, Selkirkshire and Roxburghshire; 'Western': Renfrewshire, Lanarkshire, Ayrshire, Wigtownshire, Kirkcud-brightshire and Dumfries-shire.

south-east

Counties of Bedfordshire, Buckinghamshire, Oxfordshire, Berkshire, Hampshire, Hertfordshire, Essex, (Greater London), Surrey, Kent and Sussex.

South Lancashire

Area in NE England; now Merseyside and Greater Manchester.

South Wales

'Formally' comprised of the counties: Brecknockshire, Cardiganshire, Carmarthenshire, Glamorgan, Pembrokeshire and Radnorshire.

south-west

Counties of Gloucestershire, Wiltshire, Somerset, Dorset, Devon and Cornwall.

West Country

Counties of Cornwall, Devon, Somerset and parts of Wiltshire, Gloucestershire and Dorset.

east midlands

Counties of Shropshire, Staffordshire, Warwickshire, Worcestershire and Herefordshire.

PARISHES

Ash

In Derbyshire, 8 miles SW of Derby.

Banbury

In Oxfordshire, 22 miles N of Oxford.

Blackburn

In Lancashire; 11 miles E of Preston and 210 miles NW of London; one of the principal locales of cotton manufactures.

Bottesford

In N Leicestershire, 7 miles NW of Grantham or in Lindsey, Lincolnshire, 7 miles W of Briggs.

Burslem

In Stoke-on-Trent, N Staffordshire; 20 miles NNW of Stafford by rail; most notably the birthplace of Josiah Wedgwood (1730–95).

Dawlish

In E Devonshire.

Gedling

In Nottinghamshire, 3 miles NE of Nottingham.

Morchard Bishop

In Devonshire, N of Exeter.

Odiham

In NE Hampshire.

Shepshed

In Leicestershire, 4 miles W of Loughborough.

Winlaton

In Durham on river Tyne.

RIVERS, CANALS AND GEOGRAPHIC LANDMARKS

Ayr
  River in Ayrshire, Scotland; flows 38 miles W to Firth of Clyde at Ayr.
Bristol Channel
  An expansion of the estuary of the river Severn; it is about 85 miles long and
  from 5 to 43 miles wide; rapid rising of the tide creates a *bore*, or sudden wave.
Boyne
  River in Leinster (len'ster), south-eastern province of Ireland; flows 70 miles
  through countries of Kildare and Meath to the Irish Sea; 'Battle of the Boyne'
  found James II defeated by William III on 1 July 1690.
Channel Tunnel
  Tunnel connecting Folkestone, England, and Calais, France; built beneath the
  English Channel; frequently beset by financial and political problems since the
  1960s; formally termed 'the Eurotunnel', but nicknamed 'the Chunnel'.
Clyde
  Scotland's most important river; 91 miles long; even the largest ships could
  navigate it to Glasgow; many shipbuilding enterprises built along its banks.
Culloden (Moor)
  On the border of Nairnshire, a maritime co. of NE Scotland; site of the defeat
  of Prince Charles Edward and the Highlanders (the Jacobites) by the Duke of
  Cumberland which signalled the defeat of the Stuarts.
English Channel
  Extension of the Atlantic Ocean between S England and N France; connected to
  the North Sea by the Strait of Dover; fishing grounds for mackerel and oysters;
  often simply 'the Channel'.
Humber
  Estuary of the rivers Ouse and Trent; 38 miles long and 1 to $7\frac{1}{4}$ miles across.
Kentish Weald, *see* Weald
Mersey
  North-western river formed by the confluence of rivers Goyt and Tame; empties
  into the Irish Sea; 70 miles in length; large ships could anchor there.
Thames
  Britain's most important river; navigable by a great variety of vessels; vital to
  London's import/export trade; the Thames from London Bridge to Blackwall
  was known as the 'Port of London' and the section below London Bridge was
  known as 'The Pool'.
Wear
  River in Durham; 65 miles long; barges could navigate it to Durham.
Weald
  A landmark of physical geography covering parts of Kent, Surrey and Sussex
  counties; previously it was densely forested but was largely stripped of timber to
  make charcoal for early iron making; later it supported pasturelands, hop
  cultivation and orchards, particularly in Kent.

LONDON: AREA AND LANDMARKS

East End
  Area of London generally associated with poverty and the poorer classes of
  labour; possibly so-named to contrast with the fashionable West End.

Euston Station
Station built for the London & Birmingham railway; located N central London; recognised for its architecture prior to renovations made by British Rail in the 1960s.

Greater London
1963 redesignation of the counties of London and Middlesex and parts of Surrey, Kent, Essex and Hertfordshire.

Heathrow
Formally London (Heathrow) Airport; opened 31 May 1946 to connect the United States and the United Kingdom by direct air-service; to the W of Greater London.

Spitalfields
Neighbourhood in London's East End; after 1865 French Protestants established silk weaving as an industry there.

Soho
District in W London; centre for Victorian era entertainment, reputable and disreputable alike; also recognised as a neighbourhood of immigrants.

St Pancras Station
London terminal for the midland railway; built in the centre of one of London's slum areas, Agar Town.

Sandown Park
150 acre race course, $\frac{1}{2}$ mile N of Esher Station in Surrey.

Whitehall
Formerly a royal residence; seat of the executive branch of the British government; a street between Trafalgar Square and Parliament Square, and a general designation for the area including the Prime Minister's residence, 10 Downing Street.

Index and glossary

Aberdeen, 169
Abramowitz, M., 250
absolute advantage
  Greater efficiency than someone else,
  such as Britain's greater efficiency in
  both agriculture and manufacturing in
  the nineteenth century. What is relevant
  to the question of what Britain should
  have specialised in doing, however, is
  comparative advantage (q.v.).
accelerator
  The dependence of investment on the
  amount of the product consumed, as the
  building of petrol stations depends on
  the amount of petrol sold. The
  'acceleration' refers to the speeding up
  of flow it causes in an underemployed
  economy: a rise in investment in one
  industry causes a rise in income earned
  in others by the 'multiplier' (q.v.), which
  then causes still more investment (to
  service the consumption out of the new
  income), accelerating the rise in income.
accepting houses, 170
Adams, H., 245
Africa, 183, 192, 196
age distribution, rural and urban, 339–40
age-specific rate
  The frequency of some event in
  population counting at a specific age.
  The age-specific death rate, for instance,
  is the deaths per 1,000 people of age one
  year; similar rates can be calculated for
  those ages two years, ten to fifteen years,
  etc. Marriage, birth and other rates are
  also used.
age structure
  The proportion of people at each age. In
  a rapidly growing population, for
  example, children will outnumber old
  people, and the age structure will look, if
  plotted on a graph, like a triangle with a

large base; there will be a high
proportion at ages one year, two years,
etc.
agriculture, 3–4, 96–122, 249
  arable, 1
  employment, 99–100, 105–8, 117
  exports, 188–9
  family farms, 3–4
  farm size, 97–100, 114
  inputs, 103–10, 116
  investment, 99, 116–17
  open-field system, 97–8, 115
  outputs, 100–3, 121–2
  pastoral, 1
  productivity, 10, 47, 57–8, 110–19, 252
  role in economic growth, 119–22
  shift from, 57–9
  structure of labour force, 10, 105–8
  world expansion, 324–6
  see also Corn Laws; international trade;
    tariffs
Albert, W., 57, 219
Aldcroft, D. H., 322
alertness, 267–9
Allen, R. C., 47–8, 96–122, 139, 260
America, 300, 346
  convicts, 196
  North, 183–4, 192, 195, 199
  slaves, 183
  South, 177, 192, 215, 322, 324, 326
  taxes, 198
  tobacco trade, 160, 199
  trade, 184, 192, 199, 206–7, 255, 328–9
  War for American Independence, 170,
    175, 213, 227
  see also United States
American Civil War, 175, 306
American Revolution, 187, 198, 200, 203
Amsterdam, 170, 214–15, 254
Amsterdam Wisselbank, 169
Anderson, B. L., 162–3, 167
Anderson, J., 211–12

differentials

Usually in reference to wages; differences between wages from one job to another or from one place to another. If the higher wage is compensation for worse conditions or higher skills the differentials have no tendency to disappear, and are called 'compensating' or 'equalising'.

diminishing returns

The fall in the amount of additional output as additional doses of input are applied. The nation's agriculture is subject to diminishing returns as more workers and capital apply themselves to the fixed amount of land. Output does not fall: it merely rises less than it did from previous doses.

direct investment

An investment in one's own company by contrast with investment in the bonds of other companies ('portfolio investment'). Cunard Lines, Ltd, investing in port facilities for itself in Quebec would be an example of direct investment; Cunard investing in Canadian Pacific Railway bonds would be 'indirect' or portfolio investment.

direct tax

Levied on the people on whom it is believed or intended to fall, such as the income tax. The distinction between direct and indirect taxes, however, 'is practically relegated to the mind of the legislator. What he proposes should be borne by the original payer is called a direct tax, what he intends to be borne by someone else than the original taxpayer is called indirect. Unfortunately, the intention of the legislator is not equivalent to the actual result' (E. R. A. Seligman, *On the Shifting and Incidence of Taxation* (1892), p. 183). Cf. indirect tax.

discounted value, discounted present value, present value

The amount by which one down-values income earned in the future relative to income earned today. If the interest rate were 10 per cent, for example, one would down-value £1 earned next year to 90p relative to £1 earned today; the discounted value would be 10 per cent below the money value.

discounting, *see* rediscounting

discount rate, market rate of discount

The percentage reduction of the price of a short-term IOU (e.g. a ninety-day bill) now below its value when it falls due later. For example, a bill worth £100 ninety days from now might sell for £99 today. The rate is usually expressed as the annual percentage interest rate one would earn on buying such a bill for £99 and holding it to maturity (approximately $(12/3) \times (£1/£99) = 4$ per cent; more exactly, allowing for compounding, 3·67 per cent).

diseconomies of (managerial) scale

Rises in cost as an enterprise becomes too big for the abilities of its managers to manage. Cf. economies of scale.

disintegration

vertical, 280

The breaking apart of a unified enterprise, for increased efficiency (contrast integration).

disposable income

National income (q.v.) minus personal taxes plus subsidies and payments of interest on the government debt. It is the income available in someone's bank account or pocket for spending or saving, the government having taken its share of the product earlier.

distribution of income

(1) By size: the frequency of rich and poor.

(2) Functional: how income is allotted to labour, to land and to capital.

distribution of wealth

Sometimes elegant variation for distribution of income (q.v.); sometimes, and properly, the frequency among people of wealth, not annual income, of various sizes, that is, of their market worth on some date if sold off.

The way that people are spread among the economy's tasks, as tinkers, tailors, spies.

haircuts, students at university) wish to buy.

equilibrium wage
The payment to workers that makes the amount of hours workers as a whole wish to supply equal to the amount buyers of labour (owners of cotton mills, buyers of haircuts, students at university) wish to buy.

equity, 155
(1) Titles of ownership; stock certificates.
(2) The value of ownership in a company; the right of ownership.
(3) A branch of law meant to supplement the common law.

equity interest
The value of a company. Both words are used here in uncommon senses: 'equity' to mean 'the value of ownership' (as in the phrase, 'I have £2,000 of equity in my house left after the mortgage is subtracted from the price of the house'); 'interest' to mean 'legally recognised concern or right'.

Ernle, Lord, 96, 115
Ernst, J. A., 195
estate, the rise of the, 97–100
Etruria, 143
Euler, Johann, 37
Europe, 303, 327–8, 333
Eversley, D. E. C., 93, 182

ex ante
The anticipated value; or from the point of view of before the event; or planned. For example, ex ante profits in a venture are always high – for why else would one embark on it? Ex post, alas, they may be low.

excess capacity
The amount that is not produced by producing less than one can. The British economy in 1933 had excess capacity, with millions of workers out of work and thousands of factories idle. Cf. unemployment.

excess demand
(1) In micro-economics, a situation in a market in which the amount people wish to buy is at the existing price larger than the amount (other) people wish to sell.
(2) In macro-economics, a condition in which aggregate demand (q.v., that is, what people wish to spend) is larger than aggregate supply (i.e. what they plan currently to produce).

exchange rate
The value of one country's money in terms of another, such as $4.86 per pound sterling (the rate during much of the past two centuries). An exchange rate is 'fixed' if the government of one of the countries is willing to buy and sell its currency at the fixed price, in the same way as it might fix the price of wheat.

exchange risk
The hazard that the pound's price may change unfavourably before one is able to cash a promise in pounds.

Exchequer, 171, 241
stopping of payments on, 166–7

exogenous
Caused outside the system being analysed. The weather (except smog) is exogenous to the economy: it may cause things in the economy but is not in turn caused by them. The price of housing, in contrast, *is* caused inside the economy. Cf. autonomous spending; contrast endogenous.

expected, expectation, expected value
Statistically speaking, the average of what one anticipates. If one anticipated that the profits on new cotton spindles, say, could be 4, 6 or 8 per cent, each equally likely, then the expected value would be 6 per cent.

expected lifetime income
One's anticipated income over one's remaining life. The concept is useful because decisions by income earners depend presumably on their expected lifetime income, not merely the income they happen to have this year. A surgeon, for example, would be sensible to buy more than he earns early in his career, in anticipation of high income later. Identical to permanent income.

expenditure tax
Taxes imposed only on the amounts people spend, as distinct from taxes on income, which tax what they save out of the income as well as what they spend. A tax on food would be an expenditure tax, on all income an income tax, on income from bonds a savings tax.

exponential growth
Growth at a constant percentage rate per year, in the manner of compound interest. A straight line upward sloping on an ordinary graph against time has a

Invention refers to the first
implementation of an idea, for
example a machine, on an
experimental basis; innovation to its
introduction into commercial use.
There can be a long delay between the
two.

The physical amounts or money values
of materials held for working up.
'Goods in process' is the most
illuminating term. The shoemaker's
holding of leather, the steel-maker's
holding of finished steel, the publisher's
holding of paper, ink and finished books
are all 'goods in process'.

inventory costs

The expenditure to keep goods in
storage awaiting sale, as on a
shopkeeper's shelf or in a farmer's barn.

A storehouse of funds that specialises
in loaning out its funds to business for
long-term projects. In European
economic history, the German
investment banks of the late
nineteenth century are said to have
been especially bold and important in
German growth, by contrast with the
greater caution of British banks.

A thing such as a railway or a
university education purchased to
satisfy human desires indirectly and
later, not directly and now. Contrast
consumption good. Cf. capital, which
is the accumulated pile of investment
goods.

Using up resources now to get a return
in the future, such as buildings, railways,
educating the people and so forth.
Investment at home is one of the major
parts of national income (q.v., the others
being consumption, government
spending and investment abroad). It is a
more or less productive use of the money
value of saving (q.v.) to increase future
income. More technically, it is the rate
per year at which the existing stock of
capital is added to. Cf. capital
formation.

invisible earnings

In foreign trade, a country's earnings in
providing the rest of the world with
'invisible' (i.e. intangible) services, such
as shipping, insurance, tourism.

The proposition, popular in economics
c. 1830, that the wage will never rise above
subsistence because workers will give
birth to more workers as it does. Cf.
demographic crisis; Malthusian trap;
natural price of labour.

Fresh IOUs, as distinct from ones made
in the past and now being traded.

The macro-economic theory, associated
especially with the American economist
Milton Friedman, claiming that the
money supply (q.v.) is a prime mover of
the level of prices and of income. Cf.
high-powered money; monetary policy;
quantity theory of money. Contrast
Keynesian.
The plans by governments for changing
the amounts of money in order to affect
unemployment and inflation. Cf. Bank
Rate; central bank; fiscal policy; high-
powered money; money supply.
All exchanges of which the rate of
interest is the price, that is, all borrowing
and lending. Sometimes the term is
specialised to mean all such exchanges
for short periods (such as three months)
among banks, governments and large
enterprises.
The sum of all means of payment, such
as coin, bank notes, chequing accounts
and easily cashable savings accounts. Cf.
credit creation; high-powered money;
monetary policy. Also called 'stock of
money'.
One seller. The Post Office in Britain, for
example, has a monopoly of letter post.
'One buyer', as monopoly means 'one
seller'. The single coal company in a
northern village might be a monopsonist
in buying labour.

Deaths per thousand population, or
deaths at a certain age per population of
that age.
A loan on the security of houses and
land: if the borrower cannot pay the
agreed interest, he forfeits the house to
the lender.
An average over several years, called
'moving' because as years pass the
earlier years are dropped from the
average and the mid-year of the averages
moves. It is a crude way of smoothing
out jumps in a series of, say, wheat
prices to reveal the underlying trend.
The usual pattern of buying and selling
among all countries. The word
'settlement' arises from the notion that
all must in the end settle up, paying for
purchases from country Y with receipts
from X and Z. Britain's large deficit in
trade with the United States around
1910, for example, was made up in the
multilateral settlement by a surplus with
India, which in turn ran a surplus with
the Continent, which in turn ran a
surplus with the United States.
Multilaterally – i.e. looking at it from
literally many sides – the accounts
balance.
The ratio in which new expenditure in an
underemployed economy results in a
larger rise of income. New exports of
steel in 1933, for example, would have
earned steelworkers and owners in South
Wales more income, which they would
spend on, say, bread and housing,
thereby giving more income to bread
bakers and housebuilders. The multiple
effects eventually die out, killed by
'leakages' (q.v.) that do not cause higher
British income (e.g. imports or saving).
But the flow of income is permanently
higher than it was before, at least if the
initial rise of expenditure is permanent.
The economy must, however, be well

regression analysis, regression equation, curve fitting

Techniques for fitting straight lines through a scatter of points. In finding the straight line that would best summarise the relationship during 1921–38 between consumption and income, for instance, one is said to 'regress consumption on income', i.e. fit a straight line through points on a graph of annual consumption and income for these years. The simplest and by far the most widely used of the techniques is called 'least squares' or 'ordinary least squares'. The result will be an equation for a straight line, such as: Consumption in £ million at 1938 prices equal £277 million plus 0·44 times income in £ million at 1938 prices. Symbolically, the equation is in general $C = a + bY$. The actual numerical result turns out to say that the line that best fits the scatter of combinations of consumption and income is a constant (£277 million) plus 44 per cent of whatever income happens to be. The 'slope' or 'slope coefficient' or 'regression coefficient' or 'beta' is in this case 0·44. Consumption here is called the 'dependent' variable, income the 'independent' variable, in accord with the notion that consumption is dependent on income. The technique generalises easily to more than one independent variable, in which case it is called 'multiple regression' and amounts to fitting a plane (rather than a line) through points in space (rather than through points on a plane surface). In multiple regression the coefficient 'on' (i.e. multiplying) each independent variable measures the way each by itself influences the dependent variable. The equation fitted in the case mentioned above was in fact Consumption = 277 + (0·44) Income + (0·47) Consumption Last Year, which is a multiple regression of this year's consumption on this year's income and last year's consumption. It says that for a given consumption last year each £ of income raised consumption by £0·44; and for a given income each £ of consumption last year raised consumption this year by £0·47. The technique generalises with rather more difficulty to more than one *dependent*

variable, in which case it is called 'simultaneous equation estimation'.

Reid, J. D., 184, 200–2

relative income hypothesis

The notion that one's consumption (as distinct from savings) depends on one's relative economic position, not absolute wealth. According to the hypothesis the poor will save little (i.e. consume virtually all their income) even though they are in absolute terms as wealthy as, say, the high-saving middle class of a much poorer country. Cf. permanent income.

relative price

As distinct from 'nominal' or 'money' or 'absolute' prices, the price of one good in terms of another good, rather than in terms of money. If farm labour earns 16 shillings a week when wheat sells for 8 shillings a bushel, then the price of a week of labour relative to a bushel of wheat is 2·0 bushels per week. Note the units: they are units of physical amounts, not money. Relative prices are determined by the real effectiveness of the economy, whereas money prices are determined by relative prices and by the dearness of money.

religion, nonconformity, 2

remuneration in kind, 224–5

Wages paid in food, lodging and so forth rather than in coin of the realm.

Rennie, John, 17, 25, 36–7

rent, economic rent, pure rent

The return to factors of production in excess of its next best employment. In an industry with no next best employment – for instance, land used in agriculture alone – all the return will be economic rent. A coal seam is another classical example: the seam has no employment other than for coal. Economic rent need not correspond exactly to the amount earned in 'rent' in the ordinary sense of weekly rent for a flat, or even yearly rent for land. For definitions in slightly different terms: cf. economic rent; producers' surplus.

rentier

The receiver of rent, from French (and pronounced as French). Often with an unfavourable connotation, it means the receiver of income without labour, as the owner of government bonds, for example, or the owner of urban land.

    The value of alternatives sacrificed by
    some decision, viewed from the entire
    society's point of view. A decision to pay
    one's rent of £100 on a farm, for
    example, costs the private opportunity
    cost of the money: the payer cannot then
    buy that £100-worth of goods. From the
    social point of view, however, the
    opportunity cost is zero, because the
    landlord gains what you lose. There is
    no real sacrifice entailed in using the
    land, for (suppose) it has no alternative
    use outside agriculture. Cf. opportunity
    cost; rent; Ricardian theory.
    Capital used by the whole society,
    especially in circumstances in which
    expenditure on it is large and the ability
    to charge for its use is small: roads,
    dams, schools, the diplomatic corps, etc.
    Identical to infrastructure.
    The rate of return on a project earned by
    the entire society, rather than by one
    group of beneficiaries. The social rate of
    return to the building of canals, for
    example, is not merely the return from
    fares to the owners of the canals (5 per
    cent on their invested capital, say) but
    also the return, to shippers and
    landowners, not captured by the canal
    owners (an additional 4 per cent, say),
    for a social rate of return of 9 per cent
    per year. Cf. externalities; private return.
    The benefit from a project, measured to
    include all benefits over the entire
    society. The annual social savings
    divided by the opportunity costs (q.v.) of
    the investment would be the social rate
    of return (q.v.). For purposes of
    economic history the leading example of
    calculating social savings is R. W.

    Fogel's in *Railroads and American
    Economic Growth* (1964).
    A speculative mania of 1719–20,
    unimportant in itself but important for
    the long-lasting hostility to dealings in
    shares of companies that it evoked.
    The assignment of the relatively best
    qualified person or other input to the
    best job. Cf. comparative advantage;
    efficiency.
    Inputs that are used in one industry
    alone. Skilled miners or, still more, the
    coal seams themselves are highly
    specialised factors of production. They
    receive the above-normal or below-
    normal returns to the industry, being
    unwilling or unable to move in and out
    of the industry in response to good and
    bad times. That is, their earnings are
    rents. Cf. rent.
    Giving gold or silver ('specie') in
    exchange for paper currency. When
    specie payments are made on demand at
    a fixed ratio of so much gold or silver
    per pound or dollar the currency may be
    said to be 'backed' by specie or to be on
    a specie standard. Cf. gold reserves; gold
    standard; official reserves.
    The part of the Poor Law enacted in the
    1790s in a southern village. It was not
    especially important in itself, but has
    come to stand for generous relief to the
    poor.

'worked', often at useless tasks designed to discourage them from seeking shelter at public expense.